Cinema Strikes Back
Radical Filmmaking
in the United States
1930-1942

by
Russell Campbell

UMI RESEARCH PRESS
Ann Arbor, Michigan

Produced and distributed by
UMI Research Press
an imprint of
University Microfilms International
Ann Arbor, Michigan 48106

Library of Congress Cataloging in Publication Data

Campbell, Russell.
    Cinema strikes back : radical filmmaking in the
United States, 1930-1942.

    (Studies in cinema ; no. 20)
    Originally presented as the author's thesis (Northwestern),
1978.
    Bibliography: p.
    Includes index.
    1. Film and Photo League (U.S.) 2. Nykino (Organiza-
tion : New York) 3. Frontier Films (New York) 4. Moving-
pictures—Political aspects—United States.   I. Title. II. Series.

PN1999.F48C3 1982   791.43'09'09358   82-4819
ISBN 0-8357-1330-X   AACR2

Contents

List of Plates   *vii*

Acknowledgments   *ix*

1   Social Realism, Documentary, and the Concept of Montage   *1*

2   The (Workers') Film and Photo League   *29*

3   Film and Photo League Productions   *71*

4   Breakaway: Nykino   *115*

5   Frontier Films   *145*

6   *Heart of Spain* and *Return to Life*   *165*

7   *China Strikes Back*   *193*

8   *People of the Cumberland*   *213*

9   *Native Land*   *237*

10   Conclusion   *275*

Plates   *287*

Appendix: Filmographies   *313*

Notes   *321*

Bibliography   *369*

Index   *375*

List of Plates

Following page 286

1. Julian Roffman in 1935 or 1936 filming a Mother Bloor picnic. [Photo courtesy Julian Roffman.]

2. Depression: 1932. East River dock, New York City. [Photo by Leo Seltzer.]

3. Depression: 1932. Unemployed women demonstrate at New York's City Hall. [Photo by Leo Seltzer.]

4. New York City: Harlem demonstration against lynching, 1933. [Photo by Leo Seltzer.]

5. New York City, 1933. Anti-fascist, anti-war demonstration. [Photo by Leo Seltzer.]

6. Main title, "Workers Newsreel." Produced by Film and Photo League, 1931-1935. [Photo by Leo Seltzer.]

7. Depression: 1933. Rent Strike, East Harlem, New York City. [Photo by Leo Seltzer.]

8. Depression: 1933. The Floating Hospital, East River, New York City. [Photo by Leo Seltzer.]

9. Depression: 1933. Evicted family, New York East Side. [Photo by Leo Seltzer.]

10. Depression: 1932. Unemployed worker and Salvation Army band on New York City's East Side. [Photo by Leo Seltzer.]

11. Ralph Steiner. [Photo from The Museum of Modern Art/Film Stills Archive.]

12.   Paul Strand. [Photo from The Museum of Modern Art/Film Stills Archive.]

13.   *Heart of Spain*: Stretcher-bearers at the front. [Photo from The Museum of Modern Art/Film Stills Archive.]

14.   *Heart of Spain*: Dr. Bethune gives a blood transfusion. [Photo from The Museum of Modern Art/Film Stills Archive.]

15.   *Return to Life*: Madrid barricaded and bombed. [Photo from The Museum of Modern Art/Film Stills Archive.]

16.   *Return to Life*: Emergency medical care behind the lines. [Photo from The Museum of Modern Art/Film Stills Archive.]

17.   *China Strikes Back*: Chinese civilian victims of the Japanese invasion. [Photo from The Museum of Modern Art/Film Stills Archive.]

18.   *China Strikes Back*: Red Army soldiers relax. [Photo from The Museum of Modern Art/Film Stills Archive.]

19.   *People of the Cumberland*: Appalachian poverty. [Photo from The Museum of Modern Art/Film Stills Archive.]

20.   *People of the Cumberland*: Miners organized in the UMWA. [Photo from The Museum of Modern Art/Film Stills Archive.]

21.   *People of the Cumberland*: Tennessee clothing workers become unionized. [Photo from The Museum of Modern Art/Film Stills Archive.]

22.   *Native Land*: Arkansas deputies on the offensive. [Photo from The Museum of Modern Art/Film Stills Archive.]

23.   *Native Land*: Murdered sharecropper (Louis Grant). [Photo from The Museum of Modern Art/Film Stills Archive.]

24.   *Native Land*: Labor spy Art Smith under pressure from his employers. [Photo from The Museum of Modern Art/Film Stills Archive.]

25.   *Native Land*: Virginia Stevens and other mourners of the Republic Steel dead. [Photo from The Museum of Modern Art/Film Stills Archive.]

Acknowledgments

My heartfelt thanks go to the following participants in the radical film movement of the thirties who so patiently fielded my questions, and without whose generous assistance this study could not have been made: Maurice Bailen, Tom Brandon, Michael Gordon, Leo Hurwitz, Lewis Jacobs, George Jacobson, Elia Kazan, Herbert Kline, Jay Leyda, Ben Maddow, David Platt, Julian Roffman, Leo Seltzer, and Willard Van Dyke. I am particularly indebted to Maurice Bailen, Tom Brandon, Leo Hurwitz, and Leo Seltzer, who arranged for me to see films I would not otherwise have had a chance to view.

Others who helped with reminiscences, criticisms, suggestions, sharing of information, and encouragement of diverse kinds were William Alexander, Bert Hogenkamp, Myles Horton, Michael Klein, Gordon Koster, Richard Leacock, Edna Meyers, Robert Pest, Walter and Naomi Rosenblum, Anthony Slide, Ralph Steiner, Hazel Strand, Ralph Tefferteller, Anne Tucker, and Joel Zuker. My thanks to them all.

I would also like to acknowledge the help afforded by the staffs of the Margaret Herrick Library, Academy of Motion Picture Arts and Sciences; the Archives of American Art; Media Study/Buffalo; the Film Study Center, Museum of Modern Art; the Photography Department, Museum of Modern Art; the Theatre Collection, Lincoln Center for the Performing Arts, New York Public Library; the Tamiment Library, New York University; Northwestern University Special Collections; the Paul Strand Foundation; the Wisconsin Center for Theatre Research, State Historical Society of Wisconsin; and University of Southern California Special Collections. Grants from the Graduate School, Northwestern University, enabled me to undertake travel for research.

For their careful reading, valued advice, and unfailing support, I am very grateful to the members of my committee: Jack Ellis (chairman), Paddy Whannel, Chuck Kleinhans, and Martin Maloney.

Finally, for their nurture, love, and comradeship, I would like to thank Gretchen, Dana, Serafina, Marion, Steve, Sue, Jane, and the staff of *Jump Cut*.

R.C.

1

Social Realism, Documentary, and the Concept of Montage

Nearly all the films that emerged from the radical cinema movement in the United States during the 1930s were documentaries. The statement seems obvious, unproblematic; but the films might not have been so. They could have been biting satires (one or two were); they could have been expressionist cries of rage and pain, subversive comedies, surrealist nightmares, utopian fantasies. They might have been experimental narratives, political revues, hard-hitting dramas, pointed allegories, or didactic cartoons. But they weren't.

Why not? Why has documentary been the characteristic mode of left-wing expression in the cinema, to the exclusion of other alternatives? And why, particularly, should radical documentary have flourished during the poverty-stricken decade of the thirties?

These are some of the questions that lie at the root of this investigation into the work of three American filmmaking collectives of the Depression years: the Workers' Film and Photo League (known as the Film and Photo League after 1933),[1] Nykino, and Frontier Films.

The decision to make documentaries was of course partly one of financial exigency. The radical collectives were always hard-pressed for funds, and taking a camera into the street to film a demonstration was a lot cheaper than staging a musical comedy. Yet it was always more than this. The filmmakers of the Left were drawn to documentary because it seemed the logical extension, in the medium of cinema, of the doctrine of social realism.

Left-wing writers and artists have been partial to social realism[2] since the mid-nineteenth century and the birth of "scientific" socialism as a working-class movement. A doctrine of art that embraces sober investigation of the social structure seems an appropriate accompaniment for a political doctrine deduced from the data of economic and historical research; yet there is a paradox here. For in its origins, in the novels of Stendhal and Balzac, social realism was pre-eminently a bourgeois creation.

Marx, who admired Dickens, Thackeray, and their British contemporaries, and Engels, who was deeply attached to Balzac, were keenly aware of this fact;

but for them the new aesthetic was to be valued in spite of its class perspective.[3] The strength of realism lay in its cognitive power: its fidelity to fact, its ability— seemingly not shared by other aesthetic systems—to strip bare the class structure of a society. For Engels, in particular, the effectiveness of social realism in exposing class relationships veiled by the ordinary ideological mechanisms of capitalist society outweighed its limitations as an agitational weapon. Writing to novelist Minna Kautsky in 1885, he stated:

> I am not at all an opponent of tendentious writing [*Tendenzpoesie*] as such. . . . But I believe the tendency must spring forth from the situation and the action itself, without explicit attention called to it; the writer is not obliged to offer to the reader the future historical solution of the social conflicts he depicts. Especially in our conditions, the novel primarily finds readers in bourgeois circles, circles not directly related to our own, and there the socialist tendentious novel can fully achieve its purpose, in my view, if, by conscientiously describing the real mutual relations, it breaks down the conventionalized illusions dominating them, shatters the optimism of the bourgeois world, causes doubt about the eternal validity of the existing order, and this without directly offering a solution or even, under some circumstances, taking an ostensible partisan stand.[4]

In his letter to Margaret Harkness (1888) Engels went even further. "The more the opinions of the author remain hidden," he suggested, "the better the work of art." The remark signifies not that he was prepared to sacrifice political to aesthetic values, but that for him the ideological functioning of a work of social realism—whether middle-class or proletarian, negative or positive—was inevitably subordinate. Hence he could argue in the same letter:

> That Balzac thus was compelled to go against his own class sympathies and political prejudices, that he *saw* the necessity of the downfall of his favorite nobles, and described them as people deserving no better fate; and that he *saw* the real men of the future where, for the time being, they alone were to be found—that I consider one of the greatest triumphs of Realism, and one of the grandest features in old Balzac.[5]

Social realism, then, was to be understood as a unique artistic mode enjoying a privileged relationship to reality; a method of research and analysis rather than a variety of imagination—sociology, as it were, with a human face. Though its conventions have changed through time and through the various art forms (literature, painting, drama, photography, film) in which it has appeared, social realism has retained, for its Marxist adherents, the overriding virtue of referring—in direct, unambiguous terms—to a world outside that of the art object itself. As late as the 1950s, its case was being vigorously restated in terms that could have been endorsed by left-wing theorists of a century before:

> The crucial aspect of realism is its content, the truthful thinking which engenders its form, and therefore its ability to act as a force of enlightenment. It changes life by changing people, making them aware of the conflicts in life itself and the new forces emerging among them, in terms of new yet typical human personalities and human relationships.[6]

Balzac and Flaubert, Dickens and Thackeray had adopted realism as it were unwittingly, and thereby revealed truths discordant with their own conscious world view. This was to be the case, too, for the great Russians— Dostoyevsky and Tolstoy. The latter was to become the subject of a defense by Lenin undertaken in similar terms to Engels's vindication of Balzac.[7] The first important artist of the Left to pick up the banner of realism was its founder in the visual arts, the painter Gustave Courbet.

"I am not only a socialist," Courbet declared, "but also a democrat and a republican, in a word, a partisan of revolution and, above all, a realist, that is, the sincere friend of the real truth." This yoking of revolution in politics and realism in art was made in 1851, in the period of reaction following the defeats of 1848: to paint working-class subjects at this time could well be interpreted as a radical act. "They had dissolved the National Workshops," wrote a contemporary, "they had defeated the proletariat in the streets of Paris . . . they had purged universal suffrage: . . . and here was that 'vile multitude' chased out of politics, reappearing in painting!"[8]

In works such as *A Burial at Ornans* and *The Stone-breakers* (both 1849) Courbet established one of the cornerstones of committed social realist art: the serious depiction of the sort of persons who, because of their class status, would be absent from or caricatured in the dominant—bourgeois—art of the day. "Serious depiction" here means several things, including a meticulous attention to humble detail and, in Linda Nochlin's words, a "rejection of traditional ways of generalizing and idealizing the human body."[9]

Courbet's subjects were important, too, because of their typicality. Engels wrote that, "Realism, to my mind, implies, besides truth to detail, the truthful reproduction of typical characters under typical circumstances."[10] In contradistinction to the prevailing art works of the period, Courbet's paintings, despite the high degree of specificity in their rendition, evoked a sense of the everyday, and their figures were recognizably representative of particular social strata. A perceptive contemporary critic, Champfleury, made the point when he asserted that the *Burial at Ornans* "represents *a* small-town funeral and yet reproduces the funerals of *all* small towns." And it was particularly in the depiction of people that the principle could be observed: "The triumph of the artist who paints unique entities is to . . . choose a type in such a manner that everyone thinks he has known him, and can exclaim: 'That one is real: I have seen him!' The *Burial* possesses these qualities to the highest degree. . . . "[11]

To a significant extent the air of authenticity conveyed by such paintings was achieved by their unconventional compositions. Steadfastly refusing to elevate their subjects by formal devices of grouping, balance, and perspective, the realists pioneered a new way of seeing, strongly influenced by photography. (Courbet himself used a camera in his work, as did the later realists Manet and Degas.) Composition, in their hands, became a question of painting the world "as it was," rather than disposing elements within the frame according to traditional formulas. Courbet and his followers erected the aesthetic standard of "sincerity," which entailed that rearrangement, to fulfill formal demands, of what the artist had observed and experienced in life could not be tolerated. If conservative critics then found the results unsettling, if they pleaded, "at least, let your stone-breaker not be an object as insignificant as the stone he is breaking," or averred, "The important thing is . . . to emphasize the interesting portions of such a scene," they were simply exposing the propensity to falsify inherent in their ideology.[12]

It was Edgar Degas who carried the new principles of composition the furthest. In work after work he flagrantly violated the classical norms which had characterized European easel painting since its Renaissance beginnings. Critics have often remarked upon his fondness for unusual, high- and low-angle viewpoints, resulting in unconventional foreshortening. Equally important is his penchant (shared with Manet) for severing parts of heads and bodies at the edge of the frame; his lopsided arrangement of items within the scene; his evocation of movement in multiple, opposed directions; and, most provocative of all, his collocation of depicted figures whose glances not only fail to converge, but are aimed at odd angles, into the depths of the scene or outside the picture space altogether. Degas's images, with their apparently fortuitous arrangement, established realism as a mode of accurately capturing random moments from the flux of time, while their hints at the existence of out-of-frame space suggested a new sense in which the picture could be regarded as a window on the world.

Degas also brought to the visual arts a passion for documenting in quasi-systematic series. Comparable to the desire of social realist novelists—especially Naturalists like Emile Zola and Frank Norris—to describe environments in minute detail, Degas's aspiration was to observe and record the overlooked appearances of the people, places, and things of daily life. In his notebooks, he set himself tasks such as:

> Do every kind of worn object . . . corsets which have just been taken off . . . series on instruments and intrumentalists . . . for example, puffing out and hollowing of the cheeks of bassoons, oboes, etc. . . . . On the bakery, the bread: series on journeyman bakers, seen in the cellar itself or through the air vents from the street. . . . No one has ever done monuments or houses from below, as one sees them going by in the streets.[13]

The major contributor to the realist tradition in the last decades of the nineteenth century was indubitably Zola. Linking, as Courbet had done, his politics and his aesthetics—"La République sera naturaliste," he declared, "ou elle ne sera pas"—Zola elaborated a theory of the "scientific" novel, and in the twenty volumes of the Rougon-Macquart cycle demonstrated the potentialities of a systematically deployed realism, a realism that, because of his innovations, he renamed "Naturalism."[14]

Naturalism differed from previous versions of realism in its overt claim to scientific validity. In essays such as *The Experimental Novel* (1880), Zola likened his approach to that of the chemist or physicist: "I am going to try and prove for my part," he asserted, "that if the experimental method leads to the knowledge of physical life, it should also lead to the knowledge of the passionate and intellectual life."

> In fact, the whole operation consists in taking facts in nature, then in studying the mechanism of these facts, acting upon them by the modification of circumstances and surroundings, without deviating from the laws of nature. Finally, you possess knowledge of the man, scientific knowledge of him, in both his individual and social relations.[15]

Since the method yielded truth, it was unnecessary for the novelist to take a partisan stand: in this Zola seconded Engels. "The novelist is but a recorder who is forbidden to judge and to conclude," he wrote. He distinguished his role from that of the politician, whose task it was to decide on social policies.

> I have often said that we do not have to draw a conclusion from our works; and this means that our works carry their conclusion with them. An experimentalist has no need to conclude, because, in truth, experiment concludes for him. A hundred times, if necessary, he will repeat the experiment before the public; he will explain it; but he need neither become indignant nor approve of it personally; such is the truth, such is the way phenomena work. . . .[16]

Critics have frequently pointed to the disparity between Zola's polemical endorsement of a rational, dispassionate mode of fiction writing and his own often highly colored, melodramatic, and vividly imaginative novels. There is one area, nevertheless, in which his practice was at least as important as his theory: his procedure of documentation. "In one sense," P. Martino wrote in his *Naturalisme Français (1870-1895)*, "all the novels of the Rougon-Macquart series are *documentary novels*," but there were several which particularly exhibited the trait, most significantly, perhaps, *L'Assommoir* (1877). Zola's study of the laundress Gervaise and her alcoholic husband was buttressed by the incorporation of evidence derived from nonfictional treatises such as Magnan's *De l'Alcoolisme* and Poulot's *Le Sublime*. To accusations of plagiarism, Zola replied:

> It is quite true that I took some information from *Le Sublime*. But you forget to point out that *Le Sublime* is not an imaginative work—a novel; it is a documentary work in which the author cries oral testimony and true facts. To borrow from it is to borrow from reality.[17]

Data culled from books was augmented by the results of direct observation in the field. Zola's practice of carrying out exhaustive research within the social milieus in which his novels were set was to become obligatory for subsequent realist writers.

Of especial significance for the later development of the realist aesthetic was the attenuation of plot which occurred when the tenets of the "experimental" novel were consistently adhered to. Zola's statement of this principle, contained in his article "Naturalism on the Stage," represents the first stirrings of the revolt against bourgeois narrative conventions which would preoccupy radical artists of fictional literature, and of the stage and screen, in the twentieth century:

> I have said that the naturalistic novel is simply an inquiry into nature, beings, and things. It no longer interests itself in the ingenuity of a well-invented story, developed according to certain rules. Imagination has no longer place, plot matters little to the novelist, who bothers himself with neither development, mystery, nor *dénouement;* I mean that he does not intervene to take away from or add to reality; he does not construct a framework out of the whole cloth, according to the needs of a preconceived idea. You start from the point that nature is sufficient, that you must accept it as it is, without modification or pruning; it is grand enough, beautiful enough to supply its own beginning, its middle, and its end. Instead of imagining an adventure, of complicating it, of arranging stage effects, which scene by scene will lead to a final conclusion, you simply take the life study of a person or a group of persons, whose actions you faithfully depict. The work becomes a report, nothing more; it has but the merit of exact observation, of more or less profound penetration and analysis, of the logical connection of facts. Sometimes, even, it is not an entire life, with a commencement and an ending, of which you tell; it is only a scrap of an existence, a few years in the life of a man or a woman, a single page in a human history, which has attracted the novelist in the same way that the special study of a mineral can attract a chemist.[18]

Finally, Zola's influence was felt in his selection of genuinely working-class subjects, ranging from the laundresses of *L'Assommoir* to the railroad engineers of *La Bête Humaine* and the miners of *Germinal* (1885). This last novel, dating from the beginning of the period in which Zola identified himself with socialist causes, had particular significance in dealing directly with an episode in the class struggle and in taking for its protagonist a radical union organizer. If social realism has since come to specialize, in the hands of militant writers, in the depiction of strikes, the development can be traced to *Germinal's* exposé of intolerable working conditions and the battle to right them, an exposé which, for all Zola's protestations, is suffused with passion.

In the theatre, the aesthetic of realism entered a new dimension. The painter was limited to pigments on canvas, the novelist to words on paper; but the stage director, in the campaign for an illusionistic representation of reality, had a diverse arsenal at his command: actors, costumes, sets, props, lighting, sound effects, even scents. Zola, theoretician of the new movement though not himself a major playwright, insisted that the assault on prevalent Romantic conventions in the theatre required a coordinated drive in which every weapon was pointed in the same direction: towards Naturalism.

...everything is interdependent in the theatre. Lifelike costumes look wrong if the sets, the diction, the plays themselves are not lifelike. They must all march in step along the naturalistic road. When costumes become more accurate, so do sets; actors free themselves from bombastic declaiming; plays study reality more closely and their characters are more true to life. I could make the same observations about sets as I have just made about costume.... Most of all we would need to intensify the illusion in reconstructing the environments, less for their picturesque quality than for dramatic utility. The environment must determine the character.[19]

The naturalist theatre may be dated from the opening of André Antoine's Théâtre Libre in Paris in 1887. A play adapted from a Zola story, Léon Hennique's *Jacques Damour,* was selected for the theatre's first presentation. Its effect on the audience has been recreated by Mordecai Gorelik:

We are no longer looking at some fledgling actors on a makeshift stage. Instead we have stumbled into the backroom of a Paris butcher shop. The people before us are vivid Parisian types, who go on about their daily activities unaware that they have been transplanted to a stage for us to gaze at. The furniture around them... also looks as if it had been in long contact with daily life instead of having been carried in from the property studio.

Like Courbet's stone-breakers, who are seen from behind, the principal actor "even plays whole scenes with his back turned."[20]

Within a few years the Théâtre Libre would be followed by the Freie Bühne, Freie Volksbühne (sponsored by the Social Democratic Party), and Neue Freie Volksbühne in Berlin; by the Independent Theatre in London; and by the Moscow Art Theatre. From the early 1890s David Belasco, in the United States, adopted meticulous Naturalist staging techniques, though his presentations veered toward the picturesque. The movement, for a time, attracted the greatest dramatists of the day—Ibsen, Strindberg, Hauptmann, Shaw, Chekhov, Gorky—whose plays keenly dissected bourgeois morality and occasionally entered the milieu of the working class (Hauptmann's *The Weavers,* 1892) or lumpenproletariat (Gorky's *The Lower Depths,* 1902).

The movement's most enduring legacy in the theatre was the method of acting developed by Konstantin Stanislavsky at the Moscow Art Theatre. It was dedicated to a concept of psychological realism, of the revelation of an inner truth corresponding to the outer truths embodied in authentic detail of dialogue, costumes, and sets. Though its implementation basically entailed exercises to develop concentration and relaxation, to establish easy rapport between the player's conscious will and unconscious desires, its starting point was the twofold investigation/reproduction of the world at large which lies at the root of all branches of realism. Stanislavsky defined the process in this way:

When the inner world of the man the actor is observing is revealed in his actions, thoughts, or impulses, the actor should devote all his attention to the study of those actions. He should...try to understand the character of the man. When after a prolonged and penetrating process of observation and investigation he is successful in this task, he will obtain valuable creative material for his work on the stage. It often happens, however, that the inner life of the man the actor is observing is not accessible to his reason, but only to his intuition. In that case, he should try to find a way into the innermost recesses of the man's mind and look there for the material of his creative work with the help of as it were, "the antennae of his own feelings." This process requires very delicate powers of observation of the actor's own subconscious mind.... While waiting for science to discover the practical approaches towards an understanding of a man's soul, the actor must do his best to learn how to discern the logic and consistency of its feelings and workings.[21]

It is unsurprising that Stanislavsky shared the distrust felt by Engels and Zola towards ideologically committed works. "Tendentiousness and art are incompatible," he argued: "the one excludes the other. As soon as one approaches the art of the stage with tendentious, utilitarian, or any other non-artistic idea, it withers away."[22] Since realism was considered no simple stylistic convention, but a means of discovering and expressing social and psychological truths, it seemed reasonable to conclude that the imposition of a priori schema could do harm by impeding the cognitive process. Some of the greatest battles of modern radical theatre and film were to be fought over precisely this point.

Social realism was the aesthetic most widely adopted by progressive artists and writers—liberal-democratic and socialist—in Europe in the nineteenth century. In the United States, social realism flourished somewhat later, predominantly after the turn of the century. This is no doubt related to the fact the the Socialist party was slower in developing than its European equivalents, and that the post-Civil War wave of immigration which was to contribute so greatly to the growth of the industrial proletariat and subproletariat in the cities did not crest until after 1900.[23]

Apart from Belasco's experiments in the theatre, American realism achieved its first significant expression in the novel. Works such as Stephen Crane's *Maggie: A Girl of the Streets* (1893), Frank Norris's *McTeague* (1899) and *The Octopus* (1901), Theodore Dreiser's *Sister Carrie* (1900) and *Jennie Gerhardt* (1912), and Sherwood Anderson's *Marching Men* (1917) brought American readers in contact with the brutal, unsentimental, vividly detailed Naturalist world which the French had encountered in the writings of Zola. Even more than Zola, however, the American writers had difficulty emancipating themselves from the melodramatic inheritance of nineteenth-century Romanticism; as a result, realism in the United States has tended towards uncharacteristic extremes, towards violence and death. Norris even considered this feature to be crucial:

The naturalist takes no note of common people, common in so far as their interests, their lives, and the things that occur in them are common, are ordinary. Terrible things must happen to the characters of the naturalistic tale. They must be twisted from the ordinary, wrenched out from the quiet, uneventful round of everyday life, and flung into the throes of a vast and terrible drama that works itself out in unleashed passions, in blood, and in sudden death.[24]

An important precedent was established with the publication of Upton Sinclair's *The Jungle* in 1906. Appearing at the height of the muckraking era, this study of the lives of Chicago stockyard workers came out shortly after an attempt at unionization had been crushed, and coincided with powerful lobbying campaigns for pure food legislation and antitrust indictments against large monopolists including the meat-packing firms of Armour and Swift. Sinclair's immensely influential novel secured the role of realist literature as a weapon in mobilizing public support over specific and topical political issues.

The Jungle, in accord with Sinclair's personal commitments, takes a socialist direction; a number of other less well-known novels of the period also plunged militantly into arenas of class conflict. Isaac Kahn Friedman's *By Bread Alone* (1901), for example, described a strike at a steel mill; Leroy Scott's *The Walking Delegate* (1905) investigated the struggle for power in New York locals of the Iron Worker's Union; Ernest Poole's *The Harbor* (1915) dealt with a longshoremen's strike; while both James Oppenheim's *The Nine-Tenths* (1911) and Arthur Bullard's *Comrade Yetta* (1913) were exposés of sweatshop conditions inspired by the notorious Triangle Shirtwaist fire of 1911.[25]

Such subjects understandably became rare in fiction of the twenties, when the Socialist party and the IWW had been virtually extinguished, the AFL acquiesced conservatively in the might of American capitalism, and the Communist party was a fledgling semilegal organization with only tiny pockets of support. Nevertheless something of the realist tradition survived in the work of Sinclair Lewis *(Main Street, Babbitt)* and Upton Sinclair *(Oil!, Boston).* And perhaps the culminating achievement of American Naturalism appeared during the decade: Dreiser's *An American Tragedy* (1925). Relying heavily on documentary sources, the story of Clyde Griffiths was based closely on the Chester Gillette murder case of 1906. Dreiser incorporated in the text, sometimes verbatim, statements of attorneys, witnesses, and the judge in the trial of Gillette, as well as published love letters of the victim. The result, a powerful indictment of capitalist society and its values, may be seen as vindicating Engels's belief in literature that "shatters the optimism of the bourgeois world."[26]

In painting, no strong social realist movement took root in the United States prior to the 1930s. In general, those artists who escaped the provincialism of the American art scene in the nineteenth century and were not caught up with the modernist experimentation of the twentieth devoted themselves to traditional landscapes and portraiture. An exception is Thomas P. Anschutz, whose remarkable *Iron Workers' Noon-Day Rest* (also known as *Steelworkers— Noontime,* c. 1880) combines a realism of rendition and grouping suggestive of

Degas with a defiantly working-class subject matter. Among Anschutz's pupils were Robert Henri and other Philadelphia painters—John Sloan, William Glackens, George Luks, and Everett Shinn—who would achieve brief prominence as the nucleus of an independent group, the "Eight," which exhibited in New York in 1908. The "Ashcan School," as they later came to be known, adopted a realist style modeled on Manet, Degas, Renoir, and Toulouse-Lautrec, and included in their work scenes drawn from the more mundane and seamier sides of urban life: the elevated railroad, barrooms, docks. Only Sloan, however, who was a socialist later closely associated with the *Masses,* systematically explored the tenement districts in search of subjects for his art, and his work, in the words of one critic, "reveals the strain of forging a romantic idiom around the refractory materials of the new naturalism."[27]

Social realism on the stage also made only sporadic appearances prior to the Depression. Belasco's extraordinarily lifelike settings (in *Tiger Rose,* 1917, a forest scene was embellished with pine-needles "upon which the actors trod, wafting the scent into the auditorium"[28]) were coupled to vehicles of bathetic romanticism. In the twenties, although leftward-leaning playwrights were drawn predominantly toward expressionism (exemplified, for instance, by Elmer Rice's *The Adding Machine*), there did emerge a handful of plays whose radical content was given a realistic treatment. Garland Anderson's *Appearances* (1925), the first full-length play by a black to be staged on Broadway, dealt with a bellhop falsely accused of raping a white woman and threatened with lynching. Paul Green's *In Abraham's Bosom* (1926) also broke with stereotypical representations of blacks; unexpectedly awarded the Pulitzer Prize, it gave impetus to the move for greater realism. The New Playwrights' Theatre (1927-29), an association of progressive dramatists John Howard Lawson, Michael Gold, Em Jo Basshe, Francis Edwards Faragoh, and John Dos Passos, flirted with a variety of symbolist, expressionist, and constructivist styles, but did plump for realism in several influential productions including Paul Sifton's *The Belt,* treating workers faced with speed-up on the assembly line in a company town; Basshe's *The Centuries,* a portrait of life in a lower East Side tenement house; and Upton Sinclair's *Singing Jailbirds,* based on his experiences when arrested for supporting a Marine Transport Workers strike in California in 1923.[29]

There was thus in the older arts of literature, painting, and theatre a long and continuing tradition of social realism on which aspiring radical filmmakers could draw when the stock-market crash of October 1929 plunged the nation into the Great Depression. The same could not be said of the cinema. It was true that American filmmakers had established a convention of authenticity in sets, props, and costumes which at times reached obsessive proportions, especially with historical subjects. Thus for D.W. Griffith's *The Birth of a Nation* (1915), "All properties such as weapons, uniforms, furniture, costumes . . . were carefully modeled on the best obtainable data in which every effort was made to have the picture authentic as an historical document."[30] In *America* (1924), Griffith used "the drum actually beaten at the Battle of Lexington, Major Pitcairn's pistols, flintlocks, vehicles, farming implements, and even garments of the Revolutionary period."[31] For *Old Ironsides* (1926), "the studio contracted for a seagoing replica of the *Constitution* to be constructed from the original blueprints, 'a life-size copy, perfect in every sail and sheet, and correct in every gun and timber.' "[32] That this fanatical quest for verisimilitude also manifested itself occasionally with contemporary stories may be seen from a review of the 1915 production *The Man from Oregon*, which stated, "If the Senate scenes were not photographed in the chamber itself, the set is one of the most remarkable ever constructed in a studio."[33] These films represented not exceptions, but extreme cases of the drive for realism of setting which dominated Hollywood style, whether shooting took place in the studio, on the back lot, or (as was not uncommon in the twenties) on location.

But there was nothing of *social* realism in this aesthetic. Analysis of Hollywood output of the silent era reveals a systematic evasion of working-class subjects. Of the more than 12,000 films reviewed or synopsized by *Moving Picture News* (later *Motion Picture News*) in the four years 1912-1915, fewer than sixty could be described as stories of workers, and among these many were antilabor in orientation. Similarly, of the 6,606 features listed in the *American Film Institute Catalog of Motion Pictures Produced in the United States, 1921-1930*, only about fifty deal seriously with proletarian characters, and then usually within a generic context which precludes any viewing of American society in a problematic light.[34] The few directors committed to social realism, such as Erich von Stroheim with his ill-fated adaptation of *McTeague, Greed* (1924), were lone, isolated figures. What was true of Hollywood was generally true of the rest of the world—with the exception of the Soviet Union, of course, which was a special case. It is not surprising, therefore, that budding filmmakers anxious to develop a left-wing aesthetic in the thirties looked elsewhere for their inspiration.

Their quest took the form of an abandonment of fiction for documentary. If social realism was indeed a mode of inquiry into the real world, it now began to seem that the construction of characters, the invention of plot, were superfluous to the main thrust of the operation, and perhaps even threatening to it. The extreme melodrama to which Naturalism tended in the hands of some practitioners (and *Greed* was an example of this) may have confirmed this opinion.

There was a precedent for this move away from fiction in the eyewitness reportage of such writers as the police reporter turned social reformer (and photographer) Jacob Riis. William Scott has noted, in his *Documentary*

Expression and Thirties America, that in the nineteenth century the primary literary vehicle for exploring social conditions was the novel; Riis broke with this tradition by directly describing life in the poorer sections of New York City in an influential series of exposés which included *How the Other Half Lives* (1890), *Children of the Poor* (1892), *The Battle with the Slum* (1902), and *Children of the Tenements* (1903). Avowed revolutionary socialist Jack London, whose fiction gravitated towards exotic adventure and apocalyptic fantasy, renounced the novel format for his skin-crawling account of the East End of London, *The People of the Abyss* (1903), of which the following passage sets the tone:

> I thought it was cigar and cigarette stumps they were collecting, and for some time took no notice. Then I did notice.
>   *From the slimy, spittle-drenched sidewalk, they were picking up bits of orange peel, apple skin, and grape stems, and they were eating them. The pits of greengage plums they cracked between their teeth for the kernels inside. They picked up stray crumbs of bread the size of peas, apple cores so black and dirty one would not take them to be apple cores, and these things these two men took into their mouths, and chewed them, and swallowed them; and this, between six and seven o'clock in the evening of August 20, year of our Lord 1902, in the heart of the greatest, wealthiest, and most powerful empire the world has ever seen.*

If it had occurred in a novel, the passage would have incurred charges of exaggeration for effect; it achieves credibility because it occurs in a book in which seemingly nothing is invented, in which all has been personally witnessed by the author.[35]

Though Jacob Riis used a camera for only a decade, in the years 1888-98, his impact on the documentary mode was probably as great as a photographer as it was as a writer. *How the Other Half Lives* was the first such book to be illustrated with photographs, and he used photography consistently thereafter, both in his books and newspaper articles, and (in the form of lantern slides) to assist his lectures. His shots offered a unique portrait of slum life: tenement alleys, dumps at the river's edge, half-starved babies, sweatshops, street arabs, 2¢ restaurants, police station lodgers, saloons, gang hideouts. Riis's achievement was extraordinary, considering the limitations of the equipment then available to him and the style of image-making considered acceptable at that time in the photographic salons of the United States and Europe.

The tradition of documentary photography Riis founded was followed by another lone pioneer, Lewis W. Hine. Hine, a sociologist, used photographs to illustrate articles in the *Survey Graphic* and particularly, in the pre-World War I period, to buttress the campaign against child labor. Hine's shots of Ellis Island immigrants, newsboys, slum streets, peddlers, and children and adults at work in bakeries, glass works, mills, and coal mines captured the feel of working-class life in a way no other medium could. In the twenties Hine paid tribute to the role of labor in the industrial age in more optimistic studies of men and machines, culminating with a series documenting the construction of the Empire State Building.[36]

Documentary photography as practised by Riis and Hine was "straight" photography with a vengeance. There was no manipulation of the image, no cultivation of soft-focus effects, no printing on gum paper for "texture." Though emulsions were slow, and camera and tripod bulky and cumbersome, Riis and Hine struggled to achieve a spontaneous, unstudied effect, often by means of flash. A case in point is Riis's *Hunting River Thieves—Dock Rats Pursued by the Police at Night*. Like so many of Degas's paintings, the photographs of these men are suspended moments in time, sections of the visible world detached and displayed for members of the public who cannot or will not see for themselves.

Documentary film was less advanced, certainly in the United States. Split-reel and single-reel studies of handicrafts and industrial processes had proved fascinating to prewar audiences, but these had disappeared with the ascendance of the feature-length fictional movie in 1915-16. Succeeding them were compilations of war footage, occasional special productions such as *Starvation* (1920)—a documentary on the work of U.S. food commissioners in Europe after the war—and the ubiquitous travelogues. The major productions of the twenties, ambitious expansions of the travelogue format, relied heavily on romantic exoticism, and were all shot outside the United States: *Nanook of the North* (1922) in Canada, *Grass* (1925) in Turkey and Persia, *Moana* (1926) in Samoa, *Chang* (1927) in what was then Siam. There were also the newsreels, with their weekly quota of parades, politicians, disasters, flower shows, sports, and novelties. There was nothing on which to base a radical aesthetic here. Only small quantities of left-wing newsreel and one or two labor documentaries, notably *The Passaic Textile Strike* (1926), seem to have prefigured what was to come in the thirties.

The Soviet Union was a far more fertile source of documentary ideas. In the convulsions that shook cultural circles in Moscow and Petrograd in the wake of the Russian Revolution and Civil War, a powerful tendency to bypass art and go directly to life took hold. Sergei Eisenstein recalled that everywhere, around 1920,

> there was the same frenzied assault on art: the demand that its symptomatic "figurativeness" be supplanted by blunt reality; its content by absence of subject; its laws by arbitrary rules; its very existence by a concrete, realistic reconstruction of life, without fiction or plot as intermediary.[37]

Symptomatic of the tendency was Dziga Vertov, newsreel editor, documentary director, inventor of the theory of Kino-Eye, who regularly thundered his denunciations of theatrical film as an outmoded relic of bourgeois aesthetics. "The camera hasn't had a chance," he declared. "It was invented at a time when there was no country not under the sway of capital. The bourgeoisie had the diabolical idea of using this new toy to amuse the masses, or more precisely to sidetrack workers from their main objective, the struggle against their bosses."[38]

Vertov's principles were expressed in a series of "elementary slogans" which he addressed to his co-workers, dubbed "kinoks":

1. The film-drama is the opium of the people.
2. Down with the immortal kings and queens of the screen! Long live ordinary human beings filmed from life following their normal occupations.
3. Down with bourgeois scenario-tales! Long live life as it is.
4. The film-drama and religion are deadly weapons in the hands of the capitalists. By demonstrating our revolutionary daily life, we will snatch these weapons from the hands of the enemy.
5. The present artistic drama is a relic of the old world. It is an attempt to channel our revolutionary reality into bourgeois forms.
6. Down with mise-en-scene of daily life: film people as they are, caught unawares.
7. The scenario is a tale fabricated about us by a man of letters. We live our lives without submitting to anyone's fabrications.
8. In life, we each attend to our own affairs without preventing others from working. The task of the kinoks is to film people without interfering with their work.
9. Long live the Kino-Eye of the proletarian revolution![39]

Vertov expressed more forcefully than most ideologues of the Left the conviction that bourgeois narrative film, through its emotional pull, was positively harmful to the spectator. The argument would later be applied by Brecht to the drama and developed into the theory of epic theatre. In 1924, Vertov wrote:

On the movie-house *habitué*, the ordinary fiction film acts like a cigar or cigarette on a smoker. Intoxicated by the cine-nicotine, the spectator sucks from the screen the substance which soothes his nerves. A cine-object made with the materials of newsreel largely sobers him up, and gives him the impression of a disagreeable-tasting antidote to the poison.[40]

The theory of Kino-Eye called for a distinct style of shooting which was to have a significant impact on the growth of the documentary movement. There was the idea of candid camera, of disguising the presence of the filmmaker in order to capture a record of spontaneous behavior. The camera operator was required to be constantly on the alert, ready to snatch telling images at a moment's notice. And highly importantly, the kinok's camerawork was *mobile*.

I am Kino-eye. I am a mechanical eye.
I, a machine, show you the world as only I can see it.
Today, I free myself forever from human immobility, *I am in constant motion*, I approach objects, I draw away from them, I slide under them, I perch on top of them, I keep abreast of

the nose of a galloping horse, I force my way into the middle of a crowd, I run ahead of charging soldiers, I turn on my back, I take off in airplanes, I fall and rise with falling and rising bodies.

This is I, apparatus, darting after all that happens, maneuvering in the chaos of movements, recording movement by means of movement in the most complex combinations.[41]

Vertov was an influential figure as much for his practice as for his theory. His various series of newsreels—*Kinonedielia* (43 issues, 1918-19), *Kino-Pravda* (23 issues, 1922-25), *Goskino-Kalendar* (50 issues, 1923-25)[42]—placed the worker in center screen as never before in film history. His compilations of newsreel footage—*Anniversary of the Revolution* (1919), *History of the Civil War* (1922), etc.—gave a left-wing inflexion to the subtradition of documentary as an ex post facto creation which had been initiated in capitalist countries during the war. And finally, his mature, preplanned feature-length documentaries—*Kino-Glaz* (1924), *Forward, Soviet!* (1926), *One Sixth of the World* (1926), *The Eleventh Year* (1928), *The Man with the Movie Camera* (1929), and others—the making of which often entailed intercutting footage from many teams of camera operators sent to locations all over the U.S.S.R., convincingly demonstrated the possibilities of nonnarrative thematic structure in film.

Many of Vertov's ideas were taken over by the British documentary movement which began to coalesce in 1929 around the person of John Grierson at the Empire Marketing Board. The fact that Soviet doctrines could be adopted and in some cases expanded outside the confines of a socialist society was to have a strong impact on the international growth of documentary styles. Without Vertov's revolutionary convictions, the British documentarians nevertheless shared his belief in a cinema centered on ordinary working people in their daily lives, and his abhorrence for fictional narrative and studio sets. "Let cinema attempt the dramatization of the living scene and the living theme, springing from the living present instead of from the synthetic fabrication of the studio," Paul Rotha, chronicler of the movement, was to write. "Let cinema attempt film interpretations of modern problems and events, of things as they really are today...."[43]

Vertov was intoxicated by machinery; less excitable, the British however also regarded documentary as an appropriate aesthetic response to the industrial age. Rotha argued that contemporary individualism in the fine arts was "the ultimate outcome of the refusal to face the changes brought about by the Industrial Revolution, when artists fled to ivory castles of lofty idyllism and covered their faces before the onslaught of the machine and the smoke clouds of coal...."[44] Documentary was accordingly a coming-to-terms with the facts of life of the twentieth century.

It was this confrontation with contemporary reality that the studio film was ill-equipped to accomplish. Adopting a quasi-Marxist approach, Rotha held that it was to be expected that commercial cinema should "reflect the ideology of a hypocritical society, and continue to be divorced from the realities of this world in which it is made." In less political terms, Grierson expressed the same case for documentary:

> We believe that the cinema's capacity for getting around, for observing and selecting from life itself, can be exploited in a new and vital art form. The studio films largely ignore this possibility of opening up the screen on the real world. They photograph acted stories against artificial backgrounds. Documentary would photograph the living scene and the living story.[45]

From the Soviet cinema, from Vertov and from Eisenstein's concept of the "mass hero," Grierson drew the idea of a film form in which the individual was no longer dominant; in this he broke decisively with the romantic aesthetics of Robert Flaherty, director of *Nanook of the North* and *Moana*.

> You may, like Flaherty, go for a story form, passing in the ancient manner from the individual to the environment, to the environment transcended or not transcended, to the consequent honors of heroism. Or you may not be so interested in the individual. You may think that the individual life is no longer capable of cross-sectioning reality. You may believe that its particular belly-aches are of no consequence in a world which complex and impersonal forces command, and conclude that the individual as a self-sufficient dramatic figure is outmoded.[46]

A consequence of not centering upon individual protagonists was the possibility of dispensing altogether with actors (and talented nonprofessionals). For Grierson this was all to the good. "We believe," he wrote, "that the original (or native) actor, and the original (or native) scene, are better guides to a screen interpretation of the modern world." This phase of the documentary credo had, of course, also been formulated in the Soviet Union, where Lev Kuleshov in 1929 had given it perhaps its definitive expression:

> If we simply choose a person, having no relationship to the theatre, and make him do what we need, we shall see that his work on the screen appears better than the work of a theatre actor and will give us more realistic material, from which subsequently it will be easier to construct a cinema film. If, finally, you photograph an organized process of work, this sequence—and only this sequence—will yield substantial cinematographic results. If you film a real stevedore, who is loading a bale, you will see that he strives to work in a way most advantageous to him, in order that in the shortest time with minimum effort he will complete his task. In the course of long years of work, he has developed certain habits of standardized, working gestures: he lifts the sacks deftly, drops them onto his shouders, carries them well, simply, and economically, unloads them, etc. This sort of work produces the clearest, most expressive, most efficient results on the screen.[47]

With all these tenets held in common, the British documentarians nevertheless parted from their Soviet counterparts at the crucial point of radical politics and its aesthetic consequences. Grierson, observes Alan Lovell, "never refers to class and seems content with the existing hierarchical order of Society."[48] When Grierson's exemplary first film, *Drifters* (1929), was exhibited in the U.S. in the summer of 1930, the absence of any evidence of class struggle provoked a decisive reaction from two critics of the Left who were soon to provide a major inspiration for the American radical film movement of the thirties.

"Where are the people in his film?" demanded Harry Alan Potamkin in *Close Up*. "He is more engrossed with the *independent graces* of fish in the water—well-done details in themselves, but no part of the human process which the film was to be." And Potamkin continued:

> This was a film intended to show labor. If Mr. Grierson thought to extend it to inferences beyond the facts of toil, to the total economy of exploitation, his attempts at inter-reference between sea and market, fisher and broker, were certainly too inadequate. The intention of labor is not fulfilled.[49]

In the *New Masses*, Samuel Brody drove home the same attack. Noting that there was "not a single facial close-up of the exploited fishermen in the whole film," he concluded:

> I believe that *Drifters* lacks "propaganda." Propaganda about the underpaid and exploited Shetlands fishermen. Propaganda against child labor in the fishing industry. Propaganda against the class responsible for the misery of impoverised proletarian fishermen. The class struggle is an even greater actor than the sea, Mr. Grierson, and the driving mate is fiercer than all the man-eating whales in the world.[50]

It was a question of emphasis in the shooting of the film, then: a failure to fix on the human—and political—dimensions of the herring fishermen's lives. But for Potamkin and Brody it was more than this. The fundamental weakness of *Drifters* was its lack of a montage structure. The length at which the two reviews developed this point is instructive, since the concept of montage, and the way it was understood in the United States, is a key to the radical film aesthetic as it developed in the Depression years. Potamkin declared:

> The failure to recognize the method of montage as an integral process is the explanation of the sad attempts to sovietize films outside of the U.S.S.R. I have had the opportunity of seeing Grierson's *Drifters* at last; and it is the immediate provocation for my statement. . . . Grierson has said he derived the *energies* of his film from the U.S.A. cinema, the *intimacies* from that of the U.S.S.R. If these could be joined together, the result would be hybrid. Why did Mr. Grierson not seek his energies also in the Soviet kino? Montage is an expression of

the energies as well as of the intimacies. That is to say montage is the progression and the intensive unit.... Grierson, it must be said to his credit, sought to revitalize the documentation with a structural intention. Yet he did not bring to his desire for intimacies the scrutiny— the *overtonal interplay*—which such a revitalization demands.[51]

Brody's statement was even more explicit in its critique and its appeal to the Soviet model:

In the documentary film the scenario must serve the purpose of *organizing* already existing material so that the film will progress according to a preconceived idea which will act as a guide and lend character to the whole. Any other method will result in a mere compilation of scenes having logical sequence but devoid of the cumulative effect which is the first essential in a film. Until the Russians showed us the way, this was (and in America *still is*) the way reality was filmed. That is why we have learned to look upon the documentary as an unimportant item in filmmaking while the Russians have, with films like *Shanghai Document* and *Turksib,* raised it to the highest level of cinema achievement.

In *Drifters* we have an example of a film in which the director has approached his material without organizing it in such a way as to convey a particular idea or evoke a desired reaction from the onlooker. The effect is left to chance and the power of the filmed material itself to create an impression. This is the way of the "nature study" film. It is true that here and there we find in *Drifters* an attempt to compose certain effects by juxtaposition of pieces (montage), but to use montage methods to create isolated effects rather than to impart to the film a unified and appropriate rhythm, is to abuse a method which is the recognized cornerstone of film art.[52]

It was, as they indicate, from the Soviet film theorists, and particularly from Eisenstein (whom they had recently interviewed in New York), that Potamkin and Brody derived their notion of montage.[53] The term, as used by the Russians, embraced two quite distinct ideas. The first concerned their preferred method, within a given scene, of cinematic mise-en-scene and editing: employing short takes and a variety of camera angles and graphic compositions for maximum dramatic effect. This aesthetic choice, based as it was on a study (described by Kuleshov in his *Art of the Cinema*[54]) of Hollywood films, represented no decisive break with bourgeois forms of cinematic articulation (and was to prove easily assimilable within the conservative "socialist realist" style which emerged in the mid-thirties). The second idea carried much more subversive implications. This was Eisenstein's "intellectual" montage, the notion of extra-diegetic metaphor and its extension into montage "chains" constructed with abstract, conceptual links. With their reference to montage as an "intensive" method of filmic organization imparting "cumulative effect" to a series of shots which would otherwise, though having "logical sequence," be a "mere compilation," Potamkin and Brody indicated that it was the second meaning they were primarily concerned with.

Eisenstein explained his concept of intellectual montage by analogy with the Japanese ideogram. The process, for instance, of signifying "to weep" by yoking the picture for water and the picture of an eye was, he claimed, exactly parallel to

> what we do in the cinema, combining shots that are *depictive*, single in meaning, neutral in content—into *intellectual* contexts and series.
>
> This is a means and method inevitable in any cinematographic exposition. And, in a condensed and purified form, the starting point for the "intellectual cinema."[55]

Specific examples of intellectual montage cited by Eisenstein include, from Pudovkin's work, the combination of a workers' demonstration with ice breaking on the river (*Mother,* 1926), and of the stock exchange and the battlefield in *The End of St. Petersburg* (1927); and from his own work, the intercutting of the killing of workers with the butchering of a bull (*Strike,* 1925), and particularly, several sequences in *October* (1928).

October was in fact the film in which his experiments in this direction were taken the furthest. In a 1929 article, Eisenstein singled out "the sugary chants of compromise by the Mensheviki at the Second Congress of Soviets" intercut with hands playing harps, and the sequence showing the union of the Motorcycle Battalion with the Congress of Soviets, which was "dynamized by shots of abstractly spinning bicycle wheels." He also noted the "liberation of the whole action from the definition of time and space" which was achieved, he asserted, by the juxtaposition of symbolically related shots such as that of one of Kornilov's tanks with a plaster-of-Paris Napoleon on Kerensky's desk. The sequences on which he placed most emphasis in his analysis, however, were Kerensky's rise to power ("trotting up the same unchanging flight of stairs" while titles indicating his ascending ranks were inserted), and the religious ikon segment of Kornilov's advance on Petrograd. The latter he described as follows:

> Kornilov's march on Petrograd was under the banner of "In the Name of God and Country." Here we attempted to reveal the religious significance of this episode in a rationalistic way. A number of religious images, from a magnificent Baroque Christ to an Eskimo idol, were cut together. The conflict in this case was between the concept and the symbolization of God. While idea and image appear to accord completely in the first statue shown, the two elements move further from each other with each successive image. . . . Maintaining the denotation of "God," the images increasingly disagree with our concept of God, inevitably leading to individual conclusions about the true nature of all deities. In this case, too, a chain of images attempted to achieve a purely intellectual resolution, resulting from a conflict between a preconception and a *gradual discrediting of it in purposeful steps.*

In these two experiments Eisenstein declared he had taken "the first embryonic step towards a totally new form of film expression. Towards a purely intellectual film, freed from traditional limitations, achieving direct forms for ideas, systems, and concepts, without any need for transitions and paraphrases."[56]

Eisenstein speculated further on the possibility of the intellectual film—the film constructed entirely on the basis of intellectual montage—in several other essays pul·'ished in 1929. In "The New Language of Cinema" he wrote:

> The sphere of work of the new cinematographic principles seems to be the *direct screening of class-useful conceptions,* methods, tactics, and practical watchwords, not having recourse for this purpose to the aid of the suspect trappings of the dramatic and psychological past.... Whereas in the first case [at the earlier stage of the Soviet cinema] we were striving for a quick emotional *discharge,* the new cinema must *include deep reflective processes,* the result of which will find expression neither immediately nor directly.

And in "Perspectives," he defined the intellectual cinema as

> a synthesis of the emotional, the documentary, and the absolute film.
> Only an *intellectual* cinema can resolve the discord between the "language of logic" and the "language of images." Based on a language of film-dialectics.[57].

Eisenstein's insistence (against Pudovkin) that montage was not linkage but conflict or collision defined one of the key aspects of the concept: it focused attention on the shock effect produced by juxtaposing seemingly unrelated elements. A second key aspect was the notion that those elements should themselves be *documentary* in nature—taken directly and faithfully from reality.

"*Primo*: photo-fragments of nature are recorded," Eisenstein wrote, "*secundo*: these fragments are combined in various ways. Thus, the shot (or frame), and thus, montage." The directness of this reproduction of the real world he compared favorably with the realism of the Moscow Art Theatre, which he described as "my deadly enemy":

> It is the exact antithesis of all I am trying to do. They string their emotions together to give a continuous illusion of realism. I take photographs of reality and then cut them up so as to produce emotions.[58]

It was true that Eisenstein's films of the twenties were all based on extensive historical and sociological research—observation in the field, interviews, study of newsreels, scrutiny of newspaper reports, photographs, memoirs, papers[59]—but as a practitioner of what its enemies termed the "played" film he was not in a strong position to establish the claim of montage to factual veracity. This task was accomplished by the Soviet documentarians: Esther Shub and Dziga Vertov.

Shub, who introduced Eisenstein to the practice of editing while adapting · Lang's *Dr. Mabuse* for revolutionary audiences, applied the concept of montage to the documentary compilation film. Her three visual histories of Russian life—*The Fall of the Romanov Dynasty* (1927), *The Great Road*

(1927), and *The Russia of Nikolai II and Lev Tolstoy* (1928)—were no mere aggregations of footage in chronological sequence, but structures organized to reveal social truths by means of sharp and unexpected contrast. An example of her montage technique, from *The Fall of the Romanov Dynasty,* is given by Jay Leyda:

> A crowd of elegant idlers are dancing [a mazurka on the awninged deck of a yacht].
> The dancing tires some of them. They drink wine.
> Title: "It made them sweat."
> And again they dance.
> Title: "...sweat."
> A peasant, exhaused by his work, plows a furrow.... [60]

Shub had begun to explore the possibility of using newsreel footage to depict the past after seeing *Potemkin* (1926), whose script she had collaborated on with Eisenstein. Her subsequent success led her to the conclusion that her own method, utilizing only authentic period film, was superior to that of historical reconstruction by means of dramatization. Of *The Russia of Nikolai II and Lev Tolstoy,* she wrote:

> This montage must serve as an eloquent illustration of the fact that any available acting method for the historical film, no matter how good or talented, has only an ephemeral value in comparison with the chronicle film, which possesses a conviction that can never pale and can never age. [61]

For *Today* (*Cannons or Tractors,* 1930), Shub had recourse to foreign newsreels in building a contrast between capitalist and communist systems. Here, even more than before, she had an opportunity to demonstrate the montage principle of organizing fragments of actuality to make a forceful political statement (forceful enough for the film to be seized by police when about to be shown in Newark, New Jersey, in 1932). [62] Earlier, Eisenstein had remarked, apropos his intellectual montage experiments in *October,* "I would not attempt to deny that *this form is most suitable for the expression of ideologically pointed theses.*" In explaining her technique, Shub took a like position—and in doing so challenged, by implication, Engels's view that class relationships were best exposed by means of a nontendentious aesthetic approach:

> ...what interests us here is not the usual narrative montage, a consequence and corollary of cutting, but expressive montage, above all ideological. It is no accident that compilations so flourish in the U.S.S.R. It is natural that the country where the first theories of montage were formulated accords a leading position to the compilation film as an ideological weapon. One should keep in mind that montage is not a simple succession of shots, nor even a sum of their contents, but produces something new, something original. It is a remarkable application of

the Marxist law of dialectical change from quantity to quality. Montage rests fundamentally on the interaction of the images ... *ideological* montage aims at a precise political or moral point in putting together images which have no strictly causal or temporal relationship.[63]

On the question of montage, Vertov's practice and doctrine reveal a close congruence with that of Shub. Though working, predominantly, with images secured by design rather than "found" footage, he, too, constructed montage sequences whose connective logic was political-thematic and nonnarrative. He also, at times, utilized precisely the same "cannons or tractors" oppositional motif. Thus Georges Sadoul cites the following series of shots and linking titles from the fifth reel of *Forward, Soviet!*:

> *I am speaking to you in the name of the Soviet* (a loudspeaker) *We are fighting for our economy* (automobiles of spectators in the public square) *Instead of rifles* (...) *Hammers* (...) *Axes* (...) *Shovels* (...) *Instead of bullets* (...) *Screws* (...) *Nails* (...) *Bricks* (...) AND—*Railroads* (...) *Instead of ruins* (factories in operation, with smoke) *The derailed locomotive* (Shot of the locomotive reduced to scrap iron, as in the first reel) *Repaired* (Symphony of connecting rods, jets of steam, turning wheels, rails, etc.) *Where it was impossible to get through* (an auto bogged down, dragged out of a hole in the road by two horses) *Highways* (a road being paved—a steam roller) *Instead of cannons* (a threshing machine) *Instead of machine guns* ... (theodolite of surveyors in the process of leveling a stretch of ground) *Instead of shells* (a modern plow, with turning plowshares) *Instead of tanks* ... *Peaceful means* (a caterpillar tractor) ... [64]

Vertov sharply distinguished his concept of montage from what he termed the *collage* of shots filmed separately, following a scenario, in theatrical film. "Kinoks give 'montage' a quite different meaning," he explained, "for us it means the *organization of the visible world.*" Montage was not confined to the editing process, but was the ordering principle at every phase in the production of a film:

> FIRST PERIOD: The "Montage Evaluation" of all the documents which are directly or indirectly related to the chosen theme (manuscripts, various objects, film clippings, photographs, newspaper clippings, books, etc.). As a result of this montage which consists in picking and grouping the most precious documents or those simply useful, *the plan indicated by the theme* becomes crystallized, appears more evident, more distinct, more defined.
>
> SECOND PERIOD: *"Montage Synthesis" of the human eye* concerning the selected theme (montage of personal observation or of reports by the information-gatherers and scouts of the film). *Plan of shots,* as a result of the selection and classification of the observations of the "human eye." At the moment when this selection is made, the author takes into account the indications of the thematic plan as well as peculiarities of the "machine-eye" of Kino-Eye.
>
> THIRD PERIOD: *"General Montage,"* synthesis of the observations noted on the film under the direction of the "machine-eye." Calculation in figures of the montage groupings. Unification of homogeneous pieces; constantly, one displaces the pieces, the frames, until all shall have entered a rhythm, where all the ties dictated by the meaning shall be those which

coincide with the visual ties. As a result of all these mixtures, of all these displacements and of all these reductions, we have a kind of visual equation, a visual formula. This formula, this equation, which is the result of the general montage of the cine-documents recorded on the film, is one hundred percent the cine-thing: I see, I cine-see.[65]

Early in his career Vertov had experimented, in the same vein as Kuleshov (and in the tradition of the "documentary compositions and musico-literary word-montages" he had created in his "sound laboratory" before the Revolution), with the montage of strips of film taken at different times and in different places, and had enthusiastically endorsed the results. Further research led him to the conclusion that "the extraordinary flexibility of montage construction allows for the introduction, in a film étude, of any political or economic motif"—one is reminded of Eisenstein's plan to film *Capital*. Moreover, montage as practiced according to Kino-Eye principles became a means, not only of scoring ideological points (Shub), but of structuring the insights gained by documentary camerawork so as to reveal significant truths of the social system: *Kino-Pravda,* cinema-truth.

> It is not sufficient to show on the screen isolated fragments of truth, separate images of truth; it is necessary to organize these images *thematically* so that truth emerges from the whole.

Vertov thus reaffirmed the claim to a cognitive function which has characterized the left-wing realist aesthetic since its earliest formulation.[66]

In Western Europe, Soviet documentary montage experiments had repercussions in the film societies of Antwerp, Amsterdam, and Berlin. Radical filmmakers such as Joris Ivens and Béla Balázs began a practice of recutting commerical newsreels in order to alter their class orientation, driving home a political message missing from the footage in its original form. Here, too, the dominant ordering principle became that of conflict of oppositions, for example:

> Skating rinks and the guests on the terrace of a luxury hotel. "This, too, is St. Moritz": a melancholy procession of ragged, hungry snow-shovelers and rink-sweepers . . . A "Brilliant Military Parade" was followed by disabled ex-servicemen begging in the streets.

The success achieved by this re-editing in subverting the intended meaning of the film as released was noted, and spurred similar efforts by radical organizations internationally during the Depression years.[67]

The possibilities of using montage, as here understood, as an aesthetic device were by no means confined to film. Of its various manifestations in the other arts in the period following the First World War, perhaps the most significant both intrinsically and in terms of implications for the cinema were photomontage and the political theatre of Erwin Piscator.

Photomontage was an invention of the Berlin dadaists.[68] Its aetiology is to be traced in the ruptured surface of the dada poem, which dislocated the customary flow of language to express a novel, cross-sectional perception of the world. As Richard Huelsenbeck wrote in his *Dadaist Manifesto,*

> The   BRUITIST poem
> represents the streetcar as it is, the essence of the streetcar with the yawning of Schulze the *rentier* and the screeching of the brakes.
> The   SIMULTANEIST poem
> teaches a sense of the merry-go-round of all things; while Herr Schulze reads his paper, the Balkan Express crossed the bridge at Nisch, a pig squeals in Butcher Nuttke's cellar.

It was only logical that such forms of expression should also find visual form. Raoul Hausmann, another member of the Berlin Dada Club and self-proclaimed inventor of photomontage, explained:

> The Dadaists, who had "invented" static, simultaneous, and phonetic poetry, applied the same principles to visual representation. They were the first to use photography to create, from often totally disparate spatial and material elements, a new unity in which was revealed a visually and conceptually *new* image of the chaos of an age of war and revolution. And they were aware that their method possessed a power for propaganda purposes which their contemporaries had not the courage to exploit. . . .[69]

The early dada forays into this new artistic territory resulted in kaleidoscopic jumbles of imagery, often incorporating snippets of newspaper headlines and hand-drawn graphic elements, arranged with a defiant whimsy calculated to impress on the viewer the chance nature of the grouping. John Heartfield's *Dada Photomontage,* Hanna Höch's *Cut with the Cake-Knife* (both 1919), and George Grosz's *My Germany* (1920) are good examples of this.[70] But photomontage soon left such wildness behind for a much more controlled, concentrated, purified form of juxtaposition, sometimes comprising as few as two elements, and having, often decidedly political connotations.

In Germany, the major exponent of the new trend was John Heartfield, former dadaist whose evolution towards a more directly political art was no doubt quickened by his exposure to revolutionary street fighting in 1919 (he was a founding member of the KPD—the German Communist Party—at the beginning of that year). Heartfield was associated with left-wing publishing ventures, and his photomontage designs were usually conceived for books or for newspapers and magazines, particularly the weekly *Arbeiter Illustrierte Zeitung.*

Typical of Heartfield's blunt, searing style in his *Nach Zehn Jahren: Väter und Söhne* (1924). In the lower half of the composition, a squad of young uniformed boys carrying rifles march toward us; above them, a variegated row of skeletons stand out starkly white against the black background. At the right, an elderly Junker in military attire (Hindenburg?) stands full-length and head on, dominating the arrangement. The political meaning is conveyed by a brutal, shocking contrast requiring only a simple verbal tag ("fathers and sons") for its implications to become abundantly clear.[71]

Heartfield often sought to impart a documentary quality to his work by incorporating in his compositions photographs of well-known buildings (such as the Reichstag) and public figures (particularly after the rise of fascism, when Hitler, Goebbels, von Papen *et al.* were featured frequently). Unlike a political cartoonist, "Monteur" Heartfield (as the dadaists called him) strove not to distort the individual features of his subjects—even on occasion advertising the authenticity of his representations. Thus *Goering the Executioner* (1933), which shows the Nazi minister in bloodspattered butcher's apron ferociously gripping a chopper before a burning Reichstag, carries the statement: "The face of Goering is taken from an original photograph and has not been retouched."[72]

In the U.S.S.R., a strong school of photomontage arose in the twenties around the figures of Gustav Klutsis, El Lissitsky, and Alexander Rodchenko. Centering on themes of socialist construction, their work tended to employ the style of contrast familiar from montage documentary film: thus in *Transport Achievement of the First Five-Year Plan* (1929) by Klutsis a woman on a camel is dwarfed by a steam locomotive towering behind her. (In her book *Photomontage,* Dawn Ades comments: "Klutsis's celebration of railway construction has similarities with Viktor Turin's film *Turksib,* on the building of the Turkestan-Siberian railway, which also juxtaposes the old method of transport [camel] with the new.") Photomontage undoubtedly influenced the growth of film montage theory, particularly via Rodchenko, who designed title sequences and posters for Vertov's films and was associated with Eisenstein in the LEF group: Eisenstein, in his first published article (1923), remarked that his concept of "montage of attractions" was "fully analagous with the 'pictorial storehouse' employed by George Grosz, or the elements of photographic illustration [photomontage] employed by Rodchenko."[73]

John Heartfield collaborated, as a designer, with Erwin Piscator in the creation of experimental left-wing theatre in Germany in the twenties.[74] The principle of Piscator's staging as he developed it through the decade, notably at the Berlin Piscator-Bühne in 1927-28 and again 1929-30, was that of a montage of documentary material, presented in various media, whose juxtaposition pointed to a political interpretation of the action depicted. Thus in his production of Ernst Toller's *Hoppla! Wir Leben* (1927), Piscator incorporated a compilation of newsreel footage (edited by Walther Ruttman) covering significant events in the ten-year period prior to the protagonist's release from an asylum: the Russian Revolution, Mussolini's march on Rome, the Munich *putsch,* the execution of Sacco and Vanzetti were included.[75] In *Rasputin,* which came next,

Piscator used three film projectors and two thousand meters of film. The stage setting was shaped like a segment of a globe which opened in sections and turned on revolving platforms. The globe itself formed one projection screen; another screen hung above it, while at one side of the stage a narrow filmic "calendar" kept marginal notes on the multitude of events, giving dates and footnotes.[76]

The actress Tilla Durieux recalled the effect of this technique in one scene:

I was in my boudoir with my lady-in-waiting. We were not yet fully aware of the danger, and conversed gaily. Suddenly, on the film next to the segment of the open stage on which I stood, I saw the Red Army troops on the march. I was so shaken up that I forgot my lines and couldn't go on. It is hard to understand, and then I wondered how terrifying the impression must have been to the audience at that moment.[77]

In the same production, in what was according to Brecht probably the first occasion on which records had been used in a stage performance, a recording of Lenin's voice was played, interrupting the action.[78]

But perhaps Piscator's most provocative experiment in montage theatre—because of its approximation to a strictly documentary technique—pre-dated his work at the Piscator-Bühne. This was his production of *Trotz Alledem!* (In Spite of Everything) at the Grosses Schauspielhaus in Berlin, July 12, 1925, for the opening of the KPD party convention that year. The play, collectively written, was an "historical revue of the years 1914 to 1919 in 24 scenes with interspersed films" covering political events from the outbreak of the war to the murder of Rosa Luxemburg and Karl Liebknecht. As Piscator described it:

The whole performance was a unique montage of authentic speeches, articles, newspaper clippings, proclamations, broadsheets, photographs, and films of the war and the revolution, of historical figures and scenes.[79]

In one characteristic juxtaposition, a scene showing a meeting of the Reichstag Social Democratic caucus on August 2, 1914, was immediately succeeded by the projection of newsreel footage depicting mobilization, troops on the march, and the beginning of the slaughter at the front. Piscator commented:

When, for example, the vote of the Social Democrats on war credits (played scene) was followed by film which showed a storm attack and the first deaths, this not only defined the political character of the event, but also provoked a feeling of shock, and thus created art. It proved that the strongest political-propaganda effect lay in the direction of the strongest artistic formulation.[80]

The concept of montage as used in this chapter has been defined by Ben Brewster as applying to "a work whose openness and heterogeneity is characterized by assembling (simultaneously or successively) a series of strongly homogeneous units within a deliberately incongruous frame (e.g. Heartfield's photomontages, Piscator's stagings, Eisenstein's films, particularly *October* and *The General Line*)."[81] It is clear that this represents a decisive break with certain of the conventions of social realism, as Eisenstein's vehement rejection of the Moscow Art Theatre model indicates.

In particular, montage is associated with a rupture of, or total disregard for spatial-temporal continuity; stage settings that are constructivist or functional rather than veristic; acting which is self-evidently a performance (or alternatively, the behavior of people who are playing no one but themselves) as against the psychological realism of the Stanislavsky school; in general, an attempt to incorporate the stuff of life itself, and not some counterfeit of it, within the artistic context.

The adoption of montage by avant-garde left-wing artists in the twenties can be seen as an attempt to overcome limitations which had become apparent in social realism as a Marxist aesthetic. New technologies—photography, film, sound recording—had made it possible to reproduce the surface textures of the world with greater verisimilitude than in the past, but in doing so they brought into question the political value of simple reproduction. Central to the thinking of montage artists was the belief that the apathy of spectators (they had in mind un-class-conscious workers) could only be punctured by techniques of shock and disruption, which entailed rearranging the picture of real life which was placed before them in order to disclose its contradictions. Bertolt Brecht, who opposed "montage" to "growth" and "jumps" to "evolutionary determinism" in his formulation of the principles of the new "epic" theatre, became after 1930 the foremost exponent of an aesthetic in which discontinuity and heterogeneity were deliberately employed in the hope of breaking the ideological chains of bourgeois society.[82]

Social realism had also been rendered aesthetically old-fashioned by movements in modern art which attacked its legacy, beginning with the disjunction of coherent time and space and ending with a rejection of representation itself. Following Cézanne, the cubists and futurists fractured a scene into discrete facets. In the theatre, the expressionists aggregated fragments of dialogue lacking ordinary conversational logic. The novel offered stream-of-consciousness techniques which decomposed action into fleeting subjective aperçus. By and large, Marxist artists and critics (Georg Lukács is the prime example[83]) stigmatized such modernist innovations as manifestations of bourgeois decadence; but their sway could not be entirely resisted. Part of the rationale of modern art, for example, is that it explores avenues of depicting the world in motion; clearly an art which claims to be based on dialectical materialism must make some concession to dynamism.

Montage was, then, an attempt to broach the limitations, both political and aesthetic, of social realism; but in contrast with the dominant movement of modern art in the capitalist world toward ever greater distortion and abstraction, it held fast to the principle of accurate representation of the "real" world. Ultimately it was a continuation, rather than the abandonment, of a tradition. Montage was social realism's compromise with the twentieth century; and within the new aesthetic the idea of documentary held pride of place. Pursued rigorously, montage had proved it could give shape to the construction of bold and stunning works of political art.

Yet because is was a compromise, it was unstable. There was always the possibility of older elements in the social realist tradition re-emerging to undermine the new. Within this volatile aesthetic context, American film-makers of the Left were to fight out their battles during the Depression decade.

2

The (Workers') Film and Photo League

The (Workers') Film and Photo League [(W)FPL] was part of the cultural movement sponsored by the Communist International and its affiliated national parties in the interwar period. Specifically, it was a section of the Workers' International Relief (WIR), American chapter of the Comintern-linked *Internationale Arbeiterhilfe* (IAH), which had been founded at Lenin's instigation in Berlin in 1921.[1]

The IAH's initial function was famine relief in the Volga region of the Soviet Union. After the crisis had passed, the organization—with branches established in many countries throughout the world—became an international support force for strikers and their families, and for victims of natural disasters such as the Japanese earthquake of 1923. Enlisting the endorsement of renowned artists and intellectuals including Käthe Kollwitz, Albert Einstein, George Grosz, Upton Sinclair, Bernard Shaw, Henri Barbusse, and Anatole France, and under the slogan "Not Charity, But Solidarity," the IAH undertook appeals for German workers in the wake of the uprisings of 1923-24, Chinese strikers during the Shanghai incidents of 1925, and British miners at the time of the 1926 general strike. In the United States, the WIR provided food, clothing, and shelter in the course of the Communist-led textile and cotton workers' strikes at Passaic (New Jersey), New Bedford (Massachusetts), and Gastonia (North Carolina), in 1926-29. As an extension of its relief activities the organization also ran summer camps for children, and in some places raised troops of "WIR scouts."

But the IAH's sphere of operations went far beyond relief; it grew to encompass the mass media and many cultural fields. In Germany, under the leadership of the remarkable Communist entrepreneur and propagandist Willi Münzenberg, the IAH built up a flourishing publishing empire embracing daily newspapers *(Die Welt am Abend, Berlin am Morgen),* illustrated periodicals *(Arbeiter Illustrierte Zeitung, Der Eulenspiegel),* and books (under the imprint of the Neuer Deutsche Verlag), all with a left-wing perspective. Elsewhere, with the exception of the Soviet Union (where the IAH's enterprises, particularly during the NEP period, were extensive), the organization concentrated on ventures requiring little or no capitalization. Thus in the United States, in the early thirties, the WIR sponsored the Workers' Laboratory Theatre, the Red Dancers, symphony and mandolin orchestras, bands, choirs, art workshops, etc.

Münzenberg was especially interested in film. In 1925 he published a pamphlet, *Erobert den Film!* (Capture the Film!), extracts from which were published in the U.S. *Daily Worker* of July 23, 1925. Münzenberg first drew attention to the growing significance of the cinema as a mass medium, a significance which, he claimed, might surpass that of the press in some countries:

> The total attendance in the movie theatres of England, France, and the United States is perhaps even today greater than the total number of newspaper readers in those countries.
> Even if the press were granted the greater numerical dissemination, let it not be forgotten that the film, through the medium of the visual picture, influences its patrons far more strongly and emphatically than does the printed word its readers.

He then noted the technical progress achieved in the medium, and in a passage recalling Vertov argued:

> We must develop the tremendous cultural possibilities of the motion picture in a revolutionary sense . . . the film must truthfully reflect social conditions instead of the lies and fables with which the bourgeois kind befuddles the workers, etc.[2]

Reviewing the meager efforts at film production by left-wing organizations to date, Münzenberg decried the fact that "in the main the labor organizations and even the Communist parties and groups have left this most effective means of propaganda and agitation in the hands of their enemy." Effective bourgeois exploitation of the cinema for propagandist purposes, on the other hand, had included the production of a series of monarchist and militarist movies released during the Hindenburg election campaign, and numbers of highly colored anti-Soviet concoctions.

Münzenberg concluded that the correct response was not to burn such films—as enraged Leipzig workers had done—but to turn the machinery by which they were produced to the use of the labor movement:

> One of the most pressing tasks confronting Communist parties on the field of agitation and propaganda is the conquest of this supremely important propaganda weapon until now the monopoly of the ruling class: we must wrest it from them and turn it against them.

The IAH's first motion-picture activity was in the Soviet Union, where in 1922 it began distributing German films. Two years later it made the break into production by forming the company Mezhrabpom-Russ (later Mezhrabpom-film, "Mezhrabpom" being the Russian acronym for the IAH). After turning out several movies in the pre-Revolutionary "artistic" tradition espoused by the members of the Russ collective,[3] the studio made a new departure with Yakov Protazanov's *His Call* (known in the U.S. as *Breaking Chains* or *Broken Chains*), released in 1925. Anticipating Eisenstein's *Strike* by two months, *Breaking Chains* was the first major Soviet film to be openly agitational: based on the appeal made after Lenin's death to enlarge the membership of the Communist party, it was a chronicle of life in contemporary Russia which "became, somehow, not the tale of persons but the story of a village, of a school, a Soviet meeting, to which came news of Lenin's death." Münzenberg boasted:

> This film was enormously successful throughout the world and marked a *turning point in the history of the Soviet cinema.* The systematic working influence of the IAH, which admittedly did not consult specialists in socialism, but nevertheless steered the project purposefully towards the political film, celebrated its first great victory. The proof was furnished that the great political film was not only important, but also possible, and this success pushed the other film studios in the right direction.[4]

Notable releases from the Mezhrabpom studio in following years included several other films by Protazanov, Boris Barnet's *Girl with the Hatbox* and *Moscow in October,* Pudovkin's *Mother, End of St. Petersburg, Storm over Asia,* and *Deserter,* Kuleshov's *The Great Consoler,* Vertov's *Three Songs about Lenin,* and the first Soviet sound film, Nikolai Ekk's *Road to Life.* Münzenberg was to claim credit for the IAH for the international perspective of many Mezhrabpom productions, such as *Storm over Asia,* which he termed "the first film to thrust deeply into the chaos of imperialist politics."[5]

Mezhrabpom also fostered its international aims by undertaking co-productions with IAH affiliates in Germany (Fyodor Otsep's *The Living Corpse* was one such venture), and by inviting screen writers, directors, and technicians from Western Europe to the Soviet Union to gain experience in order, as Münzenberg explained it, for them "to be able to start a germ cell of proletarian cinema within the capitalist world."[6] Among those who went were Béla Balázs, Hans Richter, Joris Ivens, and Erwin Piscator, who made his only film as director, *Revolt of the Fishermen,* for Mezhrabpom.

In Germany the IAH entered production via the Prometheus company, acquired in 1925. Prometheus produced a number of films with a working-class point of view, including: Piel Jutzi's *Hunger in Waldenburg* (which was banned for its exposé of exploitation and misery) and *Mutter Krausens Fahrt ins Glück,* a proletarian family melodrama centering on the consequences of unemployment and the housing shortage; Kurt Bernhard's *Schinderhannes,* from Zuckmayer's play about a revolt of peasants against French landowners in 1783; Leo Mittler's *Jenseits der Strasse,* a contemporary social melodrama shot on the Hamburg docks; and *Kuhle Wampe,* directed by Slatan Dudow from a script by Ernst Ottwald and Bertolt Brecht, the well-known drama of the radical workers' movement in depression Berlin.[7] Prometheus pioneered, too, in the distribution of Soviet films in Europe, scoring a big success with *Potemkin* in 1926.

Documentary filmmaking for the KPD was handled by another IAH company, Weltfilm, founded in 1928 primarily as a distribution outlet for workers' and Soviet films (this firm first popularized the use of 16mm for such screenings). Among Weltfilm's first productions (all in release during 1930) were film reports on KPD-organized demonstrations and rallies *(100,000 unter Roten Fahnen, Leipzig unter Roten Fahnen)*; a short newsreel-style film of a police attack on a May 1 demonstration *(Blutmai 1929)*; a publicity film for Red Aid—the German International Labor Defense *(Sprengt die Ketten)*; an exposé of urban housing conditions *(Zeitprobleme)*; a record of the 1930 national games and conference of Red athletes at Erfurt *(Rot Sport Marschiert)*; and a documentary on a mine disaster *(Todeszeche).*[8]

Film propaganda was a consistent preoccupation of the American IAH affiliate from its founding in 1921—despite the organization's frequent structural overhauls and changes of name. (Created as the Friends of Soviet Russia, it became the Friends of Soviet Russia and Workers' Germany in 1923, the Workers' International Relief in 1924, the International Workers' Aid in 1926, and the WIR again in 1927. Another body, the Friends of the Soviet Union, was established in 1929.) Throughout the twenties, to counteract hostile propaganda emanating from Hollywood,[9] the affiliate arranged nationwide release of documentaries about the Soviet Union: these included *Russia through the Shadows* (1922), *The Fifth Year* (1923)—described as an "historical, news, scenic, educational film depicting events in the Soviet Union, chiefly during 1922,"[10] *From Death to Life, Jewish Life in Soviet Russia* (1924), *The Russian Revolution* (1927), and *A Visit to Soviet Russia* (1929). It also organized occasional showings of Soviet dramatic features, both theatrically (until November 1926, when Amkino Corporation, which was granted a monopoly in the field, was founded), and nontheatrically, in the halls of labor unions, fraternal societies, etc.[11]

Secretary of the WIR in the mid-twenties was William F. Kruse, who was responsible for the distribution of Russian films in Canada, Mexico, and Argentina as well as the United States.[12] In September 1925, in an article in *Workers Monthly,* Kruse summarized the argument of Münzenberg's pamphlet *Erobert den Film!* and gave some data concerning the experience of his organization to date in distributing and exhibiting left-wing films in the United States:

> In about 250 cities of all sizes and compositions we have shown anywhere from one to seven film programs, to average total audiences of 100,000 for each film. On the first handsome profits were realized, on the others the costs were more than covered.

For Kruse, however this was a qualified achievement:

> Can this be called a success? If we compare our record with the failures of other branches of the labor movement on this field of [*sic*] the bankrupt "Labor Film Service," backed by yellow Socialists and Gompersites, it would seem an excellent result. But this would be sectarian gloating, and foreign to Communist reasoning. Our comparison must be made against the achievements of our capitalist enemy. Our enemy shows his films in 20,000 houses, we show in about 200. Our record receipts for one night were about $4,000 in collections and admissions, but in the same city the "Auditorium" record for its 3,600 seats for one week was $55,000—this for the vicious anti-Negro film, *The Birth of a Nation*. Our enemy produces about 700 feature films a year, several thousand short features, and a couple of hundred more are imported, few of which reach the American screen. Against this we put out two or three features at most, and a few short subjects. Our enemy reaches fifty million people a week.... We reached ten thousand a week, once.[13]

Factors inhibiting expansion of radical film distribution included capitalist hegemony over the industry ("most of the film exchanges and theatres are trust-controlled and closed against us"); the lack of trained workers to undertake the demanding job; censorship (regulations prohibiting, for example, scenes which "stir up... antagonistic relations between capital and labor" or "tend to weaken the authority of the law"); weaknesses of organization; and costs. It was the latter two which presented the most serious problems:

> ... our heaviest difficulties are still in the field of finance and organization. Our film sources are not yet sufficiently regular. The cost of preparing films for showing (duty, duplication, titling, etc.) is a strain at certain seasons because we lack a sufficiently elastic amortization policy. Our organization is not fully equal to the task of exhibiting our films extensively and intensively as well. Presentation costs are high, due to high rentals, cost of promotion, etc., and our low-cost itinerant program has not yet been adapted to overcome all obstacles everywhere.

It was Kruse's opinion, nevertheless, that the great potential of working-class cinema justified an intensified struggle for its attainment. Film was a medium uniquely suited to the Communist movement:

> Its tremendous revolutionary possibilities, among precisely those elements difficult of access by our ordinary propaganda weapons—the primitive-minded inert working masses who never go to meetings, and never read anything better than a capitalist comic page—as well as special elements like the scattered rural proletariat and semi-proletariat; the oppressed and often illiterate subject peoples; the children, and similar groups. These vast masses hold the future of the revolutionary movement in their hands—they will determine the outcome of our struggle against imperialism—we must win them. Every weapon used by the masters to hold them we must seek to turn to help set them free. And the film is by no means the least of these. We must win it for the working class.[14]

Kruse's pressing concern was with distribution. It is clear that at this time the WIR's objective was to make Soviet films available to American workers rather than to undertake production within the United States, and Kruse quotes Münzenberg favorably to the effect that "the victorious Revolution in Soviet Russia gives the world proletariat an economic and ideological base for film production," obviating the need to fight that battle in one's own backyard. But there was nevertheless a desire for some local content in workers' film programs, as a Chicago venture described by Kruse indicates.

Commercial newsreels of a strike at the stockyards had been released. The anti-labor titles "excused the manhandling and arrest of strikers on the ground that they were 'sniping' at the police from the housetops" and praised the police "for their Cossack ruthlessness." In an experiment which antedates the practice of European film societies by several years, the Workers Party[15] rearranged the footage and supplied it with new titles—"As soon as a strike is called the cop is on the corner," "The patrol wagon does its stuff in Chicago as in Berlin," "When the police are inadequate there is always the militia," "A Chicago banker is in charge of operations—his operating tools, rifles and bayonets and six-shooters, in case the machine guns fail," etc. The fact that the scenes had previously passed the censors failed to prevent banning of the new version of the film.[16]

As far as can be ascertained, no actual shooting had been carried out by WIR or other Communist groups in the U.S. by the time Kruse's article was published. But one prolabor production from earlier in the decade had set a significant precedent. This was *The Contrast* 1921), a coal-fields documentary directed by Guy Hedlund. According to Hedlund, the film as he shot it was "exposé-flavored but not Communist-inspired"; however (he later charged),

after editing by three men in New York, one American and the others apparently Russian, the film included a shot of Lenin addressing a communist throng in Moscow and a shot of Pennsylvania State Police firing into a crowd of miners. The theme music had been changed from mood compositions to the *Internationale*, the communist anthem.

The fact that *The Contrast* was distributed by the Socialist-backed Labor Film Service nevertheless suggests that its Communist orientation could not have been as blatant as Hedlund implies.[17]

The WIR was to enter the arena of production much sooner, probably, than William F. Kruse imagined. The occasion was the long-drawn-out textile workers' strike at Passaic, which commenced early in 1926 and lasted most of the year. One of the few major strikes in a lean decade for unionism, and the first to be led exclusively by Communists, it provided a focus for liberal and left-wing discontent which was expressed in the large sums of money the WIR was able to collect around the country for relief purposes.[18] Some of this money was no doubt converted to the production of *The Passaic Textile Strike,* a seven-reel documentary released by the then International Workers' Aid in October 1926. It is unfortunate that so little is known about this picture. The *AFI Catalog* states only that "According to the licensing records of the New York State Motion Picture Commission, this film contains references to the exploitation of the millworkers and to the attitude of the millowners."[19] The film (or a re-edited version of it) was later exhibited by the Workers' Film and Photo League in 1931, and there can be little doubt that (if only in the fact of its production) it was an important forerunner of the league's work.

Even less is known about *Gastonia* (1929), presumably a similar documentary covering the textile strike of that year, in which the WIR again played a crucial role as support force. The alternative title, *Volga to Gastonia,* implies that the film's focus was on the WIR's relief activities, with some reference to the history of the organization, but this cannot be confirmed from the limited information available.[20]

It is fairly clear, however, that the technical team or teams responsible for *The Passaic Textile Strike* and *Gastonia* did not form a permanent production crew able to undertake ongoing filmic coverage of working-class events. The necessity for such a group became apparent after the stock-market crash and the onset of the Depression. On March 6, 1930, a Communist-led demonstration of the unemployed resulted in probably the largest such crowds in U.S. history jamming into New York's Union Square, but the capitalist press minimized the event and commercial newsreels of the demonstration were suppressed at the behest of New York police chief Grover Whalen—no doubt partly because they exposed the savagery of his officers in action. A film laboratory worker explained in a letter to the *New Masses:*

> As a result of the police brutality of Thursday, March 6, the authorities have placed a ban on all pictures of that moral victory. In the New York demonstration, Cop Whalen had ordered all talking picture apparatus off the scene when the speakers began. . . . The day after the unemployment demonstrations, special newsreels were shipped to 250 branches throughout the world. About noon, a scene depicting one of New York's "finest" slugging and kicking a prostrated woman, was ordered out. About 4 o'clock, the reel was completely censored.[21]

In May, writing in the *Daily Worker,* Samuel Brody drew the evident conclusion. Reiterating the class analysis of motion-picture content made earlier by Münzenberg and Kruse, he affirmed the need for an adversary cinema:

> I want once more to emphasize the news-film is the important thing; that the capitalist class knows that there are certain things that it cannot afford to have shown. It is afraid of some pictures. . . . Films are being used against the workers like police clubs, only more subtly— like the reactionary press. If the capitalist class fears pictures and prevents us from seeing records of events like the March 6 unemployment demonstration and the Sacco-Vanzetti trial we will equip our own cameramen and make our own films.[22]

Less than two weeks later, again in the *Daily Worker,* the call for workers' movie production was repeated, this time by Harry Alan Potamkin. Once more, Hollywood was assailed. Brody had argued that "while whisky results in a lowering of the productive capacity of the worker, the film kills two birds with one stone by stupefying him while allowing him to retain his working efficiency." Potamkin reiterated the charge in asserting: "The movie obscures the facts of present society with pictures of luxuriance and hope that ensnare and betray the worker into a 'secondhand' life." Both Brody and Potamkin saw the situation as worsening: "The last eighteen months," said Brody, "have exceeded all possible limits in output of moronic films," and Potamkin, observing control of the motion-picture industry increasingly concentrated in institutions of high finance, asserted that, "As the workers' threat advances, the capitalist hands the workers more blarney and less truth."[23]

Potamkin's proposal for a counter-cinema spelled out the type of production a workers' film organization might concentrate on:

> The German workers have started well. There is no need to begin big. Documentaries of workers' life. Bread lines and picket lines, demonstrations and police attacks. Outdoor films first. Then interiors. And eventually dramatic films of revolutionary content. Workers' organizations should support a group to be pioneers on this important front.

Financing for production could come from showings to "workers' clubs and related organizations" of "films of merit that may not otherwise be released here, or will be mutilated by the commercial exhibitor": Potamkin cited the examples of the Workers' Film Society of London and the film leagues of Denmark and Holland.[24]

As the economic situation worsened, protest marches, rallies, and manifestations of all kinds became more frequent, and the bourgeois media continued to ignore or distort them. It was clear that there was an urgent need, at the very least, for workers' newsreels. In July, an irate correspondent of the *New Masses* complained of the commercial news film he was forced to sit through when attending a showing of the Soviet film *Turksib.* "Why must the workers of New York be forced to swallow this nonsense every time they want to see a revolutionary picture from the Soviet Union?" he asked. "Why could not some cultural organization like the WIR or ILD [International Labor Defense] or John Reed Club establish workers' movies without the additional hokum?" In a note, Potamkin responded: "Steps towards the organization of workers' film groups are being taken now." He invited readers to contact him at the *New Masses*—which they evidently did, as his remarks in the August issue indicate:

> Numerous letters have come in asking for information about workers' films. As yet no further report can be made beyond what is contained in my statement as secretary of the

John Reed Club in the previous number of the *New Masses*. When developments have reached the point where a definite move for a film group is to be inaugurated—and that may be some time in the fall—the *New Masses* and *Daily Worker* will carry detailed notices to that effect.[25]

No such notices appeared, but meanwhile the left-wing cultural organizations were quietly mobilizing their cinematic forces in moves which had their parallel on the international scene.

In Germany, as has been described above, the IAH-linked company Weltfilm expanded from its base in distribution to begin the production of workers' newsreels and short documentaries in 1929. Its initiative was followed in Britain by the Federation of Workers' Film Societies (FOWFS), which shortly after its formation established the Atlas Film Company to import Soviet and German features. Atlas commenced production of its own films in 1930: two editions of the series *Workers' Topical News* appeared in the first half of that year, providing newsreel coverage of the March 6 demonstration in London of the National Unemployed Workers' Movement, the 1930 Hunger March, and the May Day events. In the Netherlands, the *Vereeniging voor VolksCultuur* (VVVC), like the FOWFS primarily an association for the distribution and exhibition of left-wing films, also began production in 1930, with a newsreel series whose first editions included footage of the Soviet Union (apparently shot by Joris Ivens), and of activities of the Dutch International Labor Defense organization. A similar undertaking was under way in Japan, where Prokino (the Proletarian Film League) produced *The Funeral of Yamamoto,* about a Communist politician who had been murdered by terrorists, in 1929, and the following year brought out the first of a planned newsreel series, *Prokino-News No. 1,* whose content is not known. Among Prokino's other productions up to this time were films documenting the May Day demonstrations in Tokyo in 1929 and 1930, and *Earth* (1930), a tribute to the collaborative struggle of workers and peasants against the expropriation of a plot of arable land for a large factory.[26]

Although all of these groups had Communist party ties, only Weltfilm seems to have been directly linked to the IAH. In the case of the remainder, a variety of other formal and informal arrangements prevailed—the VVVC, for example, was apparently closely associated with the ILD. The IAH was, however, the major institutional support for the workers' photo leagues, which by 1930 or a little later had been established in a number of countries including Germany, the Soviet Union, Great Britain, France, Switzerland, Czechoslovakia, Austria, the Netherlands, and Japan. The purpose of these groups was to provide visual coverage of working-class subjects for the left-wing press; Münzenberg claimed that there were 102 local branches of the *Vereinigung der Arbeiterphotographen* operating in Germany alone in 1931.[27]

In the United States, a photography group with ties to the WIR had been in existence for several years. This was the (Japanese) Workers' Camera League (also known as the Workers' Camera Club and the Nippon Camera Club), based in New York. A report in the *New Masses* of February 1930 described the league as having "about 52 members," holding meetings once a week and exhibitions twice a year. The story continued:

> Only one of the members is a professional photographer. All the other photographers earn their living as food workers, in restaurants, and housework. They have all learned the art of photography in this country.
>
> Their spacious headquarters is fully equipped with a dark room, filming room and enlarging room, and all the materials used in the different processes of photography. The club also owns a moving picture projector and screen.
>
> The club was started five years ago by a group of eight people who were interested in photography as an art medium and decided to work together to develop it. When later they found they also had a mutual interest in the revolutionary labor movement, their activities were reorganized to include class-struggle propaganda, through the work they were engaged in.[28]

The Workers' Camera League was said to be "particularly interested in photographs of industrial and farm life, natural scenes, workers' homes, labor sports, machines, engines, and pictures of individual workers at their tasks." At its 4th Annual Photo Exhibition, held from December 1929 to January 1930, it displayed photographs "mainly concerned with proletarian life and the class struggle," including

> scenes of May Day, demonstrations of food workers, laborers at construction work, a factory, fishermen, etc. Class consciousness is the theme of pictures bearing the titles: *Sabotage, Movement, Workers, Speed-Up, Exploitation, Red Day, Mobilization to Work,* etc.[29]

In the spring of 1930 the Workers' Camera League combined forces with the International Labor Defense, the Communist legal-aid organization parallel to the Workers' International Relief, to form the Labor Defender Photo Group. The purpose of this new association was "to get pictures of the class struggle for use in working-class papers and magazines," particularly the ILD's *Labor Defender.* The secretary announced in July: "Our members are ready with their cameras on the picket line, demonstrations, street meetings, in factories, unemployment lines, and in the homes of workers." A spokesperson for the ILD projected "a network of worker-photo groups throughout the country" with which "we will be able to create a powerful pictorial expression of our struggles which can be used very effectively in building our organization."[30]

Of particular interest is the fact that the group reportedly possessed two motion-picture cameras, and one of its first tasks was to be "the making of a film showing the varied activities of the International Labor Defense to be shown at ILD meetings." Whether this project eventuated is not known, but the Labor Defender Photo Group did take movies of the 1930 May Day parade in New York City.[31]

It was these films, very probably, that the WIR announced for showing at the "mass celebration of the Five Year Plan, to be held at Ulmer Park, Brooklyn, this Saturday, May 31, Defend the Soviet Union Day." Other workers' newsreels followed. In September, at a "big entertainment and dance" of Communist party sections 2 and 3, films of March 6 demonstration leaders William Z. Foster, Harry Raymond, Robert Minor, and Israel Amter in jail, and of "all the later Party demonstrations," were shown for the first time. At Detroit in October, newsreels of activities at the WIR children's summer camp and of the raid on the WIR camp at Van Etten, N.Y., were scheduled for a "Gala Camp Reunion." The announcements do not reveal the source of the footage, but it would be reasonable to assume that the Labor Defender Photo Group as again responsible.[32]

Both the Defender group and its progenitor were still active late in the fall. The Workers' Camera League announced an International Photo Exhibition and Dance for November 15, and the issue of *New Masses* for that month reported that the Labor Defender Photo Group had twenty active members, enjoyed the facilities of a studio and darkroom, and conducted a regular photo exchange abroad. The address given for the Defender group was 7 E. 14th Street, New York, where the premises (described above) of the Workers' Camera League were formerly located.[33]

In the spring of 1930, Samuel Brody recently stated, he and film enthusiast Lester Balog had met with a WIR representative named Gibarti to plan an expansion of the Workers' Camera League which would include film production. The initial outcome might well have been the Labor Defender group; the plan only came to full fruition, however, in the early part of December, when the Workers' Camera League was reorganized and renamed the Workers' Film and Photo League. The new group met for the first time at WIR headquarters on December 11, 1930, and two days later it held a house-warming party with entertainment, refreshments, dancing, and a screening of the Soviet movie *In Old Siberia*. An organization had been founded under the auspices of the WIR which could sustain political filmmaking and photography on a permanent, ongoing basis.[34]

At first the WFPL continued to meet at the WIR building at 131 W. 28th Street, but by February 1931 it was operating out of 7 E. 14th Street. Since nothing more was heard of the Labor Defender Photo Group, it is likely that the personnel and facilities of that body were absorbed into the new organization.[35]

The key participants in the film section of the WFPL at the beginning were Brody, Balog, Robert Del Duca, and a little later Leo Seltzer. Of the group members Del Duca had the most practical experience, having worked as a newsreel cameraman and laboratory technician; Brody was clearly the theoretician and political overseer. Balog was "mainly an inside man—he worked on art work and editing." Seltzer, with an interest in engineering and background as an art student, became in time probably the league's single most active filmmaker. Dissemination of the group's program was enthusiastically undertaken by its unofficial spokesman, Harry Alan Potamkin. Handling the WIR's film department, and thus intimately involved with arranging distribution and exhibition of—and often finance for—the league's productions, was Tom Brandon, a former student at Syracuse University and N.Y.U. who had worked as a truck driver before becoming an organizer for the WIR.[36]

The core of the league's work was the production of newsreels. This represented a direct continuation of the work which had been carried out by the Workers' Camera League and the Labor Defender Photo Group, and conformed to the emphases both Brody and Potamkin had placed in their calls for workers' movies. Writing of the WFPL in the spring, 1931, issue of *The Left,* Seymour Stern explained that, "It has for its principal purpose the taking of newsreels of demonstrations, meetings, Party activities, and other affairs of immediate, daily concern to the American working class."[37] The first league production of which there is any record is a film report of the hunger march to the New York State Legislature at Albany in February-March 1931; and for the six years of its existence the group would continue to concentrate primarily on basic cinematic journalism.

For Leo Seltzer, this was the league's *raison d'être*. "The filmmaking and distribution activities of the league had nothing to do with what Hollywood producers or commercial distributors were doing," he argues.

> Ours was a total involvement in what was happening in the world on a very practical and realistic level. We filmed the everyday social scene, the economic struggle, and we put it together to represent a realistic, not dramatized point of view, and then we carried those heavyweight "portable" projectors and the films back to the union halls and the picket lines and showed them to an audience that was the living subject of the films.[38]

There was no money to pay the filmmakers. Funds for production came from the WIR (which usually handled raw stock and processing), donations (Sidney Howard was a prominent supporter[39]), benefits (such as motion-picture costume balls), public screenings (chiefly of European and Soviet classics), and the sale of stills. Membership dues went towards the rent on the series of cheap lofts which served as league headquarters.[40] For the more committed members, WFPL activity was a way of life. Seltzer recalls "working all day and most of the night, sleeping on a desk or editing table wrapped in the projection screen, eating food that might have been contributed for relief purposes, and wearing clothes that were donated." A later initiate, Julian Roffman, writes:

> ...if I had to sweep floors and deliver posters and rush around the city carrying almost a crushing weight of two projectors and a screen and films from one club to another then I did it because, like the streetcleaner following the elephants in the parade, I was in showbiz that way. It was all worthwhile and in retrospect I enjoyed it, even if I had 25¢ for lunch and little more for dinner sometimes.[41]

Total membership in the league, including the photo section, fluctuated (according to Brody) between 75 and 100, and was "mainly working-class with a sprinkling of middle-class intellectuals and technicians sympathetic to our progressive goals." The core group of 1931 was augmented notably by a handful of enthusiasts excited by the artistic possibilities of the film medium, including Lewis Jacobs, Leo T. Hurwitz, David Platt, Jay Leyda (for a short period prior to his departure for the Soviet Union), Irving Lerner, and Ralph Steiner. For the most part these men were less involved with the league's production work than with some of its other activities, detailed below; and Seltzer recalls something of a division between the "theoreticians" and those who did the practical filmmaking and exhibiting jobs:

> The image I have: very often, there was this little round table and there'd be a group of four or five guys sitting there, the theoreticians, sitting talking, philosophizing: "How do you...?" "Why do you...?" "When do you...?" "What's the political reason for it?" And then someone would say, "Hey, something's happening! Call Seltzer!" And I'd take the Eyemo under my arm and go out and shoot.
>
> Hurwitz, Lerner, and possibly a few other "casual" members had ambitions that leaned towards Hollywood, of doing the Hollywood thing, perhaps differently. Lerner finally made it to Hollywood. I think it was much more of an ego drive with those guys—to *be* somebody rather than to *do* something. Del [Duca] and I and Lester [Balog], we didn't have that desire. We worked on the day-to-day realistic documentary productions.[42]

Hurwitz, who came to the league in 1932 with a Harvard education and background as assistant editor of *Creative Art* magazine, concedes that there was some distinction of role, but "to make a rigid division would be wrong":

> When I came in I was immediately interested in working with the camera and did, on any occasion I could. I was also interested in the aesthetics of film, in a way that maybe at that time Leo Seltzer was not, but I didn't feel that I was separate from them [Seltzer, Balog, Del Duca]—my work joined them. I guided the whole process of making the [1932] Hunger March film, and I never in any of my work before or after functioned as a theorist without doing practical work. But I do think the mind is a very important part of practical work, mind and feelings.... It also had to do with—a guy like Irving Lerner was also a practical filmmaker but he had another job, so he didn't do very much practical work at that time. A

guy like Harry Alan Potamkin was a writer. He hoped some day to get to make films but he didn't live long enough to do it. I daresay he would have. So the distinction is a little bit mechanical, but it describes something.[43]

Inevitably, some of the divisions were political. It was not that there was any major disagreement over desirable actions and tactics—Platt knew of no member of the league "who was not in one way or another active in the movement against war, fascism, and the fight for social justice," and all were agreed, he has affirmed, on the need "to cover the bread lines, flop lines, picket lines, hunger marches, etc. etc." But there was clearly a disparity between those, like Brody and Potamkin, well versed in Marxist theory and practice, and neophytes such as Seltzer, who states he was "quite naive politically and really wasn't involved for any cause." Roffman has recalled his introduction to the League in 1934:

Thus, a very very young man, almost out of his teens, burning to learn something about films, knowing nothing about the class struggle and the name Karl Marx means nothing to him, finds that the school he came to attend does not exist and there is no place to go except attend meetings in a dingy first-floor loft with a huge banner strung across the walls THE CAMERA IS A WEAPON IN THE CLASS STRUGGLE and all sorts of voluble, articulate and verbose types hurling verbal shafts at each other across the room either in banter or in deadly serious earnest . . . little to do with filmmaking, but more about how films can be used to illuminate the plight of the unemployed, the Negro in Harlem and down South, the workers in factories and the artists seeking a chance to pursue their art. . . .[44]

At times, he observes, the discussion would enter more speculative realms:

I remember Sam Brody and Nick Bela (who was supposed to be a writer from Hollywood) sitting around on a Saturday afternoon and arguing about who would do what after the Revolution—who would be commissar or whatever title that would be in the USA—and how the film industry would function to make the real films à la Ten Days and Mother—and who would do them. Certainly not the Hollywood hacks. I remember listening to this heady idle talk which was daydreaming in outer space indeed and the newcomers and neophytes listening to these experienced articulate hands, the upperclassmen, discussing matters of grave import and allowing us to listen in and I don't know but that they were having us on and having a good time at our expense, there being nothing better to do that afternoon.[45]

"Theoreticians" and practitioners hammered out actual production decisions at committee meetings of the league. Seltzer has denied there was a committee, but both Hurwitz and Brandon attest to its existence. According to Hurwitz:

The Film and Photo League did have an executive committee, and at some point I was elected a member. . . . Brandon seemed to be a power, by virtue of the leadership he took and the way he spoke, and the fact that he raised money to buy a camera, and he got Sidney

Howard or somebody to put up dough for buying film and so forth, so he had a great deal of authority. And that was partly in his manner, in his executive ability, in his thinking about things in between meetings, when other people were thinking about shooting with a camera, or not thinking about anything at all. He seemed to be the person most in charge.

Brandon's account minimizes his own role and stresses the leeway accorded individual filmmakers within a general structure shaped by collective decision-making:

Now in general the position was that there was a production committee of the Film and Photo League which discussed what kind of projects and were generally responsible for the finish of films.... [The committee] brought in proposals for what kind of films we were tentatively scheduling, thinking about, because the scheduling was a product of what funds were available for what, what the most pressing issues were that we could cope with. And also a subjective factor of which people would like to work on what.... Everybody saw rushes and their talk about it was not necessarily talk that determined frame by frame the making of a film. But people who were in charge, the people who were actually working on the film, they made the film. There was an effort not to decimate their time and their momentum. They wanted to have the film ready, say, for three weeks from now because the unemployed want to have a giant meeting. So what may have been lost in mass discussions of group editing, group cutting, was gained by having people who were working on the film discuss what they were doing with the rest of the production committee. There might have been three people working on a film, but seven or eight were on the full committee.[46]

Distribution and exhibition of their films was handled by the league members in cooperation with the Film Department of the WIR, which was in the process of building a library of Soviet and other left-wing productions. Though the newsreels did sometimes receive theatrical screenings (particularly during 1932-33, at New York's Acme Theatre), they were more often shown in a more political context, at Party functions, in union halls, or at meetings of fraternal societies, nationality groups, workers' clubs. Particularly, Seltzer insists, they were shown during strikes:

Whenever there was a picket line we covered it and came back and showed the pickets themselves on the picket line. It was a tremendous moralebooster. Plus maybe a Russian film, or maybe the *Taxi* film [a 1935 FPL production], or the waterfront film [*Marine*, 1934, also FPL], to give them an idea other people were also struggling for better conditions. We had some footage of the Kentucky strike, and the Pittsburgh strike. I don't know who shot the Pittsburgh film, but I went back with a projector to show it to the miners who were still blacklisted. They were still living in tents for the second winter. And I remember I went into the town and we stretched this sheet between two houses—the sheriff's and the deputy's house on either side—and we expected to be shot at any minute while projecting the film.[47]

Taking films to the workers became a potent organizing device. While Film and Photo League productions could give an accurate depiction of bleak American conditions and the struggle against them, Soviet features could suggest the benefits of an alternative, socialist system. In 1932, a Communist Party unit organizer wrote:

> Our shop unit in the Caterpillar plant is only about six months old. And while we are getting new contacts on the job (the plant has been working a few days a week and is now closed down indefinitely), we found that shop-gate meetings are a great help in approaching workers on their problems.
>
> On March 1st a Party speaker held a meeting at the shop during noon hour. After the meeting the workers discussed a great deal amongst themselves on how to solve the conditions in favor of the workers. During the same time the Workers' International Relief was showing a Russian movie to which the workers were invited. And for the next few days the workers in the plant were discussing the lack of unemployment in Russia and the millions of unemployed here. These discussions among the workers gave (the Party members) the opportunity to comment and help them along and thereby find out who is who in the shop.
>
> As a result of the shop-gate meetings outside and our work inside we have now a functioning group of the Metal Trades Industrial League and have recruited seven new members to the Party unit (we started the shop unit with three members).[48]

Among the Soviet films handled by the WIR in the early thirties were, in addition to the older silent classics which had been released earlier, *Cannons or Tractors, A New World in Reconstruction, The 41st, Red and White, Road to Life, Shame (Counterplan), Jimmie Higgins,* and *Mother.*

During mass mobilizations such as the two national hunger marches (1931 and 1932) and drives of support for the major CP-led strikes, the WFPL collaborated with the WIR both in the production and in the exhibition of films which would help create radical working-class consciousness. An article in the February 1932 *Workers' Theatre* on "The Class Struggle through the Camera-Eye," devoted to the question of cinematic support for the Kentucky-Tennessee miners' strike, reveals the extent to which movies were regarded as a potential revolutionary weapon:

> The revolutionary working class must itself utilize the movie for the proletariat against the ruling class. In its hands it can and must become the strongest mobilizer, educator, and organizer for this struggle of which the Kentucky strike is the pivot. The movie will agitate for better conditions, unemployment insurance, and inevitably for the overthrow of capitalism—if the workers support their own cinema!
>
> THE FILM DEPARTMENT OF THE WORKERS' INTERNATIONAL RELIEF places at the service of workers' organizations and groups every aid to carry through successful mass movie meetings: budget advice, projectors, screens, operators, publicity material, technical advice, and what is even more important, Workers' Films and Newsreels. The Workers' Newsreels, film records of demonstrations, strikes, unemployment, police terror, hunger marches, evictions, and so forth, are especially effective in linking all phases of the class struggle. As powerful antidotes to the poison of Hollywood, and as positive assertions, are the Soviet films and productions of the German WIR, which the FILM DEPARTMENT OF THE WIR is able to supply.[49]

Success in building alternative film distribution outlets grew markedly with the introduction of 16mm in 1933-34. Using an old Ford and a collectively owned projector, for example, a Farmers' Movie Circuit was able to bring *Mother, Potemkin, Fragment of an Empire,* and *War Against the Centuries* to eighty towns and villages in Minnesota, North Dakota, South Dakota, Wisconsin, and Michigan. The next year, 1935, it was reported that *Mother* had been shown "in almost every industrial center, small town, and farming community in the country." Paradoxically, the emergence of nontheatrical distribution as a growth field weakened the Film and Photo League by loosening its ties with the WIR and taking away one of its more dynamic figures. The Film Department of the WIR became Garrison Film Distributors at the end of 1932, and in 1934 Tom Brandon became a full-time employee of the organization. Roffman records that Brandon

> was a driving force and I think a force for action on a most positive level. This we lost when he decided to move into distribution. And there was no one to replace him.[50]

It was implicit in the writings of Brody and Potamkin as early as 1930 that a radical film organization, to be politically effective, would need to be more than a small-scale production company. At the start, it was true, the shooting of newsreels was stressed; but by July 1931 the WFPL was sufficiently consolidated for Potamkin to be able to outline an ambitious multi-pronged program in which such basic filmmaking activities, though still the core of the undertaking, were integrated into a broad offensive on the movie front of the class struggle. Under the heading "Film and Photo Call to Action!" he wrote:

> The League looks forward to work in the following decisive ways:
>   1. The education of the workers and others in the part the movie plays as a weapon of reaction;
>   2. The education of the workers and others in the part the movie plays as an instrument for social purposes—in the U.S.S.R.;
>   3. The encouragement, support, and sustenance of the left critic and the left movie-maker who is documenting dramatically and persuasively the disproportions of our present society;
>   4. The creation of a chain of film audiences who morally and financially guarantee such films;
>   5. The regular publication of a periodical devoted to our purposes;
>   6. The fight against the class-abuses of capitalist censorship;
>   7. The attack upon the invidious portrayal in the popular film of the foreign-born worker, the Negro, the oriental, the worker generally;
>   8. The opposition to the interests of the institutions like the church as they participate in the shaping of the monopolized film;
>   9. The use of methods of direct action, boycott, picketing, against the anti-working-class, anti-Soviet film;
>   10. The distribution of suppressed films of importance;
>   11. The defense of artists and critics abused by reactionary elements (as in the Eisenstein case);

12. The rediscovery and presentation of neglected films of significance;
13. The education of the critic and worker by closer contact.
THE SECOND PART OF NUMBER 3 IS EVENTUALLY OUR MOST IMPORTANT
PURPOSE! Our filmmakers need more training, and that is got by more opportunity. THIS
PURPOSE IS MADE MEANINGFUL BY NUMBER 13.[51]

Considering its amateur basis and stringent resources, it is remarkable just how many of these goals the league was able, in the course of time, to pursue—and make significant steps towards accomplishing.

Initial support for the WFPL's program and clarification of its objectives came from the Workers' Cultural Federation, formed just prior to the publication of Potamkin's statement. Integrated into the federation as the major component of the "film and photo commission," the league found common ground with some 130 other working-class organizations of the New York area united in the conception of culture as a weapon and in the desire to differentiate sharply proletarian from bourgeois forms of expression. Reporting on the federation in the press, Potamkin paid particular attention to the potential role of the WFPL—that "preeminently important propaganda group"—and argued that the new organization would need to relate the league's work to "every workers' club and to the entire revolutionary press. The league must be encouraged and supported," he continued, "in its showing of films, its agitational work against reactionary movies, the making of proletarian film-documents, and in the spread of the function of the worker-photographer." And Potamkin was able to note some tangible arrangements which had already resulted from the affiliation: the WFPL had assembled an exhibit of stills by worker-photographers which, like the John Reed Club's collection of Soviet posters, would travel from club to club under the federation's auspices. Little is known about the subsequent history of the Workers' Cultural Federation or the WFPL's role within it.[52]

Potamkin's official position with the league was as a member of its National Advisory Board (also known as the National Committee, not to be confused with the league's National Organization Committee, discussed below). The board, as its name implies, had consultative status and helped formulate the league's objectives as well as lend a certain prestige to the organization. At first it was composed of a group of radical writers and artists closely associated with the John Reed Club and the *New Masses:* in addition to Potamkin, there were Whittaker Chambers, Robert W. Dunn, Hugo Gallert, Joseph North, and "Robert Evans" (Joseph Freeman). Later, in 1933-34, the board became more politically and occupationally heterogeneous, numbering among its members playwrights Sidney Howard and John Wexley, poets Langston Hughes and Robert Gessner, photographers Berenice Abbott and Margaret Bourke-White, novelists Erskine Caldwell and Lester Cohen, and filmmakers Ralph Steiner and Slavko Vorkapich. Some, such as Steiner, had close personal involvement with certain phases of the league's work; others were no doubt more distant, retaining a mere nominal attachment.[53]

The league was also sustained in its purpose by its international ties. At the beginning, it was a member of the Union of Worker-Photographers *(Vereinigung der Arbeiterphotographen)* headquartered under LAH auspices in Berlin, and several of its activities during 1931 were undertaken with a view to participating in the international conference scheduled to coincide with the tenth congress of the IAH in Germany in October. The league pressed for the inclusion of film in the conference, prepared a "Proletarian Photo" exhibit for it, and planned to send a delegate, but it is not known if it achieved its aim of being represented.[54]

After Hitler's assumption of power in January 1933, the center for international film and photo cooperation shifted to the Soviet Union. A Cinema Bureau of the International Union of Revolutionary Theatre was established under the leadership of Léon Moussinac and Béla Balázs, and following the film conference held in conjunction with the International Workers' Theatre Olympiad in Moscow in May, 1933, a program of action was promulgated. The platform gave significant endorsement to the broad range of political film activity which Potamkin had outlined which the New York league was already implementing in many areas. In addition to production in a variety of genres, and among other forms of action, the Cinema Bureau called for: a) a struggle against "war, chauvinist, pacifist, and other reactionary films," and against bourgeois censorship, to be carried out by means of satirical criticism, discussions, exposés in the press, protest demonstrations, boycotts, and the popularizing of revolutionary films; b) dissection of the concealed ideology in bourgeois newsreels and in documentary films; c) the establishment of audience organizations to be connected with the film producing groups; d) the building of a repertory of revolutionary films; e) the initiation of revolutionary film press correspondence; and f) the holding of international conferences on "creative, technical, and political film questions."[55] As with the Workers' Cultural Federation, there are few subsequent references to the organization in the press, and it is probable that financial and political difficulties precluded any substantial collaboration on an international scale.

The WFPL's campaign against reactionary movies was conducted, first of all, in the press. Frequent broadsides against the Hollywood "dope industry" were delivered in the columns of the *Daily Worker* by league founding member Samuel Brody, who as early as August 1929 had taken the extreme position that "the artistic content of the cinema in capitalist countries is almost nil." He was ably seconded by Irving Lerner, Tom Brandon, Leo Hurwitz, Julian Roffman, and especially David Platt, who became the regular *Daily Worker* film critic in 1934. Harry Alan Potamkin (prior to his death in July 1933) followed up the attack in the *New Masses* and in *Workers' Theatre*. When

Workers' Theatre became New Theatre in September-October 1933 it also became the official organ of the WFPL, and with Platt, Lerner, Brody, and Hurwitz all serving, at one time or another, as film editor, it maintained a systematic critique of rightward trends in Hollywood production. In 1934 the Film and Photo League sponsored the publication of a collation of Potamkin material (put together by Lerner) as a pamplet under the title The Eyes of the Movie: the texts focused on film as a propaganda medium in the hands of high finance. For the first few months of 1935 New Theatre was supplanted as the league's organ by its own publication, Filmfront, which carried on the battle with features such as a selection of "The Worst Anti-Labor Photoplays of 1934."[56]

WFPL critics also gave lectures and sponsored discussions aimed at "the education of the workers and others in the part the movie plays as a weapon of reaction." In January 1932, for example, it was announced that Harry Alan Potamkin would

> at a lecture on "Soviet Film versus Hollywood Film"...show the contrast between an art that is full of life and reflects the growing revolutionary tempo of the workers and peasants of the Soviet Union as against the decadent, sex-sensational plots of capitalist films.

Before a "select audience" in a private home in Hollywood, to cite another instance, Tom Brandon gave "a systematic, factual disembowelment of almost every reactionary ribbon that's appeared on American screens for the past two years," winding up with "a devastating attack on Gabriel over the White House." Robert Gessner and Nicholas Bela gave firsthand accounts of their experiences in Hollywood before an FPL audience in April 1934, while the following month Harry Podolin lectured on "Film Industry in the United States and Soviet Russia." At this time the Film and Photo League was able to offer "speakers on all aspects of the movie for your organization."[57]

Criticism in the press and from the podium led to active protest and boycott campaigns against specifically objectionable movies. The first film to receive the full brunt of a WFPL assault was the Upton Sinclair/Sol Lesser version of Eisenstein's Mexican footage, released under the title Thunder over Mexico in September 1933. League writers took the position a) that the film was a commercial vulgarization of the work of a great artist and b) that it glorified the Calles-Rodríguez "military dictatorship." Leaflets were distributed and pickets posted outside the Rialto Theatre in New York, and Sinclair was subjected to a barrage of questions when he appeared to defend the release. In organizing protest action the WFPL collaborated with the Anti-Imperialist League of America, and in doing so set a precedent for future joint campaigns against reactionary pictures. David Platt, writing in the Daily Worker, was pleased to note the effectiveness of the operation and viewed it as a model for future action:

The Film and Photo League's successful demonstrations against *Thunder over Mexico,* where they succeeded in shortening the run of the picture, proved the effectiveness of mass actions within and without theatres against films of this kind. That these protest demonstrations should be carried on against other reactionary films cannot be emphasized enough.[58]

The films which Platt particularly had in mind were militaristic features aiding in the Roosevelt administration's recruiting drive. The article from which the above quote is taken begins, "The U.S. Government is using every known vehicle at its disposal for war preparation," and citing instances of direct cooperation between the War Department and Hollywood producers, Platt outlined the film industry's growing recourse to "jingo propaganda," evidenced in such movies as *Midshipman Jack, Son of a Sailor, Hell and High Water, Come on Marines, West Point of the Air, Mandalay, Hell Below, Shanghai Madness,* and *Fledglings.* Action was called for:

It is necessary for all Film and Photo Leagues, theatre and other cultural groups and individuals to attend these in large bodies and if possible turn the theatre into a forum against the film, with militant comment accompanying jingoistic and "nationalistic" scenes as they appear on the screen, explaining and clarifying the insidious nature of the movie. Also, leaflets adequately reviewing the picture in question could be prepared and distributed outside and inside the theatre.

The opportunity for action arose several months later with the release of Columbia's *No Greater Glory.* The film, according to an FPL statement, paraded "the *worship of the military uniform*" and told the spectator that "war is inevitable" and that his/her children "can have no finer virtues than the 'virtues' of war which lead to 'honorable-patriotic death.'" The Film and Photo League accordingly called upon

all anti-war fighters to send protests to Columbia Pictures Corporation... demanding that they stop distributing *No Greater Glory;* send protests and delegations to neighborhood theatres demanding that they cancel bookings of *No Greater Glory;* issue leaflets and picket theatres showing *No Greater Glory;* raise the slogan: "Boycott All Pro-War and Pro-Fascist Films!"

The statement was endorsed by the Young Pioneers, the Young Communist League, and the American League Against War and Fascism, and these groups together with the United Council of Working-Class Women collaborated with the Film and Photo League in the campaign against the film. In September it was reported that "over twenty theatres have been picketed and thousands of leaflets exposing the film have been given out." Outdoor meetings in front of theatres were also held.[59]

The other major boycott drive in 1934 was against the Nazi import, *S.A. Mann Brand.* The FPL's ally in this campaign was the Anti-Nazi Federation of

Greater New York. After picketing at the office of the distributor (an action which, it was asserted, closed Broadway theatres to the film and forced the elimination of "most of the rabid anti-Jewish sequences including the repeated cry: 'Perish Jews!' ''), the league organized mass protest demonstrations outside the small Yorkville Theatre, where *S.A. Mann Brand* finally opened in May. The protest was announced as a "solidarity action in the fight for the freedom of Ernst Thaelmann, leader of the German working class"—then in a Nazi prison for his Communist activities. Leo Hurwitz reported:

> Each night open-air meetings were held on the corner opposite the theatre, exposing the film in speeches and leaflets to crowds of more than five hundred passers-by. At the first demonstration police aided the Nazis by breaking up a mass picket line in front of the theatre and clubbing the protesting moviegoers. Succeeding demonstrations, however, impressed the police with the mass pressure behind this protest, and pickets bearing placards were thereafter unmolested by police or storm troopers. In a short time *S.A. Mann Brand* was playing to empty houses and finally was withdrawn as a result of the forewarning given to the moviegoers by these demonstrations.

By the end of the summer it could be claimed that "the campaign led by the Film and Photo League against the showing of Nazi films in this theatre . . . has almost completely isolated the depraved Goebbels creations and the Nazi cesspool in which they were screened from the mass of moviegoers of New York."[60]

Similar protest actions were initiated by the FPL against *Black Shirts*, the Italian Fascist film; *Call to Arms* (finally released as *Together We Live)*, about the raising of a vigilante gang to break a strike and quell a "red uprising"; *Black Fury*, Warner Brothers' contorted version of a miners' strike; and *Red Salute*, an attack on radical students which encountered a mammoth boycott conducted principally by the National Students' League, with assistance from such organizations as the American League Against War and Fascism, the American Youth League, *New Theatre* magazine, and the Writers' Union. Other films which spurred angry reactions included *Riffraff*, objectionable for its depiction of a fishermen's union, and *Fighting Youth*, another attempt to malign radicalism on the campus. The FPL was frequently assisted by advance information it was able to obtain on script development from sympathizers (probably CP members) in Hollywood.[61]

The atmosphere at the Film and Photo League at the height of the drive against antilabor and fascist films has been suggested by Tom Brandon, who quotes the following story—containing "some exaggeration"—told to him by Sidney Meyers:

> I wanted to work on films, either teach or learn, and I went to the Harry Alan Potamkin Film School [run by the FPL], and every time I would go there and start to discuss the work or pull out some equipment, the head of the school would say sorry classes are called off, we're

demonstrating in front of a movie up on Broadway, class will be conducted tomorrow. Night after night I went to make a film or to teach, and night after night they said no class, there is a fascist film, or there was some kind of deadly film to counter, or some mass meeting. I never had a chance to work on any films.

If true, the story indicates the league members had taken very much to heart a reproach made in the *Daily Worker* in December 1933 by Brody, who (as "Lens") had urged "a popular movement to drive the Nazis out of Hollywood," and "something more than a boycott" against *Cradle Song,* adding: "I'm tempted to suggest that the comrades in the New York Film and Photo League are a little 'dizzy with the success' of their excellent Film School and are losing sight of the importance of struggle on an even more important front."[62]

Though such actions were naturally not publicized at the time, Brody records that "during the early Fascist films we occasionally went so far as to plant stink-bombs in the theatre."[63] Whatever the tactics employed, the league boycott campaigns were undoubtedly successful in alerting the public to the presence of reactionary propaganda in the cinema, and may well have exerted an impact on industry decisions regarding the importation and production of right-wing movies.

Equally concerted was the Film and Photo League's drive against film censorship, both that actually practiced by city and state authorities and that threatened at the federal level. Self-censorship by the industry, particularly via the Hays Office, also came under fire.

The theorists of the workers' film movement were perforce aware, from an early date, of censorship as a political weapon wielded by the bourgeoisie. William F. Kruse had devoted a substantial section of his 1925 article, "Workers' Conquest of the Films," to the subject. The theme was taken up by Brody, who in 1930 wrote:

Censorship in the United States is from day to day becoming more vicious. Despite the fact that strict control is exercised at the point of production, the great danger remains the newsreel, which for technical reasons cannot very easily be overseen. Czar Hays can, however, cause any "dangerous" newsreel to be burned at a moment's notice, as in the case of the Sacco-Vanzetti films, the movie records of which have destroyed. Also the police commissioner of any city is empowered with the privilege of ruling out whatever he may think objectionable in a newsreel. A flagrant example of this was the action of Forgery Whalen, who saw to it that the films of the March 6 demonstration in New York were not shown.[64]

There were further instances of suppression to point to by the time Potamkin wrote "Who Owns the Movie?" (in *Workers' Theatre)* in 1932. Newsreels of the May 1, 1930, demonstration and of the first National Hunger March had also been censored. (Of the latter, the *Daily Worker* reported that the Paramount sound films of the hunger march were withdrawn at the order of the Bureau of Censorship in Boston; that the Hearst-Metrotone newsreel contained "not a single scene of the Hunger Marchers demonstrating" outside Congress, although the firm had complete sound-film coverage of the event; and that managers of the newsreel companies on the scene in Washington had explained that the government was looking over their films and "probably none of them will ever be shown to the public.") In the case of feature films, Potamkin cited the banning, in Philadelphia, of *Potemkin,* and the "brutal deletions from *Seeds of Freedom* which made it impossible to release the picture"; and the New York censors' suppression of *Bed and Sofa,* "vandalistic suggestions" on *Volga to Gastonia,* and withdrawal of *China Express* after it had opened. He noted that censorship at the point of distribution, exercised through Boards of Censors, was "severer with productions from independent studios that with films from companies in the Hays organization; severer with foreign films than with domestic; much harder on pictures from Soviet Russia than on pictures from capitalist Europe; and very drastic where pictures are submitted by a working-class organization."[65]

The seizure by police in Newark of *Cannons or Tractors* prior to a scheduled WFPL/WIR showing in May 1932 led to probably the first mass protest against film censorship in this country. As the scene was reported in the *Daily Worker:*

> When the doors of the hall opened for the first showing of the picture the police threw a strong guard all along the street. Over 1,500 workers who came to see the film were denied admittance by the police.
> The crowd, however, did not disperse, but stood for hours in front of the hall in protest against the censorship. Mass organizations in Newark are arranging protest meetings to demand that the censorship be removed from the film so that the workers of New Jersey can learn the truth about the Wall Street government's war preparations against the Soviet Union.

The following day it was announced that "the illegal police censorship and suppression of the anti-war film *Cannons or Tractors* at Newark Sunday afternoon will be answered by a legal and mass fight for freedom of assemblage, speech, and other civil rights," to be conducted by the WIR with the assistance of the ILD. The outcome of the challenge to police power is not recorded.[66]

A major FPL drive against censorship was triggered by a news release of March 2, 1934. The Mayor of Chicago, Edward J. Kelly, was reported as banning from his city "all newsreel pictures of rioting or mob scenes" because "such pictures 'might incite Chicago Communists to riot.'" The National Committee of the Film and Photo League responded with a press statement linking the move (which merely made official what in fact had been the practice for years) with the Roosevelt administration's antilabor New Deal measures:

The special significance of this official public action in Chicago can only be understood in the light of the fact that the Roosevelt Government is extending its policy of smashing any attempt of working-class struggle against the NRA program to the field of motion pictures. By using the local police power of censorship on the grounds of "inciting to riot," an attempt is thus being made to suppress completely or, what is worse, to distort newsreels showing scenes of picket lines, demonstrations, mass meetings, evictions, whether they appear as hot news through the commercial companies, or through increasing mass movie showings of the Film and Photo Leagues in various cities.... Considering the existence of internal censorship (censorship by the Federal Government through the capitalist film companies themselves), the conclusion is inescapable that official political censorship in Chicago is a signal for the local governments throughout the country to openly castrate all newsreels and to particularly suppress all activities of the Film and Photo League.

The committee called on all organizations "of a cultural character particularly" to send wires of protest to Mayor Kelly and to "get in touch with the various Film and Photo Leagues for joint actions against film censorship."[67]

In May, the FPL's position on censorship was published. It read:

1. We are opposed to all governmental censorship of films. We are opposed to censorship by the local police, by State Censorship (N.Y., Penna., Ohio, Md., etc.); we are opposed to the "unofficial" censor's power placed upon the Hays organization by the film industry at the recommendation of the US Federal Government.

2. We are opposed to censorship of full-length, short and all forms of standard-size films; we are opposed with most emphasis to censorship of newsreels and 16mm film censorship (at present there are bills in the legislatures of Ohio and several other states for censorship of 16mm films).

3. We are opposed on the grounds that film censorship like newspaper and censorship of speech, is a breach of the the alleged Freedom of Speech granted by the Constitution of the US, because it is an attempt to gag the working class, to distort and suppress news and opinions, in the interests of the ruling class.[68]

Further action was called for in the latter half of 1934 as the Catholic Legion of Decency instituted a drive for federal film censorship, gaining significant endorsement from other religious groups, the Hearst newspapers, and "prominent representatives of the bourgeoisie." In a lengthy article entitled "Who are the Forces behind the Legion of Decency Drive?" first published in the *Daily Worker* in August and reprinted with variations at least twice, Brandon argued that contrary to appearances the move did not represent any serious split in the capitalist camp. "Both the Church and the movies," he asserted, "as institutions of capitalist control, have been utilized for the creation of mass support for the policies of American capitalism as expressed in the NRA." The Legion of Decency was not "at war" with the movies: "On the contrary, this drive represents the endeavors of the more reactionary section of the bourgeoisie to work out more effective methods of using this great medium of social control—the movies—in the interests of the capitalist class as a whole and against the main interests of the workers, farmers, and intellectuals of

America." The article went on to expose discrepancies in Church pronounce-
ments on what films were "indecent," and charged that the "exemplary" films—
over which there was no argument—"happen to be precisely the most
reactionary, anti-labor, anti-Communist, anti-struggle, pro-war films of the
current season!" Brandon concluded that if "hunger, war, and fascism is the
price of decency held by the Church and movies in their role as mediums of
mass control for the ruling class, it is a price the international working class will
not pay."[69]

In July, the FPL was able to enlist the support of Hollywood montage
director Slavko Vorkapich in the campaign against censorship, and in August,
King Vidor joined the fight. The following month it was reported that the
league had sent a delegation to a meeting of the Association for the
Preservation of Freedom of Stage and Screen with favorable results:

> The delegation succeeded in securing unanimous endorsement of its proposal for condemna-
> tion of the narrow perspectives of the Church Crusade and for a city-wide conference against
> federal film censorship (which is being aided by the Interfaith Church Movement). In
> cooperation with the National Council of Freedom from Censorship (of the American Civil
> Liberties Union), the League will soon hold a symposium to bring public attention to the
> danger of federal film censorship.

David Platt went on the air over station WARD in Brooklyn criticizing the
activities of the Legion of Decency, but himself became the victim of censorship
when he was cut off.[70]

As a consequence of the Legion of Decency agitation numerous bills were
introduced in Congress when it convened following the November elections.
Among them was Senator Francis Culkin's H.R. 2999, which the National
Executive Committee condemned in a statement released in February 1935.
The statement outlined the repressive provisions of the bill and concluded:

> That immediate action is to be taken against this blast of Culkin's against a free screen, needs
> no discussion. Our Film and Photo Leagues, the League of Workers' Theatres, and other
> anti-movie-censorship groups should start entering protests to Senator Culkin, Washington,
> and to President Roosevelt, condemning the bill as a fraudulent attempt to stifle independent
> production and exhibition in the name of protecting "the motion-picture industry against
> unfair trade practices and monopoly" by Wall Street interests; and, secondly, as flagrantly
> against the interests of the vast audiences of moviegoers, who alone should reserve the
> unquestioned right to pass on what films they decide is best for them to see.[71]

Such protests—along with lobbying by the motion-picture industry—succeeded in blocking passage of the bill, and stymieing all further moves for
federal film censorship.

The league meanwhile continued to wage a struggle against censorship at a
local level. In some cases it was itself the injured party. Thus in June 1934 Lester

Balog, by then a member of the San Francisco FPL, was arrested and jailed in Tulare, California, for showing *Road to Life* and the league production *Cotton-Pickers' Strike* to agricultural workers, while the New York league was taken to court in January 1935 for screening newsreels in its headquarters. Later that year banning of the Soviet film *Youth of Maxim* in Philadelphia and Detroit provoked battles for its release led by the FPL in cooperation with the ILD, the American Civil Liberties Union, the National Committee Against Censorship, the New Theatre League, and other organizations. Such united actions, long a policy of the Film and Photo League, became increasingly characteristic of its work as the Communist movement entered the People's Front phase.[72]

Complementary to the WFPL's goals, as outlined by Potamkin in 1931, of exposing the role of capitalist cinema as a weapon of reaction, combatting anti-working-class films, and fighting bourgeois censorship, were the tasks of educating "the workers and others in the part the movie plays as an instrument for social purposes—in the U.S.S.R.," and of rediscovering and presenting "neglected films of significance." As a means towards accomplishing this, the league conducted series screenings of Soviet and other films, held at its headquarters, at the Labor Temple on 14th Street, or at the New School for Social Research. At the time, these were virtually the only such programs in New York City (the Museum of Modern Art's first film screenings did not take place until 1936), and constituted, in Brandon's words, "the first organized effort at what turned out to be a base for the developing quest for world cinema culture."[73]

Series were devoted to the history of Russian cinema, educational and scientific films, "the productions of independent amateurs and experimenters," "distinguished" films, and so on. European directors featured by the League included Pabst, Lang, Clair, and Epstein, while Hollywood movies rescued from oblivion included *Hands Up* (with Raymond Griffith), *Beggar on Horseback* (Cruze), and *The Last Moment* (Fejos), as well as the early works of Chaplin. Frequently speakers accompanied the screening (Potamkin, Joshua Kunitz, or Joseph Freeman, for example, on Soviet films) or spoke at independent forums (Vorkapich on "Fundamental Principles of Effective Cinema," Iris Barry on "Film in England," Henry Allman on "Modern Art and the Film," etc.). Audiences numbered in the hundreds, and even at low admission prices (usually around 25¢), the league was able to raise healthy sums of money to keep itself solvent ("We did very well," recalls Roffman, "and the money, carefully garnered, lasted a couple of months if we didn't spend it on film stock").[74]

Program notes published by the league revealed that it was not forsaking its fundamentally political orientation. Thus in an introduction to the 1934-35 season Irving Lerner wrote (under the pseudonym "Peter Ellis"):

It has become quite the thing, in some of our "enlightened" universities, bourgeois film societies, fashionable women's clubs to recognize the cinema as a cultural medium. However, the motion picture is still one of the major sections of capitalist light industry manufactured in mass production for immediate consumption. Thus after they have had their first run on Broadway and the initial showing around the circuit they are dumped into the ash can. Not that most of the films don't deserve that fate, but the distributors and producers are indiscriminate.

Lerner was willing to concede that "there have been films made in America that are important from an artistic point of view as well as an historical one," but in general the league encouraged the viewing of films not as self-contained aesthetic objects but as "a reflection of the culture in which they were created." The note on *The Cabinet of Dr. Caligari,* for example, reminded the audience that the film had been shot in 1919, when "a Revolution and bloody counter-revolution against the workers was in progress" in Germany, "but the artists that produced this picture seemed quite unaware of this and instead, they puttered blithely around with expressionism and cubism." *The Student of Prague* (Galeen) $6 1/2 \times 11$ (Epstein) illustrated "the morbid ideology of a disintegrating postwar bourgeoisie." Likewise, the director of the unconventional *Beggar on Horseback,* "in his specialized way," was "quite as much the *parvenu* as his master. He is annoyed, however, because *he* would prefer the *master's* acquisition. At heart they are *both* 'Big Business.'"[75]

At an early stage the WFPL showed an interest in building a comprehensive training program. In the early thirties, as Julian Roffman recalls, "there were no film schools or classes either within the university structure or outside" (apart from one or two screen-writing courses), and opportunities for learning still photography were also severely limited. In July 1931 the league announced a class in photography, to be conducted by Howard D. Lester, "a member of the executive board and one of the leading American photographers," and a class in projection, taught by "comrades in charge of the film showing of the WIR and Workers' Film and Photo League." Optimistically, it was stated that, "Later classes will be organized in cinematography, the history of the photo, the history of the film, the principles of photographic criticism, the principles of film criticism." It was the courses in practical still photography which proved the easiest to organize, and these followed at fairly frequent intervals. Advertised as being given "to enable workers to use their knowledge of photography to further the interests of the working class" or "to meet the pressing need for photo correspondents [for the labor press]," they covered topics such as "camera construction, developing, printing, enlarging, copying, portraiture, press work, etc." Instruction in film, it appears, was not offered on a regular basis until the opening, in November 1933, of the Harry Alan Potamkin Film School.[76]

Though the school was conceived as a monument to their mentor, league members were quick to point out that it was in no way intended as a fulfillment of the scheme drawn out by Potamkin shortly before his death for "a school of the motion picture." Potamkin's outline (published in *Hound and Horn,* October 1933) was for a four-year course of study within a university setting for "students professionally interested in the films"; the FPL school offered training for "workers and intellectuals who have pledged to become active participants in the work of the Film and Photo League upon completion of their studies (a five-months course)." The aim was not to emulate the film academy in Moscow—as William Troy, in a column in *The Nation,* had incautiously suggested—but to fulfill "the immediately urgent need to develop trained cadres of critics, scenarists, cameramen, and directors to combat the monster Hollywood reactionary propaganda machine." In *New Theatre* (January 1934), Tom Brandon discussed in detail the training which was being offered:

> The Harry Alan Potamkin Film School will be a workshop school in the various phases of the motion picture planned so that the workers who attend the school will not sit and listen to lectures, but will be a participant. There will be a lecture-discussion class on the History of the Movie, a study of the technological, economic, and social development of the motion picture, tracing the rise of the movie from the peep-show days to the present movie palace. Special lecturers will discuss War, Banking, Labor Unions, and Censorship in relation to the film. A lecture-discussion class in the history of the Soviet film will be led by Nathan Adler assisted by Joshua Kunitz and Joseph Freeman. This class will study the movie industry of the Soviet Union from its very beginning and after the Revolution to its present status as the producer of some of the greatest films of the day.
>
> Not only the physical growth of the industry will be studied but the theories and films of Eisenstein, Pudovkin, Dovzhenko, Vertov, Barnet, and Kaufman will be discussed in their relationship to the social revolution which has made their work possible. Also, there will be practical work in movie technique and production. Study of the mechanics of the movie camera, lighting, laboratory, projection, etc., will be preparatory to the production course which will embody film structure, scenario, editing.
>
> Various theories of film construction will be analyzed, but it will do what no other school in America does, it will cooperatively produce a documentary film. The class in criticism taught by Samuel Brody and Irving Lerner, will be a thorough survey and analysis of past and present film criticism. This important phase of the movies will be studied after the students have been prepared in the classes devoted to history of the movie, technique, and production.[77]

The school opened with fifty students, and included among its instructors, in addition to those listed above, David Platt, Ralph Steiner (described at the time by Brody as "the healthiest and most sincere artist in the 'avant-garde' of the bourgeois cinema and photo"), Leo Seltzer, Barton Yeager, Leo Hurwitz, and Lewis Jacobs. The workshop film, *Waste and Want* (made under Brody's direction), was not completed. Classes met two nights a week, when there was no urgent picket duty to be performed. The Harry Alan Potamkin Film School no doubt failed to fulfill all its objectives, but it was a boldly ambitious undertaking, justifying Brandon's judgement made near the beginning of its short life:

In the opening of the Harry Alan Potamkin Film School, the New York Film and Photo League made a signal advance in the short history of its development. The Film School departs from the sporadic methods of the past. It is a declaration of the *necessity* for *organized practical study* of the problems confronting workers in the film movement.[78]

The school did not survive to accept a second intake of recruits, and after its demise the Film and Photo League reverted to its former sporadic training program. In the spring of 1934, a class in "all phases of sound recording and reproduction" conducted by Edgar Zane, "the little engineering wizard of the Film and Photo League," was offered, indicating that the league was by no means totally committed to the silent film. In the summer of the following year, joint plans were laid with the New Dance League and the New Theatre League for a school which would "have as its main object the creation of a closer relationship between the dance, the drama, and the film," but it is not known if anything came of this interesting project.[79]

The Film and Photo League also, of course, had a still photography department. Though each section of the league met separately, there was no rigid division, and film cameramen, for example, would often double as photojournalists. Since the work of the still photographers complemented and reinforced that of the filmmakers, it may usefully be outlined here.

The goals of the photo section were to provide militant workers (and the unemployed) with the skills to create photographic records of the class struggle, to assure a flow of illustrations for radical publications, to orient established professional photographers more to the Left, and to help publicize the work of the WIR, the ILD, and other Communist-led organizations. To achieve these objectives, the section provided darkroom facilities, sponsored lectures, ran training courses, held exhibitions, and created channels for the supply of photographs to publishers. In carrying out this program, the FPL gave a powerful impetus to the growth both of photo-journalism and of documentary photography, neither of which was at the time greatly developed.

The FPL photographers discovered a demand for pictures of the class struggle not only from leftist publications, but also from a range of liberal and mainstream journals. In January 1935, several months after the formation of a National Photo Exchange as a central clearing house for league photographs, it was reported:

During the past year the New York League has had an unprecedented call for photos from the workers' press, from magazines and book publishers, and from picture services. We were able to supply only an average of about sixty photos per month. The demand is so great that we feel that we could easily place three times as many pictures. This we were not able to do in the past due to the local nature of our photos. Publications soon become glutted with local material. Our photos have appeared in the *Daily Worker, Freiheit, Der Arbeiter, Labor Unity, Labor Defender, Better Times Magazine, Fortune* magazine, *Jewish Daily Bulletin, Survey Graphic,* and other publications too numerous to mention.[80]

The supply of stills to the commercial press in fact provided a much-needed source of income for league members. Leo Seltzer recalls:

Motion-picture film couldn't be sold, no one would want to buy it, the newsreels had their own crews going out. But we could sell photographs, because very often we could get things the commercial news photographers couldn't get. So I took quite a lot of photographs as well as movies, and these could be sold to the newspapers to get a few bucks. A lot of times we'd know about a picket line or something that was going to happen, we could scoop the press, and that's what made our photos valuable.[81]

FPL members were in the forefront of a struggle over what constituted the most vital subject matter of photography. They rejected, of course, the romantic scenes of the pictorialists and the glamorized products and fashion models of the commercial photographers; they also had little time for the details of nature pictured by "straight" photographers such as Alfred Stieglitz, Paul Strand, and Edward Weston.[82] In 1931, when the Proletarian Photo exhibition was planned, it was pointed out:

It is to be understood that worker-photographers intending to exhibit . . . are to concentrate on the photo of class struggle and proletarian life. No bourgeois portraiture, nudes, landscapes, still lifes, will be exhibited.[83]

In 1933, the scope of FPL work expanded to include pictorial commentary, from a leftist perspective, on Roosevelt's New Deal policies. For a major exhibition in the fall, the Workers' Film and Photo League assembled a collection of photographs intended to portray "'America Today' and all the social and economic transformations it has undergone during the last four years." Subjects which would be covered included unemployment, housing conditions, militarism, and child misery; and a later appeal for entries was even more explicit, calling for "pictures from North, South, and West, pictures of industry, of farming, of unemployment, misery, stagnation, reforestation camps, child labor, political speakers, the 'New Deal,' pictures of struggle, strikes, picket lines, demonstrations, etc." Samuel Brody, at the opening of the exhibition in November, exulted: "[it] breathes with the fire of workers' struggles and makes the pink-ribbon photographic salon displays look like the last stage of pernicious anemia."[84]

The extent to which such subjects remained of priority importance to the league is indicated by several published calls for photographs and reports of work from around the country in 1935. In January of that year, the National Photo Exchange stipulated the nature of the material it wished members to submit:

> One—General Photos of Social and Economic Implication. For example: unemployed workers, child misery, bread lines, prostitution, housing conditions, destruction of crops, manpower replacing machinery.
> Two—Labor Actions. For example: strikes, demonstrations, protest meetings.
> Three—Demonstrations Against War and Fascism.[85]

In the same month the New York FPL announced some forthcoming photo exhibitions. "The City Child"—"undoubtedly the most important photographic document the New York League has made"—was designed to show the "home, school, and recreational background of the New York City child" and would be accompanied by statistical charts. "City Streets" was scheduled for April and was envisaged as "a comparative photo exhibit on this subject" in which five photographic organizations of the Metropolitan area would be invited to participate.[86]

The Chicago FPL undertook a photographic survey of living conditions on the South Side, while the Detroit group held a photo display on the subject of the "Forgotten Man." At the same time, the San Francisco League published an intriguing "proposed plan of work" which outlined a scheme to expand from scenes of proletarian life to embrace a complete pictorial class analysis of American society:

> We want to seek subjects that are powerful and representative factors in the present struggle of social forces. We want bankers, workers, farmers (rich and poor), white-collar workers, policemen, politicians, soldiers, strikers, scabs, wandering youth, stockbrokers, and so on and so on. We want to see them in relation to those things they do, where they live, how they work, how they play, what they read, and what they think. In other words we want to see them as they are in their most significant aspects. This means seeing them in relation to each other. We want this most of all because in this period of economic crisis the whole population is shifting into groups with equally uniform demands. In this shaking down of people into more and more clearly defined classes lies the prospect of vast social change.

Subjects which were specifically suggested included: "1. Waterfront, San Francisco. 2. S.E.R.A. Work Relief. 3. White Collars. 4. The New Legislature. 5. Cold. 6. Disarmament or the Next War. 7. Section 7A [of the National Industrial Recovery Act]."[87]

Still photography formed the basis for the many local chapters of the Film and Photo League which sprang up outside New York. Strong groups were established in Boston, Philadelphia, Washington D.C., Detroit, Chicago, San Francisco, and Los Angeles, and FPL branches were also reported at one time or another in Cleveland, Hollywood, Pittsburgh, New Haven, Laredo,

Madison (Wisconsin), and Perth Amboy, Newark, and Paterson (New Jersey).[88]

The regional groups pursued the same objectives as the New York league, but on a restricted scale. Only the Detroit, Chicago, and Los Angeles leagues engaged in film production on more than a minimal basis. Membership was much smaller than in New York: there were "six or eight," for example, in the Chicago group, which had no permanent headquarters.[89] Ties with the WIR seem to have been looser; but on the other hand, there tended to be closer links with other radical cultural groups like John Reed Clubs and workers'theatres. Movie production and exhibition was done principally on 16mm; filmmaking activity was no doubt hampered by the relative absence of facilities— laboratories, etc.—outside New York and California.

In this respect the Los Angeles group was helped by the proximity of Hollywood (where it operated a theatre), and it became the second most active center in the country. A 1934 report on its activities from a column devoted to the regional FPLs is indicative:

> Los Angeles Film and Photo League—(Because this group has been engaged in so many activities for this limited space, we can only include the most recent activities.) Has produced 12 reels (16mm). Has made films in strike areas and exhibited films to the strikers and among other organizations. Has used the film of the San Diego police attack on workers in court to disprove the frame-up against the workers. After obtaining a hung jury, the defense succeeded in obtaining an acquittal largely due to the graphic undeniable evidence contained in the film. Arranged joint showings of newsreels with the TUUC [Trade Union Unity Council], the Relief Workers Protective Association, the International Labor Defense. Conducted a very successful film showing and theatrical performance jointly with the Workers' Dramatic Council. Took part in the United Workers' Press Bazaar. Circularized all workers' organizations in an effort to stimulate film showings. Held a private showing of newsreels at the home of a Hollywood screen writer and raised funds for production. Working out a plan of cooperation with the WIR.[90]

Contacts between the various FPL groups were, at first, largely haphazard. "Every once in a while," says Seltzer, "someone would come in from San Francisco, or another city, or send some film in of something that happened.... We used to do most of the editing here in New York—they'd send us their film, because they didn't have the facilities or the equipment."[91]

Attempts at systematic coordination began with the filming of the second national hunger march in December 1932, when several crews from different cities obtained coverage of the regional contingents converging on Washington, for subsequent editing into *Hunger 1932*. Efforts to establish a permanent national organization were not, however, undertaken until midway through the following year.

In July-August 1933, an "Organization Committee for a National Film and Photo League" published a manifesto in *Workers' Theatre* under the headline "A Film Call to Action." Signatories David Platt, Jack Auringer, Theodore Black, J. Buchanan, Irving Lerner, and C.O. Nelson represented the WFPLs of New York, Detroit, Chicago, and Los Angeles, and the American Section, Cinema Bureau, International Union of Revolutionary Theatre (U.S.S.R.). The manifesto, addressed "to film workers (professional and amateur), to photographers, and to all who are interested in using films and photos in the interest of a creative, dynamic movement allied with the working class in the struggle against political reaction, economic oppression, and cultural decay," and "to the millions of American and foreign-born workers who make up the bulk of the movie audience," called for the organization of *"movie and camera clubs, film forums, better film groups,* in cities and towns all over the United States, for the purpose of exposing and combatting the capitalist film industry." A class-struggle, pro-Soviet program was openly endorsed as an answer to what was seen as a growing rightward politicization of the film industy ("it no longer even makes the pretense of 'pure entertainment'"), and the manifesto concluded with a plea "to help us spread a network of film and photo groups throughout the country, which will daily counteract the Hollywood standards, which will build a genuinely creative film movement based clearly and boldly on the realities of our struggle for a better society."[92]

In subsequent months Brandon was occasionally reported as acting in the capacity of "national secretary" of the WFPL, and the anticensorship statement of March 1934 cited above was released in the name of the "National Committee of the Film and Photo League" (signatories Brandon, Platt, and Samuel Greenblatt); but otherwise little was heard of the provisional national body until the following summer, when plans were laid for a national film conference to be held in Chicago in September.

The call issued by the National Organization Committee reiterated the charges previously made against the movie industry, while taking note of new developments which made action imperative. The "recent and current strike waves" had exposed the mendacity and evasiveness of the press. Mass misery and unemployment continued, while the fifth year of the crisis was seeing the outbreak of "brutal terroristic assaults by police, militia, and vigilante-fascist bands" on workers, including cameramen and film exhibitors. In addition, the Legion of Decency movement was increasing pressure for "the production of anti-labor, jingoistic, pro-war films" and the establishment of federal film censorship.

The committee, examining the records of the existing Film and Photo League groups, had found that "the rate of growth and level of effectiveness of organizations in this field are far behind both the needs and the opportunities for the development of a genuine independent solidified film and photo movement in the United States of America." There were "great tasks and opportunities at hand" for which the movement was not as yet "in any way commensurate."

Millions of movie patrons who have rejected Hollywood because the capitalist films do not check with the experiences of their lives present an anxious audience for honest and creative films made in their interest. The country is truly a gigantic studio for the production of vital films and photos. The great masses of workers, farmers, and Negro toilers now in struggle for decent conditions of life are in need of films and photographs that actually tell their story.

The National Film Conference would accordingly "devote itself to a discussion of the economic, social, and political conditions that face the amateur and professional film and photo worker; a discussion of the organizational problems facing film and photo groups; a discussion of the elementary technical and creative problems; the collective creation of a program and plan of work for the building of a National Film and Photo League, the election of a National Executive Committee." FPL branches and affiliated groups were invited to elect two or more delegates to take part.[93]

The conference was held as planned on September 25-29, 1934, a small event with about eight representatives from the Los Angeles, Chicago, Boston, Detroit, and New York leagues attending. The major achievement was the establishment of the National Film and Photo League "as an instrument for consolidating the work of the various leagues and for conciliating and uniting the many outside film and photo groups throughout the country on a minimum program of activity." Administration was to be handled by a National Executive Committee "consisting of a National Secretary, a resident National Bureau, and the executive secretaries of the various leagues supplemented by endorsers and advisers"; David Platt was selected as national secretary, while the other National Bureau officers elected were Tom Brandon, Frank Ward, John Masek, and M. Green.[74]

In his report on the conference, Platt noted that, "Problems of production, processing and developing, distribution, organization, agitation, politics, theory, were thoroughly covered and conclusions reached." Among the most heated debates was that on the relative merits of newsreel and "enacted" film production, which was decided in favor of priority to the former: "The mandate of the conference was that the major task of the Film and Photo leagues of America in this coming period must be the continuous and widespread production of newsreels and documents of the class struggle in action principally, and secondly, whenever and wherever the occasion calls, semi- or wholly enacted film production logically developed out of the firm newsreel base."[95]

Another important policy decision was that 16mm should be "the basic stock used locally by the leagues for the coming period," while on the national level "35mm is to be used and later reduced to 16mm for mass distribution." The filmmakers thereby came to terms with the fact that silent newsreels no longer had any prospect of playing theatrically (as they had up to 1933), and that in the halls where FPL films were shown the old 35mm equipment was fast being supplanted by portable 16mm sound projectors. Sixteen millimeter, of course, was a much cheaper stock for use in original photography.

Since the National Film and Photo League was conceived initially as a coordinating body, it seems odd that it should also have been charged with production independent of its member organizations. Platt reported that "the National League was authorized to go ahead and make plans for the production of four 35mm documents on coal, steel, the farm question, the South." There was no suggestion of just how the new national body would be able to undertake its own filmmaking, however; and nothing more was in fact heard of the project. Platt recently wrote: "I cannot even guess what happened to the plans for [the] 35mm documentaries.... Since we were then concentrating on 16mm newsreels I seriously doubt they were made."[96]

Further resolutions adopted by the conference called for the institution, in every league, of a "shock production troupe of the most talented cameramen in the organization, whose main function will be the production of newsreels and documents"; and for the establishment by each FPL of a training school "to provide a constant influx of new members for this important work." Approaches were to be made to the John Reed Clubs and the League of Workers' Theatres for assistance with scripts and the provision of actors and equipment; a National Film Exchange was set up to ensure nationwide circulation of locally produced films; a Photo Exchange was established; and a monthly National Film Bulletin was proposed.

New procedures were planned for the conduct of boycott campaigns. The conference report revealed that the struggle against anti-working-class films had become a large—in fact, too large—part of league activities:

> The conference agreed that the leagues must attempt to draw more liberal pacifist anti-war, anti-fascist organizations into the fight against reactionary films and not as in the past, carelessly dissipate time and energy in conducting huge mass campaigns against films like *S.A. Mann Brand* and *No Greater Glory,* single-handedly. The Film and Photo Leagues must of course take the initiative in exposing such films, but the campaign must be conducted only in conjuction with other organizations, never alone.

The National Film and Photo League would be affiliated, it was decided, to the national WIR, and member groups were to align themselves with the local WIR "if and when established." The wording suggests the relative autonomy the leagues now possessed in relationship to the WIR, which at this time was less of a force than it had been earlier in the decade. Finally, the delegates determined to hold a second convention the following year in Hollywood.

The conference's vote in favor of continued emphasis on newsreel production spelled the end of hopes of a faction in the New York league for a shift towards more dramatic and experimental film forms. Earlier in 1934, in a development examined in detail in chapter 4, Hurwitz and Steiner had published articles urging a new direction in league activity, and had argued for the formation of a full-time group of filmmakers to undertake the work. Rebuffed in this proposal, these two, with Lerner, now broke away to form the nucleus of a film collective known as Nykino.

In the wake of the conference and the Nykino split, the New York league underwent "complete revision to facilitate planned film and photo production."[97] Leo Seltzer was now less in evidence (he soon obtained work as a filmmaker with the WPA), and the production crew was augmented by Edward Kern, Julian Roffman, and Vic Kandel, who, together with veteran Robert Del Duca, handled most of the league's filmmaking work in the last year or two of its existence. Working with the assistance of the league, and in 1935 fully integrated with it, were Nancy Naumburg and James Guy, who concentrated on the dramatized political documentary.

It was clear that there were weaknesses in the movement. In November 1934, novelist and *Daily Worker* columnist Michael Gold expressed his disappointment in the league's achievement to date:

> Our Film and Photo League has been in existence for some years, but outside of a few good newsreels, hasn't done much to bring this great cultural weapon to the working class.
> As yet, they haven't produced a single reel of comedy, agitation, satire, or working-class drama.

And invoking *Three Songs about Lenin,* he concluded: "I hope somebody in the Film and Photo League finally learns how to do a film a tenth as good for proletarian America."[98]

In response, Platt could only admit that the charge was "very true": "No one knows better how true it is than the Film and Photo League itself, which has been struggling for years to produce films on a budget and with forces that would have wrecked a similar bourgeois organization." Platt, however, pointed to the New York league's reorganization and sounded a hopeful note for the future:

> Today there is a significant ferment in the field of the film, which may yet result in bringing "this great cultural weapon to the working class." New people are coming into the Film and Photo Leagues demanding work to do and getting work to do or going elsewhere. Audiences are springing up by leaps and bounds for workers' films.... This coming year will undoubtedly mark the turning point of the revolutionary film movement in the right direction, let us hope.[99]

The New York league put into effect its new plan of action, and the results did, to some extent, justify Platt's optimism. By May 1935 he was able to report that, though there still existed "an immense and immediate need ... for careful and continuous production and distribution of workers' films," some progress has been made. Newsreels are coming out of the labs faster and in better shape than at any time in the brief history of the revolutionary film movement.[100]

Meanwhile the National Film Exchange began the task of coordinating the production and distribution of workers' newsreels on a country-wide basis. Its manager, Tischler, explained his objectives in a February 1935 issue of *Filmfront:*

> [It is] increasingly essential that we expand our own newsreel propaganda work, producing real historical documents of the time from *our* side of the picture; covering all phases of workers' lives and activities from the Atlantic to the Pacific; building up an apparatus for the distribution of such films from coast to coast. An accumulation of such reels over a period of time, and in constant exhibition in halls, barns, homes, schools, churches, stables, etc. would be of inestimable value to the cause of the working class. . . . There are a number of film and photo leagues in America. If each of these leagues would undertake to make at least fifty feet of newsreel shots a week, the cost would not exceed $2.25 for raw stock and developing. The negatives would be sent to one central league. New York would be the most suitable place.
>   The New York league would print, edit, and title the material, and attend to its distribution. The length of the reel would be equivalent to fifteen minutes showing if gotten out weekly—one hour in a monthly edition.
>   As to distribution, every single workers' organization should be contacted. . . . [101]

There is no evidence to suggest, however, that the scheme ever got very far.

The National Film and Photo League, in fact, did not have a long existence. It was hurt by the loss of Brandon and then Platt, who had to devote all his time to film coverage in the *Daily Worker.* Its organ, *Filmfront,* was discontinued in March 1935 after five issues, following criticism of it for simply reproducing articles from *New Theatre,* a charge that was only partly true. (Platt records: "There was some opposition to dropping *Filmfront* in favor of space in *New Theatre.* But we were broke and couldn't afford to print the issues except in mimeograph form. It was felt that a larger circulation could develop for a film section attached to *New Theatre.* They had the money and we were persuaded.") It seems that the National League had in effect ceased to function by mid-1935, and the planned Hollywood conference of FPLs was never held.[102]

One of the contributing factors to the National League's demise was, no doubt, the eclipse of the Workers' International Relief. Reeling under the annihilation of its German operations in the Third Reich, the IAH suffered a second grievous blow in 1935, when the CPSU abolished its Russian section. Münzenberg, now devoting himself to antifascist propaganda from Paris, was no longer with the organization. It managed to survive in several European countries (amalgamated with the ILD's parent body, the International Red Aid), but in the US its activities seem to have come to a standstill by mid-decade.

The foundering of the National FPL and of the WIR had an inescapable impact on the affiliated groups. The New York league held on for some time as an independent entity, but without the organizational backing, financial support, and political direction the WIR, in particular, had been able to provide, it was an uphill struggle.

In an effort to divest itself of many of its nonproduction responsibilities, the New York FPL collaborated with Nykino and other organizations and individuals in the creation of the New Film Alliance in September 1935. The goals of the Alliance included the setting up of "a nationwide organization of independent, experimental, and amateur film producers," and the distribution of their films—and of meritorious movies shelved by commercial distributors—to a "nationwide non-profit-making organization of audience groups reaching even to small towns and farms." The alliance also intended to present screenings of film classics, institute lecture series, "work towards establishment of a competent film school," engage in the struggle on the film front against "war, fascism, and censorship," publish a magazine—in effect to take over many of the functions presently or previously performed by the Film and Photo League. (Significantly, however, in accord with the People's Front policy now being pursued by the CP, the class-struggle emphasis of the league's program was completely dropped: Hollywood films were thus stigmatized not for their anti-working-class bias, but for their "continued reiteration of outmoded, hackneyed, and adolescent themes.") The alliance was headed by Merritt Crawford, a film journalist, producer, and distributor, and among the prominent names included in its board of directors and Advisory Board were John Howard Lawson, Clifford Odets, Herman Shumlin, Harold Clurman, J. Edward Bromberg, Gropper, G.W. Pabst, George Sklar, Albert Maltz, and Robert Gessner. Edward Kern, formerly of the FPL, was apparently one of the alliance's active workers.[103]

The New Film Alliance succeeded in holding film series screenings and lectures, and in sponsoring the visit to the United States of Dutch documentarist Joris Ivens, but that was the extent of its achievement. The FPL, finding its revenues cut into (though it did continue to hold some film screenings at the New School during the first half of 1936) and offered little in return, became, in time, understandably cool toward its creature and rival.

Meanwhile, some of the league's production activities were being taken over by a group called Vanguard Films. How it happened is unclear, but a film begun as a project of the "Harlem film unit" of the New York FPL was released several months later (April 1935) as a Vanguard production (with Samuel Brody credited as production assistant). The following year, the traditional May Day films were shot and released by Vanguard ("c/o *Daily Worker*") and not, as was customary, by the FPL, even though the league was still definitely active at that time (it held the premiere of its film *The Birth of New China* on May 13).[104]

In June 1936, the filmmakers of the New York FPL moved their headquarters to 220 W. 42nd Street, while the still photographers remained at the league's then current address at 31 E. 21st Street. The break resulted in a much strengthened photo section, which, after reorganization, became the Photo League in 1937. The film section, however, fared badly. To judge by the absence of references to it in the left-wing press, it seems to have suspended operations sometime during the summer of 1936.

In February 1937 there came an indication that, appearances to the contrary, the FPL was still in existence. David Platt reported that the league, "after many months of silence," had emerged with a description of its current activities. These included the completion of work on a new film, *Getting Your Money's Worth* (first in a planned series), the composition of a scenario "about a young man who joins the National Guard," shooting on which was to begin shortly, and the planning of two further documentary films. Also reportedly active were the Chicago league, which had covered the Flint auto strike, and the Washington league, which "has just secured some sound equipment and is ready to start work."[105]

When *Getting Your Money's Worth* appeared two months later, a further statement was issued emphatically claiming that the FPL was "still kicking around in this vale of tears." According to the director of *Getting Your Money's Worth,* Julian Roffman, however, the film "was NOT a League project, and the League . . . did not exist except as a name which we kept alive because we hated to see the others kill it off by their deeds." The film is in fact sometimes credited to Contemporary Films, a unit formed by former FPL members Roffman, Kandel, and Del Duca, and subsequently responsible for two further entries in the series. In a recent letter, Roffman explained:

> The report of the non-demise of the league via the consumer series was a whistling-in-the-dark effort and a thumbing of noses at the forces that had gutted the organization by their forming of other groups and cliques. The league was dead for all practical purposes. It had not produced the films. I didn't even know that someone had issued a statement.[106]

With this in mind, it is worth examining the statement as an expression of the feeling of the remaining league members as it fought for survival in its last months of existence. The text begins:

> Once and for all, this should be made clear—the Film and Photo League is still continuing its activities, but not on as wide a front as in the past. The task of carrying on campaigns against films, issuing a magazine, and many other organizational functions, left us too little time to do what we had really organized for—the production of films reflecting social America.
>
> For this reason, meetings were called with other film groups and, as a result, the New Film Alliance was formed—to carry on the work of organizing and coordinating the film production and audience groups. The Film and Photo League devoted much of its time and energy into getting this new organization started. And when the alliance began to function, it

was understood that the league would devote its time to production of films—and the alliance to those tasks which had hampered the league's activities.

The statement goes on to note that, "Unfortunately, for various reasons, the alliance did not live up to its announced plans," and consequently had "proven a setback to the ultimate organization of the film movement as a whole." Moreover, "people were under the impression that the New Film Alliance had taken the place of the league because of film showings which it ran at the New School."[107]

The anonymous FPL spokesman concluded by referring to *Getting Your Money's Worth,* and affirmed:

> We, for our part, will continue making films, for that should be our main function. Further, we hope to cooperate with the Associated Film Audiences, for we realize that in the main their program is our program.

It was pure bravado, and the Film and Photo League and its regional chapters were scarcely heard from again.[108] Two of its offshoots, however, deserve mention. The Photo League, under the guidance of figures such as Sid Grossman, Aaron Siskind, Sol Libsohn, and Walter Rosenblum, became a significant force in documentary photography for many years to come. Placed on the attorney general's subversive list in 1947, it did not finally succumb to witch-hunting pressure until 1951.[109] The FPL was also to some extent responsible for the creation of the organization mentioned in its statement, Associated Film Audiences. This group inherited the league's program of combatting reactionary films, but its broad base of organizational support and nonmilitant plan of action clearly mark it as a phenomenon of the People's Front era:

> Now the movement to consolidate progressive opinion on the widest possible basis has materialized in the formation of an organization to be known as Associated Film Audiences, which will furnish a detailed analysis of all films released, will maintain a Hollywood office to supply information on projected pictures, and will furnish a bi-weekly news bulletin to its member affiliates.
>
> Organizations already participating include the Federal Council of Churches of Christ in America, the American Jewish Congress, the National Negro Congress, the American Youth Congress, the Workers' Alliance, the National Urban League, the American League Against War and Fascism, the International Ladies Garment Workers Union, the United Textile Workers Union, the New Film Alliance, and many others. Reviewers from the member organizations will fill out questionnaires asking for detailed information regarding racial, militaristic, anti-labor, and fascist tendencies in the pictures they review, whether historical inaccuracies or distortions occur, whether a false impression of any particular strata of society is given.[110]

The radical Left was on the defensive. The respectable tone of this pronouncement—so far removed from the revolutionary fervor of earlier manifestoes on the subject—betrays the political shift of the mid-thirties. It is a reasonable assumption that this shift is one of the reasons why the (Workers') Film and Photo League, pre-eminently a grouping of the class-struggle period of Communist politics, was deprived of organizational backing and allowed to pass unmemorialized into oblivion.

3

Film and Photo League Productions

New York Film and Photo League

1931

New York Workers' Film and Photo League production began with a film report, *Albany Hunger March,* on an episode in the struggle for unemployment relief. In January 1931, Governor Franklin D. Roosevelt of New York had summoned the governors of six other industrial states (Pennsylvania, New Jersey, Rhode Island, Massachusetts, Connecticut, and Ohio) to a conference on what was euphemistically termed "unemployment reserve." The meager practical benefits resulting (despite representations made by the Albany Unemployed Council) spurred Communist organizations to stage a hunger march converging from various parts of New York State on the capital at Albany. One column left from New York City on February 26, and a second from Buffalo the following day (after clashes with police delayed the scheduled departure by four hours). Workers' International Relief (WIR) back-up trucks provided food and first aid for the 500 marchers.

On March 2, the two contingents joined forces at Albany, where they were greeted by 3,000 demonstrators. The next day, the marchers entered the state legislature, where their leaders (including Jack Johnstone, Sam Nessin, and Fred Biedenkapp) attempted unsuccessfully to put their case for immediate relief. The silencing of their representatives provoked an uproar from the marchers in the gallery, who were thereupon attacked by state troopers and driven from the building after a 45-minute battle. A number of demonstrators were seriously injured, and one subsequently died from a fractured skull.[1]

The march was filmed by a "worker-cameraman," according to Lester Balog's recollection a Japanese-American (presumably a veteran of the Workers' Camera League). No contemporary descriptions of the film are to be found: the *Daily Worker* notice announcing its showing under the auspices of the WIR at an "Unemployed Solidarity Evening" at New Harlem Casino on April 3, 1931, states only that it offered "a permanent record of the historic fight of New York State's unemployed for unemployment relief, on the floor of the State Legislature."[2]

Filming on what was to become the WFPL's first major production, *The Strike Against Starvation,* began in the spring of 1931. Returning from a trip to the South, where they had shot some footage on the Scottsboro case, Tom Brandon and Lewis Jacobs (accompanied by a student whose name has been lost) passed through Harlan County and adjoining areas in Kentucky where a militant strike of coal miners was in progress. Despite hostility from local authorities, they were able to obtain traveling shots of mine tipples, and shots of sheriffs and deputies going out to the field. Shortly after, Brandon went back to the area to exhibit the footage to miners at union headquarters, to Pittsburgh supporters, and to other workers' groups. Enthusiasm was such that, with the support of the WFPL and WIR, he began a continuing coverage of the strike, which spread by summer to western Pennsylvania, eastern Ohio, West Virginia, and parts of Tennessee and Alabama, chiefly under the aegis of the Communist-led National Miners Union (NMU). Brandon now acted in the capacity of a working producer, the bulk of the camerawork being done by a Ukrainian motion-picture photographer whom he had located in Pittsburgh, Joseph Hudyma. The film centered on actions such as the assembly of picket lines at dawn. When developed and printed, footage was roughly edited on a geographical and chronological basis, and then shown in ongoing fashion to strikers and supporters in the mine-fields region. Brandon recalls that approximately ninety minutes of "usable" footage was obtained. Later in the year the film was cut into a three-real documentary (running forty-five minutes at silent speed) usually referred to as *The Strike Against Starvation,* although the titles *Coal Strike, 1931* and *Western Pennsylvania and Kentucky Miners' Strike* are also found.[3]

The Albany Hunger March, and others like it held in various parts of the country throughout the year, laid the groundwork for the first National Hunger March in December. Approximately 1,600 delegates of Unemployed Councils converged on Washington, D.C., in four columns starting from Boston, Buffalo, Chicago, and St. Louis. The march was organized, William Z. Foster recalled, with "an almost military structure and discipline," with provision made for the feeding, shelter, health care, and defense of the participants at all points along the route. Film coverage was arranged by the WFPL, and the resulting production, *National Hunger March* (also referred to as *Hunger March 1931* and *Hunger 1931*), included scenes shot in Boston, Providence, New Haven, Hartford, Buffalo, New York, Cleveland, St. Louis, Indianapolis, Detroit, and Pittsburgh, as well as Washington, D.C. In Washington, the marchers were confronted by large squads of heavily armed police and troops who kept them separated from crowds of supporters and blocked them from the public buildings in front of which they congregated to dramatize their demands. March leaders William F. Dunne, Herbert Benjamin, and Ike Hawkins were rebuffed in their call for federal unemployment insurance, encountering strong resistance from Congress, President Hoover, and the conservative leadership of the AFL.[4]

National Hunger March was first shown on December 21, 1931. Some footage from the film, which was probably two reels or more in length, survives; but the current version has been re-edited to rectify what Leo Seltzer terms the "haphazard" continuity of the original. At the time, the *Daily Worker* reported:

> ... the Workers' International Relief Film and Photo League prepared a complete history of the march. The pictures include the attack by police in Hammond and the splendid resistance by the crowd of workers and the marchers. They include the scenes before the Capitol, the White House, and AFL headquarters. They show the militancy of the marchers, the singing of the *Internationale* on the Capitol grounds, and the murderous preparations of the police, armed with machine guns and gas.

The Hammond incident is missing from the extant print of the film, and the Washington scenes are less extensive than is suggested here.[5]

The WFPL apparently produced newsreels at fairly frequent intervals during 1931. (In December, it was reported that the league had completed seven newsreels in the previous two months.) Apart from *May Day in New York,* a record of the May 1st celebrations, and *W.I.R. Children's Camp, N.Y.* (which may possibly have been the film shot the previous year), the subjects of these reels are not known, though in all likelihood they included strikes, demonstrations, evictions, and other phases of the class struggle.[6]

The league seems to have begun working in the compilation film genre late in 1931 with *The New World,* a two-reel documentary on the history of workers' Russia, 1914-1931. This film was exhibited by John Ballam on his lecture tour through the U.S. in 1932, but the source of the footage, and its precise content, it not known. The league also distributed *A Short Trip to the Soviet Union,* but it is not recorded if the New York WFPL members had anything to do with the production of the film.[7]

The New York WFPL ended the year working on a highly ambitious project with the title of *Winter 1931.* Designed to "portray the struggles of American workers and poor farmers against the miserable living conditions in this third winter of the economic crisis," it was to be an eight-reel film with a script written by the league's Advisory Board: Whittaker Chambers, Robert W. Dunn, Hugo Gellert, Joe North, "Robert Evans" (Joseph Freeman), and Harry Alan Potamkin. In December, six cameramen were reported to be shooting scenes for the picture. *Workers' Theatre* described the thinking behind the project:

The newspapers will not publish news of these struggles [of coal miners, textile workers, longshoremen] for better conditions. Neither will Hollywood, even in its news "reels." Because of this conspiracy of silence, there is an urgent need for a film that will reflect the bitter struggle that will certainly take place this winter. It would picture the American scene in its true colors. It would tell the truth that Hollywood is trying so hard to hide.

Winter 1931 is to be a moving-picture exposure of this kind. It will be a unified structure composed of separate news events, each news item featuring some dramatic detail of unemployment and mass struggle. Sharply against the cold of winter will flash the flop houses, the tattered clothes, the bread lines, lonely men freezing to death, spontaneous strikes, suicides, the more and more insistent demands of the starving millions, their hunger marches and demonstrations. The leisure class will be contrasted with the underfed. The picture will be used to raise relief for strikers' families and to support the struggles of the unemployed.

The estimated budget for the film (allowing for an optimistic 1.5-to-1 shooting ratio), was $4,500, "a pitifully small sum," the Advisory Board pointed out, "compared to the cost of the commercial, usual Hollywood products." The *New Masses* asked readers to send $1 a week and to keep it up for ten weeks, but evidently the hoped-for response was not forthcoming and the project foundered through lack of funds.[8]

1932

The New York league's one major production in 1932 (if we exclude the second national hunger march film, not shown in its entirety until January 2, 1933) was *Bonus March*. Also known as *The Fight for the Bonus,* this two-reel documentary, completed in October, was a record of the journeying to Washington of more than 20,000 out-of-work veterans, their encampment in the capital, their demonstrations for immediate payment of the bonus, and finally their violent eviction by police and troops. The Bonus March was not, like the national hunger marches, Communist-led, but the party did try to extend its influence among the veterans by the participation of its mass organization, the Workers Ex-Servicemen's League (WESL).[9]

Bonus March was filmed by Leo Seltzer, who describes the experience as follows:

I went to Washington twice. The first time was when the ex-servicemen were just arriving and encamping, and I got all the marching through Washington. I don't remember how long they were there, but there was a lot of marching, a lot of demonstrating. So I got there, and the thing seemed to have settled down to some extent, nothing else was happening, so I came back to New York.

Then the eviction took place. I got there just as the bonus marchers were being run out of Washington by MacArthur and the regular army, the cavalry and the tanks, and I filmed the whole area smouldering and burning, as I walked through it. The bonus marchers were already on their way, they were going to Johnstown, Pennsylvania. I walked through this place. It looked like a premature Hiroshima. Everything smouldering, bedsteads, personal belongings. There'd been families there, ex-servicemen had brought their wives and children—it was a Hooverville, right in the middle of Washington. And there was an old building that had been partly ripped out, four stories, where the bonus marchers were settled in—there were no walls, just concrete floors and cots. And then there was this order, signed by MacArthur, telling everyone to evacuate, by order of the President—I took the order itself off the wall and sent it back to Brandon—and then I followed the bonus marchers to Johnstown, where they set up another camp. We got some commercial newsreel material of the actual eviction, and I edited that in.[10]

The film survives, and is examined in detail later in this chapter.

The bulk of the league's 1932 output was in the form of newsreels. Arrangements made by Tom Brandon had secured a regular release for WFPL short subjects at the Acme Theatre on 14th Street (where they usually accompanied a Soviet feature), and production was evidently stepped up to keep pace with demand.[11]

What was described as "the only moving picture taken of scenes in Scottsboro during the trial" was scheduled to be shown for the first time at a protest meeting in New York on January 17. This presumably consisted of footage shot by Brandon and Jacobs in Alabama the previous April, when the nine black youths accused of the freight train rape of two white women were brought to trial, and eight of them condemned to death. It is suprising that the film was not shown earlier, but it is possible that it was considered too sketchy to be of great value, the crew having been run out of town by rednecks before they had a chance to obtain much worthwhile material.[12]

In March, the league issued *Kentucky-Tennessee 1932,* a film report on the NMU-led miners' strike which, following the collapse of the strike the previous summer, had been in progress since the beginning of the year. Early May saw "a full film of the huge May Day demonstration in New York with all sections, placards, floats filmed despite the heavy downpour." This was followed several days later by a newsreel of "May Day scenes throughout the country," edited, presumably, from footage sent in from league units outside New York. Also in May, the WFPL released *Scottsboro Demonstration,* shot probably on May 7, "international day of struggle," when "four thousand Negro and white workers demonstrated at 110th St. and Fifth Ave. . . . against the infamous Scottsboro lynch verdicts, and against continued imprisonment of Tom Mooney." The same month *Rent Strikes* was advertised as being available to workers' organizations, though it may have been completed earlier.[13]

In June and July the league offered newsreels of Bonus Army scenes, probably including both the New York contingent marshalling for departure and the arrival of the "Bonus Expeditionary Force" in Washington. The footage would later have been incorporated in *Bonus March. Foster and Ford in Action* (July) was undoubtedly a campaign booster for the Communist party presidential and vice-presidential candidates, William Z. Foster and James W. Ford. In August, an antiwar demonstration was covered, and in September, the league released newsreel footage of a miners' strike, a farmers' "holiday," and a Trade Union Unity League picnic.[14]

Coverage of the campaign to secure justice for the Scottsboro defendants continued in November, when the league filmed a demonstration in Washington on the occasion of a Supreme Court hearing in the case. Once again, Seltzer was the cameraman:

> Groups of people were coming from different states to picket in front of the Supreme Court, to show their support. It was an international issue at that time. The usual thing was to get a big truck, and everybody piled in, and that's how we got to Washington. . . . There was a fairly small group of pickets, and in those days Washington was a real Southern town. . . . So they were going to beat the hell out of these pickets to teach them a lesson. I figured the only way of getting close enough to take pictures was to get into the line of marchers, and after we marched into the area in front of the Capitol Building I got out of the line and started shooting film. Then things started to happen. There were a lot of plainclothes men and police around. The cops jumped at this group and started ripping placards off, and beating people up.
>
> I was filming this one policeman. It was a rainy day, and he had on a heavy, rubberized raincoat. I was about ten or fifteen feet behind him, and two or three feet beyond him was the line of pickets, with the Capitol dome beyond that. That was the shot. And as I was shooting, the cop ran in and grabbed the placard from a black marcher, and ripped the cardboard. And there was this marcher with the stick still in his hand. The marcher looked at the bare stick, and the cop was tearing up the placard which said, "Free the Scottsboro Boys," and suddenly the marcher turned and whacked the cop left and right with his stick. And the cop was so stunned, he just stood there.

Seltzer's camera was snatched at this point by an enormous detective.

> And then they started shooting tear gas, and before I knew it this guy turned around and grabbed me by the neck, lifted me with one hand, and threw me into the police wagon. He threw my camera in after me. That gave me some elevation, so I took my camera and started shooting out of the paddy-wagon door. I got another shot or two before he took the camera away from me.

Seltzer spent two days in jail as a result, but the film was not confiscated. The footage was later included in an issue of the WFPL composite newsreel series, *America Today,* and is still extant.[15]

In December, WFPL filmmakers were preoccupied with the shooting and editing of the hunger march film, new scenes from which were exhibited daily at the Acme. They also found time, however, to secure the material for a "sparklingly brilliant strip" on the Farmers' Convention held in Washington, D.C., on December 7-10 by the Communist-dominated United Farmers League: this film was shown as part of an issue of *America Today* in February, 1933.[16]

The league is also reported to have made during 1932 a film on housing conditions for the homeless unemployed, *New York's Hoovervilles.*[17]

1933

The National Hunger March of 1932 comprised 3,000 delegates of unemployed councils, unions, and other working-class organizations from all parts of the country. Once again the WIR was involved in support work for the operation, which was planned months in advance and executed with military-like discipline. The various columns reached the capital as scheduled on December 4, but unlike the contingents the previous year they were at first blocked from the city, being confined to a hillside stretch of road on the outskirts of Washington by a large force of police equipped with machine guns and tear-gas bombs. After a day of virtual internment, however, and in response to mass pressure, the marchers were permitted on December 6 to parade through the city, and were able to present their demands—for immediate winter relief and federal unemployment insurance—to both houses of Congress.[18]

In January 1933, the *Party Organizer* assessed the success of the march as follows:

> The National Hunger March aimed to broaden the united-front struggle for federal unemployment relief and for the Workers Unemployment Insurance Bill; to involve large sections of the working class in local struggles; to dramatize the struggle in a manner that would rouse the masses throughout the country; to present the demands to the US Congress. These aims in the main were achieved....
>
> The strong points of the march must be pointed out: 1) More struggles in the cities and towns in preparations for the march 2) All the marchers were elected by definite bodies of workers 3) Good composition: a high percentage of Negro workers, men and women, especially from the South; nearly 1,000 young workers, including some homeless youth; a high percentage of native-born workers 4) Only about thirty per cent of marchers were Party and YCL [Young Communist League] members (the check-up is not yet complete) 5) Better participation of the revolutionary unions (295 marine workers) and of some outstanding union leaders—marine, mining, textile, needle 6) Splendid working-class discipline and militancy, and good division and column leadership.[19]

Newsreel coverage of many phases of the march was arranged by the New York FPL in coordination with other league units, particularly the Chicago group. The resulting footage, after exhibition while the march was in progress, was swiftly edited into the four-reel documentary, *Hunger 1932* (also known simply as *Hunger*), which incorporated, in addition, an introductory section devoted to the living conditions of the unemployed. The "long awaited film of crisis and the victorious march of the 3,000 jobless delegates to Washington" was shown from 10 a.m. to midnight on January 2, 1933, at the Fifth Avenue Theatre, New York, and thereafter was to receive nationwide distribution in both 16mm and 35mm via the National Committee of the Unemployed Councils. Some footage (derived from reels 1 and 4 of the original) is extant.[20]

In the article in the *Daily Worker* Samuel Brody, who was a cameraman with column 8 of the March from New York City to Washington, pointed to the success of the film in documenting police brutality—"We have records of workers writhing in pain from the after-effects of tear gas"—and argued that the film proved conclusively "that in no case were the marchers intimidated by the unparalleled display of weapons and bombs" or distracted by provocation from the police or the capitalist press. *Hunger 1932* also recorded, Brody noted, the widespread support the marchers received from sympathetic workers en route. "The marchers' demonstration before the doll factory in Trenton where a sympathy strike had been declared," he wrote, "and the response of the workers themselves is, in my opinion, one of the most stirring documents of the class struggle." He concluded:

> Despite certain shortcomings (failure to make a more intimate and detailed record of what transpired among the marchers during their two-day internment in Washington, etc.) we feel that our film is an invaluable contribution in our efforts to unmask the lies and provocation of the capitalist press and screen before, during, and after the march, and to disseminate among wide masses of workers and poor farmers the lessons of this phase of our struggle against hunger and for unemployment insurance.[21]

There were no further major films from the New York WFPL during 1933. Production of newsreels did, however, continue. In February, the league exhibited a number in its *America Today* series, consisting of the following items: a) the Washington Farmers' Conference (December 1932); b) Lenin Memorial at the Coliseum; c) Gibson Committee Protest; d) Anti-Jim-Crow Demonstration; e) Anti-War Demonstration in Wall Street. These reels were followed several days later by *Tom Mooney Demonstration,* a record of an episode in the continuing campaign to free the California labor leader jailed since 1916.[22]

Daily Worker readers were urged in March to "Come In and See Yourselves" in *Unemployed Demonstration,* a newsreel "showing delegations from Boro Park, Staten Island, Bronx, Pioneers, etc." There was a similar appeal, no doubt, to the traditional May Day movies, which were again shot this year by league cameramen.[23]

On May 25, Leo Seltzer filmed the police attack on New York workers who were demonstrating at the North German Lloyd pier in Brooklyn in protest against the arrival of Hans Weidemann, an emissary from Nazi Germany. The footage, which forms part of the extant issue of *America Today,* shows mounted police wielding batons and dragging off protestors and bystanders by the wrist or the neck.[24]

After May, the Acme Theatre no longer announced the inclusion of workers' newsreels in its programs, and there are no records of any further WFPL productions for the year. It could be that the league, having lost a theatrical outlet for its work, slowed down or even ceased its filmmaking activities, or perhaps its films, being shown in union halls, clubs, etc., were simply not advertised.

During the year the WFPL did begin work on a "documentary film on the misery and degradation of proletarian children under capitalism in general and the economic crisis in particular." With the working title of *Misery Among Working-Class Children* or *Child Misery,* the project was under way as early as February 1933, when it was reported that the league was holding film showings "to provide money to complete the Child Misery Film in time for the national campaign of the WIR against child misery in the United States." In October, "Lens" in his *Daily Worker* column mentioned that "a group of comrades from the Film and Photo League were holding a sort of informal round-table council the other day to discuss the problems" facing them in the making of the film. By February 1934 the league was reported to be "now completing the film . . . in cooperation with the Workers' International Relief," but in his report to the National Film Conference (*New Theatre,* October 1934), Leo Hurwitz noted that it was still unfinished. The film was never, in fact, completed.[25]

Hurwitz was responsible in 1933 for a film made in association with the Workers' Film and Photo League. This was *The Scottsboro Boys,* a one-reel documentary about the case produced by the International Labor Defense. The film apparently utilized existing footage such as that shot in Alabama in 1931 by Jacobs and Brandon, as well as new material photographed by Hurwitz himself during the Decatur trial of March-April 1933. Hurwitz explains:

> There had been some footage shot and a little film made the year before, and when somebody approached me I said yes, I'd like to do it. I met with someone from the ILD, I think someone by the name of Coleman, and Brandon was involved somehow too, getting his advice on how to get a press card and things like that. There was a still photographer along, and we drove down to Decatur, Alabama, through the South, and I shot footage both in Scottsboro and in Decatur, and came back and made a film, which ILD distributed. . . . I even shot in the courtroom. I didn't ask any permission. I had an Eyemo and I shot in the courtroom and I had footage of the judge, and the counsel on both sides, and the little toy train that Leibowitz [defense counsel] used. . . . And it was a very tough situation to shoot. The cops wouldn't let me shoot in the ghetto, but I lived opposite the court house, and in order to go there in a straight line I had to walk through the black ghetto, and for a while I shot there, then the cop cars came around and prevented me from shooting. But I continued to shoot anyway—I held my camera down by my hip, got a few shots, not as much as I wanted. They were keeping very careful track of it. There was the threat of a lynching during the time. We were ridden out of Scottsboro, actually—they wouldn't let us shoot, and they held us prisoner in some office . . . and I was sitting there for hours until several cops came up, and then we were informed that we were not wanted, and we were told to leave town, and with the cop cars following us out of town we had no option on that.[26]

The ILD used the film internationally in its campaign for the release of the Scottsboro defendants.

1934

The New York Film and Photo League's single major production using original footage in 1934 was *Marine,* first shown on December 31. Also known as *Marine Strike, Waterfront, Workers on the Waterfront,* and *Marine Workers,* this fifteen-minute documentary shot and edited on 16mm by Edward Kern and Leo Seltzer was acclaimed at the time as "the best creative short yet done by the League."[27]

Marine was "a purely documentary film, no scene or situation having been staged." It attempted "to portray the struggles of longshoremen . . . by shooting their life from the moment they awake at dawn sleeping out on the docks of New York." Particularly striking, according to Ed Kennedy in *Filmfront,* were the scenes of the bread line and of the shape-up. Seltzer recently described the latter sequence:

> *Marine* . . . had some fantastic shots of what was called the "shape-up." In those days . . . the way you got a job as a longshoreman on the docks was to show up in the morning, and the boss would stand up on a box, and he'd have these little brass discs with numbers on them. He'd stand there looking over these three or four hundred men, holding out their hands, begging, and he'd flip one out to one guy, flip one out to another guy. He flipped them out to guys who he knew would kick back some of their pay to him—it was all prearranged. But the shots of these guys during the Depression, begging for one of these little brass things which meant food. . . . I got up, again in my naivete, up there right on the box next to him, and got a shot of these longshoremen begging for their bread.[28]

The shape-up was followed by scenes at union headquarters showing the build-up of strike preparations. "A photographic record of this alone would not have been sufficient," Kennedy wrote. "It was necessary to edit it so as to maintain on the screen the atmosphere of suspense that existed at the time the film was shot."

Robert Gessner was impressed with the portrayal of the men on the waterfront: "The actors are the workers themselves, many of them not knowing they were being shot, and the result has been better than most Hollywood casting." For Kennedy, what was powerful was the film's simple, logical structure:

> *Workers on the Waterfront* . . . is . . . the type of film that we firmly believe to be our most valuable weapon at the moment. This picture doesn't shout slogans, nor rely on acting. It is a very simple piece of work, not trying to cover a large field in its appeal. . . . First, it sets out to show the conditions that exist, and then it portrays the means being taken to overcome them.

Gessner had some reservations about the film's scenario ("This is the general weakness of all creative productions of the league"), but Kennedy expressed no doubts on that score. For the *Filmfront* critic, in fact, *Marine* was a triumphant vindication of the FPL's basic commitment to the unstaged documentary form:

> In a documentary film the skeptics have no opportunity to cry "propaganda" because the factual evidence is laid before them. It cannot be denied.... The problems of a documentary film are: (1) Knowing what you want to photograph and (2) Knowing where to get it. This was greatly achieved in *Workers on the Waterfront*. An audience after seeing the picture quickly realizes the necessity for strike action, so simple is the approach and so straightforward the message. The documentary film handled with care and intelligence is undoubtedly the strongest weapon a revolutionary workers' film group can use. Time and again its value has been demonstrated. In *Workers on the Waterfront* it reaches a high mark.[29]

There are records of relatively few newsreels produced by the New York league in 1934. One of the first was devoted to the city taxi-drivers' strike of February-April, which was also to give rise to a feature-length dramatized documentary made by the league in 1935, as well as Clifford Odets's immensely successful militant drama *Waiting for Lefty*. *Taxi Strike* was advertised as being shown in May. Also that month the league produced its customary report on the May Day parade, highlighted this year by aerial shots secured by Leo Seltzer. *May Day 1934* was featured at a "Workers' Newsreel Theatre" presentation on May 20, which offered coverage, in addition, of "anti-fascist struggles"—probably including a united-front demonstration outside the Austrian Consulate, "Negroes and whites fight [ing] for democratic rights," the Soviet freighter *Kim* in New York, the Scottsboro trial (possibly *The Scottsboro Boys*), and "striking middle-Western farmers" (perhaps consisting of commercial newsreel footage). There was also a "picture of Clarence Hathaway outside Madison Square Garden after having been assaulted"—the incident having occurred during the mass meeting held on February 16 to protest the repressive measures of the Dollfuss regime in Austria, at which Socialists and Communists clashed (Hathaway was editor of the *Daily Worker*).[30]

In September, Brandon complained in *New Theatre* that the New York league had "failed to make even one reel during the entire summer," and there are no reports of newsreels shot later in the year. There was a good deal, however, of other filmmaking activity.[31]

The league continued to produce review and compilation films. The extant number in the *America Today* series was apparently first exhibited in March 1934, and included, in addition to the original FPL footage of the Washington Scottsboro demonstration and the Hans Weidemann protest already described, four items culled from commercial newsreels: a) Fascist parades and Nazi activities in Italy and Germany; b) March of workers in united-front anti-fascist demonstration and political strike, Paris, February 12, 1934; c) Attack of deputies on steel-strike pickets, Ambridge, Pennsylvania, October 4, 1933; d) Interception of scab milk shipments by striking Wisconsin dairy farmers. The section devoted to Fascist activities also incorporated (in one version) an experiment in political montage utilizing footage of Franklin D. Roosevelt, and is analyzed in detail later in this chapter.[32]

The RKO-Pathe newsreel sequence of the Ambridge massacre, which showed deputies breaking up a picket line of the Steel and Metal Workers Industrial Union with batons, tear gas, and gunfire, leaving one man dead and another wounded, had a sensational impact when first exhibited in theatres and was soon withdrawn. "Lens" (Samuel Brody), in discussing it in the *Daily Worker,* significantly saw it as buttressing the Film and Photo League's aesthetic commitment to pure documentary. The column opened with a quote from Henri Barbusse: "The writer does not necessarily have to resort to direct propaganda. It will suffice if he shows things as they are: in our times, truth is revolutionary." Brody then demonstrated how even critics from the capitalist press were compelled, by the nature of the document, to draw radical conclusions, and quoted Lenin to the effect that "the film is most convincing when it leaves the studio and its artifices and applies itself to recording 'unplayed' events." The final part of the argument is worth reproducing in full, for it indicates the extreme importance a document such as this Pathe reel held for league members, both in itself and as a model for cinematic practice:

> We comrades know this [Lenin's belief] to be true from our own experience with newsreel making. We know, for instance, that no enacted movie on the subject could have carried as directly and powerfully as our documentary record of the Scottsboro demonstration in front of the Supreme Court in Washington. We can afford to discount the criticism of many among us who think that we are handicapped because we have failed thus far to turn out a single studio film. We agree with [Richard] Watts [Jr.], who, continuing on the question of the Ambridge film, says that, "There is something terribly ominous about the simple directness of the newsreel account. The unpretentiousness, the stark simplicity of a brief episode in the class war, captured without artifice by camera and microphone, is, among many other things, so dramatic that staged incidents of industrial warfare obviously cannot be compared with it."[33]

As late as June 1935, Robert Gessner was underlining the significance of the sequence:

> The Ambridge massacre sequence is also in *America Today.* I'd like to know why this short hasn't been more widely shown, especially to workers' clubs throughout the country. And the workers will wonder too, when they've seen it, why it's been in the vault. The commercial distributors took the Ambridge shots off the screen when they saw it, believing such true "propaganda" too hot to handle. Has it been too cold for us?[34]

A third number of the *America Today* series was reportedly completed during the summer of 1934, but its contents are not known. In the latter half of the year, the league produced two complete films compiled from re-edited commercial newsreel material: *Portrait of America* (first shown in September), and *World in Review*. There were, apparently, no contemporary reviews of them, but the following comment by Gessner gives an indication of their content and the manner in which they were cut:

> In *World in Review* Hitler salutes and the Hitlerites march. Here also is a perfect montage of Mussolini speaking, where his oratory (silent) is interspersed with the cheers of the crowd: the demagogue jerking the puppet strings.[35]

There were a number of uncompleted projects. Apart from *Misery Among Working-Class Children,* commenced in 1933, the league worked at one time or another on *Unemployment Council, Waste and Want,* and *Cigarette.* The first (initially titled *Death of a Worker's Child*) dealt with the lot of an unemployed family on New York's East Side and was to be scripted and directed by Michael Gold, author of the 1930 autobiographical novel *Jews Without Money* and leading Communist intellectual. Undertaken jointly with the Unemployed Council of New York, the film was announced as "ready for production" in February 1934, but was described as "unfinished" in October, and was apparently never completed. *Waste and Want,* detailing the contradictions of capitalism under the crisis, was a documentary project undertaken by a student workshop at the Harry Alan Potamkin Film School under the direction of instructor Samuel Brody. The students were "making excellent progress" with the film in April 1934, but it too was "as yet uncompleted" in October, and work on it was evidently discontinued. *Cigarette* was a project announced in December 1934 for a one-reel film with a scenario by novelist Nathan Asch and National FPL secretary David Platt. Platt recently confirmed that *Cigarette* was never produced, and added: "It was so long ago I cannot even remember what the script was about."[36]

During the year the league was also involved in an associate capacity in the production of several films made independently by individual members and other organizations.

Sweet Land of Liberty (July) was a one-reel film on the harassment of dissenters in the U.S. made by Leo Hurwitz for a Political Prisoners Committee of the ILD. (*Sweet Land of Liberty* had been the caustic title of the 1932 annual report of the American Civil Liberties Union.) After *The Scottsboro Boys,* Hurwitz recalls, the same people "wanted me to do a film on civil liberties, so I gathered stock footage and shot some other stuff, and edited a film, which as I remember was very lively." Footage of police attacks, evictions, etc., was ironically edited in contrast to symbols such as the law courts and the Statue of Liberty. "I remember using engraved legal platitudes on the courts," says Hurwitz. Stock shots were obtained at little cost from the newsreel companies which, it turned out, "had remarkable footage shot by their cameramen which never saw the light of the silver screen."[37]

Sheriffed, premiered in the headquarters of the Film and Photo League on September 14, 1934, marked a significant departure from previous practice in the radical film movement of the United States. Produced and directed by Nancy Naumburg, a member of the league, and James Guy, of the John Reed Club, it was a 16mm silent dramatized documentary, approximately forty minutes in length, on the struggle of farmers against mortgage foreclosures. (Between 1929 and 1933 a million farmers had lost their property through foreclosure.[38]) The film was shot in Pennsylvania with a cast composed of members of the farm community. Reviews in the *New Masses* and *Filmfront* were sympathetic to the picture's aims and certain of its achievements ("It is modest and unpretentious and has its faults," wrote Irving Lerner, "but the film has a certain vitality, freshness, and honesty that spring from its revolutionary conviction"). The scripting and cinematography, however, were severely criticized. Naumburg's defense, in pointing to the conditions under which the movie was made, indicates some of the concrete problems then confronting pioneers on the "revolutionary" film front:

> The purpose of this film is to show working-class audiences what the actual conditions in the life of the American farmer are, and the necessity for militant organization. The American farm situation is so complex that we found it necessary to concentrate on only one aspect of it: the inability of the farmer to pay the interest on his mortgage and the threat of mortgage foreclosure. Consequently the film may seem over-simplified.
>
> We had no precedent in making a revolutionary American film. The scenario had to be changed as we progressed in order that it might be politically and documentarily correct. Not a single scene was shot without first consulting with and getting the advice of leading members of the United Farmers' Protective Association, among them Lief Dahl and Lew Bentzley (who also "acted" the role of the organizer in the film). The scenario was subject to constant changes after we had started to shoot because of the conditions under which it was taken: the farmers were working and could be filmed on but rare occasions. For technical and financial reasons also, it was impossible to make complicated sequences or to reconstruct scenes. As far as the photography was concerned, here too the main difficulties were financial and technical. The camera was old and temperamental, jamming in the middle of important scenes, etc. Moreover, low finances did not permit securing the kind of film best suited for this work.
>
> Revolutionary filmmaking is a painful process, as you can gather from the above....

Naumburg and Guy were not deterred by the difficulties or adverse criticism, and returned to work directly with the league the following year on another ambitious project.[39]

The final collaboration in which league members were involved in 1934 was a four-reel sound documentary, *Ernst Thaelmann: Fighter Against Fascism,* also known as *Ernst Thaelmann: Fighter For Freedom.* Compiled from newsreels smuggled out of Germany and other sources, and edited in the United States under the auspices of the Thaelmann Liberation Committee, the film documented the political life of the German Communist leader from 1924 to 1933, and incorporated scenes from the world-wide struggle to liberate Thaelmann following his imprisonment under the Nazis. Footage was included of mass May Day rallies, street fighting, Nazi terror, concentration camps, the burning of the books, the Reichstag fire trial (with Dimitrov speaking in court), underground activity of the KPD, and Dimitrov in Moscow; introductory and closing remarks by CPUSA secretary Earl Browder, who reminded spectators of the threat of native fascism in the United States, were added. A *Daily Worker* reviewer again stressed the superiority of the documentary form as a cinematic weapon: "The sponsors of the film frankly admit that the picture does not have any dramatic story acted out by professional actors imitating the various individuals, like Thaelmann, Clara Zetkin, Sen Katayama, Dimitrov, Torgler, Van Der Lubbe, Barbusse, Rolland, and others, but that instead this historical document is made up of actual newsreel films of the struggles of the German proletariat. . . . " The film had a successful theatrical run in New York in September, and was distributed by Garrison. A silent, British version of this film, entitled *Free Thaelmann* and edited by Ivor Montagu, still survives, but the American original is not known to be extant.[40]

1935

The reorganization of the New York FPL following the National Film Conference gave rise to a burst of filmmaking activity in the first half of 1935. Edward Kern, in a letter to the *New Masses* of March 19, was able to point to the recent completion of *1934*, *H.R. 2827*, and *East Side, West Side*, in addition to 1934's *Workers on the Waterfront;* and at least four more films were produced by the league by June. There was a significant slackening of filmmaking work in the summer and fall as energies were diverted to the creation of the New Film Alliance (see chap. 2).[41]

About *1934* no information exists; possibly it was a compilation of newsreel footage from the previous year highlighting important events, in emulation of the annual practice of certain newsreel companies (but with, of course, a leftward twist). (The Federal Theatre's Living Newspaper *1935* of the following year was a revue dramatizing public affairs; the Group Theatre's *1931—*, however, was closer to an ordinary dramatic narrative.)

H.R. 2827 was a three-reel documentary on the Unemployment and Social Insurance Congress which had been held in Washington in January in support of the Communist Party-sponsored Workers' Unemployment, Old Age, and Social Insurance Bill. The Lundeen Bill, as it was known, provided for workers' benefits as full "average local wages" for the total duration of unemployment or disability, and was not, of course, enacted; agitation for it, nevertheless, no doubt influenced the passage of the Roosevelt social insurance legislation.[42]

In *East Side, West Side,* a study of Manhattan, the league attempted to construct a whole film of the principle of montage conflict. The idea had been used several years before by New York independent filmmaker Irving Browning in his *The City of Contrasts* (1932)—which utilized candid camera techniques and was composed entirely of multiple exposures—and was present, at least in apolitical embryo, in Herman G. Weinberg's *A City Symphony* (1930). Robert Gessner briefly described the film in his June 1935 survey of FPL productions:

> *East Side, West Side* is a hodge-podge of interesting shots, attempting to contrast the life in New York on the opposite sides of Fifth Avenue. This is a swell idea, and should be taken up more seriously and done probably as a feature. The shots for instance, of models in expensive shop-windows and the revolving doors and the fainting Prometheus of Rockefeller Center are both humorous and pathetic alongside of West Side bread lines and evictions.

Scenario, Gessner added, was its weakest factor.[43]

Despite the National Film Conference's decision in favor of straight newsreel and documentary as priority items for Film and Photo League production, the New York league went ahead with the shooting of at least two "enacted" films in the early months of 1935. *Hollywood,* directed by Vic Kandel and Robert Del Duca, broke new aesthetic ground for the league: it was a satire. Its target, of course, was the motion-picture industry, and it was apparently two reels in length, but little else is now known about it.[44] *Taxi,* on the other hand, was a development of the dramatized documentary format essayed the previous year in *Sheriffed,* and Naumburg and Guy were again the directors.

The background was the New York taxi strike of 1934, and actual newsreel scenes were included. The film, made in cooperation with the Taxi Drivers Union of Greater New York, dramatized a strike for the reinstatement of four blacklisted drivers. Described at the time of shooting as "an exposé of the miserable conditions under which taxi drivers work and the hypocritical role of the company unions," it dealt with the life of a hackie, the benefits of a union, the necessity for militant action, and the harm being done by a scab. *Taxi* was shot over a period of four months on a miniscule budget of $250, and in its final six-reel length qualified as "the first workers' feature film produced in America." Parts were played by members of the union and by actors of the Theatre Union Studio.[45]

As with *Sheriffed,* critical reaction was not at all indulgent. "Although it is the first enacted movie by the Film and Photo League," wrote Gessner, "it will perhaps be on record as time goes on as their worst." And he spelled out its faults:

From the point of view of production, it is disappointing: the photography is erratic and amateurish; the direction is almost entirely absent, and the editing is weak, the titles misplaced and poorly worded. The scenario, if any, is so much in the background that you feel the cameraman is doing the writing while shooting.

Nevertheless, Gessner found the film interesting simply because of the class-struggle nature of the material it dealt with. "The raw meat of social reality," he concluded, "is preferable diet to the cream puffs of Hollywood."[46]

For co-director James Guy, drawing on the tradition of Vertov and Eisenstein, the film derived strength from its use of real taxi drivers in the cast—despite certain drawbacks which this entailed:

Though the members of the Taxicab Drivers Union were experienced at many things besides cab driving, acting was a new one to them....

When they were asked to take various parts in the film, they did it with...verve and realism, whether the part was that of boss or stool pigeon....

During the winter it was often so cold that work was done in five-minute periods. Naturally this all took time. Most of the minor characters were only able to come around occasionally. Therefore in *Taxi* we often see a different person portraying the same part. Sometimes the actors were unable to shave or change clothes. Consequently they often looked changed in the same scene. But then those are the peculiar problems of workers' films at the moment.... Taxi driving being at best a precarious way of earning a living, the men could not be expected to give very much to a film. Nevertheless they came through handsomely, though most of the shooting had to be done on Sundays and evenings.[47]

Gessner thought that *Taxi* was important because "it shows *what can be done*," but the FPL filmmakers were to make no more experiments in the dramatized documentary mode; that field they left to their former colleagues now grouped in Nykino.

About the same time as *Taxi,* in May, came two shorts documenting activities at Madison Square Garden. The first, *United Front,* directed and edited by Edward Kern, was devoted to a recent demonstration against "fascist" legislation. Gessner thought Kern's work was "excellent," and suggested that "this short should do much, when distributed through the American League Against War and Fascism, to gain new recruits in the fight." He praised the indoor photography both in *United Front* and in the second of the two films, a report (whose title has not been recorded) on a congress of the International Workers' Order (IWO), the Communist fraternal organization. The IWO film, however, found a less impressed viewer in critic Louis Norden, who took it as a specimen of the "objective viewpoint" being espoused by the new independent filmmakers in contrast to the "impressionism" promoted by the *Experimental Cinema* group:

This new objectivity is as impassioned as was the impressionism of an earlier day. It is, according to its devotees, in the Marxian manner, though, to me, it more nearly resembles Harpo than Karl. One of the best examples of its absolute ineffectuality was the documentary film (made to order) of a recent IWO convention in Madison Square Garden. The old Film and Photo League were the perpetrators, and they perpetrated. You saw crowds, you saw banners, you saw faces making grimaces, a conductor waving his baton, people listening, a badly lighted pageant. It was a twenty-minute perpetration, too, and at its close you didn't know what it was about (even though the camera showed you everything that had happened), you received no impression of the IWO, you merely took away a great boredom, and a great resentment against the makers of this montage who refused to be criticized (on the grounds that the film had been ordered by the IWO and had been made to specification).[48]

The only simple newsreel shot by the league of 1935 of which there is any record is *May Day 1935*. The *Daily Worker* reported that in the massive New York demonstrations that year all previous highs had been topped, 100,000 taking part in the Socialist parade and 200,000 turning out under the united-front banners of the Communists. The scene was recorded by the FPL in a short film, 200 feet of which was in color.[49]

Hands Off Ethiopia, produced by the league in November, was in all probability a compilation of war footage from commercial newsreel sources. Julian Roffman does not remember the film, but suggests:

...it may have been a quick job done in a hurry to meet the needs of organizing some support among clubs and organizations for Ethiopia and against Italy and Mussolini. At that time there were some documentary features playing in the theatres supporting Mussolini— *Camicie Neri (Black Shirts)* or some such title—which glorified the Blackshirt movement and Mussolini and had great support from some elements of the Italian community.[50]

The fact that a project announced early in 1935 by the New York FPL subsequently emerged as a production, *Harlem Sketches,* of Vanguard Films, was mentioned in chapter 2. There is no proof, of course, that one and the same film was involved, though the association of Samuel Brody with the final film as production assistant certainly suggests a connection. *Filmfront* reported on January 7, 1935, that "the Harlem film unit of the New York League has completed its scenario for a 35mm exposé of conditions in Harlem," adding, "shooting will start shortly." *Harlem Sketches* premiered as a two-reel sound film precisely three months later, and it was reported that the Film and Photo League would handle distribution.[51]

Directed by Leslie Bain, "former co-worker of Slavko Vorkapich, noted Hollywood film craftsman," and with a musical score by George Antheil, *Harlem Sketches* was a straight documentary "made without any actors, or stage sets." In his very favorable review, David Platt bluntly contrasted its depiction of life in the black ghetto with that offered in feature movies:

There have been many films about Harlem. The Harlem of Carl van Vechten or Cab Calloway is a familiar sight to moviegoers. One sees flashes of Harlem night life in five out of six musicals that hit the screen. There are even small Negro production companies in Harlem that specialize in this false species of night life, forgetting another kind of life that's expressed in flophouses rather than jazz bands. But it seems this kind of life is taboo in the films, which prefer to exploit the Negro as a clownish dice-rolling, tap-dancing servant of the boss white class. . . .

Harlem Sketches is a cross section not of the night clubs with its [*sic*] fancy ladies and dapper gents, but of the day-to-day lives of the thousands of poverty-stricken Negroes, whose pent-up fury against conditions was inevitably released during the recent events that took place around 125th and Lenox Ave.

Bain takes us right into the heart of Negro Harlem. He shows us the unbelievable misery of Negro tenement life with its sick and dying for lack of medical care. He shows us the oh so charitable slop lines, the underweight and underfed children, the Negro revivalists who dole out dubious spiritual medicines in the face of suffering that can be cured only by union of black and white against conditions.

As a counterbalance to the pestilential misery that stalks thousands of households in Harlem, Bain's alert camera shows us something of the organized expression of militant Harlem Negro and white in demonstration supporting the Scottsboro boys and against the landlord oligarchies of Harlem, winding up with a characteristic study of James Ford, Negro Communist organizer in action.[52]

Ford, invited to a preview screening, himself endorsed the film without qualification, commenting:

When one sees each detached incident in Harlem life, one fails to comprehend what the totality of that life is. Here in this picture it is all assembled, street scenes, tenement dwellings, bread lines, dance halls, church revivals, and meetings. The pictures tumble in on you, one after another, each one a part of a bitter whole.

The film was offered in evidence to the Mayor's Investigating Committee on Harlem in the wake of the recent riots, and reportedly "startled" its members. *Harlem Sketches* was clearly a significant achievement of the radical film movement, even if its genesis was obscure.[53]

1936

By 1936 the New York FPL had suffered a severe cutback in its operations, and there are reports of only two films completed under its auspices during the year.

Give Us This Day, probably the work of the New York league, was described as "the life of an unemployed Negro worker," and was announced as available for booking on June 3. Julian Roffman does not recall the film distinctly, and nothing more is known of it.[54]

About *The Birth of New China,* there is substantially more information. First shown in May, it was a six-reel compilation film edited by Roffman for the American Friends of the Chinese People, and was based on film material

supplied by partisan war lord General Fang Chen-wu. A former Army commander and state councillor of the Nationalist Government, Fang had "embarrassed" Chiang Kai-shek in 1933 by becoming a leader of the People's Anti-Japanese Allied Army and throwing some 10,000 of his troops into action against the invaders in Chahar province, in violation of the Tangku truce. Stripped of his posts, Fang was forced to flee abroad for his life.[55]
Roffman recalls:

There was an organization which published a magazine *China Today* ... and they contacted the League because they wanted someone to edit a good deal of footage which had been brought to the U.S.A. by Gen. Fang Chen-wu. ... I went to see them and of course it was a no-pay job. I undertook to do it. There was an editor of the magazine, a Mr. Phillips, who supplied a Chinese associate editor who could speak English, and who either worked at a university in New York City or was studying there, and he acted as translator for the general and as advisor about the film. The general as best as I can remember was a war lord who fought against other war lords, and this film was a record of those battles. He was also anti-Chiang Kai-shek, which I imagine made him a worthy ally. Commentary was in titles. Film was silent. No money for anything else. Chiang was the main enemy, and of course the British imperialist forces still ruling in China.[56]

Augmenting Fang's footage with material from the Soviet production *Shanghai Document* (1928) and other sources, probably including commercial newsreel, Roffman was able to construct a chronicle of struggles in China from 1924 to 1935 which was impressive in its sweep. As reported in a contemporary review, the coverage embraced: "The march of the Chinese Revolutionary Army to break the power of the Northern militarists in 1926; the betrayal of the revolution by Chiang Kai-shek, supported by the war lords and the imperialist powers in 1927; the capture of Tsinan by partisan General Fang Chen-wu (now in the U.S.) in 1928; the rise of Soviet China illustrated by charts and diagrams since no photographs or films about this mighty one-sixth of China are yet available; the Japanese invasion of Shanghai, and the burning of Chapei in 1932; General Fang's Chahar campaign; the growth of the great anti-Japanese movement; the student and mass demonstrations of present-day China; and other historic events that have shaken world imperialism in the past decade of China."[57]

Although Roffman now feels that "most of the action was in the titles" and that *The Birth of New China* was "nowhere near the stature" of the later documentaries *China Strikes Back* and *The 400 Million*—which he describes as "crafted films" in comparison with his "patch job"—the film was well received at the time. David Platt, in the *Daily Worker,* called it "a quite remarkable account of the great Chinese Liberation movement," and argued that "besides being one of the best productions of the Film and Photo League" it was "an invaluable organizer for the American Friends of the Chinese People, as it will be of tremendous help in explaining China to the thousands of misinformed who have gained their ideas about the country from capitalist movies like *Leathernecks Have Landed* and Charlie Chan."[58]

The film's useful life was no doubt shortened by political developments which transformed Chiang Kai-shek into an ally of the Communists following the Sian Incident at the end of the year.

1937

Since, at the time of its release, *Getting Your Money's Worth* was referred to as an FPL production (even if this was only an honorary gesture—see chap. 2), it deserves to be described here. It was a one-reel sound documentary on the work of the Consumers Union, and showed laboratory researchers testing milk, exposing flimsy shoe construction, and revealing the dangers of poisoning from lead toys. "The idea was not," director Julian Roffman wrote at the time, "to stress the ideas or aims of the organization, but purely to do in film what the union does in its magazine—that is to show how tests are made—offer advice— show how to guard against fraud and misrepresentations."[59]

Roffman "directed, produced, photographed, and wrote the script" with assistance from league members Robert Del Duca on camera and Vic Kandel in fund-raising, the selection of music, and the writing of the commentary. Irving Browning also collaborated on the film. The Consumers Union, under Arthur Kallet, provided technical advisors and research facilities, but did not sponsor the project financially. The money, says Roffman, "I had to find and borrow."[60]

Critic Meyer Levin, writing in *Esquire,* found *Getting Your Money's Worth* an impressive piece of work:

> It is an objective, well-made exposition of certain manufacturing frauds. It names no products, but simply educates the public as to what qualities to look for, in buying. Furthermore, I found the reel really worth attention; I think the subject was as well handled as the average episode in *The March of Time....* [61]

Despite the film's quality, Roffman encountered great difficulty securing distribution for it. As he explained to Levin:

> Theatre powers thought it was swell. But when it came to have this shown around—to make known this fraud of the manufacturers to the people—to educate people with honest, intelligent films—to let them at least gain something from the film they went to see, our film magnates began to balk. As one soft-spoken owner said, and he the owner of an art cinema, "it ain't entertainment," so what does he do but book free General Electric advertising films into his theatre, and this is his idea of "entertainment."

Getting Your Money's Worth eventually opened theatrically in New York in September, playing on a bill with *Mayerling* at the Filmarte. "The Film and

Photo League had made many good newsreels and shorts in the past several years," David Platt commented in the *Daily Worker*, "but nothing with the technical and fine professional finish" of Roffman's film. Two sequels were produced under Roffman's direction by the unit Contemporary Films in subsequent years.[62]

In February 1937, the New York FPL announced several projects which in all probability never came to fruition. Two new documentary films, subject matter not stated, were declared to be "in the offing," while the league was "busy finishing up a scenario about a young man who joins the National Guard and is called out to break a strike." Work on the latter, which was to be a sound film, was to "begin shortly," but no further references to it are to be found.[63]

Regional Film and Photo Leagues

Detroit

On March 7, 1932, several thousand unemployed Detroit workers marched to the Ford River Rouge plant in Dearborn, where they planned to present a series of demands to the management. These included: jobs for all laid-off Ford workers; immediate payment of half wages and a lump sum of $50 winter relief; reduction in the work day, slowing down of the speed-up, and more rest periods; no discrimination against blacks; abolition of service men (spies, police, etc.); and free medical care, supplies of coal or coke, and protection against foreclosure for present and former Ford workers. The march was organized under the auspices of the Detroit Unemployed Council and the Communist-led Auto Workers Union. At the Dearborn city line the marchers were met by police, and fighting broke out. The workers advanced to the plant gates, where they were assaulted with tear gas, fire-hoses, and pistol shots; as they retreated, police opened machine-gun fire. Four marchers were killed, one of them an organizer for the Young Communist League, and some fifty wounded. On March 12, 40,000 paid tribute to the dead as they were given a Red funeral.[64]

The Ford Massacre (or *Detroit Ford Massacre*) was the Detroit Film and Photo League's documentary record of the hunger march and its aftermath. Filmed (except for the funeral sequence) by Joseph Hudyma, it was one reel in length, and in its brief central sequence succeeded in conveying the terror of the attack in a series of rapidly snatched, violently moving shots. The film survives (minus its opening and closing segments, according to Brandon), and is analyzed in greater detail below.

In February 1934, it was reported that the Detroit FPL had "made a one-reel film for the Macedonian Workers Club and assisted in showing it on a tour through Michigan, Indiana, Ohio, Penn., and New York." Nothing more about it is known.[65]

By the end of 1934, the Detroit league was described as having twenty members and "four or five movie cameras," and had undertaken "two documentary, partly enacted projects with the assistance, when necessary, of the John Reed Club and the Theatre of Action—these are *Speed-Up in Auto Industry* with A.B. Magil as consultant, and *Workers' Health,* with Dr. Bicknell as consultant." Apparently these films were not completed.[66]

The Detroit FPL was probably responsible for other films, records of which have been lost.

Chicago

Information on the Chicago Film and Photo League is also sparse.

The 1932 Communist party convention was held in Chicago on May 28-30, with William Z. Foster and James W. Ford being selected as the party's candidates in the forthcoming presidential elections. The event was recorded in a newsreel, probably shot by Chicago FPL members, which was shown in New York in June, under the title *Communist Convention in Chicago.*[67]

In December 1932, Chicago FPL cameramen, including C.O. Nelson and William Kruck, took part in filming the second national hunger march, and their footage was included in *Hunger 1932.*

Nelson's *Halsted Street* (1934) was a 16mm documentary, sixteen minutes in length, recording details of life along the street, "from the city limits at the southern end to Lake Michigan on the North," as an introductory title put it. The film contrasted the various ethnic neighborhoods, and included footage of a protest march in defense of the Scottsboro Boys and for unemployment relief.[68]

The Great Depression, also 1934, by Maurice Bailen, was a documentary of hard times in Chicago, incorporating fragments of a fictional story of an unemployed worker contemplating suicide. Shot in 16mm, it originally ran about thirty minutes, but it has been re-edited and shortened by Bailen over the years; existing prints are about half that length. The climax of the film is reached when the man encounters a demonstration by the unemployed demanding work.

A film by members of the Chicago league was made on the World's Fair in late 1934, but no information about this can be discovered. During the year the Chicago FPL also completed three newsreels, the subject matter of which is not known.[69]

Criminal Syndicalist Law on Trial (1935) was a documentary on the Hillsboro case. Eleven leaders of the Unemployed Council in Hillsboro, in the mining country of southwestern Illinois, had been arrested after a demonstration on June 3, 1934, and charged with "conspiracy to overthrow the government." Their bail was at first set at $8,000 each. According to Jan

Wittenber, one of the defendants, who spent six months in jail awaiting trial, the real reason for the arrests was the Unemployed Council's publication of a forty-page pamphlet, *Hillsboro Relief Scandal,* exposing official corruption in the disbursement of relief funds; 50,000 copies of the pamphlet were distributed. The ILD was active in the defense, and eventually the heaviest sentence imposed was six months' probation for Wittenber. Nothing is known of the film beyond the fact that it was completed in January or early February, 1935.[70]

At the beginning of 1935 the Chicago FPL announced a campaign, to be undertaken jointly with the Chicago WIR, "to expose the horrible living conditions of the Negro and white workers in Chicago's notoriously impoverished South Side."

> Efforts will be made during the next weeks to make a photographic survey of the general living conditions in the district, with particular attention to the alarming effects of malnutrition on the children of the workers, both employed and unemployed.
>
> The evidence will be used in public hearings to arouse the entire working class of Chicago against the starvation program of the city and federal governments. At the same time, the Film and Photo League will consult with doctors and child-health specialists for the purpose of producing a short film to expose the real state of affairs among Chicago's unemployed, most of whom are not on the relief rolls, while those on the rolls are facing drastic cuts in their already meager relief allowance.

There is no evidence as to how far the project proceeded, but the film was evidently not completed.[71]

While in Mexico in 1935, Maurice Bailen shot a personal film which was later completed with some assistance from the Chicago league. This was *Mexico Marches On,* a study of changing conditions in that country under the presidency of the progressive Lázaro Cárdenas. The film, silent and fifteen minutes in length, is a montage of images displaying the contrasting faces of the nation. A military march in commemoration of the Mexican Revolution overshadows a Fascist parade; young boys of Spanish, *mestizo,* and Indian descent grouped together on the street reveal the presence of class differences structured on race. Emergence from the Depression is the theme of a series of shots showing people at work: printers, garment workes, lathe operators, hat makers, bricklayers, street-menders, construction laborers. Detail shots from Diego Rivera murals punctuate the film, and a homemovie flavor is imparted by the appearance of Bailen himself on several occasions, cheerfully greeting Mexican friends. The most sustained sequence shows posters and pamphlets on union organization being distributed in a village with a series of titles: *"MEXICO MARCHES ON/FOR YOUTH/FOR EDUCATION/FOR CULTURE/FOR INDUSTRY/FOR LABOR/FOR HEALTH."* A print of the picture was purchesed by the Mexican government.[72]

In 1936, Bailen shot *Chicago May Day,* a newsreel of the annual march and celebration, and *Peace Parade and Workers' Picnic,* a film record of a demonstration against world militarism and fascism. These two productions, along with *Halsted Street* and *The Great Depression,* are still extant, and are discussed more fully below.

The Chicago Film and Photo League's last recorded venture was obtaining coverage of the auto workers' sit-down strike against General Motors in Flint, Michigan, in the first two months of 1937. The cameraman responsible was Fred Lassie. No detailed information on this production is available.[73]

Los Angeles

The first production of the Los Angeles Film and Photo League on record is *Tom Mooney Run* (1932). During a session of the Olympic Games in August several radical workers ran around the track carrying signs demanding the freedom of Tom Mooney. "At the same time," it was reported, "thousands of leaflets demanding the freedom of Mooney were thrown down upon the stadium by the workers on top and a huge nine-foot sign with 'Free Tom Mooney' displayed in huge letters across it was displayed on the field in front of where Governor Rolph and other dignitaries sat." The Los Angeles FPL's film of this manifestation was described by Harry Alan Potamkin as "one of the finest of dramatic newsreel-clips I have seen."[74]

The attention of the Los Angeles League was focused at an early date on the Imperial Valley region of Southern California, just north of the border, where the exploitation of agricultural workers, particularly Mexican migrants, was acute. It was here that the Communist party centered its campaign to organize farm workers in the Agricultural Workers Industrial League, which became in 1931 the Cannery and Agricultural Workers Industrial Union (and was to be smashed in 1934 by terror tactics and judicial repressive measures employed by the growers in Imperial Valley).[75] The Los Angeles league's film *Imperial Valley,* described as "a study of labor conditions in this hell hole," was shown in New York in November 1932; it was later cited by Brody as an example of the "synthetic" documentary relying entirely upon the creative contribution of the editor.[76]

Around the time of its appearance the WIR also commissioned the editors of *Experimental Cinema,* under the direction of Seymour Stern, to "produce a film dealing with the exploitation of labor, and in particular with the tragedy of Mexican workers, in agricultural sections of Southern California, notably the Imperial Valley and adjacent territory." An editorial in the magazine in 1934 stated:

... the production itself was foredoomed to the fate of many an independent film: viz., to a fatal conflict between producers and production-manager. In this instance the conflict arose over the insistent demand of the *Experimental Cinema* staff that the film be an artistic achievement as well as a piece of agitative propaganda. The production manager, however ... relentlessly opposed making the film a *creative* effort, in which the formal qualities of cinema would share honors with the agitative drive of the film. The film, unfortunately, has been scrapped.[77]

The WIR's side of the dispute was given in the *Daily Worker* by Samuel Brody (as "Lens"), on behalf of the "Educational Committee" of the New York Film and Photo League. Brody charged the *Experimental Cinema* people with "squandering a small fortune belonging to this organization." He continued:

In order to carry out the editors' idea of what an "artistic achievement" should be, they shot 18,000 feet of film, most of which consisted of canteloupes taken from various angles ("Canteloupes at sunset" was the characterization by Sidney Howard, an eyewitness to the carnage). Our "editors" jealously concealed this part treasure in their private vaults and surrendered it to the WIR only after terrific struggle. Only about 1,000 feet of the film exposed proved to be barely usable.[78]

The episode is relevant to the history of the Los Angeles FPL, since the footage which was rescued may well have been turned over to the league for its use. In 1936, the league released a second film under the title *Imperial Valley,* reportedly devoted to "the great canteloupe strike." It was recently described by Julian Roffman as follows:

It was very well photographed and made its point succinctly and graphically. The contrast between the rich and the poor in Imperial Valley. I understand it was never really finished. We had a one-reel version. Sidney Howard was supposed to have financed it and possibly have directed it. The film was almost too glossy for its subject matter. Too slick. But it was a piece of work well made.[79]

In 1933 the L.A. league produced *Cotton-Pickers' Strike* during the summer, reinforcing its commitment to agricultural workers' struggles, and *San Diego Police Attack on Workers,* a newsreel of an antiwar demonstration, whose use in court as a defense weapon has been described in chapter 2.

Bloody Memorial Day (1934), another newsreel, also proved its value in court. Documenting the police terror during Memorial Day rallies, it was "used by a group of workers arrested for 'inciting to riot,' as a last straw in defense of their innocence. The facts of the film," David Platt wrote, "showed so clearly who the real inciters to riot were, that the jury could do nothing but bring in a verdict of not guilty."[80]

California 1934 is a film the L.A. league was reported to have completed in the summer of that year, but no other information on it is available. It was possibly a compilation drawn from the league's accumulated newsreel footage, which included, in addition to the films mentioned, coverage of the El Monte berry pickers' strike and of the Los Angeles County Hunger March demonstrations, both of which reels were exhibited in January 1934.[81]

An article entitled "Valid Criticism of Los Angeles Films" which appeared in *Filmfront* in January 1935 offered information on several 1934 productions not described elsewhere.[82]

Living Wage or Death was a dramatized documentary about the calling of a strike. *Filmfront* noted:

> Members of the New York League thought *Living Wage or Death* suffered from over-simplification of the business of getting workers out on strike, and that it was incompetently acted, and much too drawn out for comfort. A main objection was the length of titles. It was unnecessary to list all the demands of the strikers, occupying several wearisome minutes which left the audience wondering whether it was a film or a political treatise.

The New York league members complimented the L.A. FPL on "its ability to produce quantities of (on the whole) well-photographed film," but urged the West Coast filmmakers to "exercise greater care and ingenuity in the preparation of the scenario, and in the titling and editing." In a significant statement of their attitude toward dramatization, the New Yorkers said that they did not "want to discourage enacted production, but we insist that the difficulties of this type of work become multiplied when faced with the problem of inexperienced actors and directors."

The L.A. league's *Tom Mooney,* evidently a documentary on the case and the campaign to free Mooney, was castigated by members of the Philadelphia FPL, who all "thought it slow and monotonous with poor and inadequate titles, entirely lacking in editing, and not nearly enough references to the history of the case down through the seventeen years; thus losing a fine opportunity to explain the case to the audience."

Finally, *Cannon Fodder* was taken to task, also by the Philadelphia league, for its "poor job of titling." The film was evidently an antiwar compilation documentary edited from commercial newsreel footage of various world armies. J. Hillman, secretary of the Philadelphia group, reported:

> We felt that the Los Angeles league missed up on a splendid opportunity for readings against imperialist war and against the Kuomintang reaction. The American and English army shots were inconsistent with what went before and seemed cut in without any clear purpose; it appeared too much like an afterthought. The shot of the three airplanes was out of place where inserted, and broke up the continuity of the film. This film could be vastly improved by intelligent editing and incorporation of more up-to-date documentary material.

Lives Wasted (1936), probably a production of the Los Angeles league, was also an antiwar film, but that is all that is known about it.[83]

The Extant Films

Nine Film and Photo League productions which have survived (at least in part), can be discussed on the basis of recent viewing. These are the New York league's *National Hunger March, Bonus March, Hunger 1932,* and *America Today; The Ford Massacre* from Detroit; and *Halsted Street, The Great Depression, Chicago May Day,* and *Peace Parade and Workers' Picnic,* by the Chicago league.[84]

All of these films depict demonstrations, suggesting the importance which was attached by the organized Left, particularly in the early Depression years, to mass protest actions. Images of militant workers pressed around a speaker, or marching down city streets, banners and placards waving, form the core iconography of the FPL opus. Yet the role which such images play structurally within the extant films is subject to significant variations, and offers a convenient axis for comparative analysis.

At the simplest level, the demonstration is the subject of a short newsreel entirely devoted to it. This is the case with *Chicago May Day,* which is composed wholly of shots of workers parading in the rain with signs demanding (among other things) the freedom of Thaelmann and Mooney (as such it probably recapitulates, in a minor key, the annual May Day productions of the New York league). The two FPL-originated segments in *America Today* (the Washington Scottsboro rally and the Hans Weidemann protest), along with one of the commercial newsreel excerpts (the united-front antifascist demonstration in Paris), are also of this type. Each of these items is an aggregation of footage devoted to a single street action, with temporal continuity forming a possible, but not necessary, sequential ordering principle. (Seltzer recalls that in editing such footage he took liberties with the chronology of events, cutting in a wide-angle shot where needed, for example, even if it actually belonged to an earlier point in time.[85])

In several films—*Peace Parade and Workers' Picnic, National Hunger March, The Ford Massacre*—a demonstration forms the main subject of a more elaborate, but still straightforward documentation.

Peace Parade begins with some introductory images—a bank, a large department store, a church, people sleeping in doorways—before launching into its coverage of the actual parade, which features the Artists Union of Chicago, the American Student Union, the Communist Party of Illinois, and other groups in an internationally-oriented manifestation of anger at fascism and war ("Ethiopia is Still Unconquered; Help Keep Her That Way," "All War Funds for Social Security," "Down with Hitler Plans Against Czechoslovakia," "Defend Lithuania"). This is followed by workers' picnic scenes at a park, where there is softball and dancing as well as crowds gathered listening to speakers. Bailen's film thus attempts (in abbreviated style) both a suggestion of the capitalist context in which the protest takes place (the film opens with a shot of the cover of John Dos Passos's *The Big Money*), and a description of working-class culture of which the march is but one expression.

National Hunger March builds up to its coverage of the large unemployment demonstrations in Washington with footage devoted to the marchers en route from many parts of the country, together with fundraising (pennies tossed into a sheet), leafleting, and preliminary demonstrations. The film (at least in its current version) reaches a climax as the march leaders prepare to present their demands to Congress, with images of the massed assemblage of unemployed delegates against the Capitol dome in the background. Here, the demonstration is the culmination of a sustained and coordinated political action whose extensive geographical sweep is emphasized by the many shots of truckloads of marchers setting out from points all over the Northeast and Midwest. (Brandon commented at a showing of the film at the Museum of Modern Art in 1973: "To an audience today scenes of people in so many different cities seems like repetition— you say, let's get one group and let it stand for them all—but to the filmmaker at that time it was most important to reflect all the life and activities of the people who had taken that step . . . and it meant a great deal to our people on the hunger march to be able to take the film back to these towns. . . ."[86])

The Ford Massacre has several sections, the police attack at the center being flanked on one side by scenes of a rally and marching, on the other by footage of the funeral for the slain demonstrators, followed by coverage of a protest parade and then picketing outside a Ford building. The film thus documents a series of actions over a period of days, there being two threads running all the way through: the militant presence of workers and unemployed insistently brandishing placards with their demands, and the simultaneous presence of an aggressive police force. (At the opening rally, and at the funeral, the police are a passive threat; during the Dearborn massacre, and again in the final sequence—in the extant print—where they break up a picket line, they are shown in violent action against the demonstrators.) What gives this structure a dynamic thrust is the inclusion of the funeral (death as a *consequence* of raising demands for social justice), and the underlining of the political meaning of the killings in the changing slogans of the protestors' signs (at the start: "Tax the Rich, Feed the Poor," "Hoover Says Starve Don't Fight," "Hoover Wall St. Prosperity Means Poverty: Workers Organize and Strike," "We Want Bread Not Crumbs"; later: "We Shall Never Forget Bloody Monday March 7th," "Ford's City at Dearborn is Stained with Blood," "They Came for Bread, Ford Fed Them Bullets," "Smash the Terror Against the Workers").

C.O. Nelson's *Halsted Street* uses the demonstration in a rather different fashion, incorporating it as one more item in a geographic series constructed with a south-to-north progression through Chicago along the line of the title street. That the protest march is to be seen as the core of the film's signification is, however, indicated in several ways. It is the only sustained sequence in a film composed principally of isolated shots or handfuls of shots, and it is placed towards the end, as the climax of a development from the rural southern tip of Halsted Street through residential neighborhoods to the central city. (In its tail section, the film continues north to document upper-middle-class life in the environs of Lincoln Park.) The march's importance is stressed mainly, however, by the incorporation in the south-side segment of shots of an anonymous man walking briskly, and then running, towards an unknown destination: when the protestors come into view, the man waves, and then, with raised fist, advances and joins them.

Likewise, *The Great Depression* offers a demonstration as the culmination of a film which is chiefly concerned with documenting the face of a city during the slump. Bailen's movie differs from *Halsted Street* in the degree to which its fictional narrative is developed (the man played by Jacques Jacobsen figures in perhaps half the film's shots), but its placement of imagery of militant protest within a context of depressed urban life is similar. There are in fact two demonstrations featured in the film: the first, a peace rally organized by students, include brief shots of speakers Heywood Broun, Lucy Parsons, Ella Reeves Bloor, and Norman Thomas; the second, at the end of the film, is a march of the unemployed demanding "Adequate Relief" and "Jobs." The protagonist encounters the latter as the conclusion of a process in which he has come to experience the life of the jobless in the city, sleeping in the park, washing in fountains, idly paging through periodicals in public libraries, standing in bread lines, despondently considering suicide. Bailen recently described the function of the demonstration footage in relation to the narrative:

> I didn't want to overdo it and make a maudlin film about a guy that was suffering hard luck. I wanted to present an innocent person who didn't realize or know what the situation was, as if he'd just come to the city, and what happens to a person in that condition. He just keeps on walking, he observes the scenes about him, and he still doesn't understand what the problems are politically—some people were blaming themselves. And I put in the scene where he sees the demonstration—then he realizes that it's not just an individual problem, there are other people like him, and there is some hope. And I show him on a note, a close-up of him realizing that, realizing it is a national situation and there are millions of people just like him.[87]

Bonus March and *Hunger 1932* also depict demonstrations as a political response to the socioeconomic crisis, but without any individualizing of the theme. In both films the cinematic reportage of the march on Washington, culminating inevitably in mass rallies outside the seat of government, is preceded by a prologue in which the background to the action, and the reasons for it, are delineated by means of documentary montage. This consists, in

Bonus March, of an evocation of enlistment in 1917, the war, and its aftermath, followed by footage of down-and-out veterans in the third year of the Depression. In *Hunger 1932,* it is composed of images of bread lines, evictions, Hoovervilles—the desperate condition of the unemployed working class. The police (and in *Bonus March,* the Army) figure, as in *The Ford Massacre,* as brutal antagonists of the marchers; *Bonus March* in fact resembles the Detroit film in structure by incorporating footage of the demonstrators under attack, followed by scenes in which they bury their dead (two ex-servicemen were killed by police), regroup, and vow to redouble their struggle ("We Remember 1918—We Won't Forget 1932!" reads one sign, and others, "We Demanded a Debt Due to Us—They Gave Us Gas!", "Negro and White Vets: Don't Mourn, Organize!"; cut into a flashback, at the end, of troops and police setting fire to veterans' shacks is a title, "They Asked for Back Pay, FOR BREAD").

The structural placement of demonstration footage in FPL films was obviously significant in determining its impact on contemporary viewers; equally important was the manner in which it was shot. In the thirties the handheld, close-range cinematography of street actions that the league offered must have struck spectators with great novelty and force. Leo Seltzer, referring specifically to his coverage of the Washington Scottsboro demonstration, stresses the importance of his physical involvement in the events he was shooting in conveying excitement:

> I think the idea is not necessarily that I considered myself one of the pickets, or had the same motivation, it was just that in my own approach I felt I had to get right into things to shoot. I had to experience what I was filming, and that was the uniqueness of both my stills and my films. Few people had seen that point of view in films before. If I had been more politically motivated I think that would have determined where I stood almost all the time I did my shooting. But because I wasn't, I had no apprehension about going up on the cops' side as well as the pickets' side, and getting a total point of view. The commercial newsreels had those big vans for their equipment, and they set the camera up on top. They'd park about a block away with a telephoto lens, and their films never really gave you a sense of being involved. My film had that quality because I was physically involved in what I was filming, and that's what I think gave it a unique and exciting point of view.[88]

Although Seltzer denies that partisan feeling was responsible for the particular quality of his footage, it is clear that he was in strong sympathy with the general aims of the radical working-class movement. ("In those days my feelings were more emotionally motivated," he states elsewhere in the same interview, "You were involved with a group of people and what they said was right you believed was right, and what they disliked you disliked.") The point is confirmed by Hurwitz, who attests:

> Leo Seltzer had a remarkable sense for the internals of an event—he was best at that, he was extraordinary. He could go into a demonstration and shoot what was essential, shoot it

fearlessly, and come out with extraordinary stuff. And he was motivated by a strong generalized political passion that made it important for him to be there.[89]

In Samuel Brody's opinion, it was precisely political commitment which determined the unique perspective of FPL productions. After working on *Hunger 1932,* he wrote:

> Soon there will be shown to the workers of New York the evidence gathered by the keen eyes of our cameras. This evidence is totally unlike anything shown in newsreels taken by capitalist concerns. Our cameramen were class-conscious workers who understood the historical significance of this epic march for bread and the right to live. As a matter of fact, we "shot" the march not as "disinterested" news-gatherers but as actual participants in the march itself. Therein lies the importance of our finished film. It is the viewpoint of the marchers themselves. Whereas the capitalist cameramen who followed the marchers all the way down to Washington were constantly on the lookout for sensational material which would distort the character of the march in the eyes of the masses, our worker-cameramen, working with small hand-cameras that permit unrestricted mobility, succeeded in recording incidents that show the fiendish brutality of the police towards the marchers.... [90]

Strong partisanship is also Tom Brandon's characterization of the stance of the FPL filmmakers toward their subjects. Discussing the same film, he said recently:

> I want to mention my recollection of a vignette there on a knoll overlooking this encampment. There were about a dozen Capital police with guns and tear gas, but the camera people were a part of the coverage—people who came from Chicago, from San Francisco, from Los Angeles.... I always remember our camera people, one woman and about eleven men, who had their heavy Eyemos, 35mm, Debrie cameras. It was too late to shoot them, we didn't have the sort of stock then that could be used at dusk, there were no lights, but the people were frozen there, they were so a part of the march, the struggle, that when the police were there, they were going to be there. I couldn't help feeling, and I'm sure most of the marchers, that if the police fired, somehow these cameramen would swing their cameras into action. Now I cite this not because cameras are effective against armed force, but as an indication of the relationship between the people who wanted to record the surface story [and the marchers].... This was exactly the quality of their thinking: they were not in the trap of objectivity. They did not say that Hoover's program was right, or, "Let's hear Hoover's program"—we saw what that was, that people were starving. They took a position on behalf of the starving people, and their object was to tell their story.[91]

Much of the footage Brody refers to is now missing from *Hunger 1932,* but the existing FPL films do display mobile, intimate camerawork, usually with short takes and quick cutting, which, whether motivated in every case by identification with the cause of the militant protestors or not, can be sharply distinguished, as Seltzer suggests, from contemporaneous newsreel coverage of similar events. *America Today* offers just such a contrast, between the cinematography in the FPL style of the Seltzer items, and the static, tripod-mounted, high-angle, medium-range shooting of the Pathe operators in the sequence of the Ambridge police attack. The commercial companies invited spectators to look on scenes of the class struggle from a safe distance; the Film and Photo League gave them the opportunity to feel that they, too, were in there fighting.[92]

Whereas demonstrations themselves were presented on film by the FPL in a style of direct reportage, evoking the context in which they occurred offered opportunities for some striking "intellectual" montage in the Soviet manner. The technique is employed to a limited extent in the two major Chicago productions, *Halsted Street* and *The Great Depression* (Bailen's insertion of shots of the military into street scenes of the unemployed in the latter is a provocative instance), but the most sustained and impressive sequences in this manner are the prologues to *Bonus March* and *Hunger 1932.*

Bonus March, in particular, is a model of savage political comment in film. Edited by Seltzer and Lester Balog, its opening passage not only sketches in the factual background to the march, but also achieves, through skillful intercutting of documentary footage with strong iconic significations, a biting attack on imperialist war and its patriotic trimmings, on the capitalist economy, and on the pretensions of religion. The sequence is constructed as follows:

TITLE: "1917..."/ swinging sign: "Go Places with the U.S. Army"—travel photographs, picture of ship, etc. / sign: "Adventure Over the World," and doughboy picture / mass parade of troops / battlefield: tanks and troops advance / swinging sign: "Travel—U.S. Army" / cannon fires / another cannon fires / "Travel—U.S. Army" sign / shells explode, blowing up building / battlefield: shells explode / "Travel—U.S. Army" sign / tank flattens tree / soldiers leap into trench / ship on sign "Go Places with the U.S. Army, " swinging / battleship / ship on sign / battleship / ship on sign (FLASH) / ship's cannon is raised / interior of gun barrel, ZOOM IN / ship's cannons fire / another battleship / battleship / (DIFFERENT ANGLE) battleship smoking / German warplane / explosion in the trenches / soldiers advance (FLASH) / explosion in the trenches / dead on battlefield / garden party, for injured and maimed servicemen / servicemen line up to be greeted / servicemen shake hands with VIPs / man on crutches, legless man / shaking hands / nurses attend to servicemen / shaking hands / stretcher patient wheeled up / U.S. flag / cathedral / another cathedral, TILT DOWN / down-and-out unemployed man on bench, head in hands / cathedral, TILT DOWN / priest in street / heroic statuary / sign: "Catholic Charities, St. Francis Xavier's Parish" / U.S. Eagle sign on Bank of the United States building / same man on bench / sign: "The Salvation Army—Jesus for the Bowery" / CLOSE-UP, man on bench / older unemployed man / bindlestiffs in street / sign: "The Salvation Army—The Bowery for Jesus"; people walk past / sign in stones: "... body a seat and we have been setting down ever since"; Hooverville, water in background; TILT UP / same sign, on riverbank, cabin in the water behind; PAN to reveal waterside Hooverville shacks / shacks, and inhabitant / HIGH ANGLE, bread line: "Emergency Food Station, the Salvation Army" / (DIFFERENT ANGLE) bread line / STRAIGHT OVERHEAD, bread line; TILT UP revealing its length / OVERHEAD (CLOSER SHOT), men in bread line / (STREET LEVEL, MEDIUM SHOT) men in bread line, reading newspapers; PAN as they inch forward.

Following documentation of agitation by the Workers' Ex-Servicemen's League, the march to Washington, the encampment, and demonstrations, the film begins its sequence of the eviction with a quick reprise of the opening statement—a title "1917..." and shots of marching troops, tanks on the battlefield, an explosion, the wounded given a garden-party reception—then "1932..." and the U.S. infantry attacks down Pennsylvania Avenue, backed up by the cavalry, and the armored division.

The prologue to *Hunger 1932* has recourse to a smaller range of material to build its indictment of an economic system unable to sustain even a minimal standard of living for the American people. It begins with shots of the Capitol dome, a "No Help Wanted" sign, and street scenes of the unemployed. A laconic series of titles follows: "1929: 10,000,000 unemployed," "1930: 12,000,000 unemployed," "1931: 14,000,000 unemployed," "1932: 16,845,000 unemployed." The remainder of the sequence documents the living conditions of men thrown out of work by the Depression ("Where were the women?"asks Hurwitz, "crowded into the rooms of relatives?"[93])—walking the streets, queueing in bread lines, being evicted from their homes, sleeping on benches, on sidewalks, in the subway, improvising shelter out of waterfront Hooverville shacks. Intercut with these images is footage picturing the nation's resources lying idle or going to waste: deserted factories, and freight trains stilled in the railroad yards; boarded-up houses and "Apartment for Rent" signs; food dumped out into garbage cans. There are angry and satiric inserts: men picketing a fraudulent employment agency; a magazine spread, inviting readers to "Go South"; a quote from New York's Mayor McKee: "As far as the homeless are concerned, we can take care of them." The prologue concludes with shots of a gathered crowd, a speaker, and a title carrying the rousing call from the *Internationale:* "Arise, ye prisoners of starvation!"

The *Bonus March* and *Hunger 1932* montage sequences are general accusations against a system which delivers war and poverty; there is one piece of creative editing in the extant FPL opus which has a more specific target. As part of the Fascist sequence in the surviving issue of *America Today,* Leo Seltzer intercut some footage of Franklin D. Roosevelt (which actually depicted him signing legislation repealing Prohibition) with shots of warships at maneuvers, to make a political point forcefully and economically. The Communist Party line at the time was that Roosevelt was preparing for aggressive war, and that the New Deal represented incipient fascism.[94] The sequence is cut as follows:

> troops parade through streets / Mussolini salutes / troops march, give Fascist salutes / Fascist salute, PAN to reveal arm is Hitler's / U.S. battleship, TILT UP to following ship / FDR signs document, reaches for blotter, lays it down, makes a fist to blot / navy cruiser, cannons fire / (FRONT VIEW) guns are raised / interior of gun barrel / cannons fire / FDR looks up and smiles / dark cloud, DISSOLVE to NRA Eagle sign and inscription: "We Do Our Part."

The short sequence was recognized, when it appeared, as a model of what the FPL filmmakers could achieve through political montage. In his article, "The Revolutionary Film—Next Step," published in May 1934, Hurwitz cited it as a specimen of "external" montage, as compared with the "internal" montage of "any acted sequence in an ordinary film."

> The newsreel shots are sure: President Roosevelt signing a state paper and looking up at the camera with his inimitable self-satisfied smile, and a shot of fleet maneuvers—two shots taken in widely separated times and places not essentially (but *externally*) related to each other. By virtue of splicing the shot of the warships just after Roosevelt signs the paper, and following the threatening ships of war with the rest of the first shot (Roosevelt looks up and smiles), a new meaning not contained in either shot, but a product of their new relation on film, is achieved—the meaning of the huge war preparation program of the demagogic Roosevelt government.

A year later Robert Gessner, in his survey of FPL films, pronounced the section "perfect."[95]

Aesthetic and Ideology

In 1921, a movie entitled *The New Disciple* was released under the auspices of the American Federation of Labor. Directed by Ollie Sellers, it is interesting in that it provided a model for prolabor film production which would be decisively rejected in the radical cinema of the Depression years. *The New Disciple* could be located firmly within the dominant Hollywood aesthetic, as its story line indicates:

> Industrialist Peter Fanning, who amassed his wealth during the World War, continues to expand his fortune through exploitation of his factory employees. When labor troubles finally result in a strike, John McPherson, who believes that both sides are wrong, is caught in the middle; and he endeavors to persuade the capitalists and the laborers to reduce their demands. The strike prevents Fanning from meeting contract deadlines, and his competitors take advantage of his financial embarrassment and press him to sell, but the workers finally agree to accept the American Plan and to join with the farmers to purchase and operate the mill on a cooperative basis—leaving McPherson free to pursue romance with Mary Fanning.[96]

Members of the Film and Photo League would no doubt have seen a connection between this picture's bourgeois melodramatics and its class-collaborationist politics; and the aesthetic which they themselves put into practice was built on a quite different foundation.

League spokesmen were explicit in acknowledging that this foundation was the Soviet cinema, and particularly that branch of revolutionary Soviet production represented by the documentary tradition of Dziga Vertov. A statement by David Platt made after the National Film Conference in 1934 reveals how completely Vertov's repudiation of the fictional aesthetic was shared by the American filmmakers:

> ... the film, although only in its 25th year, has already been so heavily overloaded with the trappings of the previous arts that, excluding the Soviet film, it can no longer be considered film at all, but bad theatre, literature, whatever you wish. The Soviet film began with the Kino-Eye and grew organically from there on. The Film and Photo Leagues rooted in the intellectual and social basis of the Soviet film begin also with the simple newsreel document, photographing events as they appear to the lens, true to the nature of the revolutionary medium they exploit in a revolutionary way. Aside from the tremendous historical and social value of the reels thus photographed, they are also true beginning of film art.[97]

Vertov's ideas were brought to the league by Brody, who discovered the Russian theorist's writings in Barbusse's journal, *Le Monde*. Brody said recently: "Not only did they confirm my conviction that the film medium was at its most effective and powerful level when its raw material was reality itself rather than the reenactment and artifical recreation of it, but also, they revealed a new approach to filmed reality which in effect outlined a special grammar and syntax for what until then had been rather rudderless." The translations by Brody of Vertov's Paris lectures which appeared in *Filmfront* Nos. 2 and 3 in January 1935 were announced (apparently quite accurately) as being "the first of any utterances or writings by Dziga Vertov to appear in the English language."[98]

Vertov's insistence, first on newsreels and second on montage documentaries constructed from newsreel-type footage, became the guiding principle for FPL production. For Brody, the political rationale for this aesthetic choice was clear. In February 1934, he wrote:

> The question: What is the medium of revolutionary film production in capitalist countries such as America? The answer: first and foremost the filmed document. Movie reportage: reality recorded on film strips and subjected to the painstaking technical operations, montage, whereby these strips are built up into wholes embodying our revolutionary interpretation of events. This is neither a makeshift nor a degradation of the creative potentialities of the cinema. . . . Are we for the documentary simply because the studio-acted film is beyond our material reach? No. Strange as it may seem our orientation in this question is one of principle based on what we think is the most convincing and effective medium for "the camera in the class struggle." It is true that the method of the revolutionary film document will lead us miles away from the forms and requirements of the enacted studio film. This may cause many to shed a tear. It is, in fact, already causing tears. Our answer? We are forging the film into a working-class weapon.[99]

Hurwitz, writing several months later, was willing to concede that newsreel production by the Film and Photo League played a crucial political role:

The film movement in America has for some time been faced with the problem of what film forms are its true concern. The Film and Photo Leagues have up to now produced mainly newsreels. They are necessary because of the rigid censorship and the malicious distortion that the capitalist film companies use in their treatment of events relative to labor and labor's struggles. These newsreels serve an agitational and revelational function to arouse the working class, and as a corrective for the lies of the capitalist agencies. A strike, demonstration, or hunger march is shown with the full brutalities of the police, with the full heroism and militancy of the workers, without the distractive mocking comment of the bourgeois announcer.[100]

The widespread outbreak of militant strike action during 1934 underlined the necessity for such basic film coverage. A conclusion of the September 1934 National Film Conference was that, "The tremendous growth of the working-class movement coupled with the increase of strikes and class warfare makes it imperative for the Film and Photo Leagues to concentrate its [*sic*] best film and photo forces on the field of battle, adequately to record the vital events of our time."[101]

In the conception of the FPL theorists, the function of the newsreel was simply to report the facts: it was important to train working-class camera operators "whose function in the workers' film movement," Brody wrote, "will correspond to that of worker-correspondents in the field of revolutionary journalism." The power of the newsreel to reveal the truth was so great that even a commercial item like the RKO-Pathe reel of the Ambridge killing could become "a supreme example of the political value to us of motion-picture reportage." In a significant inflexion of the concept of the movie screen as a window on the world, Brody defined film reporting as "the recording of highlights in the class struggle which are of political value as events overflowing the frame, which merely acts as the carrier, Ambridge, Scottsboro, Detroit Massacre, Tom Mooney Run, etc."[102]

This belief in the power of simple newsreel drew its sustenance from the conviction of Barbusse's, which Brody was fond of quoting, that "in our times, truth is revolutionary." An anonymous FPL critic, writing the program notes for Irving Browning's *The New Legion* in 1934, further defined this idea of truth. "More and more artists are coming to realize that the only honest approach to art is TRUTH," he or she said, adding: "By truth we mean a willingness to face our problems and trying to solve them by getting down to the fundamental root   the worker, and how he can extricate himself from the web tied around him."[103]

But coming to grips with the problem of the worker required something more, in film terms, than the simple newsreel: on this the theorists of the FPL were agreed. Brody advanced the concept of the "synthetic" documentary, in which the raw material was organized by the filmmaker "into a unified revolutionary interpretation": as examples he cited the Soviet films *Shanghai Document* and *Spring,* and several FPL productions including *Hunger 1932,*

Imperial Valley, and the *America Today* coverage of the Washington Farmers' Convention. Hurwitz argued that "because newsreels are fractional, atomic, and incomplete, the revolutionary movement has required a more synoptic form to present a fuller picture of the conditions and struggles of the working class." The synthetic documentary film had therefore become important—"a form which allows for more inclusive and implicative comment on our class world than the discursive newsreel."[104]

The "synthetic" documentary in the work of the Film and Photo League typically took the form of the compilation film, either utilizing original league material, in the manner of Vertov *(Bonus March, Hunger 1932)*, or, following Shub, re-editing "found" footage *(Portrait of America, World in Review, Hands Off Ethiopia, The Birth of New China).*[105] As with the Russians, the guiding aesthetic principle for the FPL filmmakers was the concept of montage: montage which by the juxtaposition of conflicting shots would expose the veiled power relationships of society. Seymour Stern, the West Coast filmmaker and writer who influenced the radical film movement in the early thirties through his editorship of *Experimental Cinema* (one of his co-editors was David Platt), had formulated the political possibilities of montage synthesis in a 1931 manifesto, "A Working-Class Cinema for America?":

> Hence, not only this:
>> A cinema of bread lines and starvation in the streets.
>> A cinema of police clubbings and a reign of terror.
>> A cinema screaming against fascist developments in USA.
>> A cinema smashing lynch-law and gangster-rule.
>> A cinema attacking with supreme fury, vehemence, and passion the mightiest and most vicious capitalism, the most brutal class-exploiting "society," the world has ever known. . . .
> But also, most necessarily, this:
>> New montage-forms for typically American raw-material imagery.
>> Synthetic montage.
>> Synthetic imagery.

Like Eisenstein, with whom he was in close contact, Stern based his conception of montage cinema directly on Marxist principles:

> The cinema is a dialectic instrument. No other instrument has the same capacity to present the class struggle of the ages in such *concentrated perspective,* so that what was separated vastly in time and space is united, and what was externally minute but intrinsically significant can be *magnified* in the cinematic scale of *relative dimensions.*[106]

Hurwitz, likewise drawn to the synthetic possibilities of film editing, recalls that he "was fascinated by the mosaic character of film, by the capacity of documentary film to extract fragments out of the matrix of visual-sound reality, then to weave these fragments into a form very different from the reality but capable of rendering the meaning and feeling of the real event." This rearrangement of fragments of factual material was the core of the montage aesthetic—"the stuff was document, but the construction was invented, a time-collage."[107]

Though FPL filmmakers achieved considerable virtuosity in their inter-weaving of thematic material in such montage works as *Bonus March* and *The Great Depression,* the central thrust remained the idea of basic, stark juxtaposition exposing the inequities and hypocrisies of capitalist society. Bailen's film intercut society dames with student peace demonstrators, and an Americanism parade with shots of men in the gutter. As late as 1935, Tischler (manager of the National Film Exchange) was urging FPL filmmakers to "show a bunch of high hats and fur coats arriving at the Waldorf for a charity luncheon, and, in the next shot, relief workers in thin overcoats and worn-out shoes shoveling snow so that the charitable limousines can pass." Or, he suggested, "show the Sunday school teacher collecting mite-boxes for the cause of Christian love among the black heathen, and then a close-up of newspaper headlines, if not actual photographs, of the latest lynching of a Negro."[108] The choice of examples closely recalls the experiments in newsreel recutting undertaken by European film societies in the twenties, and discussed in chapter 1.

In the eyes of several of its members, the Film and Photo League could have gone further in the development of the compilation documentary than in fact it did. Irving Lerner suggested in June 1934 that the league could construct an American equivalent to Shub's *Cannons or Tractors* from its own newsreel footage. Such a film would need no commentator: "Its effectiveness would depend upon the proper selection of shots and their truthful and precise juxtaposition." And two years later, inspired by *The Birth of New China,* David Platt reiterated the proposal:

> ...we would like to recommend as a future production of the Film and Photo League a similar full feature documentary on the United States from 1929 to 1936, covering seven years of events that have seared themselves into the minds of millions. There is an unending quantity of material on America 1929-1936 waiting for some such organization as the Film and Photo League to forge into a powerful documentary of the times. A great deal of this material is rusting in the vaults of the Film and Photo League at this moment.[109]

To the category of "synthetic" documentary also belonged those films—such as *Marine, Harlem Sketches,* and *Getting Your Money's Worth*—which pointed the league most firmly in the direction which mainstream documentary would later follow. The aesthetic approach adopted here (to the extent that one can judge without having seen the films) was based less on kinetic montage than on sustained exploration of a single locale or process; emphasis was no longer placed exclusively on the visual track, but was shifted towards forms of sound-image interaction. Significantly, the directors of these films either already worked professionally in the industry (Leslie Bain), or would shortly make the transition (Seltzer, Roffman).

Beyond the newsreel and the "synthetic" documentary were two further forms essayed by FPL filmmakers: the satire, and the dramatized documentary. The former, exemplified only by Hurwitz's ILD film *Sweet Land of Liberty* and by *Hollywood,* is difficult to discuss in the absence of the films or detailed information about them; from Hurwitz's comments on *Sweet Land of Liberty* it is apparent that the idea of contrast montage here again played a significant role.

The dramatized documentary—*Sheriffed, Taxi, The Great Depression, Living Wage or Death*—brought the radical film close to the aesthetic of the Naturalist novel as outlined by Zola and quoted in chapter 1. Here was an objective "slice of life" relying little on devices of plot or dramatic narrative construction; attention was directed not towards adventurous or romantic entanglements, but towards the everyday condition of life of the protagonist. Perhaps the greatest departure from Zola's model was the emphasis on the potential for change inherent in the character's becoming involved in collective action—simply being struck by the sight of an unemployment demonstration, or, more positively, entering into a strike or a fight against eviction. Again, cinematic inspiration probably came from the Soviet Union: Kuleshov had combined acted sequences with documentary footage as early as 1920 in *On the Red Front,* and films such as Eisenstein's *Old and New* and Dovzhenko's *Earth* (or *Soil*) were no doubt considered as models.[110]

This was perhaps particularly true of the decision to avoid, for the most part, the use of actors. Bailen recalls hearing Eisenstein speak in Chicago in 1930, when the Russian director gave an account of his method of typecasting ("When he wanted a farmer, he didn't take an actor and dress him up as a farmer, he went out and used a farmer"). "This," Bailen states, "made a great impression on me, and I tried to imitate it when I was shooting *The Great Depression.*" Dovzhenko, whose "Credo of a Soviet Movie Director" was translated for the *New Masses* in February 1931 by Brody, affirmed, "I utilize actors, but more so people chosen from crowds. My documentation requires this. . . ."[111]

In the dramatized documentaries the criterion of typicality, advanced by Engels and others as a defining characteristic of the realist text, came into play. Since the stories were in no way out of the ordinary, the situation portrayed could be regarded as embodying the essential characteristics of the class struggle as it was being fought on a particular terrain. A mark of success was the ease with which reviewers could move from the singular to the plural in discussing a film's subject: thus *Sheriffed* was, for one writer, "the story of one man's attempt, assisted by his neighbors, to keep his farm when it is threatened by the bankers"; for another, the film dealt with "the poor farmers' fight against losing their homes and farms." Insofar as a film attained generality, it was able to convey social and political truths. Once more, Dovzhenko was an influence: "I work upon typical documents and apply the synthetic method," he declared, "My heroes are representative of their class."[112]

In general, Film and Photo League productions aspired to the status of accurate documents of the class struggle. Like the *Winter 1931* project, they aimed "to tell the truth that Hollywood is trying to hide"; as Ed Kennedy wrote to *Marine,* "the skeptics have no opportunity to cry 'propaganda' because the factual evidence is laid before them." Since they affected an "objective" stance (in the sense of being authentic, not of giving fair play to both sides), the films seldom directly addressed the spectator; *Marine,* Kennedy said, "doesn't shout slogans," and it was typical. Titles were terse statements of fact ("1932: 16,845,000 unemployed") rather than appeals to the audience in the manner of agitprop drama (or the titles in certain Soviet films, like the conclusion to *Strike:* "Proletarians, remember!"). Even a cry like "Arise, ye prisoners of starvation!" in *Hunger 1932* was inserted *as a line being sung by demonstrators.*

To convey a spirit of militancy while retaining this documentary status, the films became, overwhelmingly, reports of struggles in progress. They seized on concrete issues—the imprisonment of Tom Mooney, the Scottsboro case— to dramatize abstract notions of class injustice and racial oppression. They depicted workers—miners, agricultural laborers, longshoremen, cab drivers— who were involved (or had recently been involved) in strike actions. They put the unemployed on the screen in the process of fighting for relief and jobs.

Because the Film and Photo League lay within the orbit of Communist organizations, its productions inevitably reflected the particular battles being waged by the party. Especially in the early thirties, during the "Third Period" of militant class struggle in the world Communist movement,[113] the films were obviously conceived of as tools for recruitment, not so much into the Communist Party itself, as into its "revolutionary" unions (affiliated to the Trade Union Unity League) and its "mass organizations." Films like *The Strike Against Starvation* and *Imperial Valley* dovetailed into the organizing drives of the National Miners Union and the Cannery and Agricultural Workers Industrial Union; others were aimed to bolster the campaigns of the Unemployed Councils, the League of Struggle for Negro Rights, the Young Pioneers, the National Farmers League, the Friends of the Soviet Union, the WESL, the ILD, the IWO, or the FPL's parent, the WIR, itself. (In Chicago, where party links seem to have been looser, there was less immediate propaganda value to the league's productions.)

In accordance with the Third Period position of the Communist Party, the ideology of the FPL films was one of working-class solidarity in the face of its enemies. Confronted with the massive social problems caused by the Depression and widespread defeatist apathy among the workers and unemployed whose living standards had been slashed, the party tended to stress concrete demands rather than long-term socialist goals, and this was especially true of propaganda disseminated through the mass media. It is highly unlikely, therefore, that any FPL film dissected capitalism as a system, or directly advocated revolution.

The capitalist structure of American society was nevertheless subjected to attack by implication in the many indictments directed against its institutions and agents. Business came under fire (Henry Ford was blamed for the massacre at Detroit), as did the military *(Bonus March),* the churches (a priest is shown unsuccessfully attempting to preach to the marchers in *Hunger 1932*), and the judiciary *(The Scottsboro Boys)*—the themes ran throughout the FPL opus, and these are merely specimens—but the main target was the government, at federal, state, and local level.

Here the basic agitational thrust was to expose "democratic" institutions as callously unresponsive to the vital needs of the people. "For two nights and three days, the marchers heroically faced a hostile mob of police, barbarous sanitation, vile eating and drinking conditions, and cold damp pavements for beds," reads a title in *Hunger 1932;* it is followed by: "While the government ordered landlords to refuse to rent empty halls to the marchers." In the same film, Mayor McKee's claim to being able to care of New York's homeless is revealed to be an inhumane lie by the Hooverville footage which follows. The most damning indictment of the state, however, was of course the violence perpetrated by its agents—police and deputies, and sometimes soldiers—on the petitioners, protestors, and picketers of the working class.

Images of violence, in fact, carried the crucial ideological signification of FPL production; but to understand their meaning it is necessary to consider the context out of which the violence arose: the demonstration.

The purpose of the demonstration, and the reason for its replication in film, is clear. Directed towards the authorities, it was both symbolic evidence of popular feeling and the manifestation of a threat. For the participants, and sympathizers in the movie audience, it was an expression of the unity and solidarity of the working class. During the Depression, observers say, the streets were strangely empty; demonstrations filled them, and images of the demonstrations were signs of strength and builders of morale for a dispirited proletariat.

But if demonstrations gave rise to repressive violence, they could mean more than that: by offering the sight of a policeman's baton struck over the skull of a hungry man or woman they could dramatically strip bare the veiled class relationships of capitalist society to expose an ugly exploitative foundation. Given sufficient incidents, the facts of class conflict could no longer be denied, and the myth of the "disinterested" state could be laid to rest. Footage of police violence was incorporated in so many of the FPL productions—in *Bonus March,* the original versions of *National Hunger March* and *Hunger 1932, The Ford Massacre,* the Washington Scottsboro demonstration, Weidemann protest, and Ambridge massacre segments of *America Today* (and no doubt in many other films that no longer survive)—because such images had the power to stir an audience to anger, to force it to take sides, to help it become *class-conscious.*

This rhetorical function of imagery of police brutality is suggested by the fact that sequences such as those in the extant *America Today* were recuperated and shown again and again, long after they had ceased to be news. (Brody's comments on the Ambridge reel are very relevant here.) Indeed, the Weidemann protest sequence was incorporated in *Native Land,* released in 1942, and some of Seltzer's footage from this period was used as late as 1946, in the prounion documentary *For the Record* (produced by Tom Brandon and directed by Julian Roffman).

During the years (roughly 1933-35) in which the Communist party was attempting to link American captalism with international fascism, shots of police violence could bc used specifically to make the connection (analogously to the "fascist-NRA" sequence featuring Roosevelt). Thus the Weidemann protest, in particular, demonstrated visually that the city administration of New York had more sympathy for Nazi Germany than it had for its own residents. (The *Daily Worker* headline read: "Police, Under Orders to Defend German Fascism, Trample-Blackjack Workers."[114])

There was one other function which the image of violence could perform: it could show the militant demonstrator fighting back. Protestors, of course, could not be viewed as *initiating* violence: in order not to alienate potential supporters, it was necessary that they be pictured, at least to begin with, as "good citizens" exercising their right to peaceful assembly. Yet the Communist party, in the thirties, had no truck with pacifism, and it was demoralizing for workers always to be seen succumbing to the clubs, tear gas, or bullets of their adversaries. Demonstrations therefore aimed, whenever possible, to buck the superior firepower of the police and retaliate against assault; and when film was obtained of such action it became a valued document of class conflict. Thus, for example, *National Hunger March* originally contained scenes of the police attack in Hammond "and the splendid resistance by the crowd of workers and the marchers." And there was the shot in *America Today* (significantly introduced by the title, "Demonstrators in front of United States Supreme Court militantly defend the right to free assembly") which showed a Scottsboro protestor turning on his assailant with the shaft from a placard, and which was printed three times over in the final film for maximum impact. Seltzer recalls that when that sequence was shown, "the audience jumped up and said, 'Give it to him!' 'Give it to him!' "[115]

It was precisely at this effect of rousing the working class to angry but principled response to the injustices of their society that the productions of the Film and Photo League were directed.

4

Breakaway: Nykino

There was always a little ambiguity as to whether the Film and Photo League's commitment (prior to 1935) to strict documentary forms was adopted as a matter of aesthetic principle, or imposed by the group's financial and technical limitations. Harry Alan Potamkin, after all, in his 1930 call for "Workers' Films," had suggested documentaries only as a first step, holding out as an ultimate prospect "dramatic films of revolutionary content"; and in December 1932, with the WFPL specifically in mind, he still saw "enacted dramatic films" as the long-range goal, suggesting that, "When our comrades of the league are prepared for the dramatic reenactment, a film like [Pabst's] *Kameradschaft* will not be a bad pattern." Potamkin and Jay Leyda, in program notes for the league's History of Russian Film series in February 1933, remarked: "Some artists have set the documentary as the end, as well as the beginning, of the film, but this is debatable."[1]

For Samuel Brody, however there was never any doubt. Films involving staging and actors had no place on the schedule of a workers' producing organization in a capitalist country. Always a partisan of factual cinema, he argued as early as 1929, for example, in a scathing review of King Vidor's *Hallelujah,* that "any attempt to portray the American Negro in the movies will have to be as close to the documentary as possible." The following year he declared: "The film created on the basis of an artificial scenario is infinitely inferior to powerful documents like *Turksib, Shanghai Document,* or the average newsreel."[2]

In its first few years the WFPL closely followed Brody's precepts, postponing consideration of the revolutionary dramatic film as projected by Potamkin until some time in the indefinite future. But by early 1934 the question could no longer be avoided. There was dissatisfaction in the league, a yearning to break the aesthetic restraints of pure documentary; and to forestall revolt in the ranks Brody issued a statement of his position which was published in the February number of *New Theatre.*

"The Revolutionary Film: Problem of Form" outlined three possible avenues for FPL production. Two, the newsreel and the "synthetic" documentary, had already been undertaken. The third, the "frankly educational film for purposes of direct political-economic instruction," had been neglected—Brody proposed that work on it be "a joint task for the Film and Photo League and the faculty of the Workers School." There was no place in Brody's schema for anything approaching the dramatic movie: indeed, in a passage quoted in chapter 3, he specifically argued that it was a question of principle and not of money which ruled out the acted film as a possible branch of radical filmmaking.

Recognizing, perhaps, that the challenge would come from those who wished to make dramatized documentaries—that there was no desire to plunge fully into fictional filmmaking—Brody couched his opposition to staging as an aesthetic objection to mixed modes:

> In the film there exists no "happy medium" between the histrionic recreation of reality and directly recorded reality itself. "The illusion of reality in the cinema," writes Léon Moussinac, "must remain constant, even in the domain of the fantastic. In other words, in the cinema the sensation of reality is indispensable to emotion." Associate filmed reality and its reconstructed counterpart into a unified structure and you find "the sensation of reality" irremediably disrupted.[3]

The content of the workshop film, *Waste and Want,* which students at the Harry Alan Potamkin Film School were involved in at about this time under Brody's direction is not recorded. It would be fair to assume, however, that it conformed to the "synthetic" documentary mode, which Brody in his article said "represents an almost totally unexplored form calling for the highest degree of skill and talent in the realm of cinematic creation." Meanwhile, there was a group, also at the Potamkin Film School, experimenting in quite a different direction, and no doubt without any encouragement from Brody.

What this group was up to was revealed in an article by Leo Hurwitz published in the May 1934 issue of *New Theatre:*

> ...ten or twelve members of the Potamkin Film School, under the technical direction of Ralph Steiner, are working in an experimental group at the Film and Photo League. They have set themselves a series of problems, each involving the writing of a shot-by-shot continuity for the sequence to be filmed, photographing of the sequence, and the final editing. Two problems have so far been completed. The first, to render the simple act of an unemployed man entering his room after an exhausting day of job-hunting, sitting down, tired, worn out, and without hope. The second, a continuation of the first, the landlord entering the room to serve the tenant with a dispossess for non-payment of rent. This group works wholly with non-actors in order to duplicate conditions which will occur in making films later. The great task is to learn how to make the camera eloquent, how to make use of the natural acts of an untrained actor to serve the needs of the scenario.[4]

The work was directed towards gaining the practical expertise for what Hurwitz termed "The Revolutionary Film—Next Step." His challenge to Brody's strictly delimited position was forthright, although the only direct reference to the preceding article was a complimentary one. After acknowledging the rationale for the production of newsreels (the argument is quoted in chap. 3) and of "synthetic" documentaries, Hurwitz maintained that financial problems *were* at the root of the league's failure to enter the field of dramatic movie production—a field which did indeed, in his view as in Potamkin's, offer great possibilities:

> Another factor, besides its great effectiveness, has determined the preoccupation of the radical movie makers with the documentary film. At this time, with the radicalized working class as small as it is, it is almost impossible for economic and technical reasons to undertake the vast task of producing and distributing revolutionary dramatic films, which, in some ways, are capable of going beyond the document (as the synthetic document transcends the newsreel) in its [sic] width of scope, its synoptic approach, in its ability to recreate events and emotions not revealable to the camera in the document.[5]

Hurwitz made the distinction between the documentary and the dramatic film not, interestingly enough, in profilmic terms—the extent to which the scene photographed had been created or modified by the filmmaker—but in terms of montage construction. (The emphasis on editing revealed how indebted American left-wing cinematic thinking still was to the theory and practice of Soviet silent cinema.) The documentary, Hurwitz argued, was based on "*external* montage, the creative comparison, contrast, and opposition of shots, externally related to each other, to create an effect not contained in any of the shots." Vertov's *The Man with the Movie Camera* was, for this type of construction, "the textbook of technical possibilities." The dramatic film, on the other hand, involved "in its cinematography the interpretive breaking-up of the recreated reality, and, in its montage, the synthesis of these analyzed elements to recreate the event on film from a given point of view."

The two forms of montage as he defined them were by no means, Hurwitz was quick to point out, mutually exclusive. "Both may be used," he noted, "and in fact have been used frequently to complement each other—sometimes with the emphasis on the document as in *Ten Days that Shook the World,* sometimes with the emphasis on the recreated drama, as in *The End of St. Petersburg.*" It was another tilt at Brody, a refutation, by reference to acknowledged classics, of the supposed impossibility of mixing modes.

The mixed mode was not only feasible, Hurwitz declared, it was desirable—and as an immediate goal of the Film and Photo League:

> A mixed form of the synthetic document and the dramatic is the next proper concern of the revolutionary film movement: to widen the scope of the document, to add to the document

the recreated events necessary to it but resistant to the documentary camera eye—a synthetic documentary film which allows for material which recreates and fortifies the actuality recorded in the document, and makes it clearer and more powerful.[6]

There was a question of learning the skills. Revolutionary filmmakers in America had gained their experience only in the shooting and editing of newsreels and documentaries, "in the crucible of events, in preparing films of workers' struggles to be used in turn as a weapon in these struggles." This was where Steiner's workshop experiments came in, to lay the initial groundwork for the FPL's proposed new line of development. Hurwitz concluded:

It is too early to indicate the nature of the films which will be made along the lines indicated here. However, the plan is to develop this experimental group into a production group within the Film and Photo League for the purpose of making documentary-dramatic revolutionary films—short propaganda films that will serve as flaming film-slogans, satiric films, and films exposing the brutalities of capitalist society.

Here, in embryo, was the second part of the Hurwitz-Steiner plan of action— and the suggestion that responsibility for the new departure in film production should be delegated to a small, select group within the league was to prove no less controversial than the aesthetic manifesto which had been issued.

During the summer of 1934 the FPL marked time, at least in terms of production, while Ralph Steiner and Irving Lerner, together with Elia Kazan (of the Group Theatre) and Molly Day Thacher, did some shooting on a dump in Queens for an improvised satire—the film which was to become *Pie in the Sky*. In the early fall, both Steiner and Hurwitz issued statements elaborating on their position.

Steiner's "Revolutionary Movie Production," published in *New Theatre* for September, revealed how far he had come, at least publicly, since his days as representative of the bourgeois avant-garde and creator of abstract studies of the play of light on water, the movement of model gears, and patterns of seaweed. Steiner now spoke as a committed radical, attributing the failure of *Cafe Universal*—his unfinished "antiwar" film—to his "lack of understanding of the political nature of imperialist war," and arguing that a "clearly stated scenario" could only come from "political clarity," by which was meant "a basic comprehension of politics, economics, history, and sociology from a Marxist point of view."[7]

Criticizing the revolutionary film movement for its stagnation—"in relation to the exciting activity and progress in the fields of literature, theatre, music, and dance the film has not even started to move"—Steiner developed the proposition that good propaganda entails good art, and that good film art would only result from training, the abandonment of a strict documentary approach, and the concentration of resources on a full-time production unit.

Training could be effected—"since we have in this country no background of revolutionary filmmaking and no Pudovkins or Eisensteins to teach us"—by the undertaking of short production exercises, "perhaps as short as two or three minutes on the screen." Each would be directed to the solution of a single problem of the many posed by a revolutionary film project.

In his scrutiny of the limitations of documentary, Steiner was anxious to puncture the myth, as he saw it, that shooting in this mode was necessarily simpler than filming a dramatic story. "It would seem natural to assume that the documentary was an easy form," he wrote, "since the material to be photographed is already in existence, and does not have to be created by the producer." The idea, however, was "not only fallacious but very harmful." It was, in fact, a highly demanding task to select and record a segment of actuality so that it signified "clearly, accurately, and forcefully to the audience what the image in the scenario had to say."

(In pursuing this point, Steiner made an important thrust at the montage aesthetic as it had been understood—or misunderstood—in America. Insisting on the strength of each individual image even if conceived only as an element in a filmic "sentence," he asserted—"all 'montage experts' to the contrary"—"The erroneous idea that the effectiveness of the shots does not matter so much since through montage [the manner of putting them together] they could be made effective has weakened us too long.")

Steiner's objections to documentary techniques were practical ones, indicating a desire not to move into fiction, but to use creative intervention by the filmmaker in order to bolster revolutionary cinematic exploration of the real world. His arguments thus meshed well with Hurwitz's suggestion that the "next step" should be the dramatized documentary. Steiner wrote:

> One great limitation of the documentary film lies in the difficulty of photographing certain events and material: events that have happened in the past, events which happen only once, and those of which capitalist society may not be sufficiently proud to want recorded. The revolutionary cameraman may often find the police and other agents of the present order not too helpful to him in getting the best shots of strike scenes, cops "preserving the peace" and shots of what the rich do with "their" wealth. Even when these hindrances are not present there is the annoying fact that events happen in time. They will not slow up, stop, or repeat themselves to allow the cameraman to photograph them in the most dramatic manner. A documentary film of the October revolution made by the most sensitive and capable director alive could not be as effective as the created films *Ten Days that Shook the World* or *The End of St. Petersburg*. The cameraman and director would have had to be omniscient (in advance), omnipresent, free-floating, impervious to bullets, and invisible in order to photograph the events with maximum dramatic effect.[8]

The article went on to discuss the expense of filmmaking (which was, however, not as great as some had imagined, and might be defrayed by showings of Soviet and other films), and the problem of organization (leadership of the groups should have had some practical experience of the difficulties of shooting films). Finally, the need for a small, totally dedicated production unit was spelled out:

> In any large group of "enthusiasts" there are necessarily only a few with sufficient ability, energy, responsibility, and purpose for a high standard of filmmaking. The major portion of the leadership's time, energy, and thought should be concentrated on them and their work. They should be supported by the group as a whole so that they can devote their full time to production.[9]

Steiner's model for this full-time group was—significantly, in view of later developments—the "Shock Troupe" of the Workers' Laboratory Theatre. As a small group living in cooperative quarters and financed by the theatre as a whole, the Shock Troupe was able "to spend ten to twelve hours a day accomplishing an extraordinary amount of excellent work."

Leo Hurwitz's "Survey of Workers' Films" was a paper written for presentation (although not delivered in person by him) at the National Film Conference held in Chicago in the last week of September. It was published in the October issue of *New Theatre*—of which Hurwitz was, at the time, film editor. Essentially it was a reworking of Steiner's arguments (and those he had himself put forward earlier in the year) with specific application to the Film and Photo League, which Steiner had not referred to by name. Again, the formula for curing the ills of the revolutionary film movement was a) advance beyond the documentary b) establish a full-time production troupe.

Neatly forestalling objections that he and Steiner might be attempting to draw FPL production away from its role as a weapon in the class struggle towards "loftier" realms of "art," Hurwitz criticized the league's output to date in the newsreel/documentary mode for containing *too little propaganda.*

> The test of propaganda is persuasive power, and our films have not been persuasive. This is due largely to the fact that they have presupposed upon the part of the audience a knowledge and sympathy with our point of view. To a class-conscious worker, for example, our May First reels, which show hundreds of thousands of workers mobilized in the steets, may be a source of inspiration and a stimulus to militancy, but to a nonrevolutionary worker, unless we clearly and effectively dramatize why these thousands are marching, May Day is another parade of marching, marching, and marching. Certainly marching workers cannot be the only item in a one-reel film if that film is to be effective propaganda.

The league's films, said Hurwitz, "*assume* the revolutionary approach, instead of *convincing* the spectator of its correctness."[10]

The lack of persuasive power in the FPL productions was partly the result, Hurwitz maintained, of the "mechanical, schematic, and unexperimental approach in the search for the proper forms for the revolutionary movie." He wrote:

We have been insisting that the documentary form is the only true one. The importance of the document as exposé material relating to working and living conditions, police brutality, the militancy of the insurgent proletariat, etc., cannot be overemphasized; and without doubt much can be done in mounting to make effective propaganda.... But to rule out other film forms in which it is easier to build up essential sequences not accessible to the documentary camera-eye is a gross error. At least, we cannot decide until we have tried these forms. Besides the newsreel and the document, other available forms are: the trailer, the enacted short, the combined enacted and documentary, animated cartoon, satiric, and didactic.[11]

In developing his case for a full-time production unit in each branch of the league, Hurwitz drew attention to the lack of continuity in FPL output. "Our filmmaking," he declared, "has progressed by fits and starts"—largely because work was done in the evenings and on weekends. A second problem was the amateurish notions entertained by league members with regard to the training of production crew. The main cause for discontinuity of output, Hurwitz contended,

has been the prevalent conception that we can train worker-cameramen and filmmakers by giving them a few lessons in photography and sending them out to cover a demonstration or make a documentary—with the result that we have not yet trained a truly able corps of film workers. Our aim has been to develop as many such camera correspondents as possible. That this is a valid aim is not to be doubted, but the fact that in the past two years, the N.Y. League has not trained *any new cadres* in film production, and that we still have to fall back on the three or four cameramen who were with us two years ago, should be sufficient reason for us to doubt that our methods have been satisfactory, and to investigate what has held us back.[12]

The analogy between film-correspondents and worker-correspondents for the revolutionary press was a false one, he argued, because of the costs of film, scarcity of equipment, and the fact that filmmaking was a specialized craft unlike writing. It was therefore necessary to make a distinction within the league between the general membership and the active production group:

We must drop our notion that everyone interested in the Film and Photo League should become a producer of revolutionary films, and we must make organizational changes to rectify this situation. The league is larger than its production, and there is room for a mass membership of workers, not directly concerned with production, but interested in combatting the growing fascination of Hollywood, and supporting the revolutionary movies of this country and the Soviet Union. There is also room for concentrated production units whose main purpose should be to produce good revolutionary films—a unit made up of the best talent and providing for the swift training of potentialities.

Looking, as Steiner had done, to the Workers' Laboratory Theatre experience, Hurwitz argued: "That such a group, a *shock troupe* of full-time film workers would step up our production quantitatively and qualitatively can hardly be doubted." And the first of his several concluding "proposals for the immediate advance in revolutionary film production" was: "Production shock troupes and training groups to be established in every league—to be financed by the whole league by means of film showings, donations from sympathizers, affairs, etc."[13]

Ironically, by the time Hurwitz's program was published the issues had already been settled. At the national conference he gained a partial victory, but at the local level—in New York, where it really counted—his proposals were decisively rejected.

The conference came out in favor of the institution in every league of "a shock production troupe of the most talented cameramen in the organization"—but, since the semi- or wholly dramatized film was endorsed only as a second-line priority, the troupe's main function was to be "the production of newsreels and documents." (There is also no mention of financial support of troupe members by the league, and it is doubtful if this was envisaged.)[14]

In New York, Hurwitz's plan seems at first to have been given the go-ahead. Tom Brandon wrote in a *Daily Worker* column of September 14, 1934, that, "Following the example of the Workers' Laboratory Theatre, this branch is organizing a 'Shock Troop' of film producers who will carry through collectively the job of making and studying films this fall." But within a few days, apparently, the executive committee met, the scheme was rejected, and the rebels departed to pursue their goals independently of the Film and Photo League—choosing to affiliate with the organization which had been their inspiration. The *New Masses* of September 25 reported that "Ralph Steiner, Leo Hurwitz, and Irving Lerner have organized . . . a *film producing* group in connection with the Workers' Laboratory Theatre."[15]

As Hurwitz recalls:

> When I proposed the idea to the Film and Photo League it was discussed in the executive committee, it may have been discussed on the floor as well, and the objections that were raised were that it was elitist, and that it was not how a mass organization should function. And I tried to show that it was very good with a mass medium like film to have a mass organization, but you couldn't have a mass organization make films, as a mass organization. It was well to distill the most talented and interested people to make films for that organization, and to have an interacting relationship with the members of that organization. But that was put down as too elitist an idea—Brandon was one of the key figures in that, I think probably Brody felt that that would be the case too, and they were worried about a group with special privilege or something like that. I thought that was a rather childish idea, and I told them at this executive meeting when they finally turned it down, that it was inevitable that that be done, and if it weren't done in the Film and Photo League, it would have to be done elsewhere. And I was determined to do it.[16]

According to Brandon, the aims of Hurwitz and Steiner, as expressed in their *New Theatre* articles, were "held to be most laudable by most people at the league." But those were aims which the FPL was not able to underwrite:

The league was not in a position to finance a professional body to experiment with other forms of filmmaking. It was hoped that eventually something like this could be achieved, but no part of the WIR could be subsidized as a professional cultural body with a paid staff and other necessary costs. [17]

The break was not achieved without bitterness. Julian Roffman felt that by deciding to work outside the league, the Hurwitz group had "decimated the organization and left it to the 'children' and the amateurs. . . . It was not all hearts and flowers and soft music," he goes on to say, "It was harsh and jangling and there were animosities and egos and ambitions covered with a very thin layer of soft verbiage about doing good for mankind." Brody recently said that the breakaway group looked upon those who remained in the league "as the great unwashed who could not be initiated into the more lofty realms of cinema art." [18]

The split certainly involved questions of artistic aspiration. Leo Seltzer considers that Hurwitz and Lerner "had ambitions that leaned toward Hollywood, of doing the Hollywood thing, perhaps differently," and he remarks:

The FPL attracted quite a number of people with different motivations. Some stayed with it. Others who had different goals moved through the league on to other things—like Ralph Steiner, Leo Hurwitz, and Irving Lerner. It's not a question of discrediting one or the other except to straighten the record. Steiner, Hurwitz, and Lerner were not involved in the day-to-day production activities of the league. They were more involved in the theoretical and dramatic aspects of film, and they moved on to do outstanding things in other areas. [19]

In the context of developments in American radical culture in general at the time, the formation of an independent group may be seen as part of a growing trend toward greater "professionalism." The John Reed Clubs were beginning to slacken their support for novice proletarian writers, and would shortly be dissolved altogether to make way for the League of American Writers, which admitted only established authors to membership. In 1933 the Theatre Collective had been formed as an offshoot of the Workers' Laboratory Theatre with the ambition of performing full-length plays on a professional basis, and in 1935 the WLT itself, renamed the Theatre of Action, took the Broadway route. The trend was encouraged by the onset of People's Front politics, which de-emphasized class-consciousness and sought to engage progressive elements from the bourgeoisie in the struggle against war and fascism. The workers' newsreels of the Film and Photo League, exhibited to strikers on the picket line, were to share the same fate as the short agitprop dramas performed on street corners by the radical theatre groups: declared artistically "primitive," they would make way for longer, more elaborate productions designed for more traditional, theatre audiences. In time, the FPL's bastard child would supplant the FPL itself.

In late 1934, however, the new group was just a small band of enthusiasts without the financial resources to do much more than talk and dream of the shape of radical films to come. The members at the start had all been part of the league's experimental group in the spring; they included, in addition to Steiner, Hurwitz, and Lerner, Sidney Meyers, a violist, and Lionel Berman, a publicity man who was also a member of the editorial board of *New Theatre.* They called themselves "Nykino"; the "Ny" stood for New York.

"We met very frequently," says Hurwitz. "We talked, studied, and experimented." During the winter of 1934-35, he and Steiner and perhaps others in the group attended a series of classes given by Lee Strasberg, a director of the Group Theatre, and the experience had a powerful impact on their thinking about film. In February 1935, Hurwitz resigned his positions as film and managing editor of *New Theatre,* announcing that he would devote his full energies to Nykino, and the following month the collective advertised for new members: "People experienced in some phase of movie work," it was stated, "and writers interested in doing scenarios for short enacted films are needed especially."[20]

Whether in response to press announcements or otherwise (Ben Maddow says he saw an ad, "either in *The New Republic* or *The Nation,* I can't recall which"[21]), the group was, at about this time, greatly strengthened by the addition of several new members. The most experienced was Paul Strand, then age 44, who, though mostly known as a still photographer, had shot an experimental film *(Manhatta)* as early as 1921, had worked for a number of years as a freelance newsreel cameraman, and had recently completed shooting the Mexican labor film *The Wave* (which he also co-scripted and produced).[22] Ben Maddow, then known as David Wolff, was a Columbia University graduate, a left-wing poet, and an orderly at Bellevue Hospital; during the year he switched jobs to become a social worker with New York's Emergency Relief Bureau. The third new arrival was Willard Van Dyke, the young San Francisco still photographer who had, by this time, also acquired some experience with filmmaking—the previous year he had made a film about cooperatives in California. And participating in some of Nykino's work was the French photographer Henri Cartier-Bresson, who in 1935 had a joint exhibition with Walker Evans in New York.

As film division of the Theatre of Action (ex-Workers' Laboratory Theatre), Nykino was able to obtain quarters "along with the WLT's props, costumes, and scenery" at 42 E. 12th Street, though Steiner's studio in the Village was also used as a meeting place. In terms of organization there was something of a division between the daytime group, consisting of Strand, Hurwitz—who at $15 a week was the only paid member of Nykino—and Steiner, and the evening group, composed of those who earned their living at regular jobs. (Van Dyke recalls that Steiner "had a thriving still photography business, a large part of which he turned over to me when I first came to New York . . . but Ralph kept one account which took care of all his needs, and it took about three days a month to service that account.") "It was just a casual group," says Van Dyke, "it had no formal organization, there were no officers or anything like that."[23]

One of Nykino's early activities was a still photography workshop. Julian Roffman recalls that "there was still some contact and dialogue between the league and Nykino," and that he was chosen as FPL delegate to attend sessions, which were informal, and to "report back on what I learnt, if anything." Roffman describes the experience:

> I did go down and I was accepted (since I was the youngest there) as a poor relative, to be tolerated and suffered but not to be involved. I could sit and listen and learn but not ask advice, offer suggestions, or participate in the dialogue of the seniors. Others sitting in and participating were Ralph Steiner, Leo Hurwitz, Margaret Bourke-White, Irving Lerner . . . maybe Sidney Meyers. I attended about six or seven sessions in an apartment which was quite impressive. Ralph Steiner seemed to be a wealthy devotee of the art of photography. He screened some of his avant-garde films like H_2O. The classes were taken up with a project called *Park Avenue,* which stretched from the fancy area downtown all the way into Harlem and the slums. The job of the people participating was to create a photo essay of Park Avenue, the life of the people on the street, in the apartments and in the slums as a study in contrasts. There were very long involved aesthetic discussions of meaning, light and shadow, symbolism and form . . . etc. etc. ad infinitum. I remember a setup in the apartment where they were doing a tabletop still of a setting of a dining table . . . and everyone looking through the ground glass of the camera and there was endless niggling movement back and forth of cutlery and dinnerware . . . this in the midst of a damn depression. . . . I don't know that I remember learning anything except that I didn't want to wind up in this coterie. I was more action-oriented and ready to record what my eye saw and my heart felt—on the streets and in life. I don't know whether I quit or they closed the door politely.[24]

The first motion-picture work Nykino members became involved in was the editing of several films which Steiner had shot with funds from a private grant but (according to Hurwitz) had not been able to complete. Hurwitz asserts that Steiner

> had a way of shooting materials for a film and then not being able to go further. That was really . . . one of the principal reasons why he joined with me and the group, because he had a feeling that his own impulses ended too early, that he didn't have enough background to give him the passion to complete things. So when I came, started to work in Nykino, there was footage for several films. . . . I undertook to finish all these films.[25]

The most important of them was *Pie in the Sky,* already partially edited. The film was completed with title-writing assistance from left-wing movie critic Kyle Crichton, and released in March 1935 as a Nykino production; it is discussed below. The other films were *Granite* (also known as *Quarry*), a short documentary on quarrying in Vermont; *Harbor Scenes* (or *Harbor*), a study of

New York harbor for which Maddow wrote a poetic commentary ("It was a terribly dull film," he now says, "a lot of baggage strewn around"); and the ambitious but politically suspect *Cafe Universal* (now lost), a symbolic, stylized drama made with the collaboration of the Group Theatre, featuring Elia Kazan and Art Smith as war resisters, and based on the drawings of George Grosz. *Cafe Universal* was never finished. Hurwitz explains:

> The other film, about war and peace, I did not feel sympathetic with—it seemed too phoney and too poetic in a detached, sentimental, un-thought-through way. Its feeling-tones didn't stir me. . . . It was handsomely photographed, but it was all off on the wrong base, so I never finished that one.[26]

At the time he joined Nykino, Willard Van Dyke recalls, "Steiner, Strand, and Hurwitz were working full-time on the development of a script with Clifford Odets." It was the period of Odets's first flush of success: *Awake and Sing, Waiting for Lefty,* and *Till the Day I Die* were all staged by the Group Theatre in the spring, *Paradise Lost* followed at the end of the year, and *Lefty* was being performed with great excitement by workers' theatres throughout the country. As a radical (and Communist party member), Odets led a fifteen-strong writers' mission to Cuba in June, to investigate conditions under the Mendieta-Batista regime.[27]

The script Odets worked on with Nykino concerned an unemployed architect and the need for housing. It was to be a dramatic film: "Ralph [Steiner] had acquired a single-system sound camera known as an Audio Akeley," Van Dyke notes, "and we had the capacity of doing synchronous dialogue." The premise of the script, Hurwitz thinks, was:

> . . . what do you do with this internal power and external skill that you develop in a world of depression, in a world of capitalism that doesn't want your skill? That was a common theme. So that was probably, if my memory is right, at the center of the film.

It remained an unrealized project.[28]

In the summer of 1935 both Van Dyke and Strand visited the Soviet Union, though not together. Van Dyke, a former high-school actor and strongly interested in theatre (later in the thirties he would direct a settlement house group on New York's Lower East Side) spent most of his time (he says) watching plays: "It was the heyday of the great Russian theatre . . . I loved it." Regretfully, he was unable to meet any Soviet directors—"everybody was out of Moscow for the summer."[29]

Strand, who traveled with Cheryl Crawford and Harold Clurman of the Group Theatre, and was in Moscow from early May to the end of July, was more fortunate. He spent an evening with Eisenstein, who liked his photography:

I think I had a few clippings from *The Wave,* film clips, and I showed him those. He held them up to the light and, if I recall correctly, he said, "Well, I can see that you are essentially a still photographer and not a film photographer." On the basis of a few clips that he saw I thought he was a little bit over-fast. But I didn't mind.

Eisenstein later invited Strand to work with him in the Soviet Union, "but this never came off because of visa difficulties." Strand also met Dovzhenko and Nikolai Ekk, and, like Van Dyke, "went to the theatre almost every evening."[30]

On September 3, Strand, Steiner, and Hurwitz were hired by Pare Lorentz to photograph his documentary on the dust bowl for the Resettlement Administration, the film which became *The Plow That Broke the Plains.* They filmed over a seven-week period in Wyoming, Montana, Texas, and other western states. Dissatisfied with Lorentz's brief script outline, which as Hurwitz recalls was "full of personal visions and fantasy" and failed to hold the profit system responsible for the devastation of the Great Plains region, Hurwitz and Strand wrote their own version: while they were headed down to the Texas Panhandle, Hurwitz says, "we stopped off in Alliance, Nebraska, where I rented a typewriter and knocked out a script." A confrontation with Lorentz in Texas led to their proposal being rejected, but Lorentz's more idiosyncratic ideas were no doubt modified, and the writing had been a valuable experience. Hurwitz notes:

> In our script thinking on this film, we had our first full opportunity to put into practice the ideas we had been germinating: the translation of meanings into images, the fusion of images into sequence-wholes, the dramatic structuring of a documentary film on the basis of a chain of needs into a time-growing totality. We wanted our films to possess at the same time a progression of emotion and a close and true relationship to the events and their causes, direct and submerged.

And the Nykino's team handling of the cinematography added both to their professional experience and to their reputation—no doubt an invaluable asset when they began seeking, a year or so later, for financial backing for an independent film production company.[31]

At about this time Steiner collaborated with Van Dyke on *Hands,* a half-reel film for the Works Progress Administration. It consists entirely of close-ups, at first of hands which are idle, thumb-twiddling, and then of hands moving into action as a WPA check is passed around and people begin to work and prosper—typing, sawing wood, sewing, buying food, etc. The film was edited and released by Pathe in a contract agreement with the government.[32]

The New Film Alliance moved to support Nykino in January 1936 by sponsoring a prize scenario contest. The winning script, it was announced, would be published in *New Theatre* and "definitely" produced by Nykino, which also reserved "the right to produce any of the other scenarios submitted."

What was required was a twenty-minute "antiwar or antifascist" story treatment which took into account the fact that Nykino had limited producing facilities: it was stipulated that "the locale should be largely exterior with a minimum of constructed sets" and "the producing unit should be able to utilize homes, offices, or factories." There could be no synchronized dialogue, but other forms of speech, sound effects, and music could be employed. The judges were to be Paul Strand, Lee Strasberg, Ralph Steiner, James Shelly Hamilton, and Michael Blankfort, and results were to be published in the April 1936 issue of *New Theatre.* No winner was, however, announced, and it can only be surmised that the contest was cancelled owing to a lack of response.[33]

In March 1936 the Dutch filmmaker Joris Ivens arrived in New York at the invitation of the New Film Alliance, and he was to remain in the United States for most of the year. He showed his films (which were not well known in the U.S.), gave several lectures, and got to know members of the Nykino group, before moving to the West Coast to observe Hollywood in action. (His scathing appraisal of the American motion-picture business appeared in the October, 1936, issue of *New Theatre.*) The arrival of Ivens was, Irving Lerner said, "a turning point...a shot in the arm"—here was "assistance from a recognized filmmaker who confirmed the theories of Nykino." Though he did not participate actively in their work, Ivens became a powerful influence in the group's commitment to independent, left-wing documentary production, and his films—*Borinage* and *New Earth* in particular—exemplified for them an aesthetic which transcended the reportage basis of Film and Photo League work, while avoiding the thematic impersonality of a government product like *The Plow That Broke the Plains.*[34]

The Nykino filmmakers had, meanwhile, maintained their contact with members of the Group Theatre, and when, that year, they at last began production activity as a collective, it was a Group Theatre factotum whom they called upon for assistance. Michael Gordon, a graduate of the Yale Drama School, was currently a stage manager, lighting technician, assistant director, and part-time actor with the Group, though he had previously directed *Sailors of Catarro* and *Black Pit* for the Theatre Union. Gordon's participation was called for because the films which Nykino envisaged shooting were dramatic reenactments. Gordon explains how he became involved:

> ... most of these people, although they were theatregoers, and were interested in the theatre, had no direct experience themselves of working with actors, and what was perhaps even more to the point, of working with non-actors.... On the basis, I guess, of personal acquaintance, and so on, I was asked to come and see if I could give them some pointers. We set up a series of meetings—it was, in a certain sense, like a seminar class, you might say—and I was telling them what I thought would be useful approaches which would enable them to get presentable performances out of, let us say, the relatively inexperienced actors whom they might be able to enlist for their projects, and ... the non-actors, just the normal civilians who

would be in the film. And out of those sessions—they appeared to be very responsive to what I was telling them—they invited me to work with them, in effect to direct *Sunnyside*, which was the first project.[35]

The plan was to produce a *"March of Time"* from a left-wing perspective. The Nykino group had been impressed—as had many mainstream critics—with the method of dramatizing the news which Louis de Rochemont's monthly series had introduced to movie theatres in 1935, but they were disturbed by its political stance, which veered to the right. The subject they chose for their first counter-production was a battle against mortgage foreclosures being waged by white-collar workers and their families at a suburban housing development in Sunnyside, Queens. The film, a one-reel item, was shot as planned, largely by members of Nykino's "evening" division under Gordon's direction, during the spring of 1936. It was followed in the summer by another reel, made this time by the whole group, again with Gordon's assistance—a "Black Legion" sequence, exposing the activities of the native fascist organization in Detroit. The two items were shown together under the title *The World Today*, beginning in September. These films are described below.

Surviving Nykino members have only vague recollections of other production activities undertaken by the group. There were the familiar grandiose hopes ("In New York the Nykino Group . . . needs scripts for both short and feature films"), and the just as familiar collisions with the brute facts of finance. (Speaking of *The World Today*, Van Dyke says: "I think we were all pretty damn naive—the idea that we could ever . . . do that on a monthly basis or that there would be an audience for it, was very naive.") A third *World Today* segment was apparently planned ("Upon completion of a third incident, this half-hour sound film will be released in standard and 16mm size to the huge audience, in theatre, church, club, and union hall, that has been starved for this type of material," *New Theatre* reported in September 1936), but there is no record of it being shot, or even scripted, prior to the formation of Frontier Films the following year. Both Van Dyke and Hurwitz, however, recall an election film or films made probably in 1936, showing "conditions in the city." Van Dyke notes:

It seems I may have done some of the photography on a little electioneering film that was made for a liberal party or left-wing candidate on the Lower East Side. We put it on a truck. It was accompanied by a recording we played on a portable phonograph, and had a back projection on the back of this.

Though the class-struggle theme was muted, the old FPL principle of taking films to the workers was evidently not entirely dead.[36]

In the fall of 1936, the group was strengthened by the addition of one more member. Jay Leyda returned from training in the Soviet Union to take a position as assistant curator of the Museum of Modern Art film library, and at nights and on weekends joined the Nykino working group. Cartier-Bresson had meanwhile departed (in 1936 in France he collaborated as assistant director with Renoir on *La Vie est à Nous* and *Une Partie de Campagne*), but otherwise the group remained intact. In March 1937, when Frontier Films was launched, its production unit would consist entirely of Nykino alumni: Hurwitz, Strand, Steiner, Van Dyke, Berman, Meyers, Lerner, Maddow, and Leyda—with Elia Kazan and Michael Gordon participating in specific projects.[37]

Nykino was a transitional grouping—the idea of preparing the way for a full-time production company was formulated at a comparatively early date—and its total output, in terms of production, was slight. But in the scope it allowed members to assess, question, and redefine their aesthetic goals it was of great significance.

What united the group was a dissatisfaction with the idea of cinema as reportage. The Film and Photo League model, as represented by the films made prior to the split in 1934, did not excite them enough. As Paul Strand remarked of fellow group members who had been in the FPL, "They felt that filmmaking was a serious art form and that a simple kind of journalism was not sufficient to interest them for any length of time," adding, "I was completely in accord with this myself." Likewise, Van Dyke feels, "The same impulse that led those men to leave the Film and Photo League would have led me to do the same thing." He was not attracted to the idea of news photography and "just couldn't see the personal artistic expression."[38]

Hurwitz considered that the prospects of radical cinema had been harmed by overemphasis on the analogy with the function of propaganda in the print media:

> Agitational propaganda, say the making of a leaflet or poster, is a very specific problem. You want to get people out to a demonstration. In order to bring them out—let's say to a meeting of the unemployed in Union Square in 1932—you need to say certain things. That's a very different problem, getting action by means of direct and quick communication, than a film on unemployment whose basic purpose is to help organize the unemployed. With the film you're not trying to do a single specific thing. You don't even know where it's going to be shown or whether anything can be done at that moment. You're trying to alter people's consciousness by dramatizing real experience, clearing away distortions so that they begin to see events in a way that has some truth to it. Action may then follow in the specific contexts of people's lives.[39]

To *move* an audience, to change people's consciousness, it was crucial, in Hurwitz's view, to structure documentary material with a pattern at variance with the elementary additive logic of film reporting:

But if you wanted to create an experience with your film, an experience in itself which could move people or stir them to ideas and action, then the journalistic form with its primary "and" connectives was very limited. What was needed was a principle of growth, enabling the film to grow out of its parts into a whole, much as a plot functions in a fiction film. One needed in the documentary film an equivalent of plot, with connectives of "but," "against," "despite," "growing into." The key to this, we found, was that a sequence had not merely to describe or relate but to create a *need* in the audience, as in a fiction film, by identification with the characters, a feeling of want or anxiety is created in the audience. Then one could look at the structure of a film and design it—with image and word and sound—as a chain of interactive needs progressing toward a resolution. If you were handling ideas, then your ideas would also have to be woven into this progression of needs.[40]

Hurwitz, here, speaks of an *equivalent* for plot and character, but the aspiring filmmakers of Nykino were also increasingly drawn towards a form in which documentary and dramatic elements were mixed. The suspicion of fiction remained—with one or two minor exceptions, no production of the radical film movement of the thirties ever moved far away from concrete historic incident—yet there was a felt need for the greater audience engagement which could be attained by individualizing the presentation of a socioeconomic thesis. The move was towards an aesthetic of reenactment in which individual figures were allowed to emerge, and there were several significant influences impelling the Nykino group in this direction. There was, of course, the example of Soviet film, which was in the process of abandoning the "mass hero" of the avant-garde productions of the twenties for the heroic individuals of socialist realism. Closer to home, there were the experience of Paul Strand and the teaching of Lee Strasberg to call upon.

Strand had shot *The Wave (Redes,* also known as *Pescados)* in 1934 for the Department of Fine Arts in the Mexican Secretariat of Education. Aiming the film at "a great majority of rather simple people to whom elementary facts should be presented in a direct and unequivocal way," Strand and his collaborators couched in quasi-fictional form their treatment of the exploitation of fishermen of the Gulf of Vera Cruz, and the struggle to organize, achieve unity, and strike. There is, in fact, an exemplary individual, Miro, who is radicalized on the death of his child through lack of medical attention, and attempts to persuade his fellow fishermen to withhold their catch because of the miserable prices offered by the dealer. Miro becomes a martyr to the cause, gunned down by a traitorous politician, and his fate unites the fishermen on a course of militant action. The Nykino group were strongly impressed by the film when it finally reached the United States in late 1936 (Sidney Meyers wrote: "It is . . . extraordinarily beautiful and moving as few films in our experience have been"); and meanwhile its success in Mexico no doubt confirmed Strand in the direction away from strict documentary which he had taken. He later recalled:

When I came back from Mexico I also found in New York besides the Group Theatre a small group of filmmakers most of whom were making their living at something else, but who were profoundly interested in the problems of filmmaking, especially documentary film-making.... they realized that the ordinary documentary approach... is a pretty dull affair unless one finds some way of dramatizing the material. Why? Because there is no story, there is no hero, there is no heroine, there are no characters as a rule with whose lives one can identify oneself and follow a development which is their life and their destiny. In other words, the documentary film tends to have a structure, an aesthetic structure and an actual structure of simply a lot of facts strung together one after another with no development, with no conflict, with no drama.[41]

It was the hope of incorporating drama into their films that drew the Nykino members to the Group Theatre—as well as the air of artistic experimentation, excitement, and collective endeavor which surrounded the organization led by Harold Clurman, Lee Strasberg, and Cheryl Crawford. Clurman records that Steiner and Strand took part in the Group's preliminary discussion sessions as early as 1931, and Steiner has attested to the significance which the group held for him:

It was terribly, terribly important, the Group Theatre. I had a photographic studio, and every Friday night they would meet in my studio, and I would rent chairs from an undertaker and pay for them, so they called me a Group Associate.

His account of one of Strasberg's rehearsals indicates what struck him about the Group's approach:

One of the things was that they were... acting out things which were parallel to life. I remember a play they did about San Francisco shipping millionaires [*Gold Eagle Guy*], and I remember in the rehearsal they were having this meeting of a big board of directors of a company. Lee Strasberg was directing this, and... he said to them, "Well, you're all big millionaires, and you're all on your dignity. Now I want you to take ten minutes off, and improvise a scene: you're pirates and you've captured a ship full of gold and diamonds and jewels, and you're dividing the swag." The result, when they got through, was absolutely wonderful. He said, "All right, now you are directors, men with money, and big homes, and great dignity, members of the boards of your churches and all that. But you're also pirates still, dividing the swag." Well... this kind of thing, where you saw a thing in parallel, a reflection of it in other terms... I think this influenced me quite a bit.[42]

Strasberg's course in theatre direction, which Steiner and Hurwitz (and perhaps others of the Nykino group) attended during the winter of 1934-35, was the decisive factor in fixing the filmmakers' attention on an actor-centered cinema. Steiner and Hurwitz assessed the implications of Strasberg's teaching for their thinking about film in their important article, "A New Approach to Film Making," published in the September 1935 issue of *New Theatre*.[43]

There were three main factors in their development, the authors wrote, "each of which contributed influences of definite positive value but each of which also warped our basic attitude toward the film medium." The factors were their "formal revolt from Hollywood," Pudovkin's book *Film Technique,* and the documentary film.

In reacting against the superficiality, triviality, and standardization of the Hollywood product, Steiner and Hurwitz had been drawn to the unexplored formal potentials of the film medium: "angles, lens distortions, camera tricks; the play of light, the magnificence of objects and objects in motion, the eloquence of things, rhythmic possibilities, and symphonic treatment." But the accent had been on *objects*—"even people were considered externally, as objects rather than as human beings." This avant-garde experimentation failed to take into account audience response—or lack of it: "In fact, the quick demise of this movement is proof that the audience got next to nothing out of it." Continued work in this vein "could lead to nothing else but ivory-tower aesthetic films, unrelated to contemporary life."

Pudovkin's book, with its emphasis on film *technique,* had misled them into a false conception of the role of editing, or montage. Stressing the significance of the way shots were joined was damaging insofar as it taught them that the content of the shot itself was unimportant, or that the meaning of a sequence depended on the way it was cut together. "Pudovkin's concern with the end problem," the authors noted, "—the detailed shooting script, the taking of the shot, and the final editing— did not give us the basis for the primary step—the conception and rendering of the story, mood, or idea in dramatic terms (theatricalization)." Hence they had been unable to understand the point of mise-en-scene exercises sent to them from Eisenstein's classes at the Moscow Film School, not realizing that without the initial step of conceiving a situation dramatically—inventing business for the actors, designing movement in space and time, and so on—"a shooting script might result in an interesting camera and montage treatment, but would never bring the situation to life for an audience." Again, it was the effect on the audience that most strongly concerned Steiner and Hurwitz—a preoccupation, of course, properly central to a search for a *political* film aesthetic. In summarizing the effect that *Film Technique* had had on their thinking, the authors wrote: "It is easy to see what errors might flow from laying the entire emphasis, as we did, on the secondary principles of film technique without grasping or even realizing there exist the primary dramatic principles without which a theatrical art cannot affect and involve an audience."

The account of the negative influence which their experience of documentary filmmaking had exerted on their development is perhaps the most crucial passage in understanding the growth of Steiner and Hurwitz towards a new radical aesthetic. "In making a documentary film, as we then conceived it, you photographed the event and the things that were relevant to it, and then by means of clever editing you could do most anything in making the film effective"—or so they thought. The results, however, did not live up to expectations:

> You were going to do a film about the Scottsboro case, or New York Harbor. You knew what the film was going to say. Then you took your camera and attempted to capture completely as you could the most meaningful visual aspects of reality. Then, to the cutting room, where you pieced the film together in a brilliant and cogent montage to make it a moving document of life. Only somehow it was never really moving. At best it turned out to be a conceptualized statement, a film concerned with objects and the purely external manifestations of people without their emotions or motivations, a pamphlet on the screen, to which you could say "yes" with your mind, but your emotions weren't involved.

They did not realize, Steiner and Hurwitz said, that to engage a spectator's emotions, even in a documentary film, it was necessary "to use theatrical means of affecting an audience—suspense, build, dramatic line, etc."

It was Strasberg who drew these points to the attention of the Nykino filmmakers, allowing them to understand that unless this audience response was obtained, their pictures, "however profound and socially important in subject," would be "lifeless and socially ineffectual." Steiner and Hurwitz concluded:

> We learned that the film as a dramatic medium cannot merely concern itself with external happenings even though they may be revolutionary happenings, but must embody the conflict of underlying forces, causes. That to achieve this, the making of a film involves not merely: (1) knowing what you want to say, (2) a scenario, and (3) shooting and cutting it, but the intermediate steps of theatricalizing the events through the invention of circumstances and activities which transform concepts, relationships, and feelings into three-dimensional happenings that are plausible, effective, and rich in significance. Only in solving [these?] problems does it seem likely that a film conduit can be constructed which can carry our revolutionary viewpoint to an increasingly receptive audience, one that is really moved because in the life on the screen it finds its own aspirations and struggles, its own failures and successes, its own truths.

Though the article makes no direct reference to Stanislavsky, this last paragraph makes it clear that the Russian director's concept of psychological realism in acting, which had such a profound influence on the practice of the Group Theatre and of Strasberg in particular, was being blended into the new aesthetic of the Nykino group. And Strand confirms: the New York filmmakers he joined, "stimulated by the Group Theatre, had been brought into contact with the theories and methods of Stanislavsky and found them useful in trying to work out some of the problems of film which they had been running into in documentary form."[44]

The Nykino productions went only a limited way towards fulfilling in practice the newly developing radical aesthetic of the group. Tom Brandon remarks that *Pie in the Sky,* though "remarkably amusing today, was not then considered to be even a partial fulfillment of the lucid and inspiring prospectus by Hurwitz and Steiner." And *Sunnyside* and *Black Legion,* in their short length and circumscribed format, gave only hints of what might come—and did come later, in the productions of Frontier Films—from a systematic implementation of the theory of dramatized documentary.[45]

It is nonetheless instructive to examine the films—particularly those that survive, *Pie in the Sky* and *Sunnyside*—in terms of what they did achieve in the field of political cinema.

Pie in the Sky, whose running time is fourteen minutes, has already been subjected to extended exegesis in two dissertations, Vladimir Petric's "Soviet Revolutionary Films in America (1926-1935)" and Joel Zuker's "Ralph Steiner: Filmmaker and Still Photographer," and further analysis runs the danger of overkill. The film was, after all, never considered a serious contribution to left-wing cinema—certainly not by Elia Kazan, one of its principal creators, who observes: "It was a lark . . . we just horsed around." Ray Ludlow, reviewing *Pie in the Sky* in *New Theatre,* warned, "In no sense does the picture successfully solve the cinematization of a revolutionary point of view," and Nykino did not go to great pains to have the film distributed.[46]

Pie in the Sky was, in fact, an exceptional work to have come out of the radical film movement of the time, not least in the fact that the documentary impetus is minimal. Minimal, that is, unless we accept Zuker's formulation of the film as an "expositional 'documentary' about Group Theatre exercises." The remark, glib as it seems, does shed some light on the apparent anomaly of a light-hearted improvised satire suddenly appearing as the production of an organization heavily committed to (noncomic) documentary realism. Ralph Steiner, the cameraman and co-director, was the Group Theatre's photographer—his work included shooting stills of their summer workshops, rehearsals, and plays—and it is probable that his contribution did, indeed, consist of recording a pair of performances (by Elia Kazan and Elman Koolish) whose inspiration derived not from anything which was being done by the Left on film at the time, but from the theatre.[47]

This interpretation is sustained by Kazan, who recalls, "Ralph and I would discuss a scene, I'd set up the camera and then he would photograph it and I acted. In a sense," he continues, "I directed the performances and he directed the photography." And the performances—the improvised comedy around the themes of deprivation and religious mystification—came from the theatrical activity which Kazan (and other Group Theatre actors, particularly those like Kazan with radical convictions) were engaged in. As he recounts:

> Ralph and I directed another film out here in New York, at the city dump. It was just a two-reel comedy, called *Pie in the Sky.* In those days, these things were shown at fund-raising

meetings. I used to go to them and do comedy skits that didn't have much social point but were amusing. And this film was just more of that.[48]

Even the conception of the performances as "exercises" is accurate. The film's satiric strength lies in its inspired play upon the categories of fantasy and reality, in which objects are transformed through delicate mime (a twisted wire is a pretzel, a rubber cup becomes a breast, a birdcage is swung as a censer). The closeness of this make-believe acting to exercises which Kazan would perform at this period in preparation for a play is revealed by a description of the latter by Willard Van Dyke:

> One of my first New York memories . . . is the sort of preparation that Kazan used to do every day before he began to rehearse. . . . One day he was holding something tight like this—it wasn't really there—and I suddenly realized it was a straight razor he had in his hand, and he carefully stropped the thing like that, got it sharp, got the hair out of it, carefully peeled the hair—this was all done without props. He would do exercises like that by the hour.[49]

In *Pie in the Sky* two hungry tramps (Kazan and Koolish), disappointed in their hope for a handout at a Bowery mission, find themselves on a city dump, and there—"under the inspiration," as Ray Ludlow wrote, "of the gangrenous locale and its heterogeneous junk"—act out a wistful parody of relief agencies and the ethos of religion. The film's title, of course, comes from the popular Wobbly song written by Joe Hill:

> Long-haired preachers come out every night
> Try to tell you what's wrong and what's right
> But when asked about something to eat
> They will answer in voices so sweet
>
> *(Chorus)*
> You will eat, by and by,
> In that glorious land above the sky,
> Work and pray, live on hay,
> You'll get pie in the sky when you die.
> (That's a lie!)

The words of the chorus are in fact superimposed over the images in a final montage in which a pie at last appears—only to vanish as a mirage.

As a defiant endorsement of a materialist world-view against the delusions of idealism (pitched very close to Brecht's "Erst kommt das Fressen, dann kommt die Moral"[50]), *Pie in the Sky* was, for all its tomfoolery, a hardhitting film. Indeed, it struck too hard for some left critics as the radical labor movement entered the People's Front phase. Ludlow wrote:

Considered as a film experiment, which is all its producers claim for it, *Pie in the Sky* has both excellent photography and imaginative acting to recommend it. As a revolutionary film, however, it is unsatisfactory as it is not very appropriate for showings before mass audiences. The fierceness and baldness with which it ridicules the Church would prove antagonistic to an average working-class audience.[51]

But the chief reason why *Pie in the Sky* remained outside the mainstream of radical film was that it failed to conform to the aesthetic pattern which practitioners in the Film and Photo League and Nykino were in the process of marking out: a) expose socioeconomic conditions b) document the struggle to change them. According to Steiner, Communist party members and the heads of the Soviet film corporation (Amkino) in New York felt that the film's ideological conception "watered down the problem of unemployment in a vaudevillian, naive, and superficial way." And it is true that *Pie in the Sky* gives no indication of the economic causes for its protagonists' hunger; nor does it suggest any engagement in militant struggle. As Joel Zuker points out, in a criticism which probably captures thinking of the thirties:

The most important ideological indictment that can be leveled against *Pie in the Sky* is that the two characters are just as defeated and downtrodden at the end of the film as they were in the beginning. They still have no sense of history; in fact, they have reverted to a dream world in which the "pie in the sky" (their salvation) is really a mirage. We do not expect these men to organize, or become revolutionaries, but rather, we assume that they will sink deeper into self-pity and illusion. Far from offering its audience the idea that revolutionary actions must be taken to end the Depression, the film confirms the notion that nothing can be done—we are helpless, we have no voice in deciding our own destiny.[52]

It is significant, in this light, that Ludlow's review of *Pie in the Sky* (the only full-length study of the film to appear at the time) discounts its political value and concentrates on its handling of actors as a precedent for future independent productions. "It explores," he notes, "for the first time in American cinema, the application to the screen of the acting technique elaborated by Stanislavsky and the Moscow Art Theatre"—a technique which had been "used with striking results by the leading left theatres, including the Group Theatre, the Artef, and the Theatre of Action." Ludlow goes on to argue:

Though the method of Stanislavsky was conceived for the stage, it is amazing how it meets the problems of cinema acting head on. Stanislavsky asks the actor to concentrate upon an object or person he is working with, instead of playing to the audience. He trains him in the use of objects in a way which stimulates inventiveness in their use and gives significance and reality to the handling of them. In a camera close-up the theatre value of this is magnified. And finally, he stresses the system of affective memory as a means for evoking genuine and immediate emotion.[52]

But a serious application of this technique to the cinema clearly implied a break with film structures which, inspired by Russian montage experimentation, reduced the actor "to a sort of living prop." Ludlow's strong endorsement of the actor (which had its parallel with contemporary developments in Soviet film) entailed maintaining the integrity of a performance through comparatively long takes and the construction of a coherent time-space continuum: in other words, a rejection of the aesthetic of montage. His ideas undoubtedly meshed with the Nykino group's developing conception of the film as a dramatic medium; and in this, limited, sense, *Pie in the Sky* was a precursor of Nykino's next production, *The World Today.*

Why, if the participants in Nykino wished to move away from screen journalism, did they choose as the model for their only major production the film news magazine *The March of Time?* The answer seems to be twofold. Firstly, in its form—its selection and dramatization of particular news events in depth—*The March of Time* marked a significant advance over film reportage of the past, even that (in the opinion of Irving Lerner in 1935) of the Film and Photo League, most of whose newsreels, he said, had been "formless and as poorly made as the commercial reel." Secondly, *The March of Time* was having a profound influence on audiences, and from a political point of view it was necessary to counteract what was perceived as its reactionary propaganda.[54]

Something of the appeal of the *March of Time* format to the Nykino group is suggested by an article of Lerner's of 1937, in which he claimed that it had "revolutionized" the newsreels. He went on to say:

> As a matter of fact, it was very easy for *The March of Time* to advance over the conventional newsreel. It eliminated the "entertainment" values of the newsreel and presented "news" and "educational" features in a fresh manner. It proved that the reenacted newsreel, the dramatic documentary, need not necessarily detract from the *actuality* of the event. As a matter of fact, it added the welcome dramatic punch.

Yet *The March of Time*'s potential was often greater than its achievement. Writing in 1937, Lerner and Sidney Meyers observed that its subjects were "never more than sketchily documented," were "unimaginatively edited," and featured "a species of reenactment invariably wooden and unreal." The Nykino filmmakers felt they could do better. Agreeing that *The March of Time* was "awfully shoddy in its reenactment," Leo Hurwitz recently said: "*The World Today* was an attempt to do what *The March of Time* did, much better, much more truthfully, with more grasp of the fullness of the event, and the meanings of an event—and with more truthfulness in the reenactment."[55]

Part of *The March of Time*'s danger, in the opinion of the radical critics, was that its method of dramatization made it a much more efficient and deceptive carrier of right-wing values than the conventional newsreel. "In the

name of objectivity and honest reporting," Lerner said, "*The March of Time*
went the way of the rest of the *Time-Fortune-Life* enterprises: flirting with
Reaction," and he and Meyers spelled out the news magazine's political record,
as they saw it, in its initial period of existence:

> Taken all in all, the issues of *The March of Time* for the past two years run the entire gamut
> from conservatism to fascism. It has presented us with roseate pictures of the benefits of
> Japanese imperialism to the Chinese coolie. The Stavisky incident has been laid to the door
> of Communists and other criminals. Colonel de la Rocque and the Croix de Feu have been
> hailed as the hope of France. It has approved of sneaking frame-ups in ridding CCC camps of
> "discontented agitators." It has ridiculed the unemployed by malicious reenactments of their
> behavior during the occupation of the New Jersey Assembly last winter. The French
> peasants have been shown as opposed to the Popular Front. Governor Talmadge of Georgia
> has been given the guise of a working-class hero. The Nicaragua dope ring incident was
> utilized to discredit revolutionary movements.

And the authors went on to cite further examples of bias to the right.[56]

There was an evident appeal in the notion of taking *The March of Time*'s
form, improving on it, and giving it an alternative content, so that the social
and political struggles of the American people came to the fore. As early as
March 1935, in a severely critial analysis of the first *March of Time* issue, Ray
Ludlow and Eva Goldbeck suggested, instead of the items chosen, a string of
topics which might better have been included: the national unemployment
conference, the invoking of an old syndicalism law by California capitalists
against agricultural workers, department-store workers organizing and going
on strike, recent exposures of plans for "fascist mobilization of Wall Street
figures," and so on. The article, which appeared in *New Theatre,* might well
have stimulated the Nykino group towards the formulation of their *World
Today* concept.[57]

The Sunnyside mortgage interest strike began in April 1935. It was low-
cost housing, Michael Gordon recalls, but there were very high mortgage
interest rates.

> The mortgages extended over twenty years or thirty years but the houses were disintegrating,
> they were jerrybuilt, long before the mortgage payments were even nearly discharged. And
> they were not getting what was guaranteed to them in terms of materials, repairs, and so
> forth. They just decided not to pay.

Organized in the Sunnyside Gardens Home Owners' Mortgage Committee
(which represented more than 75% of the owners by the end of the year), the
residents resisted interest demands from the mortgagees, and asked for the
right to bargain collectively over the rates. Foreclosures followed—by
December, actions had been taken or were pending against nearly a hundred
owners, and the community was mobilizing in an attempt to prevent evictions.

On December 31, collective action by the Sunnyside residents thwarted an effort to evict one owner, Mrs. Corinne Thal, but on January 25, 1936, communal solidarity was overwhelmed by a force of "fifteen deputies, and the movers, plus several police cars and a cordon of police," and Mrs. Thal was thrown out of her house. The homeowners vowed to continue the struggle.[58]

In the coverage in the Communist press of the Sunnyside strike and of Mrs. Thal's eviction—particularly a feature article in the *Sunday Worker* of February 2—certain salient themes emerged. The homeowners were identified as "white-collar workers"—and now that they faced eviction, it was stated, "the 'security' of the middle class has been exposed to them as a sham." Mrs. Thal was quoted as saying that through their experience, "we'll have learned the best lesson the middle class can learn." Sunnyside was, until the trouble started, a "typical New York suburb" with its bridge club and petty community tiffs. "The suburb dwellers came to Sunnyside to get away from the smoke of New York," it was stated: "They wanted to have homes for their families, in which children could lead healthy lives." Mrs. Thal, shaken from the complacency of her "knitting, darning, and cooking," emerged as a model militant:

> I used to be an idle woman, but I'm busy now. This has been a marvelous education for all of us. When we first started, Alexander Bing, the builder, called us a bunch of reds. And you know what we answered? We said, "If we are reds you are the ones who are making us reds. Because we're fighting for our rights does that make us reds?"

The residents' concern for their homes was presented as a "deeply embedded American idea," whose roots lay firmly in national tradition:

> Walter Ludwig, a director of the Pioneer Youth of America, told the home owners that their fight was similar to that of the farmers of Massachusetts in Shay's Rebellion, when shortly after the Revlutionary War they resisted eviction from their farms. Terrorized by vigilantes from wealthy Bostonian families, the farmers went west to find free land and freedom. But nowadays there is no such escape possible, Walter Ludwig told the home owners; they have to stay and fight foreclosures and evictions.

The contemporary equivalent of the "wealthy Bostonian families" were the mortgagees—and particularly Mrs. Thal's, the Merchants' Indemnity Corporation, of which John D. Rockefeller, Jr., was a director and large shareholder. The *Sunday Worker* article was entitled "Mrs. Thal Saved and Scraped to Build a Dream Home . . . and Rockefeller Foreclosed the Mortgage," and it was illustrated by a photograph (alongside a shot of Sunnyside children with placards) of Rockefeller Center. The caption read: "Rockefeller Center in the heart of New York was built as a monument to the House of Rockefeller. It is the savings of small home owners, the blood of workers spilled in the Ludlow Massacre, that made possible this edifice."[59]

The incident of Mrs. Thal's eviction had thus been subjected to considerable ideological mediation by the time it was selected as the subject for the first *World Today* item. Clearly, its ability to sustain political reverberations long after it had ceased to be news was a factor in its suitability for the Nykino project.

The script for the film was elaborated collectively, with the participation of the Sunnyside homeowners. Shooting took place close to the original locales, at weekends, with the local residents now reenacting their role in the struggle. Willard Van Dyke was on camera, Michael Gordon directed, and Van Dyke and Gordon, together with Sidney Meyers, also played bit parts. Irving Lerner took production stills and edited the film (probably with the assistance of Meyers), and Ben Maddow wrote the commentary. "It was all right, as I remember," says Gordon; but as a director, he "knew absolutely nothing about cinema...except what one knows as a moviegoer," and hence, "fumbled and bumbled and made the most grotesque mistakes all over the place."[60]

Those mistakes are not evident in *Sunnyside,* which has a sharp visual style and a keen sense of dramatic pace, keyed to a nervous pitch in places by rapid camera movement and cutting, along with somewhat strident music. There was little chance—or need—to develop any sustained acting, but Gordon derived from his nonprofessionals creditably convincing performances: Lerner claimed that *The World Today* was "so realistic, that when this sequence was shown to the 'actors' they refused to believe their eyes—that this was *not* the actual eviction."[61]

The film opens with idyllic shots of a pleasant, tree-lined suburb: wind rustles the leaves and sun bounces off the laughing cheeks of children at play. "Sunnyside, 1926," the narration goes, "it was a paradise in those happy days...." A paradise lost with the Crash and the Depression. Suddenly the streets are empty and forlorn, and foreclosure signs appear. The young professionals, "hardpressed with obligations," are threatened by "the billion-dollar usurers, the mortgage companies, the insurance corporations."

But they band together to save their homes. A community meeting is reenacted, at which the sheriff (we see him only from the rear) reassures the homeowners that "no one will be evicted until it's warm enough to sleep on your own front lawn."

There is an abrupt cut to the following morning. In sub-zero temperatures, a bailiff bangs at Mrs. Thal's door. The community protection scheme is put into effect. Phones ring, the warning siren blows, neighbors tear away from their breakfast and rush to the defense of the threatened home. A flurry of shots intercuts people running in the street and edging into the house by the back door, with the bailiff smashing his entrance and beginning the eviction. Police and deputies come to the assistance of the movers, dragging people and furniture out of the house, beating protestors, making six arrests; despite militant defense by the community, which finally forces its way en masse into the house, the authorities are victorious. The film ends with a shot of "plucky" Mrs. Thal outside with a pile of furniture. She speaks directly to camera:

> The mortgage companies think they have us licked, but they haven't. The home owners are wonderful, and have all taken a pledge not to settle separately. The Equitable will think twice, I am sure, before they try anything like this again. My eviction hasn't been a defeat, it's been a victory, a moral victory.

The narration shapes the incident into a morality play whose outlines are familiar from coverage of the eviction in the radical press. The residents are introduced as middle-class: "the young teacher or engineer." Sunnyside Gardens was "a peaceful development twenty minutes from the glaring towers of New York City, a village beside a metropolis," where many came "as bride and groom, to raise their children in safety and sunlight, to create for themselves a home of their own—the dream of America." The pioneer tradition is once more invoked. In the people who resisted was "the force of the old American ideal, of a home and family"; "These Sunnysiders," the authoritative voice comments, "showed the traditional spirit of the American pioneers who transformed the waste land into farms, cities, and homes." And though Rockefeller is not named in person, the reference to the "billion-dollar usurers" directs audience anger in his general direction.

Ideologically, the film thus adopts a militant defensive posture. The Communist Party's attempt to win middle-class sympathies in the new People's Front era is plainly echoed in the strong endorsement given to the suburban way of life (the *Sunday Worker* had evidenced a certain equivocation about this in its allusion to "knitting, darning, and cooking"), and struggle is engaged in not to transform a fundamentally unjust economic system, but to restore a supposedly harmonious past. References to the American tradition serve to bolster a backward-looking vision (in the press the contemporary power elite would come to be painted as "economic royalists" by analogy with the enemies of the Revolutionary age), and there is even an opening toward quasi-religious piety: "Which is more sacred, the American home, or six per cent?" *Sunnyside,* in this way, introduced to the cinema that characteristic amalgam of radical and conservative values which would distinguish most "progressive" culture of the later thirties.

Black Legion was inspired by the exposure, in May 1936, of the activities of the Michigan-based secret society of that name, a northern equivalent of the Ku Klux Klan. The Black Legion directed its violence against Communists, blacks, Jews, and Catholics, and was apparently flourishing with the backing of auto industry executives alarmed at the unionization drive. (Warner Brothers' 1937 feature *Black Legion* significantly avoided any reference to the union issue.) Investigations at the time began to uncover a series of murders carried out by legion terrorists, including the slaying of a WPA worker, Charles A. Poole, allegedly because "he knew too much about the organization." The *Daily Worker* reported:

> Dayton Dean, one of the men named in the murder warrants, today confessed, according to police, that Poole was shot "because the rope didn't show up in time."
> Detectives Joe Harvill and Charles Meehan, of the homicide squad, said that Dean told them plans of the vigilantes had embraced hanging but Poole was shot because the automobile bearing the rope did not arrive at the place designated for his execution.
> "It was planned to be a one-way ride for Poole," the officers quoted Dean as saying.[62]

This killing was selected as the central incident for the second *World Today* item, but as with *Sunnyside* some background to the event was apparently included. According to publicity, the film contained "a reconstruction of the Black Legion's rise and reign of terror in the Middle West," and the legion's elaborate initiation ritual was recreated in the film in a scene which, in Lerner's estimation, was "more vivid than anything in the Warner Brothers' version of *Black Legion.*"[63]

Since Nykino's *Black Legion* has not, evidently, survived, and little was written about it at the time of its release, discussion is necessarily restricted. The action was entirely dramatized (it is not recorded who played the roles), and the main sequence, at least, was shot at night in the New Jersey woods, with light from flares and bonfires. Ralph Steiner was the cameraman (Van Dyke may also have shot some of the footage), Michael Gordon directed ("some of it," he says), and the whole group including Hurwitz and Strand apparently participated in the project. Hurwitz's recollection is that the WPA worker was not developed as a character, "although he was treated much more as a human being, and more fully within the event, than would have been the case in *The March of Time.*"[64]

The World Today premiered in New York on September 22, 1936, and was then included in a package of films "being sent to ten districts of the Communist party by the National Campaign Committee" as part of the election drive in the last week of September. (The program also included *Millions of Us,* made independently in Hollywood by American Labor Films, *The Voice of Progress,* a speech by Earl Browder, and *Who Gets Your Vote?,* the "first labor cartoon," made by Del of the *Daily Worker.*) *Sunnyside* and *Black Legion* did not, however, receive a regular theatrical run until the spring of 1937, by which time Nykino had been supplanted by Frontier Films. The filmmakers were nevertheless still hoping to continue to work within the news magazine format. Lerner wrote in the May 1937 issue of the *New Masses:*

> This first issue has its faults; to deny them would be unfair to the members of the staff of Frontier Films, since in ideas and technique they have advanced beyond this film, made

months ago. Nevertheless, it is strong enough, and exciting enough to amaze many members of the *March of Time* staff when it was shown to them. This is truly a bold new step in the field of the American movies and it is up to us to support it for all we're worth.

But the one issue of *The World Today* was to be the last; and Frontier Films was soon to set its sights on more ambitious projects.[65]

5

Frontier Films

In March 1937, the informal collective Nykino was converted into the nonprofit production company Frontier Films. The move came after a screening, attended by "some seventy-five of America's most important writers and filmmakers," of the Paul Strand/Fred Zinnemann film *The Wave (Redes)*, together with Nykino's *The World Today*. "These extraordinary works," *New Theatre and Film* reported, "settled for those present the many doubts that for years have sidetracked the progress of independent film production." Plans were immediately put into action "for the solidification of all progressive film forces in the East," and in the last week of March articles of incorporation for the new organization were filed in Albany, N.Y.[1]

The company was launched on a wave of sympathetic support from progressive individuals and organizations in cultural and political fields. Leo Hurwitz recalls:

> We had the interest of artists, writers, trade-union people, people in the city government, etc. There was a strong interest in the "new film," and a strong community among intellectuals, progressive and "left"—a strong enthusiasm for an emerging culture, opening up stereotyped forms, digging into the content of living experience, pulling up the blinds of isolated art-oriented art, making real connections with people.[2]

It was what the Nykino members had long been awaiting. According to Paul Strand, they "all were very eager to stop working at anything except filmmaking," and the attraction of a full-time group, "similar, in a sense, to the Group Theatre" was sufficient to overcome doubts about the miniscule wages they would receive—when films were in production.[3]

The statement of intent issued by Frontier Films at the time of its incorporation defined the company's composition and aims. The organization comprised "a group of forward-looking professional scenarists, directors, dramatists, and cameramen" who had combined "in response to a vital need"—"the production of films that truthfully reflect the life and drama of contemporary America." The statement continued:

> There are many aspects of American life ignored by the film industry. In the stirring events that overflow our newspapers... in the vivid reality of our everyday lives... in the rich and robust traditions of the American people... there exists a wealth of dramatic material. This is the subject matter that needs to be dramatized in America's most popular medium of entertainment. It is this America—the world we actually live in—that Frontier Films will portray.

For the first time, Frontier claimed, the "enormous power" of movies "to influence habit and opinion" would be wielded by an independent production organization "consistently on the side of progress"—in contradistinction to Hollywood, which has used the power "to mold the minds of the nation in its own image."[4]

Such progressive filmmaking required a genuinely collective organizational structure. As Strand explained in a published interview with Sidney Meyers:

> ...this collective of director-cameramen-actors-playwright and composer must be more than they are in Hollywood—merely accessories used by the producer to present reality in the interests of the box office—in the interests of providing an unhealthy escape into a world of phantasy to millions whose lives are unhappy and meager. Good films... will only be made when the technicians and artists of the films work together unified by a common agreement and strive to present truthfully the rich and dramatic material which is the very stuff and fabric of our lives.[5]

In a promotional leaflet, Frontier Films printed expressions of support from an array of well-wishers which included Harold Clurman (director of the Group Theatre), Catherin Bauer (secretary of the Labor Housing Conference), Herman Shumlin (theatrical producer and promoter of the Joris Ivens documentary group, Contemporary Historians, Inc.), Lewis Mumford (social critic and town-planning visionary), Malcolm Cowley (literary critic), and Gardner Jackson (chairman of the National Committee on Rural and Social Planning). Their statements were alive with suggestions for territory the new organization could stake out. Catherine Bauer, for example, wrote:

> Thousands of incidents and situations, which affect the lives of millions of people and have numerous dramatic possibilities, occur daily in America. The labor situation, the housing problem, the waste of natural resources and the valiant effort to conserve and utilize these resources in the public interest, are not only increasingly significant in themselves, but they have *visual* elements which make them much better material for presentation through films than by spoken or written word. But the present framework of the movie industry ignores the opportunity and would be incapable of utilizing this great new mine of material even if it were aware of the demand. The formation of Frontier Films at this time is, therefore, both welcome and strategic. It not only deserves success—but is almost certain to be successful.

Malcolm Cowley's proposals were even more concrete:

> Frontier Films could show us sit-down strikers, marching out of the Chrysler plants behind their brass bands—or they could tell the story of the union campaign in textiles, beginning with the first plans to organize more than a million workers and extending through battles in front of mill gates in South Carolina and Rhode Island down to the moment that must come when a treaty of peace is signed for the whole industry (and when the workers get their first pay envelopes under the new agreement)—or, again they could picture the struggles and sorrows (not to forget the fun) of an ordinary working-class family—in a word, they could give us living people as against the Paris clothes and Grand Rapids furniture that are the real subject of most screen dramas, or the big-business propaganda that is the real purpose of the ordinary newsreel.[6]

Frontier Films itself, to begin with, was less explicit about its plans. *Variety* reported that, "while no definite production schedule is planned immediately," the group intended to produce "feature pix" which would have "dramatic and story appeal rather than bear too heavily on 'propaganda.'" All, however, would express a "'liberal' political and social viewpoint."[7]

From the start it was the intention of Frontier to work in collaboration with other organizations of the Left. The initial press statement affirmed that the company

> places itself at the disposal of progressive organizations and agencies in all fields—trade unions, educational institutions, social welfare groups, farm organizations, cooperative societies, peace organizations, etc. For such organizations the skilled technical staff of Frontier Films is available for the production of dramatic feature films, documentary and dramatic shorts, and newsreels.

And as early as March, even before the formal constitution of the company, it was reported that "definite progress has been achieved in securing tie-ups with key labor organizations." Subsequent developments fulfilled Frontier's aspirations in this direction, but only to a limited extent.[8]

The production staff of Frontier Films, at the outset, was comprised of Paul Strand, Leo Hurwitz, Ralph Steiner, Willard Van Dyke,[9] Lionel Berman, Ben Maddow ("David Wolff"), Sidney Meyers ("Robert Stebbins"), and Irving Lerner. Jay Leyda was not mentioned in publicity releases, probably because he was still working as assistant film curator at the Museum of Modern Art, but he too formed part of the team as a spare-time volunteer. The names of a number of other people were included in press listings of Frontier's staff at this time, but they seem to have become involved in a limited capacity, if at all. Elia Kazan, for example, worked on one film, *People of the Cumberland,* but was not part of the permanent organization. Joris Ivens, also listed, was at the time in Spain, filming *The Spanish Earth,* and he was never to play an active role in Frontier Films. Others cited whose involvement was marginal—at least on the day-to-day level—included the playwrights John Howard Lawson, Philip Stevenson, Albert Maltz, and George Sklar, together with Marion O'Rourke, Kyle Crichton, and Louis Kamp.[10]

It was announced that Frontier Films had a board of directors consisting of Paul Strand, president; Leo Hurwitz and Ralph Steiner, vice-presidents; Lionel Berman, executive director; John Howard Lawson, secretary; Bernard J. Reis, treasurer; and Kyle Crichton, William Osgood Field, Jr., Elia Kazan, Mary Lescaze, Anita Marburg, Philip Stevenson and Ben Maddow. This list too, however, needs to be accepted with caution. Kazan, for instance, claimed: "They put me on their board, but I attended few meetings." And though Lawson was described as secretary, he was living in Hollywood at the time and according to Hurwitz was "not very actively" involved in Frontier. "Most of the people on the board," he recently explained, "were people who were accomplished in their own field and felt excited by what we were doing."

> On occasion we would ask for their advice. And sometimes not. I don't remember that we asked for Jack [Lawson]'s advice. I knew Jack sort of well, I liked him. . . . Maybe we said, "Hey, where can we get money, we're stuck for dough, have you got somebody we can show some films to, get some money?" Maybe, I don't remember exactly. That's about the extent of the advice.[11]

At the very beginning, before production got under way, the only full-time employees were Berman and Hurwitz, and of them only Berman was paid. Hurwitz recalls that Berman

> came to Frontier Films as a kind of executive director in the promotional end, and holding the office together. He was interested in making films, and he suspended that for a long time to do the administrative work. Although his ideas were welcomed, and he was interacted with not simply as an administrative person—I did administration, too, and so did Paul— but he was the center of that.[12]

There was also an Advisory Board, comprising a roster of left-of-center cultural talent of the late thirties: Catherine Bauer, Albert Bein, Bruce Bliven, Vera Caspary, Carlos Chavez, Aaron Copland, Malcolm Cowley, Paul de Kruif, John Dos Passos, Waldo Frank, Lester Granger, Lillian Hellman, Josephine Herbst, Arthur Kober, Max Lerner, Archibald MacLeish, Lewis Milestone, Clifford Odets, Sidney Perelman, Edwin Rolfe, Muriel Rukeyser, George Seldes, Irwin Shaw, Claire Sifton, Paul Sifton, George Soule, Virginia Stevens, Genevieve Taggard, Arthur Zugsmith.[13]

Financing for the venture came, in the main, in the form of loans and donations from liberal and left-wing sympathizers. A staunch backer was Ethel Clyde, granddaughter of the founder of the Clyde steamship line, who had a long history of involvement with progressive causes—the previous year, for example, as part of a campaign for an inquiry into the plight of southern sharecroppers, she had financed a political dinner in Washington, which led to the formation of the La Follette Civil Liberties Committee of the U.S. Senate. In the first year of Frontier's existence (April 1, 1937 to March 31, 1938), Clyde contributed, in the form of unsecured loans, $14,931.00 of the company's total receipts of $26,470.23, the remainder of the income coming from donations ($8,522.05), rental of films ($2,846.53), and sale of scripts ($170.65). Clyde's total subscription to Frontier Films over the five-year period of its existence was close to $30,000.[14]

No other individual contributed on such a scale, although substantial financial support came from persons such as Daniel S. Gillmor (approximately $5,500), William Osgood Field, Jr. ($3,500), Charles H. Frazier ($2,500), Frazier McCann ($2,000), Elizabeth Marshall ($1,500), and Corliss Lamont ($1,500). Loans or donations of $1,000 each were made by Louise Bransten, Margaret Gage, George Marshall, J. McCann, Marion R. Stern, Paul Robeson, Paul Strand, and possibly others. It was reported that Jo Davidson presented a sculpture, and Reginald Marsh a painting to be sold for the benefit of the company. Institutional backing came from the Whitney Foundation ($1,000) and the Robert Marshall Foundation ($6,000).[15]

Although the collective saw itself as closely allied to the burgeoning labor movement, underwriting documentary film production was not, at the time, a priority concern for labor unions. At one stage the United Auto Workers was interested in sponsoring a film (see below), but the project did not get off the ground. As Hurwitz recalls, "I don't think any international unions contributed anything from the international treasury, but there were local unions that did." The amounts involved were small.[16]

Potential financial backing was rejected in cases where it could interfere with Frontier's conception of the film in production. "We only went after financing by those people who would, in general, like the idea of what we were doing," says Hurwitz.

> We never submitted anything to anybody, to say "Do you think this is OK?" . . . We wanted the American Civil Liberties Union to find money—they had very good contacts with money—for *Native Land*. And one of the things they said, Roger Baldwin and Elmer Rice, was that it dealt too much with labor. What about the little library in Arkansas that couldn't have James Joyce in it? That was a good story too, but this film was about labor, that was what the La Follette Committee was about, so we never got any money through the ACLU . . . And Roger Baldwin had a hypnotic capacity to influence people with money.[17]

Much of Frontier's "unearned" income came in the form of small contributions. According to Hurwitz, money was "collected in bits and little pieces, from everywhere." It was estimated at the time of the release of *Native Land,* Frontier's major production, in 1942, that between five and six thousand persons had become "partners in the venture." Of Frontier's total receipts in the period April 1, 1937 to March 31, 1942, which amounted to $117,191.94, straight donations—principally of smaller sums—accounted for $41,680.77, or 36%. (Unsecured loans, at $31,031.95, and trustee certificates, at $25,600.00, brought the total of financial backing from sympathizers to $98,312.72, or 84% of receipts.) Frontier Films was definitely a noncommercial operation.[18]

"The chief contributor to our financing," notes Hurwitz, was "our own unpaid work-time—and the minimally paid work of actors, composers, and others who wanted to work with us." Members of the collective were paid (usually) $35 per week "applied equally regardless of different responsibilities and efforts," but there were periods when funds were low and salaries were not paid at all. "It was very much a nonprofit organization," Paul Strand said. "We had always a tough struggle to pay very minimum salaries, salaries which in Hollywood would have been absurd—in fact, they were absurd in New York, too."[19]

After the first films had been completed, distribution revenues (received through Tom Brandon's Garrison Films) began to offset some of the costs. The company was optimistic about the possibilities of opening up new exhibition outlets unexplored by Hollywood; in a statement published in November 1937, it explained:

> We have ... appealed so far to the "subway circuit" of motion-picture houses, for the most part independently owned and exhibiting the finer foreign films throughout the country. We propose now to open up new channels which will embrace the greatest potential theatrical and extra-theatrical audience for living and purposeful films that exists in America. Our facilities are already at the disposal of responsible agents which cut across the bias of modern life—the trade unions, the cooperative societies, educational institutions, social-welfare groups, peace organizations, public forums, churches of whatever denomination, schools, and the like. We hope to utilize all these channels in the regular distribution of our films. In time we expect to include an even more widely scattered audience in a program of organized road shows which will tour the farming communities and mill towns of the nation.[20]

Frontier's confidence was well-placed, but nontheatrical distribution did not expand as fast or as profitably as was hoped. Revenues from the rental and sale of films proved insufficient to sustain the organization on an ongoing basis, let alone provide the capital for a feature-length production. Sums received from the distribution of Frontier's four political shorts—*Heart of Spain, China Strikes Back, People of the Cumberland,* and *Return to Life*—for the years ended March 31 were as follows:

1938:	$2,846.53
1939:	4,149.59
1940:	486.39

1941:   285.42
1942:   77.48

In a typical month of the later period, April 1940, there were seven bookings (16mm) and one sale (16mm) of *People of the Cumberland,* and one booking (35mm) of *China Strikes Back; Heart of Spain* and *Return to Life* were apparently by now out of distribution. Garrison took 35% of the gross receipts, and the net return on *People of the Cumberland* was split 50-50 with the Highlander Folk School: Frontier's share for the month was $29.65, not enough to pay the weekly salary of a single member of the collective.[21]

Frontier's two nonpolitical productions, having neither the benefits nor the drawbacks of topicality, repaid their costs but contributed little extra to the company's coffers. The income from *History and Romance of Transportation* (cost $3,701.62) was $3,259.50, and that from *White Flood* (cost $5,722.17) amounted to $6,292.96. Even mainstream documentary was far from being a lucrative business.[22]

Nontheatrical distribution was beginning to open up, but the stranglehold of the major companies on commercial distribution made it tough to make inroads into the movie theatres. Hurwitz recently summarized their experience:

> Distribution was something we would have to break through. In the theatres there was block-booking and therefore control by the major production companies. Independent films, especially in a new form and with social content, didn't have a chance in the national circuits. The 16mm market was far more limited than it is today. We counted on an expansion of the 16mm market to the new and vital trade unions, clubs, church groups, progressive organizations, and perhaps some colleges. We hoped also to build up an independent theatrical distribution based on independently owned neighborhood theatres, in areas where a demand for our films could be stimulated. We were aware that we were tackling a vastly difficult job; we were prepared to struggle. We began to open up these fields, but our larger objective was never achieved.[23]

In their first few months of existence as a production company, the Frontier group bristled with film plans and projects. At the start (and surprisingly enough, in view of the collective's commitment to documentary film), adaptations of plays were considered. In March 1937 it was reported that "already five writers of distinguished accomplishment have turned over the film production rights to well-known plays to Frontier Films." The writers were not specified, but a number of dramatists were associated with Frontier at the time of its formation as "staff," advisors, or members of the Board of Directors, including Albert Maltz, George Sklar, Albert Bein, John Dos Passos, Lillian Hellman, Archibald MacLeish, Clifford Odets, Irwin Shaw, Claire Sifton, Paul Sifton, Philip Stevenson, and John Howard Lawson.[24]

The only play actually mentioned at this time as being a possibility for cinematic adaptation was Odets's incomplete and unproduced *Silent Partner,* which the Group Theatre had rehearsed but abandoned as unsatisfactory early in 1937. Harold Clurman's account of the script suggests the type of material which Frontier was receptive to:

> It had a great theme. Through a strike situation in an industrial area, identified as the twin cities of Apolo and Rising Sun, Odets showed an old order of benevolent capitalism that had grown lame, a new order of monopolistic capitalism that was growing vicious (or fascist), and a still unorganized and spiritually unformed working class. What Odets was trying to say was that the old world of money and power was fast becoming decrepit and desperate, while the new world of the future, which belonged to the mass of people, was in America still raw, unclear, undisciplined, mentally and morally clumsy.

After a first report, "understood Clifford Odets has okayed filming of his *Silent Partner*," however, nothing further was heard of the project.[25]

It was mentioned in chapter 4 that another issue of the planned *World Today* series was being contemplated at a comparatively late date, and this is confirmed by a report in *Variety* (April 21, 1937) noting that the second edition was "being scripted at present." The seriousness with which Frontier planned to continue shooting films in this format is indicated by the fact that when the first issue was exhibited at the Roosevelt Theatre, New York, in the first week of May, the company responsible was described as "Labor Productions, sound-newsreel division of Frontier Films." The subject chosen for the second in the series was labor's struggle to organize against insidious and brutal opposition, as revealed in the findings of the La Follette Committee. The script for a two-reel film was completed by the last week in June, and production went ahead later in the year. Another *World Today* number, however, never materialized: the "labor spy" subject would emerge five years later, after many vicissitudes, as the feature *Native Land.*[26]

The *Variety* article stated that "no definite production schedule is planned immediately," but on the same day the *New York Times* carried a different story. "The recently formed Frontier Films is planning to begin production within two weeks of a three-reel film dramatizing the problem of child labor," it reported. "Its second venture of the season, set for early summer, will be a full feature based on incidents in the lives of the founders of Bucks County, Pa., presented as a general film discussion of farm problems."[27]

The group was overly optimistic, and the "full feature" on farm problems did not progress far: Hurwitz recalls that Philip Stevenson began writing a script, but the idea was soon abandoned. The child labor project, however, was to become the furthest advanced of all Frontier's unrealized films. The subject was in the news: it was featured in the March 1937 issue of *The March of Time,* and in May, when the New York State Assembly failed to ratify the Child Labor Amendment to the U.S. Constitution, the American Labor Party declared that it would make child labor "a cardinal issue in the coming Fall elections." A script was written (in collaboration with Vera Caspary) by George Sklar, the radical dramatist who had co-authored *Merry-Go-Round* (1931), *Peace on Earth* (1933), *Stevedore* (1934), and *Parade* (1935). Described as "a warm, human story showing the effects of child labor on the life of a thirteen-year-old boy and his family," the film, then still envisaged as a three-reeler, was to have gone into production "about July 15th." Shooting did not commence as planned, but the scenario grew to feature length and was completed by mid-August.[28]

Tentatively titled *Pay Day*, the film was to have been directed by Strand, Hurwitz, and William Watts (who had had extensive experience in the workers' theatre movement). Hurwitz remembers that he and Strand, possibly with the assistance of Ben Maddow, wrote at least a partial shooting script based on the completed scenario by Sklar and Caspary, and efforts to obtain funding were set in motion. A promotional screening (of *The Wave* and *Heart of Spain*) was arranged for December 7, and in her invitational letters Ethel Clyde mentioned that "we need $20,000 for the child labor film," adding that "the National Child Labor Committee, which is supporting the production and distribution of this film, has given the script its unqualified endorsement." The requisite backing, however, was not forthcoming, and the $2,114.97 which Frontier had invested in the project had to be written off. A sidelight on the scheme is given by George Jacobson, who was hired as production manager for Frontier Films in 1937 and remained with the company for several years. Initially he collaborated with another employee, John Cornell. Jacobson recalls:

> The script called for children working at a laundry. And Cornell and I started a search for children working at a laundry in the New York area. We found nothing. It didn't exist. So that idea then was cancelled.... [29]

Another aborted project was inspired by the massive sit-down strikes in the auto industry of that year, resulting in the mushrooming growth of the United Automobile Workers of America. (Frontier may also have been influenced by John Howard Lawson's play *Marching Song*, devoted to this theme, which was presented by the Theatre Union in New York in February.) "The UAWA has expressed interest in a film which we outlined for them, and offered to appropriate a good part of the cost of the film," Lionel Berman wrote in June. "At their suggestion we are now contacting the SWOC [Steel Workers Organizing Committee] to arrange for the balance of the money necessary to start production." Apparently the steel workers were not interested, for little more was heard of the plan to portray "the unionization of John Doe, automobile worker." Several years later Frontier filmmakers were in fact able to contribute to a film on this subject, when they took over the editing of the UAW strike documentary *United Action*, discussed below.[30]

A final projected venture which did not come to fruition was of a different character. Ralph Steiner relates that he had the "brilliant idea" of asking Dashiell Hammett ("who was very left") to write a labor mystery film for Frontier. "Then we'll make some money," Steiner recalls arguing, "we'll have some fun doing it, and we can get all the left-wing actors, get a great left-wing director . . . and then we can keep on, keep making films—we get $30 a week and then when they're over there's nothing for in-between, we're getting nowhere."

> So they thought that was a good idea, so I went and talked to Hammett, and he said, "Gee, that's a great idea, I'd love to do that for you!" So we waited three weeks, four weeks, called up, and he said, "Well, I've just now found a brilliant idea, I've got a great idea, something simple that you can do." So weeks go by, weeks go by, call him up again, "Well, I'm working on it, I'm working on it." Finally after about three months I went to see Lillian Hellman, the playwright with whom he was living, and I started to explain, and she said, "I know, forget it."[31]

There were several projects which did, however, get under way in 1937. The first was *Heart of Spain,* based on footage of the Civil War which had been shot by former *New Theatre* editor Herbert Kline in the early months of the year. Kline returned to New York in June, and his material was edited at Frontier by Strand and Hurwitz, with Maddow and Kline collaborating on the commentary. *Heart of Spain* was released as a Frontier Films production in September.

About the same time, Frontier obtained film which had been taken by dancer/musician Harry Dunham in Shensi Province of northwest China, stronghold of the former Red Army (which was now united with Chiang Kai-shek in resisting Japanese aggression). The task of editing this footage, together with material from commercial newsreels, was assigned to Jay Leyda, Irving Lerner, Ben Maddow, and Sidney Meyers. The work was carried out during the summer, and the completed documentary *China Strikes Back* reached the theatres in October.

Meanwhile Ralph Steiner and Elia Kazan were shooting footage on Frontier's first original production, *People of the Cumberland.* The undertaking was made possible by a donation from Ethel Clyde as a contribution to the work of the Highlander Folk School in Tennessee, the main subject of the film. Meyers, Leyda, and William Watts also became involved, and a commentary was written by novelist Erskine Caldwell. Finally released in May 1938, *People of the Cumberland* was Frontier's first fulfillment of its aim to document "the rich and robust traditions of the American people."

Production also began, in the fall of 1937, on what was to become Frontier's culminating achievement, the feature-length *Native Land.* Although the *World Today* concept seems finally to have been dropped, the civil liberties film was still thought of as a short subject when shooting commenced. The script was written by Maddow, and the crew consisted of Michael Gordon, director, Willard Van Dyke, cameraman, and George Jacobson, production manager. Sequences which the unit filmed included a reenactment of the Republic Steel massacre, and an incident involving the murder of a militant farmer by hired thugs. It was the group's handling of the latter which precipitated a crisis in the Frontier organization.[32]

As Willard Van Dyke recalls:

> We started working on the sequence that subsequently became the farmer and his wife on the farm, and he is visited by some vigilantes and she runs through the barnyard and the chickens fly up. This was to be shot out near Newburgh, New York, and we were using Leo's brother-in-law, or cousin, or something, he was the farmer, and the actress was Mary George. By now it was late October and the days were short. We had to get up in the dark and drive out to Newburgh, and sometimes it was so cold we couldn't get the camera to run hardly, and we were up against every kind of difficulty. We cut together what we had in a sequence and showed it to Leo and Paul and Ralph—well, a general meeting—and Leo was very unhappy with what he saw, and called the thing to a halt, and said we'll not continue with this, we need to do some work on the script, and so forth and so forth.

Michael Gordon freely admits the merits of the criticisms which were made:

> When we were looking at the footage, those people who were into film said, "Well, we're not covered. We need many more close-ups," and so forth and so on. And at first I couldn't see why—everything was kind of in beautiful long shot, with the man following the plow over the brow of the hill, with the beautiful sky beyond, and all that sort of thing. . . . I was making, I thought, very pictorial setups, but then I didn't have the remotest idea of the necessity of close-up, of any concept of montage at that point. I don't think [Eisenstein's] *The Film Sense* had yet been published in this country, and I had no idea of what was adequate coverage, and so I really did a very bad job. There's no question about it.[33]

The recollection of the affair by Van Dyke and Gordon is substantially confirmed by Hurwitz, who states:

> [Gordon's] relationship to the thing was kind of tentative: he wasn't a member of Frontier Films, but he did have experience in the theatre, and he was working with this thing with only part of him. So what he did was quite good, but it really wasn't good enough. And what Willard did in the photography was OK, but it wasn't good enough. And what Ben had done in the way of a script was OK, but it really wasn't there, so we had to reorganize the whole project.[34]

Michael Gordon's departure was amicable—"I think by mutual consent I kind of withdrew from it," he says, "because I didn't know what the hell I was doing, in all honesty." But the resignation from Frontier Films of Willard Van Dyke, which was accompanied by that of Ralph Steiner and was triggered by the cancellation of shooting on the civil liberties project, was acrimonious (and attended by personal animosities which have not abated to this day).[35]

For Van Dyke, the halting of the project was "a very trying experience" and "the culmination of a number of confrontations with Hurwitz." Van Dyke asserts that he and Steiner

> just felt that it was getting too complicated for our lives. There wasn't the kind of free participation, of working together, any more. There was a *producer* there, and we didn't respect that particular producer, I didn't. That was Hurwitz.

Steiner maintains that he was "very upset" over some experiences on *People of the Cumberland,* including the editing of the film, and when he read the *Native Land* script he said, "I don't want to have anything to do with this"—he felt the treatment was overly pessimistic—and determined to leave.[36]

Hurwitz's view is that "there was a good deal of redbaiting of Frontier Films" which Van Dyke and Steiner were very nervous about.

> Their own political commitment to the kind of films we wanted to do did not develop into a strong passion as it developed in some of the rest of us, or political understanding either. So there was a good deal of nervousness.... Steiner had the nervousness right on the skin, and Willard Van Dyke, being a cooler cat, did not exhibit it quite as directly.... It may well be that Willard didn't feel he had enough voice in the development of Frontier Films, and I could go back and indicate that, or didn't have enough real commitment to his feelings.... There was considerable opportunism, that he came into this—it was the only place in America where you could make documentary films and learn about them while you were making them, and when he had thought he had learned a little bit he went off.

Steiner, says Hurwitz,

> was a man ten years older than I, very unstable in his relationships with the source of his art. He was a very good photographer, but most of his photography was spent doing commercial photographs of fruit and various things. He wanted to do films, and he had real talent, but he felt that he was nervous in his world, he had a very hard time integrating himself and finding out who he was, and he hoped to, through this political contact with the Left, and through me, and later through Paul Strand. But on the other hand he could not take the struggle that's involved in trying to hold your own, and hold your own as a growing artist, and still not accept the junk of the world, and the junk ideas of the world, and incur the dangers of limited income. So at a certain point he couldn't take any more, and I understand him very well.[37]

Both Van Dyke and Steiner affirm that one of their reasons for quitting was supposed Communist influence over the organization. Van Dyke argues:

> Nykino had no connection with the Communist party, although I assume that a couple of the people in it were probably party members—I don't know that for a fact. But with the formation of Frontier Films it appeared to me at least that it was under the direction and

influence of people who were avowedly fellow-travelers or Communist party members.

I got nervous when Frontier Films was founded, and there was a board of directors headed by John Howard Lawson, and at that point I began to feel, well now where? Up to now it's been kind of loose, and nobody got paid, and we could do our own thing and we could come and go as we wished, but when you had a board of directors headed by one of the really great ideological Communists in this country, this made me very nervous.

Similarly, Steiner claims that "everything had to be approved by the party, everthing had to finally conform."[38]

Other Frontier workers have different opinions on this point. Jay Leyda says that he never saw Lawson at any meeting or discussion, and doesn't remember submitting film at any stage for approval. The Communist party may have imagined it had an influence, he continues, but there was no real supervision, because the motion picture was too flexible a medium. Elia Kazan, who in 1952 accused the party of trying to "capture the Group Theatre and make it a Communist mouthpiece," recently denied that there was any comparable Communist party influence on Frontier Films, saying, "We all felt a certain way about America at that time, and we wanted to show it."[39]

"As far as the Communist party trying to take over anything," Michael Gordon contends, "it seems to me that is a grotesque exaggeration."

There was a protestant spirit abroad, as a consequence of the objective realities in which we lived, and that provided a tremendous energy source to a lot of manifestations in literature, in cinema, and in theatre.... All of it would certainly have to be categorized as left of center.... I think that whatever level of, shall we say, affiliation with a political party is concerned, all of the people that I knew were fundamentally theatre people, of disparate particular persuasions.... They were not politicians or political activists who said, "Now where shall we devote our energy? Shall it be in transport or the theatre?"... No, it didn't work that way. These were people who were essentially artists without, let us say, the qualitative implications of that description. We were the innocents, we were theatre people, who were actors, who were directors, whatever we were, film people, that was the primary interest.[40]

Leo Hurwitz answers the charge of Communist domination as follows:

There were people on the Left who followed mechanically various ideas, and there were people on the Left who didn't. If you look at Frontier Films you will see that there is no dictatorship from the outside. We had very little contact with party people. When we did—in one instance I sought advice of people who had experience in industrial struggles—I got very good advice. But the things were built by ourselves out of our experience and filtrations, which isn't to say that we simply rejected somebody because he was a Communist party member, or rejected somebody because he wasn't. And I think that's the heart of it myself.[41]

There is little objective evidence either to support or to refute accusations that Frontier Films was under Communist party sway. In 1938, in his report to the National Convention of the Communist party on the work of the Cultural

Commission, V.J. Jerome made reference to Frontier Films along with such organizations as the American Artists Union, the League of American Writers, and the New Theatre League, but the notes of his address do not contain a specific claim to party control over the group. Frontier was cited for its alleged Communist character by Professor John Dewey's Committee for Cultural Freedom in April 1940, by Congressman Dies in September 1942, and by the House of Representatives' Special Committee on Un-American Activities in March 1944, but the charges were inconclusive.[42]

When Steiner and Van Dyke left Frontier they combined to form American Documentary Films and undertook, as their first production, a film for the American Institute of Planners for which Frontier had been negotiating. This undoubtedly contributed to the bitterness attendant on the split, and exactly what happened is difficult at this stage to determine. Hurwitz maintains that Steiner and Van Dyke "pulled that film away to do it on their own," while Steiner's account is a little more complex. According to Steiner, he was approached, while still at Frontier, by Arthur Mayer, whose brother-in-law Clarence Stein wanted a film made on city planning for the New York World's Fair.

> So Clarence Stein through Arthur Mayer called me up, and I went to see him, and I showed him films I'd made, and he said, "All right, I want you to make the film." And I said, "Well I'm still part of Frontier Films, and I'm getting out." So I went back and resigned, and called up Clarence Stein and said, "I've resigned, and since I negotiated with you as a member of Frontier Films, I'm resigning." And by that time I'd asked Willard to work on it with me, and then Clarence Stein called up and said, "Whether you work on it or not, Frontier Films is not going to work on it." And I said, "Well in that case, if you'll put that on paper, we will work for you."[43]

On another occasion, Steiner affirmed:

> I got out of Frontier and handed the making of *The City* to Frontier. But the sponsors would not have it that way—they feared left-wing bias. Willard and I took *The City* only when we were assured that Frontier could not have it, and that it would go to others if we didn't want it.[44]

Whatever the circumstances surrounding its inception, *The City* proved indicative of the trend American documentary would take once cut loose from its left-wing moorings and reliant upon commercial or institutional sponsorship (*The City* was financed by a $50,000 grant from the Carnegie Corporation). Something of the aesthetic of montage remains in the film's juxtaposition of industrial slums and the congested metropolis with the utopian greenbelt community, but there is no class analysis, no hint of struggle, no suggestion of the *political* means by which social change might be effected. Significantly, Steiner later differentiated his own political-aesthetic position from that of

Frontier by reference to the film. "Hurwitz and Strand wanted to make what I thought were films far too gloomy-militant for my taste," he noted. "You can see this from the use of humor in *The City,* which did much to keep the film from turning out dark gray and black."[45]

Following the departure of Steiner and Van Dyke at the beginning of 1938, the *Native Land* project was restructured (to be directed, now, by Strand and Hurwitz), and, expanding to feature length, it gradually came to absorb nearly all the time and energies of the collective. (The title *Native Land* was decided upon only at a late date; for the filmmakers, it was simply *"Production #5,"* and at various times the project was referred to as *Labor Spy, Edge of the World, Listen America,* and *Civil Liberties.*) Nevertheless, the group did pursue certain other activities while fundraising and filming on the major production continued.

After the completion of *Heart of Spain,* Frontier Films was sponsored by the Medical Bureau and the North American Committee to Aid Spanish Democracy to produce a second film detailing emergency medical care in Republican Spain. Herbert Kline was entrusted with the assignment, on the understanding that he collaborate with former Nykino member Henri Cartier-Bresson, now in France. The arrangement worked out successfully, and shooting took place towards the end of 1937 (a French cameraman, Jacques Lemare, was hired for the job). The 45-minute documentary was edited in Paris, and after the preparation of an English-language commentary by Ben Maddow, it was released as *Return to Life* by Frontier in August 1938.

Frontier's next release was a commercial assignment. Produced for the Rocket Port Exhibit at the Chrysler Building at the World's Fair, *History and Romance of Transportation* (1939) was written and edited by Lionel Berman and Sidney Meyers. It was basically a compilation film drawn from library material. Describing it in an article on "Films at the Fair," Richard Griffith wrote:

> ... the film tells the story of transport from earliest times to the present. Cunningly cut on lines of accelerating movement, it builds tension which is released by the actual launching of a miniature rocket ship, the climax of the exhibit proper. In representing the development of transport as a fulfillment of human need, this short document gives the citizen an understanding of his vital stake in this commonly accepted convenience of daily life.[46]

United Action (1940) was not a Frontier production, but editing and sound were handled on behalf of the collective by Ben Maddow and Lionel Berman. The documentary, directed by Michael Martini and forty minutes in length, was in fact produced by the film department of the United Auto Workers (then CIO), and dealt with the long and finally victorious strike waged by tool and die locals of the union against General Motors in 1939. A large part of the film's footage was of picket lines (often set up in defiance of police) and mass demonstrations in a variety of Michigan locales; intercut were sequences devoted to the men at work prior to the strike, strategy committee meetings, the collection of food from sympathetic union farmers, "flying squads" of motorized pickets in action, a strike kitchen run by the women's auxiliary, the CIO negotiating committee preparing to meet with GM executives, and victory celebrations in the streets. One quasi-dramatized sequence depicted members of the women's auxiliary explaining the issues of the strike to a doubting wife; the parts were played by "the auto workers, their families and friends," but the voice-over dialogue was spoken by Earl Robinson and Virginia Stevens (an actress who appears in *Native Land* and who was a member of Frontier's Advisory Board). Robinson, with his People's Chorus, also supplied a musical background of union songs such as *We are the CIO, Joe Hill,* and *Solidarity Forever. United Action* forcefully conveyed the message that solidarity— between strikers and non-strikers, wage-earners and farmers, men and women, blacks and whites, skilled and unskilled workers—could bring victory against a powerful monopolistic corporation.[47]

White Flood was a fifteen-minute educational documentary released by Frontier in 1940. Like *History and Romance of Transportation,* it was nonpolitical in character, and is therefore not treated at length in this dissertation. Utilizing striking footage of glaciers, icebergs, and snowstorms shot in the Alaskan fiords by the geologist William Osgood Field, Jr., a board member of Frontier Films, together with a variety of stock shots, the film poetically evoked the last great ice age, explained how glaciers are formed, and speculated on the precarious existence of life on the crust of the earth. Here, in the concluding words of the commentary (by Ben Maddow), there was a hint of the Marxist stress on the human mission to shape and transform the environment:

> Living on the surface of the earth, man's life hangs in this colossal balance of air, sun, ice, and water. This is his world. Therefore he matches his brain against the changing mountains, slowly learning to control the blind movement of nature and the earth.

But since only untamed nature appears in the film, the assertion is but a tiny gesture towards the human potential. *White Flood* was scripted and edited by Berman, Maddow, and Meyers, and was particularly noteworthy for its experimental music score by Hanns Eisler.

While these films were made and production on *Native Land* continued, Frontier attempted to launch several other projects. Financial records reveal that in May 1938 Berman, Maddow, and Meyers were at work on *"Production #7,"* a "Youth Film," but of the nature of this there is no indication. The collective also hoped to obtain backing for a film about racism as it affected blacks. A circular letter sent out in April 1939 read:

Frontier Films, Inc., a nonprofit cooperative producing organization, is vitally interested in dramatizing the vast cultural contribution of Negroes to American life.

The film contemplated will be built against the background of the rich contribution of the Negro people to American history and culture.

Mindful of the gross distortions of the Negro as depicted in Hollywood productions, we are calling a conference of prominent citizens, Negro and white, to discuss the content and form of this film.[48]

Like the Film and Photo League, Frontier Films also had interests beyond motion-picture production, but shortages of time, money, and manpower prevented them from being vigorously pursued. Individual members of the collective continued to function as film and photography critics—Meyers, Lerner, Leyda, Maddow, Strand, and Hurwitz all having articles published during this period—although the group had no collective voice comparable to the league's *Filmfront* or columns in *New Theatre* magazine. It is probable that a paragraph detailing the group's nonproduction interests in a promotional leaflet of November 1938 spoke more of Frontier's aspirations than its achievements:

Other activities of Frontier Films include lectures and classes on the motion picture as an art medium and as a mirror of the life of our times; and research into the techniques and history of the film medium. We are planning at the earliest opportunity to establish a studio for the training of young people in the various crafts of the motion picture—a type of education not available elsewhere in this country in any systematic form. Of necessity, these activities have taken a secondary position to the pressing problems of production.[49]

By the time this was written, there had been some further changes in the Frontier personnel. Irving Lerner, who had worked mostly on a volunteer basis, left the group in mid-1938, pursuing an independent career in documentary film. In November of that year Lionel Berman made the transition he had long desired from administration to production, and was replaced as executive director by Arnold Perl, a law school graduate who had had a varied career as literary critic, agent, freelance writer, and managing editor, in addition to taking over Ben Maddow's orderly job at Bellevue Hospital. As work on *Native Land* recommenced, William Watts was pressed into service as associate director (handling the actors); he left when shooting was about half completed, to be replaced by another graduate of the workers' theatre movement, Alfred Saxe, who had co-directed the Theatre of Action's *The Young Go First* in 1935 with Elia Kazan. Jay Leyda was less involved with Frontier as the decade wore on.

On Frontier's board of directors, by the first half of 1939, Ralph Steiner had of course been dropped, while Mary Lescaze, Anita Marburg, and Philip Stevenson had been replaced by Ethel Clyde, A.J. Isserman (the company's attorney), and Sidney Meyers. Additional names on the roster of supporters designated as the Advisory Board indicated Frontier's broadening appeal: Congressmen John T. Bernard, John M. Coffee, J.J. O'Connell, and Henry C. Teigan; Bishop Francis J. McConnell, of the North American Committee to Aid Spanish Democracy; journalists William Allen White and Oswald Garrison Villard; Roger Baldwin of the American Civil Liberties Union; actor Melvyn Douglas; sociologist Robert Lynd; Harold Clurman of the Group Theatre; screenwriters Dudley Nichols and Donald Ogden Stewart; left-wing New Dealer Gardner Jackson; Morris Watson of the Newspaper Guild; Rockwell Kent of the artists' union; humorist Dorothy Parker; and others.[50]

Filmmakers active in or formerly associated with Frontier played a leading role in the formation of the Association of Documentary Film Producers in June 1939. Announced as "the first organization of its kind in this country and one of the first in the world," it was designed to sustain and promote "independent, creative films," and to serve as a means of communication and cooperation between documentary producers. For its first year, under the presidency of Joris Ivens, Paul Strand and Willard Van Dyke were elected first and second vice-presidents respectively, while William Osgood Field became treasurer and Lionel Berman was selected as chairman of the membership committee, in which Jay Leyda also served. Leo Hurwitz, Sidney Meyers, Ben Maddow, Herbert Kline, Irving Lerner, and Ralph Steiner became Regular Members of the Association.[51]

Production on *Native Land* advanced fitfully over a period of years. Hurwitz notes:

> We began with $7,000—and a feature-length script. Production proceeded until we ran out of money, at which point we showed rushes and raised some more money, resumed production, stopped again—many times. This is why the film took three years to make, from 1938 to 1941.

His account is confirmed by Strand, who recalls:

> At one point we had to stop for almost a year, about seven or eight months, and devote ourselves entirely to raising funds to continue. At another time we stopped for about four months and there was no production during that time either.[52]

Intensive efforts (described in greater detail in chapter 9) were made to gain sponsorship for the *Native Land* project and for the work of Frontier Films in general. Eleanor Roosevelt declined an invitation to lend her support officially to the group, but she was sympathetic, and in May 1938 attended a specially arranged screening of *Heart of Spain, China Strikes Back,* and *People of the Cumberland* at the White House. Her published reaction was not as helpful to their cause as the Frontier filmmakers would have liked, though they were encouraged; Lionel Berman wrote to Hurwitz:

> You heard about the White House showing before you left town. It was really thrilling hearing the *Heart of Spain* and *China Strikes Back* commentaries in the White House. Mrs. Roosevelt, as the enclosed clipping indicates, was really deeply moved. She had to be cagey in her column and, of course, that makes her statement less useful to us. But Pat Jackson is going to try to get her to write something specifically about Frontier Films in a future column.

Achieving the open endorsement of the First Lady, however, seems to have been a People's Front coup which the Frontier Films radicals just failed to pull off.[53]

As a method of attracting financial contributions Frontier hit on the scheme of exhibiting rushes of completed scenes to prospective "angels," usually at the Preview Theatre at 1600 Broadway, New York City. The screenings would sometimes have the added bonus of celebrity sponsors, such as Lillian Hellman, Thomas Mann, Lewis Milestone, Dudley Nichols, Dorothy Parker, and Franchot Tone (January 18, 1939), Tom Mooney (June 20, 1939), and Paul Robeson (June 30, 1939). In Strand's view the idea was a good one:

> In the raising of funds we also had to innovate and we did something that I've never heard of before or since. At a screening for fundraising we showed film as it came out of the camera, developed of course, but with the slate still on it, uncut; which was so exciting visually that it was perfectly satisfactory from the point of view of creating enthusiasm and interest on the part of the prospective fund-givers or lenders. Because at the end of the film we had a group of people who loaned money to complete the production.

One such showing (December 19, 1938) resulted in donations and pledges totalling $10,000. Some 15,000 people saw *Native Land* in various stages prior to completion.[54]

Money was a pressing necessity because of the escalating costs of the group's productions. *The World Today,* a two-reeler shot in 1936 with an unpaid crew, had required a mere $800, while *Heart of Spain*'s three reels reportedly "reached the projector's booth at a cost of only $5,000." *China Strikes Back* and *People of the Cumberland* were similarly comparatively cheap, costing approximately $5,600 and $2,600 respectively. The feature-length *Native Land,* however, with its semi-fictional format, proved to be considerably more expensive, its direct cost (excluding promotion, etc.) eventually amounting to $67,556.73. Frontier began issuing trustee certificates in large denominations during 1939-40 in an attempt to keep pace with the mounting bills.[55]

Native Land was eventually completed to answer print stage by December 1941, and was released in New York in May 1942. The war-time situation destroyed hopes the company had entertained for the film to be "a spearhead for the making and distribution of independent, progressive films." The dramatized documentary feature was Frontier's most ambitious weapon in its drive to break Hollywood's block-booking monopoly. Hurwitz explains the scheme:

> The plan was to go into workers' committees where there was a strong union membership and tell a theatre owner: "A lot of people in your area would be interested in seeing *Native Land*. If you want to be sure, ask them, talk to the trade-union people, see if they won't put out leaflets advertising the film. They'll bring the audience to your theatre and you'll make money out of it." By appealing to the neighborhood theatres in this way, we hoped to outflank the commercial restrictions of the big companies.
>
> We aimed at building up a base like this all over the country, getting the support of progressive trade unions and other organizations. When the film was shown to union audiences before it was completed, the response was very strong, and we felt sanguine about our plans.

But *Native Land*'s subject matter, interpreted as being disruptive to national unity, proved its undoing. *"Native Land,"* says Hurwitz, "was finished as far as wide distribution was concerned."

> In *Native Land* we had dramatized the conflict between the American ruling class and the unions in the thirties. Now, however, there was a need for unity within the country for the war against fascism. U.S. business had to be willing to join with the Soviet Union, to end its isolationism and drop its fierce enmity towards the Soviets. So a policy of national unity came into being. This was right and necessary but, to my mind, it was carried out wrongly.[56]

The Communist party, Hurwitz argues, could have been important "in influencing trade unionists and therefore in getting the film distributed," but, despite liking the film, party leadership offered no assistance because of the wartime policy of working-class cooperation with business and the government.[57]

Even if *Native Land* had reached wide audiences, however, the collective which brought it into existence would not have been able to benefit. Because of the war, Frontier Films had been disbanded in 1941, and its former members were mostly, by the time of *Native Land*'s release, actively engaged in various phases of the war effort. The Depression decade was over, and it would be many years before committed, left-wing filmmaking collectives like Frontier Films would be seen again in America.[58]

6

Heart of Spain and *Return to Life*

O Cities across the ocean, Hankow, Yenan, with dark steel
guard yourselves! And you, capital of the world,
Madrid, Madrid! —since your great trenches hold
death back from love; and if they hold, keep safe
our trees, our harbors, and our happiness.

> —from *The Defenses* (1938)
> by David Wolff (Ben Maddow)[1]

Frontier Films' two documentaries on the Spanish civil war, *Heart of Spain* and *Return to Life*, were propaganda weapons in a campaign to secure broad popular support for the Loyalist cause. As such they were shaped, more than most documentaries (including other Frontier productions), by immediate political exigencies. If there were divisions on the Loyalist side which the films—like Joris Ivens's contemporaneous *Spanish Earth*—failed to point out, if the political issues at stake were oversimplified, even distorted, it was because of the overriding need for unity in the face of the enemy. While analysis conducted with hindsight may detect shortcomings in the films as historical documents, it should not lose track of the fact that they were shot in the heat of battle and distributed while the bitter struggle against fascism continued. In the most limited sense, *Heart of Spain* (1937) and *Return to Life* (1938) were designed for use in fundraising drives for the North American volunteer medical services in Spain; and in this, at least, they fulfilled their purpose.

Principally responsible for the material which was assembled into *Heart of Spain* was the former editor of *New Theatre* magazine, Herbert Kline.[2] Finding himself in a policy conflict with members of his editorial board, Kline resigned his position in December 1936 and headed for Spain, with the intention of enlisting in the Republican cause. After a stopover in Paris, Kline reached Madrid in the third week of January, 1937, and soon after he became a broadcaster with the powerful government shortwave radio station, EAQ.[3] (His reports were monitored in the United States and provided material for pro-Loyalist journals covering the Spanish civil war.)

Some three weeks after commencing this work, Kline says, he was approached by the Hungarian still photographer Geza Karpathi, whom he had met in Paris. (Karpathi's real name was Kaiser; he was later to become the Hollywood actor Charles Korvin.) Karpathi had been hired—at a nominal salary—by the Canadian doctor Norman Bethune to act as cameraman on a documentary about the work of the Hispano-Canadian Blood Transfusion Institute, which Bethune had founded, and which was providing medical services for wounded Republican soldiers and civilians. At Karpathi's urging, Bethune asked Kline to write a script for the film, which would explain the Institute's newly developed method of preserving blood by the addition of sodium citrate and refrigeration.[4]

Kline agreed to do so. Although he had had no previous practical experience with film, he had written a play, and had contact with Hollywood and documentary filmmakers through his work on *New Theatre*. Kline recalls:

> So I said, "All right, I'm a screenwriter," and I wrote a script outline, and they showed it to Joris Ivens. And Ivens said it was so good that I should direct it. And I said, "What the hell do I know about directing?" He said, "Herbert, if you know enough to write with a pen cinematically, you can write with a camera." So, with a lot of help from Geza Karpathi, I became a film director.[5]

Kline's inexperience in motion pictures was equalled by that of Karpathi, who had never worked as a cinematographer, and did not even know how to load the camera. As Kline recollects, "We had to pretend that the Eyemo had broken down so we could take it to a film repair factory and count the sprocket holes (in setting the film loops) while the mechanic was testing it."[6]

Kline and Karpathi joined Bethune's medical unit and stayed with it for several months, observing and filming. "We lived right with the unit," Kline told an interviewer at the time. "Lots of times we helped unload the ambulances. Sometimes we were so concerned with the transfusions that we forgot all about pictures." Thus he apologized for the technical quality of a scene showing transfusion being given to a badly wounded soldier:

> "You know," he said, "you feel sort of humble about fussing around with lights and stuff when a fellow may be dying. That fellow was so close to death that it wasn't easy to think of just movies. I suppose we didn't get some angles that we should have gotten."[7]

At times the filmmakers were pressured to include deliberately shocking material. Kline wrote of one such incident at a hospital where they were shooting:

> [The doctor] stopped at the bedside of a woman of about forty. "Here," he said, "you must see what the Fascists have done to this woman, you must take a picture of her to show people

in America what these barbarians have done to us. Look," he said, throwing back the blanket.

The woman lay there stolidly. I saw a leg even more terribly tangled than the arm of the injured young woman. It would serve no purpose to describe how sickening the wound looked.[8]

The film's shooting took place over a three-month period in Madrid, on the Jarama front, and on other fronts in the Madrid region, sometimes with Spanish troops, and at other times with the International Brigades. Karpathi was wounded slightly while photographing a bombardment in the capital. In late spring, Kline and Karpathi left Spain for Paris—where, Kline says, directors G.W. Pabst and Max Ophuls saw the completed footage and offered to work with him on editing it.

However, Dr. Bethune was returning to the United States to raise money,

and I had reasons to return to the States if I could, before returning to the war in Spain as I intended to do. Frontier Films heard of the film only in my letters to Leo Hurwitz, and thus they did not have anything to do with the early concept or the shooting of the film. But they were friends of mine, and I was connected with them in sort of an honorary way because of my editorship of *New Theatre*. So when I showed it to them, I told them about the interest of the people in France, but I preferred to do it with old friends.[9]

The Frontier staff welcomed the footage Kline and Karpathi brought back, but found it inadequate, on its own, to convey a sufficiently powerful statement on the war. "It was interesting material," Paul Strand later said, "but was material that could not possibly have made a film unless it had been added to and edited with a very definite film structure." And Ben Maddow recently commented:

One of the troubles with *Heart of Spain* is that a lot of the material is very bad, poorly shot, and so you had to cover the bad joints with flashes of little lightning.... But you know the material was extremely important to all of us politically. I think we were far more interested in Spain than we were in our own country.[10]

In the hands of Strand and Leo Hurwitz, who edited the film in the summer of 1937, the documentation of the Blood Transfusion Institute and the Kline-Karpathi battle footage became the kernel of a broadly-based study of the struggle against fascism. The original footage was augmented with considerable supplementary material derived from other sources: commercial newsreels, film shot by Soviet cameraman Roman Karmen, outtakes contributed by Joris Ivens from his *Spanish Earth*—which he happened to be editing in an adjoining cutting room at the time.

Kline, pleased with the work of Strand and Hurwitz—he recently called it a "marvelous job"—collaborated with Maddow in the composition of the commentary, which was spoken by John O'Shaughnessy. Alex North, with help from Jay Leyda, arranged a musical score. Thirty minutes in length, *Heart of Spain* opened in New York on September 10, 1937, on a bill with Renoir's *Lower Depths (Les Bas-Fonds)*.[11]

The film achieved considerable commercial success for an independent leftist documentary, playing for seven weeks at the 55th Street Playhouse, and receiving theatrical bookings in many cities around the country. Its most widespread distribution, however, was in conjunction with the fundraising campaign conducted by the Medical Bureau and the North American Committee to Aid Spanish Democracy, the bodies which, with the Canadian Committee to Aid Spain, were the sponsors of Bethune's Institute.[12] At the time of the film's release, it was previewed in Hollywood as a preliminary to the fund drive, and on September 10, Frontier Films received the following telegram:

HEART OF SPAIN WAS RECEIVED ENTHUSIASTICALLY IN HOLLYWOOD BEFORE SELECT GROUP OF 200 LAST NIGHT STOP UNANIMOUSLY AC- CLAIMED THE MOST COMPELLING DOCUMENT EVER SHOWN OF WAR- TORN SPAIN AND THE SPLENDID WORK DONE BY AMERICAN MEDICAL UNIT THERE STOP WE ARE PROUD TO SHOW IT ON THE ROAD IN CON- JUNCTION WITH THE TRANSCONTINENTAL TOUR OF OUR TWO AMBU- LANCES DEDICATED TO LOYALIST SPAIN LEAVING HOLLYWOOD ON SEPTEMBER 10TH. SIGNED: HERBERT BIBERMAN, SIDNEY BUCHMAN, HUM- PHREY COBB, FLORENCE ELDRIDGE, LEWIS MILESTONE, DUDLEY NICHOLS, SAMSON RAPHAELSON, DONALD OGDEN STEWART, FRANCHOT TONE, EXECUTIVE BOARD, MOTION PICTURE ARTS COMMITTEE.[13]

"The most unusual road show ever seen in these United States," as it was dubbed, featured two ambulances (fully equipped for field service, and with the name of the sponsors painted on the panel body), two Hollywood writers (Martin North and Albert Kahn), two projectionists and cameramen, a nurse, and the film *Heart of Spain*. The caravan toured cross-country to New York, "stopping enroute for impromptu talks with crowds that quickly gather and for scheduled mass meetings at which the stirring film *Heart of Spain* is shown." Funds were collected for continued medical aid to the republic.[14]

In places, the tour encountered opposition, chiefly from the Catholic Church. In Albany, New York, for example, the visit of the "Hollywood stars- outfitted" ambulance was attacked by the Catholic weekly *Evangelist* as "a stunt to attract an audience to the Red propaganda film *Heart of Spain*." An editorial headlined "A Trojan Horse Comes to this Town: Spanish Reds Foist Films on 'Sucker' Audiences" denounced both the stopover of the ambulance and the film, and insinuated that scenes had been faked by "Spanish Reds, dressed in clerical garb" (there seem to be no shots in the film to which this charge could be meaningfully applied). The editorial also intimated doubt about whether the ambulance would ever reach Spain and about what percentage of money collected would be applied to the advertised cause.[15]

Heart of Spain also ran up against attempted local censorship. In Detroit, police moved to prevent showings of portions of the picture which were "uncomplimentary to dictators Adolf Hitler and Benito Mussolini," but their efforts were thwarted by legal maneuvering. It was estimated that, despite handicaps, *Heart of Spain* eventually reached audiences totalling over two million.[16]

Soon after completion of the film, Herbert Kline and Frontier Films were commissioned by the Medical Bureau to produce a second documentary on medical services in Spain. Kline welcomed Frontier's suggestion that he collaborate with the photographer Henri Cartier-Bresson (or Cartier, as he then preferred to be called) on plans for what was to become *Return to Life* (French title: *Victoire de la Vie).*[17]

Shooting for *Return to Life* took place in Madrid, at Benicasim (on the Mediterranean north of Valencia), and later in the Barcelona region, with an experienced French cameraman, Jacques Lemare, handling the photography. Kline and Cartier-Bresson had prepared a rough script outline, which they expanded and changed as they went along. "The main visual ideas," says Kline, "were Cartier-Bresson's, and the main story ideas, shooting that picture, were mine, in collaboration with both Cartier-Bresson and Lemare." A cameraman from Barcelona also accompanied Kline on a separate trip to the front, and contributed some footage to the final film.[18]

Return to Life was edited in Paris by Laura Sejour, under the supervision of Cartier-Bresson (chiefly) and Kline. A narration was written by Kline (with a French aide) and Cartier-Bresson. The composer Charles Koecklin created a musical track incorporating such elements as songs of Spanish refugee children living in Paris.

The English-language version of the film was prepared in New York by Frontier, presumably in the spring or early summer of 1938. "Frontier Films acted in the capacity of a producer on that film," Paul Strand told an interviewer, "and when the film was brought to America we put on a master track and a recorded sound track and completed the job." A new commentary was written by Ben Maddow and spoken by Richard Blaine.[19]

Return to Life, forty-five minutes in length, was first shown in the U.S. at a benefit preview screening held under the auspices of the Theatre Arts Committee (an outgrowth of the Theatre Committee for the Defense of the Spanish Republic) on July 20, 1938. (A leaflet for the occasion read: "THRILLS! ACTION! LAUGHTER and TEARS! IN THE ROMANTIC STRUGGLE FOR SURVIVAL OF A GREAT PEOPLE.") The film then opened in New York at the Cameo Theatre on August 3 (accompanying it were two films by Ivor Montagu, his recent documentary *Behind the Lines in Spain* and his 1928 comic fantasy *Day Dreams,* with Charles Laughton and Elsa Lanchester).[20]

National distribution, theatrical and nontheatrical, followed. Handled through Garrison Films, it seems to have been less extensive than for *Heart of Spain.* The phasing out of the international volunteers in Spain, and moves by some elements on the Republican side for an accommodation with Franco, made *Return to Life* less topical than it would have been a few months earlier (though Paul Strand's recollection that the film "was no longer needed for its purpose and . . . was never shown" is clearly at fault). Censorship problems were again encountered: in Chicago, for instance, police ordered the deletion of references to international fascism, including mentions of Hitler and Mussolini and the phrases "Fascist forces," "against Italian troops," "a piece of metal made in Italy," "Rome-Berlin Axis," "fifteen Italian bombers," and "back to face German artillery and Italian bombs."[21]

Propaganda for the Spanish Republicans in the United States was compelled to take into account two discouraging factors: a public unwilling to become involved, and a rigidly neutral government policy.

The two to three thousand Americans (many of them Communists) who volunteered and fought for the Republic in the Abraham Lincoln and George Washington Battalions were not at all representative of public sentiment at large. Fearing entanglement in another European war, most Americans expressed no sympathy for either side in the civil war: in one poll (taken in February 1937), as many as 67% of respondents were neutral. As late as January 1939, 79% of those who expressed an opinion on the question, "Should Congress change the Neutrality Act to permit the shipment of arms to the Loyalists in Spain?" answered "No." Any call for commitment, therefore, which urged support for the Loyalist government and its embattled citizenry in other than strictly humanitarian terms could be expected to encounter stiff resistance.[22]

In accord with this popular isolationist feeling, the Roosevelt administration, abetted by Congress, followed a stringent noninterventionist line throughout the Spanish civil war. The president himself, together with Eleanor Roosevelt and prominent cabinet members such as Henry Morgenthau, Henry Wallace, and Harold Ickes, was sympathetic to the Republican cause (he invited Ivens and Hemingway to the White House to screen *The Spanish Earth*), but every government move was in the direction of cutting off any potential aid to Spain. The 1935 Neutrality Act did not apply to civil wars, but, as Hugh Thomas notes, "the American government acted from the start of the Spanish conflict as if it did." Secretary of State Cordell Hull discounted reports of massive German and Italian violations of the Non-Intervention Agreement which had been signed by the European powers, and consistently opposed any breach of neutrality in the American position. In January 1937, at Roosevelt's urging, Congress—with only one dissenting vote—passed the Embargo Act, prohibiting the export of arms to either side in the Spanish war. The provisions of the measure were incorporated in the revised Neutrality Act of May 1937, and the embargo remained in force for the duration of the conflict, despite the clearly discriminating character it took on as the war progressed. (On the one occasion when it seemed there might be a possibility of it being lifted, in May 1938, Roosevelt acted decisively to squelch the move.) Neutrality was enforced by regulations which prohibited the collection of funds for either side in the war except for *bona fide* relief purposes. Even a project to bring Basque refugee children to the United States was dropped as a possible violation of neutrality, and under the Embargo Act the State Department refused permission, for a time, for doctors and nurses to go to Spain.[23]

"Neutrality" was also the line which Hollywood productions about the civil war ostensibly followed, although the right-wing sympathies of *The Last Train from Madrid* (Paramount, 1937) and left-wing commitment of *Blockade* (United Artists, 1938) were nonetheless evident. In the former, there was "subtle glorification of the fascists," wrote Irving Lerner of Frontier Films: "This is accomplished by making the Loyalist commander a louse and a boob, glorifying the deserters and reactionaries, and representing the political prisoners (those who were executed by the Loyalists, of course) as nice, gentle, and cultured old men." *Blockade* (written by Frontier Films board member John Howard Lawson) was, on the other hand, received enthusiastically by the Left. Lerner called it "a modern miracle" and declared:

> Against a conventional spy melodrama-plot Lawson and Dieterle have given us a profound indictment of totalitarian war. It condemns the Fascist slaughter of innocent civilians, of women and children. "The world can stop it," says Henry Fonda. It cries out against the inhumanity of our so-called democratic nations which stand by and allow Italian and Nazi pirates to torpedo relief and food ships. "Where is the conscience of the world?" is the final accusation of the film.... Hollywood had given us a film which will be seen by millions of people and which, in effect, shouts LIFT THE EMBARGO!

Neither film, however, veered far from the customary studio sets, star performers, and romantic narrative of the motion-picture industry in its attempt to dramatize a contemporary political crisis. For suggestions of a direct, unequivocal approach to cinematic coverage of the Spanish civil war, the Frontier documentarians would have to look elsewhere.[24]

The struggle was, of course, being recorded in newsreels shot on both sides of the lines, and it became a common practice to compile such footage into medium-length and feature-length documentaries, after the manner of Dziga Vertov during the civil war in Russia. For the Soviet Union, Roman Karmen and his associate Boris Makaeyev filmed a long series of weekly reports under the general title *What is Happening in Spain,* and these were edited into the documentary *Spain* by Esther Shub in 1939. (Karmen's footage was occasionally shown in the U.S.: thus in August 1937 Lerner reported that "the exciting newsreels of present-day Loyalist Spain which were shown at the Cameo in New York last week under the title *Forward!* indicated again that the Soviet newsreelmen, who made them, knew what they were about.") In Britain, the left-wing Progressive Film Institute assembled *News from Spain* and *Crime Against Madrid* during 1937.[25]

The first compilation of Spanish civil war footage to be exhibited in the United States was apparently *Hell Rains on Spain,* a documentary incorporating scenes of warfare (two cameramen were reportedly killed during its production) which was shown in Chicago (and possibly elsewhere) in December 1936. It was followed in January by *The Defense of Madrid,* a silent 16mm film (with titles by Muriel Rukeyser) detailing life in the city under siege and the organization of resistance, and *Spain in Flames,* a feature-length assemblage which traced the background of the army revolt and dealt with "the bombardment of Madrid, evacuation of children, German and Italian ships in Alicante, training of the defense militia, the struggle for Guadarrama hills, women and youth fighting side by side with the men." *Madrid Document,* a three-reeler distributed in February 1937, was advertised as depicting "actual bombardment" of the city and the International Brigade in action; writers from Madrid acted as commentators. In March, a thirty-minute documentary with Spanish commentary on the activities of the People's Front in Catalonia was favorably reviewed in the *Daily Worker,* although its title was not recorded. Also focusing on the early struggle in Barcelona and the surrounding region was *Fury Over Spain* (sixty minutes, July 1937), which contained what an otherwise hostile reviewer termed "some of the most vivid war photography ever filmed." *With the Lincoln Battalion in Spain* (May 1938) offered "intimate scenes of the American volunteers at the front."[26]

Some of the newsreel compilations strikingly anticipated, in their imagery and structural patterns, the later Frontier productions. *Spain in Flames,* for example, included shots of the training of raw recruits—"young men, green kids of sixteen stand together with men of sixty learning about guns and how to shoot"—while the Spanish-language film from Catalonia incorporated "scenes of soldiers at the front, nurses caring for the wounded, farmers preparing food for the hungry, wives and mothers on the march, youth in the front ranks, and one splendid scene showing a screen full of upraised fists of defiance to the fascists (photographed against the sky)." An especially close parallel to *Heart of Spain* and *Return to Life* was offered by *The Defense of Madrid:*

> First we are introduced to Madrid in peace time, a quiet, beautiful city, clean and rich with the traditions of centuries. Children play happily at the squares, and young girls go about

their work, drawing water from the wells and washing clothes. In outward appearances the city is the Spain of the picture post cards. But a People's Front government has been elected and appearances are deceiving.

July 18, 1936, fascist generals with the support of the fascists in Germany and Italy stage a revolt. Franco, backed by the regular army and German and Italian munitions, sweeps on against the poorly organized militia of the people to the gates of Madrid....

Madrid builds barricades of heavy pavement bricks and sandbags, builds trenches protected by machine guns. The fascists will have to fight for each street and each house. Shelters are built for air raids. Food and coal are rationed. Queues of patient women and children wait for their allotment of coal and bread, while their husbands build trenches, erect barricades.

Anti-fascists from all over the world come to aid the defenders of Madrid. We see the International Column, the fighters from all over the world who are helping to save Spain from fascism....

And while Madrid holds off the fascists, we see the ravages and destruction caused by the German Junkers and Heinckel planes. Women and children are moved down. Coffins stand row on row in the government quarters, some of the dead still awaiting identification. One minute a house is seen whole, the next it is in smoldering ruins, from an incendiary bomb dropped by foreign airplanes. A woman rushes out of a house, and as she reaches the street the house crumbles behind.

But the spirit of the Madrilenos has not been broken. As we watch the militia training in an open square we realize that. The tide of the battle has turned. They still need aid, and it is up to us to see that we do our part in helping them.[27]

The majority of these compilation documentaries reflected a Communist interpretation of events, depicting Soviet steamers bringing foodstuffs and medical supplies to the beleaguered Republicans, concentrating on the activities of the Communist-organized Fifth Regiment, or showing Communist leaders such as Hans Beimler, Ludwig Renn, Jose Diaz, and Dolores Ibarruri ("La Pasionaria") in action. A film such as *Madrid Document,* whose showings were sponsored, like those of *Heart of Spain* and *Return to Life,* by the Medical Bureau, would undoubtedly have followed this line.[28] The only exception seems to have been *Fury Over Spain,* which was severely criticized in the Communist press for being "corrupted by a narrow partisan political viewpoint" and "top-heavy propaganda for the CNT and FAI, the Anarchist groups."[29]

Although several of these films, particularly *Spain in Flames*, were successful with audiences and proved invaluable as propaganda weapons, there were limitations to newsreel compilation as a documentary technique. The editor of *Spain in Flames,* Joris Ivens's collaborator Helen van Dongen, ran up against some of them when she was given the assignment, in late 1936, to edit existing newsreel footage "into a documentary whose aim was to give the background of the war, and explain the issues to the American public." Ivens elaborates:

Helen's job was not simple: most of the newsreel footage given her turned out to be taken on the Franco side, with the Franco point of view; the costs of a feature-editing job were greater than the backers expected. After watching a particularly painful session in the cutting room, and listening to the sponsoring committee complain about results, I remarked that it would be cheaper and more satisfactory in every respect to make such a documentary film on the spot, instead of being at the mercy of newsreel costs and newsreel attitudes.

The result was that the compilation was completed at minimal additional cost, and plans were then made and funds raised to send Ivens to Spain to shoot an original documentary film.[30]

The Spanish Earth has been extensively discussed by Ivens and others,[31] and it is not necessary here to analyze it in detail. But since Ivens was in contact with the Frontier filmmakers both in New York and in Spain, and is known to have exerted considerable impact on their thinking (though Maddow recently said that Ivens "had less influence on all of us than he should have had"), some aspects of his approach in documenting the conflict should be pointed out. Initially, he planned to shoot a quasi-dramatized film depicting events in a Spanish village beginning in 1931, the year of King Alfonso's abdication, and covering the war only in a culminating final section. Ivens soon discovered that such a conception, relying heavily on reenactment, was totally unrealizable in the existing conditions in Spain. The propaganda authorities were unequipped to deal with a "subtle half-fictional, half-documentary film," and villagers in the teeth of battle could not be expected to be concerned with reconstructing the atmosphere of the prewar period: "One could not possibly ask people who were engaged in a life and death struggle to be interested in anything outside that struggle." Thus circumstances propelled Ivens toward a direct documentary form, in which, however, certain ideas from the earlier outline were retained. On a thematic level, the relationship of agriculture to the military struggle, through the irrigation scheme and the supply of food to the defenders of Madrid, remained a central concern; and in terms of structure the notion of individual characterization survived in an attenuated way in the provision of what Ivens terms a "thin continuity line" through the portrayal of the young peasant, Julian, at the front and at home in his village.[32]

Heart of Spain embodies an approach to its subject which is comparable in many ways to that of *The Spanish Earth*. It rejects, of course, any suggestion of Hollywood melodrama. It is more tightly and logically organized—around the operation of the blood bank and the metaphor of civilian support for combatants in a people's war—then any newsreel compilation could be. Like Ivens's film, it deals only with the contemporary struggle and does not attempt, other than in a few words of commentary, to fill in the historical background. And it has recourse to a minor narrative thread involving two slightly-developed individual characters (in addition to Dr. Bethune) in order to personalize the action and help link scenes filmed in different locales.

The film may be divided into three sections. The first two document phases of the struggle in general, concentrating on civilian, and then military life in war-torn Spain. The third section forges a symbolic bond between the preceding two in dealing specifically with the work of the Blood Transfusion Institute.

The opening images of *Heart of Spain* are of Madrid: buildings half-reduced to rubble by rebel bombardment. "Silent," the narration begins. "Blood has been spilled here." The ruins give way to shots of daily life going on in the beleaguered city—and then the mood is abruptly shattered by an enemy attack. Amid explosions, smoke, and falling masonry, the dead lie in the street, and citizens run for cover. When the shelling ceases, life returns to "normal": the wounded are treated, volunteers train in empty lots after work, boys play at war, trenches are dug, barricades are built. The film moves to the countryside, where the land is irrigated and plowed, and food produced for the front. A group of children play a skipping game, oblivious to danger. Then there is another eruption of violence, as planes overhead conduct a bombing raid, and there is a flurry of shots of explosions, flaming buildings, fires being fought, women weeping, corpses, anxious crowds, children being dug out from under collapsed walls. The final sequence of the "civilian" section of *Heart of Spain* shows refugees—women, children, old people—living in a primitive cave settlement (Alcala de Henares) in the mountains.

The "military" section opens with footage of the cemetery of the International Brigades, the gravestones of men who have "come from all corners of the world to fight for the idea of democracy, to make Madrid the tomb of fascism." We then see Spanish and foreign combatants on the march, troop trucks, cannons firing, followed by a group of soldiers being addressed by Commandant Enrique Lister. His talk forms a prelude to battle scenes filmed at the front, with infantry, cavalry, aircraft, tanks, and artillery in action. The section concludes with a series of shots detailing the treatment of the wounded, carried from the trenches by stretcher-bearers, given first aid, transferred to ambulances, and speeded to base hospitals where operations can be performed.

A transition to the final section is provided by an image of a soldier and his mother together: he has been shot while at the front, she has been bombed in her home. The vulnerability of both military and civilian populations is made manifest, and the need for mutual support implied. This part of the film shows how blood is donated and stored at Dr. Bethune's Institute, and then depicts a blood truck moving up under fire towards the front lines, as a battle rages and injured troops are brought out and given treatment. The truck arrives at a front hospital, the staff greet Dr. Bethune, and then the transfusions take place. A woman donor meets the soldier who has received her blood—"A new kind of friendship begins, strengthened by blood." There is a brief glimpse of a joyful peasant dance, and *Heart of Spain* ends with a montage in which shots of blood pouring into a phial and arms outstretching for the needle to be inserted are intercut with scenes of troops marching, in a visual assertion of solidarity in the defense of the Spanish Republic.

Return to Life does not boast such a neat tripartite structure, but its subject matter and organization are nevertheless close to that of its predecessor. The film has four main divisions, focusing, after the general pattern of *Heart of Spain,* on civilian and military life, and on the medical care being provided by the Republic for each of the two main sectors of the population. Separating noncombatants from combatants is a transitional section, and inserted into the long final part on the treatment of military casualties is an interlude.

The opening section is devoted to street scenes in Madrid. At first we see children playing, vendors at their stalls, crowds on the sidewalk, streetcars, theatres: the face of daily life, apparently normal. Next, there are images of troops on guard, of the barricades, of a billboard urging "EVACUAD MADRID." The streets are empty. "City of barricades," says the narrator, "but you can't barricade the sky." A series of shots documents bomb damage: a gutted building, a flattened church. The consequences of the long siege on living conditions within the city now become apparent, as grim-looking citizens wait in lines for rationed food, and others scavenge in the streets. Several further views of war-scarred Madrid conclude the section on a note of bitter determination, with the voice-over commenting, "The people wanted a republic, the aristocrats wanted a king."

The film now shows medical services being provided for the civilian population, concentrating on care for women and children. The operation of a maternity hospital in Madrid is depicted, followed by scenes of a children's seaside clinic, where the patients are victims of tuberculosis, shrapnel wounds, typhus.

A transition is provided by the next section, which draws attention to two vital services being performed for the support, in particular, of the troops in the field. These are bandage manufacture—being carried out chiefly by women workers—and food production by peasants.

The military segment, which follows, again brings the medical theme to the forefront by singling out, in its coverage of recruits being trained, those learning to be stretcher-bearers. We see them parade through the streets, and then troops in the countryside, on the move up to the front lines. Tanks advance, artillery is maneuvered into position, men take their positions in trenches, machine guns are fired. The scenes of actual battle, however, are relatively brief, and *Return to Life* moves quickly into its fourth major division, for which the previous sections have been introductory, and which occupies two-thirds of the film's total running time.

Documentation of the injured soldiers' "return to life" begins with their being carried from the battle field and given emergency first aid care at a post immediately behind the lines. Meanwhile, at base positions, ambulances are loaded with supplies: cotton, bandages, serum. Needles, syringes, anti-toxins are prepared at the forward post as a camouflaged ambulance makes its way, under shell-fire, toward the front. The rendezvous is made, casualties are loaded on to ambulances, an urgent operation is performed on the spot. The scene than shifts to the city, where the wounded are transferred from the trains on which they have arrived to various hospitals. A group of shots shows men in pain and the care they receive from nurses and doctors, many of them international volunteers. The opportunity for political comment is not lost: "Spain called to the world for help," the narrator informs us, "The governments were deaf, but the people answered." We are shown patients recuperating, trying to adjust to the loss of a limb: a man with both feet blown off, another minus a leg.

The interlude, introduced at this point, consists of footage of a village fiesta, ostensibly held to celebrate the first anniversay of the foundation of a nearby American hospital. The town crier bangs his gong, and peasants converge from the countryside on foot, in trucks, on donkeys. Festivities commence, and the wounded watch local men perform a traditional dance, the Aguachadilla. The Americans dispense bread and chocolate to village children, who then take part in folk dances and games (as singing by Spanish refugee children is heard on the soundtrack).

The final portion of *Return to Life* depicts the last stages in the convalescence of a group of injured servicemen at a seaside treatment center at Benicasim. They are shown walking on crutches, studying, undergoing physiotherapy with the aid of mechanical devices, boxing, playing ball. Then, recovered, they clamber aboard a truck in the first stage of their return to the front. "They're going back, perhaps to die," intones the narrator, "that the Republic may live, that freedom may not perish from the earth."

In their structuring, both *Heart of Spain* and *Return to Life* reveal an attempt to organize documentary material according to montage principles, incorporating, as Leo Hurwitz expresses it, "opposition, conflict, and contradiction" into their image assembly. The cuts, for example, in the opening sequence of *Return to Life,* from bustling streets to barricades to ruins, shock the viewer with a nonsequential logic which, when understood, carries potent political signification. Life goes on as normal, *and yet* the city is barricaded: the civil war is a defensive struggle to protect ordinary people from outside attack. The city is barricaded, *and yet* much of it lies in ruins: the citizens of Madrid are in acute need of support to help them withstand fascist assaults.

In *Heart of Spain,* in particular, contrast editing is deployed in a conscious effort to mold a political aesthetic. Hurwitz asserts that it was the first sound film in which he was able to carry through to completion (with Strand's assistance) the idea of "dialectical structure" of documentary, which he had first incorporated into his shooting script (rejected by Pare Lorentz) for *The Plow That Broke the Plains.* "In documentary films," he explains, "where you don't have a person within a plot to identify with, the problem is to evoke needs, a sense of empathy, a process of growth of feeling without these devices." The solution he arrived at was to "create the equivalent of plot—that is, the process of growth and involvement—rather than simple exposition, or declaratory statement."[33]

The working out of this concept in *Heart of Spain* resulted, according to Hurwitz, in "a feeling of interior dramatic growth" and a steadily solidifying audience identification with the struggle of the Spanish Loyalists. (One is reminded of his objection to May Day newsreels which failed to involve an audience not already committed to radical objectives, to films which "*assume*[*d*] the revolutionary approach, instead of *convincing* the spectator of its correctness."[34] In a recent interview, Hurwitz analyzed in detail how, in his view, the "dialectical" structure of *Heart of Spain* operated:

> The film opens with bombed buildings, Madrid in ruins—"Blood has been spilled here." The war is treated in its effect on people, the spilling of blood. Then a sequence of normal living in the midst of war—people walking around, carts going by. This creates a need for life to go in spite of the torn city. Then there is an explosion and the first scenes of the fascist attack on Madrid—people running through the smoke-filled streets, children dug out of bomb craters. Again you return to a scene of a "normal" city during war—recruits being trained, children playing at defense. Positive and negative needs are created in the audience. You want people to live on without threat; you don't want their lives torn apart. You want them to be able to defend themselves against attack from the sky. Such feelings derive from the actual experience of life in a city during war. In this way, as when you have a plot which actuates needs and empathy, one moves through the film identifying with the needs of the Spanish people to renew life in their fight against the fascists. When the actual blood transfusion sequence begins, a thematic basis for the film has already been constructed, which weaves together the specifics of medical aid with the social struggle. From this point on, the detailed events—what happens to the blood from donor to wounded soldier—carry with them the larger metaphor.[35]

For Hurwitz, then, the film's narrowing down in reference, from the war in general to the work of Dr. Bethune's Institute in particular, is not anticlimactic: on the contrary, since this ordering allows the symbolic as well as material significance of the blood bank to be understood, *Heart of Spain* remains concerned throughout, he would argue, with the total struggle. As he has expressed it:

> The nature of war, and the nature of *the* war in Madrid is developed at great lengths, at the beginning, before you begin to touch what the film's about. You have to understand the nature of that war before you can understand the meaning of the blood transfusion—then it takes on an entirely different meaning by virtue of its connection with the fascist invasion.

And when you have defined that, then the relation of people in the blood episode becomes much more meaningful, because the nature of working together, of comradeship, becomes symbolized by the blood transfusion service, so it's the same thing fundamentally. [36]

There was, of course, a Hegelian/Marxist component to Hurwitz's thinking about structure. The pattern of thesis-antithesis-synthesis may clearly be discerned in the tripartite arrangement of *Heart of Spain* as outlined above, in which civilian and military are opposed, and the opposition transcended in their symbolic fusion in the final section. Stripped to essentials, one can see the film as yielding, through the counterposing, or contradiction, in Hegelian terms, of "civilian populace" and "army (at war)," the new, higher concept of "people's war," in which the purposes and actions of both sectors of the population are interlocked. [37]

Evidence that the film was perceived in such terms at the time of its release is offered by an interesting review by Elizabeth Noble which appeared in the *New Masses*. Her interpretation closely paralleled the construction Hurwitz places on the editing which he and Strand carried out:

Thus war and blood transfusion are the scenario's core. With this tool, the editors imposed the superior reality of human reason and feeling on the unrelated atoms of reality seen by the camera. Cutting in the silent film's best tradition, Strand and Hurwitz were able—by building on the tension of opposites—to produce powerful relations between sequences and to create not only the sense of historic fact but also the sense of drama, of conflict, moving and beautiful, poignant and heroic.

In analyzing the form of *Heart of Spain,* it should be emphasized that the sequences are not thematic variations but true developments growing out of previous situations, and in turn causing new situations to arise. The film's dramatic progression falls into three divisions: (1) Spain is torn by shells of international fascism; (2) to save the land and the people, the army moves into battle; there is frightful loss in shattered limbs and broken bodies, blood spilled; (3) behind the lines, the people create a vast reservoir of blood to renew the life of those who fight for Spain and freedom.

Internally, a similar pattern is found. The first section, for example, is developed as follows. Blood has been shed in physically torn Spain, the ruins silently declare. Yet—life must go on. Go on it does, almost as usual. A sudden explosion, and people run in the streets to escape death. Still life goes on, soberly, heroically. Another explosion, an aerial bomb—Italy and Germany are invading Spain—and babies buried in flames. From fascist threats, men and women flee the city.... [38]

Moreover, for Noble, as for Hurwitz, such structuring represents an attempt to infuse documentary film with the emotional charge of fictional narrative. "Unlike the enacted film," she wrote, "in which the audience becomes emotionally involved in the internal life of the characters, their needs and their hopes, the documentary film is made up of disconnected fragments of reality—of people, places, and events which the audience does not know specifically in relation to dramatic plot. The documentary film"—she concluded—"must therefore find equivalents by means of which the audience can be involved in what is happening on the screen. . . . "[39]

It is on this question of the emotive power (and consequently, for Hurwitz, the political efficacy) of "dialectical" film structure that controversy has arisen. Hurwitz's experimentation gained strong endorsement from Noble, who argued that *Heart of Spain* possessed "emotional intensity not usually found in the documentary film or short," which it achieved "by virtue of a dramatic integration not customarily found in the form, by a dramatic impact made possible because of its makers' method of approach." The critic of *Film Survey News Release* (organ of the progressive Associated Film Audiences) was not, however, as enthusiastic, finding *Heart of Spain* "not so moving as *Spanish Earth.*" And Ben Maddow, collaborator of Hurwitz and Strand on the project, had doubts about the viability of the editing structure which was being imposed on the material:

> Leo Hurwitz had such a dominating influence theoretically. . . . His notions . . . essentially derived from a form of Hegelian dialectics, filtered through Marx. Thesis, antithesis, and then synthesis. . . . And I often would argue that this was too schematic, I've since thought it was far too schematic, although it had a certain value, it was something to think about. But Leo Hurwitz, I don't think—now this is my judgement—ever had a firm grip of that instinctive aesthetic, how things should be built as a whole. Without any thinking, because you could feel it. He would have to know precisely, intellectually, where to go from Sequence A to Sequence B. And so Sequence A would be the thesis and Sequence B would be the antithesis and so on.[40]

Such a critique brings the specific content of images, as well as their ordering, into question; and it is difficult now to believe that the rather prosaic imagery of bottles of blood, refrigerators, and ambulances which dominates the final section of *Heart of Spain* could ever have carried (except perhaps for those already strongly committed to the Loyalist cause) either the emotional force or the political significance which Hurwitz attributes to it. (In the absence of concrete evidence, however, any judgement as to the impact of *Heart of Spain* on 1937 audiences must necessarily be speculative.)

But the "dialectical" structure of *Heart of Spain* was not its only experimental feature. The dramatization of the documentary footage by the introduction, in the last section, of a limited amount of individual characterization was not, strictly speaking, an innovation—the device had been used in several Film and Photo League productions such as Maurice Bailen's *The Great Depression,* and was, of course, employed in *The Spanish Earth.* Nevertheless it was a comparatively unusual trait in American cinema at the time; and it was to become an important part of the developing Frontier Films aesthetic. As such, it deserves some comment.

Heart of Spain follows the actions of a woman named Hero Escobedo. We see her at the institute, donating her blood and having the scheme explained to her by Dr. Bethune. Later, we see her at a hospital visiting the young soldier who has received a transfusion with the blood she gave. (Kline notes that we also see her several times earlier, walking in the street, but since she has not at this point been introduced as an individual character we have no particular reason to notice her.) We know little about her beyond the fact that she has a fifteen-year-old daughter, who also appears. Of the soldier recipient, we learn virtually nothing, except that his name is Enrico Gallan. Kline comments on this mini-narrative as follows:

> Without knowing for sure how to combine story and documentary, my instinct was to write the story. Now if I had known then as much as I'm supposed to know now, I would have expanded the wounded soldier's story, that she gave her blood to. But within the limitations of the money . . . We didn't have enough money to shoot it, or other scenes that Karpathi and I planned to do with her. Both Geza and I wanted money to shoot more in Spain. I would have developed more characters simply by having more film.[41]

It is likely that Kline, playwright and lately editor of *New Theatre* magazine, Hurwitz, the former student of Lee Strasberg, and Strand, associate of the Group Theatre, were reluctant to relinquish the dramatic possibilities latent in individual characterization. At the same time all three rejected for political and aesthetic reasons the fully dramatized film as produced in Hollywood. Kline says, "We were torn between straight documentation and striving for story values." The result, then, was a compromise, a strictly limited, quasi-fictional narrative which was never allowed to dominate the objective, general, cognitive aspects of the documentary mode. Hurwitz, clearly trying to reconcile conflicting strands in the realist aesthetic which had emerged from twentieth-century experimentation (see chap. 1), appealed to both Brecht and Stanislavsky in support of the Frontier position:

> [Brecht's] idea of distance does not mean lack of involvement of audience, and in fact that's where he's immensely brilliant. That is, you do get dramatic involvement, but you don't get dramatic involvement so that you are sucked away from the ideas that are involved. And that's what he's after, he's after the break into the empathic response which is an audience's response, so that it doesn't get lost in an island of self, into sentimentality, into the consideration of the individual as apart from other individuals, but becomes part of the texture and contour of the forces of the world you're in. And there is no distinction between what I'm saying there in terms of how you can use the ideas of Stanislavsky for dramatic involvement, and this form of using your dramatic involvement for illumination of your world and illumination of the audience's world. *Native Land* and *Heart of Spain* both are built upon those principles, and they relate very much to what Brecht wanted to do, and did in his work, in an entirely different form.[42]

In *Native Land,* and in *People of the Cumberland,* with shooting conditions directly under their control, Frontier filmmakers would permit characters to emerge in greater depth than in *Heart of Spain,* but again each would be strictly confined to a single segment of the film. In this way individual figures—drawn from fiction or real life—were presented as typical rather than extraordinary, exemplars like Hero Escobedo whose social role was more important than their personal psychology.

Both *Heart of Spain* and *Return to Life* are composed of a large number of short shots, many no more than a few seconds in duration. Partly the reasons for this were technical. Synchronous-sound shooting, which would inevitably have entailed longer takes (and would have made character development considerably easier), was not feasible on location in Spain, and the cameras that were used were not equipped for continuous running. The Eyemo, employed on *Heart of Spain,* for example, was spring-driven and was good for shots with a maximum length of ten seconds.[43] But there were also aesthetic considerations involved.

Elizabeth Noble speaks of Strand and Hurwitz cutting in the tradition of the silent film, and it is evident that the Soviet montage style, based on the short take, continued—despite its eclipse in the U.S.S.R.[44]—to exercise a powerful influence over documentary filmmakers in the later thirties. The reductionism implicit in Soviet theory, whereby each shot was regarded as having a single content which took on meaning only within the context of an image chain, was reflected both in the nature of the footage incorporated in *Heart of Spain* and *Return to Life,* and in the manner in which it was edited.

It was, in a sense, a still photographer's style, and it may be no coincidence that of the men who worked on the two films, Karpathi, Strand, and Cartier-Bresson were all primarily accomplished in still photography.[45] Shots, as Noble suggests, could be considered "unrelated atoms of reality" which would be shaped into sequences in the cutting room. In this respect a major U.S. precedent had been set by *The Plow That Broke the Plains.* On that film Strand and Hurwitz (together with Steiner) had been assigned, almost as if they were still photographers in Roy Stryker's unit at the Resettlement Administration, to make a series of shots illustrating certain themes—wheatlands, cattle country, erosion etc.—which were then organized into significant patterns by Pare Lorentz and his editors in Washington. Neither of Frontier's Spanish films were made in quite this way, but there was a similar attitude towards the pliability of filmic raw material, particularly in the case of *Heart of Spain*—on which Strand and Hurwitz, confronted now with the task of editing a mass of footage from heterogeneous sources into a meaningful whole, found their positions reversed from what they had been on *The Plow*.

Heart of Spain, of course, as a quasi-compilation documentary, was especially susceptible to image manipulation in accordance with montage conceptions. None of the sequences, except for those parts of the final section detailing the operation of the Blood Transfusion Institute, appears to have been conceived and executed in conformity with conventional principles of spatio-temporal continuity from shot to shot. (In some cases, as in the bombing raid, attempts were obviously made to fake such continuity in line with Kuleshov's concept of "creative geography,"[46] but inconsistencies in locale and camera positioning, as well as disparities in the grain and contrast of the images, render the synthetic quality of such sequences apparent.[47]) In general, images are grouped together on an abstract, conceptual basis (a diverse handful of shots, for example, of peasants forking hay, a draft horse drawing water, plows, flocks of sheep, and donkeys signifying "agriculture behind the lines"); and this form of construction, while stripping the film of the solidity of a more carefully preplanned and visually coherent work like *The Spanish Earth*, makes it more capable of being shaped into a "dialectical" pattern of political argument.

The sequence depicting the International Brigades cemetery in *Heart of Spain* illustrates how, in this method of filmic argumentation, shots are cut off at the point where they have yielded their (singular) item of information. The shot of the grave marked "Inconnu, Canadien," for instance, is held just long enough for us to register the fact that an anonymous fighter has given his life; if it were longer, we might begin to notice the texture of the stone. It is by montage that the argument is built: that in the struggle many nationalities are united (there are separate images of the graves of Polish, Italian, French, American, English volunteers); and that though these are dead, the cause for which they fell lives on ("by cutting in close-ups of living soldiers in the International Cemetery sequence," wrote Elizabeth Noble, "the mood was established that men die, but other men will take their place, until Spain is free").[48]

Neither *Heart of Spain* nor *Return to Life,* however, uses montage as boldly as the Workers' Film and Photo League had done in films such as *Bonus March* and *Hunger 1932*. There are only a few minor experiments in Eisensteinian "intellectual" montage, and two of these do not stand on their own, but are bolstered by explanatory comments on the soundtrack. In *Heart of Spain,* in the bombing-raid sequence, images of Hitler and Mussolini are inserted between footage of the bombs being dropped and shots of the explosions on the ground. There is a similar resort to extradiegetic material in *Return to Life*'s battlefield sequence, in which, interposed between shots of artillery and machine guns being fired, are images (connected by swish pans) of Italian, Nazi, and Moorish insignia. In both cases the meaning of such unconventional cutting is pointed to by the narrator, who in *Heart of Spain* comments, "Germany and Italy want Spanish steel for guns, Spanish coal for warships, copper, lead, mercury, zinc..." and who remarks, in *Heart of Spain:* "Fascism speaks only one way, with lead and steel, and Spain had to reply with the same weapons, against the Italian troops, the swastika, the Moorish legions...."

The most ambitious attempt at political comment through montage is the finale of *Heart of Spain,* in which already familiar shots are recapitulated in a new and provocative order. Images of a blood bottle filling up, Republican troops on the march, the arms of donors reaching out to give their blood, and of soldiers and civilians giving the clenched-fist salute are intercut in an affirmation of strength through interdependence. The symbolic point is pressed hard, since there is a close graphic similarity between the arms of the blood donors and the arms of those giving the Loyalist salute. The film's final image is of the bottle of blood superimposed over marching soldiers.

As sound films, *Heart of Spain* and *Return to Life* relied heavily, for their political and aesthetic impact, on the narration. The writer responsible in each case (with the collaboration, on *Heart of Spain,* of Herbert Kline) was Frontier's resident "word man," Ben Maddow, who was accepted into the group initially on his reputation as a poet. There was something of a convention at the time that commentaries for documentaries have poetic qualities: W.H. Auden, for example, had written verse for *Coalface* (1935) and *Night Mail* (1936), while Lorentz's narration for *The River* (1937) was cadenced and repetitive in a Whitmanesque manner. Maddow did not attempt anything so close to self-sufficient poetry, but his writing was nevertheless far from a simple prose expository style.[49]

In 1936, inspired by *The March of Time,* Maddow had speculated on the notion of a continuous narration which would function "as a sort of ground-bass to the images on the screen." The musical analogy was intriguing but probably misleading, given the impossibility of listening to grammatical speech as if it were, simply, rhythmical accompaniment. Working with Hurwitz, Maddow soon reached a more sophisticated understanding of word and image interaction in the cinema. Hurwitz was particularly pleased with the results on *Heart of Spain,* and later, *Native Land*:

> What these films introduced ... is a marriage of narration and image so as to form one complex structure of meaning. So the writing, and the distillation of the writing, which is a very important part of it, which I did with Ben, and the laying in of the text, and the recording of the narration, is done in relation to that marriage, so that there is in truth no such thing as narration: the words are part of the image-word continuum.... The whole attitude towards the person who speaks is not as a narrator, it's as a person who is a part of the context of living that is being built.[50]

The final voice track was arrived at through a collaborative process which Hurwitz describes as ultimately very satisfactory:

> [Maddow] was a word man, it took him a long time to become a film man, he was a poet, and my problem in working with him—it was not a problem I had great difficulty with—was to prevent the substantiality of the word from becoming the substantiality of the film. In other words, we worked very closely and in a marvelous relationship, but I was always aiming

toward the most sensitive, clear, vivid use of language that did not stand by itself, but that stood in relation to a complex and chemical interaction with the development of image. And when I took those words that we recorded, when I directed the recording, and when I then edited the film, then transformations took place that in a sense he could know nothing about while in the writing phase, but the writing was directed to lead to that.[51]

"Chemical interaction" is a difficult concept to demonstrate, but analysis of patterns of word-image conjunction in *Heart of Spain* and *Return to Life* does in fact reveal a varied set of relationships. The commentary often relates to the picture in quite straightforward fashion, while in other cases there is an expressive indirectness. It is most frequently explicatory, elucidating what is in the image ("Food must be rationed" over people lining up in the streets). It may be simply interpretive ("*Primero Libro*—First Book" over a book titled *Primero Libro*), or it may serve as a reportorial substitute for synchronized speech, as with Lister's address in *Heart of Spain* and the town crier's announcement in *Return to Life*. In a special case, it may directly appeal to the audience to observe what is on the screen ("Don't turn away," says the narrator of *Heart of Spain,* as the stump of an arm appears). On the other hand, the commentary may engage in political proselytizing ("Spaniards, Americans, and Canadians march under General Miaja against the fascists who attacked an elected government" over Republican army columns). It may also be ironic ("Hitler wants iron, Mussolini wants coal" over coffins and weeping women) or anecdotal (a pan round a bombed building with the accompaniment: "It was Sunday..they were having breakfast..the old couple on the top floor..the watchmaker eating with his three daughters..the baby at the window..one bomb, one hundred wounded, thirty-seven dead..a hand blown off..").

Likewise, the style of writing varies, from the matter-of-fact ("The blood is preserved by adding sodium citrate, and it will remain good for use for two weeks, when kept in refrigerators at two degrees Centigrade") to the rhetorical ("They have the traditional courage of men who fight for freedom and for bread"), the accusatory ("Who brought death to the Spanish people? Reichs Chancellor Hitler..Il Duce Mussolini..Generalissimo Franco.."), and the poetic ("One day of fiesta..there's sun in the dust..the road is clear as the powder of jewels..").

Critical reaction to the functioning of the commentary at the time of the films' release was mixed. The narration in *Return to Life,* for example, was termed "fairly intelligent" *(Variety),* and praised for showing "a further development in the embryo art of expository dialogue in film" *(New Masses).* Howard Barnes of the *New York Herald Tribune,* on the other hand, found it "random and repetitive," while Frank S. Nugent remarked in the *New York Times:*

> ...now familarized to the point of banality is the doom-voiced narrative commentary by
> David Wolff [Ben Maddow], who keeps reminding everyone that the Loyalist heroes are
> pitting flesh and blood against the steel of the Fascists. Except for that accusingly dramatic
> voice which turns every crutch into a propaganda weapon, the picture might very easily have
> been simply a photographic report of a medical group to its patrons. We prefer to forget Mr.
> Wolff's part in it.... [52]

There is some justice to Nugent's complaints. *Return to Life*'s narrator, Richard Blaine, tends to be oratorical in his delivery, and projects a certain professional distance from the subject. Similarly, the voice of John O'Shaughnessy, in *Heart of Spain,* is slow-paced, solemn, and a little pedantic. Both may be contrasted with the equally serious, yet rough-edged, restrained, and personally felt commentary of Ernest Hemingway in *The Spanish Earth*.[53]

There is also, as Nugent charges, some reiteration of the flesh vs. steel opposition ("flesh and bone against machine and cannon," "flesh and bone against bits of steel," "this peasant...who placed himself, his flesh and his organs, against steel and lead," etc.). At the time it may have seemed important from a propagandistic standpoint that such a strong image be repeated for effect. Yet it typified a slightly hollow, rhetorical quality to be found in both the writing and the speaking of the commentaries (were not the Nationalists also, even if professional soldiers, pitting flesh against steel?). Maddow recently remarked:

> I think the rhetoric that's in those films that we did is a sort of self-indulgence, which often
> appeared in the poetry that I published too. It was over-rhetorical and it wasn't tempered by
> irony because I didn't understand what irony was. I didn't see anything ironic at all. Nor
> would it have been understood by the group.[54]

Maddow now feels (an opinion not shared by Hurwitz) that the commentaries were simply too long—though they were far from the continuous "ground-bass" he had earlier envisaged. Not counting pauses, there is approximately 8 minutes of voice-over in *Heart of Spain* (27% of the running time), and 17 minutes in *Return to Life* (38%). A relevant comparison is *The Spanish Earth,* in which the figure is 10 minutes (19%). *Heart of Spain,* Maddow argues, "could easily suffer a fifty percent cut in words," while the narration to *Return to Life,* he considers, is "far over-written": "It was essentially Cartier-Bresson's film, and I don't think he knew English really well enough to be able to judge the narrative, otherwise he would have cut at least two-thirds of it out." The judgement highlights a dilemma of documentary in general and political cinema in particular, where there is always a tendency to anchor the meaning of an image by the addition of language, whatever the aesthetic drawbacks of such a procedure may be.[55]

It is the commentary (together with some introductory titles in *Return to Life*) which determines, in each film, the specific ideological stance (in fact, as

Nugent suggests, *Return to Life,* stripped of its commentary, would scarcely continue to function as political propaganda, and the same is true of *Heart of Spain*). This stance is very nearly the same in the two films (and is close to that of *The Spanish Earth*), and is characterized as much by what is omitted as by what is said.

The positive statement is that the war in Spain is being fought between the forces of "democracy" and "fascism." The international volunteers, in *Heart of Spain,* have come "to fight for the idea of democracy, to make Madrid the tomb of fascism." The Loyalist soldiers, in *Return to Life,* are "going to the trenches to stop the fascists before they attack the world . . . they're going back, perhaps to die, that the Republic may live, that freedom may not perish from the earth." The fascists "attacked an elected government" *(Heart of Spain);* they "lost an election, and they began a war" *(Return to Life).*

The "fascists" are identified primarily as German and Italian troops at the command of Hitler and Mussolini, and only secondarily as Spanish monarchists. Franco is not even mentioned in *Heart of Spain,* and must take his place third in line behind the Axis powers in *Return to Life:* "They know what they're going to face . . the German artillery . . the Italian bombers . . the tanks and troops that Franco was able to buy."

The war is thus one of defense against foreign invasion. In *Heart of Spain,* scenes of bomb attacks are accompanied by comments such as, "This is the kind of thing the fascist dictators do very well." "The Spanish people did not ask for war," we are told in *Return to Life,* "their land was invaded"; and the three prefatory titles to the film make this analysis explicit:

> After centuries of tyranny, in February 1936, the people of Spain created a democracy. But within the army General Franco organized treason, and in July 1936, began an insurrection.

> Hitler and Mussolini came to the aid of the Spanish rebels. They sent commanding officers, regular troops, and overwhelming supplies of armaments. So treason became civil war and civil war became invasion.

> . . It is more than two years—and the Republic of Spain still blocks the road of the fascist invaders.[56]

The Western democracies, it is implied, have been pusillanimous in failing to counter this fascist aggression. There is no explicit mention of the embargo and the nations enforcing it, but the commentary in *Return to Life* states that when Spain appealed for aid, "the governments were deaf"; and most crucially, Spain "was denied the right to buy arms, denied the right to self-defense." A convalescent soldier is reported as saying: "If only we had more tanks, planes— American planes, that's what we need."

References to divisions within the Spanish population are very limited and guarded. The only Spaniards referred to as being aligned with the enemy are the landlords and generals *(Heart of Spain)* and the aristocrats *(Return to Life)*; those supporting the Republican cause are repeatedly alluded to as, simply, "the people."

The films' demarcation of the opposing sides inscribes fascism as a nonhuman, mechanical force associated with aircraft, bombs, armaments, and the metals used in their manufacture; we are never shown the faces of enemy soldiers, nor do we learn anything of them other than the fact they are foreigners or troops "that Franco was able to buy." There is nothing in either the Frontier productions approaching the characterization, in *The Spanish Earth,* of the opposing soldiers, described over a shot of University City outside Madrid:

> Living in the cellars of that ruined building are the enemy. They are Moors and Civil Guards. Brave troops, or they would not have held out.... But they are professional soldiers, fighting against a people in arms. Trying to impose the will of the military on the will of the people. And the people hate them, for without their tenacity, and the constant aid of Italy and Germany, the Spanish revolt would have ended six weeks after it began.

The opposition in *Heart of Spain* and *Return to Life* is more rigidly defined as one of people against machines, flesh against steel.

Thus care is taken to strip the Republican soldiers—who were not, in fact, regular soldiers like Franco's—of conventional militaristic associations. They constitute an army "sprung out of the people...peasants' sons, young men from the university, workers from the machine shops." There are close ties between the army and the peasantry: we see "the sons of...peasants on leave from the trenches for a week come to help with the harvest." The defenders of Madrid are drawn from the ranks of the workers and petty bourgeoisie, a cross-section of ordinary citizens: "carpenters, storekeepers, bakers, machinists, bootmakers...." The composite character of the Republican forces denotes a spirit of proletarian internationalism: there are "Spanish and Slavic peasants," "Spanish and Polish miners," etc. These troops are ideologically motivated, fighting "that freedom may not perish from the earth"; they are unassuming and courageous, making "a joke of their bravery, claiming they joined the army to get a cup of chocolate."

This verbal portrait of a unified, democratic people in arms against a treasonable elite and foreign fascist invaders, abandoned to its fate by governments which should have been sympathetic, but supported by freedom-loving private citizens of many nations, is buttressed by imagery and music. Visuals acting as concrete illustrations of generalized concepts voiced on the soundtrack are of course the chief prop for the ideological structure of the films, but there are also elements which function partly or fully independently of political themes articulated in words.

Both *Heart of Spain* and *Return to Life,* for example, resort, as Nykino's

Sunnyside had done in its denunciation of mortgage foreclosures, to iconography of children at play, to connote an original state of harmony and innocence soon to be shattered by the forces of evil. In *Heart of Spain* a soldier turns a skipping rope, and various shots depict boys and girls absorbed in the game, one laughing, another making an effort to smile. Intercut are shots of planes overhead, and then the bombing begins. After the raid, children are disinterred from the rubble. In *Return to Life,* children appear in the opening sequence, again skipping rope, and there are boys digging in the street. The narration is close to *Sunnyside*'s opening words, evoking an idyllic mood associated with bright sun, trees, and children's games: "A day in April, about ten in the morning. Sunlight, the scent of green leaves. . . . " In this case the mood is ruptured by a shift to imagery of barricades, empty streets, and then ruins, while the narration continues, "This is Europe, this is the Republic of Spain, a city where people live and work, where steel may drop from the sky."

Children recur in *Return to Life*'s fiesta sequence, where they bolster the film's celebration of indigenous Spanish culture in their folk dancing and songs, which follow hard upon the male peasants' performance of the Aguachadilla, "a dance a thousand years old that began when they were serfs in the middle ages, when they bowed to the lords and were bought and sold with the land." The sequence typifies the People's Front policy of preserving rather than transcending the class-bound culture of the past, and was singled out for its symbolic reverberations by some critics at the time of the film's release, as the following quotation (from the *New York World-Telegram*) indicates:

> One of the sequences of the film will show a performance of the Aguachadilla, a dance a thousand years old. This dance, like many dances derived from primitive, tribal times—as exemplified by the dances of American Indians—is traditionally participated in only by men and has a symbolical and ceremonial character.
>
> *Return to Life* is the pictorial record of the slow recovery from their wounds of soldiers in the Spanish war, and the Aguachadilla is introduced in a sequence showing a village fiesta participated in by some who are almost well again. While the dance has almost always been performed in Spanish villages by men in rough peasants' clothes, it is here performed by men in military uniforms and there is as much significance as one chooses to find in the fact that this age-old dance is acted out by men whose bodies only recently have been torn by the most modern instruments of warfare.[57]

Heart of Spain has no comparable sequence, but the film's use of Spanish musical themes to a certain extent fulfills the same function, and was also noted by contemporary reviewers. Elizabeth Noble, for example, wrote:

> For the hospital, two guitars playing a sad and gentle Spanish folk air. At the end, renewal, new life: a soldier handing another a cigarette, a nurse smiling, an elderly woman coming to see the wounded soldier to whom her donated blood had been given, and over all a woman's throaty voice singing a heroic fandaguilla. By such an apparently simple device, the film builds to a resolution of hope and invincible courage.[58]

In both films, the incorporation of Spanish dancing and music represents a recuperation of popular national traditions and their reassertion in a political context.

Determined as it was by the nature of the sponsoring body, the concentration in each film on themes of medical care, healing, and recovery was straightforward and predictable, but it also held metaphorical significance in a wider, ideological context. Particularly, it reinforced the argument that the civil war, for the Loyalists, was a defensive struggle for survival against heavily armed aggressors. The producers at Frontier may well have calculated that in such a humanitarian emphasis lay their best hope of reaching an American audience then still strongly pacifist and isolationist in its sympathies.[59]

It is unsurprising that this focusing on medical care also carried with it the subtle implication that it was the fascists who were responsible for all the wounding and destruction, the Republicans who were concerned with healing and rebuilding. In propaganda committed to the Republican cause, such a slanting was perhaps inevitable. It was also one more factor contributing to the extremely schematic (and thereby misleading) presentation of the conflict in the two films, which resulted chiefly from the significant elisions made in the analysis of the situation.

Heart of Spain and *Return to Life* obscured the fact that it was in essence a *civil* war which was being fought in Spain, by omission of the historical background to the hostilities, and of any serious class analysis of the line-up of Nationalist and Republican supporters. In particular, the films' understandable reluctance to mention attacks by peasants and workers on the Church blocked any disclosure of the highly important religious dimension to the conflict.[60] By neglecting to allude to the supplies of arms which the Republic received from the U.S.S.R. (and, to a lesser extent, from France and Mexico), while laying heavy emphasis on the role of Germany and Italy, *Heart of Spain* and *Return to Life* confused the aspects of international intervention. Moreover, in their anxiety to establish the pure democratic legitimacy of the Republican government, the films chose to ignore the revolutionary situation which existed in many parts of Spain prior to, and during the war (paradoxically, the word "revolutionary," which had been bandied about freely on the Left during the nonrevolutionary early years of the decade, was now taboo). Similarly, there was no acknowledgment that the Loyalist forces were predominantly led by Socialists, Communists, and Anarchists—or that there was fierce internecine feuding in the ranks, and in the regional and national administrations. Finally, the two Frontier productions suppressed the role which the Communist International and its affiliated parties were playing in the dispute, a point which deserves to be considered in greater detail.

In a sense, of course, the omission of party identifications in a Communist-promoted production can be interpreted as a gesture of goodwill towards allies in the anti-fascist struggle. (It was for flaunting the exploits of its anarchist fighters the *Fury Over Spain* was criticized.) Yet systematic elision of any reference to the Communist presence in a situation—such as the organization of civilian and military resistance in Republican Spain—where it is of cardinal significance, can only be mystificatory. It is not stipulated, for example, that the International Brigades were entirely created and led by Communists—and that without the organization which the Comintern was able to provide the participation of international volunteers in the conflict would have been negligible. Again, a military leader like Enrique Lister is presented, described as "formerly a stone mason in Galicia"—without reference to the fact that, as a Communist, he had studied at the Frunze military school in the Soviet Union. (Lister also appears in *The Spanish Earth*, where it is stated that "in six months of fighting he rose from a simple soldier to the command of a division," again without mention of his Communist affiliations.)[61] Such omissions give a vague and inaccurate impression of things happening spontaneously which in fact were highly organized to calculated effect. In general, the fact that the word "Communist" is not used in either of the two films (along with the words "Anarchist," "Socialist," "Trotskyist," or the names of the political parties) makes them of extremely limited value as documents of the *political* struggle being waged in Spain.

The fear of redbaiting was no doubt a potent factor in the suppression of explicit Communist identifications. Ivens notes of the commentary to *The Spanish Earth* that, "to forestall any of the expected accusations of purveying red propaganda, Hemingway had to be careful not to use any tendentious material." According to Ben Maddow, there were various reasons for withholding Communist references:

> One was a feeling that the films were intended for a wider audience, and therefore to say "Communist party" immediately prejudiced the audience, because being a Communist was a rather risky thing, and it had been for a long, long time. If you go back to 1877 and read the accounts of the railroad strikes you'd think it was all the doing of the Commune, direct from Paris! The second was the fact that Earl Browder, head of the American Communist Party at the time, was really a Popular Frontist, and his slogan was "Communism is Twentieth Century Americanism." Well, if you just turn that around you don't have to mention Communism, you just say Americanism, and you've said it. I think that attitude really made possible Frontier Films, for example, because otherwise what would be the point of doing this kind of films? You wanted to bring in the middle classes, and so on. And the other thing you have to realize is the history of the trade-union movement in this country. It was very strongly anti-communist. It may have been left, but it was anti-communist, all the way along. So we didn't want to spoil that connection either.[62]

Overall, *Heart of Spain* and *Return to Life* steered clear of any material which could prove at all controversial. Kline notes that "at that time we weren't going into the divisions between the political groups because they were cooperating with each other—the Socialists, the Communists, the fellow travelers, the in-between parties, even the ultraliberal Republicans were cooperating, and since we were trying to make a statement against a whole world of hostility in the newspapers, on the radio, among the governments which were against Loyalist Spain, including the American government refusing to send arms to the duly elected government of the Republic of Spain in violation of our international obligations, I suppose it's only human that we erred on the side of positive statements." And he argues in retrospect that if they had had the extra film and money needed to shoot some of the ideas they had on paper, they would have incorporated in *Heart of Spain* some critical thinking—such as that which emerged in an article Kline wrote for the *New York Times* based on an interview with the playwright Jacinto Benavente y Martínez.

> His interview, while it wasn't Fascist, was certainly not as sympathetic to the Republic as our more strident statement of my feeling, of Geza's feeling, of Strand's feeling, of Hurwitz's feeling. In retrospect I could agree it was necessary, like Hemingway in his novel on Spain, *For Whom the Bell Tolls,* to refer to early excesses on both sides, as in our own country's Civil War. I think the picture would have been better if it had shown that there were some differences of opinion, showing the reality of conflicts on our side too. But at that time Spain was fighting for its life, Franco had his bayonets, bombs, and bullets at the jugular of Spanish democracy, and frankly we weren't too broadminded. We wanted to say something that would help raise money for ambulances and medical aid to Spain—and the funds we raised saved many lives. I think it would have done so, however, somewhat better, if there had been some human differences expressed. Nobody is ever 100% right. I happen to think we were 95% right, and that the history of fascism rising to great power followed our defeat in Spain.[63]

Maddow suggests that the filmmakers were both unaware of some of the complexities of the struggle in Spain, and unwilling to credit any interpretation which differed with their own, especially one which might accord the Republicans a less than fully heroic stature:

> "Didn't the Spanish Republicans murder quite a number of people?" No one would ever ask such a question. We had no Hugh Thomas, you know. We would have driven him out with whips.[64]

For the moment, the Spanish people on the Loyalist side *were* fighting grimly for survival, and if, in the Frontier gestures of support, there was no room for some of the niceties of political analysis, that was a sacrifice which Kline and Cartier-Bresson, Strand and Hurwitz and Maddow were no doubt willing to make.

7

China Strikes Back

I was in Yenan-Fu, the capital of Soviet China, in 1937, just after the Communists had achieved their first great victory, the end of all civil war, the unity of 400 million people.

—Harry Dunham, 1938[1]

In terms of relative political importance the development of the national contradiction between China and Japan has demoted the domestic contradictions between classes and between political groupings to a secondary and subordinate place. But they still exist and have by no means diminished or disappeared.

—Mao Tse-tung, 1937[2]

China Strikes Back was made at a crucial moment in Chinese history. In 1936 the Red Army under the command of Mao Tse-tung and Chu Teh was reunited after the Long March in Shensi province, in the northwest, and a strong guerilla base established. A capital of the Liberated Areas was set up, first at Pao-an, and then, from January 1, 1937, at Yenan. In December 1936, in the Sian Incident, Chiang Kai-shek was kidnapped by the pro-Communist Marshal Chang Hsueh-liang and held until he agreed to a Kuomintang-Communist united front against the Japanese. The civil war was halted, and during 1937 moves toward unification proceeded: the Chinese Soviet territory became the Special Administrative District, and in September the Red Army in Shensi was reorganized as the Eighth Route Army and integrated into the national defense forces. Japan resumed its invasion of China in July 1937, and in November-December overran key cities including Shanghai and Nanking.

Harry Dunham secured his "several hundred feet of film" of the Communists in Shensi in late 1936 and/or early 1937. According to a report in the *Daily Worker* at the time of the picture's release,

> *China Strikes Back* traces its origins back to a day in Paris last winter when Harry Dunham, adventurous young cameraman, arrived in France. The first paper he picked up told him that big news was about to break in China. Unity between Chinese Communists and the Nanking government seemed on the way.

Dunham had thought of going into Spain for pictures, but the news from the Orient set him off on a new goal. He had given himself one of the most difficult photographic assignments in the world. He was going to photograph China's famous Red Army.

Variously described as a ballet dancer, musician, editor, still photographer (he had had pictures published in *Life* magazine), as well as an amateur cameraman, Dunham achieved his scoop, becoming the first filmmaker to penetrate to the remote Shensi region, then blockaded by Chiang's troops, and obtain detailed coverage of the Communist forces. (The author Edgar Snow had previously taken some shots of Pao-an on 16mm which he used to illustrate his lectures in the United States.) Until this time, even still photographs of the Red Army had been rare: reportedly "the first photographs of rank and file Chinese Red Army men and of all the liberation forces in China ever to be published in America" appeared in the September 1936 issue of the magazine *China Today*, and it will be recalled that the Film and Photo League's compilation documentary, *The Birth of New China*, completed a few months earlier, had had to resort to charts and diagrams to illustrate life in the Chinese Soviet areas.[3]

Dunham returned to the U.S. in May 1937 (smuggling his film out, it was rumored, in Chinese ginger jars), and the footage was turned over to Frontier for editing. Jay Leyda, Irving Lerner, Ben Maddow, and Sidney Meyers worked on this project during the summer, at about the same time as Strand and Hurwitz were editing *Heart of Spain*. Dunham's material was augmented with newsreel and stock footage to document the course of Japanese aggression since 1931 and the oppression of the Chinese people under the occupation, and Willard Van Dyke shot some scenes for an introductory montage. It became a problem keeping pace with the swift turn of events in China:

> *China Strikes Back* was four months in preparation. In that time, the Chinese situation altered to such an extent that Frontier had to change the scenario several times in order to keep up with events. They had to add scenes, drop others, change the spoken commentary. The tempo of living history even forced them to modify the original conception of the film.... It was going to be a film about Chinese unity. It still is a film about Chinese unity. But since the beginning of research in July and the completion of the film early this month [October], there has been an important change in the treatment of the material.

As a result of the unification finally concluded in the face of the Japanese invasion,

> the producers had to make a happy change in the theme of *China Strikes Back*. It was no longer a film showing the Chinese people moving towards unity. It became a pictorial history revealing the how and why behind a realized unity.[4]

A musical score was arranged by Alex North (a Chinese "folk song" which was featured later turned out to be the theme from *Song of the Fishermen*, a movie produced in Shanghai in 1934).[5] With a narration written by Maddow and spoken by John O'Shaughnessy, the 23-minute documentary was released through Garrison in October 1937.

Probably because of its novelty and topicality, *China Strikes Back* met with an unexpectedly strong public response. "That film started in Brooklyn as a small, secondary film to a feature in a neighborhood house," Paul Strand recalled: "It grew from then so quickly that *China Strikes Back* got the big headline on the marquee very quickly, and it ran in some eighty-odd theatres." A program note from the Museum of Modern Art, where the film was shown some two years later, confirms its popularity:

> *China Strikes Back* was successful with audiences. It was the first documentary to fight its way into the ordinary commercial theatres purely on its merits as an interpretation of the news. On the strength of this appeal alone, it was featured on the marquees of many theatres above the fiction film which it accompanied. It has had wide nontheatrical distribution also, being principally sponsored by organizations supporting the cause of China.[6]

Leyda writes that "its unique material and the adventure of its cameraman gained it more circulation and attention than any other film we made." *China Strikes Back* achieved some foreign showings—in Britain, for example, it was released by the radical 16mm distributor Kino following a Left Book Club selection of Snow's *Red Star Over China*. It also had an impact in Moscow, where it was influential in informing a public hitherto very ignorant of Communist developments in China, and in persuading newsreel cameraman Roman Karmen, on his return from Spain, to go to Shensi himself.[7]

There is no record of of censorship difficulties encountered by *China Strikes Back* in the United States, but in British Columbia, in February 1938, it was banned (3,000 people reportedly waited in vain for a screening arranged by the League for Peace and Democracy in Vancouver).[8]

As had been the case with *Heart of Spain,* the major task facing the Frontier filmmakers as propagandists was to confront the isolationist spirit of the American public. In a poll taken on August 2, 1937, shortly after the renewal of Japanese attacks, 55% of respondents answered "No" to the question, "In the present fight between Japan and China, are your sympathies on either side?"; and two months later, when Japan's brutal aggression had become increasingly apparent, 40% of those polled were still neutral. It is true that those who favored one side or the other were overwhelmingly supportive of China (43% to 2%, and 59% to 1%, in the two polls); but that this was a measure of sympathy only, and did not imply a readiness to become even minimally involved in the conflict, was indicated by a follow-up question which was asked of supporters of China in the October poll. To the query, "Is your sympathy for China great enough to keep you from buying goods made in Japan?", 63% of respondents replied "No."[9]

The American government sought to steer a middle path. Although President Roosevelt did not apply the neutrality laws, he declared on September 14 that government vessels would not transport munitions to either belligerent; and in a statement by Secretary of State Cordell Hull offering American assistance in conciliation, there was no suggestion at all that any concerted pressure would be applied upon Japan to dissuade it from further incursions into Chinese territory. A two-to-one majority in Congress—fearful of foreign entanglement but also mindful of the profitability of Japanese trade, particularly in scrap iron and oil—was opposed to sanctions in any form. At an ineffectual international conference on the war held in Brussels in November 1937, attended by the United States, the only nation to advocate stringent measures against Japan was the Soviet Union.[10]

The Communist press strongly urged the adoption by the United States of a policy of collective action against the aggressor. If the Kellogg Peace Pact and the Nine Power Naval Treaty, which Japan had violated, were to be collectively enforced by the U.S., the Soviet Union, Britain, and France, it was argued, China's territorial integrity would be safeguarded. How this would be achieved without involving the country in war was not specified, and the U.S., like Britain, was concerned at this time to avoid any possible military entanglement.[11]

If *China Strikes Back* could not hope to make a dent in the rigidly noninterventionist line of the Roosevelt administration, it could at least aim to counteract the distorted images of China's Communists which had been purveyed, for a number of years, by Hollywood. Against a variegated tapestry of sinister war lords (*The Bitter Tea of General Yen,* 1933), stalwart peasants (*The Good Earth,* 1937), devious opium smugglers (*Charlie Chan in Shanghai,* 1935), wealthy but tragic Eurasians (*Shanghai,* 1935), and panicking refugees (*Lost Horizon,* 1937), the revolutionaries were depicted, in the studio movies, as the catalysts of China's chaos. Rebel leader Warner Oland in *Shanghai Express* (1932)—greasy, lecherous, sadistic—was a portent of things to come. In *Shanghai Madness* (1933), Communists misguidedly murder two U.S. sailors and then attack a mission where heroine Fay Wray has been set ashore; cashiered lieutenant Spencer Tracy is fortunately on hand to go to the rescue. There is a similar imperialist coloring to *Oil For the Lamps of China* (1935, loyal employee saves oil company from pillaging Communists), *The Leathernecks Have Landed* (1936, "demonstrates graphically how really devastating a mere handful of marines can be when American lives and property are to be protected from Chinese insurgents"), and *West of Shanghai* (also released as *War Lord* and *Cornered,* 1937, rival American oil men seek field in the heart of territory ruled by rebel general Boris Karloff).[12]

The line between bandit and revolutionary in these movies—as it was in Chiang Kai-shek's rhetoric—was thin to nonexistent. Irving Lerner (then of the Film and Photo League) wrote of *Shanghai Madness* that it was "the first

American motion picture actually calling 'those dirty yellow bandits' Communists," and remarked:

> In fact the words "Communist" and "Soviet" are heard from the screen about a dozen times. The plot of this film is no different from that of *Shanghai Express, The Roar of the Dragon,* etc. The Red Chinese leaders are Harvard graduates and wear Russian caps, Russian blouses, and even long Russian beards! The followers are dirty, wild looking, unorganized mobs of coolies. Our American (Spencer Tracy) hero wins a medal from the U.S. Navy and the daughter of an American captain for wiping out a Soviet fortress, with a three-inch cannon.

Likewise, a reviewer commented on *The Leathernecks Have Landed:* "There seems to have been an honest doubt in the minds of those responsible for the picture over whether the forces of General Chang should be called bandits or rebels, but, under either label, the leathernecks disposed of a lot of them in the process of protecting an oil company and a mining company in the interior of China."[13]

Particularly interesting, for its direct opposing of American capitalist to Chinese Communist, was *Oil For the Lamps of China.* Andre Sennwald wrote in the *New York Times:*

> The photoplay tries to be a glowing tribute to the Atlantis Oil Company and its high-minded crusade to bring light to the Chinese barbarians.... It presents the Chinese Communist movement not as the struggle of a tragic people to find a path out of their degradation, but as a vulturous gangsterism preying on organizations like the Atlantis Oil Company, which stand for honor and decency in their relations with China's masses. Far from hinting that China may be a little less than enthusiastic about being exploited by foreign countries and bending the neck to war lords of the counterrevolution, the photoplay affirms that China looks upon American commercial intercession with eagerness and hope.

New Theatre magazine charged that last-minute doctoring of the film to whitewash the image of the corporation had been done at the behest of William Randolph Hearst, whose Cosmopolitan unit at Warner Brothers was responsible for the production.[14]

The one Hollywood movie in which Chinese rebels appeared in a favorable light was *The General Died at Dawn* (1936), written by Nykino ally, and later Frontier Films associate Clifford Odets. This film, however, succeeded only in offering a benign variation on the imperialist motif, omitting reference to Communists (and, of course, the Kuomintang dictatorship), and presenting Gary Cooper as an American with a firm belief in democracy and a hearty dislike of oppression assisting the suffering Chinese to rid themselves of rapacious war lord Akim Tamiroff.

U.S. newsreel reporting on the Chinese situation tended to ignore the civil war, while offering powerful visual evidence of Japanese aggression, as in the famous coverage of the bombing of Shanghai in 1932, and again in 1937.

Reviewing Universal's newsreel *Bombing of Shanghai* in the *Daily Worker* in September 1937, David Platt acknowledged the value of the grisly footage in cementing anti-Japanese sentiment, while objecting to the isolationist stance which was adopted. The film said "not a word about the guilt of the Japanese fascists.... All the commentators have to offer are misleading tidbits like... America must stay as far away from the Far East as possible." Platt noted that "this erroneous isolationist policy is also expressed in the film by General Smedley Butler."[15]

On the other hand, a pacifist organization thought that an issue of *The March of Time* for September 1937 veered towards an interventionist line—in support of American business interests:

> Most of the footage in [*The March of Time*] Vol. 4, No. 1, is given over the the Far Eastern War. It is treated from the angle of how Chiang Kai-shek's program of industrialization and Chinese independence is endangered by the Japanese invasion. The commercial interests of the United States, Great Britain, and other foreign governments are emphasized. The significance of the struggle in the U.S., and the years and dollars spent in development of private enterprise in China are loudly stressed. Secretary Roper speaks in behalf of American business, followed by Senator Bennett Champ Clark's plea against our involvement for any reasons or under any circumstances.
>
> Obviously the film is calculated to build up anti-Japanese sentiment and to encourage Americans to insist upon their "rights" in China.[16]

Alternative, left-wing film versions of the struggles in China were, prior to 1937, very rare. Soviet interest had subsided following the crushing of the Communist movement in the cities in 1927, Yakov Blyokh's *Shanghai Document* (released in 1928) and Ilya Trauberg's fictional *Blue Express* (or *China Express,* 1929) being the last major Russian films to deal with the Chinese situation. The only immediate predecessor of *China Strikes Back* was the Film and Photo League's compilation *The Birth of New China* (1936), which was hampered by a paucity of relevant footage and achieved only very limited distribution.

A significant documentary was, however, released almost simultaneously with *China Strikes Back*. Photographed by Eric Berns and with a commentary by Jack Foster, *This Is China* was a record of a "12,000 mile film expedition across China" which (although stigmatized in the *New Masses* as a "travelogue masquerading as documentary") stressed China's unity against Japanese aggression and incorporated images and editing strategies comparable to those of the Frontier production. Thus, "in the streets of Peiping, the ancient capital of China, the camera caught Japanese soldiers seizing a young Chinese, binding him to a post, and whipping him while his Chinese friends stood powerless to help him." A *Daily Worker* review described the content of the film:

The opening shots show the life of the Chinese peasants of Mongolia. They stress the peacefulness of the existence of these hard working people, poverty-stricken to the extreme, yet carrying on their work in tranquillity.

Then, boom! Japanese guns. The piecing together of these contrasting scenes is splendid; Japanese aggression stands out in bold relief.

The scene shifts to the cities. Men carry wooden cases twice their size on their backs; others push heavily laden carts, straining every muscle as they turn the heavy spokes of the wheels by hand. . . . There are many other scenes which show the misery of the Chinese people; there are others which show their new-born strength, source of their unified resistance to the invader.

And there are scenes of destruction. One town is shown pursuing its daily schedule, and then, blown to bits, while men pick charred remains of humans from the debris. [17]

China Strikes Back was to spark a renewal of interest in the subject among radical filmmakers in both the United States and the Soviet Union. Garrison Films backed the production of a documentary short, *Stop Japan* (originally titled *Death Follows the Rising Sun*), which was released in early 1938 and was described as "recording the rise of the anti-Japanese boycott movement in the U.S. and sketching the historical background of Japanese aggression in China." [18] Joris Ivens, sponsored by essentially the same group that had underwritten the production of *The Spanish Earth,* went to China in 1938 to film *The 400 Million,* and Roman Karmen obtained extensive coverage of guerilla fighting and life in Yenan in 1938-39. (Karmen's news report were shown in the U.S.S.R. in a series entitled *China in Battle*—a selection from which was exhibited as the documentary *China Fights On* in New York in August 1939— and they were later compiled into the feature-length film *In China,* released in 1941.)

China Strikes Back has a six-part structure. It opens with a prelude conveying the interest of the American public in the Sino-Japanese conflict via the excited attention of the mass media: the war is a hot news item. The second section fills in the background to the current fighting, outlining the history of Japanese aggression in the East since 1931. Harry Dunham's footage is introduced in section three, which depicts the life of revolutionary soldiers, students, and peasants in Shensi. A song sung by soldiers forms the pretext for the fourth part, a montage illustrating the oppression of the Chinese people resulting from the Japanese invasion. Further coverage of Shensi activities, including troop maneuvers and mass meetings addressed by Chu Teh and Mao Tse-tung, follows in the next section; and the final part shows, by means of montage, a united China gearing up for concerted military defense.

The opening sequence is a curious experiment in rapid-fire montage of the variety practiced by Slavko Vorkapich in Hollywood. According to Willard Van Dyke, who planned the sequence in collaboration with Sidney Meyers, and who did the shooting, the idea was to give "the impression of a newsreel, the introduction to a newsreel, a kind of *March of Time* opening." The shots are edited as follows:

Radio being switched on (DOLLY IN) / announcer and microphone / Times Square lighted news bulletin (DIAGONAL COMPOSITION): it reads, "200 DEATHS WERE.... " / announcer / Times Square bulletin: "THE SEVEN HOUR BOMBING OF NANKING.... " / newsreel theatre, advertising "complete new show today—new Chinese bombings" (DIAGONAL COMPOSITION) / newspapers flop down onto conveyor belt / hands grasp newspaper bundle / headline: "JAPS MOBILIZE FOR CHINA WAR" / headline: "CHINA RESISTS JAP DEMANDS" / headline: "JAPAN CALLS WAR COUNCIL" / headline: "INVADERS BOMB SHANGHAI" / headline: "THREAT TO BOMB ALL OF CHINA" / Times Square bulletin: "... FOR THE U.S. GOVERNMENT CHARGING JAPAN WITH 'WILLFUL SLAUGHTER OF NONCOMBATANTS.' "[19]

Accompanying the images are the voices of radio announcers. The first, after an irrelevant teaser ("... is five feet six inches in height and weighs 103 pounds"), reports the incident of July 1937 which marked the reopening of Sino-Japanese hostilities:

Tokyo. Japanese sources charged that their troops near Peking were fired on near the Marco Polo bridge and replied with machine-gun fire. The Japanese foreign minister stated that his government expected an early adjustment of this difficulty. He attributed this incident to lack of discipline among the Chinese garrison, and Japan will ask fullest apologies for....

The second brings news of a more recent development:

We interrupt this program to bring you a last-minute flash. One hour ago the Japanese dreadnought Estilvo [?] and five destroyers which were anchored in the Whangpoo River opened fire on the native quarter of Shanghai. Aid is being directed from the International Settlement. It is feared that casualties will run to the hundreds.

The voice becomes overlaid with other sounds, such as the tapping of a Morse key; and the track then dissolves into an indistinguishable melange of high-keyed news reports, developing to a pitch of frenzied excitement.

The sequence is curious because it tends to assimilate *China Strikes Back* to a mode of journalism—superficial, nervous, sensational—that it elsewhere repudiates. The *March of Time* model had, of course, exerted a powerful influence over the Frontier filmmakers during the Nykino period; but it was of waning importance now that the group was concentrating on longer, reflective documentaries in which immediate news value was of subordinate significance. The montage may certainly be understood as stating, in effect, "Here are the headlines," and implying, "the film will take you behind the headlines"; yet the apolitical presentation, the subject matter (U.S. media), and the pace and tone so much at variance with the remainder of the picture mean that the sequence fits uneasily into the total structure.

The second section consists of newsreel compilation, in which the principles of juxtapositional cutting are used sparingly, but to telling effect. The pattern is set in the opening few shots. China: we see corpses strewn on the street. There is a direct cut to Japan: the army on parade, and the Emperor on horseback, resplendent, at the head of his troops. Even the disparities in photographic quality contribute to the impact, the Japanese footage having a glossy sheen absent from the rough-looking Chinese material. The narration commences: "A nation of islands is too small for the Emperor of Japan . . . . "

The sequence goes on to chronicle the fall of Manchuria, the bombing of Shanghai, and the loss of Jehol, Chahar, and Hopei to the invader. Shots of Chinese and Japanese continue to be intercut: Chinese civilians under attack, fleeing explosions and burning buildings, carrying their wounded, becoming refugees—or lying dead in the street; Japanese troops on the march, running through villages, advancing in armored cars, parading, searching pedestrians, engaging in ground fighting—"advancing over the bodies of a weak and divided China."

Graphics show the extent of the Japanese incursion: on a map of China the conquered provinces go black, and then a map of the United States is superimposed for comparison. The narrator explains: "China was paying the price of her disunity. . . . Politically and economically it meant the death of China, as if the Atlantic seaboard of the United States had been conquered by foreign troops. As if the iron and coal of Pennsylvania, the timber of Maine and the Carolinas, the mills of New York and New England had been torn away and their millions of men and women placed in subjection."

The final part of the film's second section is a brief series of images—a worker, a political speaker, military planes—to illustrate the thesis that "At last the patriotism of the Chinese people began to unify them under Chiang Kai-shek" and "China began to form around itself the armor of modern industry."

Harmony rather than conflict is the defining characteristic of the third section of *China Strikes Back*. Dunham's footage depicts a variety of activities in the guerilla stronghold of Shensi province, all of them flowing easily one into another. A detachment of Red Army troops makes its way through a rocky valley; soldiers assemble for a class at the Anti-Japanese University; cavalrymen train their horses in guerilla tactics; students play basketball; nurses at the university treat peasants. The narration stresses the impregnability of these districts ("They are safe against guns; planes crack up against the stone edges of their mountains"), and the social changes that have been wrought ("The people of this region have a popular government, many newspapers, factories, printing presses, and a university . . . The health of every peasant is a direct concern of the government").

In the midst of this section is a title introducing the Communist leaders—though they are not described as such. "Mao Tse-tung," it reads, "president of the Special Administrative District, and Chu Teh, commander-in-chief of the army, inspect the work of the university." There follow several shots of Mao and Chu at a table, receiving a report. The atmosphere is informal, unceremonial, reinforcing the image of Mao and Chu at this phase of their careers created by journalists such as Edgar Snow and Agnes Smedley—or Harry Dunham himself, who in an article the following year described the two men attending a theatre performance as if they were simply two ordinary members of the audience:

> The house, filled with soldiers who are now members of the Eighth Route Army, applauded and cheered. Mao Tse-tung and Chu Teh, in the row ahead of me, applauded and smiled.[20]

In the film, the commentary further defines the response we are to have toward the "president" (Mao's power, of course, derived from his—unspoken—position as chairman of the Chinese Communist Party) and the commander-in-chief:

> Mao Tse-tung, on the left, quiet, resolute, modest, a man whose political insight is respected in the capitals of Europe and Asia. Chu Teh, hero of a thousand escapes. In the songs of China his name has become a legend.

Scenes from life in the liberated areas then continue: a patrol of soldiers in rugged terrain; the painting of slogans by the roadside urging peasants to stiffen their resistance to Japan; classroom instruction of recruits; and finally, soldiers enjoying peasant hospitality in a local village, smoking, eating, playing games, borrowing straw to make a bed for the night, and then gathering round to sing.

The images which follow, constituting the fourth section of the film, accompany the "Song of the Chinese Soldier" which is heard on the soundtrack. The music is actually the theme composed by Jen Kuang for Tsai Chu-sheng's *Song of the Fishermen,* and if it was not exactly a folk song at the time *China Strikes Back* was made, it has since, Jay Leyda informs us, virtually acquired that status.[21] English words are spoken on the soundtrack as if in translation of the Chinese (the poem was in fact an original creation of Maddow, who was not working from a pre-existing text):

> Brothers, it is midsummer, the hours are still warm,
> and the fields are gathered in the North.
> I remember our life, the shining grain in the sunlight,
> the dogs in our village quarreling far off.
> The dogs are silent, greedy and fat in the ruins.
>
> The village is dead in the summer sunlight.
> The crop is gathered in the black barns. The crop of ashes.
> The fruits of death lie on the endless road.
>
> We have no homes. The Japanese stand on Manchuria.
> The men without mouths, that speak out of guns.
> Where their voice is heard there are many
> peasants already dead.

With words and tears we assailed the enemy,
the Japanese, the locusts with human faces.
Brothers, the wind as we fled was bitter with smoke.
Scattered are the families, the children without care.
The homeless people scattered like leaves,
the children like dead leaves on the freezing stream.

I have heard that many are locked in the Japanese mills.
Where are you, O younger sister? Where are you?
The families walk in slavery,
toiling till moonlight for a cup of rice.
Hunger moves them, hunger makes them weak.

Stand up brothers, do not stoop!
As you bend, the Japanese climb on your back.
Stand up, look, a lion roars in the sky.
It is me, flying.
Look up, I am armed, my hands are friends to the rifle.
Look up, brothers and sisters, I am coming with planes to defend you.

The lines provide cues for a diverse selection of imagery, illustrating three stages of the Japanese invasion. At first, there are shots evoking a happy life prior to the attack: expanses of grain, and close-ups of it waving in the sun; peasants drawing water for cattle, and at work in the fields. Secondly, the invasion itself is pictured: Japanese troops advancing, explosions, burning buildings, refugees, soldiers (presumably Japanese) marching down the Great Wall, young Chinese children with babies strapped to their backs, shells exploding in open country, Chinese traveling by punt down a river (this series of images forms a reprise to the second section of the film.). The third part is devoted to life under the occupation, and shows oppressed Chinese working as dishwashers, threshing rice, racing with a rickshaw, hauling a cart, drawing a barge—bent over with toil; and interspersed are shots of figures praying. The sequence concludes with a dissolve back to the singing Red Army soldiers in a Shensi village, and a fade-out.

In the fifth section of *China Strikes Back,* Dunham's material is returned to. The morning routine in the village at which the soldiers have spent the night is documented in some detail: the men getting up to the bugler's call, washing, cleaning their teeth, eating breakfast, and then sweeping, returning their straw, paying for a broken plate. The next sequence shows the troops at maneuvers in the rough mountain country of the province, rehearsing an attack on an imaginary Japanese position. The squads are highly mobile foot soldiers, armed only with rifles and machine guns. The section concludes with footage introduced by a title, "At mass meetings throughout the countryside, the citizens assemble to take part in a momentous decision." Groups of civilians and military detachments wind through the valleys in long columns, pennants aloft, and gather at large assemblies. Among the speakers we see addressing the crowds are a female student from Shanghai, Chu Teh, and Mao Tse-tung. The narration over this fifth section describes in matter-of-fact fashion the Red Army activities, paying particular attention to the close relationship fostered between soldier and peasant, and waxes more poetic toward the end:

> The 400 million of China beginning to move. The single idea, the idea of a nation, of China as a country with one twisting boundary and one people. The 400 million moving with a single purpose, marching many miles, a great wall of people who are ready to defend their own fields.

The final part of the film is a montage of images triggered by references in the supposed speech of Mao Tse-tung, which continues on the soundtrack. It begins with a dissolve from the listening crowd to old newsreel footage of Sun Yat-sen making a public speech, as Mao comments that he has seen the tomb of China's first president in Nanking. The subsequent images are of crowds in the street, Chiang Kai-shek on horseback, Chinese foot troops advancing over rubble, a student speaking, a large group of women marching, a woman addressing a crowd, more speakers, soldiers on the march, cavalry, artillery, armored cars, tanks, troop trucks, military aircraft, rotating propellers, watching crowds, a plane taking off, and formations of planes in the air. The narration, ostensibly in the words of Mao, pays tribute to the courage of the men and women who resisted the Japanese in 1932, while insisting that "the methods of 1932 will save the honor of China but will not bring victory." For victory is needed weapons equal to those used by the enemy: "shells, battleships, planes that fly like a bullet, bombs that can destroy a battalion of enemies . . . rifles, machine guns, trench mortars, tanks, field guns that can shoot twenty miles"—most of all, in the final words of the film, "planes, planes!"

Structurally, *China Strikes Back* has an alternating negative-positive pattern with cumulative impact which is roughly equivalent to the "dialectical" arrangement of *Heart of Spain*. Its parts may be tabulated as follows:

Section	Subject	Geographical Level
1	Overture: War News	—
2	Defeat	National
3	Organizing Resistance (civilian emphasis)	Provincial
4	Oppression	National
5	Organizing Resistance (military emphasis)	Provincial
6	Preparing Counterattack	National

Built into this structure are a series of divisions and "contradictions." An overriding opposition of America to Asia, of observers to participants, is contained in the break between section 1 and the remainder of the film. What Mao terms the "national contradiction between China and Japan" is expressed by means of the opposed emphases of sections 3, 5, and 6 (Chinese) versus sections 2 and 4 (Japanese), and by means of contrast editing within sections 2 and 4 themselves. The domestic division between Communist and Nationalist forces is given formal recognition by cutting between Shensi province (sections 3 and 5) and other, unspecified parts of China (sections 2, 4, and 6). The division between the civilian and military population of China is reflected in a stress on the former in sections 2, 3, and 4, and on the latter in 5 and 6; this is not a rigid separation, however, since significant time is allotted to Red soldiers in section 3, peasants in section 5, and urban civilians in section 6. Finally, there is a distinction between the human and nonhuman components of a defense force, soldiers being emphasized in sections 3 and 5, and military hardware in section 6.

Each of these oppositions contains, in Hegelian-Marxist fashion, the potential of being transcended, and the film is so organized as to make this dynamic possibility the vehicle for its ideological strategy. The core of the film's message is, precisely, the attainment of unity and strength through the overcoming of divisions.

The America / Asia division is perhaps the least well worked out in terms of its political implications. Its resolution is reliant upon a metaphoric interpretation being placed upon the film's final images, and it is not easy to judge if contemporary audiences would have read the sequence in the way it was apparently intended. Specifically, the United States and China are presented in the opening montage as worlds apart; for Americans a foreign war means titillation through the mass media. The main portion of the film details the suffering and death which are the reality of the war for the Chinese. Symbolically, the concluding images of military aircraft represent a potential bridging of the gap between the United States and China by evoking the possibility and desirability of American military aid to the Chiang Kai-shek government. "The planes at the end," Leo Hurwitz recently said, "were symbolic of the need for American aid to defeat Japan."[22]

Within the prevailing political context, *China Strikes Back* certainly seems to have been designed as an appeal for direct military assistance in a way that Frontier's Spanish films were not. President Roosevelt's failure to invoke the Neutrality Act meant that shipments of arms to the Chinese were not ruled out a priori; and the *March of Time* issue described above reveals the existence of considerable business sentiment in favor of intervention in the war on the Chinese side. A further factor which may have predisposed the U.S. government towards support for China was the American presence in the International Settlement in Shanghai. At the resumption of fighting in 1937 Roosevelt had in fact sent in additional Marines to guard American nationals and property, bringing the total force in China to some 2,500 men.[23] That the film refrained from making an explicit call for U.S. assistance is probably best understood as the result of a desire not to directly affront the sensibilities of the many American individuals and organizations that in 1937 were still strongly pacifist and isolationist in orientation, even if sympathetic to the Chinese cause.

The Chinese/Japanese opposition is, of course, central to *China Strikes Back*. It is part of the propagandistic functioning of the film that the presentation is asymmetrical, more time being allotted to China than to Japan. Discussing the alternation of scenes of daily life and fascist attack in *Heart of Spain,* Leo Hurwitz argues that "positive and negative needs are created in the audience,"[24] and a similar logic operates here. In sections 2 and 4, we are shown the Chinese in defeat and subjection, the Japanese in triumph. In sections 3, 5, and 6, we see a strong, revitalized Chinese people; the Japanese are absent. The images which would be needed to complete this pattern are of the Japanese subdued; these images do not exist because, in life, the task of winning the war lies ahead. Thus the film sets up in audiences a desire for the aesthetic scheme to be fulfilled; it can be fulfilled only through action.

The possibility of a successful countermove against Japan is suggested by a discontinous yet progressive shift in the depiction of Chinese as the film proceeds. In the section chronicling the Japanese advance, they are corpses in the street, blood flowing from their heads, or harried, stumbling refugees. In the images accompanying the "Song of the Chinese Soldier," they are half-starved slave laborers. By contrast, in the Shensi sections they are shown in active training, and in the final montage they are mobilized, with heavy weaponry.

The political implications of this shift in imagery, connoting a stiffening resistance to Japanese invasion, are reinforced by the rhetoric of the narration, which insists that only if the Chinese match the armored strength of the enemy will they be able to overcome. In section 2, an unarmed people is opposed to a war machine: "The Japanese rulers begin their cold plan to take China province by province—a march of iron, mile by mile.... The dead were buried in the captured provinces." The conclusion of this section points in the direction the nation was compelled to move: "China began to form around itself the armor of modern industry." After a diversion to the rural-based, lightly-armed Communist troops of sections 3 and 5, the film reverts to this theme in full force in section 6, where it is stated that, "While China still lives it must begin to prepare.... Let us meet the Japanese with exactly the same weapons they use"— and the arms needed for national defense are listed.

The Communist/Nationalist split, which is the crucial division to be overcome if China is to be united against Japan, is partially repressed. There are no direct references to the Communist party or the Kuomintang, and the civil war is mentioned only in passing; the fact that the Red Army has been driven to a remote corner of the nation as a result of a series of extermination campaigns waged against it by Chiang Kai-shek is not alluded to. As in *Heart of Spain* and *Return to Life,* the reality of class conflict is brushed aside. But it must necessarily be acknowledged that China has been internally divided, even if the causes are conveniently passed over in silence, and the film does this chiefly in the narration.

China is described in section 2 as "weak and divided...confused and desperate"; under the Japanese onslaught, she was "paying the price of her disunity." Yet "at last the patriotism of the Chinese people began to unify them under Chiang Kai-shek," and "the dead became a force for unity." In section 3, a poster hung by students at the Anti-Japanese University "represents the traditional giant of strength—he stands for China United, crushing Japan in one hand, and Chinese betrayers in the other." The theme is reprised in section 5, where the newfound unity—"the single idea, the idea of a nation..."—is now paramount, and divisions are consigned to the past. Mao's speech clinches the issue:

> People of Shensi.... Your leaders met with the national government. There will be no more civil wars, no more divisions. We are proclaimed a province of the Republic of China. I have been to Nanking, where I saw the tomb of Sun Yat-sen, the first president of China. After he died, his words were nearly forgotten. Our shame was that we stood aside and quarreled with ourselves, while a thief came and took the land. Our shame was the loss of Manchuria, the theft of the northern provinces, while we could not agree to resist the enemy.

The speech goes on to celebrate a mobilized nation, "a whole people marching": a historic dialectic advance has been made.

The civilian-military opposition, and its overcoming in the concept of a people's army, is familiar from Frontier's *Heart of Spain.* In *China Strikes Back* the interlocking of interests of soldiers and peasants, in particular, is strongly emphasized, predominantly, of course, in the Shensi sequences. The introductory words of the narration accompanying Dunham's footage point to the distinctive character of the Red Army: "And 1,500 miles away, in the northwest, in the secret interior of China, another force for unity, an army growing among the people." The way the Communist forces differ from those of Chiang Kai-shek's government or of the war lords is not explicitly stated, but the idea of a revolutionary peasant-based army as demonstrated in the film must have been sufficiently novel for American audiences in the thirties for the implications to have been abundantly clear. In a remark directed at the American media presentation of Chinese Communists (especially, perhaps, Hollywood films), the narrator insists: "This is no force of bandits, but the army of the peasants themselves."

The interweaving of civilian and military activities in the sections documenting Shensi life gives substance to the claim. Soldiers and students from all parts of China attend the university, which also caters to peasants in its capacity as a medical treatment center. "As a regular part of their training," we are told, in a title, "the students are assigned to a local patrol of soldiers and participate in military maneuvers." The army appears to be intimately involved in the administration of the region, though the exact nature of governmental functioning is not made clear because of the film's repression of the role of the Communist party.

The Red Army's relationships with the civilian populace were governed by a series of simple precepts contained, at the time of *China Strikes Back*'s release, in the "Seven Rules of the Army," and later reissued by Mao as the "Three Main Rules of Discipline" and the "Eight Points for Attention." Among the injunctions were: "Don't take a single needle or piece of thread from the masses," "Speak politely," "Pay fairly for what you buy," "Return everything you borrow," and "Don't take liberties with women."[25] The sequences in sections 3 and 5 depicting a Red Army squad being billeted at a village for the night seems specifically designed to illustrate these rules in action. A soldier fondles a baby carried on its mother's back, while others relax and smoke tobacco offered by a villager "with the traditional gestures of Chinese courtesy." A strong rapport between civilian and noncivilian is evidenced or strongly suggested in the scenes showing the games which are played (one is called "The Seven Rules of the Army"), the meal cooked by the peasants, and the singing session. In the morning, the army men are shown sweeping up, returning the straw borrowed for the night, and making recompense for a plate which has been broken (the owner is reluctant to accept payment). The commentary makes it explicit: "What is borrowed must be returned, whatever is broken must be paid for."

In sequences such as this, the Shensi sections demonstrate the implementation of policies consciously adopted to overcome any potential rift between army and peasantry through a fusion of interests and a pooling of resources. The narration sums it up:

> The men of this army were born in the villages, nourished in the villages, and are trained to defend them. The peasants feed the army and the army teaches the peasants. This contact forms the unity of China.

Solidarity in the cities between the military and civilians is pointed to in the final section, which intercuts shots of Chiang in uniform and Chinese troops with speakers addressing crowds and citizens marching in rallies. The narration in fact bridges the gap by applying militaristic language metaphorically to the actions of civilians: "The spirit of . . . resistance has strengthened the whole nation—it is in the speech of the students, in the women marching with flags of battle, in the whole people marching, shouting the slogans of strength." *China Strikes Back* does not, however, show workers actively involved in the defense effort, as *Heart of Spain* and *Return to Life* do.

There is one further opposition contained structurally within the film: that between soldiers and weapons. The narration to section 6, in which this theme is climaxed, is primarily concerned with arguing that, unless heavily armed, a "great wall of people" will not prevail against the Japanese invader. The film implies that successful resistance will be made possible by a coming together of the highly trained and motivated troops of sections 3 and 5 with the artillery, tanks, and aircraft of section 6. The final four lines of the "Song of the Chinese Soldier" in section 4 point forward to this conclusion, poetically heralding the supply of military hardware to the Chinese troops: " . . . Look up, brothers and sisters, I am coming with planes to defend you."

According to the Museum of Modern Art program note cited earlier, *China Strikes Back* was "praised by critics for its brilliant editing, which was planned around a poem by David Wolff." The reference is evidently to the fourth ("Song of the Chinese Soldier") section: the note adds, "The poem was written specifically for the film and is one of the first instances in which poetry has been used consciously in relation to structure and editing." The encomium now seems overstated, but the section is worth examining in the light of an aesthetic polemic, "Film Into Poem," Ben Maddow (as "Wolff") had written a year earlier for *New Theatre* magazine. It was probably the first chance Maddow had to put his ideas into effect, and though he and his fellow editors were obviously constricted by the limited range of stock footage available to them, the results are interesting.[26]

In his article, Maddow asked why it was that even in the greatest of films one did not experience the "close emotion, the extreme passionate lucidity" that one found in the other arts.

> Is it not possible that the lack is not in craftsmanship, but in form? That a new form of cinema must be conceived? A form which would correspond to the scope and concentration of poetry?

He went on to suggest some of the features which would characterize, in his view, such a "cine-poem." For a start, it would not be "poetic": it would refuse "the dreamy, the vague, or the pictorial," and reject "triple exposures as well as rivers seen under an archway." It would be "real, exact, not dripping with the perfume of Jean Cocteau's *Sang d'un Poète*."

Acknowledging the speed and shock of contemporary life, the new form would capture the "abrupt sensations" and "complex patterns" of our lives with "a sharp, concise, and shattering emphasis." Freed from fixed temporal continuity and inspired by the "juxtaposed and concurrently developing images" of modern poets, the cine-poem, unlike any other form of art, would be able to "encompass modern events, their violent compressions and simultaneities."

The fourth section of *China Strikes Back* corresponds to this projected aesthetic in its abrupt cuts (patterned after the imagery of the poem) from peasants peacefully at work, to explosions, to refugee columns, to oppressed and exploited slave laborers. Moreover, the development follows a thematic logic, in accordance with Maddow's suggestion that "a cine-poem might be constructed on the movement of a single idea, or on an abstract declarative concept, or on some fertile metaphor." In this case, the "single idea" is the fate of the Chinese population when subjected to Japanese invasion. What distinguishes the sequence from an orthodox documentary presentation of such a theme is its high degree of compression (the section is three minutes long), and its employment of visual metaphor. Maddow wrote that "the common devices of montage are often the equivalent of metaphor," and in this sequence the series of shots depicting physically stooped workers—hauling rickshaws, carts, barges—intercut with images of Chinese bent over to pray, serve to connote submission before the conqueror—an interpretation made explicit (perhaps over-explicit) in the line of the poem, "As you bend, the Japanese climb on your back." The interlude thus offers an example of the type of political montage construction Maddow and his co-workers were capable of when freed from the usual editing restraints of discursive argument and narrative flow.

When Joris Ivens's *The 400 Million* was released, in March 1939, the relationship of the Sino-Japanese conflict to the worldwide alignment of hostile forces could be stated quite openly. A prefatory title read:

> ...On one side, the Japanese military machine, ally of the Rome-Berlin axis, brutal and merciless. On the other side, just as in Europe, the peaceful masses of humanity—victim of fascist attack. Europe and Asia have become the western and eastern front of the same assault on democracy.

No such equations are made in *China Strikes Back,* and indeed the rhetoric of "democracy" and "fascism" is not employed at all. Explanations for this can only be speculative, but it is possible that the Frontier filmmakers believed that to picture Chiang Kai-shek's dictatorial and corrupt administration as "democratic" would be to stretch an audience's credulity too far, particularly considering that it was only a few months since Chiang had been an object of left-wing vilification in the press and in films such as *The Birth of New China.*

If in this respect *China Strikes Back* departs from the ideological model presented by *Heart of Spain* and *Return to Life,* it resembles the Spanish films in several significant ways. The film depicts a people in arms against a foreign invader, is sparing in its use of political identifications, particularly of Communists, and represses almost all evidence of class conflict and civil war.

It is the last two features which render *China Strikes Back* problematic as a piece of political analysis. A contemporary reviewer wrote that one could "perhaps gain a fuller realization of China's struggle to unify its defenses,"[27] but since the audience is not informed of the obstacles to unification, this is not at all certain. To omit, as the film does, all reference to Chiang's slaughter of urban Communists in 1927 and of the bitter nine-year war of annihilation then waged against Red forces in the provinces is to totally obfuscate the nature of the alliance entered into in 1937 by Chiang and Mao; failure to explain the Long March renders the presence of the Red Army in remote Shensi province virtually unintelligible; neglecting to allude to the semi-feudal conditions of life still subsisting in China under Kuomintang rule obscures the revolutionary nature of the Communist party's social program; and the absence of any discussion of the Sian Incident deprives viewers of an understanding of how the civil war has come (temporarily) to a halt.

While the film presents Mao as proclaiming, "There will be no more civil wars, no more divisions," he was in fact stressing in public statements at the time that the basic conflict between the Communist Party and the Kuomintang was by no means resolved. The argument quoted at the head of this chapter is evidence of this, as is his report to the Communist party in Yenan in April 1937, an extract from which was included in Edgar Snow's *Red Star Over China:*

> The Communist party retains the leadership on problems in the Soviet districts and the Red Army, and retains its independence and freedom of criticism in its relations with the Kuomintang. On these points no concessions can be made.... The Communist party will never abandon its aims of Socialism and Communism, it will still pass through the stage of democratic revolution of the bourgeoisie to attain the stages of Socialism and Communism. The Communist party retains its own program and its own policies.[28]

China Strikes Back may be accused, then, of underplaying the still-existing contradictions of the Chinese situation for the sake of a desired unity. And in fact this is substantially the judgement which, with hindsight, Leo Hurwitz makes of the film:

> The symbolic ending was also a reflection of the fact that a united front against the Japanese invasion had developed between the Kuomintang and the Chinese Communist Party, after the Sian Incident. The film shows the alliance between Mao's and Chiang's forces, which is often forgotten today. The Red Army became the Eighth Route Army of the Chinese Army. The nature of that alliance is very interesting and, as you know, was never fulfilled. Chiang was more interested in suppressing the Communists than in fighting Japan. The film's ending is of course naive in a way that Mao was not. For while he fought for a united front against Japan, he did not allow the weakening of the strength, initiative, and principles of the Communist movement—which was the reason why the Communists were successful in both the war against Japan and in the civil war provoked by Chiang.[29]

8

People of the Cumberland

In the thirties, the Cumberland Plateau region of Tennessee was one of the most poverty-stricken areas of a generally impoverished nation. The industries which had once flourished had been in decline for several decades, and the mountain people, no longer capable of eking out an existence amid the mined-out coal fields and cut-over timberlands, were being drawn into the valleys in the hope of finding work in the mines and mills that thrived on cheap labor. *People of the Cumberland* was a film about this situation, and about an institution, the Highlander Folk School, which had been established to combat poverty and exploitation in the area.

The Highlander Folk School was founded in 1932 by Myles Horton, a young graduate of Cumberland University who had studied sociology in Chicago and come under the radicalizing influence of Reinhold Niebuhr at New York's Union Theological Seminary. Rejecting pressure to enter the ministry, he concluded that the best method to help the people of his home region improve their condition was to run an adult education center where they could learn the skills necessary to organize themselves. In 1931-32 he spent several months in Denmark studying folk schools, from which he derived some ideas concerning nonauthoritarian teaching methods and the role of local popular culture in building class consciousness.[2]

The school was funded with donations solicited by an advisory committee, whose members included Niebuhr and Socialist leader Norman Thomas. A 1932 circular letter from Niebuhr appealing for contributions stated:

Our project is the organization of a Southern Mountain School for the training of labor leaders in the Southern industrial areas. The Southern mountaineers who are being drawn into the coal and textile industries are completely lacking in understanding of the problems of industry and the necessities of labor organization. We believe that neither AF of L nor Communist leadership is adequate to their needs. Our hope is to train *radical* labor leaders who will understand the need of both political and union strategy. Without local leadership a labor movement in the South is impossible.[3]

Highlander, located at Monteagle, Tennessee, quickly drove roots into the mountain community. Horton immediately offered the school's support to labor unions of the area, and was personally involved in assisting the miners' strike at Wilder, in the north of the state, during the winter of 1932-33. (Strike leader Barney Graham was murdered by vigilantes, an incident which was to be dramatized in *People of the Cumberland.*) The school's instructional programs, offered in the form of short live-in workshops and seminars, and later in extension classes, concentrated on local problems, and their underlying political and economic causes, from a socialist perspective.

After the smashing of the Wilder strike, the school helped the ousted miners to obtain work with the new TVA project. It then assisted in the organization of striking bugwood cutters into a Cumberland Mountain Workers and Unemployed League, and from 1935 was instrumental in campaigns to obtain fair treatment in allocation of funds for the region from the WPA. In 1937, when *People of the Cumberland* was made, Highlander placed all of its resources at the disposal of the Textile Workers' Organizing Committee (CIO) for its unionizing drive in the South, and Horton himself took a leave of absence to become a full-time organizer.

Meanwhile Highlander was dedicated to the rediscovery and renewal of local folk culture. Ralph Tefferteller, another young Tennessean who had attended Union Theological Seminary, joined the school's staff in 1936 and introduced a lively program devoted to the "songs and dances and tall tales of the southern mountain hill regions." Also on the staff was Horton's wife Zilphia, who specialized in the dissemination of labor songs from the South (Leadbelly and Pete Seeger were to become frequent visitors at the school).

Although Niebuhr was a prominent Socialist party member, and Horton had invited Norman Thomas to speak to miners during the Wilder strike, the Highlander Folk School was not aligned with the Socialist party to an extent which precluded cooperation with Communists. "Highlander could be classified as a united-front school at the time," Horton recently wrote. The school maintained its political independence by abstaining from formal ties with either party of the Left: thus in 1934 it was stated that "the school is in no way connected with any political party, either in an official capacity, or as a recipient of financial aid."[4]

The principal instigator of *People of the Cumberland* was the executive director of Highlander at the time, James Dombrowski. (Dombrowski, a graduate of the Union Theological Seminary who had received a Ph.D. at Columbia University with a dissertation devoted to the early days of Christian

Socialism in America, had been on the staff of Highlander since 1933.) Horton recalls that Dombrowski "arranged for the film to be made," and Tefferteller notes:

> By 1937 the school had been in operation ... for some five years, and it was through the efforts of staff at Highlander, principally Myles Horton and Jim Dombrowski, [that the film was made]. Jim ... was performing pretty much as the administrator, fiscal manager and so on of the school, seeking to enlarge the school's image, and all the while trying to develop a solid base of financial support for the school. He felt it would be very helpful to have an audio-visual presentation of the school, at that time.[5]

Tefferteller goes on to explain that "in order to bring this about, there had to be some kind of financial angel who could make it possible." Horton and Dombrowski turned to Ethel Clyde, who had been an early supporter of the school's work, and was also a sponsor of Frontier Films. She agreed to back the project, and contributed, Horton recalls, $2,000 towards the making of the film.[6]

Frontier accepted the assignment, no doubt with alacrity, probably in the late spring of 1937, and Ralph Steiner and Elia Kazan traveled south in the last week of June to begin shooting on what was at first conceived of as a one-reel film. There was little initial scripting. According to Kazan:

> We made it up as we went along. It was mostly a matter of going in there and photographing the things we found. Then we made up the script afterwards.[7]

What they found was probably what was suggested to them by the Highlander staff. "The concept, of course," states Ralph Tefferteller, "came from the persons who were most responsible for the directions that the school was taking, the staff and the small board of directors." Scenes were selected to illustrate the range of the school's activities and involvements, and Tefferteller became the film crew's liaison man with the local community:

> It was only logical that I should become a sort of legman for the filming operation ... taking "Gadget" Kazan and others to possible locations where they might shoot series of scenes for the film. So the film kind of developed as we went along, whether it was with some of the millworkers down in the valley off the mountain, or whether it was in a mountain shack with underfed, illclothed children and their parents ....[8]

Kazan had not spent much time in the South before, although he had hitchhiked a lot around the country and, as he recalls, "had friendships with the Communist leaders in the South, particularly with one of them who lived in Chattanooga, in Tennessee." He felt that "the residents of that community resented our photographing them because they thought we were New York Jews making fun of them." It thus became Tefferteller's task to smooth the relationship between the film unit and the local people featured in the film:

Wherever . . . we went I was always trying to prepare the persons who were to be filmed for this intrusion into their lives. . . . Persons in the mountains, going back forty years ago, they were pretty shy . . . and if a familiar personality sort of paved the way it made the director's job a lot easier. Kazan never impressed me as having a very pleasing personality—pretty rough in handling people back there years ago.[9]

Tefferteller himself appeared in two scenes of *People of the Cumberland*. In the more important, he was filmed calling the square dance on one of the regular social occasions at Highlander which he had helped initiate. At the time the school was founded, square dancing was banned as irreligious in much of the Cumberland region, and reviving it had become part of Highlander's program of renewing the pride of local people in their folk cultural traditions. Tefferteller had been involved for several years in seeking out and learning the dances of the Southern Appalachians, and at the school he taught them to local residents:

I had been working with young people in the community, doing recreation work, and I'd taught a group of them the square dance as I knew it over in the eastern part of Tennessee, further east, and across the mountain in North Carolina. They had been exposed to some square dancing, but it was a kind of haphazard sort of experience. So we began holding regular socials, once a week, and I would handle the calling and the instruction, and we'd get local musicians to furnish the hoe-down music . . . .[10]

It was thus easy to stage a performance for the benefit of the Frontier crew. Kazan has since remarked:

I got great confidence in my ability to go into an environment and get drama and color and entertainment out of the most ordinary people. I was able to make them act and dance.

Tefferteller notes in response:

I was in a good position, and well prepared to help with the group of young people from the Summerfield community in putting on a demonstration of the mountain style of square dancing. Kazan didn't have anything to do with that. True, he might have gone into some community and have been able to find a natural leader and do a filming that would be effective, but in this case Highlander had within its staff the resources, whether it was my being fully prepared to set up the square dance sequences and call the dances, or Zilphia Horton leading the singing, all he had to do was to set up his cameras and do the shooting . . . .[11]

The other scene in which Tefferteller appeared was a brief one, and was part of the film's coverage of the work of Highlander staff in supporting union organization. He recalls the type of activity which was involved:

I was doing a good deal of work with unemployed coal miners in the little, almost ghost towns, communities, where the coal mines had been worked out years ago. There was only one coal mine operating at the time, and that was further along on the Cumberland Plateau at Palmer,

Tennessee, at the other end of Grundy County. These unemployed coal miners, of course, became WPA workers on farm-to-market roads and so forth, and I helped their leaders in organizing a union. They had brought in a charter of the common laborers' union, and they held their regular meetings. I attended those meetings, also helped them in organizing committees to go into the nearest WPA administrative headquarters in Chattanooga.

Tefferteller was filmed with a group of miners outside a UMWA hall:

> I became sort of the silent organizer, as it were. I remember one of the scenes that we shot on the mountain was in front of a little log meeting place—that's where one of the locals of the coal miners met—and I sat with a group of them on the outside, and the filming of course was from my rear, but the idea was that here was the organizer, the business agent working with his members of the union. [12]

Not all of the shooting proceeded without incident. Local business interests were hostile to the film crew, as they were to the Highlander Folk School itself. Tefferteller relates what occurred on one occasion:

> I remember one incident in Tracy City where the Tennessee Coal Mine Company had its headquarters, or one of their offices, and while Gadget was directing a scene showing a piece of paper blowing across a vacant lot, one of the people rushed out of the office, and I feel sure if he'd had a gun he would have blown our heads off. He was of course interested in having us film the beautiful mountain views and waterfalls and so on, and felt we were misrepresenting the life and physical landscape of his native Cumberland mountains. [13]

Ralph Steiner recalls a more serious attempt to interfere with the filming:

> I remember once we were shooting some lime workers, and were chased off the plant grounds . . . they came after us with guns. The whole town was owned by the plant. These were company towns, the stores, everything was owned by the company. So, we had to shoot the union meeting on the road—right in the middle of the road—because that belonged to the county, and not the company. [14]

No actual violence erupted in the course of filming, but the Frontier unit did recreate for the camera the slaying of the president of the Wilder miners' union local, Barney Graham, in 1933. According to Horton, the scene showing the murder "was based on and was an accurate portrayal of a real incident in which I was involved." The Highlander director had brought food and publicized the condition of the miners, who, striking against a wage cut, were near starvation and receiving minimal help from the (then weak) United Mine Workers. On one occasion he had been arrested by the National Guard for "getting information and going back to teach it." When the company brought in hired thugs who talked brazenly of their plans, Horton tried to avert the threatened danger:

We told Barney he was going to get killed. I told him who these people were and that they were brought in to kill him. He knew they were going to kill him.

He was that tough kind that wouldn't quite, you know. So I went to work to try to get pressure to expose this before it happened, thinking that might bring enough pressure on the company and on public opinion that it might save his life. And that's when I tried—tried everything I could, put everything in the paper, the names of these guys, their history, said they were going to kill Barney Graham, and I couldn't move anybody.[15]

Graham was murdered on April 30, 1933. A historian records that he was shot in the back, about sunset, as he went to fetch a doctor for his wife. He was felled in front of the company store; the killers bashed in his head and "stood guard over his body, refusing to let anyone take it away until about 10:00 P.M." Details of the death were later recalled by a striker:

And so we went up to where Barney was shot. And his gun lying under him. He'd managed to get his gun out. He was shot, he had eleven bullet holes in him, with his brains leaking in three places. And there was a gun there with the handles off of it where they had beat him.[16]

"Of course the Barney Graham tragedy highlighted the very sharp conflicts that had already taken place in the coal fields, and in organizing efforts in other industries in the southeastern part of the country," says Ralph Tefferteller; "But here was a graphic, dramatic incident, and Myles had been involved in it, close to it, and it was natural, very natural, that the story of Highlander would include such an incident." The murder of the labor organizer (he is not identified by name) in *People of the Cumberland* is the one major sequence which was reenacted.[17]

One other event may, however, have been staged at least partially in the knowledge that it would be filmed. The Fourth of July Labor Rally held on July 5, 1937, in La Follette, Tennessee, was the culmination of a major five-week extension program which had been conducted by the Highlander Folk School in the small town some 120 miles northeast of Monteagle. Union education classes were held in conjunction with the Amalgamated Clothing Workers of America for a shirt-workers' local, and for a nearby miners' group. Typically for Highlander, there was instruction in labor songs (Zilphia Horton), "How to run a union meeting" (Tefferteller), and trade union history (Dombrowski). The closing event for the school was the Independence Day parade and picnic, in which 4,000 workers and their families marched with flags and banners demonstrating union solidarity, and then assembled in the local fairgrounds for festivities with a working-class flavor, all of which was recorded by Steiner's camera. Tefferteller remarks that "Jim and Myles's wife Zilphia and I had been very active in La Follette, Tennessee, another coalmining town, but where there were some cotton garment workers, two factories were located there, and we were doing a workers' education project, so that again it was only natural that some of the scenes would be located there."[18]

When Steiner and Kazan returned to New York with their footage there was some dissatisfaction in the Frontier camp. Leo Hurwitz records that he was not involved in the actual production of *People of the Cumberland,*

> but I had to do with all the films in the sense of talking over the ideas, considering scripts, looking at rushes, giving my advice as to whether it should be done. In that case Steiner and Kazan brought back a very fragmented set of rushes that couldn't possibly be put together. So then the problem was who should go and finish it, and we sent Sidney Meyers down to do that. It seemed clear, too, then that the script which we had left people alone with was too ill-thought-out, so we counselled work on the script.

Jay Leyda, who was brought in with Meyers to supervise the production, also felt that there was a problem of digging out a system from unsystematic material.[19]

Steiner has since charged that he and Meyers were sent back to Tennessee "with the specific purpose of putting more Karl Marx into the film." He objected to such a directive because, he argues, "the school was a very sweet, innocent, and socially minded, but certainly not Communist, organization." The three men who ran Highlander—he is referring to Horton, Dombrowski, and Tefferteller—"were saints, and we saw it as that and nothing more." Hurwitz, however, had said: " 'Let's make it in terms of black revolutionaries,' and all that stuff."[20]

It is very possible that Hurwitz urged the filmmakers to put a sharper political edge to their material, but in general Steiner's recollections seem unduly colored by his subsequently adopted anti-Communist beliefs. The three Frontier staffers had obviously advanced politically far beyond their common training at the Union Theological Seminary, and in any case the final version of the film, in accordance with the nonaligned position of Highlander and the People's Front values then being promulgated by the Communist party, does not go, ideologically, beyond a generalized affirmation of union organization and working-class solidarity. A contemporary critic actually commented that *People of the Cumberland* "started as a bitter document of the miserable life of the people in that section of the country and became a rather sweet one of the newly founded Highlander Folk School."[21]

Steiner, in any event, returned to the Cumberland with Meyers in order to pick up more shots. (Kazan, Steiner notes, "was in a play and couldn't go back"—he was probably rehearsing for his part in the Group Theatre's *Golden Boy.*) As Steiner recalls:

> I remember saying to Sid Meyers, as we were driving down, he was reading Karl Marx on the way down, and I said, "Sid, if you're going to revolutionize these people, you better look out the window once in a while and see what they look like!"[22]

It is not clear precisely what footage was obtained on this second trip, but it may have included the scenes featuring Myles Horton, who remembers that "a couple of shots of me were dubbed in later." Steiner and Meyers were accompanied by the former workers' theatre director William Watts, who is credited, along with Kazan, as an "assistant" on the film, and who directed the action in association with Meyers.[23]

People of the Cumberland has no separated credit for editing, which implies that it was cut chiefly by Meyers and Leyda. Steiner, who at around this time left Frontier Films, was disturbed by what he felt to be (at least in retrospect) the Communist bias which was being imparted to the material, particularly by the addition of newsreel footage:

> After we got back, the boys in New York stuck in all sorts of revolutionary shots of workers in factories giving the Communist salute out of the windows, and so forth. Well, the Highlander Folk School wasn't very Communist-oriented, and Frontier Films upset me a great deal.[24]

A narration was written by novelist Erskine Caldwell, who at this time was receiving praise for his successful exposé documentary book *You Have Seen Their Faces,* a study of southern sharecroppers done in collaboration with the photographer Margaret Bourke-White. Assisting him was Frontier's regular writer, Ben Maddow. The content of the commentary was shaped by the perception which the Highlander staff themselves had of their work, as Tefferteller explains:

> The staff of the school of necessity had to work very closely with those who were putting the film together. The staff . . . had to present a sort of complete rundown on the school's work and activities, and then the commentary would sometimes be taken from the information of staff people, so it was a joint effort, a cooperative effort, involving those who were on the spot, the staff persons at Highlander Folk School, and those who were coming in from the outside to put together an audio-visual presentation of what the school had been doing and was all about.[25]

The narration was spoken by Richard Blaine.

Alex North, who had arranged the music for *Heart of Spain* and *China Strikes Back,* was called upon to compose a score. Aided by Earl Robinson, who supplied choral arrangements and introductory music, North provided an accompaniment for the images which drew on eclectic sources including black-Baptist style chanting, labor songs such as *Sit Down,* and American folk and traditional tunes. The sound editing was handled by Helen van Dongen, editor of *Spain in Flames* and *The Spanish Earth.*

Eighteen minutes in length (and thus almost twice as long as originally planned), *People of the Cumberland* was first shown at a screening for Congressional Liberal Bloc members and others in Washington, D.C., on March 29, 1938. (*Heart of Spain* and *China Strikes Back* were also shown, the intention being to interest progressive legislators in Frontier's civil liberties project.) The film received its public premiere at the New School in New York on

May 2, and the same week it was shown to Eleanor Roosevelt in the White House, and to supporters of the Highlander Folk School in Washington. Lionel Berman reported:

> The Washington trip was exciting and useful. We showed *Cumberland* (16mm) at the United Mine Workers to Katherine Lewis, Len De Caux, Hetzel, and other UMWA and CIO people. In spite of the fact that the sound was terrible (a huge room, full of echoes), they liked it and will help us with publicity in the *CIO News* and the *Mine Workers Journal.*

The film received the approbation of the Highlander directors and staff, who, as Tefferteller recalls, "were pretty well pleased with it as a portrayal of some of the work" that was done by the school.[26]

Handled, as was now customary with Frontier productions, by Garrison Film Distributors (apparently under an arrangement whereby half the net proceeds were paid directly to the Highlander Folk School), *People of the Cumberland* opened theatrically at the Cameo in New York City in the first week of June, accompanying the Soviet feature *Country Bride.* It subsequently played in a limited number of theatres around the country. Getting the film exhibited required active campaigning: a favorable review in *Film Survey* pointed out that "as it is an independent production, it will not be shown in your local theatre UNLESS YOU ASK YOUR NEIGHBORHOOD THEATRE TO SHOW. *THIS YOU MUST DO.*"[27]

People of the Cumberland achieved its major exposure, however, through nontheatrical distribution, mainly on 16mm. Acclaimed as "the first American trade-union picture" and endorsed by Labor's Non-Partisan League, the United Mine Workers, the Amalgamated Clothing Workers, and the International Ladies Garment Workers Union, the film received wide circulation through sale and rental of prints to labor organizations, including the CIO. A Museum of Modern Art program note confirmed that in its first two years of release *People of the Cumberland* had been booked extensively by unions, churches, colleges, scientific societies, and the Y.M.C.A. Writing in 1940, critics asserted that Frontier's first domestic production had been seen by "several millions" and was "the most popular labor film ever made."[28]

The author of the MoMA program note observed that the film had "evoked remarkable audience response, particularly in regions where people live under the conditions represented in the film itself." This was true of the fifty or so showings arranged by the West Virginia Labor Film League, many held in remote mountain communities where children had never seen a film before, or where, for lack of a hall, the screen had to be pinned to the back of the company store. *People of the Cumberland* inspired "a new hopefulness, and desire for better things," the organizer of the film tour wrote to Ethel Clyde.[29]

By 1937, the plight of the sharecroppers of the South, both black and white, was well known to Americans: it had been the subject of numerous articles, photo-essays, and books, and of several films, both fictional and documentary. The comparable poverty being experienced by the mountain people of the southern Appalachians was not nearly as widely publicized, and *People of the Cumberland* was clearly designed to draw the conditions in the region to the attention of a broad public. But the film went far beyond the typical "exposé" piece of the period by depicting the residents of the area, victims of exploitation and a faltering economy, actively organizing to transform their way of life.

The picture was one diametrically opposed to that which had emerged in the few Hollywood movies to deal with the life of miners or the old mountain communities. Films such as Warner Brothers' *Black Fury* (1935) and *Mountain Justice* (1937), ostensibly liberal "social problem" tracts boldly documenting issues other Hollywood producers resolutely steered clear of, in fact created extraordinarily negative and distorted images of the working-class characters who were their subjects.[30]

Black Fury, in particular, called for refutation. This study of a coal-miners' strike which whitewashed working conditions, turned a blind eye to evictions, evaded the truths of destitution among strikers, showed the mine operators in a favorable light, neglected to portray the organization and militancy of the miners, and belittled the role of radicals, was fiercely attacked in journals such as the *Daily Worker* and *New Theatre*. Albert Maltz, for example, the author of *Black Pit* (and later to become an associate of Frontier Films), sardonically commented, "Here, then, is the Hollywood truth," specifying: "Strikes are started by racketeers; militant workers are paid stool pigeons; strikes are unwarranted; miners are stupid sheep; mine operators are fair-play boy scouts who counsel their hired thugs not to use violence!"[31]

Mountain Justice depicted a backward hillbilly community with a fundamentalist morality wreaking savage retribution on a young woman, a nurse, who has dared to challenge the patriarchal law. The mountaineers resist any manifestation of enlightenment or progress, eventually descending on the local township as a hooded mob out to lynch her. The only hope for liberation afforded by this film is escape to another state in which more civilized values prevail.

Except for the Workers' Film and Photo League cameramen who ventured into Kentucky during the coal strikes of 1931 and 1932, documentary filmmakers had scarcely approached the southern Appalachian region before *People of the Cumberland* was made. Pare Lorentz's cameramen (including Frontier's Willard Van Dyke) had, however, shot in Tennessee for *The River* (1937), and both this film and its predecessor, *The Plow That Broke the Plains* (1936), offered instructive models in terms of a documentary approach to rural poverty. It was an approach which the Frontier group by and large rejected.

When *The Plow* was released in May 1936, Irving Lerner, writing in *New Theatre,* remarked on the film's failure to dramatize the human story of the Dust Bowl.

> But where is the major tragedy—the vain sacrifices that generations of struggling men had made to build homes for themselves and their children in the Great Plains? As *Variety* says, speaking of how the farmers are portrayed in the film, "... they aren't called upon for any histrionics other than staring at the sky or whittling sticks to indicated complete resignation to fate."

Lerner was particularly scornful of the upbeat conclusion:

> There is an epilogue, unnecessary and a little silly (done in the standardized manner of the regular commercial film) which makes a sorry attempt to show what the Resettlement Administration wants to do—and has done. Millions of people are homeless; and by means of an animated map you are informed that 4,500 families have been resettled![32]

Reviewing Lorentz's second production, Lerner made similar objections. He argued:

> You cannot make a dynamic and meaningful film about the tragedy of erosion and the lack of planning unless you include the people. You cannot hope to show what the new projects, the Norris Dam, the Pickwick Dam, and the rest of the Tennessee Valley projects mean by merely stressing the formal beauties of the structures.[33]

Lorentz's films epitomized the outlook of the liberal New Deal administrators implementing policies from Washington, D.C. People—when they appeared—were depicted as passive victims of natural disasters—droughts and floods—and subsequently the equally passive beneficiaries of federal relief projects. Lerner, as a radical and member of the staff of Frontier Films, clearly articulated the group's response to the government school of documentary in his reviews, and it was to be expected that when Frontier came to make its first domestic film it would focus not on the landscape, natural or manmade, but on the people. *People of the Cumberland* would move, not from the top down, but from the bottom up, and its protagonists would be shown in active struggle, themselves, for a better life.

People of the Cumberland conforms to the familiar Frontier pattern of alternating negative and positive sections. In this case there are four main divisions, each of which is broken up into smaller self-contained sequences, as follows:

Section	Subject	Subdivisions	
1	Devastation	a)	Mountain
		b)	Valley
2	Organization	a)	Highlander Folk School: community activities
		b)	Nationwide unionizing
		c)	ACWA
		d)	Highlander Folk School: square dancing
3	Threat	a)	Hired thugs
		b)	UMWA
		c)	Murder of organizer
4	Triumph	a)	Labor rally
		b)	Recapitulation

The first section documents conditions of life in the depressed Cumberland region. After shots of clouds above wooded hills and of the thinned forest, come images of a rotting lumber mill, the foundations of a house which is long gone, an abandoned mine entrance. We see the unemployed miners entering the disused shaft in the hope of digging out enough coal to keep them alive: "Tons of slate and rock, pounds of coal," says the narrator, "But those few pounds meant food, so they went down again into mud and darkness, the rotting timbers and the smell of dynamite smoke." In the next series of shots are depicted the "ruined people" of the mountain: idle figures gathered on sagging verandahs or standing in the doorway of an old shack; a wrinkled, elderly woman; ragged, dirty children eating from cans; a young woman with a baby at her breast; gaunt men and scraggy adolescents. The photography captures them in immobile moments with fixed expressions signifying a determination to hang on despite the extinction of hope; in style it is strongly reminiscent of the Resettlement Administration/Farm Security Administration work of Walker Evans or Dorothea Lange. Intercut are images of stony cornfields and of graves decorated with broken pieces of crockery.[34] The narration to the sequence stresses both the destitution of the people—"No food . . . years of hard work and hunger . . . the earth that failed to keep them alive"—and their ancestry—"Yet they're the stock of the pioneers, the tough Scots and the English. . . . " The final "mountain" shot is a pan around meager timber huts on a hillside.

"Some of the families went down into the valley hearing there was work down below," the voice-over tells us, as the image dissolves to a mud street and a large timber building, followed by town houses and shacks—"work and food, work and life, maybe a new start and a decent pair of shoes, and maybe electric light." But conditions here aren't much better: we are shown tumbledown cabins in stony fields, while the narrator observes caustically that exploitation in the valley is not much preferable to unemployment in the mountains:

> Plenty of work, eleven hours a day, six dollars a week. The trees torn out, the mines ruined to make a dividend, the people drawn into the towns and robbed there. The same greed rules the valley and the mountain.

Section 2 is a counter-attack launched against section 1, a people's offensive with the Highlander radicals in the vanguard. A simple, factual title serves as introduction: "In 1932, a group of teachers aware of conditions in the Cumberland, organized the Highlander Folk School." After shots of the school building (a two-story converted farmhouse set amid trees) and of Myles Horton (the pipe-smoking intellectual, reading, with shelves of books behind him), there follow an array of scenes depicting Highlander activities. Teachers are shown instructing small informal groups: lumbermen in the forest, laborers beside a pile of bugwood.[35] A sample of the school's educational approach is given by means of live dialogue in a sequence featuring men and women at work tilling a field. "What are the advantages of labor unions?" asks the instructor.

> "They give us shorter hours."
> "An increase in wages."
> "They protect your job."
> "Clyde?"
> "Education."
> "Vacations with pay."
> "What else, Mac?"
> "Brotherhood."
> "Good. Ruby, anything else?"
> "Increases prosperity."

The theme is reiterated in a further outdoor sequence, showing a workers' class under way alongside a barn. In this case the teacher employs visual charts illustrating the forces arrayed against the unions, and those in support. ("Who's against us? The associations of manufacturers, the no-strike injunctions, the men who won't look and won't listen, the thugs hired in Memphis, the unions faked by the company. Who's for us? The government. The Wagner Act. The Constitution backs us up.")

Interspersed are scenes picturing work at the school itself. We see a folk dance class in action, students taking down books from the library shelves and studying together under the shade of a tree, a mock union meeting in progress. Subjects of instruction, we are informed, include "the principles of organization, history, science, economics, what are the problems of the world, how to unite the Cumberland people, why there is poverty and why there is war."

The film up to this point has confined its range geographically to the southern Appalachian region. The second part of the "Organization" section resorts to newsreel footage to demonstrate that the struggle of the folk of the Cumberland to organize is paralleled nationwide. In an upbeat transition, the narrator proclaims:

> It's a new idea. You hear it in the Cumberland in Tennessee, in the big mills of the South. Ten million voices. Get wise, organize!

And the soundtrack segues into a chorus of voices singing the new labor song, *Sit Down:*

> Sit down, just take a seat
> Sit down and rest your feet
> Sit down, you've got 'em beat
> Sit down! Sit down!
>
> When they tie a can to a union man
> Sit down! Sit down!
> When they give 'im the sack they'll take 'im back
> Sit down! Sit down! . . . [36]

The images are those objected to by Ralph Steiner: men and women workers on sit-down strike laughing and waving from the windows of factories they have occupied (a sign announces "6 DAYS NOW"), parades of strikers (some identified as auto workers by a UAWA banner, others showered with bits of paper in a working-class version of a ticker-tape celebration), massive street demonstrations, more strikers happily greeting their supporters, more parading. The series of shots encapsulates the tremendous wave of union organizing of 1937 stemming from the success of the Michigan sit-down strikes. The singing voices are muted for the narrator to comment: "Chattanooga and Minneapolis, New York to San Francisco, do you hear them? Seattle and Pennsylvania, it's in the air, coast to coast." And again: "Get wise, organize!"

The third part of section 2 documents one phase of the organizing drive in Tennessee: the activities of women garment workers belonging to an Amalgamated Clothing Workers local (actually in the town of La Follette, although this is not specified). The workers are pictured at their machines, sewing: a series of close-ups individualizes them, asserts their dignity. (These, and several other shots cut in here, of women shearing cloth and at work in a textile mill, seem indebted to the pioneering photographic work of Lewis Hine in the South.) "Men and women are more than machines," the narrator asserts, "they've got a union"—and we cut to women leaving the offices of the ACWA with copies of their union paper *Advance;* a group doing organizing work, sitting round a table with a typewriter; others playing table tennis with their union banner behind them.

The fourth subdivision of this optimistic section of the film returns us to the Highlander Folk School, where a square dance session is in progress, under the high-spirited guidance of Ralph Tefferteller. "Swing 'em high, swing 'em low," he sings, "Swing your girl and let her go..." as the fiddler and guitarist energetically attack the old-time music. The dancers, forming a single circle with clasped hands, create a pattern fitly symbolic of the theme of labor unity. And the gusto with which they join in is an appropriate note on which to conclude a filmic celebration of newfound solidarity through education and organization.

There is an abrupt shift in mood as section 3 commences. Silence, and a title reading: "But there were powerful forces that still denied the right of these people to a happy life." Then a low-key, backlit scene of a group of men being supplied with guns, accompanied by tense music and a voice heavy with menace: "There's talk the unions are getting organized again, want more money—we hear they're having a meeting some place." A revolver is loaded.

The line provides a cue for the cut to a United Mine Workers meeting, at which new members are being sworn in. In front of the American flag, a miner is asked, "Are you willing to take an obligation which binds you upon your honor as a man.... To keep the same as long as life remains, and sincerely promise to bear true allegiance to the United Mine Workers of America, and to help all brothers in adversity, to have all mine workers join our union, that we may all enjoy the fruits of our labor?"

The film cuts back to the conspirators. A message is penned: "Warning: we're giving you 24 hours to get out of town." The paper is wrapped around a bolt, passed to a thug who drops off the running board of a car and hurls it through a window. "It's kind of a craze, that union stuff," we hear, "first the mines, then the girls down at the knitting mills, and then this Folk School on the mountain."

The dramatic climax of the film follows. The organizer is shown walking the streets of the town, a marked man, closely observed by the gangsters lying in wait for him. A breathless, subjective stream-of-consciousness narration accompanies his movements:

> Sooner or later I knew it was coming. First the note and then it was deadly quiet for about three days. I knew they were up in the hotel watching me. I went up Carey Street in a hurry. I knew it was coming. It was on Carey Street. I knew it would be this way. I've got to get to Jeff's place. They killed Frank last month, shot in the stomach four times. I've got to get out. No chance. They'll wonder where I am. It's here. I've got to get out!

Ambushed in an alley by two gunmen, he is cornered, makes a dash, struggles, is shot dead. There is a straight cut to a grave, and then, after a fade, the section concludes with scenes demonstrating that organization proceeds despite the murderous violence: miners conferring outside their union hall; lime workers discussing the situation. In this transitional segment, the narration compresses into a few phrases the negative-positive political aesthetic of the film, marked even in the speaker's sharp shift in tone as he moves from the grave to the meeting, death to life, past to present:

> Death for one man, a stone for memory. But the miners were organized! Americans are too tough to frighten. The school went on with its work....

The fourth section rejoices in the victory of an organized working community over threats and intimidation. A sign announces the Fourth of July Labor Rally and Parade, the list of speakers including William Turnblazer, president of District 19 of the UMWA; Dr. Arthur E. Morgan, chairman of the TVA; and Dr. James Dombrowski, "educator." A short series of shots shows the sign posted in the window of a shoe shop, a furniture store, an ice cream parlor, and then coverage of the parade commences—a carload of waving youths, bands, baton twirlers, men of the UMWA and women of the ACWA on the march through the streets of La Follette. The narrator ensures that there can be no mistaking the meaning of the sequence:

> A new kind of Independence Day. No more terror. No more insecurity. No more gangsters. No more fear in the streets. The people are the unions, the unions are the people.

In the fairgrounds, the celebration continues: a three-legged race, a long jump contest, piggyback competitions, tug of war ("a miners' local against the boys from the mill"), boxing, the oldest married couple, and—most distinctively— "the oldest American sport," hog calling. The games are interrupted for a few brief shots of an assembled crowd and speakers: a miners' representative, a teacher from the Highlander Folk School (presumably Dombrowski) who "promises the people of La Follette that the school will continue to answer their needs, will continue despite financial difficulties, that the school is answerable only to the people of Tennessee." The final speaker shown is a woman textile organizer "who was a graduate of the school." The film then reverts to its imagery of Fourth of July picnic contests—an egg and spoon race, a sack race, shot-putting. This part of the final section concludes with an affirmation on the soundtrack of newly-found power:

> Youth takes over, a new generation. Daughters of miners, daughters of lumbermen. They've got strength and they've got nerves. The children of union men in a union town. They've got courage and hope and clear heads. And they're going to need them.

A shift in tone is signalled with a transition from the upbeat martial rhythms of the labor rally sequence to the mournful choral music which had accompanied the opening evocation of devastation on the Cumberland Plateau. And the imagery of the first section is recapitulated: sky over the hills, huts among the trees, a poor woman and her child, a crockery-strewn grave, a deserted mine entrance. "For the badlands remain," we are told, "the rotting houses on the mountains." But it is only a short reminder of the poverty to be overcome; there follows a montage of activity, movement and change, men at work in the forests and reclaiming soil, and then a series of images of the new dams in the Tennessee valley, with their spillways and turbines, interspersed with shots of a farmer plowing, and miners pledging allegiance to the UMWA. Finally, we see a young worker at the Fourth of July rally putting the shot, his fist thrust toward the camera in a gesture of might which recalls union power through its association with the Communist salute. The commentary summarizes the film's conception of material transformation of conditions of life in the region through working-class unity:

> The people must be fed. No more routine of birth and death and scurvy. The land must give life. There is so much work to do, so many riches lost under the ground. There's work for a hundred thousand men, to clear away the years of neglect, to put back the flooded soil, to bring out of the stony ground, life. TVA, light for the dark valley. A good beginning, but only a beginning. This land can be rich, can bring forth wheat and fruit and hope for these American people. Union towns, good wages, decent food, a new kind of life, rich and abundant. The people stand together. Their union is their power. A new kind of America is beginning to rise, a land of the free. Power, light, a new morning for America, for the folk of the Cumberland.

People of the Cumberland shares with *Heart of Spain* and *China Strikes Back*, the two Frontier films which preceded it, a structure of contrast and opposition, of sections charged alternately with negative and positive emotions. Yet unlike its predecessors it cannot truly be considered "dialectical" in the sense in which Hurwitz understood the term. While in *Heart of Spain* the wounds inflicted by enemy shelling and bombing are mended by the organization of joint civilian-military resistance, and in *China Strikes Back* Japanese invasion is countered by the unified mobilization of the Chinese nation, in *People of the Cumberland* there is no such inner logic. It is not readily apparent how the hunger and economic stagnation of section 1 can be overcome by the studying and folk dancing of section 2, or how the gangsterism of section 3 can be thwarted by the fun and games of section 4. The various parts in fact interact only loosely, displaying both stylistic and semantic discontinuities.

Stylistically, the most striking departure from the predominant documentary pattern adhered to in most of the film occurs in sections 3(a) and 3(c), the dramatized incident of the murder of the labor organizer by thugs. The thinking which lay behind the incorporation of this two-part sequence can be traced back to the aesthetic position papers published in 1934 and 1935 by Ralph Steiner and Leo Hurwitz, and discussed in chapter 4. The influence of Lee Strasberg was perhaps the dominant factor. Strasberg had made them realize—Steiner and Hurwitz wrote—that film is "*theatrical*—that is, it communicates its meaning by the recreation of dramatic situations in filmic time and space, and depends for its effectiveness on the emotional involvement of the audience in these situations." The killing of Barney Graham was an event which in itself made dramatically evident the conflict of progressive and reactionary forces; and its recreation on film afforded the opportunity of experimenting with mise-en-scene, montage, and sound for maximum emotional impact, in a way denied the filmmakers in the documentary segments of the work. The incident was in fact a classic example of the type of factual material which in Steiner's opinion (expressed in his 1934 article, "Revolutionary Movie Production") should be included in documentary films, but for technical reasons had to be restaged: "events that have happened in the past, events which happen only once, and those of which capitalist society may not be sufficiently proud to want recorded."[37]

The sequence is put together, as Vladimir Petric observes, in a "histrionic manner ... which places it in total stylistic dissonance with the strongly documentary fashion of recording reality in the remaining portion of the film." The low-key lighting, ominous chords, and threatening voices heighten to a melodramatic pitch the series of quick shots of thugs receiving and loading their revolvers, and subsequently delivering their "Get out of town" note. The continuation, in which the organizer is ambushed, departs furthest from the rest of the film in that it employs "voice-over from the grave"—the first-person stream-of-consciousness conveying awareness of impending doom ("I knew it was coming"), justified aesthetically, perhaps, by the fact that Barney Graham, according to Horton, had been aware of the danger he was in, and yet unwilling to ward off his fate. The scene of stalking, struggle, and shooting is constructed from a large number of short takes, "on the montage principle of analyzing the event by its division into smaller visual units"—which is, as Petric argues, "the method frequently used by revolutionary Soviet directors to heighten the conflict on the screen, to lengthen it and to aid in the characterization of the personages involved," though it is also not far removed from the fast-paced cutting of a climactic sequence in a Hollywood suspense thriller.[38]

The stylistic disjunction of the murder sequence was, perhaps, less evident to contemporary audiences than it is today. Critics reviewing *People of the Cumberland* at the time of its release did not single the episode out, and it is possible that viewers did not find the dramatic tension contrived, just as they accepted the reenactments of *The March of Time* (and *The World Today)* as legitimate aesthetic devices for heightening documentary realism. (It was a period, of course, before television and widespread sync-sound shooting on location had made the resort, in documentary, to staging techniques derived from narrative cinema less common and, when used, less convincing.) Some degree, at least, of audience acceptance is implied in the fact that the sequence was a direct continuation of the experiments in dramatizing real-life incidents conducted by Nykino in *Sunnyside* and *Black Legion,* and was a forerunner of several similar, and more fully developed sequences in *Native Land.*

What characterizes such sequences is their strict delimiting of the degree of individualization permitted. Just as Hero Escobedo and Enrico Gallan in *Heart of Spain* are "characters" only in a very restricted sense, so the hired killers and the labor organizer in *People of the Cumberland* scarcely emerge from their anonymity. Although the victim's voice-over invites audience identification, emotional involvement with the man is circumscribed by the fact that he is depicted only in the one sequence in which he meets his death. No detail of his personal life, nor—perhaps more significantly—of his working life as a union leader is permitted to emerge; and hence *People of the Cumberland* is a long way from the thirties' Soviet aesthetic of socialist realism and its embrace of the exemplary individual. Hurwitz's interpretation of the Brechtian approach to political drama, which he applied to *Heart of Spain* and *Native Land,* is here equally applicable to *People of the Cumberland:* the audience "doesn't get lost in an island of self, into sentimentality, into the consideration of the individual as apart from other individuals, but becomes part of the texture and contour of the forces of the world you're in."[39]

Consideration of the film's aesthetic thus leads inevitably to an examination of its semantic dimension, its ideology. Whether more or less accidentally or by conscious design, *People of the Cumberland* is situated squarely within the boundaries of the People's Front political analysis and tactical line adopted by the CPUSA in the latter half of the thirties. Communist parties internationally demoted class struggle in favor of an alliance with sections of the middle classes against fascism, and—in case these sections of the middle classes should become alarmed—placed a virtual interdiction on the discussion of socialism. In Europe, where strong fascist movements existed, the rationale for this strategy was readily apparent; it was less clear in the United States, where the most openly fascist elements—the Silver Shirts and the Christian Front—were also among the most laughably innocuous. Party orthodoxy, nonetheless, called for a recasting of the terms of the political contest, and in the ensuing ideological debate of the period, when "democracy" and "civil liberties" became Communist watchwords and capitalism not a fit subject for attack, the thrust of allegedly radical social criticism was somewhat blunted. *People of the Cumberland* reflects the People's Front position in its conception of the alignment of forces in the current struggle, its promotion of various manifestations of "Americanism," and in its commitment to short-term trade-union goals.

The Communist party continued, of course, to endorse working-class solidarity, and the montage in section 2(b) of *People of the Cumberland* of sit-down strikers and union demonstrators from across the nation is an inspiriting visualization of the concept. But for what purpose this unification was to be achieved—whom the workers were to be aligned *against*—was less clear in 1938 than it had been earlier in the decade. The Highlander teaching session depicted in section 2(a), and described above, names those forces which are to be considered enemies and allies of the working people of Tennessee. A pertinent factor here is that the state—in the form of the Roosevelt government with its labor legislation, and the Constitution—is no longer viewed as an arm of the ruling class (as it was, for example, in the productions of the Film and Photo League), but as a supporter of workers in their drive to unionize. Moreover, the chief enemy of the working class is not defined as the bourgeoisie itself, the owners of the means of production, but as a particular right-wing faction of that class, the "associations of manufacturers"—a reference principally to the National Association of Manufacturers, repeatedly denounced by radicals at the time for its strike-breaking policies and anti-union activities. "No-strike injunctions" are identified as things to be fought, but it is not explained who they are obtained by—the employers—and how they are obtained—through the state's legal apparatus—and thus no conclusions are drawn on this subject. Likewise, the "thugs hired in Memphis" are classified as antagonists, but the question of who hired them is unanswered. (It remains a mystery in the dramatized sequence, in which the "powerful forces that still denied the right of these people to a happy life" are not named.) In general, despite its apparent concreteness (and its visual charts), the lesson—or what we see of it in the film— serves to obfuscate more than explicate the nature of the capitalist system and the oppression of the worker under it.

People of the Cumberland contains various manifestations of that Americanism with which the rhetoric of Party-influenced organizations in the later thirties became permeated, in line with the People's Front slogan "Communism is Twentieth-Century Americanism." In Communist parades the red flag was replaced by the Stars and Stripes, and various junctures in *People of the Cumberland* the American flag is prominent: at the meeting of Highlander students at which the rules of debate are taught, during the visual-charts session, in one of the workers' parades from elsewhere in the country, during the UMWA meeting when new members take the oath of allegiance, at the La Follette rally, and (with special emphasis) in the final montage.

With the People's Front philosophy came a new attention to patriotic lineage. "The Communist party did not neglect genealogy," a pair of anti-Communist historians sardonically observed, "and since by happy chance Earl Browder could trace his line back to pre-Revolutionary Virginia, many were the descriptions in Communist literature of the covered wagons that had been ridden by his always forward-looking ancestors. A campaign biography," they continued, "...declared that 'The Browders have a right to say that they are among the founders of America.'"[40] *People of the Cumberland* similarly takes pride in the fact that the mountain folk of Tennessee put down their roots long ago (unlike the members of Frontier Films, who were, for the most part, first-generation Americans). The narration tells us:

> Yet they're the stock of pioneers, the tough Scots and the English, descendants of the people who came here two hundred years ago with hope and a few grains of seed. These are the same faces, the fifth generation.

And again:

> For they are the stock of the first pioneers. Tough, clear-headed, brave.

And yet again:

> The daughters of pioneers... Brave, a crackerjack speaker. The leaders of the Cumberland, the people of tomorrow.

The radicals responsible for the script apparently failed to notice that in conferring moral qualities on the protagonists on the basis of genetics they were guilty of mysticism, if not racism.

A happier aspect of the sudden Communist interest in national traditions was the stress attached to the recuperation of folk culture. If a dance, for example, was old, it was considered worth preserving—like the Aguachadilla, featured in a celebrated sequence in *Return to Life,* "a dance a thousand years old that began when they were serfs in the middle ages, when they bowed to the lords and were bought and sold with the land." *People of the Cumberland* depicts the American equivalent, folk dances almost as venerable but dating, allegedly, from better times: "dances that their fathers had forgotten, the dances of a long time ago when the community was happy and prosperous." The shift in emphasis from the earlier years of the decade, when "revolutionary" dance, a new proletarian form of artistic expression, was being forged, is striking.

Reclaiming the Fourth of July from the right-wing patriots was a crucial part of the Americanism campaign. As early as February 1936, a Communist party writer had argued that the celebration by workers and peasants of Bastille Day in France offered an inspiration, if not a precise model, for giving Independence Day commemorations a working-class slant. "While we cannot adopt for ourselves the pattern of work of the French party," he cautioned, "nevertheless, within time, proper mass agitation can arouse the American workers against the American Legion fanfare of patriotism and anti-Communist poison on the anniversary of the American Revolution." The shift towards such a symbol of mainstream American life was in accord with the new line adopted at the Eighth Communist Party Convention in 1935: it would "hardly be in the spirit of the United Front and of our new tactical orientaton to ignore the traditions of July 4," the writer declared, asking: "How can we realize this need to translate and transform the tradition of July 4? How can we make of this day one of struggle and demonstration instead of a nightmare of blatant patriotism?"[41] *People of the Cumberland* responds. The answer is to make July 4 an occasion for a union parade and a labor rally, to invite as speakers not Legionnaires and Daughters of the American Revolution, but union officials, radical teachers, and New Deal administrators. "A new kind of Independence Day," the narrator informs us, twice. Sealing the spirit of the event is the musical track, which offers a brassy rendition of a medley of traditional tunes including *I've Been Working on the Railroad, Old MacDonald had a Farm, Goodnight Ladies,* and *Mary had a Little Lamb.*

The film's adherence to trade-unionist values is evident throughout, not least in the audacious claims of the commentary ("the people are the unions, the unions are the people"). In the final montage of the film the position is summed up—and inadvertently subjected to a subversive critique.

Following the short series of images which remind the audience of the still depressed condition of the mountain areas, there is a wipe which introduces a coda consisting of 24 brief shots:

> men at work in forest, thinning / workers reclaiming soil / earthmover grabbing soil / power station and dam / CLOSER SHOT, LOW ANGLE, dam with water pouring from below / INTERIOR of power station, hydroelectric turbines / water falling down spillway / farmer plowing / miner (#1) taking UMWA oath / dam with spillway / falling waters / miner (#2) taking UMWA oath / miner (#3) taking UMWA oath / miner (#4) taking UMWA oath / water spilling from dam / OVERHEAD SHOT, water falling / US flag / spillway with jet of water / shot-putting at Labor Rally / spurting waters / power transformers / dam with cascading water / two colliding jets of water / young shot-putter, fist TOWARD CAMERA.[42]

Somewhat in the manner of Lorentz's *The River,* the shots of the dams symbolize work, power, abundance—an optimistic future for the region. Unlike Lorentz, however, the Frontier filmmakers introduce footage of the workers and farmers who create the wealth and who will, supposedly, benefit from it. Additionally, they repeat a series of medium close-ups of miners pledging allegiance to their union, while once more affirming their patriotism by means of the Stars and Stripes. Finally, images of shot-putters signify the youthful strength which will transform the life of the people of the Cumberland. The montage ordering associates unionism with the concrete solidity of dams and the dynamic force of jets of water; the last image concludes the film on a note of free-spirited vigor.[43]

The ideological statement is easily read, even without the expository narration ("Union towns, good wages, decent food . . . "etc.). Yet there are holes in it, which correspond in some respects with the logical gaps between sections of the film as a whole. The give-away is the sudden introduction, at this late point in the picture, of the TVA power project, which has not received even the briefest of mentions hitherto. Recourse to this *deus ex machina* which will bring prosperity to Tennessee betrays the fact that the film has presented no evidence to suggest that union organizing, in itself, can deal with the economically depressed condition of the Cumberland area. (In fact, it may prove counter-productive, with millowners who had established themselves in the region to take advantage of cheap labor moving elsewhere.) An authentic analysis of the problems of the Cumberland and their potential solution would have to take account of such issues as public and private investment, regional planning, and the ownership of land and industry—no matter how awkward politically it might be to do so. *People of the Cumberland,* failing to give outright endorsement to the New Deal project as a model for economic development in the region, and outlining neither the hazards of capitalist investment nor the prospects of socialist planning, remains bound within the tight ideological constraints of the People's Front line. One leaves Frontier's first domestic production with the impression that square dancing and hog calling, delightful as they are, are no substitute for serious political thinking.

9

Native Land

Although not released until 1942, *Native Land* was conceived and largely filmed in the years 1937-39, and is quintessentially a product of the People's Front era. CPUSA leader Earl Browder had declared, in conformity with decisions promulgated by the Communist International at its Seventh World Congress in 1935, that the crucial political struggle of the day was not socialism vs. capitalism, but democracy vs. fascism. And democracy in the United States was to be preserved, the Communist argument ran, by a vigorous defense of those civil liberties which were the heritage of the revolutionary history of the American people, and which were now menaced by powerful reactionary forces with fascist tendencies.

The immediate inspiration for the film was the series of hearings conducted in Washington was the series of hearings conducted in Washington by the La Follette Civil Liberties Committee (a subcommittee of the Senate Committee on Education and Labor), which was established by Senate resolution in June 1936 and continued in existence for four years. Like several investigating committees which had preceded it, such as the Pecora Committee (1932-33), which laid bare the unethical practices of bankers, the Nye Committee (1934-1936), which dissected the munitions industry, and the Black Committee (1935), which exposed the utilities lobby, the La Follette Committee was a political instrument in the hands of congressional liberals. It was created in reponse to pressure from two main sources: from organizations (such as Gardner Jackson's National Committee on Rural and Social Planning and Benjamin C. Marsh's People's Lobby) concerned about the plight of sharecroppers in the South; and from the National Labor Relations Board, frustrated by right-wing industrialists in its efforts to enforce the 1935 Wagner Act and thus guarantee the right of collective bargaining.[1]

Partly because of entrenched opposition to such an inquiry in the Senate, the La Follette Committee never paid much attention to sharecroppers, and soon gave up all investigations that touched on the Deep South. Instead, it narrowed its focus—at least until 1939—to anti-union activity, mostly in industrial regions of the North. Taking as its yardstick labor's right to organize, it painstakingly revealed the widespread violations of that right by employers. In particular, the committee exposed corporation techniques of union-smashing by the employment of labor spies, and strike-breaking by means of munitions stockpiling and vigilante force.[2]

The La Follette Committee became both a prop to the National Labor Relations Board, as had been foreseen, and a powerful adjunct of the CIO in its unionizing drives. The committee afforded assistance to the UAW's General Motors organizing campaign, was influential in U.S. Steel's decision to sign a contract with the CIO in 1937, directed a glare of publicity on "Little Steel's" anti-union tactics, particularly the Republic Steel Massacre of May 30, 1937, and triggered FBI investigations into Harlan County's reign of terror that led eventually, after court cases, to the UMW unionization of Kentucky mine fields in 1938. The CIO's general counsel Lee Pressman wrote a letter to senators commending the committee for uncovering "a vast conspiracy against the civil rights of workers throughout broad sections of American industry" and arguing that, "The exposure of this conspiracy has been of great assistance not only to organized labor, but to all democratic and progressive forces in the United States."[3]

Some of the committee's most important work was in detailing and denouncing the lucrative and treacherous business of labor espionage. Spy agencies such as the Railway Audit and Inspection Company attempted to destroy their own records, but committee agents rescued fragments from wastebaskets and pieced them altogether so that the damning evidence was not lost. As a result of exposure, two of the biggest detective agencies in the field, Pinkerton's and Corporations Auxiliary Co., went out of the business of labor spying in 1937. This phase of the committee's work was given popular treatment in Leo Huberman's *The Labor Spy Racket,* published in September 1937 and an acknowledged stimulus for *Native Land.*[4]

The chairman of the committee, Senator Robert M. La Follette, Jr., at times seemed lukewarm in his commitment to its work, and there seems little doubt that the aggressiveness with which inquiries were pursued can be attributed to the presence of radicals on the committee's team of investigators. Key staff members such as counsel John J. Abt (until mid-1937) and Charles Kramer (or Krivitsky) were later revealed to have been Communist party members, and others were strongly left-wing. Historian of the committee Jerold S. Auerbach writes:

> With a nucleus of at least half a dozen staff members sympathetic to Communist party doctrine, it is not surprising that incidents were selected, witnesses chosen, and reports drafted that stressed the theme of class warfare and placed responsibility for it squarely on the shoulders of the American capitalists. Industrial tyranny was a fact—and the La Follette Committee performed a genuine service in exposing it. Yet the committee, by producing a composite portrait of the American industrialist as an armed practitioner of class violence,

probably did more to buttress the Communist party line than any other New Deal institution.[5]

The decision to base a film on the findings of the La Follette Committee may have been one of the Frontier collective's first decisions, although other projects, such as the Bucks County farming story and the child labor film, were initially given more publicity. As early as June 26, 1937, at any rate, Lionel Berman was able to write to Roger Baldwin of the American Civil Liberties Union: "We have just completed the script for another *World Today* release—a two-reel progressive *March of Time* based on the findings of the La Follette Senate Committee."[6]

Ben Maddow was responsible for the script, and as recounted in chapter 5, production began in the fall under the direction of the Group Theatre's Michael Gordon, with Willard Van Dyke on camera. The flavor of shooting at this early stage is suggested in production manager George Jacobson's account of the filming of a Republic Steel Massacre sequence (the footage, like most— perhaps all—of the material shot by the Gordon-Van Dyke unit was scrapped after the restructuring of the *Native Land* project early in 1938):

One of the big scenes called for restaging the Republic Steel strike in Chicago, where the Chicago police massacred many working people, union people. And the newsreel film of that was untouchable. There was film of it, and it was quite bloody, and it was kept in secret by Congress I guess . . . they wouldn't release the film, and neither would the companies who made the film. And so we had, we thought, to accommodate the script that Ben had written, to restage it. Well, we had no organization really—I was the production manager, but what was I managing—just the crew. So I found a location in Green Point that was a Republic Steel plant, had "Republic Steel" written on it, and a big empty lot alongside of it, and it was the location we were going to use to restage the massacre. So I made arrangements with some union, I forget which now, to have a lot of people out at the location on that date, or to meet me here in New York, and I would get them out there. The date came, the crew was out there waiting, Mike Gordon had these khaki riding breeches on, and puttees—or was that Willard Van Dyke? Either one of them, I forget which it was. But they were really laying it on. When I got to the union hall to pick up the people here in New York there was nobody there. No one. So I went down to Sixth Avenue, where they had a lot of employment agencies, and people standing out looking at the signs, and I said, "Anyone who wants a job, follow me." And I had about a couple of hundred people following me, and I got a lot of nickels and went into the subway, I paid their fares, and got them out to Green Point, to the location. We got on to the location, and they all wanted to know how much they were going to get, and what they were going to do. And so I had to call New York, Lionell was in the office, and I said, "I need a lot of money, fast." I had to pay these people. And we'd also had lunch catered, and all that. And then I had hired costumes, policemen's uniforms, and so on and so on. So they started to shoot with these people, and meanwhile the money was coming, and then we had to line them up and pay them the money, ahead of time, before they would do too much. But when I saw the rushes of what we had done . . . I began to have my doubts that we were on the right track.[7]

In November, laboratory invoices indicate, the unit was at work shooting a labor meeting and scenes in Bronx Park, as well as the disputed farm sequence; in January 1938, it obtained footage of Jersey City's notorious Mayor Frank Hague. The latter was intended for an exposé of the Hague "dictatorship," which as late as April 1939 was planned as a "major episode" of the film, though it was not included in the final version. Hague was a natural target for a documentary on civil liberties: he was quoted as saying, "As soon as they begin to shout about 'free speech' and 'free press' and 'civil rights,' I know they are Communists. They are not really fighting for rights, but raising this cry as a subterfuge." On January 6, 1938, the *New York Post* addressed a warning to him:

> Mayor Hague: Frontier Films, which incurred the wrath of Japan for screening a pro-China movie, and the wrath of Germany for producing a Spanish Loyalist film, is completing the Rome-Tokyo-Berlin-Jersey City axis. It will take movies of your anti-labor meeting tonight.[8]

The circumstances under which production on the film was halted and the whole project restructured have been discussed in chapter 5. For Leo Hurwitz, the footage Gordon and Van Dyke had shot for the farm sequence was "just too bare . . . it had more the character of the *Sunnyside* eviction sequence. For a *March of Time* kind of thing," he contends, "it would have been OK, but for something that had to get in and really pull up the quality of life that was in it, it simply was not rich enough or intense enough." He explains the thinking which led to the reorganization:

> That was a situation in which work had been done, a group had been given an idea for a film to do, and then when we looked at it, a certain part of the work, it was clear to me and to Paul—and to others as well, but we were the leaders, and were the ones who were most outspoken and clear—that the concept behind it was too ill-thought-out, that the work on the shooting was only fair and not great, as it should be, and that the work was done with a tangential control rather than that deep inner control that a work of art needs to have. We decided to reshape the whole production, and then we put aside this footage and started production all over again by going to the script and writing a long shooting script, which was based loosely on the script that Ben Maddow did, which he never fully developed before this fully enough. Then we reorganized the production, and Paul and I decided to co-direct it, with the agreement of the rest of the group. We had been putting off our involvement in it because we were involved in the child labor film, and we felt that this was an important enough project for us to get into right away, in light of the fact that the first footage was too weak.[9]

With the rewriting of the script, it became clear that rather than a two- or three-reeler, *Native Land* would have to be a feature-length film. This, in turn, necessitated a rethinking of the budgetary considerations. Funds were low at this point, but by April 1938 the group had amassed a starting capital of $7,000 for the production and, soon after, shooting recommenced. "I am happy to be able to tell you that we are going to begin photography of the civil liberties film within a short time," Paul Strand wrote to a supporter on April 21. "Although we haven't yet raised the full amount of the budget, we have sufficient funds to begin the work and we feel confident that the balance needed can be raised during the course of production." A total outlay of approximately $40,000 was envisaged at this point.[10]

Meanwhile attempts were made to gain endorsements which would lend prestige to the project and thus make it a magnet for contributors. Among those who were informed of the civil liberties film and who, for various reasons, declined invitations to become sponsors of Frontier Films were Secretary of Agriculture Henry Wallace, Secretary of the Interior Harold Ickes, and Eleanor Roosevelt. Frontier had more luck with congressmen and trade unions. Following a screening for Congressional Liberal Bloc members of *People of the Cumberland, Heart of Spain,* and *China Strikes Back* on March 29, 1928, Congressman John M. Coffee wrote to Strand: "I shall join with Congressman O'Connell in urging sponsorship by as large a number of House and Senate members as possible of the Civil Liberties film." At least four members of the House of Representatives became members of Frontier's Advisory Board as a result. Unions, particularly those with militant leadership, were also quick to endorse *Native Land.* By April 1938, expressions of support had been received from the American Newspaper Guild, the Transport Workers Union, the United Federal Workers of America, the State, County, and Municipal Workers, the National Maritime Union, the United Office and Professional Workers of America, and the Textile Workers Organizing Committee; among related bodies endorsing the film were the League of Women Shoppers and the Labor Housing Conference.[11]

Frontier was not, however, successful in securing the endorsement of the American Civil Liberties Union. The ACLU was active in its support of the La Follette Committee (and occasionally critical of the committee's self-imposed limitations in its field of investigation). An officer of the ACLU, playwright Elmer Rice, had apparently contributed to the development of the *Native Land* screenplay: in November 1937, Hurwitz wrote to thank him for his "help on the Civil Liberties script," adding, "We're planning to take you up soon on your offer to cooperate with us." In April 1938, however, the secretary of the ACLU wrote to say that its Committee on Educational Propaganda had found the latest version of the script unsatisfactory: "The manuscript of the film," it was stated, "as the last seen by Mr. Carmer and Mr. Rice and read to the committee at the March meeting, was not considered easily susceptible to satisfactory revision, and therefore the committee did not wish to give it its endorsement." The reasons for the rejection, which were not specified, may well have been the script's concentration on incidents in labor's struggle to organize, at the expense of other violations of civil liberties, as Hurwitz contends (see chap. 5); it should be noted, however, that as late as April 1939 it was intended that the film should include, in addition to material from the La Follette Committee investigations and a treatment of Mayor Hague's regime, "major episodes" documenting "an academic freedom case, and discrimination against racial minorities."[12]

"The great advantage to me in this kind of work," Ben Maddow has said of his period at Nykino and Frontier Films, "was that the writer was not artificially separated from all the other work." The script for *Native Land*, like that for other Frontier productions, was not the creation of an isolated individual, but was "hammered out in arguments and endless conferences." Discussion would center, according to Maddow, on "issues of structure" and on "what material should be used, and how people would go into it, and whether additional shooting had to be done, and how to raise money—all these things were always intermingled." About the political line to be adopted there seems to have been no serious dispute, at least after the departure of Steiner and Van Dyke. "That was a minor part of the question," says Maddow, "because I think that we were more or less agreed."

Factual incidents, which had in most instances been the subject of ACLU or La Follette Committee investigations, formed the core of the screenplay. They included the murder of a union farmer in Michigan in 1934, and of a labor organizer in Cleveland in 1936; the shooting down of two Arkansas share-croppers (one black, one white) by deputies, again in 1936; the infamous Shoemaker killing of November 30, 1935, in which the Ku Klux Klan tarred and feathered progressive candidates in a local Florida election; and the Republic Steel Massacre of 1937. A lengthy central sequence exposing the *modus operandi* of spies in a labor union was a dramatized version of acts revealed in the Senate committee hearings. Interwoven with the portrayal of these selected events, the *Native Land* script called for documentary sequences illustrating the themes of the historical legacy of the Bill of Rights and the modern transformation of American life through industrialization.

In determining the structure of the *Native Land* script, Hurwitz had a decisive impact. Its "dialectical" pattern followed Marxist principles which he had earlier elaborated and applied to *Heart of Spain* (see chap. 6). Maddow, now, has misgivings about this structure, thinking it overly schematic, with "peculiar shifts" and a "lack of surprises." At the time, however, he did not formulate any strong objections, and in case of any difference of opinion on the script would generally yield to Hurwitz. The "dialectical" structure, Maddow says, was

one of the things that we would talk about. And I would generally lose. Because I wasn't quite certain of my own theoretical ground, nor did I have anything to point to. I couldn't say, "Well, I've made this film or that film on an instinctive basis." ... I don't even know that I objected very violently to this kind of structure. I didn't feel secure in myself as to how it should be done. I think that if we discussed it we didn't discuss it very violently, otherwise I would have quit I guess.[14]

According to Maddow, Hurwitz made a greater contribution than Strand at the scripting stage:

Strand was a very, very bright man, particularly when he was young, but he got sort of locked into a political stand, he couldn't yield. He was a very proud man. He could never admit he was in error last week, or anything of this kind. He was certain he was quite right all the way along. So he was simply not flexible to be able to work this thing out.... Hurwitz really dominated both of us, because he'd thought his way around these things, he had theoretical conceptions which most of us hadn't given any thought to.[15]

Maddow continued to form part of the production crew throughout the shooting of the film. "The writer was expected to be around," he says, "in case I had to make changes in dialogue or whatever." (Besides, he adds, "they required extras every once in a while—it was useful to have a writer's anonymous face somewhere.")[16]

Most of the filming of *Native Land* after the reorganization seems to have taken place in two major spurts, in the late spring and summer of 1938, and again of 1939. Financial records indicate major outlays at these two times, with a fallow spell in the fall and winter of 1938, when a fundraising drive was undertaken. Shooting was described as being "about half finished" in the early months of 1939, "nearly two-thirds completed" in July 1939, and "almost completed" on August 29 of that year (when it was noted that "our funds are close to exhausted"). There followed a sustained period of lesser activity from fall 1939 to winter 1941, during which final photography, editing, and preparation of the soundtrack were carried out.[17]

To assist in handling the actors in the shooting of dramatized sequences, William Watts and subsequently Alfred Saxe were hired as "associate directors." Watts had gained acting and directing experience in workers' theatres in San Francisco and in the "Shock Troupe" of the Workers' Laboratory Theatre (later Theatre of Action) of New York; he had previously assisted Frontier in the production of *People of the Cumberland,* and later was employed as stage manager with the Group Theatre. Saxe had attended the University of Wisconsin and worked in the Little Theatre of Chicago before coming to New York, where he had become an actor and director with the Theatre of Action (among his productions were the outstanding agitprop *Newsboy,* and the group's first full-length play *The Young Go First*); he was also a member of the National Executive Board of the New Theatre League and an instructor in Acting Production at the New Theatre School.

Hurwitz explains that Watts and Saxe were given credit as associate directors, "and they functioned as associate directors, with Bill working part of the film, and Al working after Bill had to leave."

They had had considerably more experience with actors than either Paul or I, and that was the basic reason for bringing them on. In Hollywood they would have been described as "dialogue directors," "dialogue coaches," or whatever. But what happened by and large was that I worked with them this way: I would conceive the action in collaboration with Paul, we cast it together, and we developed the action of the scene, we'd lay that out while Paul and I were examining setups as to where it would be shot, and Bill or Al would work with the actors, maybe on a scene that moved through various shooting angles, and then we would look at that. I would generally, but not always, work through the associate director to the actors, so as not to confuse his relationship to them, where there were acting problems involved, or behavior problems, or action problems, or whatever. And then, when we'd had a setup, and decided what part of the action, and what the movements were, we would then adapt the thing that had been built up between the actors and Bill, for example, directly, which we then remolded, and cast into this particular shot. And the holding of the scene as between one shot and another and another... was basically my role. To some extent Paul's, too. The basic work with the actors was either Bill or Al.... [18]

For George Jacobson, the working setup on *Native Land* was frustrating.

It was making film by a committee of two people. They had a director, it was Bill Watts, but Bill was to direct the actors, and Paul and Leo were to direct the film, really. And they did, by a committee of two. And adding Bill Watts for his advice sometimes it was three.... The wait between shots, when we were shooting, was interminable. We had to wait while they discussed and discussed and discussed, and so on. Paul was very much under Leo's influence. Although he had ideas of his own, he generally conceded the point to Leo. And Leo is the kind of man who—there's nothing spontaneous in his work, in my opinion. He gets something, he may come close to something, and then he doesn't quite make it. And then he goes back and does it again, and again, and again. And reshoot it all the time so that it loses whatever life it had, and becomes a technical thing... it's an abstraction, it has no meaning, it doesn't fit together. He's expressing something inside of him that makes him re-do all the time, re-do. I know in films you make a number of takes, but somehow there comes a point where perhaps the first take you've made is the best one you've done, or the fifth take, but not the twentieth. By then you've washed it all up, I think. [19]

Jacobson considers that Hurwitz and Strand did not consult with other members of the collective as fully as they might have done. They were expressing "very personal, deepfelt ideas," as they were entitled to, Jacobson allows—"but to use *us* to do it.... "

I mean film is a collaboration to a certain extent, and we were all working for nothing, and working like crazy, under hard circumstances, and we wanted to participate. We think maybe we might have contributed some more ideas, or something like that. Or at least, if it was film by committee, perhaps they should have enlarged the committee. We sort of felt left out on a lot of things. And the result was we acted bored in many cases, where they wanted adoration. I guess some of us didn't give it to them. [20]

Strand's camerawork on the film was very methodical. "He was very careful about the composition," Maddow reports. "For example, if there was a pan, a man comes out of a door and runs along a path—there were a lot of running shots in the film—he would very carefully frame that doorway, so that itself could be a Strand photograph, and he would pan to a point with a tree on the left behind which the runner went past, and the shot ended, he would end the shot on such a frame that it was, again, a Strand photograph." The deliberate way in which Strand set up his shots did not, however, slow down shooting, according to Jacobson:

> Strand had been a newsreel cameraman at one point, he had shot football games for the newsreels. He was adaptable. He was extraordinarily adaptable.

Strand himself, it was said, resented "as if it were a canard the hint that he is a perfectionist and that that may have had something to do with the prolonged production period."[21]

Locations for filming were chosen mostly in and around New York City, with some trips further abroad when necessary. The Ku Klux Klan sequence was shot at the Communist party's Camp Unity in Wingdale, New York, "with vacationers acting out the script in Klan robes." Episodes of the labor spy sequence were filmed in a union hall of the United Wholesale and Warehouse Employees of New York, Local 65 of the United Retail and Wholesale Employees of America (CIO). Disguised as newsreelmen, a Frontier camera crew (operating from their 1935 Ford station wagon with a platform on top) filmed a May Day parade in the city. Industrial scenes were shot at Jersey Meadows, and the funeral of a victim of the Republic Steel Massacre was staged in a cemetery on Staten Island. New England gravestones and town halls were filmed by Hurwitz and Strand on a separate trip, as were waves crashing on the Atlantic coast in Maine for the "Plymouth Rock" opening montage.[22]

No sets were used. "Although low-ceilinged interiors posed unique lighting problems," it was reported, "Strand found it unnecessary to sacrifice any desired effect for studio flexibility." The documentary look was heightened by the employment of actors who, though mostly professional (with the significant exception of Staten Island grocer James Hanney, who played a union president), were little known to moviegoers, and who wore no makeup. Despite Hurwitz's alleged penchant for retakes, a fairly economical shooting ratio of less than 9-to-1 was achieved.[23]

Although it was stated that "editing was done as the film progressed," itemized accounts detailing expenditure for cutting room and screening facilities indicate that the great bulk of the work was done after principal shooting had been completed, in 1940 and 1941. In addition to footage shot by the Frontier crew, the editors had to gather together and integrate a variety of other visual material: an animated sequence (commissioned from Ted Eshbaugh Studios), stills (of the Republic Steel massacre), workers' newsreel scenes (including Leo Seltzer's coverage of police violence on the Brooklyn docks in 1933), and stock shots (embracing items such as "crowds," "riots," "moving train," "strikes," "Trans-America," "rails from traveling train," and "Capitol at night"). Leo Hurwitz took charge of the editing process, with the help of Julia Milch, Lionel Berman, and Sidney Meyers; sound editing was handled by Meyers and a newcomer to the unit, Ralph Avseev. Richard Leacock, then a physics student at Harvard anxious to learn about film, remembers being allowed to assist Milch, and spending a summer (probably 1940) "sitting in the narrow hallway of Preview Theatre, waiting for a reel of film to splice (Griswold spit and razor blade—God, did they stink)."[24]

Selected to create a score for *Native Land* was the left-wing composer Marc Blitzstein, whose steel-town opera *The Cradle Will Rock,* inspired by Brecht, had caused a sensation in 1937. The music, which included songs with original lyrics for Paul Robeson and chorus as well as orchestral accompaniment for the picture, was composed in the cutting room, probably towards the end of 1940. Blitzstein worked closely with the members of the Frontier team:

> On *Native Land* my work with Paul Strand and Leo Hurwitz is constantly in the best spirit of give-and-take. I have even worked harmoniously with a poet (David Wolff) for the first time in my life.[25]

To speak the commentary, which was written by Ben Maddow (as "David Wolff"), the group "never had anybody in mind but Robeson. We knew it was a task for him," Hurwitz said, "—and he agreed immediately." Robeson, an outspoken opponent of racism and reaction in the United States, was then nearing the peak of his career as screen and stage star and opera singer. It was reported that "Robeson rehearsed the commentary for weeks before it was recorded, as if it were a part in a play." The narrator was offscreen throughout the film except for a final speech delivered to camera (deleted from prints of *Native Land* currently in distribution), arguing that American labor's victory over its enemies at home had strengthened it for the task of fighting "the greatest enemy of our liberty—the Hitler Axis."[26]

Native Land was premiered at the World Theatre in New York (as a benefit for the Newspaper Guild) on May 11, 1942, just five years after the idea of a film on civil liberties and labor's right to organize had first been mooted. General critical reaction was strongly favorable. Bosley Crowther in the *New York Times* labelled it "one of the most powerful and disturbing documentary films ever made," adding that Hurwitz and Strand had "selected their material with care and . . . placed it upon the screen with such bite and dramatic intensity as would make the best directors of films take solemn note." Writing in the *New York Herald Tribune,* Richard Watts, Jr., declared that the film had "a savagery, a power, and a persuasively factual quality that are coldly impressive." *Time* magazine called it "an eloquent indictment of acts of injustice and intolerance" with "a fine feeling for suspense and violence." The trade papers were lavish in admiration of its technical qualities: *Variety* asserted that "the production is refreshing on many angles, often almost brilliant," displaying "remarkably intelligent" direction, while *Film Daily* averred that "Messrs. Hurwitz and Paul Strand have done a superb job of producing, directing, photography, and editing." Joining in the paean of praise was Eleanor Roosevelt, who in her published column described *Native Land* as "a beautiful piece of photography and most artistically produced."[27]

Many reviewers, however, had reservations about the suitability of the film for release in time of war. For Archer Winsten of the *New York Post*, it "would have spoken to more people and fulfilled a more timely function before the United States was at war with foreign nations"; he argued that "despite the use of timeless conflicts, the film sounds dated already, at its premiere." Echoing these sentiments, William Boehnel in the *New York World-Telegram* wrote:

> As propaganda, then, *Native Land* seems as feeble and dated as a film showing the evils of Nazism before the war. Moreover, it can be questioned whether opening up old wounds is prudent at a time when every effort is being made to seek unity between labor and capital.

And a similar view was expressed in the *New York Daily News*. "Since it is not the type of picture to make converts of those the film calls fascist, and since it serves only to revive the wrongs inflicted upon the 'little people,'" wrote Dorothy Masters, "there seems little argument for its release... at a time when national unity is paramount."[28]

The left-wing press countered by stressing the connection, implicit in the film, between native and foreign fascists. "*Native Land* is Powerful Exposé of America's 'Little Hitlers,' " David Platt's review in the *Daily Worker* was headlined, "Indicts Spirit of Klan and Appeaser Elements in U.S." Quoting Robeson's final speech, in which it was asserted that "no appeasers, fifth columnists, or native fascists can divide us," Platt maintained: "If today plant charts are shooting up and labor everywhere is producing for victory against the Axis, it is because this conspiracy to stop the onward march of unionism was nipped in the bud by the mass action of labor." The film, therefore (he implied) would strengthen rather than sap national morale.

Radicals found support for this point of view in the column of Richard Watts, Jr.:

> ... my chief interest in the picture lies in a point it brings up concerning all forms of expression in this day of total war which is also a war of ideas. To a certain extent the story told by *Native Son* [*sic*] is dated. Begun, as it was, several years ago, it deals with a state of

affairs that took place in the preceding decade. Since Pearl Harbor we have been chiefly concerned with other things, including national solidarity. Is, therefore, a work that brings up these ugly issues of the past an unnecessary raking-over of old coals? Is it unwittingly giving aid and comfort to the enemy, as it shows with considerable conclusiveness that the American record is not in all ways a pretty one? Since the one important thing in the world today is to win a war against a savage foe, is it wise to remind ourselves of such domestic unpleasantness as the film describes? . . .

It is my own impression that the showing of *Native Land,* rather than providing a depressing or subversive spectacle, is an encouraging sign of the national courage and the excellence of the national morale. The facts of incipient fascism in American life have, by almost common consent, always been present, and it strikes me that the most wholesome thing imaginable is to bring them out and face them, if only for the warning they present. It is a little difficult to imagine Germany or Japan facing such self-criticism as the Strand-Hurwitz picture offers, and it is an indication of our strength that we can do so. It would be pretty foolish to beat the fascists abroad and to fail in striking at the fascists at home. *Native Land* is one-sided and strictly partisan, but it is fiercely American in spirit and there is no doubt in its heart about the vital necessity of American victory. It merely reminds us that it is good to be on our guard here, too.[29]

Despite such arguments, the Communist party declined to assist in the promotion of the film through labor unions. Hurwitz explains:

They said, "We like the film but we can't help at this time because we're in a period of national unity." I went to see [William Z.] Foster and he told me had had written a book which he had to keep in his desk until the end of the war, for the same reasons. Foster had seen the film and I think he liked it very much. "Don't worry," he said, "the class struggle will be back." He seemed to have a patience I didn't have. I think it was a mistaken patience. You can't have a period of national unity which forgets history. Not without eroding basic principles. I wasn't able to quote Mao on the question of independence and initiative in the united front, but that's the basic argument I made.[30]

The Communist party's decision was a contributing factor in *Native Land's* failure to achieve a widespread release after its successful run at the World Theatre. Distribution of the film was also hampered by censorship, its status as an independently produced feature, its unfamiliar quasi-documentary form, its lack of a major star, doubts about its topicality, as well as its leftist political stance. *Native Land* gained only a few sporadic showings, mostly in major cities, during 1942 and 1943. Revived briefly after the war, it then sank into oblivion as the Cold War intensified. The film was taken out of distribution by the trustees, and attempts were made to round up all prints. Those who had made loans or purchased trustee certificates never fully recouped their investment.[31]

In the early seventies, however, *Native Land* reemerged from obscurity. Control and ownership of the film were transferred by the trustees to Strand and Hurwitz, and in 1974 it was returned to distribution. Several comparatively recent articles attest to a renewed interest in the culminating achievement of Frontier Films and radical cinema of the Depression years.[32]

Native Land has a complex structure, and mixes material in an unusual variety of cinematic modes. Table 1 represents the basic breakdown of subject matter, and provides an indication of the dominant mode within each subdivision. (The term "drama" refers to sequences in which individualized characters emerge, "staged documentary" to those in which actions have evidently been performed for the camera, but whose linear logic is thematic rather than narrative; the line between these, and between both of them and straight "documentary," is sometimes difficult to draw.) The table makes apparent the film's alternating pattern of light and dark, advance and setback, which is the cornerstone of the "dialectical" structural aesthetic developed consistently in Frontier productions.[33]

Section 1. The film opens with a series of three titles:

Since the founding of our country the American people have had to fight for their freedom in every generation.

Native Land is a document of America's struggle for liberty in recent years.

It was in this struggle that the fascist-minded on our own soil were forced to retreat. And the people gained the democratic strength essential for national unity and victory over the Axis.

There follows a sustained montage, about seven minutes in length, illustrating the theme that liberty was the ideal on which the United States of America was founded and developed. The section is divisible into two main parts, the first covering the pioneering phase from 1607 to the late nineteenth century, the second devoted to the subsequent period of industrialization.

In the initial series of shots, images of the natural landscape—stormy seas, rocks, sky, mountains, clouds, woods, swollen rivers, trees, fields—are interwoven with images of tombstones, of New England churches and town halls, of statues (Washington, Jefferson, Lincoln, the Statue of Liberty, and others), and of American flags. The photography imparts an austere grandeur to the subject matter; camera movements are uniformly slow. A specific montage effect is achieved by intercutting two shots (both tilting up) of a Greek column and a massive tree trunk: "We built liberty into the beams of our houses," says the narrator. The statues, in conjunction with the commentary, evoke the War of Independence and the Civil War—battles to preserve and extend freedom—and the graveyard shots recall the cost in lives lost of creating a "new world... with liberty and justice for all."

Section 1(b) has a faster, more nervous rhythm. The imagery is of molten iron, locomotive wheels, steam engines, trains, girders, bridges, factories, pylons, high-tension wires, smokestacks, oil tanks, cranes, pipelines, sky-scrapers—and again, the Stars and Stripes and the Statue of Liberty. "New

Table 1.
Structure of *Native Land*

Section	Subject	Subdivisions	Mode
1	The Forging of Liberty	(a) Pioneering, Revolution, Civil War	Documentary
		(b) Industrialization	Documentary
2	Vigilante Violence	(a) The Michigan Farmer	Drama
		(b) The Cleveland Union Man	Drama
		(c) The Arkansas Sharecroppers	Drama
		(d) Transition: Night	Documentary
3	The Working Day	(a) Waking, Breakfast, Going to Work	Staged documentary
		(b) Work	Documentary
		(c) Union Meeting	Documentary
4	Labor Espionage	(a) The Industrial Service Agency	Staged documentary
		(b) The Labor Spies	Drama
		(c) The Blacklist	Staged documentary
5	Union Upsurge		Documentary
6	Repression	(a) The Memphis Grocer	Drama
		(b) The Murdered Organizer	Drama
		(c) Police Violence	Documentary
7	Anger: The Militant Clergyman		Drama
8	Brutality: The Ku Klux Klan .		Drama
9	Democracy in Action	(a) Public Protest	Documentary
		(b) Destruction of Evidence	Staged documentary
		(c) Reconstruction of Evidence	Staged documentary
		(d) The Conspiracy Exposed	Animation
10	Official Violence: The Republic Steel Massacre	(a) Memorial Day Holiday	Documentary
		(b) The Police Attack	Stills
		(c) The Funeral	Drama
11	The Defense of Liberty		Documentary
12*	The Present Crisis		Direct address

*Not included in prints of the film currently in circulation.

resources, new power," is the motif of the narration, which assures us that as the face of the nation has been transformed the ideal of liberty stays alive: "The old words, the historic documents, we built them into bridges and dynamos, and concrete cities." The historical prelude to the film is concluded with the line: "We struggled three hundred years and took freedom as our inheritance."

Section 2. The generality of the first section is answered with the specificity of the second; to the past is opposed the present; victories are succeeded by defeats. Three incidents of murder are dramatized, all supposedly factual, all occasioned by the victims' becoming engaged in union activity. A short epilogue shadows forth a symbolic night in which the violence is blotted out, wiped from memory.

There is a lyrical quality to the first sequence of section 2, set on a Michigan farm: sturdy white draft horses, a rude plow cutting the soil, billowy clouds in a blue sky, an excited boy, his mother happy in her work. Fred Hill, who "spoke up at the farmers' meeting last night," goes unsuspectingly to consult with a team of swankily-outfitted hit men—and is found several minutes later by his panicked wife, battered and bloody and dead. "A man's farm invaded," the narrator comments, "his liberty attacked, the right of free speech denied to an American."

The second sequence also depicts violence obliquely. A young maid washing the windows of the rooming house where she works smiles at a boy playing with a paddle ball on the sidewalk, laughs and sings with a fluffy dog on her lap. Then she knocks on a door to do her cleaning, gets no response, tries her key and can't turn it. In the room, her banging shakes the dresser propped against the door, and torn curtains sway at the open window. Alarmed, she forces her way in, discovers the body of a man lying in a pool of spilled ink (or blood?) on the floor. It is Cleveland, Ohio: "A spring day in 1936. Again, it happened again. They say he was a union man."

The scene shifts to Fort Smith, Arkansas. Sharecroppers meeting at a church hall ("they wanted ten cents more for their cotton, just enough to live on") are attacked by rifle-toting deputies. Two men, one black, one white, race away through the swamps. The black man is hit in the leg by gunfire; his companion stops to bind up the wound. Then they walk on, arm in arm. The voice of Paul Robeson breaks into a mournful spiritual, *Dusty Sun.* A deputy, unseen by the croppers, cocks his rifle, fires, and the black man falls dead. There is more firing. The white man runs for his life, reaches a barbed wire fence, is shot, falls. A torn rag of his shirt remains pinned to the wire. "The South in July, cotton country," the narrator says; "Two men, dead on a road in Arkansas."

A short transitional sequence follows: a moving shot from a roadway, a farmhouse, a pine cone falling, water flowing, the countryside at night. "The long afternoon kept moving across America," we are told, and the violent acts of vigilantes are unknown or unremembered: "Night erased them all for 130 million Americans."

Section 3. A new day, a new mood: America wakes up to the cheerful strains of a Blitzstein song ("Open the window hear it coming / Here's another new day..."). A montage of details of early morning life in an American city: raising the shades, brushing teeth, stirring porridge, a girl skating, the newsboy on his bicycle, the family breakfast, bouncing balls on the street, a baby in a carriage, and so on. And then the "little people, unaware of powerful enemies" are seen on their way to work, crowding the streets, clocking in at the factories.

Section 3(b) depicts Americans at work: steelworkers, longshoremen, garment workers, drill-press operators, sign painters, auto workers, ditch diggers, fruit packers, farm workers, fishermen. As the sequence progesses, the men and women are pictured more and more in groups, in collaborative work. "They learned to work together," we learn of the employees in the new industries of twentieth-century America, "and therefore they had to learn to think together, to move together, to act together."

Logically, the film proceeds to document union meetings: long shots and close-ups of workers—both men and women—voting, clapping, speaking, listening, laughing. "They put the Bill of Rights into action," the voice-over tells us. "Here's what they wanted with the Bill of Rights: bread and butter, and old-age pensions, and health insurance, and the forty-hour week." And then, encapsulating the positive-negative pattern of the film: "Yes, they were confident—over-confident."

Section 4. The La Follette Committee had made sweeping investigations into a number of labor espionage agencies (including the Railway Audit and Inspection Co., National Corporation Service Inc., the Corporations Auxiliary Co., Pinkerton's National Detective Agency Inc., and the William J. Burns International Detective Agency Inc.) It had also exposed the operations of industrial munitions manufacturers (such as the Lake Erie Chemical Co., and Federal Laboratories Inc.,), for which the spy firms sometimes also acted as agents. Section 4, a major portion of the film (nearly 26 minutes in length), demonstrates how labor espionage succeeds in smashing workers' attempts to organize.

The first part is a fast-cut montage showing that the agencies offering "a complete line from undercover men to riot guns" operate, on the surface, just like other businesses: name board on the office door ("Industrial Audit Service," "American Service Bureau"), switchboard, phones, filing cabinets. Pages are stapled, shorthand taken, letters typed, mail stamped. The sound-track recalls the "Voices of Commerce" section of Basil Wright's *Song of*

Ceylon—"Hullo, good morning, good afternoon, Dear Sir, My dear Sir, we trust, we firmly believe... "—until the perversion of this particular business becomes apparent:

> Two dozen giant gas grenades, triple X. One Thompson submachine gun, with three additional magazines.... Entirely confidential. The phone rang and a man was bribed. Traps for weak men. Good openings for criminals. Behind the front of everyday business, conspiracy against the lives of innocent men.

In the long second part, a narrative involving penetration of a labor union by such an agency on behalf of the employer is developed. With scenes alternating between the union hall, the agency office, the home of the union president, and the apartment of a stool pigeon (played by Art Smith), the story is told. At a union meeting a "No. 1 rat"(Jim) is exposed, apparently through the vigilance of a sharp member (Harry Carlisle). But Harry, too, is in the pay of the spy firm, as we learn in the next scene: he has been "hooked," and despite his reluctance to continue providing reports, cannot now back out. Through his action in nailing Jim, Harry is promoted to union vice-president, and in that capacity is entrusted with the all-important membership book. Threatened with the disclosure of his spying activities to the union, Harry is induced to pass on the book to the agency; he is bandaged up and his apartment ransacked to make it look as though he has been the victim of force.

The final part of section 4 details the consequences of a union membership list falling into the hands of an employer, as a shift back from drama to quasi-documentary is made. Bosses speak into dictaphones, dismissal notices are typed, workers are notified that they are fired, laid-off employees disconsolately pace empty streets. "Steelworker, salesman, bookkeeper, month after month without a job," says the narrator. "New Orleans longshoreman, Detroit tool and die man. It's all over. You're through. Blacklisted. Where was the right to organize? Where was the Bill of Rights?"

Section 5. The music shifts from the elegiac to the martial, and an assembly of newsreel-type shots shows "how we tore up the blacklist." Union members proudly parade in the streets: the Irish American Trade Unionists, the National Maritime Union, the Amalgamated Meat Cutters. Banners proclaim: "Knowledge is Power: Workers' Education," "Education for Democracy," "Our Aim 100% Union." As in *People of the Cumberland,* the power of organization has triumphed over the anti-union forces: "No more fear in the streets... We carried our names in the open air... Two and a half million new people never organized before." The film goes on to show that unions mean "life, liberty, yes, but also the pursuit of happiness"—we see members of a Laundry Workers Union go on a boat ride, dancing on the decks in a joyful expression of good fellowship and interracial solidarity. Then, we return to public demonstrations:

huge union crowds in the streets and squares of various American cities, ending with a rally in Union Square, New York—"millions of little people banded together to protect each other."

Section 6. The alternating pattern continues: repression sets in. Three short sequences illustrate varied ways in which attempts are made to stem the wave of organizing.

The first part is a dramatized incident involving "Frank Mason, a grocer in Memphis, Tennessee." Frank's neighbors were union people, we are told; he "shared their interests, helped them organize, contributed money when he could." A little girl is in his store playing with a balloon as the sequence begins; it pops, and he laughs and giggles with her. He is weighing out some cheese when a thug with pockmarked face enters, crowbar in hand. "This is an open-shop town," the thug snarls, "You don't seem to learn." He smashes a crate of eggs, terrorizes the girl, and orders the grocer to pay his bills and get out of town. "Twenty years in Memphis," is the narrator's comment; "Raised a family here. Pay him a little visit. Teach him what's what."

The second part is the tail end of what was evidently conceived of as a longer sequence. George Jacobson recalls that he played a small role in a scene in which Karl Malden and Martin Ritt played gangsters.

> It was a gas station sequence.... Those two were gangsters and they drove up in a car. I was a gas-station attendant and they asked for gas, and while I was putting the gas in, I see a body in the car. And then I look up at them and they pull out of the station and leave me flopping in a mud puddle or something like that.[34]

The film omits this, but shows a country road and a body tossed from a truck. Wrapped in a sack, it rolls down a slope to a railroad bed as a train passes (Jacobson played the corpse). "Find the key man," the voice-over explains tersely: "The best organizer, the man you can't buy."

In the third portion of section 6, newsreel footage of attacks by police and deputies on demonstrators and pickets in various parts of the U.S. is assembled. The material includes, notably, the Pathe newsreel of violence against steel strikers in Ambridge, Pennsylvania, in 1933 (previously incorporated in the extant issue of the Film and Photo League's *America Today*); the FPL coverage of police brutality during the Hans Weidemann protest in Brooklyn, also 1933; shots of police using tear gas against crowds at the time of the San Francisco general strike, 1934; and documentation of policemen beating and dragging off demonstrators in Florida. The tone of the commentary becomes acid:

> Murder one man, frighten a thousand. It's technique. Get the whole county in the palm of your hand. Pick up the poolroom sharks. Give 'em a badge. Citizen's committee. Plenty of

whisky. Brand new riot guns. Break up the unions once and for all.... That's the stuff. That's the technique. The open shop's the American way. Mobilize the respectable elements of the community. Rights? We've got to have action. We've go to have law and order in this fair city of ours. Anybody talk about rights, slap him down.[35]

Section 7. Repression provokes outcry among liberal sectors of the community: a minister speaks out. The section consists of a single, low-angle medium shot of the minister delivering a sermon from his pulpit:

In our own town, on our own streets. There are two men dying in the county hospital. But we cannot turn our faces aside. They are our brothers. They were gathered in peaceful assembly. That was their right. They were unarmed and unafraid. They were met with cold-hearted brutal attack. I've been advised to say nothing. Powerful and respectable people in this community have come to me, have phoned to me repeatedly, have urged me not to deliver this sermon. That would be easy, perhaps, but I will not be guilty of such silence.... There are men with high office in this community who would silence brave teachers, violate our free elections, write injustice into law, all in the name of patriotism. Men with great names have hired criminals, have paid weak men to spy on their brothers, have expended secret money to set Christian against Jew, and white against colored, to brand every immigrant a dangerous enemy.... We must grapple with this evil thing, before the forces of darkness arise with fire and sword to break down the very doors of our church. Today, now, we must speak, act, vote, protest, before it is too late!

Section 8. In Tampa, Florida, in 1935, a group known as the Modern Democrats, with a progressive platform, had entered candidates in elections and, as the commentary to this section tells us, had "pledged to smash the political machine" of the Ku Klux Klan. Two of their leaders, Joseph Shoemaker and Eugene Poulnot, together with a Dr. Sam Rogers, were seized by police at a meeting on November 30, 1935, held without charge, and then turned over to the Klan. They were tarred and feathered, and Shoemaker later died from his wounds.

Section 8 dramatizes this incident. At night, around a fire, about twenty Klansmen drag their victims from a car, strip them, tie them to a tree trunk, flog them, and then dip their bodies in molten tar and coat them with feathers. The members of the KKK wear masks and robes; one, who is unmasked, is revealed to be a woman transfixed by the scene of cruelty. The narration relates the incident to other manifestations of native fascism:

Here was treason in America. The face of fascism. KKK. Black Legion. Associated Farmers. Silver Shirts. Christian Front. Lies. Torture. Blackmail. Lynch law. Dr. Rogers tarred and feathered. Ministers, teachers, forced from their profession. Open terror. And secret persecution. Whatever their mask, these forces hated one thing, the practice of democracy.

Section 9. Again the pendulum swings. Public anger results in the formation of the Senate Civil Liberties Committee, whose patient inquiry exposes the "conspiracy" aimed at denying ordinary Americans their rights.

In the first sequence, a montage of documentary material portrays an outpouring of public sentiment. Images of mass meetings, of crowds in the streets, give way to shots of letters, of the Post Office handling mail, of trains and airplanes speeding the message of protest to Washington. "It was we the people, speaking out loud." the narration tells us: "We were sick, and bitter, and angry. We wanted facts, we wanted action." The montage (Hollywood rather than Soviet in inspiration) culminates in a shot of a floodlit Capitol dome at night.

Section 9(b) offers an impressionistic rendering of the evasive tactics employed by the labor spy agencies and industrial munitions companies when threatened with Senate subpoenas. A glass of wine is spilt, an automobile races out of an alleyway, telegrams and letters are burnt, files are torn up and dumped out. The voice-over explains the formation of the Senate Civil Liberties Committee and comments on the stonewalling it encountered:

> Bad news. Bad news for the big shots, for the spy agents. Rumors of Senate subpoena. Bad news for the tear-gas salesmen. Not in today. Out of town. Correspondence? Never keep it. Business? Strictly cash. Don't answer unless you have to. Strikebreaking? Never do it. Stool pigeons? Never use them. We'll never know the full story. We'll never know all the facts. They destroyed the dates, the names, the figures.

"But they were too late." A staged documentary sequence illustrates the process by which torn fragments of partially destroyed documents were reassembled by the La Follette Committee's staff to provide incontrovertible evidence of the underhand attacks on labor of the firms under investigation.

In the fourth part, animation is used to illustrate the film's contention that a "conspiracy entangled the whole United States . . . an immense conspiracy, directed by a handful of fascist-minded corporations . . . to undermine the Bill of Rights, to weaken the strength of America"—a criminal scheme kept secret until the Senate committee "turned on the light." The chief graphic components of the sequence consist of close-up drawings of an eye and an ear (representing spying), and a map of the United States with arrows indicating the locales of union-smashing activity; the arrows move together and interlock, becoming a cobweb over the country. The committee's work of investigation and publicity meant that "the American people had won again: their enemies could no longer operate in disguise."

Section 10. The Republic Steel Massacre is selected as the culminating incident of the film. Its brutality is highlighted by bracketing which places the violence between scenes of contrasting mood: celebration on the Memorial Day holiday, and subsequently the funeral for a slain victim of the police attack.

The first sequence is awash with patriotic imagery: flags, and saluting at a memorial service; parading to honor the dead, Boy Scouts, the laying of wreaths, a salvo of rifles. According to the narration, Memorial Day is "a moment in the history of the Bill of Rights." This more solemn segment is followed by a portrayal of relaxation in the parks. Children provide the dominant motif—riding bicycles and tricycles, sailing model boats, skating, playing on swings and slides and merry-go-rounds. There are shots of lovers, of pigeons, of bears and seals at the zoo. "What do people want out of life?" the narrator asks. "Not very much. Not too much. Enough to eat, and a family, pay the rent, some kind of future."

There is a sudden shift: "At that moment, out in Chicago, two thousand people, walking toward the Republic Steel plant, were blocked by the police." News photographs of the attack (amid clouds of tear gas, police with batons raised and pistols drawn pursue fleeing demonstrators) are accompanied by sound effects of gunfire, a siren, cries. "These facts were proved," the voice-over informs us, alluding to the La Follette Committee investigation (a volume of the published hearings is pictured): "An act of fascism, ten killed, ninety injured."[36]

The third part of section 10, a dramatized sequence, depicts the burial of one of the ten dead. A group of men and women is gathered round a grave site; smokestacks in the background are a reminder of the industrial milieu. Earth is shoveled; the dead man's widow, weeping, collapses under the strain and has to be helped to her feet. The music picks up the sacrificial dance motif of Stravinsky's *Rite of Spring,* suggesting that new life will arise from martyrdom. One of the mourners delivers a simple eulogy, concluding with the words:

> To take away a man's life! They shouldn't get away with a thing like that. He had a right to go on that line. He was the kind of man who stood up for his rights. We don't forget that. Never.

Flowers are tossed in the grave.

Section 11. The closing montage is a reprise of the opening section, reiterating the imagery and the verbal rhetoric of liberty, while placing an intensified emphasis on the necessity for its defense in every generation. The shots are familiar: statues of Jefferson and Lincoln, the hills and valleys of the "raw continent" out of which "we created a new world," New England town halls, old gravestones—and then the smokestacks, steam engines, steel bridges, and skyscrapers of twentieth-century America, followed again by the Stars and Strips and the Statue of Liberty. The narration sums up the film's message:

> We set the foundations of our cities on the rock of the Bill of Rights. And yet today our liberty is in danger. The freedom we have won from enemies abroad must be saved again from enemies within. Once more the old enemy rises to threaten the four freedoms, the rights of all Americans, every creed and every color, to a job, a home, adequate food and medical care, the right to bargain collectively, to act for the greatest good of the greatest number, the

right to live at peace, unthreatened, threatening no one. Today these words must become deeds. For there has never been a moment in our history when Americans were not ready to stand up as free men and fight for their rights.

The argument is clinched by a close-up of the speaker at the funeral (repeated from section 10) vowing, "We don't forget that. Never."

Section 12. The above are the concluding words and images of *Native Land* as it now stands, and as it was probably originally conceived. As a contemporary account indicated, however, "The events at Pearl Harbor necessitated a slight change in the ending of the film."[37] The emphasis on "enemies within" had, in fact, to be reversed. Evidently an epilogue was appended, consisting of a shot or shots of Paul Robeson delivering the following speech to camera:

> This end is our beginning. Today, as never before, we must stand up for our rights as Americans. Together with the peoples of the world we are fighting the greatest enemy of our liberty—the Hitler axis. This scourge of mankind must be destroyed. We Americans have had to fight for our liberty in every generation.
> *Native Land* shows this struggle in our own times. A great and intense conflict. There were many casualties, many wrongs. Yet American labor and the American nation are stronger for having passed through this fire. Labor is producing for victory. We are becoming an organized people, a united people. No appeasers, fifth columnists, or native fascists can divide us. With the united power of field and factory and arms, we will deliver the blows to crush fascism.
> For only absolute victory over Hitler and Japan can safeguard our democratic gains and preserve the independence of America.[38]

Native Land's alternating, episodic structure was not arrived at haphazardly: on the contrary, it was the result of careful and deliberate calculation. Hurwitz's earlier thinking on the notion of "dialectical" film form, and Frontier's experimentation with structures of this type in their short political films, have been described. In *Native Land* this political aesthetic was applied to a full-length work.

Central to the dialectical concept was that the situation dealt with in the film was not fixed but fluid; history was in the process of being shaped, and there were not crippling defeats to mourn nor final victories to celebrate. In Hurwitz's view, such a conception ruled out the possibility of a conventional dramatic climax and resolution. Moreover, concern with an abstract notion—liberty—as the driving force of the film required that the individual dramas, though factual, be subordinated to an overall pattern in which discursive documentary segments would also have a place.

Hurwitz himself had described the thinking behind the structure of *Native Land* as follows:

... what we were doing, rather than defining an abstract political line, was taking a series of events that came out of experience, analyzing them, and finding a line—a line of film and a line of idea.... I wrote on the flypage of my shooting script a little paragraph that was a modernization of the idea that the price of liberty is eternal vigilance. I translated this idea into current terms: in contemporary working-class and union struggles there are no wars won or lost, only battles.

That was the key premise behind the political and emotional development of the film. The emotional development of the film is toward the resolution of a problem; that resolution then becomes a problem itself. That's the reason the film can end with a funeral.... Having come from other defeats, the speaker saying: "We don't forget that, never," is enough to indicate what the line of growth is. I saw it as dialectical—the reforms, defeats, and victories are all part of one developing process, towards a radical social transformation.... even after you have won a victory, the forces and contradictions shape up again, on a different level.[39]

Hurwitz considers that the form of the film, intercutting dramatized episodes and documentary sequences, "added up in practice the years of study and experiment in film" which the Frontier group had undertaken. It was an attempt to come to grips in cinematic terms with the contemporary rise of the labor movement, making the struggles, defeats, and triumphs vivid and emotionally moving for an audience, while at the same time elucidating the underlying social forces at work. "At the time we were writing the script and preparing the production," Hurwitz recently commented, "the militant trade-union movement had made tremendous gains, had fought its way through government and employer repression, and had succeeded in making union organization a right confirmed by law." The form of *Native Land* arose from a transmutation of factual material contained in the reports of the La Follette Committee:

The many volumes of committee testimony contained essential data on the class struggle of the thirties in its wide social aspect as well as in the individual stories of its participants. To weave together the large social design with the human details required thinking in terms of a new film form. This combined the enactment and the document, the lyrical and the statistical, the overall social pattern and real story episodes.

"The function of the technique," Hurwitz wrote on another occasion, "was to bring together seemingly unrelated events into the real coherence they possessed and so dramatize underlying forces and conflict."[40]

The desire to make acted episodes the core of the film arose from the belief, which had been held by members of the Frontier collective since the Nykino days, that straight documentary, failing to touch an audience's emotions, was inefficient as an agitational weapon. Paul Strand, speaking at the Third American Writers' Congress in June 1939, when a completed portion of *Native Land* was exhibited, declared that the film was "designed to arouse the public to the danger of the curtailment of their constitutional rights and to the assaults on democracy being made in various sections of the country by adherents of the Ku Klux Klan, the various 'shirt' groups, and similar organizations." Such a result could best be achieved by a film form which went beyond a conventional newsreel or documentary format, he argued:

> Strand pointed out that the term documentary was vague and often led to a narrow approach. In making the civil liberties film Strand and Hurwitz felt that though the famous Shoemaker case in Tampa, Fla., startled the nation into a horrified awareness of the flagrant violation of civil liberties, it would be necessary to make members of the film audience identify themselves with the harassed and beaten workers and small business men who are menaced by reactionaries. A number of little-known incidents involving violation of civil liberties were dramatized—all leading up to the more notorious Shoemaker case. Such treatment of the problem, Strand said, would be far more adequate than only superficial hit or miss treatment necessitated by spot news reporting.[41]

Hurwitz, of course, concurred. His belief that methods of dramatic involvement as developed by Stanislavsky could be reconciled with Brechtian distancing, segmentation, and sociopolitical didacticism had been mentioned in the discussion of *Heart of Spain*. In *Native Land* the function of the dramatic/documentary form was to maintain a tension between the emotional experience afforded by the individual story episodes and the intellectual understanding which would hopefully be communicated when these were situated within a carefully constructed aesthetic framework and linked by discursive documentary passages. As Hurwitz expresses it:

> A film is built of episodes that deal with individual human responses within social forces which also act on other individuals. Now then, if one limits one's concept of an event to what happens between a small number of people, you have the story film, the Hollywood film, and the basic forces (which in truth are commanding) are not part of the event at all.
>
> The larger event in *Native Land*, not evident in particular episodes, is not unlike a political conspiracy. There is an interlocking of interests out of which things happen: a farmer is shot down, a union organizer is killed, black and white sharecroppers are flushed out of a church, a spy is planted in a union local. The idea of the film and its dramatic growth are built on the principle that these individual events by themselves are not understandable. It therefore forces you into building up the larger event.... That's how the social concept is arrived at, and that's how the fresh structural form of the film is arrived at ... to meet the needs of this content.[42]

The form developed in *Native Land* was thus a reaction, in part, against the individualism of Hollywood films ("One of the reasons I didn't go to Hollywood," says Hurwitz, "is because I wasn't interested in that kind of thing, that however well made would be an isolation of a dramatic situation from real situations"). It was also, of course, influenced by the Soviet cinema—the documentary/montage school of the twenties, rather than the contemporaneous Socialist Realist style. The latter, as exemplified by *Chapayev* (1934) and its successors, placed a heavy emphasis on the individual, in stark contrast to the subordination of the individual to the mass in the early films, for example, of Eisenstein. Maddow recalls that *Chapayev* "really hit all of us tremendously hard, because it upset all our ideas, about personalities, particularities. . . . Maybe it didn't throw Hurwitz."[43]

The fact that the acted segments in *Native Land* were curtailed in length did not imply that attempts were not made to engage the audience by traditional dramatic means. The mise-en-scene in these sequences adhered fairly closely to the codes of conventional narrative cinema, and the actors strove for a style of low-key psychological realism close to that which was developed in Hollywood during the thirties, and which was then being fostered on the stage by the Group Theatre. Several of the actors in *Native Land* were, in fact, associated with the Group, including Art Smith (who played the largest role as the "hooked" union vice-president), Howard Da Silva (labor spy), Mary George (farmer's wife), and Bert Conway (union member). Paul Strand later observed:

> We found that the actors that were the most helpful to us, and the ones we always sought, were the actors who had been trained by the Group Theatre and the Stanislavsky Method. Although we also used, and had to use, actors who were simply theatre actors of that time, along with many people who were not actors at all.[44]

Reviewers were impressed with the quality of the acting, *Variety* observing that "there are several worthwhile performances contributed—good mainly because so lifelike," and Bosley Crowther in the *New York Times* remarking: "The actors—Art Smith as the labor spy, Howard Da Silva as a 'stool pigeon,' Fred Johnson as the farmer, and many more—portray such believable characters that one is inclined toward relaxation when they are off the screen." The intention was to integrate the performances within the documentary texture of the film as a whole: as Hurwitz expressed it, "Hollywood sells personalities, not actors. We tried to achieve personality of film." For at least one critic, their goal was achieved. Arthur Pollock of the *Brooklyn Eagle* headed his review, "In *Native Land* are Actors who Act as if they didn't Know they were Acting," and wrote:

> There is a scene in which a Negro and a white man are hunted in a swamp. You would swear as you watch that that Negro was someone the directors picked up in the fields where he lived—persuaded to act out a part of his life as he had lived it. Everything he does is true. It happens, however, that he is a professional actor.[45]

For Hurwitz, the form of *Native Land* was dictated by its subject matter—which had such a broad sweep that an unusual variety of filmic modes were felt necessary to encompass it. A question of unity inevitably arose. Shortly before the release of the film, an interviewer reported:

> Mr. Hurwitz says that despite, or rather through, the multitude of devices used—narration, dialogue, music, factual sequences, enacted sequences, straight documentary treatment, and even the insertion of several stories—they have tried to achieve a complete unity of meaning, a singleness of purpose that will leave the audience with a "tight fistful of emotion."

Likewise, Strand insisted that, "The episodic stories . . . of typical citizens are each complete in themselves and woven together in the feature-length script which, before we shot a scene, was completely organized." Contemporary reviewers had sharply differing opinions of the degree to which the diverse materials of the film were, in fact, unified.[46]

Thus William Boehnel of the *New York World-Telegram* found *Native Land* a "sketchy, patchwork piece of business," and the otherwise-laudatory Bosley Crowther contended that "as a whole, the picture lacks the cohesion of its truly superb episodes." On the other hand, the *Christian Science Monitor*'s John Beaufort declared: "Everything about the production—its photography, narrative, music, acting, editing, Paul Robeson's delivery in speech and song of the commentary—combines to produce a kind of realism which has seldom been achieved and possibly never surpassed in American motion pictures." And in the *Documentary Film News,* Herman G. Weinberg was adamant that *Native Land*'s heterogeneous composition was an unqualified success:

> Slowly, steadily the American documentary film movement, insofar as it was a movement, through the sporadic work of Ivens, Van Dyke, Lerner, Stebbins, Lorentz, Cartier[-Bresson], Kline, Steiner and Hurwitz and Strand, has been experimenting with indigenous forms—utilizing the newsreel, the reenacted film, the "straight documentary," stills, maps, animation, dialogue, commentary, music, sound. Always the forms of these films derived from their material and were shaped by them. In *Native Land* a more felicitous fusing of all these elements has been achieved towards a more pure expression of statement and comment than has heretofore reached the screen. It has its own form, but it is not a formula. Other themes might require other treatments. But it says what it has to say with eloquence, power, and conviction. That is the triumph of its form.
>
> Its theme is the Bill of Rights . . . and its chief problem was to create out of its diverse material . . . a simple, emotional unity—to find the equivalent for its own purposes of the way the plot of a straight fictional film unifies its audience. That *Native Land* emerged as a highly integrated single thing made out of these many elements is a tribute to the awareness of Hurwitz and Strand that the film is a progressive medium, that it is always evolving, and that the driving force of a film's idea can be solidified out of many elements, as molten steel is solidified in the crucible. . . .
>
> The texture of the film is the texture of America. Although we are a heterogeneous people, we are Americans all in this great melting pot. Although each reel of *Native Land* has an average of 250 separate scenes (as contrasted with the average of 70 for a Hollywood film), the spectator is unaware of this unusual diversity. There is no "fast cutting" in the film—it is, rather, a mosaic, composed of many pieces, which form an all-over pattern. So subtly has the film been cut, so carefully have the shots been chosen with the cutting in mind that the film moves with the precision of a well-oiled, complex piece of machinery. Le Corbusier described a house as "a machine for living." *Native Land* could be described as "a machine for putting an idea across."[47]

It is on this single "idea" which is put across, the concept of liberty, that the film's claim to unity resides. Consideration of the aesthetic form of *Native Land* is thus inextricably tied to an examination of its denotative and connotative content, its ideology.

Like the Frontier films which preceded it, *Native Land* emerged from a political and cultural context shaped by the Communist People's Front program, whose coordinates will by now be familiar. Yet while it is necessary to point to a congruence between the visual and verbal rhetoric of *Native Land* and the propaganda slogans adopted by the CPUSA in the period 1935-39, it must also be recognized that the film has its own specific slant, its distinctive political posture determined by the particular function it was designed to fulfill and by the personal preoccupations of its creators.

Characteristic of the period was the line drawn in *Native Land* between contending forces in the contemporary struggle. The film reflects the Communist party's continuing focus of attention on the industrial working class, as well as its longstanding attempts to forge an alliance which would also include farmers (the Michigan sequence) and—as they were then termed—the Negro people (the Arkansas sequence). But, in addition, it depicts as allies of the workers representatives of two social elements which earlier in the decade would have definitely been viewed with hostility: organized religion, and small business.

The party's attitude toward religion in the early thirties could be gauged from a comment made by William Z. Foster in his *Toward Soviet America* (1932). "In the U.S.S.R., as part of the general cultural revolution, religion is being liquidated," he wrote; "Religion is the sworn enemy of liberty, education, science." By 1936, however, Earl Browder was declaring: "We can well say that the cessation of ineffective, rude, and vulgar attacks upon religion is a positive improvement in our work." In the new phase, church leaders became important figureheads for party-sponsored organizations: thus the Rev. Harry F. Ward headed the American League Against War and Fascism, and Bishop Francis J. McConnell was chairman of the North American Committee to Aid Spanish Democracy. Frontier Films played its part in drawing liberal churchmen into the anti-fascist coalition, and in fact Bishop McConnell and Bishop Robert L. Paddock were supporters of the *Native Land* project. The dramatically flat and seemingly anomalous sequence of the minister's sermon (delivered by an actual clergyman, the Rev. Charles Webber) may thus be seen as performing the tactical propagandistic function of affirming the place of progressive church leaders (and by extension, churchgoers) within the democratic alliance.[48]

In similar fashion, the inclusion in the film of a self-employed businessman, the Memphis grocer, is symptomatic. During the class-struggle period of the first years of the decade persons in this category were regarded, in Communist circles, as particularly unstable elements easily drawn toward fascism, and the despised petit-bourgeois politics of the Socialist party were characterized by referring to it derisively as a party of shopkeepers. The portrayal of the victimized grocer is a clear expression of the Communist party's reaching out to segments of the population it had prevously shunned.

In an important development, noted in the analysis of *People of the Cumberland,* the state was also now viewed as a potential ally. The prominence accorded the work of the La Follette Committee in *Native Land* is indicative of the Communist party's newfound attachment to the system of bourgeois democracy now that, on a world scale, it was threatened with annihilation. Asked recently if he felt the way the committee functions in the film obscures the role of the state in capitalist society, Hurwitz replied:

> No, I don't. I think this criticism involves an oversimplification. The state is not available for dissolution except at certain key moments in history. The struggle goes on at times when the state is not available for dissolution, in forms that involve using the contradictions within the ruling class and their state. The fact is that the acceptance of the trade-union movement as part of the legal structure of American life was forced by American workers, and the staff of the La Follette Committee did a good job of exposure.[49]

Who, then, was the enemy? Certainly at the outset of the People's Front era, the CPUSA was not at a loss to name those it considered the oppressors. Accepting nomination as his party's presidential candidate in June 1936, Earl Browder declared:

> Our enemy is Wall Street—the reactionaries, the enemies of the people. The battle is difficult and complicated. The enemy is strong, ferocious, and unscrupulous, an octopus with a thousand poisonous arms.

Several days later, on July 4, an editorial in the *Daily Worker* took the opportunity to remind readers that "in 1776 the Tories sought by every vicious means to defeat the revolutionary movement," and continued:

> One hundred and sixty years later, it is the Hearsts, the "Liberty" League, and the Republican party who seek once more the destruction of the liberties of the American people. They bring forward the black menace of fascism.[50]

Native Land is less specific in its accusations. Among those responsible for the antilabor outrages it portrays, it of course names the Ku Klux Klan, along with its brother organizations, the Black Legion, Associated Farmers, Silver Shirts, and Christian Front. The police departments of Chicago, New York, San Francisco, and other cities are by implication held liable for their violent attacks on demonstrators, and the sheriff and his deputies of Fort Smith, Arkansas, are flagrantly guilty of murder. But on the crucial questions of who is behind the smooth hit men who leave Fred Hill dead on his Michigan farm, who hired the unseen killer of the organizer in Cleveland, who employed the treacherous labor spies or the pockmarked thug of Memphis, the film is evasive. One might, at a guess, assign the responsibility to a miscellaneous bunch of reactionary corporations of various sizes scattered around the country, each resisting violently but independently to labor demands for collective bargaining, were it not that *Native Land* specifically rules out this possibility. Recasting the class struggle into terms of democracy vs. fascism meant, for the filmmakers, that the people be confronted by a single monolithic menace.

"CONSPIRACY" screams a title superimposed over the image in the animated sequence of the film, and the narration explains: "A plan with a single aim, backed by millions of dollars, by the resources of the biggest corporations." To this point, the analysis seems close to the general indictment of monopoly capitalism implied in Browder's attack on "Wall Street." But as the section continues, it becomes clear that this is not what is meant: the guilty party is not a typical, but an exceptional representative of American business. The conspiracy, whose "secret connections" and "interlocking parts" have been exposed by the Senate, is under the direction of "a handful of fascist-minded corporations"—which remain unspecified.

The charge of conspiracy arising from the investigations of the La Follette Committee was not a new one. Lee Pressman had used the term in his letter of commendation quoted earlier in this chapter, and historian Auerbach observes: "Congressional investigating committees during the New Deal years invariably assumed that one person, or a tiny but omnipotent interest group, had devised a diabolical plot to do evil.... Each committee discovered a conspiracy; each, perhaps, needed to find one in order to justify its existence and to command the attention of a large audience."[51] In questioning the validity of the conspiracy hypothesis, one is not doubting that the machinations of the labor spy agencies and the employers who used them were kept secret, but that the violations of civil liberties all originated from a single source: in terms of the film, it may be doubted if the pattern linking the sporadic outbursts of violence depicted is explicated by a drawing of a cobweb over a map of the United States.

Native Land in fact invites audiences to become angry, but the specific target of this anger—the "old enemy" rising to threaten the four freedoms of Americans—remains mysteriously elusive. "And yet today our liberty is in danger," the narrator asserts towards the end of the film, but just where the threat is coming from (apart from Hitler, who is introduced only in the epilogue) is obscure. The labor espionage conspiracy has been dealt with; what remains? Are the fascist-minded corporations still in the business of negating the Bill of Rights, and if so how? The *Daily Worker* critic identified the villains as America's "Little Hitlers"—but the film is hardly about Huey Long or

Father Coughlin or the other native demagogues to whom this term was normally applied. Among contemporary reviewers who found *Native Land* perplexing on this score were John Beaufort of the *Christian Science Monitor* and Bosley Crowther of the *New York Times*. Beaufort wrote:

> In a film of shocking incidents, it was incumbent upon the producers to name names, dates, places. They could probably have been more specific than they are. . . . [The film] will leave many a spectator emotionally thrashed and intellectually puzzled.

In Crowther's view, *Native Land* was

> to put it bluntly, a sharp indictment of certain subversive elements in this land—elements which are never precisely identified, other than by such terms as "the big shots," "the interests," and "powerful corporations". . . . Of course, a fundamental question might be raised as to what point this picture makes without naming the actual oppressors, other than that oppression is an evil thing.

And he reiterated on another occasion:

> [*Native Land*] carelessly neglects to mention whom it is arguing against. It literally sends shivers down your spine and brings a tight feeling to your chest with its vivid reenactments of some actual violations of civil liberties. . . . But it is never clearly stated, either in the commentary spoken by Paul Robeson or in the pictures themselves, who it is that has provoked these vicious deeds. Thus, a foreword says something about the "fascist-minded on our soil," and Mr. Robeson frequently mentions "the big shots," "the corporations," and such vague terms. But that is as close as it comes. It leaves you wondering with whom you should be mad—and just a bit uncertain as to whether the producers know whom either.[52]

The weakness of the film in this respect can be traced to the CPUSA's single-minded insistence on finding a menace to American democracy to which the tag "fascist" could be applied, so that a grid which fit for Germany, Italy, or Spain could be forced to fit the totally different situation in this country. For example, the Republic Steel Massacre could be easily understood in the context of a history, in the United States, of company violence against strikers which stretched back three quarters of a century or more. To call it, as *Native Land* did, "an act of fascism," or to write, as Browder did, "The spirit which prepared those guns is exactly the same as that of the barbarities of Franco in Spain, of Italian submarines sinking Spanish boats, of Nazi battleships bombarding Almeria, of Hitler's airplanes destroying Guernica,"[53] was to draw a specifically modern parallel with a rhetorical intent which could only confuse the issue. The fact of the matter (perhaps easier to recognize with hindsight) was that in the U.S. Roosevelt had effectively liquidated any serious fascist threat; to assert that American democracy was at peril from "fascism"—be it in the guise of Wall Street, the Liberty League, William Randolph Hearst, the

Republican Party, the Ku Klux Klan, Arkansas deputies, labor spies, "the biggest corporations," or the Chicago Police Department—was to characterize imprecisely the nature of the various struggles which had to be waged.

If *Native Land*'s model of fascism is derived from foreign experience, its concept of democracy is drawn very much from within the American tradition. The film focuses on the Bill of Rights, and particularly the rights to free speech and assembly which were being violated as employers mobilized to thwart the militant unionizing drive of the thirties. The conservative strand of People's Front politics is reflected in the fact that the struggle to organize is seen not as a fight for a new society based on new class relationships, but as a battle to preserve a heritage of liberty supposedly handed down by the founding fathers of the nation. "More than a dream, more than a document," runs the introductory comment on the dramatized episodes of section 2, "the Bill of Rights meant a way of life, a way of life for all Americans." The working class, in this depictment, enters history to defend the prerogatives granted to it by a set of constitutional amendments adopted 150 years previously.

Hurwitz has explained in some detail the rationale behind this appeal to the bourgeois ideals of the past. His argument is worth quoting at length:

> In the film itself and in the social thinking behind it, the historic realities are important to the present. First of all, the idea that American history reflects a continuous struggle between oppressors and oppressed, the idea that liberty has to be fought for in every generation. Social development was very uneven. You could have a slave owner who could state important democratic concepts and understand the nature of revolution (Jefferson said that the tree of liberty has to be watered with the blood of tyrants every twenty years). The complexity in a historical situation is that a given class, when it makes its revolution, has to state its own needs in much broader terms to get wide support. The American bourgeoisie interested in freeing themselves from the colonial restrictions of England couldn't say, "All people who have so much property are created equal." They had to say *everyone* is created equal, each with the right to pursue happiness. This is the way in which the class which becomes the new ruling class gives ammunition to the new oppressed class, because they can't live up to their own supposed objectives....
>
> Remember, *Native Land* begins with a foreword that says, "This is the story of the struggle for liberty in our own time." Now that's a very daring idea. One isn't "patriotic" if one says we have to struggle for liberty in every generation. We inherited a set of ideas and feelings which the film shatters—it shatters the idea that freedom and freedom of speech are monolithic and constant, which is the "patrioteering" approach. Freedom of speech has to be fought for in the new context of organizing labor, in which the oppressor is fighting you by saying that you are un-American. So you are trying to reverse what is called "un-American" into American.
>
> The Declaration of Independence and the Bill of Rights, although they contain within them the strategy and objectives of the ruling class—of the landowners and growing bourgeoisie of the time—contain ideas that are not restrictive. The masters weren't going to get the farmers and workers to fight for them except under the banner of liberty and equality and the pursuit of happiness. When you say that, you create a contradiction and give weapons to the oppressed class; then they can say, "We want some of what you promised." That contradiction is one of the causes of the oppressor's destruction.[54]

While some of the cogency of this class analysis is contained within *Native Land,* much of it is obscured because of the broad nature of the anti-fascist alliance the film was prompting. Overall, *Native Land* refutes the notion of an oppressed class within American society by demonstrating that temporary grievances can be redressed by having recourse to the democratic process—writing letters to Congress.

Much of the conservative flavor of the film is imparted by its copious patriotic imagery—the Stars and Stripes fluttering from an eagle-topped mast, the Statue of Liberty (photographed in slow pans so that it glides across the screen), the statues of Washington, Jefferson, Lincoln, the floodlit dome of the Capitol building—many of them shots which are multiply repeated. ("One of the difficulties with Hurwitz's approach," observes Maddow, "was that he simply could not let go of a film after he got it to the editing room, so that a shot I think that he invented—I saw it later in the preface to the BBC *Masterpiece Theatre*—very close on the rolling movement of a flag, there must have been hundreds of feet of that, he used every last foot of it.") There is no doubt that the intention was to reclaim the symbols of national tradition for the working class and the more progressive elements in American society, just as in *People of the Cumberland* the Fourth of July Labor Rally was calculated to subvert established right-wing celebrations of Independence Day. Hurwitz notes that "*Native Land* takes the symbols of the old Americanism and turns them into something else," and at the time of the film's release in 1942 he told an interviewer:

> . . . we wanted to get away from the clichés that obscure our thinking about the flag, about the Declaration of Independence and the Bill of Rights. We wanted to look at our heritage freshly and see what it means in terms of life as it is lived now in New York or Tampa or Fort Smith, Arkansas.[55]

The patriotic symbols are, indeed, invested with new significance by being placed, through montage, within an unfamiliar context: a shot of the Statue of Liberty, for example, inserted between images of sparks of molten iron and a locomotive wheel in a foundry (sec. 1). Yet they do not thereby lose their conservative connotations: they cannot express a desire for change. To display an American flag is to assert pride and contentment in the country as it has been and as it is; only in the case of rule by a foreign oppressor could the act become a call for radical social transformation.

Part of the pride in country which *Native Land* attempts to engender is respect for the westward expansion of settlement, which (the commentary would have it) was a matter of high ideals:

> We came in search of freedom, but there were dangers in the deep woods, and nowhere to put in a plow. Our only road a flooded river. We were alone. But we took hold.

> In the name of liberty we opened the roads to the West. We crossed the blue Alleghenies, the Ohio, the Mississippi, the last ranges of the Rockies. We took freedom with us.
>
> Out of a raw continent we created a new world, we, the people, laboring all these years, pushing the frontier back from ocean to ocean, plowing freedom into the dark soil. We defended our valleys against all enemies. We fought to make America the name for liberty.

At no point is there any mention (except implied, as one of the "enemies") of the Native American population—which for a film entitled *Native Land* is something of an omission. As Ernest Callenbach rightly observes in a recent review, the film "assumes (as virtually all white Americans then did) that the continent was empty—or populated only by savages, which came to the same thing—when the settlers came, and that their occupation of it was thus a glorious chapter in the march of civilization, and not at all the bloody and unscrupulous genocide we now know it to have been." Hurwitz's defense of the film on this score is somewhat less than adequate:

> The Indians are left out of the film. Not because we didn't know of their history and didn't feel strongly about it, but it became difficult to place within the specific context of this film. Perhaps it should have been worked in....

The issue, of course, is not simply that the Indians are neglected, but that by their omission the whole presentation of American history is distorted in a romantic, white-chauvinist, and imperialist direction.[56]

Despite its tributes to the triumphant struggles waged by "the plain people" of America, *Native Land*—and this is one of its most striking characteristics—is a film which dramatizes defeats. Hurwitz and Strand were "obsessed by blood and bodies," says Jacobson. We learn that Fred Hill spoke up at a farmers' meeting, but we are not shown the meeting (nor do we discover what he spoke about); we see him hoisting his son on to a horse, washing up, chatting with his wife—and then his murdered body. The Cleveland labor organizer is merely a corpse: the film's focus is on the maid who finds him. The important movement to organize sharecroppers during the mid-thirties is represented by the shooting down of two activists. Likewise, the labor espionage section concentrates on the destructive maneuvers of the spies; the Memphis grocer is shown, not helping unionists, but being driven out of town for doing so; the socialist leaders of the Modern Democrats in Florida, active opponents of the Ku Klux Klan, are depicted only in their role as the recipients of torture; the Republic Steel strikers and their supporters are simply massacre victims.

Of contemporary reviewers, only William Boehnel remarked critically on this aspect of the film. His comments, though far from representing a radical point of view, perceptively pinpoint the rhetorical posture of a motion picture which, he claims, is "entirely negative in its thinking."

Not once does it show how labor organized itself and used its strength to fight back at its oppressors. Instead, it shows the workers forever being beaten up without the guts to slash back with both fists. Watching the film one wonders how labor gained what it has gained.

In almost the very first episode, where a Negro and white sharecropper are hounded by a posse and shot down like dogs because they dared to ask for a small increase for the products of their labor, nothing is done to show how the workers fought against such brutality. Nor is any effort made to show how labor struck back at the Klan or any of its other oppressors in these dramatized incidents.

To this writer, at least, this prevailing note of defeatism makes labor seem less the powerful, patriotic body it is than a sulking child trying to take revenge on its elders for all its past grievances.[59]

While labor's defeats are pictured concretely, the fight back is conveyed only in the abstract, via the commentary and sequences of generalized montage. "Here's how we tore up the blacklist," the narrator says, and we are shown unionists parading in the streets: the steps of the process by which the reversal is brought about, from the destruction to the triumph of organization, are omitted. The desire to portray American workers as eminently law-abiding citizens (the CPUSA specifically repudiated violence at its 1936 and 1937 conventions[58]) results in curious gaps in the film's structural logic: just as, in *People of the Cumberland,* gangsterism is answered by a Fourth of July rally, here police brutality is met by a moralistic sermon from the pulpit. (A revealing contrast is offered by *Heart of Spain* and *China Strikes Back,* in which the Frontier filmmakers could impose a clear, meaningful dialectic on their material—display the force of the enemy, and then reveal the anti-fascists organizing a militant defense and counter-attacking with equivalent strength.)

Except for the angry unionists who are restrained by their president from assaulting the exposed labor spy (for fear of adverse publicity), the protagonists of *Native Land* are not fighters but passive victims—"little people," the "innocent ones" who "never hurt anyone, never could." Like those of *People of the Cumberland,* these working people are shown mostly at play: ping pong and checkers at the union hall, a steamboat excursion, visiting the parks and the zoo. The film fails to trace the source of working-class strength: the power to strike. Strikes, in fact, are not even mentioned on the soundtrack—an extraordinary omission in a film celebrating the victories of the union movement in the thirties.

But it is again the defeats which have the most powerful emotional impact. Ben Maddow has discussed this preoccupation of the Frontier productions, and particularly *Native Land,* with violence and death:

I think that death is a form of rhetoric. It's part of the suspense. Martyrdom. And the use of martyrdom is true of any growing religion that wants converts. I don't know why that is. And it was true of the Russian films too. In a way it was a depot of powerful emotional experience. . . . The gravestone, graveyard theme was a cliché of American photography long before *Native Land.* A lot of early Van Dykes are photographs of gravestones, and I think that Paul Strand was tremendously fond of those New England folk art gravestones up there in the snow. And he had to use them. It *is* very much a part of American life, if you read labor history, the amount of death and destruction is tremendous. So I think that death as the price of progress...In short it was a rhetorical or romantic view of America.

Maddow feels that there is a connection between this thematic concern and the uprooted personal life which the numbers of the Frontier collective experienced as intellectuals during the Depression:

> ...there was a tremendous amount of morbidity and inner depression, from your experiences. Because you didn't know quite where you were going when you got out of college. There were no jobs, and it was very tough on you spiritually. And this emotion of sadness, of loneliness outside society, just built up a residue which, I guess, was inexhaustible finally. And I think that a lot of the morbidity is partly expressed in these works.[59]

The fact that *Native Land* centers, in it major dramatized segment, not on the strong union man (the president) but on the weak (the vice-president) may also be related to the personal situation of the filmmakers. Interestingly, the labor spy episode revives the moral crisis which was at the heart of Albert Maltz's 1935 drama of the coal fields, *Black Pit*. Both film and play dissect the existential struggle of a worker, a union member, tempted, pressured, and finally blackmailed into betraying his comrades to the class enemy. It is significant that this figure was resurrected in the film despite the severe criticism which Maltz's play had received from some sections of the Left for making a sympathetic character of a stool pigeon. Art Smith's Harry Carlisle is the most fully realized individual in *Native Land,* and the sequence in which he hoodwinks the union, wrestles with his conscience, and finally capitulates by releasing the membership book to the spy agency forms the longest and most elaborate narrative portion of the film.

The choice of such a protagonist, in place of a more positive figure—a union organizer, for instance, who succeeds in uprooting treachery in the ranks—suggests an impatience with the more facile, optimistic formulas of proletarian literature and drama. It also reflects a need to balance mass action with individual "psychology" in the tradition of the bourgeois realist stage and novel. Of course, Harry Carlisle's role in relation to the total structure of *Native Land* is much smaller than that of Joe Kovarsky to *Black Pit*. The intriguing fact, however, that both works focus their attention on such a weak, vacillating, and ultimately destructive figure indicates the difficulty their creators must have had in closely identifying with the labor movement. (Maltz, Maddow, and Hurwitz shared a similar Jewish-immigrant, petit-bourgeois background, and all three had graduated into the Depression in 1930, Maltz and Maddow from Columbia, Hurwitz from Harvard.) One might almost see the alienated Kovarsky/Carlisle, tempted by the prospect of material gain and individual advance to sell out his fellow workers, as a surrogate for the left-wing intellectual allured by the idea of success—escape from poverty, at least—in the commercial world.[60]

A product of the diffuse progressivism of the People's Front period, *Native Land* is revealingly cautious in political content. Perhaps the film-makers believed that to openly promulgate a socialist alternative was to invite rejection and repression—not to speak of jeopardizing the support of the wealthy liberals who, for the most part, bankrolled the project. The film speaks profusely of liberty and freedom, and not at all of communism, socialism, capitalism, public ownership, the proletariat, class struggle, or revolution. Leo Hurwitz argues that nevertheless *Native Land* carries unequivocally radical implications:

> The film *is* about capitalism, the film *does* dramatize very clearly how capitalist relations result in the repression of workers, their difficulties of organization. It does deal with how workers come together in order to struggle against capitalism. Now it's true that the film does not result in, does not anywhere talk about the theoretic diagrams of what capitalism is, or what the nature of the class struggle is. But it's directly in the middle of that class struggle, and all the forces that are involved in capitalism are there, the main forces. . . .
> I defy you to read Gorky's *Mother* and find in it a diagram of capitalism. You won't. I'm not saying one can't do that in a work of art. One can. And I would like to do such a film. But one of the characteristics of that recreation of experience that we call a work of art is that out of its own inner tensions you can draw conceptual conclusions. And I think it's there in *Native Land.*[61]

The difficulty in Hurwitz's argument is that *Native Land* employs some political concepts—"liberty," "fascism,"—and not others. The audience is thereby led to interpret the conflict it views in terms of the words which the film applies, while screening out analyses built on alternative conceptual frame-works. If the labor spy system is directed by "a handful of fascist-minded corporations," then it is possible to assume that business in general has the interests of workers at heart. If freedom is "a way of living and of looking at life" and the steel rigger and the sailor are declared to be "part of it," then there is no room to consider the alienation of labor under capitalism.

In general, *Native Land* takes a working-class conservative-defensive line. The democratic system (the Bill of Rights, the Senate committee, the administration of Roosevelt—whose portrait appears almost as an icon on the walls at union headquarters) is pictured as responsive to labor's needs. Soviet ideology was associated with the collectivization and mechanization of agriculture: as if to remove any hint of contamination by it, *Native Land*'s first hero/martyr is a family farmer who works his own land with a horse plow— and is manifestly content. Work is seen as fulfilling. The mass unemployment of the Depression years (in 1939, there were still nine and a half million jobless) is scarcely alluded to. No change in life style is proposed: the film celebrates in happy imagery and upbeat song the working family's morning routine, the pastimes of a summer holiday. People, we are told, don't want very much out of life.

It is overstating the case to claim, as Ernest Callenbach does, that the film "assumes a prior Golden Age—apparently the heroic pioneer period—when men were men, invented liberty and equality, and lived happily without oppression."[62] On the contrary, *Native Land* insists that Americans have had to fight for their freedom in every generation. Yet the myth of a pre-existent harmony lingers in sequences such as the early morning montage and the Memorial Day holiday. Central to both is the iconography of children at play, that stereotypical imagery of an untroubled age. These sequences, like those (in previous productions of the Frontier group) of Sunnyside Gardens prior to the Crash, or Madrid before the shells and bombs explode, represent the calm before the storm: they propose that American working people are basically and normally happy and satisfied with their lives, that they have moderate desires, and that they have done nothing to deserve the murderous repression exercised upon them. If their demands (like those of the Arkansas sharecroppers) are modest, it is all the more outrageous that they should be shot down for making them.

Such a rhetorical structure has the effect of making *Native Land* appear, in some respects, backward-looking beside, say, Van Dyke and Steiner's *The City* (1939), which is saturated with naive American optimism. It is true that *The City* also turns to the past—in fact recreates a supposed prior harmonious age in some detail—but its major emphasis is on the transformation of living conditions prevalent in contemporary industrial society in the utopian community to come. Its solution is of course politically fanciful, as the Frontier filmmakers were quick to point out. *Native Land,* being more "realistic," is concerned with protecting the gains of the past rather than projecting a future of radical social change.

At a time when the Nazis were on their way to subjugating Europe, it was an understandable preoccupation. The question which *Native Land* provokes— and it is relevant to the People's Front strategy as a whole—is whether America's "native fascists" were seriously comparable to Hitler; whether, in fact, the situation justified the sacrifice of radical working-class initiatives in the interests of a broad-based defensive coalition whose political goals were vague and whose unity would be welded by fervent invocation of the patriotic ideals of a bygone age.

10

Conclusion

The criteria that must be applied in assessing the strengths and weaknesses of the radical film movement of the thirties are ultimately political. One may inquire to what extent the productions of the Film and Photo League, Nykino, and Frontier Films were effective in promulgating progressive political values and in lending support to particular struggles being waged on the Left. One may also question whether the operating decisions made by the filmmaking collectives were correct—whether, by adopting other strategies, more and stronger films might possibly have been produced and exhibited.

The greatest achievement of the Film and Photo League productions was at the level of manifestation. Hollywood feature films had ignored the working class; commercial newsreels either did not offer coverage of actions such as demonstrations and strikes, or if they did were censored or supplied with a right-wing commentary. As socialist artists had done previously in painting (Courbet), literature (Zola), and drama (Gorky), the FPL filmmakers depicted workers (and the unemployed) seriously and systematically. Aid for the Forgotten Man was Roosevelt's campaign slogan in 1932, and "Remember My Forgotten Man" a hit number about unemployed veterans in the Warners musical *Gold Diggers of 1933;* the protagonists of FPL newsreels and documentaries were the working people of the country refusing to be forgotten, announcing their entrance on the stage of history. The demonstration, a visible token of class solidarity and militancy, was the ideal icon for FPL films.

Much of the political value of the league productions, too, lay in their normally being conceived and executed as part of a specific campaign or organizing drive. In this respect the league's connection with the Workers' International Relief provided a definite impetus and direction; coverage of the hunger marches, for instance, took shape from its being one of a number of support functions which the parent organization performed for the demonstrators. The immediacy of the demand which league productions fulfilled led to a directness of manner which at its best (one imagines) was highly effective: as the *Filmfront* critic wrote of *Marine,* "An audience after seeing the picture quickly realizes the necessity for strike action, so simple is the approach and so straightforward the message."[1]

The FPL fostered the growth of social documentary cinematography in undertaking or assisting the production of films on the life of miners *(The Strike Against Starvation)*, agricultural workers *(Imperial Valley)*, stevedores *(Marine)*, farmers *(Sheriffed)*, cab drivers *(Taxi)*, and ghetto blacks *(Harlem Sketches)*; in doing so it extended the range of American documentary far beyond the limits it had reached to that point. In addition, FPL cameras vividly recorded innumerable scenes of the Depression years: parades, picket lines, bread lines, Hoovervilles, fights against eviction, and so on.

At times, the FPL filmmakers deployed montage boldly and provocatively, as in the sequences analyzed from *Bonus March, Hunger 1932,* and *America Today*. Unconstrained by any need to adapt their style to the demands of the sound film, league members such as Leo Seltzer and Leo Hurwitz were able to apply the concept of montage as it has been developed in the Soviet Union in experimental filmic constructions embodying corrosive political commentary. Ideologically, such sequences went beyond the presentation of immediate issues to convey biting attacks on business, the Roosevelt government, the churches, the law courts, and the army.

In terms of organization, the Film and Photo League (in New York) gained strength by virtue of its being a society of some 75 to 100 members capable of sustaining the small core of actual filmmakers in their work. The league's equal commitment to still photography, which required much smaller financial outlays than film and in fact could be a source of income, made this comparatively large membership possible. FPL work was also furthered by the establishment of branches in many cities of the country: these provided mutual encouragement and their existence enabled coordinated activities to take place.

The league's production work was also buttressed by the many other functions carried out by members. The exhibition of Soviet films, quite apart from its fruitful impact on the filmmaking styles of the league members, complemented the FPL showings by holding out the model of a socialist society against which the chaos of American capitalism could be measured. The FPL practice of taking films directly to the workers, at union halls or on the picket line, immeasurably increased the political effectiveness of their productions. Campaigns against reactionary and fascist films heightened audience awareness of ideological content in motion pictures and made them more receptive (probably) to the progressive alternative offered by the league. Similarly, battles against political censorship directed the attention of audiences to the structure of governmental power within which their film viewing took place. The filmmaking skills of FPL camera operators and editors were sharpened by their participation as teachers or students in training programs conducted by the league; these programs, in addition, broadened their understanding of film history and culture, as did the league's film series screenings, and the various publishing activities of members.

But the Film and Photo League had its weaknesses. Evidence of its organizational shortcomings was its failure to sustain film production at a continuing high level. Filmmaking took place in fits and starts, periods of months went by without (evidently) any shooting being done at all, and projects were abandoned before completion. The accounts of participants suggest that much of the filmmaking program was on an ad hoc basis, without long-term planning or principled allocation of resources. An over-ambitious program of nonproduction activities may also have served to dissipate the group's energies.

Despite the FPL's fraternal ties with "revolutionary" unions and the Communist party's mass organizations, in conjunction with which it often produced films, distribution and exhibition seem at times to have been surprisingly haphazard. Thus Hurwitz charged that *Hunger 1932* had never been shown outside New York, although "the three thousand delegates on the march were eager to have the film shown to their organizations all over the country."[2] Reports of workers' and farmers' exhibition circuits operating successfully in some parts of the country exist, but overall the efficiency of the WIR Film Department (and later Garrison Film Distributors) in making FPL productions available to organizations outside New York is not known.

In promoting his scheme for a "Shock Troupe" of full-time filmmakers in the league, Hurwitz in 1934 claimed that the FPL had "not yet trained a truly able corps of film workers," and his remark is given credence by the rather amateurish technical quality of some of the extant FPL footage. Hurwitz's insistence that filmmaking was a skilled craft which only the most talented and committed members of the league should be entrusted with probably contained valid criticism of an overly casual approach to filmmaking assignments which had been prevalent in the New York FPL up to that time. (The reorganization which the league underwent in the last months of 1934 may well have been addressed partly to this problem.)[3]

On the question of aesthetics, the objection of the Hurwitz-Steiner group to the FPL's concentration on strict newsreel and documentary forms has been discussed in detail. Some league members, of course, like Sam Brody, viewed the league's policy not as a weakness but as a source of strength. Arguments may be made on both sides, but the two factions would probably have agreed, at the time of the Nykino split, that too much of the league's production was in the form of simple reporting (Hurwitz's "another parade of marching, marching, marching"), with too little analysis or exploration of the "synthetic documentary" mode. Providing workers with minimally mediated images of themselves was a valuable first step in building morale, but repeated without variation this pattern of production could only lead to recircuiting (ritual gestures being performed for the camera), and ultimately validation of the status quo. The league itself seems to have recognized this problem with its stepped-up program of filmmaking in late 1934-early 1935, embracing work in a variety of forms including the straight documentary, the dramatized documentary, and the satire.

When the FPL did move in the direction the Nykino group had earlier wished it to go, with the production of the dramatized documentary *Taxi* in 1935, its failure was evidently so egregious that not even politically sympathetic critics were willing to downplay the film's faults. To handle successfully such an enacted project required talents and training in scriptwriting and direction which the FPL crew obviously lacked. Before committing itself to the support of James Guy and Nancy Naumburg, who had previously failed with *Sheriffed*, the FPL might well have sought some skilled assistance (as the Nykino group did) from persons with experience in workers' theatre.

Perhaps the league's greatest weakness, though it was not one which could be readily overcome, was its strictly amateur basis. Since no one was paid, filmmaking of necessity had often to be relegated to evenings and weekends, and there was no opportunity to perform the intense collective work which, as Hurwitz and Steiner indicated, the Shock Troupe of the Workers' Laboratory Theatre was able to carry out. The league was probably only able to retain the services of such skilled filmmakers as Del Duca, Seltzer, and Roffman because of the Depression situation and the underdeveloped state of the documentary film industry in the United States, which made regular jobs in the profession virtually impossible to obtain for some years. The amateur nature of the FPL was very likely the one major reason for its sporadic output. In reaction, Frontier Films was to be established on a professional basis, which would make continuous work possible, at the cost of introducing a major new problem— that of fundraising.

Prior to this, however the Frontier group met for several years, unpaid, as Nykino. Nykino's strengths were those of a loose collective sharing radical political convictions, consumed with the desire to shape the new art of film, and dedicated to working together on common projects. They were serious, carrying out systematic study of the aesthetics of drama and photography; they were intellectual, basing their developing theory of radical cinema on carefully considered philosophical foundations.

Pie in the Sky, though owing its success more to the Group Theatre actors who performed in it than to the Nykino members who did the photography and editing, was an inspired thrust along a line—that of improvised satire—which radical filmmakers in the United States would not pursue. Because its imaginative parody could not be squared with the commitment of the Nykino group to documentary filmmaking, the forcefulness of *Pie in the Sky*'s political attack was underrated and the possibilities which it suggested were discounted. The decision to move in other directions is understandable in view of the heavy reliance of satiric skits of this kind on performing talents not possessed by any of the Nykino members themselves, and considering the opportunities which the newly developed field of documentary was only just beginning to open up. What is regrettable is that after *Pie in the Sky* the left-wing film movement of the thirties lost all trace of a sense of humor.

Instead of satire, Nykino explored the potentials of dramatic reenactment in *The World Today*. The convincingness of *Sunnyside,* in particular, proved that dramatized sequences (even using nonactors) could be handled with an authority that previous efforts, such as *Sheriffed* and *Taxi,* totally lacked. Enabling the episode of Mrs. Thal's eviction to be placed on screen with maximum emotional force and political clarity, the technique of reenactment as utilized in *Sunnyside* paved the way for future development of combined dramatic-documentary forms.

Nykino's limitations as a political film group lay in its rupture from a working-class organizational base. While independence from the Film and Photo League, and consequently the WIR, left the Hurwitz-Steiner associates free to pursue their own aesthetic preoccupations unhindered by externally imposed guidelines, it also propelled them into an isolation from day-to-day struggles, with the result that a sense of urgency and political proportion could be lost. This was especially true in view of the fact that the group members were all of petit-bourgeois background. Julian Roffman's recollection of "endless niggling movement back and forth of cutlery and dinnerware" in the *Park Avenue* photographic project suggests the dangers of such a group developing into an ingrown coterie.[4]

Nykino also lacked the financial resources to become actively productive. Optimistic announcements from time to time that it was ready to undertake ambitious projects were devoid of any realistic assessment of its capabilities. Moreover, when films *were* produced, only minimal efforts were made to obtain distribution for them, with the result that this potential source of income was lost.

Overall, while it was apparently understood that Nykino was to be only a transitional grouping, one has the sense that there was too much marking time. *Pie in the Sky,* which Nykino completed, was actually photographed earlier. The fact that in the two-and-a-half years of its existence (which encompassed momentous historical developments both internationally and on the domestic scene) Nykino as able to shoot and edit only about fifteen minutes of film which it initiated itself must be seen as an indictment of its organizational structure and policies.[5]

It is perhaps unjust to be too harsh on Nykino's lack of productivity, however, since much of the collective's time was spent in laying the groundwork for a permanent organization which would overcome the difficulties the group was experiencing. The establishment of Frontier Films with enough no-strings-attached financing to make possible ongoing political filmmaking on a professional basis was an impressive achievement. The time-consuming nature of film production makes spare-time shooting a long-drawn-out process, and, lest topicality be lost, effective political cinema, in particular, demands full-time commitment from at least some members of the film crew. Frontier's ability to provide the members of the collective with an income (if barely at subsistence level) during its five years of existence was perhaps its major source of strength.

Frontier's second operational accomplishment was an extension of its Nykino method of work, fostering collective creativity on a groundwork of principled discussion. Both Hurwitz and Maddow have testified to the value of such an approach. A warning note, however, is sounded by George Jacobson, who as production manager seems to have been excluded from the decision-making process. Jacobson feels that he and others "wanted to participate" in the creative work on *Native Land* but were not able to; he charges that Strand and Hurwitz "used other people as tools perhaps, but not as intellects."[6] Jacobson's complaint raises a critical question about the extent to which, in radical filmmaking, a collaborative team may be expanded without becoming unwieldy—one is reminded of the extreme reluctance of Jean-Luc Godard and Jean-Pierre Gorin to enlarge the Dziga Vertov collective beyond its member-ship of two, or occasionally three, active filmmakers. Arbitration of the issue in the Frontier Films case is not possible in view of that fact that detailed knowledge of the group's internal dynamics cannot now be obtained.

Frontier Films (in cooperation with Brandon's Garrison company and other organizations) was successful in disseminating its pictures to a much larger audience than had been reached by either the Film and Photo League or Nykino. The estimates of several million spectators for films such as *Heart of Spain* and *People of the Cumberland* attest to a very high potential political impact. This was perhaps particularly true of *Heart of Spain,* many of whose showings were held under the auspices of the Medical Bureau in the context of broad educational and propaganda work on behalf of Republican Spain. Although for various reasons revenue accruing to Frontier from screenings of its films was comparatively small, it greatly exceeded that received by either of its predecessor organizations, and pointed to the possibility of a political film group becoming at least partly self-sufficient on the strength of its earnings.

Another major achievement of Frontier was the high professional quality of its output. Acting, and the direction of actors, was strikingly good, particularly in *Native Land.* Photography, notably that done by Paul Strand, was in a sharp documentary style that occasionally achieved great beauty. Editing, in general, imparted to the films an appropriate pace and emphasis. And the musical scores, especially that composed by Marc Blitzstein for *Native Land,* were of a high standard. Frontier productions, designed to break into theatres and compete with the product of the commercial industry, were certainly able to do so on technical grounds.

Yet this striving for professionalism, with a fraction of the resources available to Hollywood, may also have weakened Frontier. No longer were films turned out, as they had been at the Film and Photo League, in the heat of the moment, to serve pressing political needs. High aesthetic aspirations occasioned delays at every stage of the production process (some three or four months' work on *Native Land,* it will be recalled, was discarded on the grounds of its slightly inferior quality). Although *Heart of Spain* and *China Strikes Back* were completed with admirable dispatch, the excessively long production periods of *People of the Cumberland, Return to Life,* and especially *Native Land* were definitely harmful in terms of the films' political effectiveness.

In this respect the decision to make a feature film, understandable in view of the hopes of the Frontier group of establishing themselves as artists, must be considered a mistake. Committing the organization to the production of a full-length movie with a starting capital of only $7,000 meant that virtually every other project of a political nature had to be suspended for the remaining three to four years of the company's life, many months of valuable production time were to be wasted in the process of chasing funds, and the element of topicality, so crucial to political cinema, would be quite lost in the finished film. Hurwitz and Strand were right in believing they would somehow be able to find the money to finance a feature-length production; they were wrong in their estimates of how long it would take. George Jacobson reasons with hindsight:

> We had no right to make a feature film at that time, without considering whether Frontier Films would exist after that. I think more importantly Frontier should have gone on making short films until they reached a point where they could finance, really finance a feature on a social subject. . . . [7]

The high cost of its pictures, and particularly *Native Land,* meant that Frontier became dependent, for the bulk of its income, on donations and soft loans from wealthy supporters. Although Hurwitz insists that no money was accepted in cases where the contributor wished to influence the production along lines not acceptable to the filmmakers, the source of financing cannot but have had some impact. The eminent respectability of the Frontier films, their emphasis on democracy and liberty and failure to speak of socialism or revolution, is surely partially attributable to the nature of their backing—even though it also coincided with the People's Front strategy of the Communist party. In any event, the shift away from the pattern of support (by a radical working-class organization) enjoyed by the Film and Photo League is significant, and discomfiting.

Associated with the artistic aspirations of the Frontier group, and the need to appeal to monied backers, was a recrudescence of elements in the older social realist aesthetic. Particularly noticeable were a weakening of the documentary impetus, the attenuation of montage, and a partial assimilation in dramatized sequences to the Hollywood model.

The bulk of *Native Land* consists not of documentary, but of staged incidents portrayed with what might be termed "documentary realism." There is a certain similarity, in the employment of location shooting, little-known actors, and sociological themes, to the "semi-documentaries" produced by Louis de Rochemont in the years immediately following World War II. In the actual documentary sections, such as those depicting America's industrialization or the upsurge of union organization, stock footage and material previously shot by newsreel companies or the Film and Photo League is heavily resorted to. In emphasis, like the American Naturalist novels, *Native Land* moves away from the documentation of everyday life towards the extremes of violence and death. Richard Leacock remarks:

> The film was truly a series of narrative sequences performed by actors. Looking back to this period, I think of it as the beginning of the dark ages of documentary, the hopeless period where synchronous sound necessitated the adoption of studio techniques and led to the acted docu-drama.[8]

Though the point has no bearing on the political value of *Native Land*, it may be remarked parenthetically that the film holds less fascination for an audience today than much genuine documentary of the period (such as Farm Security Administration photography).

The lessening use of montage for political argumentation in the films of the later thirties has been discussed. With the introduction of sound, the burden of conveying specific ideas was shifted to the commentary, which could express with the directness and exactitude of language whatever message the film-makers wished to put across. Though many sequences were still composed of short shots aggregated on an abstract basis, the chief ordering principle became, not shock and contrast, but thematic similarity. While the Frontier filmmakers were right to explore the potential of spoken narration, the abandonment of "intellectual" montage with its intense subversive power cannot be easily justified. Paralleling as it does a trend in the Soviet Union, it is the mark of an increasing aesthetic and political conservatism.

Also signifying a rejection of left-wing avant-garde experimentation of the twenties was the style of acting favored by Frontier Films. Derived from Stanislavsky via the Group Theatre, it was a variety of "psychological realism" adapted for film—and for the miniature roles which the actors were called upon to play. As it worked in practice, the style was almost indistinguishable from much Hollywood acting, particularly as it had been developed in genres such as the gangster film of the thirties. As has been suggested, the mise-en-scene, too, adhered to conventional patterns of spatio-temporal continuity, and was evolved in terms of ordinary dramatic tension and climax. The result was that in the compromise Hurwitz hoped to effect between Stanislavsky and Brecht, Stanislavsky won out: the audience in *Native Land,* for example, is invited to identify emotionally with the labor spy portrayed by Art Smith, rather than led to a deeper intellectual understanding of the operation of labor espionage and how it may be combatted.

But it is at the ideological level that the weaknesses of the Frontier productions are most apparent. There were, it is true, tactical reasons for the unsophisticated defensive stance which is taken in the films devoted to the international situation. If *Heart of Spain, Return to Life,* and *China Strikes Back* bypassed the existence of revolutionary struggle and impressed a binary model of "the people" and "the invader" on the tangled conflicts of Spain and China, it was because, at the time, the ultimately decisive battle lines were between Loyalist and Franco forces, between Chinese and Japanese troops. War imposed its overriding simplifications, its savage dualism of We and They; and help was needed for the imperiled defenders of Madrid and Shanghai. Yet the results of taking such a position, for a radical film collective, were corrosive. For the effect of presenting the Spanish Civil War as simply a battle for the preservation of democracy, of picturing the Chinese revolution as merely part of national defense against foreign invasion, was to reinforce, not subvert, the dominant ideology—corporate liberalism—of American capitalist society.

With *People of the Cumberland* and *Native Land*, not even utilitarian justifications could be invoked. No war was being fought in the streets and farms and factories of the Unites States, merely sporadic skirmishes whose antagonists could only with the greatest of intellectual straining be consigned to two (and no more than two) opposing camps. It was as if, having once adopted their melodramatic schema (with its "dialectical" pattern), of having deliberately checked their insights the better to serve the needs of the moment, the Frontier filmmakers could not shake free of the Manichaean vision with which they passionately interpreted events abroad.

Thus, forced to identify an enemy of the American people (but forbidden to employ the concept of class struggle), they settled on a right-wing faction of the bourgeoisie: the "associations of manufacturers," the "handful of fascist-minded corporations." But in rightly delivering these elements of reaction, the worst offenders among the capitalists, up to obloquy, the filmmakers quite omitted to touch on the general structure of capitalism and the necessity of its abolition. Offering no challenge to peaceable businesses which agree to bargain collectively, *People of the Cumberland* and *Native Land* do not confront the power of monopoly capital, and ultimately, like the other Frontier films, fail to break with corporate liberal ideology.

A guiding principle of any left-wing activity, whether in the political or cultural sphere, must be that a long-range perspective is not lost. This has been, perhaps, the greatest failing of the Left in the United States. American capitalism's enormous capacity to absorb protest means that radical initiatives are quickly blunted unless the sense of a Socialist alternative is kept alive. The greatest danger lies at the point at which government and business begin to make concessions: here there is a temptation for militants, in their anxiety to foster the move and protect the gains which have been made, to cease their articulation of revolutionary goals—particularly when they themselves, former outsiders, enjoy a taste of power.

During the Depression decade, this point was reached in 1935-36. The WPA was established, putting millions of the unemployed to work (not least in cultural fields). The Social Security Act was passed, and the Wagner Act, despite its wayward career in the courts and tribunals, conferred collective bargaining rights. In discouraging the use of force against sit-down strikers, the New Deal administration leant just enough to the left to make the mushrooming growth of the CIO possible.

Coinciding with these events was the entry of the Communist party into its People's Front phase. The "revolutionary" unions and the Trade Union Unity League, which had been unremitting in their attacks on the conservatism of the AFL, were dissolved. The party's mass organizations of the early thirties (of which the WIR was one) were phased out, to make way for more broadly-based bodies in which Communist leadership was disguised. The Communist party soon gave up a plan to build an independent farmer-labor party, and threw its weight, effectively, behind the Roosevelt government.

Justifying their action by reference to the fascist threat—which was, of course, real in Europe, but greatly exaggerated in the United States—radicals affiliated with the Communist party dropped the class-struggle approach of the early years of the decade. The Bill of Rights was made a rallying cry around which it was hoped to build a defensive coalition of workers and middle-class liberals, and all socialist analysis and advocacy was soon suspended.

These historical developments are clearly reflected in the work of the Film and Photo League, Nykino, and Frontier Films. It is suggestive of the changing situation that Leo Seltzer of the FPL was jailed for filming a demonstration in Washington, D.C., while Lionel Berman exhibited Frontier productions in the White House—to an appreciative First Lady. The shift may perhaps best be seen in the differing uses to which patriotic symbols and images of governmental power were put.

Thus in the hunger march films and Seltzer's newsreel of the Washington Scottsboro demonstration, the Capitol building signifies an alien, repressive force, unresponsive to popular pressure; in *Native Land* it represents the organized power of the people. The Statue of Liberty, in *Sweet Land of Liberty,* is deployed ironically to highlight the harassment of dissenters in the U.S.; in *Native Land,* it performs a complete about-face to symbolize the freedoms Americans enjoy. Likewise, in the extant *America Today*, Roosevelt is equated with fascist dictators Mussolini and Hitler, while in the culminating production of Frontier Films his portrait is reverently hung on the walls of union headquarters.[9]

Hence the radical filmmakers played their part in the dilution of progressive thought that occurred in the latter half of the decade. While, of course, it was necessary to recognize the role Roosevelt had played in conferring legality upon the CIO's tremendous unionizing drive, adopting an uncritical attitude to a president in power and the symbols of constitutional government, as *Native Land* did, implied the repression of any vision of a socialist future. In a similar way, the taboo which operated in *People of the Cumberland* on the discussion of the capitalist system inhibited any realistic analysis of the problems of the region and their potential solution.

In the union movement, concentration on short-range bread-and-butter issues had harmful results. The enormous energies generated by the wave of sit-down strikes were quickly dissipated once the immediate goals of union recognition and higher wages were achieved. A loss of impetus followed, and in the long run, as rank-and-file militancy receded, bureaucracy became entrenched, corruption seeped in—and despite their moderation, officers aligned with the Communist party were ousted. Labor's fervid proclamation of its loyalty (evidenced in the images of the Stars and Stripes which pervade *People of the Cumberland* and *Native Land)* proved no defense against Cold War attacks: on the contrary, in the form of the Loyalty Oath adopted under pressure from the Chamber of Commerce, it was turned into a tool to destroy left-wing union leadership.[10]

One of the factors contributing to the case with which Communist officers were purged was the secretiveness they had employed in not admitting their party affiliation. The policy of dissimulation was one which dated from the People's Front era, and was reflected in the productions of Frontier Films, none of which used the term "Communist" either to refer to their protagonists (not even Mao Tse-tung), or to designate any aspect of the political situation under review. While this was of minor significance in the films dealing with the United States, it proved a source of mystification in those devoted to Spain and China, where Communist parties played a major role in events. It may be argued that Communists colluded in their own repression by adopting a system of concealed membership; whether or not this is true, it is certainly the case that *Heart of Spain, Return to Life,* and *China Strikes Back* are less valuable as political documents because of their failure to acknowledge a Communist presence.

To hide one's connection with the Communist party one had also, in many instances, to refrain from advancing a radical point of view. And here a crucial issue is raised. For if one declines to employ a socialist perspective for fear of its not being sufficiently popular, one is helping ensure that left-wing values will never, in fact, gain wide-spread support. (It is an undialectical, mechanistic Marxism that proposes that the economic crisis of capitalism will in itself produce radicalization of consciousness.) What operated in Communist culture of the later thirties was a process of self-censorship which hamstrung militant expression just at the time when it might well have found a large and receptive audience.[11]

As part of that culture, the productions of Frontier Films must share in the general indictment. Polished and professional as they are, they lack the subversive edge of the rough but vital footage of the Film and Photo League; failing to make a decisive rupture with the ruling ideology of bourgeois society, they tend ultimately to reinforce that ideology by invoking its own symbolism. As a film like *Bonus March* reminds us, a radical cinema must and can be something other than an affirmation of trade-union or "democratic" values within the context of corporate liberalism.

1. Julian Roffman in 1935 or 1936 filming a Mother Bloor picnic.
[Photo courtesy Julian Roffman.]

2. Depression: 1932. East River dock, New York City. [Photo ©1977 by Leo Seltzer.]

3. Depression: 1932. Unemployed women demonstrate at New York's City Hall. [Photo ©1977 by Leo Seltzer.]

4. New York City: Harlem demonstration against lynching, 1933.
    [Photo ©1977 by Leo Seltzer.]

5. New York City, 1933. Anti-fascist, anti-war demonstration.
[Photo ©1977 by Leo Seltzer.]

6. Main title, "Workers Newsreel." Produced by Film and Photo League, 1931-1935. [Photo ©1977 by Leo Seltzer.]

7. Depression: 1933. Rent Strike, East Harlem, New York City. [Photo ©1977 by Leo Seltzer.]

8. Depression: 1933. The Floating Hospital, East River, New York City. [Photo ©1977 by Leo Seltzer.]

9. Depression: 1933. Evicted family, New York East Side. [Photo ©1977 by Leo Seltzer.]

10. Depression: 1932. Unemployed worker and Salvation Army band on New York City's East Side. [Photo ©1977 by Leo Seltzer.]

11. Ralph Steiner. [Photo from The Museum of Modern Art/Film Stills Archive.]

12. Paul Strand. [Photo from The Museum of Modern Art/Film
Stills Archive.]

13. *Heart of Spain*: Stretcher-bearers at the front. [Photo from The Museum of Modern Art/Film Stills Archive.]

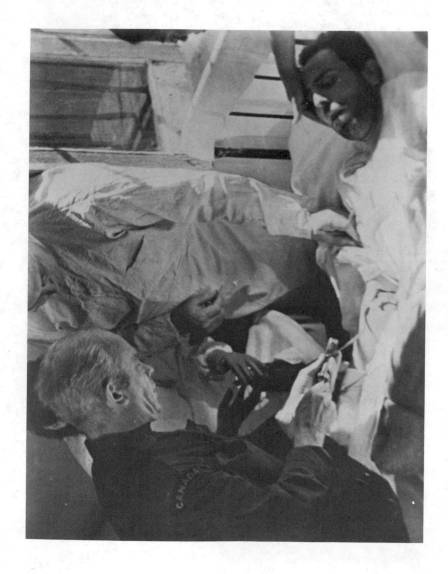

14. *Heart of Spain:* Dr. Bethune gives a blood transfusion. [Photo from The Museum of Modern Art/Film Stills Archive.]

15. *Return to Life*: Madrid barricaded and bombed. [Photo from The Museum of Modern Art/Film Stills Archive.]

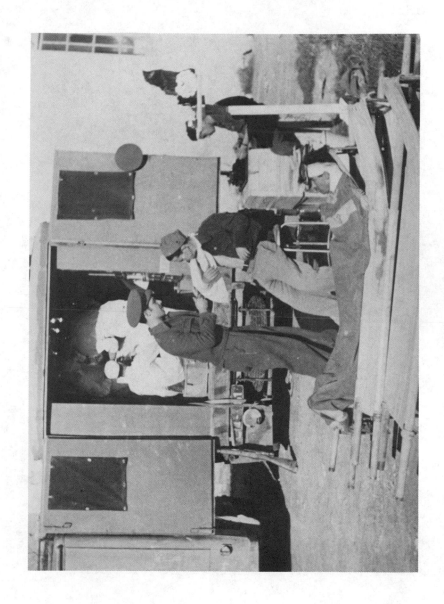

16. *Return to Life*: Emergency medical care behind the lines. [Photo from The Museum of Modern Art/Film Stills Archive.]

17. *China Strikes Back*: Chinese civilian victims of the Japanese invasion. [Photo from The Museum of Modern Art/Film Stills Archive.]

18. *China Strikes Back*: Red Army soldiers relax. [Photo from The Museum of Modern Art/Film Stills Archive.]

19. *People of the Cumberland*: Appalachian poverty. [Photo from
The Museum of Modern Art/Film Stills Archive.]

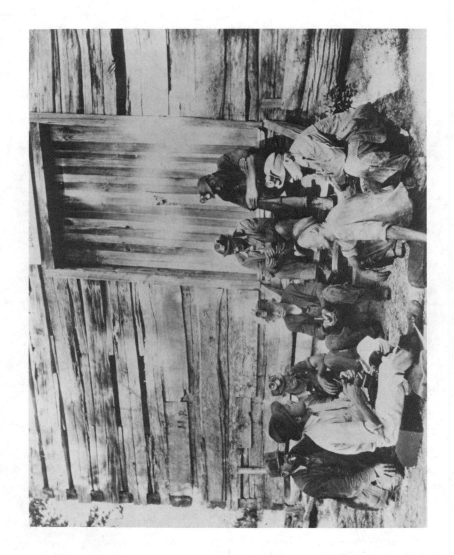

20. *People of the Cumberland:* Miners organized in the UMWA.
[Photo from The Museum of Modern Art/Film Stills Archive.]

21. *People of the Cumberland:* Tennessee clothing workers become unionized. [Photo from The Museum of Modern Art/Film Stills Archive.]

22. *Native Land*: Arkansas deputies on the offensive. [Photo from The Museum of Modern Art/Film Stills Archive.]

23. *Native Land*: Murdered sharecropper (Louis Grant). [Photo from The Museum of Modern Art/Film Stills Archive.]

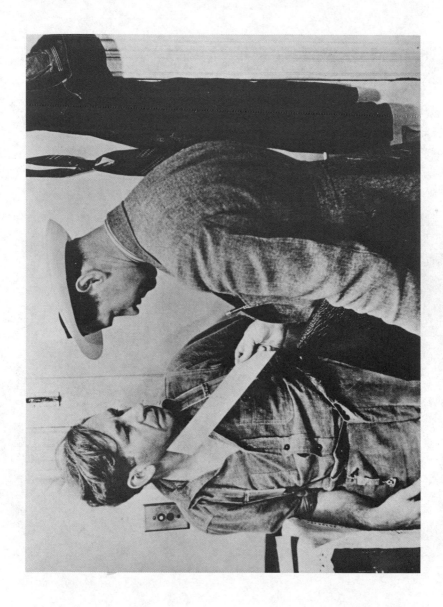

24. *Native Land*: Labor spy Art Smith under pressure from his employers. [Photo from The Museum of Modern Art/Film Stills Archive.]

25. *Native Land:* Virginia Stevens and other mourners of the Republic Steel dead. [Photo from The Museum of Modern Art/Film Stills Archive.]

Appendix

Filmographies

Unless otherwise stated, the films listed below are (or were originally) in 35mm, black-and-white, and silent, and may be assumed to be one reel (fifteen minutes at silent speed) or less in length. Dates cited are those of first known exhibition. Production credits are given where the information exists. Films known to have survived are so identitifed.

Annotating the newsreel footage presents special problems. Particular reels might be referred to by a variety of titles, or by none at all. Footage—such as that of the hunger marches—could be exhibited in various shifting combinations, subjected to recutting, cannibalized for later productions. In general, newsreel subjects have been listed as individual films where the nature of the material or the prominence of references to the footage seems to justify it. Occasionally a title has been supplied, in which case it is enclosed within square brackets.

As explained in the text, some New York Film and Photo League newsreels were grouped together and exhibited, sometimes with significant commercial newsreel footage, under the series head *America Today*. No. 3 in this series was announced as being completed in September 1934, but it is not known how many issues were produced in all, and the assignment of numbers in this list is only tentative.

This filmography was first prepared for publication in *Jump Cut*, No. 14 (1977), with the assistance of William Alexander.

Abbreviations used in this appendix: *add ph* additional photography, *assoc d* associate director, *asst* assistant, *d* director, *dist* distributor, *ed* editor, *m* music, *p* producer, *p.a.* production assistant, *ph* photography, *prod mgr* production manager, *sc* screenplay.

New York Film and Photo League

1931

Albany Hunger March (April).

May Day in New York (May). ph/Irving Lerner [?], Ralph Steiner [?]

National Hunger March / *Hunger March 1931* / *Hunger 1931* (December). ph/ Sam Brody, Robert Del Duca, Kita Kamura, Leo Seltzer, Alfredo Valenti *et al.* Approx. 2 reels. Some footage survives.

The Strike Against Starvation / *Coal Strike, 1931* / *Western Pennsylvania and Kentucky Miners' Strike.* ph/Joseph Hudyma, Tom Brandon, Lewis Jacobs. 3 reels.

W.I.R. Children's Camp, N.Y.

Workers Newsreel—Unemployment Special. ph/ Robert Del Duca, Leo Seltzer. ed/ Leo Seltzer. Extant.

The New World. 2 reels.

A Short Trip to the Soviet Union.

In December, it was reported that the league had produced seven newsreels in the previous two months. The subject matter of these reels is not known.

1932

[*Scottsboro Trial*] (January). ph/Lewis Jacobs, Tom Brandon. Some footage was probably later incorporated in *The Scottsboro Boys.*

Kentucky-Tennessee 1932 (March).

[*May Day Demonstration*] (May).

[*May Day Scenes*] (May).

Scottsboro Demonstration (May).

Workers Ex-Servicemen's Bonus Demonstration / Workers Ex-Servicemen's Bonus Parade (June). Footage later incorporated in *Bonus March.*

Foster and Ford in Action (July).

Bonus March / The Fight for the Bonus (October). ph/Leo Seltzer. ed/Leo Seltzer, Lester Balog. 2 reels. Extant.

Washington Scottsboro Demonstration (November). ph/Leo Seltzer. Later incorporated in the extant *America Today.*

Rent Strikes (Spring?).

New York's Hoovervilles.

Other Newsreel Subjects: a) Bonus Army scenes (later included in *Bonus March*) (June-July), b) Antiwar demonstration (August), c) Miners' strike (September), d) Farmers' holiday (September), e) TUUL picnic (September), f) National Hunger March scenes (later incorporated in *Hunger 1932*) (December).

1933

Hunger 1932 / Hunger (January). ph/Leo Seltzer, Leo T. Hurwitz, Robert Del Duca, Sam Brody, C.O. Nelson, William Kruck, Irving Lerner, Alfredo Valente. ed/Leo T. Hurwitz, Robert Del Duca, Leo Seltzer, Norman Warren. 4 reels. Some footage survives.

America Today No. 1 [?] (February). Contents: a) Farmer's Conference (held Washington, D.C., December 7-10, 1932, by the United Farmers League), b) Lenin Memorial at the Coliseum, c) Gibson Committee Protest, d) Anti-Jim-Crow Demonstration, e) Antiwar demonstration in Wall St.

Tom Mooney Demonstration (February).

Unemployed Demonstration (March).

May Day Celebration / May Day Demonstration / May Day 1933 (May).

Hans Weidemann Protest (May). ph/Leo Seltzer. Later incorporated in the extant *America Today.*

1934

America Today No. 2 [?] (March). Contents: a) Hans Weidemann protest, May 25, 1933 (FPL footage), b) Washington Scottsboro demonstration, November 7, 1932 (FPL footage), c) Fascist parades and Nazi activities in Italy and Germany (with FDR montage in one version) (commercial newsreel), d) March of workers in united-front anti-fascist demonstration and political strike, Paris, February 12, 1934 (commercial newsreel), e) Attack of deputies on steel strike pickets, Ambridge, Pennsylvania, October 4, 1933 (commercial newsreel), f) Interception of scab milk shipments by striking Wisconsin dairy farmers (commercial newsreel). ph (FPL footage)/Leo Seltzer. ed/Leo Seltzer. Extant.

Taxi Strike (May). Some footage possibly later included in *Taxi*.

May Day 1934 (May). ph (aerial)/Leo Seltzer.

Portrait of America (September).

America Today No. 3 [?] (September). Contents not known.

Marine / Marine Strike / Marine Workers / Waterfront / Workers on the Waterfront (December). d/Edward Kern. ph/Leo Seltzer. add ph/Julian Roffman. ed/Leo Seltzer. Approx. 15 min. 16mm. *Note*: The credits for this film are disputed. See chap. 3, n.27.

World in Review.

W.I.R.

The Land of the Free.

Other Newsreel Subjects: a) "Anti-fascist struggles," probably including united-front demonstration outside the Austrian Consulate (May), b) "Negroes and whites fight for democratic rights" (May), c) Soviet freighter *Kim* in New York (ph/Leo Seltzer) (May), d) Striking middle-western farmers (May), e) "Clarence Hathaway [editor of *Daily Worker*] outside Madison Square Garden after having been assaulted" (May).

1935

H.R. 2827 (March). ed/A. Tish. 3 reels.

1934 (March?).

East Side, West Side (March?).

May Day 1935 (May). Partly (200 ft.) in color.

Taxi (May). d/Nancy Naumburg, James Guy. Approx. 80 min. 16mm [?].

United Front (May?). d/Edward Kern. ed/Edward Kern.

I.W.O. [?] (May?). 2 reels.

Hands off Ethiopia (November).

Hollywood (Spring?). d/Vic Kandel, Robert Del Duca. 2 reels.

1936

The Birth of New China (May). ed/Julian Roffman. 6 reels.

Give Us This Day (Spring?).

1937

Getting Your Money's Worth (April). d/Julian Roffman. sc/Julian Roffman. ph/Robert Del Duca, Julian Roffman, Irving Browning. ed/Julian Roffman, Vic Kandel. consultant/Arthur Kallet for Consumers Union. dist/Lenauer International Films. Sound. 8 min.

Independent Films Made in Association with the New York FPL

The Scottsboro Boys / Scottsboro (1933). p/International Labor Defense. d/Leo T. Hurwitz. ph/Lewis Jacobs, Leo T. Hurwitz, Leo Seltzer. ed/Leo T. Hurwitz.

Sweet Land of Liberty (July, 1934). p/Political Prisoners Committee of International Labor Defense. d/Leo T. Hurwitz. ed/Leo T. Hurwitz.

Sheriffed (September, 1934). p/Nancy Naumburg, James Guy. d/Nancy Naumburg, James Guy. ph/Nancy Naumburg. cast/Lew Bentzley (organizer), Mr. and Mrs. John Cummings and their four children, members of the United Farmers Protective Association. Approx. 40 min. 16mm.

Ernst Thaelman: Fighter Against Fascism / Ernst Thaelmann: Fighter for Freedom (September, 1934). p/Thaelmann Liberation Committee. dist/Garrison Film Distributors. supervisor/Tom Brandon. ed/George Moscov. Sound. 4 reels.

Harlem Sketches (April, 1935). p/Vanguard Films. d/Leslie Bain. p.a./Samuel Brody. m/George Antheil. dist/New York FPL. Sound. 2 reels.

Unfinished Films

Winter 1931 (1931-32). sc/Whittaker Chambers, Robert W. Dunn, Hugo Gellert, Joe North, Robert Evans [Joseph Freeman], H.A. Potamkin.

Misery Among Working-Class Children / Child Misery (1933-34).

Unemployment Council / Death of a Worker's Child (1933-34). d/Michael Gold. sc/Michael Gold.

Waste and Want (1934). d/Samuel Brody.

Cigarette (1934-35). sc/Nathan Asch, David Platt.

Detroit Film and Photo League

1932

The Ford Massacre / Detroit Ford Massacre (March?). ph/Jack Awringer, Robert Del Duca, Joseph Hudyma, John Shard, Leo Seltzer. ed/Lester Balog, Joseph Hudyma. et al. Some footage survives.

Unfinished Films

Speed-Up in Auto Industry (1934-35). consultant/A.B. Magil.

Worker's Health (1934-35). consultant/Dr. Bicknell.

In February 1934, it was reported that the Detroit FPL had made a one-reel film for the Macedonian Workers Club. The title of this film is not known.

Chicago Film and Photo League

1932

Communist Convention in Chicago (June).

1934

World's Fair (Fall).

Halsted Street (Fall?). d//C.O. Nelson. sc/C.O. Nelson. ph/C.O. Nelson. ed/C.O. Nelson. 16 min. 16mm. Archive print in the collection of the Film Center, School of the Art Institute of Chicago.

The Great Depression. d/Maurice Bailen. sc/Maurice Bailen. ph/John Freitag, Maurice Bailen. ed/Maurice Bailen. cast/Jacques Jacobsen (man in the street), Nettie (prostitute). 15 min. 16mm. Archive print in the collection of the Film Center, School of the Art Institute of Chicago.

1935

Criminal Syndicalist Law on Trial (February).

1936

Chicago May Day (May?). ph/Maurice Bailen. ed/Maurice Bailen. 6 min. 16mm. Extant.

Peace Parade and Workers' Picnic (Summer?). sc/Maurice Bailen. ph/Maurice Bailen. ed/ Maurice Bailen. 10 min. 16mm. Extant.

Independent Film Made in Association with the Chicago FPL

Mexico Marches On (1935). p/Maurice Bailen, in association with Chicago FPL. d/Maurice Bailen. sc/Maurice Bailen. ph/Maurice Bailen/ ed/Maurice Bailen. 15 min. 16mm. Extant.

The Chicago FPL was also responsible for at least three newsreels not mentioned above whose content is not known. In January 1935 a project was announced for a film which would expose the real state of affairs among Chicago's unemployed, through consultation with doctors and child health specialists. The film was not completed. In early 1937 a documentary (whose title is not known) covering the Flint auto workers' strike was shot for the Chicago league by Fred Lassie.

Los Angeles Film and Photo League

1932

Tom Mooney Run (August?).

Imperial Valley (Fall?).

1933

Cotton-Pickers' Strike (Summer).

San Diego Police Attack on Workers.

1934

Bloody Memorial Day (June?).

California 1934 (Summer).

Cannon Fodder.

Living Wage or Death

Tom Mooney.

Other Newsreel Subjects: a) El Monte berry-pickers' strike (January), b)Los Angeles County Hunger March demonstrations (January).

1936

Lives Wasted (Spring?).

Imperial Valley (Spring?).

The Los Angeles FPL was also responsible for other films, the subject matter of which is not known.

Nykino

Pie in the Sky (1935). p/Nykino, d/Elia Kazan, Ralph Steiner, Irving Lerner, Molly Day Thacher, ph/Ralph Steiner, ed/Ralph Steiner, Leo Hurwitz, titles/Robert Forsythe [Kyle Crichton]. cast/Elia Kazan *(tramp)*, Elman Koolish *(tramp)*, Russell Collins *(minister)*. 14 min. 16mm. First shown March 23, 1935. Archive print at Museum of Modern Art, New York.

The World Today (1936)—*Sunnyside.* p/Nykino, d/Michael Gordon, sc/Ben Maddow, ph/ Willard Van Dyke, commentary/Ben Maddow, narrator/Michael Gordon [?], ed/Irving Lerner, Sidney Meyers [?]. cast/residents of Sunnyside *(themselves)*, Michael Gordon *(deputy)*, Willard Van Dyke *(young husband)*, Sidney Meyers *(policeman)*. 9 min. 35mm. Extant. First shown September 22, 1936.

The World Today (1936)—*Black Legion.* p/Nykino, d/Michael Gordon, sc/Ben Maddow, ph/Ralph Steiner, Willard Van Dyke [?], commentary/Ben Maddow, narrator/Michael Gordon [?], ed/Irving Lerner. cast/actors not known. Approx. 10 min. 35mm. First shown September 22, 1936.

Frontier Films

Heart of Spain (1937). p/Frontier Films, in cooperation with the Canadian Committee to Aid Spain and the Medical Bureau to Aid Spanish Democracy, d/Herbert Kline, sc/Herbert Kline, Paul Strand, Leo Hurwitz, ph/Geza Karpathi, commentary/David Wolff[Ben Maddow], Herbert Kline, narrator/John O'Shaughnessy, ed/Paul Strand, Leo Hurwitz, music arranged by/Alex North, assisted by Jay Leyda, dist/Garrison Film Distributors. 30 min. 35mm. First shown September 10, 1937. Archive print at Museum of Modern Art, New York.

China Strikes Back (1937). p/Frontier Films, sc & ed/Eugene Hill [Jay Leyda], Peter Ellis [Irving Lerner], David Wolff [Ben Maddow], Robert Stebbins [Sidney Meyers], ph/Harry Dunham, narrator/John O'Shaughnessy, music arranged by/Alex North, dist/Garrison Film Distributors. 24 min. 35mm. First shown October 11 [?], 1937. Archive print at Museum of Modern Art, New York.

People of the Cumberland (1938). p/Frontier Films, in cooperation with the Highlander Folk School, d/Robert Stebbins [Sidney Meyers], Eugene Hill [Jay Leyda], asst d/Elia Kazan, William Watts, ph/Ralph Steiner, commentary/Erskine Caldwell, assisted by David Wolff [Ben Maddow], narrator/Richard Blaine, music/Alex North, Earl Robinson, choral arrangements/Earl Robinson, conductor/Elie Siegmeister, sound ed/Helen van Dongen, dist/Garrison Film Distributors. 18 min. 35mm. First shown May 2, 1938. Archive print at Museum of Modern Art, New York.

Return to Life (1938). p/Frontier Films, in cooperation with the Medical Bureau and North American Committee to Aid Spanish Democracy, d/Henri Cartier [-Bresson], in collaboration with Herbert Kline, sc/Henri Cartier [-Bresson], Herbert Kline, ph/Jacques Lemare, commentary/David Wolff [Ben Maddow], narrator/Richard Blaine, ed/Laura Sejour, music/Charles Koecklin, dist/Garrison Film Distributors. 45 min. 35mm. First shown August 3, 1938. Archive print at Museum of Modern Art, New York.

History and Romance of Transportation (1939). p/Frontier Films, for Chrysler Motor Corp., sc & ed/Robert Stebbins [Sidney Meyers], Lionel Berman, David Wolff [Ben Maddow]. 35 mm.

White Flood (1940). p/Frontier Films, sc/David Wolff [Ben Maddow], Robert Stebbins [Sidney Meyers], Lionel Berman, ph/W.O. Field, Jr., Sherman Pratt, commentary/David Wolff [Ben Maddow], narrator/Colfax Sanderson, ed/David Wolff [Ben Maddow], Robert Stebbins [Sidney Meyers], Lionel Berman, music/Hanns Eisler, conductor/Jascha Horenstein. 15 min. 35mm. Archive print at Museum of Modern Art, New York.

Native Land (1942). p/Frontier Films, d/Leo Hurwitz, Paul Strand, assoc d/Alfred Saxe, William Watts, sc/David Wolff [Ben Maddow], Leo Hurwitz, Paul Strand, ph/Paul Strand, prod mgr/George Jacobson, p.a./Julia Milch, Ruth Miller, commentary/David Wolff [Ben Maddow], narrator/Paul Robeson, songs/Paul Robeson, ed/Leo Hurwitz, sound ed/Robert Stebbins [Sidney Meyers], Ralph Avseev, asst ed/Lionel Berman, Robert Stebbins [Sidney Meyers], animation/Ted Eshbaugh Studios, music/Marc Blitzstein, conductor/Lehman Engel, asst in orchestrations/Henry Brant. cast/Fred Johnson *(Fred Hill, farmer)*, Art Smith *(Harry Carlisle, labor spy)*, Housely Stevens *(white sharecropper)*, Louis Grant *(black sharecropper)*, Howard Da Silva *(Jim, labor spy)*, Tom Connors *(Joseph Shoemaker)*, Mary George *(Mrs. Hill, farmer's wife)*, John Rennick *(farmer's son)*, Amelia Romano *(slavey)*, James Hanney *(John McComb, union president)*, Bert Conway *(union member)*, Richard Bishop *(spy executive)*, Charles Jordan *(contact man)*, Vaughn King *(Mary McComb, wife of union president)*, Robert Strauss *(Frank Mason, grocer)*, Dolores Cornell *(little girl)*, John Marlieb *(thug)*, Harry Wilson *(Poulnot)*, Rev. Charles Webber *(minister)*, Virginia Stevens *(widow)*, Clancy Cooper *(speaker)*, Tom Pedi *(union member)*. 83 min. 35mm. First shown May 11, 1942. Archive print at Museum of Modern Art, New York.

Film Made in Association with Frontier Films

United Action / United Action Means Victory (1940). p/Film Department of UAW-CIO, d/Michael Martini, ph/Michael Martini [?], commentary/David Wolff [Ben Maddow], narrator/Charles Gordon, additional voices/Virginia Stevens, Earl Robinson, ed/David Wolff [Ben Maddow], Lionel Berman, sound ed/David Wolff [Ben Maddow], Lionel Berman, music/Earl Robinson, songs/American People's Chorus. 40 min. 35mm. First shown March 8, 1940. Distributed by United Auto Workers, Detroit.

Notes

The following abbreviations are used:

DW   *Daily Worker*
NM   *New Masses*
NT   *New Theatre* (in 1937, *New Theatre and Film*)
NYT   *New York Times*
SW   *Sunday Worker*

Chapter 1

1. The discussion will concentrate primarily on the New York league, which was the original group and the most productive. Some reference will be made to other units, particularly the Detroit, Chicago, and Los Angeles leagues. The local groups were loosely federated in the National Film and Photo League, a coordinating body, in 1934-35.

2. "Realism" refers to a mode of representation, "social" to a choice of (lower- and middle-class) subject matter. In the period with which I am dealing, the two were often, but not always, associated. Social realism, which adopts a critical stance within capitalist society, is of course to be distinguished from "socialist realism," the aesthetic of optimism promulgated in the Soviet Union in the 1930s and thereafter.

3. See Karl Marx, *The English Middle Class* (1854) and Friedrich Engels, letters to Laura Lafargue (1883) and Margaret Harkness (1888), in Lee Baxandall and Stefan Morawski, eds., *Marx and Engels on Literature and Art* (St. Louis and Milwaukee: Telos, 1973), pp. 105, 112, 115-16.

4. Engels, letter to Minna Kautsky, November 26, 1885, in Baxandall and Morawski, p. 113. The views expressed in this letter, and the one to Harkness (see n.5, below), must, however, be taken with caution. The letters were not public statements, and they were composed in the special context of encouraging two aspiring socialist writers. Neither Marx nor Engels ever fully elaborated an aesthetic position.

5. Engels, letter to Margaret Harkness, April 1888 (draft), in Baxandall and Morawski, p. 116.

6. Sidney Finkelstein, *Realism in Art* (New York: International Publishers, 1954), p. 41.

7. See Vladimir Ilyich Lenin, "Leo Tolstoy as the Mirror of the Russian Revolution," "L.N. Tolstoy," and "Leo Tolstoy and his Epoch," in Maynard Solomon, ed., *Marxism and Art: Essays Classic and Contemporary* (New York: Vintage, 1974), pp. 169-78.

8.   Gustave Courbet, quoted in Arnold Hauser, *The Social History of Art* (London: Routledge & Kegan Paul, 1962), IV, 62; Jules Antoine Castagnary, quoted in Linda Nochlin, *Realism* (Harmondsworth: Penguin, 1971), p. 47.

9.   Nochlin, *Realism*, p. 119.

10. Engels, letter to Margaret Harkness, in Baxandall and Morawski, p. 114.

11. Champfleury, letter to George Sand, September 1855, in Nochlin, ed., *Realism and Tradition in Art, 1848-1900* (Englewood Cliffs, N.J.: Prentice-Hall, 1966), pp. 42-43.

12. See Nochlin, *Realism*, pp. 36, 44. The critics are Charles Perrier and Louis de Geoffroy, quoted p. 35.

13. Edgar Dagas, quoted in *ibid.*, p. 19.

14. Emile Zola, quoted in Hauser, *The Social History of Art*, IV, 62. The issue lies beyond the scope of this survey, but it should be noted that Marxist critical orthodoxy of the twentieth century, as represented e.g. by George Lukács, is hostile to Naturalism because of its supposed pragmatic and empirical tendencies, resulting in a "weakening of the relation between ideological principle and individual fact," and because it "deprives life of its poetry, reduces all to prose." See Lukács, *Realism in Our Times: Literature and the Class Struggle* (New York: Harper & Row, 1971), pp. 119, 125.

15. Zola, *The Experimental Novel and Other Essays* (New York: Cassell, 1893), pp. 2, 9.

16. *Ibid.,* pp. 125, 30.

17. P. Martino, *Naturalisme Français (1870-1895)* (Paris: Colin, 1923), p. 70; Zola, quoted in Haskell M. Block, *Naturalistic Triptych: The Fictive and the Real in Zola, Mann, and Dreiser* (New York: Random House, 1970), p. 25.

18. Zola, *The Experimental Novel*, pp. 123-24. Ideas such as these later became the aesthetic foundation of Italian neorealism. A very close restatement of Zola's argument is to be found in Cesare Zavattini, "Some Ideas on the Cinema," *Sight and Sound*, XXIII, No. 2 (October-December 1953), pp. 64-69.

19. Zola, "Naturalism in the Theatre," in Eric Bentley, ed., *The Theory of the Modern Stage: An Introduction to Modern Theatre and Drama* (Baltimore: Penguin, 1968), p. 369.

20. Mordecai Gorelik, *New Theatres for Old* (New York: French, 1940), p. 129. The Théâtre Libre also did symbolist and verse drama.

21. Konstantin Stanislavsky, quoted in David Magarshack, "Stanislavsky," in Bentley, p. 243.

22. Ibid., pp. 268-69.

23. The peak year was 1907, when 1,285,000 immigrants landed. See Maldwyn Allen Jones, *American Immigration* (Chicago: University of Chicago, 1960), p. 179.

24. Frank Norris, quoted in Block, *Naturalistic Triptych*, p. 9.

25. For a study of left-wing literature of the period, see Walter Rideout, *The Radical Novel in the United States, 1900-1954: Some Interrelations of Literature and Society* (Cambridge: Harvard University, 1956), chap. 2, 3, and 4.

26. See Block, *Naturalistic Triptych*, pp. 58-59.

27. Sam Hunter, *Modern American Painting and Sculpture* (New York: Dell, 1959), p. 37.

28.   Gorelik, *New Theatres for Old,* p. 164.

29.   For an analysis of left-wing drama of the twenties, see Jay Williams, *Stage Left* (New York: Scribner's, 1974), chap. 2.

30.   Frank Woods, quoted in A. Nicholas Vardac, "Griffith and *The Birth of a Nation,*" in Harry M. Geduld, ed., *Focus on D.W. Griffith* (Englewood Cliffs, N.J.: Prentice-Hall, 1971), p. 85.

31.   Frederick Roche, quoted in Patrick McGilligan, "Thomas Jefferson Still Survives," *The Velvet Light Trap,* No. 8 (1973), p. 44.

32.   Tom Flinn, "*Old Ironsides:* The Influence of Seapower Upon Hollywood," *The Velvet Light Trap,* No. 8 (1973), p. 5.

33.   *Motion Picture News,* September 8, 1915, p. 90.

34.   Data from research undertaken by the author for a forthcoming book by Thomas J. Brandon. See Kenneth W. Munden, ed., *The American Film Institute Catalog of Motion Pictures Produced in the United States, Feature Films, 1921-1930* (New York: Bowker, 1971), I.

35.   William Scott, *Documentary Expression and Thirties America* (New York: Oxford University, 1973), pp. 75-76; Jack London, *The People of the Abyss,* in Upton Sinclair, ed., *The Cry for Justice: An Anthology of the Literature of Social Protest* (Philadelphia: Winston, 1915), pp. 127-28. On Riis, see Alexander Alland, Sr., *Jacob A. Riis: Photographer and Citizen* (New York: Aperture, 1974).

36.   See Lewis W. Hine, *Men at Work: Photographic Studies of Modern Men and Machines* (New York: Dover, 1977) (originally published 1932); Judith Mara Gutman, *Lewis W. Hine and the American Social Conscience* (New York: Walker, 1967), and *Lewis W. Hine, 1874-1940: Two Perspectives* (New York: Grossman, 1974); and Walter Rosenblum *et al., America and Lewis Hine: Photographs 1904-1940* (New York: Brooklyn Museum/Aperture, 1977).

37.   Sergei Eisenstein, quoted in Yon Barna, *Eisenstein* (Boston: Little, Brown, 1973), p. 47.

38.   Dziga Vertov, "Instructions provisoires aux cercles 'Ciné-oeil,' " *Cahiers du Cinéma,* No. 228 (March-April 1971), p. 12. Translation by author.

39.   Ibid., p. 14. Translation by author.

40.   Vertov, in Luda and Jean Schnitzer and Marcel Martin, eds., *Cinema in Revolution: The Heroic Era of the Soviet Film* (London: Secker & Warburg, 1973), p. 81.

41.   Vertov, quoted in Georges Sadoul, *Dziga Vertov* (Paris: Champ Libre, 1971), p. 81. Translation by author.

42.   The figures are those given by Sadoul, *Dziga Vertov,* pp. 148-60; slightly different figures are cited by other authorities. Vertov did not work personally on every newsreel issue.

43.   Paul Rotha, *Documentary Film* (New York: Hastings House, 1952), p. 69.

44.   Ibid., p. 67.

45.   Ibid., p. 68; John Grierson, in Forsyth Hardy, ed., *Grierson on Documentary* (New York: Praeger, 1971), pp. 146-47.

46.   Grierson, in Hardy, *Grierson on Documentary,* p. 147.

47.   Ibid.; Lev Kuleshov, in Ronald Levaco, ed., *Kuleshov on Film: Writings by Lev Kuleshov* (Berkeley and Los Angeles: University of California, 1974), p. 57.

48.   Alan Lovell, in Lovell and Jim Hillier, *Studies in Documentary* (New York: Viking, 1972), p. 19.

49.   H.A. Potamkin, "Movie: New York Notes," *Close Up,* VII, No. 4 (October 1930), p. 250, reprinted in Lewis Jacobs, ed., *The Compound Cinema: The Film Writings of Harry Alan Potamkin* (New York: Teachers College, 1977), pp. 396-97.

50.   Samuel Brody, in *NM,* VI, No. 3 (August 1930), p. 14.

51.   Potamkin, "Movie: New York Notes," pp. 249-50.

52.   Brody, *NM,* VI, No. 3 (August 1930), p. 14.

53.   See Tony Safford, "The Camera as a Weapon in the Class Struggle: Interview with Samuel Brody," *Jump Cut,* No. 14 (1977), p. 28. Brody had also heard Eisenstein speak a few months before in Paris, and reported the event in *Close Up,* VI, No. 4 (April 1930), and *NM,* V, No. 11 (April 1930).

54.   Kuleshov, in Levaco, *Kuleshov on Film,* pp. 43-50.

55.   Eisenstein, "The Cinematographic Principle and the Ideogram," in *Film Form: Essays in Film Theory and The Film Sense,* ed. Jay Leyda (Cleveland and New York: World Publishing, 1957), p. 30.

56.   Eisenstein, "A Dialectic Approach to Film Form," in *ibid.,* pp. 58-63.

57.   Eisenstein, "The New Language of Cinema," in *Film Essays and a Lecture,* ed. Leyda (New York: Praeger, 1970), p. 34, and "Perspectives," in ibid., p. 45.

58.   Eisenstein, "Through Theatre to Cinema," in *Film Form: Essays in Film Theory and The Film Sense,* p. 3, and quoted in Marie Seton, *Sergei M. Eisenstein* (New York: Grove, 1960), p. 115.

59.   See Barna, *Eisenstein,* pp. 78, 117.

60.   Leyda, *Films Beget Films* (New York: Hill & Wang, 1971), p. 28.

61.   Esther Shub, quoted in ibid., p. 26.

62.   *DW,* May 9, 1932, p. 2.

63.   Eisenstein, "A Dialectic Approach to Film Form," p. 62; Shub, quoted in *Films Beget Films,* p. 27.

64.   Sadoul, *Dziga Vertov,* p. 92, translation by author.

65.   Vertov, "Instructions provisoires," p. 14 [translation by author], and "Dziga Vertov on Kino-Eye, Lecture II," *Film Culture,* No. 25 (Summer 1962), p. 65 (originally published in *Filmfront,* 1, No. 3 [1935], translation by Brody).

66.   Vertov, in Schnitzer and Martin, *Cinema in Revolution,* p. 79, and quoted in Sadoul, *Dziga Vertov,* pp. 86, 142 (translation by author). See also Sadoul, p. 76.

67.   Béla Balázs, quoted in *Films Beget Films,* p. 29. Ivens writes: "Up to this time my experience in *idea* editing had been rather sparse. My earliest experience was sometime in 1929 when I was given charge of the film programs for a series of workers' cultural and educational Sunday mornings. On Friday nights we would borrow a number of commercial newsreels. On Saturday we would study the material in the newsreels in relation to the international and national situation of the week, re-edit them with any other footage we happened to have available to us giving them a clear political significance, print new subtitles (the films were still

silent) showing relationships between events which newsreel companies never thought of, and which would certainly have shocked them if they had ever seen our uses of their 'innocent' material. For example, we could relate the injustice of an American lynching with the injustice of the Japanese aggression in Manchuria, making a general statement about injustice which we would then localize with a current event in our own country. Previously miscellaneous material was knit together into a new unity, sometimes with the addition of a spoken word on the public address system or some cartoons, photographs, or photostats of an editorial from the Dutch conservative press. After our Sunday morning show was finished we would take the film apart again, restore its original form, and return it to the newsreel companies who were none the wiser!" Joris Ivens, *The Camera and I* (New York: International Publishers, 1969), pp. 96-97. See also Bert Hogenkamp, *Workers' Newsreels in the 1920s and 1930s* (London: History Group of the Communist Party, n.d. [c. 1977]), p. 6.

68.   Or more precisely, a re-invention. During the Paris Commune, in 1871, photomontage had been employed by reactionary forces in order to discredit the revolution by means of falsified "documents." See Willi Lüdecke, *Der Film in Agitation und Propaganda der Revolutionären Deutschen Arbeiterbewegung (1919-1933)* (Berlin: Oberbaumverlag, 1973), p. 23.

69.   Richard Huelsenbeck, quoted in Hans Richter, *Dada: Art and Anti-Art* (New York: Abrams, 1965), p. 106; Raoul Hausmann, quoted in ibid., p. 116.

70.   These photomonages are reproduced in Dawn Ades, *Photomontage* (New York: Pantheon, 1976).

71.   Reproduced in John Heartfield *et al., John Hearfield: Fotomontör* (Stockholm: Moderna Museet, 1967), # 10.

72.   See Ades, #27. The first exhibition of Heartfield's montages in the U.S. was held by the Photo League in 1937. Among American documentary filmmakers who were influenced by Heartfield were Lewis Jacobs, who was "much excited" by Heartfield's work, and "did some photos of a similar nature about the Depression in America, photomontages and things" (interview with author, April 13, 1977), and Paul Strand, whose cover for *TAC* magazine in January 1939—a skeleton on a swastika—was inspired by similar anti-fascist images of Heartfield which he "greatly admired" (see Michael E. Hoffman, ed., *Paul Strand: Sixty Years of Photographs* [New York: Aperture, 1976], p. 161).

73.   Ades, #51, and p. 111; Eisenstein, "Montage of Attractions," in *Film Form: Essays in Film Theory and The Film Sense*, p. 231.

74.   Piscator in fact called Heartfield the "founder of Epic Theatre" after the occasion in 1920 when he arrived late with the scenery for a play being performed by the Proletarian Theatre and argued, in the presence of the audience, that the show—which had already started— should not continue until the sets were in place. See Erwin Piscator, *Das Politische Theater* (Hamburg: Rowohlt, 1963 [first published 1929]), pp. 48-49n, and Maria Ley-Piscator, *The Piscator Experiment: The Political Theatre* (New York: Heinemann, 1967), pp. 11-12.

75.   Ley-Piscator, *The Piscator Experiment*, pp. 80-81; see also Piscator, *Das Politische Theater*, pp. 146-59.

76.   Gorelik, *New Theatres for Old*, p. 421.

77.   Tilla Durieux, quoted in Ley-Piscator, *The Piscator Experiment*, p. 85.

78.   Bertolt Brecht, in John Willett, ed., *Brecht on Theatre* (New York: Hill & Wang, 1964), p. 102.

79.   Piscator, *Das Politische Theater*, p. 73. Translation by author. Heartfield was designer of the production.

80.   Ibid., p. 75. Translation by author.

81.   Ben Brewster, quoted in James Pettifer, "Against the Stream—*Kuhle Wampe*," *Screen*, XV, No. 2 (Summer 1974), p. 64n.

82.   Brecht, in Willett, p. 37. Brecht was an associate of both Piscator and Heartfield (with whom he once co-edited a sports paper, *Arena*). Brecht's conception of the possibilities of montage in the cinema is suggested by this description (by Bernard Eisenschitz) of his contributions to the script of *Kuhle Wampe:* " 'Foreign elements' were to abound: informative and ideological inserts, which are simultaneously indications, allusions, and rhythmic pauses. . . . Montage here means the very process by which a new dramatic art relocates actors and story within a chain of causality, and the spectator's interest is no longer aroused by harmonizing with his emotions, but through recognition—of reality—and of what is at stake in that reality. The cinematic process itself is but one of the modalities of that construction principle, its most frequent application being the inclusion of material that resists the fiction: legal paragraphs, news items, an agitprop scene miming the family being evicted, and also the sequences of 'intellectual montage' that were to develop in the film and determine its new economy: 'self-contained pieces of music accompanied by images of apartment blocks, factories, and landscapes.' " Eisenschitz, "Who Does the World Belong to? The Place of a Film," *Screen*, XV, No. 2 (Summer 1974), pp. 70-71.

83.   See Lukács, *Realism in Our Time.*

Chapter 2

1.   Some of the material in this and the following chapter appeared in an article by the author, "Film and Photo League: Radical Cinema in the 30s," *Jump Cut*, No. 14 (1977), pp. 23-25. Information on the IAH is derived principally from Willi Münzenberg, *Solidarität: Zehn Jahre Internationale Arbeiterhilfe, 1921-1931* (Berlin: Neuer Deutsche Verlag, 1931), and Babette Gross, *Willi Münzenberg: A Political Biography* (Michigan: Michigan State University, 1974).

2.   Münzenberg, "Capture the Film!," *DW*, July 23, 1925, p. 3. *Erobert den Film!* is reprinted in Willi Lüdecke, *Der Film in Agitation und Propaganda der Revolutionären Deutschen Arbeiterbewegung (1919-1933)* (Berlin: Oberbaumverlag, 1973).

3.   The "Artistic Collective of Russ" had been formed in the early months of 1918. Under a special agreement with Lunacharsky, "all films were to have primarily artistic and not political aims," and because of its composition, Jay Leyda writes, the collective "could be justly called the film branch of the Moscow Art Theatre." The group was committed to conventionally dramatized, narrative film, as exemplified by its first production, *Polikushka*, from the short story by Tolstoy. See Leyda, *Kino: A History of the Russian and Soviet Film* (London: Allen & Unwin, 1973), p. 146.

4.   Ernestine Evans, quoted in Leyda, ibid., p. 187; Münzenberg, *Solidarität*, p. 511 (translation by author).

5.   Münzenberg, *Solidarität*, p. 513.

6.   Ibid., p. 515.

7. After ninety per cent of the shooting on *Kuhle Wampe* had been completed, Prometheus failed, and the movie was taken over by Praesens-Film. See *Screen,* XV, No. 2 (Summer 1974), p. 47n, and interview with George Hoellering, "Making *Kuhle Wampe,"Screen,* XV, No. 4 (Winter 1974-75), pp. 71-79. *Jenseits der Strasse* was released by the WIR in the US as *Harbor Drift.*

8. Lüdecke, *Der Film,* pp. 48-49.

9. See Russell Campbell, "Nihilists and Bolsheviks: Revolutionary Russia in American Silent Film," *The Silent Picture,* No. 19 (1974), pp. 22-31.

10. Kenneth W. Munden, ed., *The American Film Institute Catalog of Motion Pictures Produced in the United States, Feature Films, 1921-1930* (New York: Bowker, 1971), I, 236.

11. Soviet features handled by the WIR in the U.S. during the twenties included *Polikushka* (Sanin, 1922), *The Ultimatum* (Bassaligo, 1923), *Breaking Chains* (Protazanov, 1925), and *Hirsch Leckert/Seeds of Freedom* (Rosal, 1928).

12. Gross, *Willi Münzenberg,* p. 168.

13. William F. Kruse, "Workers' Conquest of the Films," *Workers Monthly,* IV, No. 11 (September 1925), p. 503.

14. Ibid., p. 526.

15. The Workers Party was formed in December 1921 as the legal front of the undergound Communist Party of America, which had resulted from the merger earlier that year of the two Communist parties founded in September 1919. In April 1923 the undergound party was dissolved. The Workers Party became the Workers (Communist) Party in 1925 and the Communist Party, U S A., in 1929.

16. Kruse, "Workers' Conquest," p. 503.

17. "Reds Tried Film Entry 30 Years Ago," *Hollywood Citizen News,* May 7, 1951, p. [?]. According to Philip Sterling ("A Channel for Democratic Thought," *Films,* No. 2 [Spring 1940], p. 15), *The Contrast* was produced by the AFL, which, if true, also tends to cast doubt on the possiblity of Communist propaganda being inserted.

18. According to Benjamin Gitlow, a Communist leader at the time, the party's Political Committee "exercised jurisdiction over the American branch of the International Workers' Aid and all Communist relief activities. During the Passaic textile strike when hundreds of thousands of dollars rolled in to offices of the Passaic Textile Workers Strike Relief Committee, it was not unusual for the Polcom to make decisions ordering the relief committee to turn over large amounts of the relief money to the party." Gitlow, *The Whole of Their Lives* (New York: Scribner's, 1948), p. 129.

19. Munden, *The American Film Institute Catalog,* p. 591.

20. See, e.g., House of Representatives, Special Committee to Investigate Communist Activities in the United States, *Investigation of Communist Propaganda* (Washington, 1930), Part 5, IV, 620.

21. Sandor Parlagi, letter, *NM,* V, No. 11 (April 1930), p. 21.

22. S[amuel] B[rody], "The Movies as a Weapon Against the Working Class," *DW,* May 20, 1930, p. 4.

23. Ibid.; Harry A. Potamkin, "Workers' Films," *DW,* May 31, 1930, p. 3.

24. Potamkin, ibid., p. 3. The London Workers' Film Society, affiliated to the Federation of Workers' Film Societies (FOWFS), the *Forenigen for Filmskultur,* and the *Vereeniging voor VolksCultuur* (VVVC) had all been founded in the late twenties, principally for the purpose of exhibiting Soviet films uncensored to workers. Comparable organizations were the *Volksfilmverband* in Germany and the quickly suppressed *Amis de Spartacus* in France. See Bert Hogenkamp, *Workers' Newsreels in the 1920s and 1930s* (London: History Group of the Communist Party, n.d. [c. 1977]), pp. 4-14, 21-22.

25. Michael Friedman, letter, *NM,* VI, No. 2 (July 1930), p. 22; Potamkin, in *NM,* VI, No. 3 (August 1930), p. 20.

26. Hogenkamp, *Workers' Newsreels,* pp. 6-15; Eckart Jahnke *et al., Dokumentarfilm in Japan: Seine Demokratische und Kämpferische Traditionen* (Berlin: Staatliches Filmarchiv der DDR, 1976), pp. 7, 34.

27. Münzenberg, *Solidarität,* p. 87. At one time an "official Comintern publication" asserted: "A special field of activity of the WIR is the production of proletarian movie pictures. For this purpose the WIR has its own movie picture organizations in the U.S.S.R., Germany, Italy, Norway, America, France, Sweden, and other countries." (See Witold S. Sworakowski, *The Communist International and its Front Organizations* [Stanford: Hoover Institution on War, Revolution, and Peace, 1965], p. 456.) The existence of these organizations outside the Soviet Union, Germany, and the United States has, however, not been authenticated. Hogenkamp writes: "The evidence that I have gathered so far suggests that the kind of relationship that existed between the [Film and Photo] League and the American section of the WIR was rather unique." Hogenkamp, letter to *Jump Cut,* February 19, 1978.

28. Frances Strauss, "Workers' Photo Exhibit," *NM,* V, No. 9 (February 1930), p. 20.

29. *NM,* V, No. 8 (January 1930), p. 20; Strauss, *"Workers' Photo Exhibit,"* p. 20.

30. Isabelle A. Kleinman, in *NM,* VI, No. 2 (July 1930), p. 22; *Labor Defender,* April 1930, p. 76.

31. Kleinman, ibid., p. 22; *Labor Defender,* ibid.

32. *DW,* May 28, 1930, p. 1, September 6, 1930, p. 2, and October 16, 1930, p. 2.

33. *NM,* VI, No. 6 (November 1930), p. 20.

34. Brody, letter to Anne Tucker, June 10, 1977, cited in Tucker, "Photographic Crossroads: The Photo League," *Journal of the National Gallery of Canada,* No. 25 (April 6, 1978), p. 3; *DW,* December 11, 1930, p. 2. Elsewhere Brody asserts: "I was the founder of the Workers' Film and Photo League in 1931" (Tony Safford, "The Camera as a Weapon in the Class Struggle: Interview with Samuel Brody," *Jump Cut,* No. 14 [1977], p. 28). Balog's name was originally spelt "Balogh." The last meeting of the Workers' Camera League was held at the WIR building (131 W. 28th Street) on December 4, 1930 (*DW,* December 4, 1930, p. 2). *In Old Siberia* was probably *Katorga* (Raizman, 1928).

35. *DW,* December 18, 1930, p. 2, and February 4, 1931, p. 2.

36. Leo Seltzer, in Russell Campbell, " 'A Total and Realistic Experience': Interview with Leo Seltzer," *Jump Cut,* No. 14 (1977), p. 25; Tom Brandon, interview with author, November 4, 1976.

37. S[eymour] S[tern], "A Working-Class Cinema for America?", *The Left,* I, No. 1 (Spring 1931), p. 71.

38. Seltzer, in Campbell, " 'A Total and Realistic Experience,' " p. 26.

39. Sidney Howard was a successful Broadway dramatist whose plays included *Marseilles* (1930), *The Late Christopher Bean* (1932), *Yellow Jack* (1933), *Alien Corn* (1933), *Dodsworth* (1934), *Ode to Liberty* (1934), *Paths of Glory* (1935), and *The Ghost of Yankee Doodle* (1937). Among his screen credits were *Raffles* (1930), *Dodsworth* (1936), and *Gone with the Wind* (1939).

40. The (Workers') Film and Photo League was located successively at the following addresses in New York City. Earliest and latest found references for each address are given.

    131 W. 28th St. (WIR), December 1930.

    7 E. 14th St., February 1931; March 1931.

    131 W. 28th St. (WIR), May 1931.

    799 Broadway (WIR), June 1931.

    16 W. 21st St. (WIR), December 1931.

    13 W. 17th St., November 1932; April 1933.

    220 E. 14th St., August 1933; November 1933.

    116 Lexington Ave., November 1933; January 1934.

    12 E. 17th St., February 1934; September 1934.

    31 E. 21st St., December 1934; May 1936.

    220 W. 42 St., Rm. 1203 (Film Section), June 1936; February 1937.

41. Seltzer, Campbell, "'A Total and Realistic Experience,'" p. 26; Julian Roffman, letter to author, October 26, 1977.

42. Brody, in Safford, "The Camera as a Weapon," p. 28; Seltzer, in Campbell, "'A Total and Realistic Experience,'" p. 25. Lewis Jacobs, formerly an art student in Philadelphia, had made several experimental short films, and was a founding editor, in 1930, of *Experimental Cinema*. In 1931 he obtained work as production manager of a New York motion-picture trailer company, and thereafter was not an active WFPL participant. Leo T. Hurwitz graduated from Harvard in 1930, and was a freelance journalist and portrait photographer. David Platt, a former Philadelphia poet, was co-editor of *Experimental Cinema*. Jay Leyda, from Ohio, had worked as an assistant to Ralph Steiner and had made a short experimental film, *A Bronx Morning*. Irving Lerner, born in New York, had attended Columbia University and was a commercial still photographer. Ralph Steiner, from Cleveland, was a still photographer and award-winning experimental filmmaker (H_2O, *Mechanical Principles*, etc.).

43. Leo Hurwitz, "One Man's Voyage: Ideas and Films in the 1930's," *Cinema Journal*, XV, No. 1 (Fall 1975), pp. 2, 6, and interview with author, April 14, 1977.

44. David Platt, letter to William Alexander, July 30, 1975, and letter to author, July 19, 1977; Seltzer, in Campbell, "'A Total and Realistic Experience,'" p. 26; Roffman, letter to author, October 16, 1977.

45. Roffman, letter to author, October 26, 1977. Nicholas Bela, born in Hungary, had lived and worked in Hollywood since 1928. Primarily an actor, he also claimed to have been employed as a writer, though I have not been able to locate any screen credits for him. Testifying before the House Un-American Activities Committee on December 14, 1954, he recalled his passing association with the Film and Photo League, and particularly Tom Brandon, who epitomized, he said, "the typical Communist organizer—cold, calculating opportunist who would only get whatever he can [*sic*] from you and never, if possible, give you anything in return except driving you on to study and work; you did not know enough." See House of Representatives, Committee on Un-American Activities, *Communist Methods of Infiltration (Entertainment—Part 2)* (Washington, 1954), pp. 7242-47.

46.   Seltzer, in Campbell, " 'A Total and Realistic Experience,' " p. 25; Hurwitz, interview with author; Brandon, in Fred Sweet et al., "Pioneers: An Interview with Tom Brandon," *Film Quarterly*, XXVII, No. 1 (Fall 1973), p. 19.

47.   Seltzer, in Campbell, p. 27. The Acme Theatre was on 14th Street in Union Square. FPL films were also occasionally shown at the New Star Casino (Park Avenue and 107th Street), the Fifth Avenue Theatre (Broadway and 28th Street), and later at the Cameo Theatre (42nd Street).

48.   *Party Organizer*, V, No. 8 (August 1932), p. 27.

49.   *Workers' Theatre*, February 1932, p. 30.

50.   *NT*, October 1934, p. 5; Henry Hart, ed., *American Writers' Congress* (New York: International Publishers, 1935), p. 180; Roffman, letter to author, October 26, 1977. It seems likely, given the CP pattern of control over its mass organizations, that the shifting of resources and manpower into film distribution was the result of a conscious political decision. However I have no detailed information regarding the formation or operation of Garrison Film Distributors (which was eventually dissolved in October 1941, to re-emerge as Brandon Films in January 1942).

51.   Potamkin, "Film and Photo Call to Action!," *Workers' Theatre*, July 1931, pp. 5-6. A different version of this article (perhaps an earlier draft) is published as "A Movie Call to Action!" in Lewis Jacobs, ed., *The Compound Cinema: The Film Writings of Harry Alan Potamkin* (New York: Teachers College, 1977), pp. 583-86. Potamkin had been a founder of the New York John Reed Club, the Communist writers' and artists' group, in 1929, and was a delegate to the Kharkov Conference of the International Union of Revolutionary Writers in November 1930.

52.   Potamkin, "What is the Program of the Workers' Cultural Federation?", *DW*, July 18, 1931, p. 4.

53.   The board is referred to, e.g., in *NM*, VII, No. 7 (December 1931), p. 27; "S. Vorkapich, Cinema Technician, Backs Film-Photo League Program," *DW*, July 27, 1934, p. 5; "Film-Photo League Protests Expulsion of Hughes from Carmel," *DW*, August 16, 1934, p. 5.

54.   Potamkin, "Film and Photo Call to Action!", p. 5; *NM*, VII, No. 1 (June 1931), p. 22.

55.   "Program of the International Cinema Bureau," *NT*, May 1934, pp. 15-16; Walter S. Steele, "Communistic 'Cultural Front,' " *National Republic*, XXII, No. 2 (June 1934), pp. 21-22. See also Maria Baker, "Film Conference," *NT*, September-October 1933, p. 24, and Béla Balázs, "Let Us Create an International Union of Revolutionary Cinema," *International Theatre*, No. 4 (1933), pp. 6-8.

56.   S[amuel] B[rody], "*Hallelujah* at Embassy Don't Portray Real Negro," *DW*, August 30, 1929, p. 4; Potamkin, *The Eyes of the Movie* (New York: International Pamphlets, 1934), reprinted in *The Compound Cinema*, pp. 243-69; *Filmfront*, I, No. 2 (January 7, 1935), p. 2. For several years in the early thirties Brody wrote a *Daily Worker* column under the pen name of "Lens." *Filmfront* was issued by the National Film and Photo League. The films it listed were *The President Vanishes, Flirtation Walk, The First World War, Man of Courage, British Agent, The Merry Frinks, Friends of Mr. Sweeny, No Greater Glory, World in Revolt, House of Rothschild, Come on Marines, S.A. Mann Brand, Stand Up and Cheer,* and *I Believed in You.*

57.   *DW*, January 4, 1932, p. 2; "Lens," "Flashes and Close-Ups," *DW*, September 11, 1933, p. 5; Ibid., April 18, 1934, p. 5. Potamkin also presided at a symposium on "American vs. Soviet

Movies" in February 1931, and the same month gave a lecture on "Film in the Class Struggle" (*DW,* February 21, 1931, p. 2, and February 4, 1931, p. 2). Robert Gessner's documentary book on the oppression of American Indians, *Massacre,* was filmed by Warner Brothers in 1934 (see his account of the carnage, "Massacre in Hollywood," *NT,* March 1934, pp. 16-17). At this time, he declared: "We revolutionaries . . . are interested, or should be if we are at all revolutionary, in perfecting our writing as a force aiding the proletariat in a Communist revolution" (*NM,* July 3, 1934, p. 29). Also a highly-regarded poet (his *Cross of Flame* on the Reichstag Fire Trial was published in *Proletarian Literature in the United States: An Anthology,* 1935), Gessner pioneered academic film study in the United States as Professor of Cinema at New York University in the late thirties.

58. Platt, "War Department Takes Over Movies for Jingo Propaganda," *DW,* February 12, 1934, p. 5. On the *Thunder over Mexico* campaign, see 'Lens," "Flashes and Close-Ups: Thunder Over the Rialto," *DW,* September 26, 1933, p. 5; "Mexican Movie Evokes Thunder Over Sinclair," *DW,* September 26, 1953, p. 5; Platt, "The New Film Smokescreen Over Mexico: The Sinclair Distortion at the Rialto Theatre," *DW;* September 26, 1953, p. 5; Brody and Brandon, "A Mexican Trailer," *NM,* IX, No. 1 (September 1933); p. 28; Stern, letter, *DW,* August 31, 1933, p. 5; Workers' Film and Photo League of Detroit, "Resolution," *Close Up,* X, No. 3 (September 1933), p. 254. See also *Experimental Cinema,* I, No. 4 (1932), and I, No. 5 (1934). The intensified campaign, beginning in early 1934, against reactionary Hollywood films and fascist imports, with its draining effect on the FPL's other activities (particularly production), was possibly the result of an important policy decision, but according to Tom Brandon no conscious change in program was made (letter to author, July 8, 1978).

59. "Film-Photo League Calls for Protest Against War Picture," *DW,* May 21, 1934, p. 5; Hurwitz, "No Greater Treachery," *NT,* June 1934, p. 13; Brandon, "The Movie Front," *NT,* September 1934, p. 30, and "What's Doing in the Film and Photo League Branches," *DW,* September 14, 1934, p. 5. Brandon's *New Theatre* article cites a figure of "1,800" theatres, a probable misprint. Prior to the Popular Front period, Communist parties opposed military build-up in the democratic (as well as fascist) capitalist countries, since it was feared they would form a hostile alliance against the Soviet Union.

60. Hurwitz, "Hisses, Boos, and Boycotts," *NT,* July-August 1934, pp. 10-11; Brandon, "The Movie Front," *NT,* September 1934, p. 30. See also Brody, "*S.A. Mann Brand,* Vicious Nazi Film, Opens in New York," *DW,* May 30, 1934, p. 5; "Mass Demonstration Tonight in Yorkville to Protest Nazi Film," *DW,* May 30, 1934, p. 5; "Picket Nazi Movie *S.A. Mann Brand* in Yorkville Tonight!", *DW,* June 7, 1934, p. 5; "Iris," "Flashes and Close-Ups," *DW,* June 11, 1934, p. 5; T.J. B[randon], in *NT,* June 1934, p. 22.

61. On *Black Shirts,* see "Iris," "Flashes and Close-Ups," *DW,* May 12, 1934, p. 7. On *Call to Arms,* see "Lens," "Flashes and Close-Ups," *DW,* October 18, 1934, p. 5; *DW,* October 23, 1934, p. 5, November 20, 1934, p. 5, and January 12, 1935, p. 7; Platt, "Flashes and Close-Ups," *DW,* July 5, 1935, p. 5; Platt, "The Movie Front," *NT,* December 1934, p. 25; and *Filmfront,* I, No. 2 (January 7, 1935), p. 17. On *Black Fury,* see Platt, "Film *Black Fury* is Vicious Attack on Militant Unionism in Coal Fields," *DW,* April 15, 1935, p. 5, and Albert Maltz, "Author of *Black Pit* Calls for Boycott of Vicious Anti-Union Film *Black Fury,*"*DW,* April 22, 1935, p. 5. On *Red Salute,* see *DW,* August 9, 1935, p. 5, and November 19, 1935, p. 3. See also Lauren Adams, "Hollywood is on the Run: Nothing Gives Film Men Jitters Like Pickets—And for Good Reason," *DW,* February 6, 1936, p. 7.

62. Sidney Meyers, quoted in Sweet et al., "Pioneers," p. 15; "Lens," "Flashes and Close-Ups," *DW,* December 1, 1933, p. 5.

63.   Brody, in Safford, "The Camera as a Weapon," p. 29.

64.   Kruse, "Workers' Conquest," p. 503; Brody, "The Movies as a Weapon Against the Working Class."

65.   "Censorship Clamps Down on Films of the Hunger March," *DW,* December 19, 1931, p. 5; Potamkin, "Who Owns the Movie?", Part II, *Workers' Theatre,* April 1932, pp. 18-19.

66.   *DW,* May 9, 1932, p. 2, and May 10, 1932, p. 2.

67.   "Open Censorship of Movies Shown in News Release," *DW,* March 21, 1934, p. 7.

68.   "Truth is Forbidden: The Mayor of Chicago as Film Censor," *NT,* May 1934, p. 22.

69.   Brandon, "Who are the Forces Behind the Legion of Decency Drive?", *DW,* August 17, 1934, p. 5; Platt, "Flashes and Close-Ups," *DW,* December 17, 1934, p. 5; Editorial, *Filmfront,* I, No. 1 (December 24, 1934), pp. 1-3.

70.   *DW,* July 27, 1934, p. 5, and August 17, 1934, p. 5; Brandon, "What's Doing in the Film and Photo League Branches"; "Lens," "Flashes and Close-Ups," *DW,* October 25, 1934, p. 5.

71.   Platt, "Flashes and Close-Ups," *DW,* February 23, 1935, p. 7.

72.   "Iris," "Flashes and Close-Ups," *DW,* June 11, 1934, p. 5; "WIR Protests Arrest of Cameraman Lester Balog in California," *DW,* June 21, 1934, p. 5; Brandon, "The Movie Front," *NT,* July-August 1934, p. 19; Platt, "Flashes and Close-Ups," *DW,* January 28, 1935, p. 5, and July 5, 1935, p. 5; *DW,* October 4, 1935, p. 5, October 19, 1935, p. 2, and October 22, 1935, p. 3.

73.   Brandon, in Sweet et al., "Pioneers," p. 20. For several months in 1933 the Film Forum, an organization formed under the presidency of Sidney Howard, held similar screenings. A WFPL member, according to Brandon, was executive director of the group, and it dedicated "all proceeds above expenses" to independent film-producing enterprises, "notably to workers' newsreel organizations." See *NM,* VIII, No. 7 (February 1933), p. 29, and *NYT,* December 1, 1932, p. 25.

74.   Roffman, October 16, 1977. Details of league screenings and meetings have been compiled from notices in the press, particularly the *Daily Worker,* for the years 1931-36.

75.   Irving Lerner (as "Peter Ellis"), FPL Program Notes, October 13, 1934, in Clippings File, Theatre Collection, Lincoln Center for the Performing Arts, New York Public Library; FPL Program Notes, October 13, November 10, and December 22, 1934, all at Lincoln Center. Comments on *The Student of Prague* and *6 1/2 x 11* are by Lerner, on *Beggar on Horseback* by Allen Chumley.

76.   Roffman, October 16, 1977; *NM,* VII, No. 2 (July 1931), p. 21; *DW,* October 12, 1934, p. 5, and April 4, 1935, p. 5.

77.   "Lens," "Flashes and Close-Ups," *DW,* November 29, 1933, p. 5; William Troy, "An Academy of the Film," *The Nation,* November 22, 1933, p. 605; Brandon, "Workers Study the Film," *NT,* January 1934, pp. 14-15. Potamkin's "Proposal for a School of the Motion Picture" is reprinted in *The Compound Cinema,* pp. 587-92.

78.   "Lens," "Flashes and Close-Ups," *DW,* November 13, 1933, p. 5, and November 29, 1933, p. 5; *Experimental Cinema,* I, No. 5. (1934), p. 54; Brandon, "Workers Study the Film," p. 5.

79.   "Lens," "Flashes and Close-Ups," *DW,* April 9, 1934, p. 7; *DW,* July 9, 1935, p. 5.

80.   "Send Photos to the National Exchange!", *Filmfront,* I, No. 2 (January 7, 1935), p. 12.

81. Seltzer, in Russell Campbell, " 'A Total and Realistic Experience,' " p. 26.

82. In 1933, Brody reported in the *Daily Worker* that Edward Weston had informed the New York Workers' Film and Photo League that he saw no sense in contributing to the "America Today" exhibition (see below), "unless you could use the social relations of trees and rocks." Brody commented, "No Ed, we can't use 'em . . . Might spoil your business with the fat dames at twenty dollars a print if we did." Two weeks later Brody retracted the remark. "Your Lens hereby reports itself completely out of focus in its crack about Edward Weston a couple weeks ago . . . Permit me to eat dirt in full view of all my readers and take it all back . . . Tom Brandon, National Secretary of the Workers' Film and Photo League, is good and sore and wants me to inform you that Weston reads the *Daily* and is a friend. . . . " "Lens," "Flashes and Close-Ups," *DW*, September 5, 1933, p. 5, and September 19, 1933, p. 6. Strand, who became radicalized during the thirties, was later to be an enthusiastic and valued supporter of the Photo League.

83. *NM*, VII, No. 1 (June 1931), p. 22.

84. *DW*, August 15, 1933, p. 5, and October 21, 1933, p. 7; "Lens," "Flashes and Close-Ups," *DW*, November 13, 1933, p. 5. Among the members of the sponsoring committee of the "America Today" exhibition were Margaret Bourke-White, Joseph Freeman, Ralph Steiner, Berenice Abbot, David Platt, and Irving Lerner.

85. "Send Photos to the National Exchange!"

86. "New York Photo Activities," *Filmfront*, I, No. 3 (January 28, 1935), p. 14.

87. "The Fight Against South Side Misery in Chicago," *Filmfront*, I, No. 2 (January 7, 1935), p. 13; *Filmfront*, [I, No. 5] (March 15, 1935), p. 9.

88. Brandon, in Sweet et al., "Pioneers," pp. 23-24, alludes also to groups in Baltimore and Seattle, but I have found no other reference to FPL organizations in those cities. Information on league chapters outside New York is derived from the *Daily Worker, New Theatre*, and *Filmfront*, and from interviews. For the Chicago league I am particularly indebted to Maurice Bailen, a former member.

89. Bailen, interview with author, March 6, 1977. Bailen lists the following, apart from himself, as key members of the Chicago FPL: C.O. Nelson (whose real name was Frieberg), John Frietag, Gordon Koster, William Kruck, John Masek, Dr. J. Twigg, Mishkin. Bailen recalls, "We used to meet in different places in Chicago . . . wherever we could find a room." League headquarters were reported located at one time at 1703 West Madison St., Room 8 (see *DW*, December 31, 1934, p. 5), and Koster remembers a meeting place on Division Street. The Chicago league evidently grew out of a workers' camera club organized by Nelson as early as April 1930 (see *DW*, April 12, 1930, p. 3), and was still operative in 1937.

90. *NT*, February 1934, p. 23. The theatre was reportedly at 5225 Harold Way, Hollywood. See House of Representatives, Special Committee on Un-American Activities, *Investigation of Un-American Propaganda Activities in the United States* (Washington, 1938), I, 541.

91. Seltzer, in Campbell, " 'A Total and Realistic Experience,' " p. 27.

92. "A Film Call to Action," *Workers' Theatre*, July-August 1933, p. 9.

93. "Film-Photo League Issues Call for National Film Conference in September," *DW*, August 29, 1934, p. 5. See also *NM*, September 4, 1934, p. 30.

94. Platt, "The Movie Front: National Film Conference," *NT*, November 1934, p. 30; Bailen, communication with author.

95. Platt, ibid.

96. Platt, letter to author, January 10, 1977.

97. Platt, "Flashes and Close-Ups," *DW,* December 10, 1934, p. 5.

98. Michael Gold, "Change the World!", *DW,* November 5, 1934, p. 7.

99. Platt, "World of the Movies—A Reply to Michael Gold," *DW,* November 16, 1934, p. 5.

100. Platt, "Flashes and Close-Ups," *DW,* May 10, 1935, p. 5.

101. Tischler, "Towards a Workers' Newsreel," *Filmfront,* I, No. 4 (February 15, 1935), pp. 19-20, reprinted in Hogenkamp, pp. 31-32.

102. *NT,* March 1935, p. 26; Platt, letter to author. *Filmfront,* the organ of the National Film and Photo League, was published between December 1934 and March 1935, its circulation rising from 500 to 3,500 copies in that period (*DW,* March 23, 1935, p. 7). The first four issues were mimeographed, the last offset printed. It was collectively edited with a board consisting of David Platt, Julian Roffman, Sam Brody, and one or two others. *Filmfront* contained political analyses of Hollywood and Soviet features, documentaries, and American left-wing productions, news of FPL activities, attacks on the Legion of Decency movement and Hollywood-Washington tie-ups, translations of writings by Dziga Vertov, a column "Technically Speaking" by Leo Seltzer, coverage of the formation of the Screen Actors Guild, etc. The five numbers have been reprinted (together with the Photo League's publication, *Photo Notes)* by the Visual Studies Workshop, Rochester, N.Y.

103. "The New Film Alliance," *NT,* September 1935, p. 29; Platt, "Flashes and Close-Ups," *DW,* September 14, 1935, p. 7; Josephine Danzel, "Group to Produce Film Against War," *DW,* December 24, 1935, p. 7; Roffman, October 16, 1977.

104. *Filmfront,* I, No. 2 (January 7, 1935), p. 14; Platt, in *DW,* April 10, 1935, p. 5; *DW,* May 4, 1936, p. 5, and May 13, 1936, p. 7. A film of the 1937 May Day parade (16mm, silent, 45 min.) was made by the Education Department of the International Workers' Order (IWO) (see *DW,* April 30, 1937, p. 9, May 5, 1937, p. 7, and May 31, p. 7).

105. Platt, "Fanning with Platt," *SW,* February 21, 1937, p. 13.

106. "Film and Photo Demise Greatly Exaggerated," *DW,* April 30, 1937, p. 9; Roffman, October 16 and October 26, 1977.

107. "Film and Photo Demise Greatly Exaggerated."

108. On August 23, 1937, the Film Section of the "Film-Photo League" billed Frontier Films $24.25 for "97 feet of dupe neg film of Chinese stock shots of Sun Yat-sen and Chiang Kai-shek" (presumably for use in *China Strikes Back).* The invoice, which is in the Frontier Films Collection, Paul Strand Foundation (New York), bears no address. On September 17, 1937, Platt reviewed *Getting Your Money's Worth* in the *Daily Worker,* referring to it as a League production and concluding: "The Consumers Union and the Film and Photo League will be rendering an invaluable service to the public by producing such films regularly" (Platt, "*Getting Your Money's Worth* Excellent Service to Consumers," *DW,* September 17, 1937, p. 9). This is the last contemporaneous reference to the league I have found.

109. See *Photo Notes;* Tucker, "Photographic Crossroads"; and Tucker's book, *Photographic Crossroads: the Photo League* (Knopf). For background information on the Photo League I am indebted to Walter Rosenblum.

110. *NT,* April 1937, p. 16.

Chapter 3

1. *NYT,* January 25, 1931, pp. 1, 30; *DW,* January 26, 1931, pp. 1, 3, February 12, 1931, p. 2, February 14, 1931, p. 1, February 19, 1931, pp. 1, 2, February 25, 1931, p. 2, February 26, 1931, pp. 1, 2, February 28, 1931, p. 1, March 3, 1931, p. 1, March 4, 1931, p. 1, and March 6, 1931, pp. 1, 3; Willi Münzenberg, *Solidarität: Zehn Jahre Internationale Arbeiterhilfe, 1921-1931* (Berlin: Neuer Deutsche Verlag, 1931), p. 482.

2. Lester Balog, as told to William Alexander, *DW,* March 31, 1931, p. 2.

3. Tom Brandon, interview with author, November 4, 1976, and letter to author, April 11, 1978; Lewis Jacobs, interview with author, April 13, 1977. The student's first name, Brandon recalls, was Eugene.

4. William Z. Foster, *Pages from a Worker's Life* (New York: International Publishers, 1939), pp. 187-91; *DW,* October 12, 1931, p. 1, and December 12, 1931, pp. 3-4.

5. "Censorship Clamps Down on Films of the Hunger March," *DW,* December 19, 1931, p. 5. The print I saw, courtesy of Leo Seltzer, was being re-edited by him in preparation for the re-release of a batch of FPL films.

6. *NM,* VII, No. 7 (December 1931), p. 27. Irving Lerner told Alexander that he and Ralph Steiner were responsible for some of the shooting on *May Day in New York* (1931), but these men's names are not otherwise linked with the league until some time later. The short film recently restored by Leo Seltzer and designated by him *Workers Newsreel—Unemployment Special 1931* is probably one of this group, although I have not had an opportunity to confirm this.

7. Information supplied by Alexander.

8. *NM,* VII, No. 7 (December 1931), p. 27; *Workers' Theatre,* January 1932, pp. 22-23. H. Longview and Lewis Jacobs were slated to work on the editing.

9. The Bonus March has been extensively documented. For contemporary accounts, see Mauritz A. Hallgren, "The Bonus Army Scares Mr. Hoover," *The Nation,* July 27, 1932, pp. 71-73, and Paul Y. Anderson, "Tear Gas, Bayonets, and Votes," *The Nation,* August 17, 1932, pp. 138-40, in addition to newspaper reports. Books on the march include W.W. Waters, as told to William C. White, *B.E.F.: The Whole Story of the Bonus Army* (New York: John Day, 1933), Jack Douglas, *Veterans on the March* (New York: Workers Library, 1934), and Roger Daniels, *The Bonus March* (Westport, Connecticut: Greenwood, 1971).

10. Leo Seltzer, in Russell Campbell, " 'A Total and Realistic Experience': Interview with Leo Seltzer," *Jump Cut,* No. 14 (1977), p. 26.

11. Brandon, interview with author. See also Fred Sweet et al., "Pioneers: An Interview with Tom Brandon," *Film Quarterly,* XXVII, No. 1 (Fall 1973), p. 22.

12. "Writers to Speak on Scottsboro Case Sunday," *DW,* January 16, 1932, p. 1; Brandon, interview with author; Jacobs, interview with author.

13. *DW,* May 4, 1932, p. 2, May 10, 1932, p. 2, May 9, 1932, p. 1, and May 19, 1932, p. 2.

14. *DW,* June 8, 1932, p. 2, July 14, 1932, p. 2, August 4, 1932, p. 2, and September 8, 1932, p. 2.

15. Seltzer, in Campbell, " 'A Total and Realistic Experience,' " p. 26. The demonstration took place on November 7, and the film was shown on November 28. See *DW,* November 8, 1932, pp. 1, 3, and November 28, 1932, p. 2.

16. *DW*, December 2, 1932, p. 2, December 5, 1932, p. 2, and February 10, 1933, p. 2; Samuel Brody, "The Revolutionary Film: Problem of Form," *NT*, February 1934, p. 22, reprinted in *Jump Cut*, No. 14 (1977), p. 32.

17. Bill Nichols, "The American Photo League," *Screen*, XXIII, No. 4 (Winter 1972-73), p. 109. I have found no contemporaneous references to this title.

18. *DW*, October 24, 1932, p. 3, December 5, 1932, p. 1, December 6, 1932, p. 3, and December 7, 1932, p. 1; Edward Dahlberg, "Hunger on the March," *The Nation*, December 28, 1932, pp. 642-44.

19. *Party Organizer*, VI, No. 1 (January 1933), pp. 1-2.

20. *DW*, December 28, 1932, p. 2, and January 25, 1933, p. 2. In 1934, Leo Hurwitz wrote: "A film as important as *Hunger 1932*, was seen by a few thousand people mostly in New York, despite the fact that the three thousand delegates on the march were eager to have the film shown to their organizations all over the country. Being a topical and timely film, it was necessary to distribute it quickly. This was not done, with the consequence that it has in a short time become so much celluloid." Hurwitz, "Survey of Workers' Films: A Report to the National Film Conference," *NT*, October 1934, p. 28.

21. Brody, "The Hunger March Film," *DW*, December 29, 1932, p. 4.

22. *DW*, February 10, 1933, p. 2, and February 13, 1933, p. 2.

23. *DW*, March 9, 1933, p. 2, and May 6, 1933, p. 5.

24. See *DW*, May 26, 1933, p. 1.

25. *DW*, October 26, 1933, p. 5, and February 23, 1933, p. 2; *NT*, February 1934, p. 23, and October 1934, p. 27.

26. Hurwitz, interview with author, April 14, 1977.

27. Robert Gessner, "Movies About Us," *NT*, June 1935, p. 20, reprinted in Lewis Jacobs, ed., *The Documentary Tradition: From Nanook to Woodstock* (New York: Hopkinson & Blake, 1971), p. 96. See also David Platt, "Flashes and Close-Ups," *DW*, December 31, 1934, p. 5. According to Gessner, and Ed Kennedy ("Three Workers' Films," *Filmfront*, I, No. 2 [January 7, 1935], p. 11), *Marine* was directed by Kern and photographed by Seltzer. Seltzer states: "Ed Kern was the one who probably initiated the film, and I think he paid for the raw stock. He came along for moral support, but not directing. There was no such thing as a separate director on our documentary filming, and Ed had no background in directing." Seltzer, in Campbell, " 'A Total and Realistic Experience,' " p. 27. Julian Roffman recalls that he did some shooting on the film (letter to author, October 16, 1977), but this is disputed by Seltzer. "Ed Kennedy" was a pseudonym.

28. Kennedy, "Three Workers' Films," Gessner, "Movies About Us," Seltzer, in Campbell, " 'A Total and Realistic Experience,' " p. 27. The *Daily Worker* claimed in 1933 that racketeering on the docks netted huge sums for Tammany Hall and International Longshoremen's Association figures. See H.J. Farmer, "$25,000,000 a Year in Graft on Waterfront," *DW*, May 27, 1933, p. 5.

29. Gessner, "Movies About Us," Kennedy, "Three Workers' Films."

30. *DW*, May 12, 1943, p. 7, and May 19, 1934, p. 7; Seltzer, communication with author.

31. Brandon, "The Movie Front," *NT*, September 1934, p. 30.

32.   The prints of *America Today* I have seen (courtesy of Tom Brandon and Leo Seltzer) differ slightly in their editing, and the Roosevelt sequence is missing from one.

33.   "Lens," "Flashes and Close-Ups," *DW*, October 20, 1933, p. 5.

34.   Gessner, "Movies About Us."

35.   Brandon, "The Movie Front," *NT*, July-August 1934, p. 19; Gessner, "Movies About Us."

36.   *Unemployment Council:* "Lens," "Flashes and Close-Ups," *DW*, December 4, 1933, p. 5; *NT*, February 1934, p. 23; Hurwitz, "Survey of Workers' Films," p. 27. *Waste and Want: NT*, April 1934, p. 22; Hurwitz, "Survey of Workers' Films," p. 27. *Cigarette: NT*, December 1934, p. 25; Platt, letter to author, January 10, 1977.

37.   Hurwitz, interview with author, and "One Man's Voyage: Ideas and Films in the 1930's," *Cinema Journal*, XV, No. 1 (Fall 1975), p. 10.

38.   Richard O. Boyer and Herbert M. Morais, *Labor's Untold Story* (New York: Marzani & Munsell, 1955), p. 260.

39.   Irving Lerner (as "Peter Ellis"), in *NM*, September 25, 1934, p. 30; Kennedy, "Three Workers' Films," pp. 10-11; Nancy Naumburg, quoted in Kennedy, ibid., p. 11. See also *DW*, September, 14, 1934, p. 5.

40.   *DW*, September 17, 1934, p. 2. See also *DW*, September 14, 1934, p. 3; Platt, "Powerful Indictment of Fascism in Vivid 'Free Thaelmann' Film," *DW*, September 20, 1943, p. 5; Lerner (as "Ellis"), in *NM*, October 2, 1934, p. 46; *NT*, October 1934, pp. 27, 29. *Ernst Thaelmann* was edited by George Moscov under the supervision of Tom Brandon. See Bert Hogenkamp, "Thaelmann's Trail," *Jump Cut*, No. 21, (1979), p. 27. A French version was possibly also made; see Jonathan Lewis, "Before Hindsight," *Sight and Sound*, XLVI, No. 2 (Spring 1977), p. 73.

41.   Edward Kern, letter, *NM*, March 19, 1935, p. 21.

42.   *DW*, January 19, 1935, p. 1; Platt, "Flashes and Close-Ups," *DW*, April 17, 1935, p. 5; *NM*, April 2, 1935, p. 20, and June 18, 1935, p. 13. The Unemployment Congress, held on January 5-6, was attended by 2,506 elected delegates representing an extremely broad range of American working-class organizations. See Albert Prago, "The Organization of the Unemployed and the Role of the Radicals, 1929-1935" (unpublished Ph.D. dissertation, Union Graduate School, Ohio, 1976), pp. 242-46.

43.   Gessner, "Movies About Us," p. 20. There are references to *The City of Contrasts* in *Experimental Cinema*, I, No. 5 (1934), p. 54, and Vladimir Petric, "Soviet Revolutionary Films in America (1926-1935)" (unpublished Ph.D. dissertation, New York University, 1973), p. 426. Harry Alan Potamkin scathingly reviewed *A City Symphony* in *Close Up*, VII, No. 4 (October 1930), pp. 251-52, reprinted in Lewis Jacobs, ed., *The Compound Cinema: The Film Writings of Harry Alan Potamkin* (New York: Teachers College, 1977), pp. 397-98.

44.   *Filmfront*, I, No. 2 (January 7, 1935), p. 14; Platt, "Flashes and Close-Ups," *DW*, May 10, 1935, p. 5.

45.   *Filmfront*, I, No. 2, p. 14; *NM*, May 14, 1935, p. 31. See also *NYT*, May 6, 1935, p. 22; Platt, "Flashes and Close-Ups," *DW*, June 17, 1935, p. 5; Edward H. Shustack, *The Documentary Film: History and Principles* (New York: Film and Sprocket Society of the C.C.N.Y. Art Department, 1938), pp. 21-22. There were actually two New York taxi strikes in 1934, the first (in February) over the split of a five-cent fare surcharge, and the second (in March) over union recognition. See Gerald Weales, *Clifford Odets: Playwright* (New York: Pegasus, 1971), pp. 40-45.

46.   Gessner, "Movies About Us," p. 20. The fact that *Taxi* was the first "enacted" movie by the New York FPL (if we exclude *Sheriffed,* which was an independent production, and *Hollywood,* released about the same time) makes nonsense of Petric's claim that, *"During their initial stage of production in the early 1930s,* the filmmakers of the New York Film and Photo League were overwhelmingly inspired by the cinematic theory which relied on the documentary style with feature characteristics; they introduced plot and 'enacted' sequences into factually recorded social events." Petric, p. 457 (emphasis added).

47.   James Guy, quoted in Platt, "Flashes and Close-Ups," *DW,* May 10, 1935, p. 5.

48.   Gessner, "Movies About Us," p. 20; Louis Norden, "Experiment in Film Criticism," *Pacific Weekly,* June 29, 1936, p. 380. It is possible, considering the date, though not likely, that Norden was speaking of a second IWO film.

49.   *DW,* May 2, 1935, p. 1; Platt, "Flashes and Close-Ups," *DW,* May 10, 1935, p. 5.

50.   Information supplied by Alexander; Roffman, letter to author.

51.   *Filmfront,* I, No. 2, p. 14; James W. Ford, "Miserable Conditions of Negro Life Portrayed in Harlem Film," *DW,* April 3, 1935, p. 5.

52.   Ford, "Miserable Conditions"; Platt, in *DW,* April 10, 1935, p. 5.

53.   Ford, "Miserable Conditions"; *NM,* April 16, 1935, p. 23.

54.   "The Film section has available for booking three new films, one produced by the N.Y. League, two by the Film and Photo League of Los Angeles. They are *Imperial Valley... Lives Wasted... Give Us This Day....* " (Platt, in *DW,* June 3, 1936, p. 7); Roffman, letter to author, October 26, 1977.

55.   *SW,* May 3, 1936, p. 6; *DW,* May 13, 1936, p. 7. On Fang Chen-wu, see H.E.W. Woodhead, ed., *China Year Book, 1934* (Shanghai: North-China Daily News and Herald, 1934), p. 678; Israel Epstein, *The Unfinished Revolution in China* (Boston: Little, Brown, 1947), p. 78; and James E. Sheridan, *Chinese Warlord: The Career of Feng Yü-hsiang* (Stanford: Stanford University, 1966), pp. 271, 273.

56.   Roffman, October 16, 1977.

57.   Platt, "Flashes and Close-Ups," *DW,* June 3, 1936, p. 7.

58.   Roffman, October 16, 1977; Platt, "Flashes and Close-Ups," *DW,* June 3, 1936, p. 7.

59.   Roffman, quoted in Meyer Levin, "The Candid Cameraman," *Esquire,* August 1937, p. 162. See also "Film and Photo Demise Greatly Exaggerated," *DW,* April 30, 1937, p. 9; and *NM,* September 21, 1937, p. 29. The Consumers Union was formed as a breakaway group following a strike at Consumers' Research in 1935 led by Arthur Kallet. The Union was later cited as a Communist front "headed by the Communist Arthur Kallet (whose party name is Edward Adams)." See House of Representatives, Special Committee on Un-American Activities, *Report* (Washington, 1944), p. 153.

60.   Roffman, October 16 and October 26, 1977.

61.   Levin, "The Candid Cameraman," p. 162.

62.   Roffman, quoted in ibid.; Platt, *"Getting Your Money's Worth* Excellent Service to Consumers," *DW,* September 17, 1937, p. 9. Subsequent films were devoted to cold cream, razor blades, and hosiery (1938), and used cars (1939).

63.   Platt, "Fanning with Platt," *SW,* February 21, 1937, p. 13.

The listing of the New York FPI films in this section is undoubtedly far from complete, particularly in respect to more topical newsreel productions. Two films I did not mention in the text because there is so little information about them: *The Land of the Free,* cited by Brody ("The Revolutionary Film: Problem of Form") as an example of the "synthetic documentary, the effect and intent of which is one hundred percent cent dependent on the intervention of the 'editor,'" and W.I.R. (1934), a reference to which was discovered by William Alexander.

A "Workers' Animated Film Group" of the WIR was formed by A. Prentis and Leo Hurwitz in 1934. "The purpose of the group," it was stated, "is to get together a number of artists, writers and film technicians who will work collectively to bring out revolutionary animated cartoons." The unit's first project was a cartoon version of Helen Kayes' story *Battle in the Barnyard,* to be directed by Prentis and Leonard Barnes, and distributed by the Film and Photo League. The film was probably never completed. See *NT,* April 1934, p. 22, and September 1934, p. 30; and *DW,* August 27, 1934, p. 5.

64.   *DW,* February 8, 1932, p. 2, and March 8, 1932, p. 1; Maurice Sugar, "Bullets—Not Food— for Ford Workers," *The Nation,* March 23, 1932, pp. 333-35; *NM,* VII, No. 10 (April 1932), p. 10, and VII, No. 11 (May 1932), p. 13.

65.   *NT,* February 1934, p. 23.

66.   Platt, "The Movie Front," *NT,* December 1934, p. 25.

67.   *DW,* June 6, 1932, p. 2.

68.   *Halsted Street* was dated 1931 by Brandon in his retrospective programs, but internal evidence suggests the film was shot in late 1934. The running time is sixteen minutes at silent speed, eleven minutes at sound speed.

69.   Brandon, "What's Doing in the Film and Photo League Branches," *DW,* September 14, 1934, p. 5; *Filmfront,* I, No. 3 (January 28, 1935), p. 15.

70.   Percy Shostac, "Hillsboro, A Symbol," *NM,* July 17, 1934, pp. 21-23; *Filmfront,* I, No. 3 (January 28, 1935), p. 15; information from Jan Wittenber. Bail was reduced after a six-day hunger strike by the defendants, who were mostly members of the militant union, the Progressive Miners of America. The arrests followed recent Communist election victories in nearby Benld and Taylor Springs. Wittenber was a founder of the Chicago John Reed Club; he appears in fictional guise as Jan Erlone in Richard Wright's *Native Son* (1940).

71.   "The Fight Against South Side Misery in Chicago," *Filmfront,* I, No. 2 (January 7, 1935), p. 13.

72.   *Mexico Marches On* is extant. I am indebted to Maurice Bailen for the opportunity to view it, as well as his other films.

73.   Platt, "Fanning with Platt"; Maurice Bailen, interview with author, March 6, 1977.

74.   *DW,* August 17, 1932, p. 1; Potamkin, "Movies and Revolution," *NM,* VIII, No. 5 (December 1932), p. 21, reprinted in *The Compound Cinema,* p. 513.

75.   See, e.g., Jerold S. Auerbach, *Labor and Liberty: The La Follette Committee and the New Deal* (Indianapolis and New York: Bobbs-Merrill, 1966), pp. 183-87.

76.   *DW,* November 28, 1932, p. 2; Brody, "The Revolutionary Film: Problem of Form."

77.   "Notes on Activities of *Experimental Cinema* during 1933," *Experimental Cinema,* I, No. 5 (1934), inside front cover.

78.   "Lens," "Flashes and Close-Ups," *DW,* January 17, 1934, p. 5.

79.   Platt, in *DW,* June 3, 1936, p. 7; Roffman, October 26, 1977.

80.   Platt, "*The Unknown Soldier Speaks* Reveals the Power of Newsreels," *DW,* July 26, 1934, p. 5.

81.   Brandon, "The Movie Front," *NT,* September 1934, p. 30; information supplied by Alexander.

82.   "Valid Criticism of Los Angeles Films," *Filmfront,* I, No. 2 (January 7, 1935), pp. 12-13.

83.   See n. 54.

84.   A short film by the New York WFPL, designated by Brandon *Workers Newsreel No. 12,* is also extant, although I have not seen it. It deals with the National Hunger March of December 1931, and the footage may be incorporated, in whole or in part, in *National Hunger March.* See Sweet et al., "Pioneers," p. 15. This may possibly be the same film as *Workers Newsreel—Unemployment Special 1931.* See n. 6.

85.   Seltzer, communication with author.

86.   Brandon, at Museum of Modern Art, New York, May 6, 1973.

87.   Bailen, interview with author.

88.   Seltzer, in Campbell, " 'A Total And Realistic Experience,' " p. 27.

89.   Ibid., p. 26; Hurwitz, interview with author.

90.   Brody, "The Hunger March Film."

91.   Brandon, May 6, 1973.

92.   The style of shooting was also a function of the equipment available to the filmmakers. The Eyemo, which was most commonly used by FPL crew, was a spring-driven 35mm camera capable of running a maximum of fifteen seconds (at silent speed) per take, and had to be frequently reloaded. It was light enough to be handheld, unlike the cameras favored by the commerical newsreel teams, which, being power-driven and magazine equipped, could run continuously for minutes at a time. The commercial crews were able to record synchronous sound, which was easier to handle if takes were relatively long.

93.   Hurwitz, "One Man's Voyage," p. 5.

94.   See, e.g., Earl Browder, "The Roosevelt 'New Deal' and Fascism," *DW,* July 8, 1933, p. 5.

95.   Hurwitz, "The Revolutionary Film—Next Step," *NT,* May 1934, p. 14; Gessner, "Movies About Us."

96.   Kenneth W. Munden, ed., *The American Film Institute Catalog of Motion Pictures Produced in the United States, Feature Films, 1921-1930* (New York: Bowker, 1971), I, 541.

97.   Platt, "The Movie Front: National Film Conference," *NT,* November 1934, p. 30.

98.   Brody, in Tony Safford, "The Camera as a Weapon in the Class Struggle: Interview with Samuel Brody," *Jump Cut,* No. 14 (1977), p. 28; *Filmfront,* I, No. 2 (January 7, 1935), p. 6, and I, No. 3 (January 28, 1935), p. 7.

99.   Brody, "The Revolutionary Film," p. 21.

100.   Hurwitz, "The Revolutionary Film—Next Step."

101. Platt, "The Movie Front," p. 30.

102. Brody, "The Revolutionary Film," pp. 21, 22.

103. FPL Program Notes, December 22, 1934, in Clippings File, Theatre Collection, Lincoln Center for the Performing Arts, New York Public Library.

104. Brody, "The Revolutionary Film," p. 22; Hurwitz, "The Revolutionary Film—Next Step."

105. Shub's *Cannons or Tractors* was perhaps the major influence in the development of these "synthetic" forms, particularly the compilation film made from commercial newsreel clips, but several other precursors of the FPL productions may be noted. In 1930 the ILD distributed in the U.S. *The Road to Freedom*, a four-reel film of "the workers' struggle in all sections of the world." The first three reels were compiled in Germany; the fourth, put together in America (presumably by the Labor Defender Photo Group), included scenes from the demonstrations for Sacco and Vanzetti, the Pennsylvania miners' strike, and the March 6 demonstrations. *Cry of the World* (1932), edited by Louis de Rochemont from the Fox newsreel files, offered "a vivid picture of the people of all nations in their struggle against hunger, unemployment, and war"—particularly in the "rearranged" version which was shown at the Acme Theatre. Footage was prominently devoted to mass demonstrations in the Soviet Union, France, England, and the United States, to the revolt in India, and to the Japanese attack on Shanghai. Gilbert Seldes' *This Is America* (1933) was "an ambitious compilation of newsreel shots" which covered "the economic history of the United States from the First World War to the Depression," and included documentation of living conditions during the slump by ex-FPL cameraman Lewis Jacobs. In addition, there were the World War compilation films: *Der Weltkrieg* (1927), *Forgotten Men* (1933), *The First World War* (1934), and so on. *NM*, VI, No. 5 (October 1930), p. 20; *DW*, September 13, 1932, p. 2; John Howard Lawson, *Film: The Creative Process* (New York: Hill & Wang, 1967), p. 127; Jacobs, interview with author; Jay Leyda, *Films Beget Films* (New York: Hill & Wang, 1971), pp. 33-36.

106. S[eymour] S[tern], "A Working-Class Cinema for America?", *The Left*, 1, No. 1 (Spring 1931), pp. 70, 72.

107. Hurwitz, "One Man's Voyage," p. 12.

108. Tischler, "Towards a Workers' Newsreel," *Filmfront*, I, No. 4 (February 15, 1935), p. 19, reprinted in Bert Hogenkamp, *Workers' Newsreels in the 1920s and 1930s* (London: History Group of the Communist Party, n.d. [c. 1977]), p. 32.

109. Lerner, "A Dry Martini with Cyanide," *NM*, June 19, 1934, p. 30; Platt, "Flashes and Close-Ups," *DW*, June 3, 1936, p. 7. A great deal of FPL footage was, however, lost in a storage fire at a studio in Fort Lee, N.J. Brandon puts the date of the fire at 1935. Seltzer, in Campbell, "'A Total and Realistic Experience,'" p. 26; Brandon, May 6, 1973.

110. Ron Levaco, ed., *Kuleshov on Film: Writings by Lev Kuleshov* (Berkeley and Los Angeles: University of California, 1974), p. 8; Leyda, *Kino: A History of Russian and Soviet Film* (London: Allen & Unwin, 1973), pp. 150-51. Leyda also mentions a "semi-documentary," *Uprising*, directed by Alexander Razumni and completed in 1918 (p. 132).

111. Bailen, interview with author; Alexander Dovzhenko, "Credo of a Soviet Movie Director," *NM*, VI, No. 9 (February 1931), p. 23.

112. Kennedy, "Three Workers' Films," p. 10; Lerner (as "Ellis"), in *NM*, September 25, 1934, p. 30; Dovzhenko, "Credo," p. 23.

113. The "Third Period" followed the phase of support for armed insurrections internationally in the first years after the Revolution, and the mid-twenties policy of legal, moderate, united-front activity. The ultra-left era was ushered in at the Sixth Congress of the Communist International, held in Moscow in July-September 1928, which declared, for example, that the socialist parties were "a particularly dangerous enemy of the proletariat, more dangerous than the avowed adherents of predatory imperialism."

114. *DW,* May 26, 1933, p. 1.

115. Seltzer, in Campbell, " 'A Total and Realistic Experience,' " p. 27.

Chapter 4

1. Harry A. Potamkin, "Workers' Films," *DW,* May 31, 1930, p. 3, and "Movies and Revolution," *NM,* VIII, No. 5 (December 1932), p. 21, reprinted in Lewis Jacobs, ed., *The Compound Cinema: The Film Writings of Harry Alan Potamkin* (New York: Teachers College, 1977), p. 514; Jay Leyda and Potamkin, Program Notes, WFPL, February 25, 1933, in Clippings File, Theatre Collection, Lincoln Center for the Performing Arts, New York Public Library.

2. S[amuel] B[rody], "*Hallelujah* at Embassy Don't Portray Real Negro," *DW,* August 30, 1929, p. 4, and "Television—A New Weapon for the New Imperialist War," *DW,* June 14, 1930, p. 3. In the 1929 piece Brody defended Pudovkin's documentary *Mechanics of the Brain,* noting that when it was recently shown, "Mordaunt Hall, of the *New York Times,* expressed the moronic opinion that such films, although of some educational value, were not fit for exhibition in theatres because they are not strictly 'entertainment.' Feed your audiences on *Fox Movietone Follies, Hollywood Revue, Broadway Melody.* Damned be your *Mechanics of the Brain!* The third largest industry in the country can live and prosper only on 'mechanics' of bare legs, frisky musical comedies (filmed ones), and no 'brains' necessary, either." A fellow reviewer on the *Daily Worker* staff had remarked a few days earlier that *Hollywood Revue* was "being wildly received twice daily by enthusiastic audiences . . . crammed full of entertainment sketches, catchy songs, and dynamic dancing. . . . The ordinary motion-picture fan will eagerly welcome this kind of entertainment." *DW,* August 19, 1929, p. 4.

3. Brody, "The Revolutionary Film: Problem of Form," *NT,* February 1934, p. 21. Brody was never to be converted from his position in favor of strict documentary, which was boosted (in his view) by the release of Vertov's *Three Songs About Lenin* in November 1934. In an enthusiastic review, in which he pointed out that the film did not contain "a single foot of film that is not actual," he wrote (as "Lens"): "We know that Vertov has freed the film from the literary and theatrical trappings which Soviet cinematography inherited from the bourgeois film. No actors, no artifice, no illusion. The movie camera is the great documentary revealer that must plunge headlong into the turbulent currents of life itself, must become a fearless visual reporter, must expose, must unearth, must praise and condemn. 'We must transfer the cinema from the arena of the stage to the arena of life itself,' says Vertov. And that is of pivotal importance to all workers in the revolutionary film movement, because among us there are still some who maintain that '100 per cent factual' in the film means limitations and artlessness. The work of Vertov is therefore something that we must observe and study tirelessly because it bears directly on our own orientation in the Film and Photo League." (*DW,* November 1, 1934, p. 7.) Brody's recent statements about Vertov's importance are quoted in chap. 3.

4. Leo T. Hurwitz, "The Revolutionary Film—Next Step," *NT*, May 1934, p. 15. Steiner now claims: "The Film and Photo League certainly didn't interest me. I was supposed to teach a course there and got thrown out at the second session because I couldn't see life and the world through the thick volume of Marx's *Das Kapital.*" Ralph Steiner, in Judith Gerber, "Ralph Steiner: Enjoying the Interval," *Afterimage* (US), V, No. 9 (March 1978), p. 19.

5. Hurwitz, "The Revolutionary Film—Next Step," p. 14.

6. Ibid., p. 15.

7. Steiner, "Revolutionary Movie Production," *NT*, September 1934, p. 22. According to William Alexander ("Frontier Films, 1936-1941: The Aesthetics of Impact," *Cinema Journal,* XV, No. 1 [Fall 1975], p. 17n), Hurwitz collaborated with Steiner on the article. Steiner has since disowned some of the opinions expressed in his writings of this period. In 1975, he told Joel Zuker: "I, and others, found in the Left the only place to make films and to be with other filmmakers. The Party hacks took advantage of our need by using those of us who weren't very left, but needed the Left. They rewrote magazine pieces to slant them toward their needs. I, who loathed the crappy Party clichés, could never have written some things attributed to me. In all my life, I never went in for the word 'revolutionary.' " Quoted in Joel Zuker, *Ralph Steiner: Filmmaker and Still Photographer* (New York: Arno, 1978), p. 332.

8. Steiner, "Revolutionary Movie Production," pp. 22-23.

9. Ibid., p. 23.

10. Hurwitz, "Survey of Workers' Films: A Report to the National Film Conference," *NT*, October 1934, p. 27.

11. Ibid., p. 28.

12. Ibid.

13. Ibid.

14. David Platt, "The Movie Front: National Film Conference," *NT*, November 1934, p. 27.

15. Tom Brandon, "What's Doing in the Film and Photo League Branches," *DW*, September 14, 1934, p. 5; *NM*, September 25, 1934, p. 30. The author of the *New Masses* piece was Irving Lerner (as "Peter Ellis"), who, naturally, welcomed the move: "Revolutionary films must have high artistic quality in addition to their message if they are to have the most popular appeal. But only continued production, or as Ralph Steiner points out in the current *New Theatre*, a school based on production is the only way we can train the necessary forces for the kind of films the revolutionary movement demands. Therefore it is good to learn that Ralph Steiner, Leo Hurwitz, and Irving Lerner have organized such a *film producing* group in connection with the Workers' Laboratory Theatre."

16. Hurwitz, interview with author, April 14, 1977.

17. Brandon, interview with author, November 4, 1976.

18. Julian Roffman, letter to author, October 16, 1977; Brody, in Tony Safford, "The Camera as a Weapon in the Class Struggle: Interview with Samuel Brody," *Jump Cut,* No. 14 (1977), p. 30.

19. Leo Seltzer, in Russell Campbell, " 'A Total and Realistic Experience': Interview with Leo Seltzer," *Jump Cut,* No. 14 (1977), p. 25.

20. Hurwitz, in Michael and Jill Klein, "*Native Land:* An Interview with Leo Hurwitz," *Cineaste*, IV, No. 3 (1974), p. 4; Steiner and Hurwitz, "A New Approach to Film Making," *NT*, September 1935, pp. 22-23; *NT*, February 1935, p. 30, and March 1935, p. 13.

21. Ben Maddow, interview with author, March 17, 1977.

22. Hurwitz had first met Strand when laying out an article on his work for *Creative Art* magazine. See Hurwitz, "One Man's Voyage: Ideas and Films in the 1930's," *Cinema Journal*, XV, No. 1 (Fall 1975), p. 6.

23. Jay Williams, *Stage Left* (New York: Scribner's, 1974), p. 163; Hurwitz, "One Man's Voyage," p. 11; Willard Van Dyke, interview with author, October 15, 1976. The Workers' Laboratory Theatre had severed its connection with the WIR in 1932. According to Van Dyke there was another member of Nykino's evening group, a certain Herman Truboff, "who seems to have disappeared."

24. Roffman, letter to author, January 10, 1978.

25. Hurwitz, interview with author. Steiner records: "A Mrs. Elmhurst, who'd been a Whitney...gave me $14,000 to make films, and that lasted five or six years." Steiner, interview with James Blue, July 12, 1973 (Media Study/Buffalo).

26. Hurwitz, interview with author; Maddow, interview with author; Steiner, interview with James Blue. On Steiner's films see Zuker, *Ralph Steiner*. Kyle Crichton also wrote under the name "Robert Forsyth."

27. Van Dyke, interview with author; Daniel Aaron, *Writers on the Left* (New York: Avon, 1961), p. 319. See also Carleton Beals and Clifford Odets, *Rifle Rule in Cuba* (New York: Provisional Committee for Cuba, 1935).

28. Van Dyke, interview with author; Hurwitz, interview with author.

29. Van Dyke, interview with author, and interview with James Blue, August 2, 1973 (Media Study/Buffalo).

30. Paul Stand, interview with Milton Brown, November 1971 (Archives of American Art, New York), pp. 32-34.

31. Richard Dyer MacCann, *The People's Films: A Political History of U.S. Government Motion Pictures* (New York: Hastings House, 1973); Hurwitz, quoted in Calvin Tomkins, "Profiles," *New Yorker*, September 16, 1974, pp. 72, 74, and "One Man's Voyage," p. 13. See also Robert L. Snyder, *Pare Lorentz and the Documentary Film* (Norman: University of Oklahoma, 1968), pp. 28-31.

32. See MacCann, *The People's Films*, pp. 50-51, and Zuker, *Ralph Steiner*, pp. 231-40, where the film is described in detail. Contrary to the contention of both authors, the film could not have been made in 1934, since the WPA was not established until the spring of 1935.

33. "A Prize Scenario Contest," *NT*, January 1936, p. 42.

34. Alexander, "Frontier Films," pp. 18-19; Joris Ivens, "Notes on Hollywood," *NT*, October 1936, pp. 8-10, 28; Lerner, quoted in Alexander, "Frontier Films," p. 18. See also Alexander, "*The March of Time* and *The World Today*," *American Quarterly*, XXIX (Summer 1977), pp. 182-83.

35. Michael Gordon, interview with author, March 25, 1977.

36. *NT*, August 1936, p. 21, and September 1936, p. 3; Van Dyke, interview with author; Hurwitz, interview with author.

37. Jay Leyda, interview with author, October 12, 1976, and letter to author, May 13, 1978. Leyda employed the pseudonym "Eugene Hill" on his work for the group. Renoir is usually cited as either sole director, or one of several directors, of *La Vie est à Nous* (shown in the U.S. in 1937 as *People of France*); however, Leyda writes (letter to author): "Renoir was the producer, not the director of *La Vie est à Nous*—he has made that very clear to me. But Henri Cartier-Bresson assisted Renoir on *Les Bas-Fonds;* I visited him on that set in '36."

38. Strand, interview with Milton Brown, p. 39; Van Dyke, interview with author. Van Dyke's attraction to non-journalistic documentary photography was evidenced in an appraisal he made in 1934 of the work of Dorothea Lange. He wrote: "In an old Ford she drives to a place most likely to yield subjects consistent with her general sympathies. Unlike the newspaper reporter, she has no news or editorial policies to direct her movements: it is only her deeply personal sympathies for the unfortunates, the downtrodden, the misfits, among her contemporaries that provide the impetus for her expedition. She may park her car at the waterfront during a strike, perhaps at a meeting of unemployed, by sleepers in the city square, at transient shelters—bread lines, parades, or demonstrations. Here she waits with her camera open and unconcealed, her mind ready." Van Dyke, "The Photographs of Dorothea Lange—A Critical Analysis," *Camera Craft*, XLI, No. 10 (October 1934), p. 464.

39. Hurwitz, in Klein, *"Native Land,"* p. 4.

40. Hurwitz, "One Man's Voyage," pp. 12, 13.

41. Strand, quoted in Sidney Meyers (as "Robert Stebbins"), *"Redes," NT*. November 1936, p. 21; Meyers, ibid., p. 20; Strand, interview with Milton Brown, pp. 34-35. *The Wave* was scripted by Henwar Rodakiewicz from a story by A. Velazquez Chavez and Strand, and directed by Fred Zinnemann, assisted by Emilio Gomez Muriel. English titles were by John Dos Passos and Leo Hurwitz.

42. Harold Clurman, *The Fervent Years: The Story of the Group Theatre and the Thirties* (New York: Knopf, 1945), pp. 32, 45; Steiner, interview with James Blue.

43. Steiner and Hurwitz, "A New Approach to Film Making."

44. Strand, interview with Milton Brown, p. 34.

45. Brandon, interview with author.

46. Vladimir Petric, "Soviet Revolutionary Films in America (1926-1935)" (unpublished Ph.D. dissertation, New York University, 1973), pp. 446-53; Zuker, *Ralph Steiner*, pp. 191-211; Elia Kazan, interview with author, April 13, 1977; Ray Ludlow, *"Pie in the Sky," NT*, May 1935, p. 19; Brandon, interview with author.

47. Zuker, *Ralph Steiner*, pp. 210, 198.

48. Kazan, in Michel Ciment, *Kazan on Kazan* (New York: Viking, 1974), p. 17, and in Stuart Byron and Martin Rubin, "Elia Kazan Interview," *Movie*, No. 19 (Winter 1971-72), p. 1, quoted in Zuker, p. 209.

49. Van Dyke, interview with James Blue.

50. Literally, "Grub comes first, then comes morality." The line occurs in the Second Threepenny-Finale of *The Threepenny Opera*. Macheath sings:

> Now all you gentlemen who wish to lead us
> Who teach us to desist from mortal sin
> Your prior obligation is to feed us:
> When we've had lunch, your preaching can begin.

> All you who love your paunch and our propriety
> Take note of this one thing (for it is late):
> You may proclaim, good sirs, your fine philosophy
> But till you feed us, right and wrong can wait!

Bertolt Brecht, *The Threepenny Opera* (English lyrics by Eric Bentley) (New York: Grove, 1964), pp. 66-67.

51. Ludlow, *"Pie in the Sky,"* p. 19.

52. Steiner, letter to Joel Zuker, March 15, 1972, quoted in Petric, p. 452; Zuker, *Ralph Steiner,* pp. 207-08.

53. Ludlow, *Pie in the Sky,"* pp. 19, 20.

54. Lerner (as "Ellis"), in *NM,* July 9, 1935, p. 30, quoted in Alexander, *"The March of Time,"* p. 189.

55. Lerner (as "Ellis"), in *NM,* May 11, 1937, p. 29; Lerner (as "Ellis") and Meyers (as "Stebbins"), "Are Newsreels News?", *NT,* April 1937, p. 45; Hurwitz, interview with author.

56. Lerner, in *NM,* May 11, 1937, p. 29; Lerner and Meyers, "Are Newsreels News?"; Alexander, in *"The March of Time* and *The World Today,"* contests the view that *The March of Time* was consistently right-wing, arguing that "critics on the Left incorrectly saw *The March of Time's* political tendency as fascistic or as only fascistic" (p. 184). *March of Time* historian Raymond Fielding writes: "Within the huge, conservative bureaucracy of Time, Incorporated, the *March of Time* and its films were considered moderately left-wing. Indeed, there were a substantial number of liberal and leftist filmmakers on the payroll. Louis [de Rochemont] himself could not by the wildest stretch of the imagination have been considered part of any left-wing persuasion. And yet, the films that he created were consistently liberal, progressive, and militantly anti-fascist at a time when it took courage to attack 'prematurely' the totalitarian adventures then under way in Germany, Italy, Spain, and Japan. His films were critical, though somewhat less vigorous in their treatment of Soviet communism.... His films consistently championed the racially oppressed and doggedly exposed theatre audiences to the emerging horrors of anti-Jewish persecution and genocide." Raymond Fielding, *The March of Time, 1935-1951* (New York: Oxford University, 1978), pp. 35-36.

57. Ludlow and Eva Goldbeck, "Time Marches Where?", *NT,* March 1935, p. 19.

58. Gordon, interview with author; *DW,* December 18, 1935, p. 4, December 31, 1935, pp. 1, 2, and May 20, 1936, p. 4; Sidney Streat, "Mrs. Thal Saved and Scraped to Build a Dream Home...and Rockefeller Foreclosed the Mortgage," *SW,* February 2, 1936, p. 3.

59. Streat, "Mrs. Thal"; *DW,* December 31, 1935, p. 2.

60. Lerner, in *NM,* May 11, 1937, p. 29; Alexander, *"The March of Time,"* p. 190; Gordon, interview with author.

61. Lerner, in *NM,* May 11, 1937, p. 29.

62. "Scores Held Victims of Black Legion," *DW,* May 26, 1936, pp. 1, 2; see also "Black Legion Plot to Rule Sifted," *DW,* May 27, 1936, p. 1.

63. *DW,* September 28, 1936, p. 7; Lerner, in *NM,* May 11, 1937, p. 29.

64. Van Dyke, interview with author; Gordon, interview with author; Hurwitz, interview with author. Prints of *Black Legion* may possibly still be in existence, but I have not been able to confirm this.

65.   *DW,* September 28, 1936, p. 7; Lerner, in *NM,* May 11, 1937, p. 29.

Chapter 5

1.   *NT,* March 1937, p. 50; "Films for Progressives is New Company's Plan," *DW,* April 6, 1937, p. 9. Frontier Films established an office at 10 E. 40th St., New York City. It subsequently moved, in January 1938, to 723 Seventh Ave., and in April 1939 to 250 W. 57th St., where it remained until final dissolution of the company in 1942.

2.   Leo Hurwitz, "One Man's Voyage: Ideas and Films in the 1930's," *Cinema Journal,* XV, No. 1 (Fall 1975), p. 13.

3.   Paul Strand, interview with Milton Brown, November 1971 (Archives of American Art, New York), p. 39. In his history of the Group Theatre, Harold Clurman wrote: "Paul Strand and Ralph Steiner derived much from us in the formation of Frontier Films" (*The Fervent Years: The Story of the Group Theatre and the Thirties* [New York: Knopf, 1945], p. 96). Relationships between Frontier and the Group are discussed in William Alexander, "Frontier Films, 1936-1941: The Aesthetics of Impact," *Cinema Journal,* XV, No. 1 (Fall 1975), pp. 23-25.

4.   "Films for Progressives is New Company's Plan."

5.   Strand, quoted in Sidney Meyers (as "Robert Stebbins"), "Paul Strand's Photography Reaches Heights in *The Wave,*" *DW,* May 4, 1937, p. 7.

6.   Frontier Films, leaflet, in Clippings File, Theatre Collection, Lincoln Center for the Performing Arts, New York Public Library.

7.   " 'Liberal' News Reel Frankly Propaganda," *Variety,* April 21, 1937, p. 27.

8.   "Films for Progressives is New Company's Plan"; *NT,* March 1937, p. 50.

9.   During the winter of 1936-37 Van Dyke was employed by Pare Lorentz as a cameraman on *The River.* Van Dyke recalls: "After *The Plow,* it's a matter of history that Lorentz disagreed with his cameramen on that film and especially Strand and Hurwitz, and so when *The River* came along he asked Steiner to go with him as a cameraman, and since Steiner was working in this Nykino coop kind of thing, Strand and Hurwitz said, "You can't go unless we go—all three of us were on *The Plow.*" And so Steiner reluctantly told Lorentz no, and they all three of them recommended me as a cameraman on it, and that's how I got that position with Lorentz." Willard Van Dyke, interview with James Blue, August 2, 1973 (Media Study/ Buffalo).

10.   "Films for Progressives is New Company's Plan."

11.   Ibid.; Elia Kazan, quoted in House of Representatives, Committee on Un-American Activities, *Communism in Hollywood Motion-Picture Industry,* Part 7 (Washington, 1952), p. 2410; Hurwitz, interview with author, April 14, 1977.

12.   Hurwitz, interview with author.

13.   "Films for Progressives is New Company's Plan."

14.   Jerold S. Auerbach, *Labor and Liberty: The La Follette Committee and the New Deal* (Indianapolis and New York: Bobbs-Merrill, 1966), p. 46; Bernard Reis & Co., *Treasurer's Report to Frontier Films Inc. from Inception to March 31, 1942* (Frontier Films Collection, Paul Strand Foundation, New York), pp. 2, 3-4, 5.

15. *Treasurer's Report to Frontier Films,* pp. 3-4, 5; Bernard Reis, letter to Frontier Films, December 29, 1938 (Frontier Films Collection); Frontier Films, *Account of Income and Expenditures from February 1939 to August 1939* (Frontier Films Collection); *Congressional Record,* LXXXVIII, Part 6 (September 24, 1942), p. 7450; Theodore Strauss, "Homesteading Our 'Native Land,' " *NYT,* May 3, 1942, p. X3. The figures quoted refer only to unsecured loans, trustee certificates of $1,000 or more, and donations of which there is a record; the total sums contributed by the individuals cited may well have been greater. Elizabeth Marshall (wife of George Marshall) worked for a time as script girl on *Native Land.* The Robert Marshall Foundation was established under the terms of the will of Robert Marshall (himself a Frontier Films benefactor during his lifetime), who died in 1940; some $768,000 was set aside for "the promotion and advancement of an economic system in the United States based upon the theory of production for use and not for profit." The Foundation made its contribution (in two installments) to Frontier in August 1941; among trustees of the fund were Frontier Films Advisory Board members Gardner Jackson and Jerry J. O'Connell, and previous donor George Marshall (brother of Robert Marshall). Louise Bransten, a substantial supporter of Communist publications for many years, subsequently married Lionel Berman of Frontier. The financial records of the company fail to substantiate the recollection of Joseph Goodwin, hired as an overseer in the last few months of work on *Native Land,* that Corliss Lamont (son of the Wall Street banker) contributed over $25,000 to the production (Joseph Goodwin, "Some Personal Notes on *Native Land,"* *Take One,* IV, No. 2 [1974], pp. 11-12).

16. Hurwitz, interview with author. Frontier records at the Paul Strand Foundation note contributions from the United Office and Professional Workers of America and Local 65 of the United Retail and Wholesale Employees of America.

17. Hurwitz, interview with author.

18. Ibid.; Strauss, "Homesteading," *Treasurer's Report to Frontier Films,* p. 2.

19. Hurwitz, "One Man's Voyage," p. 14; Strand, interview with Milton Brown, p. 41. The $35 wage did not apply to office workers (except for the executive director), production assistants, or editing assistants, who were paid less. George Jacobson, who received $25 as production manager, handed in his resignation in October 1939 when he asked for, and was not granted, a raise.

20. Quoted in Ben Belitt, "The Camera Reconnoiters," *The Nation,* November 20, 1937, pp. 557-58.

21. Data derived from *Treasurer's Report to Frontier Films* and other financial records, Frontier Films Collection. I have not been able to discover the precise financial arrangements under which HEART OF SPAIN and RETURN TO LIFE were produced and distributed. Tom Brandon recalls that Frontier "was never the owner of rights or negatives" and that distribution revenues were split between the sponsoring Spanish aid agencies and Garrison (letter to author, July 8, 1978).

22. *Treasurer's Report to Frontier Films,* p. 2.

23. Hurwitz, "One Man's Voyage," p. 14.

24. *NT,* March 1937, p. 50.

25. Clurman, p. 185; " 'Liberal,' " *Variety,* April 21, 1937, p. 27. A scene from *The Silent Partner* was published in *New Theatre and Film,* March 1937, pp. 5-9.

26. " 'Liberal,' " *Variety,* April 21, 1937, p. 27; David Platt, "Newsreel with Punch in *The World Today,"* *DW,* May 6, 1937, p. 7; Lionel Berman, letter to Roger Baldwin, June 26, 1937, and letter to Rockwell Kent, July 9, 1937 (Frontier Films Collection). As always,information derived from press releases must be treated with caution. The announcement of the existence of a "sound-newsreel division of Frontier Films" may possibly have been less an indication of seriousness than bluff in the attempt to attract investors, arrogance, or self-delusory wishful thinking.

27. *NYT,* April 21, 1937, p. 18.

28. Hurwitz, communication with author; *DW,* March 18, 1937, p. 9; "Child Labor Key Issue Next Fall, Says ALP," *DW,* May 11, 1937, p. 1; Berman, letters to Roger Baldwin and Rockwell Kent; Ben Compton, "Social Theatre in Action with New Fall Program," *SW,* August 22, 1937, p. 10. Vera Caspary was a Hollywood screenwriter whose credits to 1937 included *The Night of June 13th, Such Women Are Dangerous, Private Scandal, I'll Love You Always,* and *Easy Living.*

29. Belitt, "The Camera Reconnoiters," p. 558; Hurwitz, interview with author; Ethel Clyde, invitational letters for December 7, 1937, screening, Frontier Films Collection; *Treasurer's Report to Frontier Films;* George Jacobson, interview with author, April 17, 1977.

30. Belitt, "The Camera Reconnoiters," p. 558; Berman, letter to Roger Baldwin.

31. Ralph Steiner, interview with James Blue, July 12, 1973 (Media Study/Buffalo). Hellman writes: "I am fairly sure that Hammett joined the Communist Party in 1937 or 1938" (Lillian Hellman, *Scoundrel Time* [New York: Bantam, 1977], p. 41).

32. Jacobson, interview with author.

33. Van Dyke, interview with author, October 15, 1976; Michael Gordon, interview with author, March 25, 1977.

34. Hurwitz, interview with author.

35. Gordon, interview with author.

36. Van Dyke, interview with author; Steiner, interview with James Blue. For an account of one of Van Dyke's confrontations with Hurwitz, see chap. 7, n. 18. The halting of work on the project probably occurred in the latter half of January 1938; a laboratory invoice for "Voice Test, Production #5 [*Native Land*]" in Van Dyke's name is dated January 13, 1938. The last invoice on which Steiner's name appears is for "Highlander Folk School" *(People of the Cumberland)* on December 27, 1937. Invoices are in the Frontier Films Collection.

37. Hurwitz, interview with author.

38. Van Dyke, interview with James Blue, and interview with author; Steiner, interview with James Blue. Willard Van Dyke qualifies his charge of Communist domination by pointing out: "I never personally witnessed control over any of the films by the Communist party" (letter to author, May 20, 1978). Ralph Steiner gave the following account in 1973 of his break with Frontier: "And then there was terrible trouble with Frontier Films. Rocks were thrown through my window, people I'd known intimately for years didn't know me when they saw me on the street, and there were all sorts of things written that I was a Trotskyite. And I finally had to say something. 'I know who Leon Trotsky was, but what is a Trotskyite?' I was that brilliant politically. So finally I got a really wonderful person, a person I worked with when I was in Hollywood, really one of the fine left-wing writers, Albert Maltz, and he was the Communist party's I guess top artistic guy, and he listened to me and he listened to them, and

he just said, 'Ralph is not getting out for political reasons, he thinks everything you want to do is black and dull'—he told this to all the Frontier people—and he said, 'You're being Boy Scouts.' And so that was the end of my dealing with Frontier Films." Steiner, interview with James Blue.

39. Jay Leyda interview with author, October 12, 1976; Kazan, quoted in Robert Vaughn, *Only Victims: A Study of Show Business Blacklisting* (New York: Putnam, 1972), p. 160; Kazan, interview with author, April 13, 1977. By his own admission, Kazan was a Communist party member in 1934-36.

40. Gordon, interview with author. Gordon, after having been named by Edward Dmytryk and Frank Tuttle in testimony before the House Committee on Un-American Activities in 1951 as a member of a Communist party group in Hollywood, declined to testify before the Committee on grounds of possible self-incrimination. See House of Representatives, Committee on Un-American Activities, *Communist Infiltration of Hollywood Motion-Picture Industry,* Part 4 (Washington, 1951), pp. 1482-87.

41. Hurwitz, interview with author. Because of the Communist party's policy of confidentiality in this regard, any identification of party membership can only be tentative. From information derived from a variety of sources (including interviews, testimony before the House Un-American Activities Committee, public statements and endorsements, and published memoirs), I have concluded that of the Frontier group the following were either members of the Communist party or very close to it: Paul Strand, Leo Hurwitz, Lionel Berman, Ben Maddow, Sidney Meyers, Irving Lerner, Jay Leyda. Of those who worked in an associate capacity, Herbert Kline and Michael Gordon were also probably connected with the Communist party, while Elia Kazan by his own account had left the party in 1936.

42. Eric Bentley, ed., *Thirty Years of Treason: Excerpts from Hearings Before the House Committee on Un-American Activities, 1938-1968* (New York: Viking, 1971), p. 227; Vaughn, p. 303; *Congressional Record,* LXXXVIII, Part 6, pp. 7450, 7452. Hurwitz relates (interview with author) that when John Howard Lawson came to New York, "I talked to him about all kinds of things, and maybe about the rigidity of a person named V.J. Jerome, who was important culturally in the Communist party." Rep. Martin Dies, chairman of the Special Committee on Un-American Activities, called Frontier Films "an out-and-out Communist organization," but his credibility is impaired by his mistaken claim that *Native Land* was based on Richard Wright's *Native Son.*

43. Hurwitz, interview with author; Steiner, interview with James Blue.

44. Steiner, letter to Richard H. Platkin, March 26, 1968, quoted in Platkin, "The American Documentary Film: Its Origin and Early Development" (unpublished senior history thesis, The University of Michigan, 1968, in Film Study Center, Museum of Modern Art, New York), p. 52.

45. Ibid. Hurwitz says of *The City:* "It was a romantic and wish solution that fitted in well into the demagogy of the New Deal, but its elements were not at all analyzed, so it was not structurally a built film relating to the world around" (interview with author). According to Jacobson, "Everybody up at Frontier derided *The City*" (interview with author).

46. Richard Griffith, "Films at the Fair," *Films,* I, No. 1 (November 1939), pp. 70-71.

47. *TAC,* II, No. 7 (March 15, 1940), p. 4. The film, which is still in distribution by the UAW, is also known as *United Action Means Victory.* Virginia Stevens was, at the time, married to Paul Strand. Though not credited specifically on the film, Maddow evidently wrote the commentary (see Mary Losey, ed., *Living Films* [New York: Association of Documentary Film Producers, 1940], p. 54).

48. Frontier Films financial records, and Arnold Perl, circular letter, April 24, 1939 (both in Frontier Films Collection).

49. Frontier Films, promotional leaflet, November 1938 (Frontier Films Collection). Sidney Meyers (as "Robert Stebbins") was a regular film critic for *New Theatre*, and later *TAC* magazine (editied by his wife Edna Ocko), while Irving Lerner, as "Peter Ellis," wrote frequently until 1938 for the *New Masses*. Jay Leyda composed Museum of Modern Art program notes and published occasional articles such as "A Guide to the Social Study of the Film" (with "Ellis," *Theatre Workshop,* April-July 1937), and "Joris Ivens: Artist in Documentary" (with Meyers, *The Magazine of Art,* July 1938). Among other pieces, Ben Maddow (as "David Wolff") wrote reviews of the Walker Evans exhibition at the Museum of Modern Art (*NM,* October 4, 1938), of *Confessions of a Nazi Spy* (*Films,* November 1939), and of *Shors* (*Films,* Spring 1940). Paul Strand reviewed Morris Engel's photographic exhibition (*Photo Notes,* December 1939) and Dorothea Lange's *An American Exodus* (*Photo Notes,* March-April 1940). Hurwitz was less active as a writer than he had been earlier in the decade, but his introduction to Paul Strand's *Mexican Portfolio* (1940) was an important critical statement. The Frontier group were also active in an editing capacity. Meyers was film editor of *TAC;* Hurwitz, Lerner, Leyda, and Kline were contributing editors of *Theatre Workshop;* and Leyda and Meyers were on the editorial board of *Films.* In 1938, as members of the Photo League's advisory board, Strand and Hurwitz helped prepare a syllabus and reading list for courses in Advanced Photography and Documentary Workshop, and themselves lectured to the classes. See Anne Tucker, "Photographic Crossroads: The Photo League," *Journal of the National Gallery of Canada,* No. 25 (April 6, 1978), p. 5.

50. Names taken from a Frontier Films letterhead of April 1939. Other new members of the Advisory Board were Leroy Bowman, Jerome Davis, Paul J. Kern, E.C. Lindeman, Ernest L. Meyer, and Rose Schneiderman. Only three persons originally announced as members of the board were no longer listed: John Dos Passos, Claire Sifton, and George Soule.

51. "Documentary Makers Form National Unit," *Motion Picture Herald,* June 24, 1939, p. 56.

52. Hurwitz, in Michael and Jill Klein, "*Native Land:* An Interview with Leo Hurwitz," *Cineaste,* VI, No. 3 (1974), p. 5; Strand, interview with Milton Brown, p. 46. Hurwitz's figure of $7,000 as the starting capital for the (revamped) *Native Land* production is substantiated by the bank statements of Frontier Films, which reveal that deposits of $3,000 and $4,000 respectively were made on March 25 and April 13, 1938, in a new account, "Special Account B" (financial records, Frontier Films Collection).

53. Berman, letter to Leo [Hurwitz], May 6, 1938 (Frontier Films Collection). Gardner ("Pat") Jackson played an active part in Frontier's fundraising schemes. Eleanor Roosevelt's column read: "I returned to a swim in the pool, supper in the rose garden, and three short movies sent down expressly for me to see. One movie was on the war in Spain, one on the war in China, and one on conditions in our Cumberland Mountains, which might almost be termed a war on our own economic conditions. I could hardly bear to look at some of the pictures. I found myself closing my eyes in utter disgust and horror that human beings can do such things to each other." Eleanor Roosevelt, "I was Haunted by the War Pictures," *Washington Daily News,* May 4, 1938, p. [?].

54. Financial records, Frontier Films Collection; Strand, interview with Milton Brown, p. 46; Bernard Reis, letter to Frontier Films; Strauss, "Homesteading." Tom Mooney had been freed from jail by New Deal Governor Oken of California in January 1939.

55. " 'Liberal,' " *Variety,* April 21, 1937, p. 27; Belitt, "The Camera Reconnoiters," p. 558; *Treasurer's Report to Frontier Films,* pp. 2, 11-12. According to the accounts, the exact cost

of *China Strikes Back* was $5,634.87 and of *People of the Cumberland* $2,591.17. No figures are given for *Heart of Spain* or *Return to Life*. The figure for *Native Land* refers to costs incurred to May 15, 1942, after the film had opened in New York. Joseph Goodwin's claim that *Native Land* cost some $125,000 is hard to credit in the light of the *Treasurer's Report*.

56. Hurwitz, in Klein, *"Native Land," Cineaste*, VI, No. 3 (1974) pp. 5-6.

57. Ibid., p. 6.

58. Most of the Frontier personnel continued filmmaking careers after their participation in the group. Ralph Steiner and Willard Van Dyke, after *The City*, went their separate ways, Steiner to Hollywood for a frustrating period as a "producer" before finding his way back to commercial photography and filmmaking, Van Dyke continuing in sponsored documentary production *(Valley Town, The Year's Work, The Children Must Learn)* before wartime film work for the Foreign Policy Association *(The Bridge)* and the Overseas Motion Picture Branch of the Office of War Information (OWI). Irving Lerner, after sponsored documentary work, became chief editor and producer for the OWI's Overseas Branch. Ben Maddow worked with Van Dyke on *The Bridge* before war service as a documentary scriptwiter in Army production. Sidney Meyers became American editor for the British Ministry of Information in New York, and subsequently chief film editor for the OWI. Lionel Berman, prevented for reasons of health from continuing film work, apparently became a Communist party section organizer for New York artists and professionals. Jay Leyda, after some work as an editor in documentary, moved into film scholarship (as translator of Eisenstein, etc.). Arnold Perl later became a TV scriptwriter. Leo Hurwitz worked on documentaries for the OWI before attaining the position of chief of news and special events for CBS TV. Paul Strand, frustrated in his attempts to work on wartime government film production (apparently as the result of a blacklist), reverted to still photography.

Chapter 6

1. *TAC*, I, No. 1 (July 1938), p. 12.

2. Herbert Kline, from Davenport, Iowa, had been associated with workers' theatres and the John Reed Club in Chicago, and was the author of the play *John Henry*. He became managing editor of *New Theatre* in April 1934 and editor three months later. Beginning in 1935, he served as a member of the executive board of the Theatre of Action. In 1936 he visited France, England, Germany, Czechoslovakia, Poland, and the U.S.S.R., writing articles, soliciting material for *New Theatre*, and attending the Soviet theatre festival. Information on the shooting of *Heart of Spain* is principally derived from Herbert Kline, interview with author, April 16, 1977, and letters to author, February 23, 1978, and April 25, 1978.

3. Press reports from later in 1937 refer to the station as "EAR" or "EAR-2."

4. Kline, interview with author. Norman Bethune was a distinguished surgeon and (secret) member of the Communist Party of Canada. After returning from Spain to North America in 1937—he looked in on the *Heart of Spain* editing team in the lab where they were at work, and reportedly appeared at several screenings of the finished film—he was sent by the Communist parties of the U.S. and Canada to China, where he arrived at the head of a medical team in the spring of 1938. He worked serving the army and the people of the Liberated Areas in the Shansi-Chahar-Hopei region until his death from blood poisoning on November 12, 1939. See Mao Tse-tung, *In Memory of Norman Bethune* (Peking: Foreign Languages Press, 1966).

5. Kline, interview with author.

6. Ibid.

7. Kline, quoted in unidentified newspaper clipping, September 13, 1937, in Clippings File, Theatre Collection, Lincoln Center for the Performing Arts, New York Public Library. Kline states that in fact neither Karpathi nor he "lived" in Bethune's quarters.

8. Kline, "Hospitals in Spain," *DW*, June 29, 1937, p. 7. According to Kline, the doctor referred to was Bethune.

9. Kline, interview with author.

10. Paul Strand, interview with Milton Brown, November 1971 (Archives of American Art, New York), p. 41; Ben Maddow, interview with author, March 17, 1977. There was reportedly 10,000 feet (about 100 minutes) of film devoted to the Blood Transfusion Institute (see Elizabeth Noble, *"Heart of Spain," NM*, October 5, 1937, p. 18).

11. Kline, interview with author; Alfred Hirsch, "*Heart of Spain* Film Tribute to Bravery," *DW*, August 4, 1937, p. 7; David Platt, "*Heart of Spain* Film Remarkable," *DW*, September 15, 1937, p. 7.

12. The Medical Bureau to Aid Spanish Democracy was at first attached to the American Friends of Spanish Democracy (AFSD), but later gained greater autonomy. Its national chairman was Dr. Walter B. Cannon of Harvard, and its general secretary Roger Chase, who was succeeded by Dr. William J. Crookston. Both the Medical Bureau and the AFSD were affiliated to the umbrella organization, the North American Committee to Aid Spanish Democracy (NACASD), which was headed by the Methodists Bishop Francis J. McConnell as chairman and Rev. Herman F. Reissig as executive secretary. Information on the activities of these groups may be found in F. Jay Taylor, *The United States and the Spanish Civil War* (New York: Bookman Associates, 1956).

13. "Hollywood Stars Send Two Ambulances to Spain," *DW*, September 17, 1937, p. 9. The Hollywood group was usually referred to as the Motion Picture Artists' Committee. Ivens's *The Spanish Earth* was also used in the campaign to buy ambulances, $20,000 having been raised in Hollywood for that purpose at screenings on July 11, 12, and 13, 1937 (see John T. McManus, "Down to Earth in Spain," *NYT*, July 25, 1937, p. X4).

14. "Movie-Sponsored Roadshow for Spain Gets Wide Response," *SW*, October 3, 1937, p. 10.

15. Unidentified clipping, December 8, 1937, in Clippings File, Film Study Center, Museum of Modern Art, New York.

16. *New York Herald Tribune*, September 11, 1937, p. 2; *NM*, September 21, 1937, p. 29; Richard Griffith, Museum of Modern Art Program Note, "Special Program," [January 6, 1940], p. 2.

17. There is some confusion over the production dates of *Return to Life*, but the preponderance of evidence suggests it was filmed in late 1937. Kline believes it was shot earlier, during the summer.

18. Kline, interview with author.

19. Ibid.; Strand, interview with Milton Brown, p. 45. Frontier Films laboratory invoices indicate that Kline screened "Spain" in New York on April 20 and 27, 1938 (Frontier Films Collection, Paul Strand Foundation, New York). Kline was not able to assist in writing the English commentary since he left for Czechoslovakia to film CRISIS.

20. Theatre Arts Committee, leaflet, July 20, 1938; Platt, "*Return to Life,* Stirring Spain Film at Cameo," *DW,* August 5, 1938, p. 7.

21. Strand, interview with Milton Brown, p. 45; Censorship Files, Film Review Section, Chicago Police Department.

22. Taylor, *The United States and the Spanish Civil War,* p. 137; Hadley Cantril, ed., *Public Opinion 1935-1946* (Princeton, N.J.: Princeton University, 1951), p. 808. According to Earl Browder, speaking in June 1937, over 60% of the Lincoln Battalion were members of the Communist party (Browder, *The People's Front* [New York: International Publishers, 1938], p. 182). After the war, the American contingent became popularly known as the "Abraham Lincoln Brigade," but the designation "Battalion" was most often used at the time of fighting. In the 1939 poll cited, a majority (52%) was opposed to changing the Neutrality Act in order to permit shipment of foodstuffs to Loyalists in Spain. Except among the Catholic hierarchy, support for Franco in the United States was muted, and no American is known to have volunteered for the insurgents during the course of the war.

23. Joris Ivens, *The Camera and I* (New York: International Publishers, 1969), pp. 130-31; Hugh Thomas, *The Spanish Civil War* (New York: Harper & Row, 1963), pp. 233, 338-39, 536, 393; Taylor, *The United States and the Spanish Civil War,* pp. 157, 133. See also Thomas, pp. 260, 293.

24. Irving Lerner (as "Peter Ellis"), *NM,* June 22, 1937, p. 29; Lerner (as "Ellis"), *TAC,* I, No. 1 (July 1938), p. 8. *The Last Train From Madrid,* directed by James Hogan, starred Gilbert Roland and Dorothy Lamour. *Blockade* was a Walter Wanger production, directed by William Dieterle, starring Henry Fonda and Madeleine Carroll. The only other Hollywood movie, apparently, to deal with the Spanish civil war while it was in progress was *Love Under Fire* (Twentieth Century-Fox, 1937). In this film the war served as an "insignificant background" for a boy-meets-girl romance, and David Platt wrote that "no one will take the ridiculous Spanish angle seriously" ("Boy Meets Girl in False Background," *DW,* August 30, 1937, p. 7). In 1937, Darryl F. Zanuck of Twentieth Century-Fox dropped plans to make a film (based on a script by Hearst correspondent H.R. Knickerbocker) on the siege of the Alcazar from a Franco perspective, in response to protests from the Left (see *DW,* January 16, 1937, p. 7, and *NT,* March 1937, p. 27).

25. Leif Furhammar and Folke Isaksson, *Politics and Film* (New York: Praeger, 1971), p. 53; Lerner (as "Ellis"), in *NM,* August 3, 1937, p. 29; Bert Hogenkamp, "Film and the Workers' Movement in Britain, 1929-39," *Sight and Sound,* XLV, No. 2 (Spring 1976), p. 74.

26. *DW,* December 28, 1936, p. 2; Dorothy Gates, "First Pictures Portray Brave Madrid Defenders," *DW,* January 25, 1937, p. 7; Gates, "*Spain in Flames* Details History of Fascist Coup," *DW,* January 28, 1937, p. 7; *DW,* February 2, 1937, p. 7, and April 30, 1937, p. 9; J.B. Thomas, "*Spain in Flames* a Tragic Document of Immortal Heroes," *SW,* February 21, 1937, p. 13; *NM,* February 16, 1937, p. 26; Platt, "Spanish Film a Scoop Packed with Spirit," *DW,* March 3, 1937, p. 7; Howard Rushmore, "*Fury Over Spain* Fails to Present the Truth," *DW,* July 20, 1937, p. 7; *DW,* May 20, 1938, p. 7. Kline, Lemare, and Cartier-Bresson shot *With the Lincoln Battalion in Spain* during a day off from filming *Return to Life.*

27. Gates, "*Spain in Flames*"; Platt, "*Spanish Film*"; Gates, "First Pictures Portray Brave Madrid Defenders."

28. The Medical Bureau and the North American Committee to Aid Spanish Democracy were not officially Communist-sponsored bodies, but they received much of their support from Communist organizations, and never deviated, in their public statements and actions, from

the party position on the Spanish conflict. In a Tag Day for NACASD in December 1936, almost $5,000 of the $5,897 collected was contributed by the Communist party, the Young Communist League, and the Communist-dominated organizations American League Against War and Fascism, Icor, ILD, and IWO (*DW*, December 29, 1936, p. 2). Hugh Thomas writes: "By this time, organizations for aid to the Republic had sprung up in nearly every country of the world. Friends of Spain, Spanish Medical Aid Committees, Committees for Spanish relief were set up everywhere. Behind them all lurked the shadow of the Comintern or of the local Communist parties." Thomas, *The Spanish Civil War*, p. 305.

29. Rushmore, *"Fury Over Spain"*; Lerner, (as "Ellis") in *NM*, August 3, 1937, p. 29.

30. Ivens, *The Camera and I*, p. 103. A review stated, in apparent contradiction with Ivens's recollection, that *Spain in Flames* was "photographed by Government and Soviet cameramen" (Gates, *"Spain in Flames"*).

31. See, e.g., Ivens, *The Camera and I*, pp. 103-38, and Furhammar and Isaksson, *Politics and Film*, pp. 111-15.

32. Maddow, interview with author; Ivens, *The Camera and I*, pp. 104-06, 107, 124. The original script was written by Lillian Hellman and Archibald MacLeish. Kline says, "The main influence on my work in Spain was Joris Ivens" (communication with author).

33. Leo Hurwitz, in Michael and Jill Klein, *"Native Land:* An Interview with Leo Hurwitz," *Cineaste*, VI, No. 3 (1974), p. 5. The first theorist to speak of "dialectical" form in the cinema was probably Sergei Eisenstein, in his essay "A Dialectic Approach to Film Form"(1929) (see chap. 1). The concept was adopted by Harry Alan Potamkin to describe the structure of certain Soviet films such as *The End of St. Petersburg, Storm over Asia, Fragment of an Empire, China Express, Ten Days that Shook the World*, and *Old and New*. Potamkin wrote: "Dialectics as drama is conflict—and that is its structure in the film. There is the THESIS— the status quo. The ANTITHESIS asserts itself—the proletariat (combatant, antagonist-protagonist) or the new force. The result is the SYNTHESIS—the new order. The idea-dynamics of the Soviet film is dialectics." Potamkin, "Populism and Dialectics," *Experimental Cinema*, I, No. 2 (June 1930), p. 16, reprinted in Lewis Jacobs, ed., *The Compound Cinema: The Film Writings of Harry Alan Potamkin* (New York: Teachers College, 1977), p. 176.

34. See chap. 4, n. 10.

35. Hurwitz, in Klein, "Native Land," Cineaste, p. 5.

36. Hurwitz, interview with author, April 14, 1977.

37. I am here employing the concept of the dialectical triad as it has been popularly understood on the Left. The extent to which the separate conceptions of Hegel and Marx are compatible is an important question which is beyond the scope of this study.

38. Noble, *"Heart of Spain,"* p. 18. According to Hurwitz's recollection, Elizabeth Noble was the photography critic Elizabeth McCausland. He writes, "I remember talking to her at great length about *Heart of Spain*, and showing her my work notes" (letter to author, June 14, 1978).

39. Ibid.

40. Ibid.; *Film Survey News Release*, No. 4 (October 1937), p. 3; Maddow, interview with author. In an undated interview (c. 1970) with Richard MacCann, Maddow argued: "The closer to this kind of inexplicable, irrational poetry a film is, the closer to a film poem it is, then the

better the documentary film it is, the closer it is to true documentary." Maddow, interview with Richard MacCann, Tape T68, University of Southern California Special Collections.

41.   Kline, interview with author. Kline expected that in the earlier street scenes the woman would be introduced by name in the commentary. The part was played by a volunteer nurse. Kline and Karpathi planned scenes of Hero and the man meeting after he was able to get around and walk with her aid.

42.   Hurwitz, interview with author.

43.   At sound speed, 24 frames per second. See chap. 3, n. 92.

44.   Under official pressure, Eisenstein clung to the concept of montage, but in so modified a form that it became almost unrecognizable. Thus in 1939 he wrote: "It is entirely incorrect to assume that if an actor acts in a single unbroken strip of film, uncut by the director and cameraman into different camera angles, that such a construction is untouched by montage! By no means!" Sergei Eisenstein, "Word and Image," in *Film Form: Essays in Film Theory and The Film Sense*, ed. Jay Leyda (Cleveland and New York: World Publishing, 1957), p. 23.

45.   Hurwitz had also worked as a still photographer, and both he and Maddow became pioneering, and perceptive, photographic critics.

46.   Kuleshov argued that "through montage it was possible to create a new earthly terrain that did not exist anywhere." See Lev Kuleshov, "Art of the Cinema" [1929], in Ronald Levaco, ed., *Kuleshov on Film: Writings by Lev Kuleshov* (Berkeley and Los Angeles: University of California, 1974), p. 52.

47.   The bombing raid, for example, appears to begin in a rural village, continue in the streets of a city, and conclude with shots of dead bodies in a wooded area. It is true that some of the synthetic continuity would not have been evident to audiences viewing the film for the first time.

48.   Noble, *"Heart of Spain,"* p. 18.

49.   Irving Lerner later commented: "Our writers mostly came from the field of poetry, because the theory was that the art of writing narration had to be not merely descriptive of the picture—as a matter of fact it shouldn't be that at all—it had to be a counterpoint, and of course had to be very concise, and with a few words in a sentence capture a great deal of meaning, in an emotional way." Lerner, interview with Arthur Knight, April 7, 1970, Tape T309, University of Southern California Special Collections. Kline comments on the *Heart of Spain* narration: "Maddow and I worked closely, as I provided him with actual words said by Lister to the troops, by Bethune to the wounded, and to coworkers in the blood bank. This gave the truth of the real experience of the war in Spain, which neither Maddow nor Hurwitz had seen or taken part in." Kline, letter to author, April 25, 1978.

50.   Maddow (as "David Wolff"), "Film Into Poem," *NT,* November 1936, p. 36; Hurwitz, interview with author.

51.   Hurwitz, interview with author.

52.   *Variety,* August 10, 1938, p. 27; James Dugan, in *NM,* August 16, 1938, p. 30; Howard Barnes, in *New York Herald Tribune,* August 4, 1938, p. L15.

53.   *The Spanish Earth* was originally narrated by Orson Welles. Ivens wrote: "As proposed by Archibald MacLeish we asked Orson Welles to read it and it seemed like a good job; but there was something in the quality of his voice that separated it from the film, from Spain, from the

actuality of the film.... In any case, when I took the film to Hollywood, the other people in Contemporary Historians—Herman Shumlin, Lillian Hellman, Dorothy Parker—sensed what was wrong and suggested that Hemingway try reading it himself. That was right. During the recording, his commentary sounded like that of a sensitive reporter who has been on the spot and wants to tell you about it—a feeling that no other voice could communicate. The lack of a professional commentator's smoothness helped you to believe intensely in the experiences on the screen." Ivens, *The Camera and I*, pp. 128-29.

54. Maddow, interview with author.

55. Ibid.; Hurwitz, interview with author. The narration times of the other Frontier productions are 13 minutes/57% *(China Strikes Back)*, 11 minutes/61% *(People of the Cumberland)*, and 23 minutes/28% *(Native Land)*. Kline notes that Cartier-Bresson had no control over the U.S. version of *Return to Life*.

56. The first statement is slightly misleading. Democratic elections had been held in Spain, following the establishment of the Republic, in June 1931, and several times thereafter. The elections of February 1936 returned a Popular Front government to power.

57. *New York World-Telegram*, July 14, 1938, p. [?].

58. Noble, *"Heart of Spain,"* p. 18.

59. Some indications of widespread pacifist and isolationist sentiment in the mid-thirties were the strong support and favorable publicity gained by Senator Nye's investigating committee into the munitions industry; the one-day antiwar strikes conducted on campuses across the country each year, beginning in 1934 (in 1937 the number of students participating reached one million); the substantial following achieved by the American League Against War and Fascism (a Communist-sponsored organization which in 1937 changed its name to the American League for Peace and Democracy and its programmatic emphasis to collective security); and the almost unanimous vote in Congress to apply an arms embargo against Spain (see above).

60. Hugh Thomas records that at the outbreak of the war, "throughout Republican Spain, churches and convents were indiscriminately burned and despoiled," and "thereafter the churces, whether gutted or still usable as a store or refuge, were as firmly closed...as were right-wing political party offices." He goes on to cite an estimate of some 8,000 religious persons—bishops, nuns, priests, monks, and novices—murdered or executed by Republicans during the war, mostly in its early phases. Thomas, *The Spanish Civil War*, pp. 171-172, 173. The only occasion on which the religious issue is raised in either of the films is a sequence in *Return to Life* detailing the destruction of a church, with damaged statuary and crucifix, which has been bombed by Franco.

61. Kline comments: "We regarded him as one of many heroic commanders of a fight against Franco, Hitler, and Mussolini—at a time Communists, Socialists, and just plain antifascist Spaniards had joined together in a 'Popular Front.' We didn't go into Lister's history, and I didn't even know he'd studied at the Soviet Military Academy until two years later when he fled to the U.S.S.R. for refuge." Kline, letter to author, May 11, 1978.

62. Ivens, *The Camera and I*, p. 128; Maddow, interview with author.

63. Kline, interview with author.

64. Maddow, interview with author.

Chapter 7

1. Harry Dunham, "Theatres of Victory," *TAC*, I, No. 2 (August 1938), p. 3.

2. Mao Tse-tung, "The Tasks of the Chinese Communist Party in the Period of Resistance to Japan" (May 1937), in M. Rejai, ed., *Mao Tse-tung on Revolution and War* (Garden City, N.Y.: Doubleday Anchor, 1970), p. 53.

3. Jay Leyda, *Dianying: An Account of Films and the Film Audiences in China* (Cambridge: MIT, 1972), p. 150; Richard Ross, "Documentary Film Tells Why and How of China Unity," *SW*, October 17, 1937, p. 11; Erik Barnouw, *Documentary: A History of the Non-Fiction Film* (New York: Oxford University, 1974), p. 126; *DW*, August 26, 1936, p. 4. According to Leyda, Dunham's footage was shot in 1936 (*Films Beget Films: A Study of the Compilation Film* [New York: Hill & Wang, 1964], p. 118). Harry Dunham was born in Cincinnati in 1910 and attended Princeton University. After his return from China he went to Spain as a freelance cameraman, and he later worked for the RKO-Pathe newsreel unit. He was killed in the Pacific during World War II.

4. Barnouw, *Documentary,* p. 126; Willard Van Dyke, interview with author, October 15, 1976; Ross, "Documentary Film." A Frontier Films promotional leaflet published in November 1938 stated that, "*China Strikes Back* was prepared in consultation with the Institute of Pacific Relations and other American educational organizations conceded to be the best informed on the history and facts of the present situation in China." Some of the stock footage was obtained from the Film and Photo League: it had presumably been used in *The Birth of New China* (see chap. 2, n. 108). An animated map sequence was supplied (for $100) by Technifilm Laboratories.

5. Leyda, *Dianying,* p. 150.

6. Paul Strand, interview with Milton Brown, November 1971 (Archives of American Art, New York), p. 44; Museum of Modern Art, Program Notes, *Non-Fiction Films: From Uninterpreted Fact to Documentary,* Program IX: History in the Making (n.d. [c. 1939]), p. 2. It is possible, as Strand maintains, that *China Strikes Back* opened in Brooklyn, but it was first reviewed when it played at the Squire Theatre, west of Times Square. (The Squire was a new movie house managed by former FPL member Edward Kern. See Charles E. Dexter, "Excellent Movie Bill at Squire," *DW,* October 13, 1937, p. 7.) One report states that *China Strikes Back* eventually played in 45 theatres in New York City (see John H. Winge, "Some New American Documentaries: In Defense of Liberty" [1939], in Lewis Jacobs, ed., *The Documentary Tradition: From Nanook to Woodstock* [New York: Hopkinson & Blake, 1971], p. 134). According to a later article, "when Frontier Films produced *China Strikes Back* and had it turned down by every house in New York, Strand and Hurwitz by getting the support of progressive organizations were able to book the film in 65 local neighborhood theatres" (Ralph Ellison, in *NM,* June 2, 1942, p. 29). Yet another figure is cited by distributor Tom Brandon, who stated in 1973: "We showed *China Strikes Back* in 204 theatres out of 700 something in the New York area." Revenue, according to Brandon, was minimal at $3.00 per rental. Tom Brandon, in Fred Sweet et. al., "Pioneers: An Interview with Tom Brandon," *Film Quarterly,* XXVII, No. 1 (Fall 1973), p. 23.

7. Leyda, *Dianying,* pp. 150-51; Bert Hogenkamp, "Film and the Workers' Movement in Britain, 1929-39," *Sight and Sound,* XLV, No. 2 (Spring 1976), p. 74.

8. *New York Herald Tribune,* February 15, 1938, p. 13.

9. Hadley Cantril, ed., *Public Opinion 1935-1946* (Princeton, N.J.: Princeton University, 1951), p. 1081.

10.   Foster Rhea Dulles, *China and America: The Story of their Relations Since 1784* (Princeton N.J.: Princeton University, 1946), pp. 207, 210, 211.

11.   See, e.g., *SW,* August 22, 1937, p. 6, and August 29, 1937, p. 6, and *DW,* August 27, 1937, p. 2. David Platt gave expression to the CPUSA line on the Sino-Japanese conflict in his *Daily Worker* review of the Universal newsreel *Bombing of Shanghai:* "The pictures constitute a vivid lesson and a warning to the American people against fascism; above all, a warning that unless the Roosevelt administration stops its middle-of-the-road maneuvers in the Far East situation and takes a decisive stand favoring collective action against Japanese aggression, as certain as night follows day, we will be embroiled in the conflict along with the rest of the world before many weeks have passed." Platt, "Shanghai Bombing Film Ghastly," *DW,* September 11, 1937, p. 7.

12.   John T. McManus, in *NYT,* March 23, 1936, p. 22.

13.   Irving Lerner, "March of the Movies," *NT,* January 1934, p. 13; McManus, ibid.

14.   Andre Sennwald, in *NYT,* June 6, 1935, p. 25; "Film Front," *NT,* June 1935, p. 27. The *New Theatre* article was an example of documentary montage—it juxtaposed a quotation from the *Hollywood Reporter* of May 6, noting that Hearst was insisting the name of Cosmopolitan Productions be removed from the credits of *Oil for the Lamps of China* "because of its attack on corporations," with an extract from a *Daily Variety* story of May 8, which read: "To soften what some previewers and Warner's execs regarded as unsympathetic treatment of a fictitious but typical corporation in the production of *Oil for the Lamps of China,* a few added scenes have been inserted in the final reel. New takes are designed to show corporation in less callous attitude toward its outpost employees than was the case in the first assembly of film made from Alice Tisdale Hobart story."

15.   Platt, "Shanghai Bombing."

16.   Albert Benham, in *Bulletin on Current Films* (National Council for Prevention of War, Moving Picture Department), No. 45 (September 22, 1937), pp. 1-2.

17.   Alfred Hirsch, "Japanese Invasion of China on Screen," *DW,* October 6, 1937, p. 7; *DW,* October 2, 1937, p. 7; *NM,* October 19, 1937, p. 28; "Unity of China Shown in Film," *SW,* October 3, 1937, p. 10.

18.   *Film Survey News Release,* Nos. 7-8 (January-February 1938).

19.   Van Dyke, interview with author. On this sequence Van Dyke had one of the disillusioning experiences which, he maintains, led to his break with Frontier Films: "Sidney Meyers and I . . . shot it, shot for shot, with the idea of exactly the way we wanted it edited, and planned to edit it, and we did it. There wasn't any money in those days, so we couldn't waste film. And we got it all shot, got it into the lab, and I had to do something in the morning, so I went around to the cutting room in the afternoon and Hurwitz had it all broken down and was editing it in his own way. I thought that this was such a contemptuous act toward a fellow worker, without even discussion of what was in our minds." In the final version the editing, Van Dyke says, is Hurwitz's; one of the voices is Van Dyke's.

20.   Dunham, "Theatres of Victory," p. 11.

21.   Leyda, *Dianying,* p. 93.

22.   Leo Hurwitz, in Michael and Jill Klein, "*Native Land:* An Interview with Leo Hurwitz," *Cineaste,* VI, No. 3 (1974), p. 4.

23.   Dulles, *China and America,* p. 208.

24. Hurwitz, in Klein, *"Native Land,"* *Cineaste*, p. 5.

25. Mao, in Rejai, *Mao Tse-tung*, p. 255.

26. Museum of Modern Art, Program Notes, p. 2; Ben Maddow (as "David Wolff"), "Film Into Poem," *NT*, November 1936, pp. 23, 26.

27. *New York Post*, October 12, 1937, p. [?].

28. Mao, quoted in Edgar Snow, *Red Star Over China* (New York: Grove, 1961), p. 488.

29. Hurwitz, in Klein, *"Native Land,"* *Cineaste*, pp. 4-5.

Chapter 8

1. Earl Browder, *What is Communism?* (New York: Vanguard, 1936), p. 20. The passage formed part of a pamphlet, *Who are the Americans?*, selections from which were frequently reprinted in the *Daily Worker*, e.g. as "Communists the Heirs of the Revolution of '76" (February 22, 1937, p. 2), and "Communism is the Americanism of the Twentieth Century" (July 3, 1937, p. 7).

2. Information on the Highlander Folk School is derived from Aimee I. Horton, "The Highlander Folk School: A History of the Development of its Major Programs Related to Social Movements in the South, 1932-1961" (unpublished Ph.D. dissertation, University of Chicago, 1971); Frank Adams with Myles Horton, *Unearthing Seeds of Fire: The Idea of Highlander* (Winston-Salem, N.C.: Blair, 1975); Myles Horton, letter to author, June 22, 1977; and Ralph Tefferteller, tape recording for author, August 17, 1977. The school is still in existence as the Highlander Research and Education Center, New Market, Tennessee.

3. Reinhold Niebuhr, quoted in Aimee I. Horton, "The Highlander Folk School," p. 332.

4. Myles Horton, letter to author; Aimee I. Horton, "The Highlander Folk School," p. 363. Highlander's long period of collaboration with the CIO was ended in 1949 when it would not make the ritual declaration of opposition to "totalitarianism" which was being employed in the campaign to destroy Communist leadership in the unions. At that time a report to Highlander Executive Council members stated that "both the Socialist and Communist Parties have made strenuous efforts to influence our policy and have retaliated by blocking contributions when rebuffed." See Aimee I. Horton, "The Highlander Folk School," p. 363.

5. Myles Horton, letter to author; Tefferteller, tape recording for author.

6. Tefferteller, tape recording for author; Myles Horton, letter to author.

7. Lionel Berman, letter to Roger Baldwin, June 26, 1937 (Frontier Films Collection, Paul Strand Foundation, New York); Elia Kazan, interview with author, April 13, 1977.

8. Tefferteller, tape recording for author. Tefferteller "had met Ralph Steiner in New York City and had a great deal of respect and fondness for him. He was an excellent photographer and a fine person." On the other hand he knew very little about Kazan personally before filming commenced. "We called him 'Gadget.' That was a nickname that was current at the time—I don't know how long it continued. But he was a little short guy, cocky, he was kind of like a bantam rooster. And giving the appearance of being very sure of himself, and so on."

9. Kazan, *Kazan par Kazan: entretiens avec Michel Ciment* (Paris: Stock, 1973), pp. 34-35 (translation by author); Kazan, in Stuart Byron and Martin Rubin, "Elia Kazan Interview," *Movie*, No. 19 (Winter 1971-72), p. 1, quoted in Joel Zuker, *Ralph Steiner: Filmmaker and Still Photographer* (New York: Arno, 1978), p. 254; Tefferteller, tape recording for author.

10. Aimee I. Horton, "The Highlander Folk School," p. 44; Tefferteller, tape recording for author.

11. Kazan, in Michel Ciment, *Kazan on Kazan* (New York: Viking, 1974), p. 23; Tefferteller, tape recording for author. Summerfield, near Monteagle, was the immediate community in which the Highlander Folk School was located.

12. Tefferteller, tape recording for author.

13. Ibid.

14. Ralph Steiner (1974), quoted in Zuker, *Ralph Steiner*, p. 253. The incident, which was observed by Ethel Clyde, had a comic sequel. As Steiner tells it: "When we got done with the scenes, the union boys said: 'They might stop you on the way back up the road, so we're going with you.' They got about six cars, three in front, three in back. They all had horse pistols with them—tremendous guns. Ethel Clyde had a chauffeur who had a pearl-handled revolver; when the union boys saw that gun, they just laughed. We finally made it out of there and to the top of the mountain. Ethel bought them all ice-cream cones. If I'd only had a still camera with me to take a picture of these tall mountaineers with all their hunting rifles and horse pistols, all licking ice-cream cones—it was wonderful."

15. Myles Horton, letter to author; Roger M. Williams, "A New Role for Old Radicals," *Highlander Reports*, n.d., reprinted from *World*, II, No. 16 (July 13, 1973); Myles Horton, quoted in Fran Ansley and Brenda Bell, "Davidson-Wilder 1932: Strikes in the Coal Camps," *Southern Exposure*, I, Nos. 3-4 (Winter, 1974), p. 129.

16. Adams, p. 34; anonymous witness, quoted in Ansley and Bell, "Davidson-Wilder 1932," p. 128.

17. Tefferteller, tape recording for author.

18. Ibid.; Aimee I. Horton, "The Highlander Folk School," pp. 131-37.

19. Leo Hurwitz, interview with author, April 14, 1977; Jay Leyda, interview with author, October 12, 1976.

20. Steiner (1974, 1973), quoted in Zuker, *Ralph Steiner*, pp. 255, 265.

21. John H. Winge, "Some New American Documentaries: In Defense of Liberty" (1939), in Lewis Jacobs, ed., *The Documentary Tradition: From Nanook and Woodstock* (New York: Hopkinson & Blake, 1971), p. 134.

22. Steiner (1973, 1974), quoted in Zuker, *Ralph Steiner*, pp. 256, 255.

23. Myles Horton, letter to author.

24. Steiner (1973), quoted in Zuker, *Ralph Steiner*, p. 260. Zuker's claim that Frontier "sabotaged" Steiner's work (p. 256) needs to be supported by something other than Steiner's (somewhat jaundiced) reminiscences.

25. Tefferteller, tape recording for author.

26. Aimee I. Horton, "The Highlander Folk School," pp. 135-36n; Berman, letter to Leo [Hurwitz], May 6, 1938 (Frontier Films Collection); Tefferteller, tape recording for author. For Eleanor Roosevelt's response to the film, see chap. 5, n. 53.

27. *Film Survey* Special Release No. 11, n.d., p. 5.

28.   *DW*, June 6, 1938, p. 7; Edward H. Shustack, *The Documentary Film: History and Principles* (New York: Film and Sprocket Society of the CCNY Art Department, 1938), p. 23; Museum of Modern Art, Program Notes, *Non-Fiction Films: From Uninterpreted Fact to Documentary*, Program VII: Labor (n.d. [c. December 1939]); Herbert Levine, "Independent of Hollywood," *Direction*, III, No. 4 (April 1940), p. 17; Mary Losey, "Joris Ivens's *Power and the Land*" (1940), in *The Documentary Tradition: From Nanook to Woodstock*, p. 192.

29.   Harold W. Houston, letter to Ethel Clyde, March 20, 1939 (Frontier Films Collection). *People of the Cumberland* is still being shown in a political context. Myles Horton recently wrote (letter to author): "I was in Canada [in 1977] working with the Cree Indians and the film was being used there. In fact, one old-timer said that for some reason the film had been banned in Canada, but they had gotten hold of and worn out two copies."

30.   Both films were directed by Michael Curtiz. *Black Fury* starred Paul Muni and Karen Morley, *Mountain Justice* Josephine Hutchinson and George Brent.

31.   Albert Maltz, "Coal Diggers of 1935," *NT*, May 1935, p. 9. See also David Platt, "Film *Black Fury* is Vicious Attack on Militant Unionism in Coal Fields," *DW*, April 15, 1935, p. 5, and Maltz, "Author of *Black Pit* Calls for Boycott of Vicious Anti-Union Film *Black Fury*," *DW*, April 22, 1935, p. 5.

32.   Irving Lerner (as "Peter Ellis"), *"The Plow That Broke the Plains," NT*, July 1936, pp. 18-19. The epilogue is not part of the film currently in distribution.

33.   Lerner (as "Ellis"), in *NM*, January 18, 1938, p. 30.

34.   Walker Evans photographed such graves for the Resettlement Administration in the southeastern U.S. in 1936. See *Walker Evans: Photographs for the Farm Security Administration, 1935-1938* (New York: Da Capo, 1975), Nos. 409-11.

35.   "Bugwood" is used in distilling wood alchohol.

36.   *Sit Down*, with words and music by the Detroit labor lawyer Maurice Sugar, was published in the *United Automobile Worker*, January 1937.

37.   Steiner and Hurwitz, "A New Approach to Film Making," *NT*, September 1935, p. 22; Steiner, "Revolutionary Movie Production," *NT*, September 1934, p. 22.

38.   Vladimir Petric, "Soviet Revolutionary Films in America (1926-1935)," (unpublished Ph.D. dissertation, New York University, 1973), p. 483; for a shot analysis of the sequence, see ibid., pp. 480-83.

39.   Hurwitz, interview with author.

40.   Irving Howe and Lewis Coser, *The American Communist Party: A Critical History* (New York: Praeger, 1962), p. 340.

41.   Louis Baron, "Communists Should Use Revolutionary Heritage of America," *DW*, February 1, 1936, p. 6.

42.   In the detailed description of the sequence in Petric, "Soviet Revolutionary Films," pp. 484-85, five shots are omitted.

43.   Petric remarks (ibid., p. 483) that the sequence "is conceptualized in the Vertovian manner, almost as a replica of the montage-depicted construction of the water power station on the river Don in Vertov's *Eleventh Year* (1928), or of the final sequence in his *Enthusiasm* (1931)."

Chapter 9

1. Information on the La Follette Civil Liberties Committee is derived principally from Jerold S. Auerbach, *Labor and Liberty: The La Follette Committee and the New Deal* (Indianapolis and New York: Bobbs-Merrill, 1966), and the volumes of testimony and exhibits, published as U.S. Senate, Committee on Education and Labor, *Hearings Before a Subcommittee of the Committee on Education and Labor: Violations of Free Speech and Rights of Labor* (Washington, 1936-41).

2. In 1939 and 1940 the committee investigated conditions in California agriculture.

3. Lee Pressman, quoted in Auerbach, *Labor and Liberty*, p. 153.

4. Leo Huberman, *The Labor Spy Racket* (New York: Modern Age, 1937); Leo Hurwitz, in Michael and Jill Klein, "*Native Land:* An Interview with Leo Hurwitz," *Cineaste*, VI, No. 3 (1974), p. 5. Hurwitz recalls (communication with author) that the Frontier filmmakers had a great deal of personal contact with Huberman.

5. Auerbach, *Labor and Liberty*, p. 169.

6. Lionel Berman, letter to Roger Baldwin, June 26, 1937, in Frontier Films Collection, Paul Strand Foundation (New York).

7. George Jacobson, interview with author, April 17, 1977. Ten people were killed and scores wounded when Chicago police fired on peaceful demonstrators outside the Republic Steel plant on Memorial Day, 1937. The La Follette Committee made a detailed investigaton and subpoenaed the Paramount newsreel of the attack, which at the time was suppressed by the producers, allegedly under pressure from the Chicago Police Department. The committee allowed journalists to view the film, and thus its contents became public; it was subsequently given limited distribution (the claim, frequently reiterated in later years, that the newsreel was never shown publicly, is evidently in error). Paramount, however, refused to grant Frontier Films access to the footage. See *Film Survey News Release*, No. 1 (July 1, 1937), p. 3, and No. 2 (August 1, 1937), p. 1, and "Mass Protests Released Film," *DW*, July 8, 1937, p. 7.

8. Invoices, Frontier Films Collection; circular letter, signed Quincy Howe, Bishop Francis J. McConnell, Corliss Lamont, Mary Van Kleek, and Lillian Hellman, February 17, March 14, and April 26, 1939 (Frontier Films Collection): Frank Hague, quoted in William E. Leuchtenburg, *Franklin D. Roosevelt and the New Deal, 1932-1940* (New York: Harper & Row, 1963), pp. 275-76; *New York Post*, January 6, 1938, p. [?].

9. Hurwitz, interview with author, April 14, 1977.

10. Paul Srand, letter to Cornelia Bryce Pinchot, April 21, 1938 (Frontier Films Collection); Theodore Strauss, "Homesteading Our 'Native Land,' " *NYT*, May 3, 1942, p. X3.

11. Information derived from correspondence in the Frontier Films Collection, and particularly Michael N. Straus, letter to Leo Hurwitz, April 1, 1938, and John M. Coffee, letter to Paul Strand. April 13, 1938. For the names of congressmen supporting Frontier Films, see chap. 5.

12. Hurwitz, letter to Elmer Rice, November 29, 1937; Lucille B. Milner, secretary, American Civil Liberties Union, letter to Paul Strand, April [?], 1938; Howe et al., circular letter (all in Frontier Films Collection).

13. Ben Maddow, interview with author, March 17, 1977.

14. Ibid.

15.   Ibid.

16.   Ibid.

17.   Financial records, Frontier Films Collection; Howe et al., circular letter; United Trade Union Committee for Frontier Films' Civil Liberties Film, letter to unions, July 24, 1939 (Frontier Films Collection); Strand, circular letter, August 29, 1939 (Frontier Films Collection).

18.   Hurwitz, interview with author.

19.   Jacobson, interview with author.

20.   Ibid.

21.   Ibid.; Maddow, interview with author; Strauss, "Homesteading."

22.   John T. McManus, "*Native Land,* Dramatic Civil Liberties Film, Warns Hitler: Americans Will Fight to Death to Safeguard their Liberties," *PM,* May 12, 1942, p. 8; financial records, Frontier Films Collection; Jacobson, interview with author; Irene Thirer, "Paul Strand and Leo Hurwitz Offer Data on *Native Land,*" *New York Post,* May 9, 1942, p. 13.

23.   Herman G. Weinberg, "*Native Land*—The Texture of America," *Documentary Film News,* II, No. 1 (April 1942), p. 7; Thirer, "Paul Strand and Leo Hurwitz"; Strauss, "Homesteading." When *Native Land* was released, *Variety* observed: "There's hardly a name in the cast that will be recognized by film audiences" (May 13, 1942). Of the actors, only Howard Da Silva had previously been featured extensively in Hollywood productions, with ten films to his credit, including *Abe Lincoln in Illinois, The Sea Wolf,* and *Sergeant York* (all were made subsequent to his work on *Native Land*); Charles Jordan had appeared in *Penrod and His Twin Brother.* Art Smith, Fred Johnson, Bert Conway, Richard Bishop, Robert Strauss, Clancy Cooper, and Tom Pedi later appeared in Hollywood films.

24.   Weinberg, "Native Land"; financial records, Frontier Films Collection; Richard Leacock, letter to author, December 2, 1977. George Jacobson says of the editing of *Native Land* (interview with author): "Then it went into the cutting room, and there Leo had total command, and his personality expressed itself in there. Julia Milch worked with him as an assistant editor, and he had her in tears most of the time." (It should be borne in mind that Jacobson left Frontier Films in October 1939.) Richard Leacock, of course, was to become a distinguished documentary filmmaker and pioneer of cinema-verite in the United States. He recalls: "At the end of the summer Paul [Strand] invited me and my girlfriend (later, my wife) to a steak dinner; he also paid our subway fare (5¢ each) and showed us still photos. . . . He was a very nice man."

25.   Marc Blitzstein, in "Music in Films: A Symposium of Composers," *Films,* I, No. 4 (Winter 1940), p. 18. *The Cradle Will Rock,* produced by John Houseman and directed by Orson Welles, was scheduled to open in June 1937 as a Federal Theatre production. Shortly before opening night, WPA officials in Washington cancelled the show. In a celebrated maneuver, Houseman, Welles, and Blitzstein staged *The Cradle Will Rock* under independent auspices, and it subsequently became a hit as a production of the new Mercury Theatre. Blitzstein had studied with Nadia Boulanger and Arnold Schoenberg in Europe and was the composer of concert works, musical plays, and revue sketches, as well as operas and film scores.

26.   Hurwitz, quoted in Thirer, "Paul Strand and Leo Hurwitz"; Weinberg, "*Native Land*"; David Platt, "*Native Land* is Powerful Exposé of America's 'Little Hitlers,' " *DW,* May 12, 1942, p. 7.

27. Bosley Crowther, in *NYT,* May 12, 1942, p. 16; Richard Watts, Jr., in *New York Herald Tribune,* May 15, 1942, p. 12; *Time,* June 8, 1942, p. 50, reprinted in Lewis Jacobs, ed., *The Documentary Tradition: From Nanook to Woodstock* (New York: Hopkinson & Blake, 1971), p. 200; *Variety,* May 13, 1942, pp. 8, 16; *Film Daily,* May 12, 1942, p. [?]; Eleanor Roosevelt, "My Day," *New York World-Telegram,* July 1, 1942, p. [?]. The *Time* reviewer was probably James Agee.

28. Archer Winsten, "*Native Land* is Shown at the World Theatre," *New York Post,* May 12, 1942, p. [?]; William Boehnel, "World Theatre Shows *Native Land,*" *New York World-Telegram,* May 12, 1942, p. [?]; Dorothy Masters, "*Native Land* Films Abuses Against Labor," *New York Daily News,* May 12, 1942, p. [?].

29. Platt, "*Native Land*"; Watts, in *NY Herald Tribune.*

30. Hurwitz, in Klein, "*Native Land,*" *Cineaste,* p. 6.

31. Michael Klein, "*Native Land:* Praised Then Forgotten," *The Velvet Light Trap,* No. 14 (Winter 1975), p. 16; Hurwitz, communication with author. The film was evidently banned for a time in Chicago. Hurwitz explains that "the 'trustees,' specifically Bernard Reis, tried to round up the prints . . . of *Native Land.* They were already in control of the negatives. [Reis] wrote letters e.g. to Cinémathèque Française to send their print back, but Henri Langlois refused." Hurwitz, letter to author, June 14, 1978.

32. Hurwitz, communication with author. Recent articles on *Native Land* include Michael and Jill Klein, *Cineaste,* Michael Klein, *The Velvet Light Trap,* and Ernest Callenbach, "*Native Land,*" *Film Quarterly,* XXVII, No. 1 (Fall 1973), pp. 60-62.

33. The breakdown into sections in the table follows to some extent that made by Michael Klein, "*Native Land,*" pp. 14-15.

34. Jacobson, interview with author.

35. Much of the La Follette Committee's time in late 1937 and early 1938 was devoted to the investigation of so-called "citizens' committees."

36. Records in the Frontier Films Collection indicate that the stills were obtained from International News Photos.

37. Strauss, "Homesteading."

38. Quoted in Platt, "*Native Land.*"

39. Hurwitz, in Michael and Jill Klein, "*Native Land,*" p. 7.

40. Hurwitz, "One Man's Voyage: Ideas and Films in the 1930's," *Cinema Journal,* XV, No. 1 (Fall 1975), p. 15, and in Michael and Jill Klein, "*Native Land,*" p. 5.

41. *NYT,* June 4, 1939, Section 1, p. 31: S[id] G[rossman], "Documentary Film Problems Discussed at Writers' Congress," *Photo Notes,* June 1939, p. 4.

42. Hurwitz, in Michael and Jill Klein, "*Native Land,*" p. 6.

43. Hurwitz, interview with author; Maddow, interview with author.

44. Strand, interview with Milton Brown (Archives of American Art, New York), November 1971, p. 47.

45. *Variety,* May 13, 1942, p. 16; Crowther, *NYT,* May 12, 1942, p. 16; Hurwitz, quoted in Weinberg, "*Native Land,*" p. 6; Arthur Pollock, in *Brooklyn Eagle,* May 17, 1942, p. [?].

46.   Strauss, "Homesteading;" Strand, quoted in Thirer, "Paul Strand and Leo Hurwitz."

47.   Boehnel, *NY World-Telegram*, May 12, 1942, p. [?]; Crowther, *NYT*, May 12, 1942, p. 16; John Beaufort, "Violence of Industrial War Pictured in *Native Land*," *Christian Science Monitor*, May 12, 1942 [?], p. [?]; Weinberg, *"Native Land,"* p. 6.

48.   William Z. Foster, *Toward Soviet America* (New York: Coward-McCann, 1932), p. 113; Earl Browder, *What is Communism?* (New York: Workers Library, 1936), p. 148.

49.   Hurwitz, in Michael and Jill Klein, *"Native Land,"* p. 7.

50.   Browder, *What is Communism?*, p. 11; "Communists are Inheritors of Revolutionary Traditions of '76," *DW*, July 4, 1936, p. 1.

51.   Auerbach, *Labor and Liberty*, p. 3.

52.   Beaufort, *Christian Science Monitor*, May 12, 1942 [?], p. [?]; Crowther, *NYT*, May 12, 1942, p. 16, and "What's Above All?", *NYT*, May 17, 1942, p. X3.

53.   Browder, *The People's Front* (New York: International Publishers, 1938), p. 179.

54.   Hurwitz, in Michael and Jill Klein, *"Native Land,"* p. 6.

55.   Maddow, interview with author; Hurwitz, in Michael and Jill Klein, *"Native Land,"* p. 6, and quoted in Strauss, "Homesteading."

56.   Callenbach, *"Native Land,"* p. 61; Hurwitz, in Michael and Jill Klein, *"Native Land,"* p. 7.

57.   Boehnel, *NY World-Telegram*, May 12, 1942, p. [?].

58.   Irving Howe and Lewis Coser, *The American Communist Party: A Critical History* (New York: Praeger, 1962), p. 339.

59.   Maddow, interview with author, and quoted in William Alexander, "Frontier Films, 1936-1941: The Aesthetics of Impact," *Cinema Journal*, XV, No. 1 (Fall 1975), p. 25.

60.   In 1953, as a Hollywood screenwriter, Maddow was summoned before HUAC. He refused to testify, invoking the Fifth Amendment, and was blacklisted. Some four years later he reversed his position and gave the Committee the names of his former associates in the Party. Maltz went to prison as one of the Hollywood Ten, and was blacklisted throughout the fifties and early sixties, as was Hurwitz. By way of contrast with *Native Land,* the prototypical protagonist of proletarian fiction of the thirties is a worker who attains greater class consciousness as the action progresses. The leading character of *Salt of the Earth* (1953) is a union leader who is a positive figure despite faults which the film exposes.

61.   Hurwitz, interview with author.

62.   Callenbach, *"Native Land,"* p. 61.

Chapter 10

1.   Ed Kennedy, "Three Workers' Films," *Filmfront*, I, No. 2 (January 7, 1935), p. 11.

2.   Leo T. Hurwitz, "Survey of Workers' Films: A Report to the National Film Conference," *NT*, October 1934, p. 28.

3.   Ibid.

4.   Julian Roffman, letter to author, January 10, 1978.

5.   The figure of fifteen minutes excludes the election footage mentioned in chap. 4, about which no concrete information exists.

6.   George Jacobson, interview with author, April 17, 1977.

7.   Ibid.

8.   Richard Leacock, letter to author, December 2, 1977.

9.   In 1943, Strand and Hurwitz, together with Robert Riley, mounted a tribute to Roosevelt at the Vanderbilt Gallery in New York. It consisted of an eighty-foot montage of photographs covering the history of his administration, with sections entitled "Lest We Forget," "America Gets New Leadership," "The Strength of the Nation Lies in the Well-Being of its People," "The President Warns the Nation," "The United States is Attacked," and "Forward to Peace." Strand was chairman of the Committee of Photography of the Independent Voters Committee of the Arts and Sciences for Roosevelt. See Michael E. Hoffman, ed., *Paul Strand: Sixty Years of Photographs* (New York: Aperture, 1976), p. 162.

10.   The UMWA, featured so glowingly in *People of the Cumberland,* was one union that became corrupt. Implicated in the conspiracy directed by UMWA president Tony Boyle to murder rival union leader (and militant reformer) Jock Yablonski in 1969 were William Turnblazer, president of UMWA District 19 (son of the man who had held that position in the thirties, and who spoke at the July 4 Labor Rally portrayed in *People of the Cumberland),* and Silous Huddleston, president of a UMWA local at La Follette, Tennessee. See Bryan Woolley and Ford Reid, *We Be Here When the Morning Comes* (Lexington: University Press of Kentucky, 1975), pp. 63-64.

11.   For a powerful critique of the Communist party's policy of maintaining invisibility within the labor movement, and the related failure to keep a socialist tradition alive, see James Weinstein, *The Grand Illusion: The Communist Party and Trade Unionism* (Somerville, Massachusetts: New England Free Press, n.d. [c. 1976]), originally published in *Socialist Revolution,* No. 24 (June 1975).

Bibliography

Books

Aaron, Daniel. *Writers on the Left.* New York: Avon, 1961.

Adams, Frank, with Myles Horton. *Unearthing Seeds of Fire: The Idea of Highlander.* Winston-Salem, N.C.: Blair, 1975.

Ades, Dawn. *Photomontage.* New York: Pantheon, 1976.

Alexander, William. *Film on the Left.* Princeton: Princeton University, 1981.

Auerbach, Jerold S. *Labor and Liberty: The La Follette Committee and the New Deal.* Indianapolis and New York: Bobbs-Merrill, 1966.

Barnouw, Erik. *Documentary: A History of the Non-Fiction Film.* New York: Oxford University, 1974.

Barsam, Richard Meran. *Nonfiction Film: A Critical History.* London: Allen & Unwin, 1973.

Baxandall, Lee, and Stefan Morawski, eds. *Marx and Engels on Literature and Art.* St. Louis and Milwaukee: Telos, 1973.

Boyer, Richard O., and Herbert M. Morais. *Labor's Untold Story.* New York: Marzani & Munsell, 1955.

Browder, Earl. *The People's Front.* New York: International Publishers, 1938.

————. *What is Communism?* New York: Vanguard, 1936.

Ciment, Michel. *Kazan on Kazan.* New York: Viking, 1974.

Clurman, Harold. *The Fervent Years: The Story of the Group Theatre and the Thirties.* New York: Knopf, 1945.

Dennis, Peggy. *The Autobiography of an American Communist: A Personal View of a Political Life, 1925-1975.* Westport, Connecticut: Lawrence Hill, 1977.

Douglas, Jack. *Veterans on the March.* New York: Workers Library, 1934.

Eisenstein, Sergei. *Film Essays and a Lecture,* ed. Jay Leyda. New York: Praeger, 1970.

————. *Film Form: Essays in Film Theory and The Film Sense,* ed. Jay Leyda. Cleveland and New York: World Publishing, 1957.

Fielding, Raymond. *The March of Time, 1935-1951.* New York: Oxford University, 1978.

Foster, William Z. *Pages from a Worker's Life.* New York: International Publishers, 1939.

————. *Toward Soviet America.* New York: Coward-McCann, 1932.

Frank, Waldo, *et al.,* eds. *America and Alfred Stieglitz: A Collective Portrait.* Garden City, N.Y.: Doubleday, Doran, 1934.

Furhammar, Leif, and Folke Isaksson. *Politics and Film.* New York: Praeger, 1971.

Gorelik, Mordecai. *New Theatres for Old.* New York: French, 1940.

Gross, Babette. *Willi Münzenberg: A Political Biography.* East Lansing: Michigan State University, 1974.

Hardy, Forsyth, ed. *Grierson on Documentary.* New York: Praeger, 1971.

Hart, Henry, ed. *American Writers' Congress.* New York: International Publishers, 1935.

Hicks, Granville, *et al.,* eds. *Proletarian Literature in the United States: An Anthology.* New York: International Publishers, 1935.

Hoffman, Michael E., ed. *Paul Strand: Sixty Years of Photographs.* New York: Aperture, 1976.

Hogenkamp, Bert. *Workers' Newsreels in the 1920s and 1930s.* London: History Group of the Communist Party, n.d. [c.a. 1977].

Howe, Irving, and Lewis Coser. *The American Communist Party: A Critical History.* New York: Praeger, 1962.

Huberman, Leo. *The Labor Spy Racket.* New York: Modern Age, 1937.

Hurley, F. Jack. *Portrait of a Decade: Roy Stryker and the Development of Documentary Photography in the Thirties.* Baton Rouge: Louisiana State University, 1972.

Ivens, Joris. *The Camera and I.* New York: International Publishers, 1969.

Jacobs, Lewis. *The Rise of the American Film: A Critical History.* New York: Teachers College, 1968.

_____, ed. *The Compound Cinema: The Film Writings of Harry Alan Potamkin.* New York: Teachers College, 1977.

_____, ed. *The Documentary Tradition: From NANOOK to WOODSTOCK.* New York: Hopkinson & Blake, 1971.

Jahnke, Eckart, Manfred Lichtenstein, and Kazuo Yamada. *Dokumentarfilm in Japan: Seine Demokratische und Kämpferische Traditionen.* Berlin: Staatliches Filmarchiv der DDR, 1976.

Kazan, Elia. *Kazan par Kazen: entretiens avec Michel Ciment.* Paris: Stock, 1973.

Lens, Sidney. *The Labor Wars.* Garden City, N.Y.: Doubleday, 1974.

Leuchtenburg, William E. *Franklin D. Roosevelt and the New Deal, 1932-1940.* New York: Harper & Row, 1963.

Levaco, Ronald, ed. *Kuleshov on Film: Writings by Lev Kuleshov.* Berkeley and Los Angeles: University of California, 1974.

Leyda, Jay. *Dianying: An Account of Films and the Film Audience in China.* Cambridge: MIT, 1972.

_____. *Films Beget Films: A Study of the Compilation Film.* New York: Hill & Wang, 1964.

_____. *Kino: A History of the Russian and Soviet Film.* London: Allen & Unwin, 1973.

Losey, Mary, ed. *Living Films.* New York: Association of Documentary Film Producers, 1940.

Lovell, Alan, and Jim Hillier. *Studies in Documentary.* New York: Viking, 1972.

Lüdecke, Willi. *Der Film in Agitation und Propaganda der Revolutionären Deutschen Arbeiterbewegung (1919-1933).* Berlin: Oberbaumverlag, 1973.

Lukács, Georg. *Realism in Our Time: Literature and the Class Struggle.* New York: Harper & Row, 1971.

Lyons, Eugene. *The Red Decade: The Stalinist Penetration of America.* New York: Bobbs-Merrill, 1941.

MacCann, Richard Dyer. *The Peoples' Films: A Political History of U.S. Government Motion Pictures.* New York: Hastings House, 1973.

Münzenberg, Willi. *Solidarität: Zehn Jahre Internationale Arbeiterhilfe, 1921-1931.* Berlin: Neuer Deutsche Verlag, 1931.

Munden, Kenneth W., ed. *The American Film Institute Catalog of Motion Pictures Produced in the United States, Feature Films, 1921-1930.* 2 vols. New York: Bowker, 1971.

Nochlin, Linda. *Realism.* Harmondsworth: Penguin, 1971.

Patterson, Haywood, and Earl Conrad. *Scottsboro Boy.* New York: Collier, 1969.

Piscator, Erwin. *Das Politische Theater.* Hamburg: Rowohlt, 1963.

Preis, Art. *Labor's Giant Step: Twenty Years of the CIO.* New York: Pathfinder, 1972.

Rejai, M., ed. *Mao Tse-tung on Revolution and War.* Garden City, N.Y.: Doubleday, 1970.

Richter, Hans. *Dada: Art and Anti-Art.* New York: Abrams, 1965.

Rideout, Walter, *The Radical Novel in the United States, 1900-1954: Some Interrelations of Literature and Society*. Cambridge: Harvard University, 1956.

Rosenblum, Walter, *et al. America and Lewis Hine: Photographs 1904-1940*. New York: Brooklyn Museum/Aperture, 1977.

Rotha, Paul, Sinclair Road, and Richard Griffith. *Documentary Film*. New York: Hastings House, 1952.

Schnitzer, Luda and Jean, and Marcel Martin, eds. *Cinema in Revolution: The Heroic Era of the Soviet Film*. London: Secker & Warburg, 1973.

Shustack, Edward H. *The Documentary Film: History and Principles*. New York: Film and Sprocket Society of C.C.N.Y. Art Department, 1938.

Snow, Edgar. *Red Star Over China*. New York: Grove, 1961.

Snyder, Robert L. *Pare Lorentz and the Documentary Film*. Norman: University of Oklahoma, 1968.

Solomon, Maynard, ed. *Marxism and Art: Essays Classic and Contemporary*. New York: Vintage, 1974.

Stott, William. *Documentary Expression and Thirties America*. New York: Oxford University, 1973.

Strand, Paul. *The Mexican Portfolio*. New York: Da Capo, 1967.

Taylor, F. Jay. *The United States and the Spanish Civil War*. New York: Bookman Associates, 1956.

Taylor, Karen Malpede. *People's Theatre in Amerika*. New York: Drama Book Specialists, 1972.

Thomas, Hugh. *The Spanish Civil War*. New York: Harper & Row, 1961.

Ulam, Adam B. *Stalin: The Man and his Era*. New York: Viking, 1973.

Vaughn, Robert. *Only Victims: A Study of Show Business Blacklisting*. New York: Putnam, 1972.

Weinstein, James. *The Grand Illusion: The Communist Party and Trade Unionism*. Somerville, Massachusetts: New England Free Press, n.d. [c.a. 1976].

Willett, John, ed. *Brecht on Theatre: The Development of an Aesthetic*. New York: Hill & Wang, 1964.

Williams, Jay. *Stage Left*. New York: Scribner's, 1974.

Zuker, Joel. *Ralph Steiner: Filmmaker and Still Photographer*. New York: Arno, 1978.

Articles

Alexander, William. "Frontier Films, 1936-1941: The Aesthetics of Impact," *Cinema Journal*, XV, No. 1 (Fall 1975), pp. 16-28.

_____. "THE MARCH OF TIME and THE WORLD TODAY," *American Quarterly*, XXIX (Summer 1977), pp. 69-73.

Anon. "Film and Photo Demise Greatly Exaggerated," *Daily Worker*, April 30, 1937, p. 9.

_____. "Program of the International Cinema Bureau: Summary of the Decisions of the Film Conference Held in Moscow Recently to Plan a Program for the Cinema Bureau of the International Union of Revolutionary Theatre," *New Theatre*, May 1934, pp. 15-16.

_____. "The Class Struggle Through the Camera Eye," *Workers' Theatre*, February 1932, pp. 29-31.

Belitt, Ben. "The Camera Reconnoiters," *The Nation*, November 20, 1937, pp. 557-58.

Brandon, Tom. "Survival List," *Film Library Quarterly*, XII, Nos. 2/3 (1979), pp. 33-40.

_____. "Who are the Forces Behind the Legion of Decency Drive?", *Daily Worker*, August 17, 1934, p. 5.

_____. "Workers Study the Film," *New Theatre*, January 1934, pp. 14-15.

Brody, Samuel. "The Hunger March Film," *Daily Worker*, December 29, 1932, p. 4.

_____. "The Movies as a Weapon Against the Working Class," *Daily Worker*, May 20, 1930, p. 4.

_____. "The Revolutionary Film: Problem of Form," *New Theatre,* February 1934, pp. 21-22.

Callenbach, Ernest. "NATIVE LAND," *Film Quarterly,* XXVII, No. 1 (Fall 1973), pp. 60-62.

Campbell, Russell. " 'A Total and Realistic Experience': Interview with Leo Seltzer," *Jump Cut,* No. 14 (1977), pp. 25-27.

_____. "Film and Photo League: Radical Cinema in the 30s," *Jump Cut,* No. 14 (1977), pp. 23-25.

Fishbein, Leslie. "A Lost Legacy of Labor Films," *Film and History,* IX, No. 2 (May 1979), pp. 33-40.

Gerber, Judith. "Ralph Steiner. Enjoying the Interval," *Afterimage* (US), V, No. 9 (March 1978), pp. 18-21.

Gessner, Robert. "Movies About Us," *New Theatre,* June 1935, p. 20.

Hoberman, J. "Breadline Eyes: Radical Newsreels of the '30s," *The Village Voice,* October 30, 1978, p. 65.

Hogenkamp, Bert. "Film and the Workers' Movement in Britain, 1929-39," *Sight and Sound,* XLV, No. 2 (Spring 1976), pp. 68-76.

Hundley, Patrick. "PEOPLE OF THE CUMBERLAND: An Attempt at Synthetic Documentary," *Film and History,* VI (September 1976), pp. 56-62.

Hurwitz, Leo T. "Hisses, Boos, and Boycotts," *New Theatre,* July-August 1934, pp. 10-11.

_____. "One Man's Voyage: Ideas and Films in the 1930's," *Cinema Journal,* XV, No. 1 (Fall 1975), pp. 1-15.

_____. "Survey of Workers' Films: A Report to the National Film Conference," *New Theatre,* October 1934, pp. 27-28.

_____. "The Revolutionary Film—Next Step," *New Theatre,* May 1934, pp. 14-15.

Kennedy, Ed. "Three Workers' Films," *Filmfront,* I, No. 2 (January 7, 1935), pp. 10-11.

Klein, Michael. "NATIVE LAND: Praised Then Forgotten," *The Velvet Light Trap,* No. 14 (Winter 1975), pp. 12-16.

Klein, Michael and Jill. "NATIVE LAND: An Interview with Leo Hurwitz," *Cineaste,* VI, No. 3 (1974), pp. 3-7.

Kruse, William F. "Workers' Conquest of the Films," *Workers Monthly,* IV, No. 11 (September 1925), pp. 502-03, 525-26.

Ludlow, Ray. "PIE IN THE SKY," *New Theatre,* May 1935, pp. 19-20.

Maddow, Ben [as "David Wolff"]. "Film Into Poem," *New Theatre,* November 1936, pp. 23, 26.

Mitchell, Louise. " 'Broadcasting American' Returns with Spanish Film," *Daily Worker,* June 22, 1937, p. 7.

Münzenerg, Willi. "Capture the Film!", *Daily Worker,* July 23, 1925, p. 3.

Nichols, Bill. "The American Photo League," *Screen,* XXIII, No. 4 (Winter 1972-73), pp. 108-15.

Noble, Elizabeth. "HEART OF SPAIN," *New Masses,* October 5, 1937, p. 18.

Organization Committee for a National Film and Photo League. "A Film Call to Action," *Workers' Theatre,* July-August 1933, p. 9.

Platt, David. "Flashes and Close-Ups," *Daily Worker,* May 10, 1935, p. 5.

_____. "The Movie Front: National Film Conference," *New Theatre,* November 1934, p. 30.

Potamkin, Harry Alan. "Film and Photo Call to Action!", *Workers' Theatre,* July 1931, pp. 5-7.

_____. "Who Owns the Movie?", *Workers' Theatre,* February 1932, pp. 27-29, and April 1932, pp. 18-20.

_____. "Workers' Films," *Daily Worker,* May 31, 1930, p. 3.

Rosenzweig, Roy. "Working-Class Struggles in the Great Depression: The Film Record," *Film Library Quarterly,* XIII, No. 1 (1980), pp. 5-14.

Safford, Tony. "The Camera as a Weapon in the Class Struggle: Interview with Samuel Brody," *Jump Cut,* No. 14 (1977), pp. 28-30.

Seltzer, Leo. "Documenting the Depression of the 1930s: The Work of the Film and Photo League," *Film Library Quarterly,* XIII, No. 1 (1980), pp. 15-22.

Steiner, Ralph. "Revolutionary Movie Production," *New Theatre*, September 1934, pp. 22-23.
———, and Leo T. Hurwitz. "A New Approach to Film Making," *New Theatre*, September 1935, pp. 22-23.
S[tern], S[eymour]. "A Working-Class Cinema for America?", *The Left*, I, No. 1 (Spring 1931), pp. 69-73.
Strauss, Theodore. "Homesteading Our 'Native Land,' " *New York Times*, May 3, 1942, p. X3.
Sweet, Fred, Eugene Rosow, and Allan Francovich, "Pioneers: An Interview with Tom Brandon," *Film Quarterly*, XXVII, No. 1 (Fall 1973), pp. 12-24.
Thirer, Irene. "Paul Strand and Leo Hurwitz Offer Data on NATIVE LAND," *New York Post*, May 9, 1942, p. 13.
Tucker, Anne. "Photographic Crossroads: The Photo League," *Journal of the National Gallery of Canada*, No. 25 (April 6, 1978), pp. 1-8.
Vertov, Dziga. "Dziga Vertov on Kino-Eye, Lecture I," *Film Culture*, No. 25 (Summer 1962), pp. 58-60.
———. "Dziga Vertov on Kino-Eye, Lecture II," *Film Culture*, No. 25 (Summer 1962), pp. 60-65.
———. "Instructions provisoires aux cercles 'Ciné-oeil,' " *Cahiers du Cinéma*, No. 228 (March-April 1971), pp. 12-17.
Wegg-Prosser, Victoria. "The Archive of the Film and Photo League," *Sight and Sound*, XLVI, No. 4 (Autumn 1977), pp. 245-47.
Weinberg, Herman G. "NATIVE LAND—The Texture of America," *Documentary Film News*, II, No. 1 (April 1942), pp. 6-7.
Zavattini, Cesare. "Some Ideas on the Cinema," *Sight and Sound*, XXIII, No. 2 (October-December 1953), pp. 64-69.

Unpublished Dissertations and Theses

Horton, Aimee I. *The Highlander Folk School: A History of the Development of its Major Programs Related to Social Movements in the South, 1932-1961*. Unpublished Ph.D. dissertation, University of Chicago, 1971.
Petric, Vladimir. *Soviet Revolutionary Films in America (1926-1935)*. 2 vols. Unpublished Ph.D. dissertation, New York University, 1973.
Platkin, Richard H. *The American Documentary Film: Its Origin and Early Development*. Unpublished Senior history thesis, University of Michigan, 1968.

Index

Abbott, Berenice, 46, 333 n. 84
Acme Theatre, 43, 330 n. 47, 75, 76, 79
Adding Machine, The (Rice), 10
Adler, Nathan, 57
AFL (American Federation of Labor), 9, 327 n. 17, 73, 214, 284
ALBANY HUNGER MARCH, 40, 71-72
Amalgamated Clothing Workers of America (ACWA), 218, 224, 226, 228
Ambridge massacre, film of, 82, 113, 254
AMERICA (Griffith), 11
American Civil Liberties Union (ACLU), 54, 55, 83, 149, 239, 241-42
American Documentary Films, 158
American Federation of Labour. *See* AFL
American Friends of the Chinese People, 89-90
American League Against War and Fascism, 49, 50, 69, 87, 357 n. 59, 263
American Tragedy, An (Dreiser), 9
AMERICA TODAY: No. 1 [?], 78, 108; No. 2 [?], 76, 81-83, 98, 100-01, 102, 113, 166 n. 32; No. 3 [?], 83; montage in, 104, 276, 285
Amkino Corporation, 32
Anderson, Garland, 10
Anderson, Sherwood, 8
ANNIVERSARY OF THE REVOLUTION (Vertov), 15
Anschutz, Thomas P., 9, 10
Antheil, George, 88
Antoine, André, 7
Appearances (Anderson), 10
Arbeiter Illustrierte Zeitung, 24, 29
Asch, Nathan, 83
Ashcan School, 9-10
Associated Film Audiences, 69, 180
Association of Documentary Film Producers, 162
Assommoir, L' (Zola), 5, 6
Atlas Film Company, 37
Avseév, Ralph, 246

Bailen, Maurice, 333 n. 88, 333n. 89, 110. Films: THE GREAT DEPRESSION, 93, 98, 100, 103, 109, 110, 180; MEXICO MARCHES ON, 94; CHICAGO MAY DAY, 95, 98; PEACE PARADE AND WORKERS' PICNIC, 95, 98
Bain, Leslie, 88-89, 110
Bálazs, Béla, 23, 31, 47
Baldwin, Roger, 149, 162, 239
Ballam, John, 73
Balog, Lester, 54-55, 103; founder of Film and Photo League, 40, 41, 328 n. 34, 71
Balzac, Honoré de, 1-3
Barbusse, Henri, 85, 106, 107
Barnet, Boris, 31, 57
BAS-FONDS, LES. *See* LOWER DEPTHS, THE
Basshe, Em Jo, 10
BATTLESHIP POTEMKIN, THE. *See* POTEMKIN
Bauer, Catherine, 146
BED AND SOFA (Room), 52
BEGGAR ON HORSEBACK (Cruze), 55, 56
Bela, Nicholas, 42, 48, 329 n. 45
Belasco, David, 7, 10
Belt, The (Sifton), 10
Berman, Lionel, 124, 159, 160, 162, 348 n. 15; member of Frontier Films, 130, 147, 148, 153, 160, 165; describes White House screening, 162-63; and Communist Party, 350 n. 41, 352 n. 58; reports on PEOPLE OF THE CUMBERLAND screening, 220-21; and NATIVE LAND, 339, 246
Bernhard, Kurt, 31
Bête Humaine, La (Zola), 6
Bethune, Norman, 166-67, 174-75, 176, 181, 352 n. 4, 356 n. 49
BIRTH OF A NATION, THE (Griffith), 10-11, 33
BIRTH OF NEW CHINA, THE, 67, 89-91, 108, 109, 194, 198

BLACK FURY (Curtiz), 50, 222
BLACK LEGION (Nykino), 129, 135, 142-43, 346 n. 64, 230
BLACK LEGION (Mayo), 142-43
Black Pit (Maltz), 128, 271
BLACK SHIRTS (CAMICIE NERE), 50, 88
Blaine, Richard, 169, 186, 220
Blitzstein, Marc, 246, 252, 364 n. 25, 280
BLOCKADE (Dieterle), 171, 354 n. 24
BLOODY MEMORIAL DAY, 96
BLUE EXPRESS. *See* CHINA EXPRESS
BLUTMAI 1929 (Weltfilm), 32
Boehnel, William, 247, 269-70
BOMBING OF SHANGHAI (Universal), 198, 359 n. 11
BONUS MARCH, 75, 98, 108, 112, 113, 286; production of, 74-75; structure of, 100-01; montage in, 103-04, 105, 109, 276
BORINAGE (Ivens), 128
Bourke-White, Margaret, 46, 333 n. 84, 125, 220
Brandon, Thomas J., 333 n. 34, 329 n. 45, 333 n. 82, 79, 92, 99, 122; and WIR film department, 40; and Film and Photo League, 42-43, 62, 63, 66, 122-23; as film distributor, 45, 150, 348 n. 21; film critic for *Daily Worker,* 47; as lecturer, 48; describes Harry Alan Potamkin Film School, 50-51, 57-58; analyses Legion of Decency, 53-54; produces THE STRIKE AGAINST STARVATION, 72; shoots Scottsboro footage, 72, 75, 79; describes shooting of HUNGER 1932, 102
Bransten, Louise, 149, 348 n. 15
BREAKING CHAINS. *See* HIS CALL
Brecht, Bertolt, 26, 326 n. 82, 32, 136, 346 n. 50, 246; dramatic theory of, 14, 27, 181, 283
Brody, Samuel, 42, 45, 57, 59, 333 n. 82, 96; critical of DRIFTERS, 17-18; calls for workers' films, 35-36; founder of Film and Photo League, 40, 41, 42, 328 n. 34; film critic for *Daily Worker,* 47, 330 n. 56, 342 n. 2, 343 n. 3; film editor of *New Theatre,* 48; and action against fascist films, 51; attacks film censorship, 51; teaches at Harry Alan Potamkin Film School, 57; directs WASTE AND WANT, 57, 83; on *Filmfront* editorial board, 334 n. 102; cameraman on HUNGER 1932, 77-78; assistant on HARLEM SKETCHES, 67, 88-89; analyses Ambridge newsreel, 82; and Imperial Valley film dispute, 96; and Film and Photo League camerawork, 102; discovers Vertov's writings, 106; champions documentary aesthetic, 106, 107, 108, 115-16; translates Dovzhenko, 110; theoretical stance criticized by Hurwitz, 117-118;

opposes paid Film and Photo League production group, 122; criticizes attitude of Nykino group, 123
BROKEN CHAINS. *See* HIS CALL
BRONX MORNING, A (Leyda), 329 n. 42
Browder, Earl, 213, 232-33, 263, 264, 266; in ERNST THAELMANN: FIGHTER AGAINST FASCISM, 84-85; in THE VOICE OF PROGRESS, 143; as advocate of People's Front, 191, 237
Browning, Irving, 86, 91, 107
Bullard, Arthur, 9
Burial at Ornans, A (Courbet), 3
By Bread Alone (Friedman), 9

CABINET OF DR. CALIGARI, THE (Wiene), 56
CAFE UNIVERSAL (Steiner), 118, 126
Caldwell, Erskine, 46, 154, 220
CALIFORNIA 1934, 96-97
Callenbach, Ernest, 269, 273
CALL TO ARMS. *See* TOGETHER WE LIVE
CAMICIE NERE. *See* BLACK SHIRTS
CANNON FODDER, 97
CANNONS OR TRACTORS (TODAY, Shub), 21, 44, 52, 109, 341 n. 105
Cartier, Henri. *See* Cartier-Bresson, Henri
Cartier-Bresson, Henri, 345 n. 37, 124, 130; and RETURN TO LIFE, 159, 169, 182, 186-87, 192, 357 n. 55
Caspary, Vera, 153, 349 n. 28
Censorship of films, 35, 51-55, 168-69, 170, 248, 365 n. 31
Centuries, The (Basshe), 10
Cézanne, Paul, 27
Chambers, Whittaker, 46, 73
CHANG (Cooper/Schoedsack), 13
CHAPAYEV (Vasiliev/Vasiliev), 260-61
Chekhov, Anton, 7
Chiang Kai-shek, 193, 194, 196, 197, 210, 211; in THE BIRTH OF NEW CHINA, 90; in CHINA STRIKES BACK, 201, 204, 205, 206-07, 208, 211
Chicago Film and Photo League, 60, 63, 68, 77; organization of, 61, 333 n. 89; productions of, 93-95, 111-12. *See also* Film and Photo League, The
CHICAGO MAY DAY, 95, 98
CHILD MISERY. *See* MISERY AMONG WORKING-CLASS CHILDREN
CHINA EXPRESS (Trauberg), 52, 198
CHINA FIGHTS ON (Karmen), 199
CHINA IN BATTLE (Karmen), 199
CHINA STRIKES BACK, 90, 195, 198-99; stock shots used in, 334 n. 108, 358 n. 4; revenue from, 150-51, 358 n. 6; screenings

of, 162-63, 195, 358 n. 6, 220; cost of, 163, 352 n. 55; production of, 193-95; structure of, 199-206, 229; political stance of, 205-09, 210-11, 270, 283, 285; editing of, 209-10, 359 n. 19

CIGARETTE, 83

CIO (Congress of Industrial Organizations), 238, 284

CITY, THE (Steiner/Van Dyke), 158-59, 273

CITY OF CONTRASTS, THE (Browning), 86, 337 n. 43

CITY SYMPHONY, A (Weinberg), 86, 337 n. 43

Clair, René, 55

Clurman, Harold, 67, 126, 132, 152; and Frontier Films, 146, 162, 347 n. 3

Clyde, Ethel, 148, 153, 161; and PEOPLE OF THE CUMBERLAND, 154, 215, 221, 361 n. 14

COAL STRIKE, 1931. *See* STRIKE AGAINST STARVATION, THE

Cocteau, Jean, 209

Cohen, Lester, 46

COMMUNIST CONVENTION IN CHICAGO, 93

Communist International (Comintern), 29, 342 n. 113, 191, 355 n. 28, 237

Communist Party of Germany. *See* KPD

Communist Party of the Soviet Union, 31, 66

Communist Party, USA, 9, 39, 327 n. 15, 85, 343 n. 7, 352 n. 58; and WIR, 62-63, 330 n. 50; and Film and Photo League, 75, 93, 104, 111-12, 113, 277; and THE WORLD TODAY, 141, 143; and Frontier Films, 156-57, 349 n. 38, 350 n. 41, 350 n. 42; and NATIVE LAND, 164, 248; and HEART OF SPAIN, 191; and RETURN TO LIFE, 191; sends Bethune to China, 352 n. 4; and Lincoln Battalion, 354 n. 22; and Highlander Folk School, 214, 360 n. 4; supports Roosevelt government, 284, and union movement, 285-86. *See also* People's Front

Comrade Yetta (Bullard), 10

Consumers Union, 91, 338 n. 59

Contemporary Films, 68, 92

CONTRAST, THE (Hedlund), 34, 327 n. 17

Conway, Bert, 261, 364 n. 23

COTTON-PICKERS' STRIKE, 55, 96

COUNTERPLAN. *See* SHAME

Courbet, Gustave, 3-4, 7

Cowley, Malcolm, 146-47, 148

CRADLE SONG (Leisen), 51

Cradle Will Rock, The (Blitzstein), 246, 364 n. 25

Crane, Stephen, 8

Crawford, Cheryl, 126

Crawford, Merritt, 67

Crichton, Kyle, 125, 148

CRIME AGAINST MADRID (Progressive Film Institute), 172

CRIMINAL SYNDICALIST LAW ON TRIAL, 93-94

Crowther, Bosley, 246, 261, 266

CRY OF THE WORLD (de Rochemont), 341 n. 105

Dadaists (Berlin), 23-24

Daily Worker, 47, 81, 222, 264

Da Silva, Howard, 261, 364 n. 23

DEATH FOLLOWS THE RISING SUN. *See* STOP JAPAN

DEATH OF A WORKER'S CHILD. See UNEMPLOYMENT COUNCIL

DEFENSE OF MADRID, THE, 172-73

Degas, Edgar, 3, 4-5, 10

Del Duca, Robert, 40, 41, 65, 86, 278; and Contemporary Films, 68; and GETTING YOUR MONEY'S WORTH, 91

de Rochemont, Louis, 341 n. 105, 346 n. 56, 282. *See also* MARCH OF TIME, THE

DESERTER (Pudovkin), 31

Detroit Film and Photo League, 60, 61, 63, 92-93. *See also* Film and Photo League, The

DETROIT FORD MASSACRE. *See* FORD MASSACRE, THE

Dombrowski, James, 214-15, 219, 228

Dos Passos, John, 10, 99, 345 n. 41, 148, 151, 351 n. 50

Dovzhenko, Alexander, 57, 110, 111, 127

Dreiser, Theodore, 8, 9

DRIFTERS (Grierson), 17-18

DR. MABUSE DER SPIELER (Lang), 20

Dunham, Harry, 202, 358 n. 3; films in China, 154, 193-94; footage used in CHINA STRIKES BACK, 199, 201, 203, 207

Dunn, Robert W., 46, 73

Durieux, Tilla, 26

EARTH (SOIL, Dovzhenko), 110

EARTH (Prokino), 37

EAST SIDE, WEST SIDE, 85, 86

"Eight," The, 10

Eisenstein, Sergei, 13, 23, 57, 87, 133; and mass hero, 16, 261; concept of montage of, 18-20, 21, 25, 27, 108, 183, 356 n. 44; and Paul Strand, 126-27; and "dialectical" film form, 355 n. 33. Films: STRIKE, 19, 111; POTEMKIN, 21, 32, 45, 52; OCTOBER, 19-20, 21, 42, 119, 119; OLD AND NEW, 27, 110

Eisler, Hanns, 160

Ekk, Nikolai, 31, 127

ELEVENTH YEAR, THE (Vertov), 15
Ellis, Peter. See Lerner, Irving
END OF ST. PETERSBURG, THE
    (Pudovkin), 19, 31, 117, 119
Engels, Friedrich, 1-3, 5, 8, 9, 21, 321 n. 4, 110
Epstein, Jean, 55, 56
ERNST THAELMANN: FIGHTER
    AGAINST FASCISM, 84-85
ERNST THAELMANN: FIGHTER FOR
    FREEDOM. See ERNST THAELMANN:
    FIGHTER AGAINST FASCISM
Evans, Robert. See Freeman, Joseph
Evans, Walker, 124, 351 n. 49, 224, 362 n. 34
Experimental Cinema, 329 n. 42, 87-88, 95-96
Expressionism in theatre, 10, 27

FALL OF THE ROMANOV DYNASTY,
    THE (Shub), 21
Fang Chen-wu, 90
Faragoh, Francis Edwards, 10
Federation of Workers' Film Societies, 37
Field, William Osgood, Jr., 148, 149, 160, 162
FIFTH YEAR, THE (Friends of Soviet
    Russia), 32
FIGHT FOR THE BONUS, THE. See
    BONUS MARCH
Film and Photo League, The (known as
    Workers' Film and Photo League, 1930-
    33), 1, 35, 329 n. 40, 341 n. 109, 138;
    organization of 321 n. 1, 29, 40-45;
    founding of, 39-40; production by, in New
    York, 43, 71-92; financing of, 40-41, 94;
    membership of, 41; committee of, 43; film
    distribution and exhibition by, 43-45;
    program of, 45; still photography activities
    of, 46, 58-61, 68, 94; National Advisory
    Board (National Committee) of, 46, 52, 54,
    62, 63, 73-74; international ties of, 47;
    campaigns against reactionary films
    conducted by, 47-55, 64, 331 n. 58;
    publications of, 48, 64, 66, 334 n. 102;
    lectures and discussions sponsored by, 48;
    drive against film censorship by, 51-55; film
    series screenings held by, 55-56; training
    activities of, 56-58, 64; local chapters of, 60-
    61, national coordination of, 61-64;
    National Film Conference of, 62-64, 107,
    120, 122; National Film Exchange of, 64,
    66; reorganization of, in New York, 64-67,
    85; suspension of operations of, 67-70;
    commitment to documentary aesthetic in,
    105-11, 115-17, 130; ideology of films by,
    111-13; mixed documentary-dramatic
    forms proposed for, 117-18, 120-22; split of
    Nykino group from, 122-24; achievements
    of, 275-76; weaknesses of, 277-78. See also
    Chicago Film and Photo League; Detroit

Film and Photo League; Los Angeles Film
    and Photo League; National Film and
    Photo League; San Francisco Film and
    Photo League
Film Forum, 332 n. 73
Filmfront, 48, 66, 330 n. 56, 334 n. 102
Flaherty, Robert, 13, 16
Ford, James W., 76, 89, 93
FORD MASSACRE, THE, 98, 99, 101, 112,
    113; production of, 92
FOR THE RECORD (Roffman), 113
41ST, THE (Protazanov), 44
FORWARD! (Karmen), 172
FORWARD, SOVIET! (Vertov), 15, 22
Foster, William Z., 39, 72, 76, 93, 248, 263
FOSTER AND FORD IN ACTION, 75
400 MILLION, THE (Ivens), 90, 199, 210
FRAGMENT OF AN EMPIRE (Ermler), 45
Franco, General Francisco, 173, 174, 188;
    support for, in US, 354 n. 22; and HEART
    OF SPAIN, 187, 192; and RETURN TO
    LIFE, 170, 185, 186, 187, 188, 357 n. 60
Freeman, Joseph [pseud. Robert Evans], 46,
    55, 57, 333 n. 84, 73
FREE THAELMANN (Montagu), 85
Friedman, Isaac Kahn, 9
Friends of Soviet Russia, 32
Friends of Soviet Russia and Workers'
    Germany, 32
Friends of the Soviet Union, 32, 111
Frietag, John, 333 n. 89
FROM DEATH TO LIFE, JEWISH LIFE IN
    SOVIET RUSSIA (Broms), 48
Frontier Films, 143, 347n. 1; staff of, 130, 147,
    161; founding of, 145; aims of, 145-47, 150,
    161; structure of, 147-48; financing of, 148-
    51, 162-63, 348 n. 15; Advisory Board of,
    148, 161-62; distribution of films by, 150-
    51; film projects of, 151-56, 159-61, 162;
    resignation of Van Dyke and Steiner from,
    156-59; and Communist Party, 156-58, 349
    n. 38, 350 n. 41, 350 n. 42; disbanding of,
    164; achievements of, 279-80; weaknesses
    of, 281-83. See also CHINA STRIKES
    BACK; HEART OF SPAIN; HISTORY
    AND ROMANCE OF
    TRANSPORTATION; NATIVE LAND;
    PEOPLE OF THE CUMBERLAND;
    RETURN TO LIFE; UNITED ACTION;
    WHITE FLOOD
FUNERAL OF YAMAMOTO, THE
    (Prokino), 37
FURY OVER SPAIN (Modern Film Corp.),
    172, 173, 191

GABRIEL OVER THE WHITE HOUSE (La
    Cava), 48

Garrison Film Distributors, 85, 199, 277;
  founding of, 45, 330 n. 50; Frontier films
  distributed by, 150-51, 348 n. 21, 170, 195,
  221, 280
GASTONIA. *See* VOLGA TO GASTONIA
Gellert, Hugo, 46, 73
GENERAL DIED AT DAWN, THE
  (Milestone), 197
GENERAL LINE, THE. *See* OLD AND NEW
George, Mary, 261
Germinal (Zola), 6
Gessner, Robert, 67, 331 n. 57; and Film and
  Photo League, 46, 48; reviews Film and
  Photo League productions, 81, 86, 87-88,
  104-05
GETTING YOUR MONEY'S WORTH, 68,
  69, 91, 109, 338 n. 62; reviewed by David
  Platt, 334 n. 108, 91-92
GIRL WITH THE HATBOX (Barnet), 31
GIVE US THIS DAY, 89
Glackens, William, 10
Godard, Jean-Luc, 280
Goering the Executioner (Heartfield), 25
Gold, Michael, 10, 65, 83
Gorin, Jean-Pierre, 280
Gordon, Michael, 157, 350 n. 40, 350 n. 41;
  directs SUNNYSIDE, 129, 139-42, directs
  BLACK LEGION, 129, 143; and NATIVE
  LAND, 130, 155-56, 239
Gorelik, Mordecai, 7
Gorky, Maxim, 7, 272
GOSKINO-KALENDAR (Vertov), 15
Graham, Barney, 214, 217-18, 230
GRANITE (Steiner), 125
GRASS (Cooper/Schoedsack), 13
GREAT CONSOLER, THE (Kuleshov), 31
GREAT DEPRESSION, THE, 93, 98, 103,
  109; dramatization in, 100, 110, 180
GREAT ROAD, THE (Shub), 20
GREED (Stroheim), 11
Green, Paul, 10
Grierson, John, 15-19
Griffith, D.W., 10
Grosz, George, 24, 25, 29, 126
Group Theatre, 126, 128, 137; and Nykino, 124,
  132, 134; and Frontier Films, 145, 152, 261
Guy, James, 65, 84, 86-87, 278

H2O (Steiner), 329 n. 42
Hague, Frank, 240
HALSTED STREET, 93, 98, 99-100, 103, 339
  n. 68
Hammett, Dashiell, 154, 349 n. 31
HANDS (Steiner/Van Dyke), 127, 344 n. 32
HANDS OFF ETHIOPIA, 88, 108
Hanney, James, 245
HANS WEIDEMANN PROTEST, 78, 81, 98,

113, 245, 254
HARBOR. *See* HARBOR SCENES
Harbor, The (Poole), 9
HARBOR SCENES (Steiner), 125-26
HARLEM SKETCHES, 67, 88-89, 109, 276
Harry Alan Potamkin Film School, 56-58, 88,
  116
Hathaway, Clarence, 81
Hauptmann, Gerhart, 7
Hausmann, Raoul, 24
Hays, Will H., 51, 52, 53
Hearst, William Randolph, 197, 264, 266
Heartfield, John, 24-25, 325 n. 72, 325 n. 74,
  326 n. 82
HEART OF SPAIN, 163; revenue from,
  150-51, 348 n. 21; screenings of, 153, 162,
  168-69, 173, 352 n. 4, 220, 280; production
  of, 154, 165-68; structure of, 174-76, 177-81,
  204, 207, 229; dramatization in, 180-81,
  231; editing of, 182-84; narration of, 184-
  88, 356 n. 49; ideology of, 187-92, 207, 270,
  283, 285
Hedlund, Guy, 34
Hellman, Lillian, 148, 151, 154, 163, 349 n. 31,
  355 n. 32, 357 n. 53
HELL RAINS ON SPAIN, 172
Hemingway, Ernest, 171, 186, 191, 192, 357 n.
  53
Henniquc, Léon, 7
Henri, Robert, 10
Highlander Folk School, 360 n. 2, 360 n. 4; and
  PEOPLE OF THE CUMBERLAND, 151,
  154, 213-21, 225, 227, 228
Hill, Eugene. *See* Leyda, Jay
Hine, Lewis W., 12-13, 226
HIS CALL (BREAKING CHAINS,
  Protazanov), 31, 327 n. 11
HISTORY AND ROMANCE OF
  TRANSPORTATION, 151, 159
HISTORY OF THE CIVIL WAR (Vertov), 15
Hitler, Adolf, 47, 83; and AMERICA TODAY,
  104, 285; and HEART OF SPAIN, 169,
  187; and RETURN TO LIFE, 187; and
  NATIVE LAND, 258, 273
Höch, Hannah, 24
HOLLYWOOD, 86, 110, 338 n. 46
Hoppla! Wir Leben (Toller), 25
Horton, Myles, 213-15, 217-18, 219, 225
Horton, Zilphia, 214, 216, 218
Howard, Sidney, 40, 42-43, 46, 329 n. 39, 332 n.
  73, 96
H.R. 2827, 85-86
Huberman, Leo, 238, 363 n. 4
Hudyma, Joseph, 72, 92
Huelsenbeck, Richard, 24
Hughes, Langston, 46
100,000 UNTER ROTEN FAHNEN

(Weltfilm), 32
HUNGER IN WALDENBURG (Jutzi), 31
HUNGER MARCH 1931. *See* NATIONAL
   HUNGER MARCH
HUNGER 1931. *See* NATIONAL HUNGER
   MARCH
HUNGER 1932, 98, 107-08, 111, 112-13, 276,
   285; production of, 41, 61, 77-78, 102;
   montage in, 101, 104-05, 183, 276;
   distribution of, 336 n. 20, 277
Hurwitz, Leo T., 329 n. 42, 79, 345 n. 41, 162;
   member of Film and Photo League, 41-43,
   101-02, 276, 277; film and photography
   critic, 47, 161, 351 n. 49; film editor of *New
   Theatre*, 48, 120, 124; reports on S.A.
   MANN BRAND campaign, 49-50; teaches
   at Harry Alan Potamkin Film School, 57,
   116; founder of Nykino, 65, 122-24, 129;
   makes THE SCOTTSBORO BOYS, 79-80;
   makes SWEET LAND OF LIBERTY, 83,
   110; discusses montage, 105, 108-09, 117-
   18; discusses newsreel production, 106-07;
   forms animated film group, 339 n. 63;
   theorist of radical film, 117-18, 120-22, 130-
   31, 132-34, 343 n. 7, 229-31; proposes
   filmmaking "shock troupe," 121-23, 277;
   attends Strasberg classes, 124, 132; in
   Nykino photography workshop, 125; edits
   Steiner films, 125-26; collaborates on Odets
   script, 126; works on THE PLOW THAT
   BROKE THE PLAINS, 127, 182; founder
   of Frontier Films, 130, 145, 148, 153; and
   THE WORLD TODAY, 138, 143-44;
   meets Strand, 344 n. 22; and Frontier Films
   financing, 149-50; and film distribution,
   151, 163-64; edits HEART OF SPAIN,
   154, 168, 177-82, 184-85, 186, 192; calls for
   halt on NATIVE LAND production, 155,
   240; and departure of Van Dyke and
   Steiner, 156-58; and Communist Party,
   157, 350 n. 41; co-directs NATIVE LAND
   159, 162, 240-47, 258-62, 267-69, 271-72,
   364 n. 24; and THE RIVER, 347 n. 9; and
   John Howard Lawson, 350 n. 42; and THE
   CITY, 350 n. 45; gives classes in
   photography, 351 n. 49; subsequent career
   of, 352 n. 58; and CHINA STRIKES
   BACK, 205-06, 211, 359 n. 19; and
   PEOPLE OF THE CUMBERLAND, 219-
   20; blacklisted, 366 n. 60; mounts Roosevelt
   tribute, 367 n. 9

IAH (Internationale Arbeiterhilfe), 29-32, 37,
   47, 66
Ibsen, Henrik, 7
ILD (International Labor Defense), 36, 66, 94,
   341 n. 105; and Labor Defender Photo

Group, 38-39, and film censorship, 52, 55;
   and Film and Photo League, 55, 58, 61,
   111; and THE SCOTTSBORO BOYS, 79;
   and SWEET LAND OF LIBERTY, 83
IMPERIAL VALLEY (1932), 95, 108, 111, 276
IMPERIAL VALLEY (1936), 96
In Abraham's Bosom (Green), 10
IN CHINA (Karmen), 199
IN OLD SIBERIA (? KATORGA, Raizman),
   39
Internationale Arbeiterhilfe. *See* IAH
International Labor Defense. *See* ILD
International Workers' Aid, 32, 35, 327 n. 18
International Workers' Order. *See* IWO
International Red Aid, 66
International Union of Revolutionary Theatre,
   47, 62
International Workers' Theatre Olympiad, 47
Iron Workers' Noon-Day Rest (Anschutz), 9
Ivens, Joris, 37, 146, 162, 173; re-edits
   newsreels, 23, 325 n. 67; visits USSR, 31;
   visits USA, 67, 128; and Frontier Films,
   147; and HEART OF SPAIN, 166, 167.
   Films: BORINAGE, 128; NEW EARTH,
   128; THE 400 MILLION, 90, 199, 210. *See
   also* SPANISH EARTH, THE
IWO (International Workers' Order), 334 n.
   104, 87-88, 111
I.W.O., 87-88
IWW (Industrial Workers of the World), 9

Jackson, Gardner ("Pat"), 146, 162, 163, 348 n.
   15, 351 n. 53, 237
Jacobs, Lewis, 325 n. 72, 41, 329 n. 42, 341 n.
   105; teaches at Harry Alan Potamkin Film
   School, 57; shoots footage for THE
   STRIKE AGAINST STARVATION, 72;
   shoots Scottsboro footage, 72, 75, 79
Jacobsen, Jacques, 100
Jacobson, George, 153, 348 n. 19, 281; and
   NATIVE LAND, 155, 239, 244-45, 254,
   269, 364 n. 24
Jacques Damour (Hennique), 7
Japanese Workers' Camera League. *See*
   Workers' Camera League
JENSEITS DER STRASSE (Mittler), 31
JIMMIE HIGGINS, 44
John Reed Clubs, 36, 37, 330 n. 51, 123; and
   Film and Photo League, 46, 61, 64, 84, 93
Jungle, The (Sinclair), 9
Jutzi, Piel, 31

Kallet, Arthur, 91, 338 n. 59
Kandel, Vic, 65, 68, 86, 91
Karmen, Roman, 167, 172, 195, 199
Karpathi, Geza, 166-67, 181, 182, 192, 356 n.
   41

Kaufman, Mikhail, 57
Kazan, Elia, 126, 147-48, 157; and PIE IN THE SKY, 118, 135-36; and PEOPLE OF THE CUMBERLAND, 130, 147, 154, 214-17, 219, 220, 360 n. 8; and Communist Party, 350 n. 39, 350 n. 41
Kennedy, Ed., 80, 111
KENTUCKY-TENNESSEE 1932, 75
Kern, Edward, 65, 67, 80, 85, 87, 336 n. 27
Kino-Eye, theory of, 13-15, 106
KINO-GLAZ (Vertov), 15
KINONEDIELIA (Vertov), 15
KINO-PRAVDA (Vertov), 15
Kline, Herbert, 162, 350 n. 41, 351 n. 49, 352 n. 2, 353 n. 19; and HEART OF SPAIN, 154, 165-68, 180-81, 184, 191-92, 356 n. 41, 356 n. 49; and RETURN TO LIFE, 159, 169, 191-92, 353 n. 17
Klutsis, Gustav, 25
Koecklin, Charles, 169
Koolish, Elman, 135-36
Korvin, Charles. *See* Karpathi, Geza
Koster, Gordon, 333 n. 89
KPD (German Communist Party), 24, 26, 32, 85
Kruck, William, 333 n. 89, 93
Kruse, William F., 32-34, 51
KUHLE WAMPE (Dudow), 326 n. 82, 31, 327 n. 7
Kuleshov, Lev, 18, 31, 110, 356 n. 46; and nonprofessional actors, 16; and "creative geography," 23, 183, 356 n. 46
Kunitz, Joshua, 55, 57

Labor Defender, 38
Labor Defender Photo Group, 38-39, 341 n. 105
Labor Film Service, 34
La Follette, Robert M., 238
La Follette Civil Liberties Committee, 149, 152, 241, 259, 365 n. 35; formation of, 149, 241, 255-56; investigates anti-union activity, 238-39, 242, 252, 256, 257, 265
Lamont, Corliss, 149, 348 n. 15
LAND OF THE FREE, THE, 339 n. 63
Lang, Fritz, 20, 55
Lange, Dorothea, 345 n. 38, 224
Lassie, Fred, 95
LAST MOMENT, THE (Fejos), 55
LAST TRAIN FROM MADRID, THE (Hogan), 171, 354 n. 24
Lawson, John Howard, 10, 67, 153, 171; and Frontier Films, 148, 151, 157, 350 n. 42
Leacock, Richard, 246, 364 n. 24, 282
League of American Writers, 123, 157
League of Workers' Theatres, 54, 65
LEATHERNECKS HAVE LANDED, THE,

91, 196, 197
Legion of Decency, 53, 54, 62
LEIPZIG UNTER ROTEN FAHNEN (Weltfilm), 32
Lemare, Jacques, 159, 169
Lenin, Vladimir Ilyich, 3, 26, 31, 82
Lerner, Irving [pseud. Peter Ellis], 55-56, 329 n. 42, 333 n. 84, 109, 138, 162; member of Film and Photo League, 41, 62; film critic, 47, 161, 351 n. 49; film editor of *New Theatre,* 48; edits *The Eyes of the Movie,* 48; teacher at Harry Alan Potamkin Film School, 57; founder of Nykino, 65, 122-23, 343 n. 15; works on PIE IN THE SKY, 118; in Nykino photography workshop, 125; describes Ivens visit, 128-29; member of Frontier Films, 130, 148; works on SUNNYSIDE, 141; edits CHINA STRIKES BACK, 154, 194; leaves Frontier Films, 161; and Communist Party, 350 n. 41; subsequent career of, 352 n. 58; comments on film narration, 356 n. 49. Film reviews: SHERIFFED 84; THE MARCH OF TIME, 138-39; THE WORLD TODAY, 143, 144; THE LAST TRAIN FROM MADRID, 171; BLOCKADE, 171; SHANGHAI MADNESS, 196-97; THE PLOW THAT BROKE THE PLAINS, 222-23; THE RIVER, 222
Lesser, Sol, 48
Lester, Howard D., 56
Levin, Meyer, 91
Lewis, Sinclair, 10
Leyda, Jay [pseud. Eugene Hill], 326 n. 3, 329 n. 42, 157, 350 n. 41, 351 n. 49, 202; describes Shub's technique, 20-21; member of Film and Photo League, 41; joins Nykino, 130; member of Frontier Films, 130, 147, 161; edits CHINA STRIKES BACK, 154, 194, 195; co-directs PEOPLE OF THE CUMBERLAND, 154, 219, 220; as critic, 161, 351 n. 49; in Association of Documentary Film Producers, 162; subsequent career of, 352 n. 58; works on HEART OF SPAIN, 168
Lissitsky, El, 25
Lister, Enrique, 175, 185, 191, 356 n. 49, 357 n. 61
LIVES WASTED, 97
LIVING CORPSE, THE (Otsep), 31
LIVING WAGE OR DEATH, 97, 110
London, Jack, 12
Lorentz, Pare: and THE PLOW THAT BROKE THE PLAINS, 127, 128, 347 n. 9, 178, 182, 222-23; and THE RIVER, 347 n. 9, 184, 222-23

Los Angeles Film and Photo League, 61, 63, 95-97. *See also* Film and Photo League, The
LOVE UNDER FIRE (Marshall), 354 n. 24
Lower Depths, The (Gorky), 7
LOWER DEPTHS, THE (Renoir), 168
Ludlow, Ray, 135, 136-38, 139
Lukács, Georg, 27, 322 n. 14
Luks, George, 10

McConnell, Bishop Francis J., 162, 353 n. 12, 263
McTeague (Norris), 8, 11
Maddow, Ben [pseud. David Wolff], 161, 165, 174, 245, 261, 268; joins Nykino, 124; writes HARBOR SCENES commentary, 125-26; member of Frontier Films, 130, 147, 153, 160; writes SUNNYSIDE commentary, 141; writes HEART OF SPAIN commentary, 154, 166, 169, 184-87, 191, 192; edits CHINA STRIKES BACK, 154, 194, 209-10; writes NATIVE LAND script, 155, 239, 240, 242-43, 270-71; writes RETURN TO LIFE commentary, 159, 184-87, 191; works on UNITED ACTION, 159, 350 n. 47; works on WHITE FLOOD, 160; as critic, 161, 351 n. 49; in Association of Documentary Film Producers, 162; and Communist Party, 350 n. 41, 366 n. 60; subsequent career of, 352 n. 58; on dialectical structure, 180; on film poetry, 355 n. 40; writes CHINA STRIKES BACK commentary, 195, 202, 209; assists with PEOPLE OF THE CUMBERLAND commentary, 220; writes NATIVE LAND commentary, 246
MADRID DOCUMENT, 172, 173
Malden, Karl, 254
Maltz, Albert, 67, 148, 151, 349 n. 38, 222, 366 n. 60; and *Black Pit,* 271-72
Manet, Edouard, 3, 10
MAN FROM OREGON, THE, 11
MANHATTA (Strand), 124
MAN WITH THE MOVIE CAMERA, THE (Vertov), 15, 117
Mao Tse-tung, 193, 205, 208, 248, 285; in CHINA STRIKES BACK, 199, 201-02, 203-04, 207, 211
Marching Song (Lawson), 153
MARCH OF TIME, THE (de Rochemont), 91, 152, 184, 199-200, 230; as model for THE WORLD TODAY, 129, 138-39, 200; political slant of, 139, 214 n. 56; China featured in, 198, 205
MARINE, 43, 80-81, 109, 111, 336 n. 27, 275, 276
MARINE STRIKE. *See* MARINE

MARINE WORKERS. *See* MARINE
Marshall, Elizabeth, 149, 348 n. 15
Marshall, Robert, 348 n. 15
Martini, Michael, 159
Marx, Karl, 1, 321 n. 4, 180, 355 n. 37
Marxism, 286; and art, 1, 2, 27-28, 322 n. 14; and film, 16, 108-09, 178-80, 205, 242-43
Masek, John, 333 n. 89
MAY DAY CELEBRATION, 78
MAY DAY DEMONSTRATION (1932), 75
MAY DAY DEMONSTRATION (1933). *See* MAY DAY CELEBRATION
MAY DAY IN NEW YORK, 73
MAY DAY 1933. *See* MAY DAY CELEBRATION
MAY DAY 1934, 81
MAY DAY 1935, 88
MAY DAY SCENES, 75
MECHANICAL PRINCIPLES (Steiner), 329 n. 42
MEXICO MARCHES ON, 94
Meyers, Sidney [pseud. Robert Stebbins], 50, 162, 350 n. 41, 351 n. 49; founder of Nykino, 124; in Nykino photography workshop, 125; member of Frontier Films, 130, 147, 160, 161; reviews THE WAVE, 131; reviews THE MARCH OF TIME, 139; works on SUNNYSIDE, 141; edits CHINA STRIKES BACK, 154, 194, 199, 359 n. 19; co-directs PEOPLE OF THE CUMBERLAND, 154, 219-20; works on WHITE FLOOD, 160; as critic, 161, 351 n. 49; subsequent career of, 352 n. 58; edits NATIVE LAND, 246
Mezhrabpomfilm, 30-31
Mezhrabpom-Russ, 30
Milch, Julia, 246, 364 n. 24
MILLIONS OF US (American Labor Films), 143
MISERY AMONG WORKING-CLASS CHILDREN, 79, 83
Mishkin, 333 n. 89
Mittler, Leo, 31
MOANA (Flaherty), 13
Montage, concept of, 17-28, 107-10, 356 n. 44
Montagu, Ivor, 85, 169
Mooney, Tom, 163, 351 n. 54; in Film and Photo League productions, 75, 78, 95, 97, 98, 111
Moscow Art Theatre, 7, 20, 326 n. 3, 137
MOSCOW IN OCTOBER (Barnet), 31
Mother (Gorky), 272
MOTHER (Pudovkin), 19, 31, 42, 44, 45
MOUNTAIN JUSTICE (Curtiz), 222
Moussinac, Leon, 47, 116
Münzenberg, Willi, 29-31, 37, 66
Mussolini, Benito: in Film and Photo League

productions, 83, 88, 104, 285; and HEART
OF SPAIN, 169, 187
MUTTER KRAUSENS FAHRT INS
GLUCK (Jutzi), 31

Nach Zehn Jahren (Heartfield), 24
NANOOK OF THE NORTH (Flaherty), 13
National Film and Photo League, 321 n. 1,
63-64, 66-67. *See also* Film and Photo
League, The
NATIONAL HUNGER MARCH, 98, 99, 113,
340 n. 84, 285; production of, 72-73
National Miners' Union (NMU), 72, 75
NATIVE LAND, 357 n. 55, 237-39; Hans
Weidemann footage incorporated in, 113,
245, 254; financing of, 149-50, 163, 164, 351
n. 52, 240-41; subject of, 152, 238-39, 242;
scripting of, 153, 154-55, 239, 242-43;
production of, 154-55, 159, 162, 349 n. 36,
239-47; cost of, 163, 352 n. 55; release of,
164, 246-48; dramatization in, 181-82, 231,
259-61, 280, 282; and People's Front, 237,
264-69, 270, 271-73; musical score of, 246,
251-52, 253, 257, 280; censorship of, 248,
365 n. 31; structure of, 249-59, 261-62;
ideology of, 262-73, 283, 284-85
Naturalism, 4-7, 322 n. 14, 110
Naumburg, Nancy, 65, 84, 86-87, 278
Nelson, C.O., 62, 333 n. 89, 93
New Dance League, 58
NEW DISCIPLE, THE (Sellers), 105
NEW EARTH (Ivens), 128
New Film Alliance, 67, 68-69, 85, 127-28
NEW LEGION, THE (Browning), 107
New Masses, 38, 39, 46
New Playwrights' Theatre, 10
NEWS FROM SPAIN (Progressive Film
Institute), 172
Newsreels, commercial, re-editing of, 23, 324n.
67, 34, 81-82, 83, 109
New Theatre, 48, 50, 66, 222
New Theatre League, 55, 58, 158
NEW WORLD, THE, 73
NEW WORLD IN RECONSTRUCTION, A
(? PLAN VELIKIKH RABOT, Room), 44
New York Film and Photo League, 71-92, 339
n. 63. *See also* Film and Photo League, The
NEW YORK'S HOOVERVILLES, 77
Niebuhr, Reinhold, 213-14
1934, 85
Nine-Tenths, The (Oppenheim), 9
Nippon Camera Club. *See* Workers' Camera
League
Noble, Elizabeth, 179-80, 182, 183, 189, 355 n.
38
NO GREATER GLORY (Borzage), 49, 64
Norris, Frank, 4, 8

North, Alex, 168, 194, 220
North, Joseph, 46, 73
Nugent, Frank S., 185-86, 187
Nykino, 92, 87, 156; formation of, 64-65,
122-25; structure of, 124-25; still
photography workshop of, 125; film
projects of, 125-26, 127-29, 134-43; film
aesthetics of, 130-34; strengths of, 278-79;
limitations of, 279-80

OCTOBER (TEN DAYS THAT SHOOK
THE WORLD, Eisenstein), 19, 21, 42, 117,
120
Odets, Clifford, 67, 81, 126, 148, 151, 197
OIL FOR THE LAMPS OF CHINA (LeRoy),
196, 197, 359 n. 14
OLD AND NEW (THE GENERAL LINE,
Eisenstein), 27, 110
OLD IRONSIDES (Cruze), 11
ONE SIXTH OF THE WORLD (Vertov), 15
ON THE RED FRONT (Kuleshov), 110
Ophuls, Max, 167
Oppenheim, James, 9
O'Shaughnessy, John, 168, 186, 195
Otsep, Fyodor, 31

Pabst, G.W., 55, 67, 167
PASSAIC TEXTILE STRIKE, THE
(Russack), 13, 34-35
PEACE PARADE AND WORKERS'
PICNIC, 95, 98
People of the Abyss (London), 12
PEOPLE OF THE CUMBERLAND, 147,
156; revenue from, 150-51; production of,
154, 214-20; screenings of, 162, 220-21, 362
n. 29; cost of, 163, 352 n. 55; dramatization
in, 181-82, 229-31; narration of, 357 n. 55;
subject of, 213, 214, 222; ideology of, 219,
231-35, 283, 285; structure of, 223-29; and
People's Front politics, 231-35
People's Front (of Communist Party), 67, 69,
163, 284, 285; and anti-censorship
campaigns, 55; and formation of Nykino,
123; and PIE IN THE SKY, 136-37; and
SUNNYSIDE, 142; and RETURN TO
LIFE, 189, 191; and HEART OF SPAIN,
195; and PEOPLE OF THE
CUMBERLAND, 219-20, 231-35; and
NATIVE LAND, 237, 262-69, 270, 271-73
Perl, Arnold, 161, 352 n. 58
PESCADOS. *See* WAVE, THE
Petric, Vladimir, 338 n. 46, 135, 230, 362 n. 42,
362 n. 43
Photo League, The, 68, 69, 351 n. 49
Photomontage, 24-25, 325 n. 68, 325 n. 72
PIE IN THE SKY, 118, 125, 135, 278-79
Picator, Erwin, 25-27, 325 n. 74, 326 n. 82, 31

Piscator-Bühne, 25
Platt, David, 329 n. 42, 333 n. 84, 96, 108, 109;
  member of Film and Photo League, 41-42,
  61, 62; film critic for *Daily Worker*, 47, 48-
  49; film editor of *New Theatre*, 48; radio
  speech censored, 54; teaches at Harry Alan
  Potamkin Film School, 57; national
  secretary of Film and Photo League, 63-64,
  66; comments on Film and Photo League
  productions, 65-66; on *Filmfront* editorial
  board, 334 n. 102; reviews GETTING
  YOUR MONEY'S WORTH, 334 n. 108,
  92; collaborates on CIGARETTE script,
  83; reviews HARLEM SKETCHES, 88-89;
  reviews THE BIRTH OF NEW CHINA,
  90; describes Film and Photo League
  indebtedness to Soviet film, 105-06; reviews
  BOMBING OF SHANGHAI, 198; reviews
  NATIVE LAND, 247
PLOW THAT BROKE THE PLAINS, THE
  (Lorentz), 127, 128, 347 n. 9, 178, 182, 222-
  23
POLIKUSHKA (Sanin), 326 n. 3, 327 n. 11
Pollock, Arthur, 261
Poole, Ernest, 9
PORTRAIT OF AMERICA, 83, 108
Potamkin, Harry Alan, 42, 46, 330 n. 51, 337 n.
  43; critical of DRIFTERS, 17-18; calls for
  workers' films, 36, 115; reports on progress
  towards workers' film group, 36-37;
  disseminates Film and Photo League
  program, 40, 45-47; film critic for *New
  Masses* and *Workers' Theatre*, 47;
  pamphlet *The Eyes of the Movie* published,
  48; as lecturer, 48, 55, 330 n. 57; analyses
  film censorship, 51-52; outlines scheme for
  motion picture school, 56-57; scriptwriter
  for WINTER 1931, 73; describes TOM
  MOONEY RUN, 95; develops concept of
  dialectical structure, 355 n. 33
POTEMKIN (THE BATTLESHIP
  POTEMKIN, Eisenstein), 21, 32, 45, 52
Prentis, A., 339 n. 63
Prokino, 37
PROKINO-NEWS NO. 1 (Prokino), 37
Proletarian Film League, 37
Prometheus company, 31-32
Protazanov, Yakov, 31, 327 n. 11
Pudovkin, Vsevolod, 19, 20, 57, 133

QUARRY. *See* GRANITE

Rasputin (Piscator production), 25-26
Realism, 1-11, 27-28, 321 n. 2
RED AND WHITE, 44
Red Dancers, 30
REDES. *See* WAVE, THE

RED SALUTE, 50
Reis, Bernard J., 148, 365 n. 31
Renoir, Jean, 130, 345 n. 37, 168
Renoir, Pierre Auguste, 10
RENT STRIKES, 75
Republic Steel Massacre, 238, 363 n. 7; in
  NATIVE LAND, 239, 242, 245, 246, 256-
  57, 266
RETURN TO LIFE, 357 n. 60; revenue from,
  150-51 n. 21; production of, 159, 165, 169,
  353 n. 17; release of, 169-70, 173; structure
  of, 176-77; editing of, 182-84; narration of,
  184-89; ideology of, 186-92, 207, 283, 285
REVOLT OF THE FISHERMEN (Piscator),
  31
Rice, Elmer, 10, 149, 241
Richter, Hans, 31
Riis, Jacob, 11, 12-13
Ritt, Martin, 254
RIVER, THE (Lorentz), 347 n. 9, 184, 222-23,
  234
ROAD TO FREEDOM, THE (International
  Labor Defense), 341 n. 105
ROAD TO LIFE (Ekk), 31, 44, 55
Robeson, Paul, 149, 163; and NATIVE LAND,
  246, 247, 251, 258, 262, 266
Robinson, Earl, 160, 220
Rodchenko, Alexander, 25
Roffman, Julian, 56, 88, 89, 110, 113, 278;
  member of Film and Photo League, 41-42,
  45, 65; film critic for *Daily Worker*, 47;
  directs GETTING YOUR MONEY'S
  WORTH, 68, 91-92; on *Filmfront* editorial
  board, 334 n. 102; edits THE BIRTH OF
  NEW CHINA, 90-91; describes
  IMPERIAL VALLEY, 96; works on
  MARINE, 336 n. 27; comments on Nykino
  breakaway, 123; describes Nykino
  photography workshop, 124-25
Roosevelt, Eleanor, 162, 351 n. 53, 170, 221,
  241, 247
Roosevelt, Franklin D., 49, 53, 59, 86, 266, 275;
  as Governor of New York, 71; in
  AMERICA TODAY, 81-82, 104, 113, 285;
  policy towards Spain of, 170-71; policy
  towards China of, 195-96, 205; labor
  legislation of, 232; in NATIVE LAND, 272,
  285; supported by Communist Party, 284;
  Strand/Hurwitz tribute to, 367 n. 9
Rotha, Paul, 15-16
ROT SPORT MARSCHIERT (Weltfilm), 32
Rukeyser, Muriel, 172
Russ collective, 30-31, 326 n. 3
RUSSIAN REVOLUTION, THE, 32
RUSSIA OF NIKOLAI II AND LEV
  TOLSTOY, THE (Shub), 21
RUSSIA THROUGH THE SHADOWS
  (Broms), 32

Ruttman, Walther, 25-26

Sadoul, Georges, 22
SALT OF THE EARTH (Biberman), 366 n. 60
S.A. MANN BRAND (Seitz), 49-50, 64
SAN DIEGO POLICE ATTACK ON
    WORKERS, 61, 96
San Francisco Film and Photo League, 54, 60.
    See also Film and Photo League, The
SANG D'UN POETÈ, LE (Cocteau), 209
Saxe, Alfred, 161, 243-44
SCHINDERHANNES (Bernhard), 31
Scott, Leroy, 9
SCOTTSBORO BOYS, THE, 72, 75, 79-80,
    81, 112
Scottsboro case, 72, 75, 81, 93, 111; Hurwitz
    film on, 79-80, 81; Washington
    demonstration concerning, 76-77, 81, 113-
    14
SCOTTSBORO DEMONSTRATION, 75
SEEDS OF FREEDOM (HIRSCH
    LECKERT, Rosal), 52, 327 n. 11
Sejour, Laura, 169
Seltzer, Leo, 65, 102, 110, 113, 276, 278;
    describes experience in Film and Photo
    League, 40-43, 61; teaches at Harry Alan
    Potamkin Film School; as still
    photographer, 59; author of *Filmfront*
    column, 334 n. 102; re-edits NATIONAL
    HUNGER MARCH, 73; films BONUS
    MARCH, 74-75; films Washington
    Scottsboro demonstration, 76, 101-02;
    films Hans Weidemann protest, 78; makes
    MARINE, 80, 336 n. 27; films MAY DAY
    1934, 81; edits BONUS MARCH, 103;
    footage used in 1940s productions, 113,
    246; comments on Nykino breakaway, 123
SHAME (COUNTERPLAN, Ermler/
    Yutkevich), 44
SHANGHAI DOCUMENT (Blyokh), 18, 90,
    107, 198
SHANGHAI EXPRESS (Von
    Sternberg), 196, 197
SHANGHAI MADNESS, 49, 196-97
Shaw, George Bernard, 7, 29
SHERIFFED, 84, 110, 338 n. 46, 276
Shinn, Everett, 9-10
Shoemaker, Joseph, 242, 255, 260
SHORT TRIP TO THE SOVIET UNION, A,
    73
Shub, Esther, 20-21, 23, 108, 109, 341 n. 105,
    172
Sifton, Paul, 10, 148, 151
Silent Partner (Odets), 151-52
Sinclair, Upton, 9, 10, 29; and THUNDER
    OVER MEXICO, 48-49
Singing Jailbirds (Sinclair), 10
6-1/2 x 11 (Epstein), 56

Sklar, George, 67, 148, 151, 153
Sloan, John, 10
Smith, Art, 126, 253, 261, 271, 364 n. 23
Social Democratic Party (Germany), 7, 26
Socialist Party (USA), 8, 9, 34, 214, 360 n. 4, 264
Socialist realism, 321 n. 2
Social realism, 1-12, 26-28, 321 n. 2
SOIL. *See* EARTH
SONG OF CEYLON (Wright), 252-53
SONG OF THE FISHERMEN (Tsai),
    194-95, 202
SPAIN (Shub), 172
SPAIN IN FLAMES (van Dongen), 172,
    173-74, 355 n. 30
SPANISH EARTH, THE (Ivens), 165,
    170-71, 180, 183, 191, 199; outtakes from,
    167; scripting of, 174; dramatization in,
    174, 180; narration of, 186, 188, 191, 356 n.
    53; fundraising screenings of, 353 n. 13
SPEED-UP IN AUTO INDUSTRY, 93
SPRENGT DIE KETTEN (Weltfilm), 32
SPRING (Kaufman), 107
Stanislavsky, Konstantin, 27, 282-83; theory
    of acting of, 7-8, 134, 137-38, 181, 260-61
STARVATION, 13
Stebbins, Robert. See Meyers, Sidney
Steiner, Ralph, 329 n. 42, 333 n. 84, 126,
    127-28, 162; and Film and Photo League,
    41, 46; teaches at Harry Alan Potamkin
    Film School, 57, 116, 118, 343 n. 4; founder
    of Nykino, 65, 122-24; as theorist of radical
    film, 118-20, 132-34, 343 n. 7, 343 n. 15,
    229-30; attends Strasberg classes, 124, 132;
    in Nykino photography workshop, 125;
    works on THE PLOW THAT BROKE
    THE PLAINS, 127; member of Frontier
    Films, 130, 148; associated of Group
    Theatre, 132, 347 n. 3; photographs
    BLACK LEGION, 143; as experimental
    filmmaker, 344 n. 25; describes Hammett
    project, 154; photographs PEOPLE OF
    THE CUMBERLAND, 154, 214-15, 217,
    218-20, 226, 360 n. 8, 361 n. 14; resigns
    from Frontier Films, 156-59, 161, 349 n. 38;
    and THE RIVER, 347 n. 9; subsequent
    career of, 352 n. 58. Films: H2O, 329 n. 42,
    125; MECHANICAL PRINCIPLES, 329
    n. 42; GRANITE, 125; HARBOR
    SCENES, 125-26; CAFE UNIVERSAL,
    118, 126; PIE IN THE SKY, 118, 125, 135-
    38; HANDS, 127, 344 n. 32; THE CITY,
    158-59, 273
Steelworkers—Noontime (Anschutz), 9
Stern, Seymour, 40, 95, 108
Stevens, Virginia, 148, 160, 350 n. 47
Stevenson, Philip, 148, 151, 152, 161
Stone-breakers, The (Courbet), 3, 7
STOP JAPAN (Garrison), 199

STORM OVER ASIA (Pudovkin), 31
Strand, Paul, 128, 156, 159, 243, 269, 364 n. 24;
    inspired by Heartfield, 325 n. 72; as still
    photographer, 59, 351 n. 49; supporter of
    Photo League, 333 n. 82; joins Nykino, 124;
    collaborates on Odets script, 126; visits
    Soviet Union, 126-27; works on THE
    PLOW THAT BROKE THE PLAINS,
    127, 182; founder of Frontier Films, 130,
    145, 146, 147, 148, 153; on film aesthetics,
    130, 134; produces THE WAVE, 131-32;
    works on BLACK LEGION, 143; meets
    Hurwitz, 344 n. 22; edits HEART OF
    SPAIN, 154, 167, 177, 179, 181, 182, 192;
    and Frontier Films finances, 149, 150, 162,
    163, 240-41, as critic, 161, 351 n. 49; in
    association of Documentary Film
    Producers, 162; and Group Theatre, 347 n.
    3; and THE RIVER, 347 n. 9; and
    Communist Party, 350 n. 41; married to
    Virginia Stevens, 350 n. 47; subsequent
    career of, 352 n. 58; on RETURN TO
    LIFE, 169; on CHINA STRIKES BACK,
    195; co-directs NATIVE LAND, 240, 244,
    259-60, 261, 262, 271; photographs
    NATIVE LAND, 245; mounts Roosevelt
    tribute, 367 n. 9
Strasberg, Lee, 124, 128, 131-32, 134, 229-30
STRIKE (Eisenstein), 19, 111
STRIKE AGAINST STARVATION, THE,
    43, 72, 111, 276
Strindberg, August, 7
Stroheim, Erich von, 11
STUDENT OF PRAGUE, THE (Galeen), 56
SUNNYSIDE, 129, 135, 140-43, 189, 230, 279
SWEET LAND OF LIBERTY, 83, 110, 284

TAXI, 43, 81, 86-87, 110, 276, 278
TAXI STRIKE, 81
Tefferteller, Ralph, 214-18, 220, 221, 227, 360
    n. 8
TEN DAYS THAT SHOOK THE WORLD.
    See OCTOBER
Thacher, Molly Day, 118
Thaelmann, Ernst, 50, 84-85, 98
Theatre Collective, 123-24
Théâtre Libre, 7, 322 n. 20
Theatre of Action, 93, 123, 124-25, 137
Theatre Union, 86, 128, 153
THIS IS AMERICA (Seldes), 341 n. 105
THIS IS CHINA (Berns), 198
Thomas, Hugh, 192, 355 n. 28, 357 n. 60
Thomas, Norman, 213, 214
THREE SONGS ABOUT LENIN (Vertov),
    31, 65, 342 n. 3
THUNDER OVER MEXICO (Sinclair/
    Lesser/ Eisenstein), 48-49
Tiger Rose (Belasco production), 10

Tischler, 66, 109
TODAY. *See* CANNONS OR TRACTORS
TODESZECHE (Weltfilm), 32
TOGETHER WE LIVE (Mack), 71
Toller, Ernst, 25
TOM MOONEY, 97
TOM MOONEY DEMONSTRATION, 78
TOM MOONEY RUN, 95
Toulouse-Lautrec, Henri de, 10
Trade Union Unity League, 76, 111, 284
*Transport Achievement of the First Five-Year
    Plan* (Klutsis), 25
Trotz Alledem! (Piscator production), 26
Turin, Viktor, 18, 25
TURKSIB (Turin), 18, 25, 36
Twigg, Dr. J., 333 n. 89

Unemployed Councils, 72, 77-78, 83, 92,
    93-94, 111
UNEMPLOYED DEMONSTRATION, 78
UNEMPLOYMENT COUNCIL, 83
Union of Worker-Photographers. *See*
    Vereinigung der Arbeiterphotographen
UNITED ACTION, 153, 159-60, 350 n. 47
UNITED ACTION MEANS VICTORY. *See*
    UNITED ACTION
United Automobile Workers of America
    (UAW), 149, 153, 159, 350 n. 47, 226
UNITED FRONT, 87
United Mine Workers of America (UMWA),
    221, 238, 367 n. 10; in PEOPLE OF THE
    CUMBERLAND, 217, 224, 227, 228, 229,
    232, 234

van Dongen, Helen, 173-74, 220
Van Dyke, Willard, 136, 345 n. 38, 162; joins
    Nykino, 124-25; describes Nykino
    activities, 126, 129; visits Soviet Union, 126;
    co-directs HANDS, 127; member of
    Frontier Films, 130, 147; on film aesthetics,
    130; photographs SUNNYSIDE, 141;
    collaborates on BLACK LEGION, 143;
    works on NATIVE LAND project, 155-56,
    239; resigns from Frontier Films, 156-59,
    349 n. 38; co-directs THE CITY, 158-59,
    273; photographs THE RIVER, 347 n. 9,
    222; subsequent career of, 352 n. 58; shoots
    footage for CHINA STRIKES BACK, 194,
    199, 359 n. 19; as still photographer, 270-71
Vanguard Films, 67, 88
Vereeniging voor VolksCultuur, 37, 328 n. 24
Vereinigung der Arbeiterphotographen, 37, 47
Vertov, Dziga, 323 n. 42, 57, 334 n. 102, 87, 108,
    171; theory of Kino-Eye of, 13-15, 106;
    theory of montage of, 22-23 106; and
    Rodchenko, 25. Films: KINONEDIELIA,
    15; ANNIVERSARY OF THE
    REVOLUTION, 15, HISTORY OF THE

CIVIL WAR, 15; KINO-PRAVDA, 15; GOSKINO-KALENDAR, 15; KINO-GLAZ, 15; FORWARD, SOVIET!, 15, 22 ONE SIXTH OF THE WORLD, 15; THE ELEVENTH YEAR, 15; THE MAN WITH THE MOVIE CAMERA, 15, 117; THREE SONGS ABOUT LENIN, 31, 65, 342 n. 3
VICTOIRE DE LA VIE. *See* RETURN TO LIFE
Vidor, King, 54
VISIT TO SOVIET RUSSIA, A (WIR), 32
VOICE OF PROGRESS, THE (CPUSA), 143
VOLGA TO GASTONIA (WIR), 35, 52
Vorkapich, Slavko, 46, 54, 55, 88, 199
VVVC. *See* Vereeniging voor VolksCultuur

Waiting for Lefty (Odets), 81
Walking Delegate, The (Scott), 9
WASHINGTON SCOTTSBORO DEMONSTRATION, 76, 82, 98, 101, 112, 113
WASTE AND WANT, 57, 83, 116
WATERFRONT. *See* MARINE
Watts, Richard, Jr., 82, 246-47, 247-48
Watts, William, 153, 154, 161, 220, 243-44
WAVE, THE (Zinnemann/Strand), 124, 127, 31, 145, 153
Webber, Charles, 263
Weinberg, Herman G., 86, 262
Welles, Orson, 356 n. 53, 364 n. 25
Weltfilm, 32, 37
WESTERN PENNSYLVANIA AND KENTUCKY MINERS' STRIKE. *See* STRIKE AGAINST STARVATION, THE
Weston, Edward, 59, 333 n. 82
Wexley, John, 46
WFPL (Workers' Film and Photo League). *See* Film and Photo League, The
WHAT IS HAPPENING IN SPAIN (Karmen), 172
WHITE FLOOD, 151, 160
WHO GETS YOUR VOTE? (Del), 143
WINTER 1931, 73-74, 119
WIR (Workers' International Relief), 36, 39, 72, 111; activities of, 29-30; film distribution and production in 1920s by, 32-35; relationship of Film and Photo League to, 39, 58, 61, 64, 328 n. 27, 123; film department of (1930s), 40, 43-45, 56, 327 n. 11, 277; action against censorship by, 52; demise of, 67, 284; support for hunger march by, 77; and MISERY AMONG

WORKING-CLASS CHILDREN, 79; and Imperial Valley film, 95-96; and Workers' Animated Film Group, 339 n. 63
W.I.R., 339 n. 63
W.I.R. CHILDREN'S CAMP, N.Y., 73
WITH THE LINCOLN BATTALION IN SPAIN, 172
Wittenber, Jan, 93-94, 339 n. 70
Wolff, David. *See* Maddow, Ben
Workers' Animated Film Group, 339 n. 63
Workers' Camera Club. *See* Workers' Camera League
Workers' Camera League, 38, 328 n. 34
Workers' Cultural Federation, 46
WORKERS EX-SERVICEMEN'S BONUS DEMONSTRATION, 76
WORKERS EX-SERVICEMEN'S BONUS PARADE. *See* WORKERS EX-SERVICEMEN'S BONUS DEMONSTRATION
Workers' Ex-Servicemen's League (WESL), 74, 104, 111
Workers' Film and Photo League, The. *See* Film and Photo League, The
WORKERS' HEALTH, 93
Workers' International Relief. *See* WIR
Workers' Laboratory Theatre, 30, 120, 121-22, 122, 123-24, 344 n. 23
WORKERS NEWSREEL NO. 12, 340 n. 84
WORKERS ON THE WATERFRONT. *See* MARINE
Workers Party, 34, 327 n. 15. *See also* Communist Party, USA
Workers' photo leagues, 38
Workers' Theatre, 44, 47-48
WORKERS' TOPICAL NEWS, 37
WORLD IN REVIEW, 83, 108
WORLD'S FAIR, 93
WORLD TODAY, THE, 138-39, 145, 163; SUNNYSIDE, 129, 135, 139-44, 189, 230, 279; BLACK LEGION, 129, 135, 143, 346 n. 64; projected third number, 151-52, 239
Wright, Basil, 252-53

Yeager, Barton, 57
Young Communist League, 49, 78
Young Pioneers, 49, 111
YOUTH OF MAXIM (Kozintsev/Trauberg), 55

Zane, Edgar, 58
ZEITPROBLEME (Dudow), 32
Zola, Émile, 4, 5-6, 7, 8, 110
Zuker, Joel, 135, 137, 343 n. 7